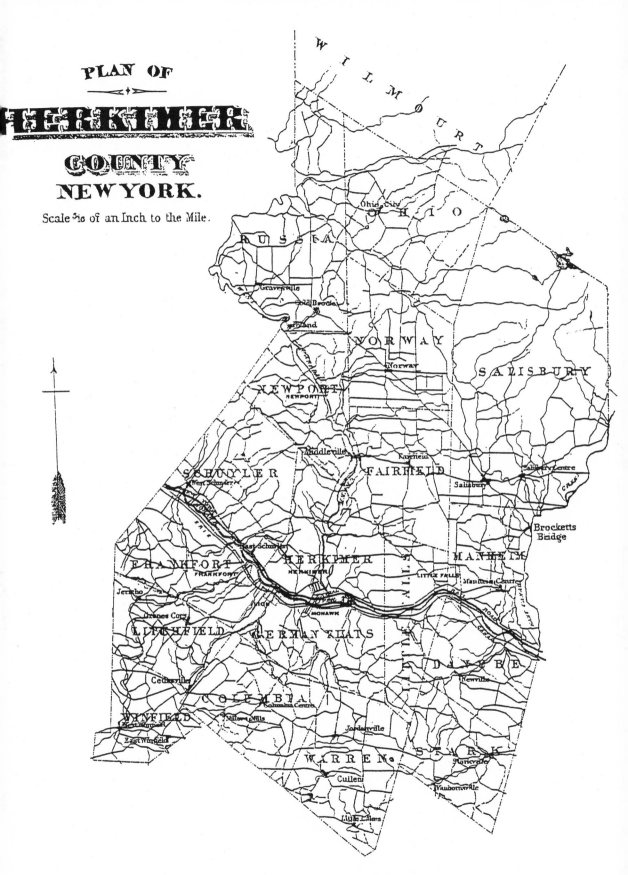

PLAN OF

HERKIMER

COUNTY

NEW YORK.

Scale ⅜ of an Inch to the Mile.

Atlas of Herkimer County New York, 1868, Nichols

DISTANT DRUMS

Herkimer County, New York
in the War of the Rebellion

David P. Krutz

North Country Books
Utica, New York

DISTANT DRUMS

ISBN 0-925168-42-4
Printed in the United States of America

Cover Photo: Officers and Colors of the 34th New York.

Cover Art by John Mahaffy

Library of Congress Cataloging-in-Publication Data

Krutz, David P., 1950 -
  Distant drums : Herkimer County, New York in the War of the
Rebellion / by David P. Krutz.
    p. cm.
  Includes bibliographical references (p. 391) and index.
  ISBN 0-925168-42-4
  1. Herkimer County (N.Y.)—History, Military. 2. New York
(State)—History—Civil War, 1861-1865—Regimental histories.
3. United States—History—Civil War, 1861-1865—Regimental
histories. I. Title.
F127.H5K78   1997   97-3193
973.7'447—dc21   CIP

Published by
NORTH COUNTRY BOOKS, INC.
PUBLISHER—DISTRIBUTOR
311 Turner Street
Utica, New York 13501

To the memory of my father, Edward Krutz

CONTENTS

FOREWORD

In almost every corner of Herkimer County one can easily find reminders of the great impact that the Civil War had on the people of our area. In the center of Eastern Park in Little Falls the statue of a Union soldier gazes across the valley, in front of the courthouse in Herkimer a memorial stone bears a plaque that pays tribute to the 34th New York, and in Dolgeville, Spofford and Faville Avenues recall the names of two hometown officers from the 97th New York. In many of Herkimer County's larger graveyards especial plots are dedicated to Civil War veterans, and most all of our cemeteries are dotted with the distinctive five-pointed GAR star that marks the final resting place of one of the boys in blue. Yet these remembrances go largely unnoticed for most people either relegate the Civil War to the realm of ancient history or else fail to realize the magnitude of the war's influence on our Mohawk Valley predecessors.

Men, who not so long ago, walked our streets, travelled our byways and in short, lived their lives in the same spaces that we now occupy, contributed heavily to the Union war effort. These men are an integral part of the heritage of Herkimer County and it is my intention in putting together this book to bring their contributions once more into the light.

As it should be, I've let the fighting men of Herkimer County tell their own story. At a quick glance, the reader will note that the majority of this book is drawn from either the letters of Herkimer County soldiers, *Herkimer County Journal* articles, or from regimental histories. In most instances, excerpts were copied verbatim, with an eye towards presenting quotations in the vernacular of the time. Errors in spelling and punctuation, for the most part, have been ignored and the notation "sic" has not been employed. I have only intruded on these writings to help tie the story together or to add swatches of local color to the narrative. Wherever possible, I've attempted to include the names of Herkimer County men who gave their all for their country. For any omissions in this regard I truly apologize. I also ask pardon if it appears that I dwell too heavily on the happenings in Little Falls and seemingly disregard the rest of the county. My source for Herkimer County affairs was the *Herkimer County Journal*, which was published in Little Falls, and ignoring its masthead, reported primarily on events in that village. (There are no other local newspaper files available for this time period.)

A word about the county itself. During the Civil War years, 1861-1865, Herkimer County occupied the same boundaries as it does today and was composed of nineteen towns. These towns, with their populations per the 1860 census,[1] were: Columbia, 1,893; Danube, 1,711; Fairfield, 1,712; Frankfort, 3,247; German Flatts, 3,940; Herkimer, 2,804; Litchfield, 1,520; Little Falls, 5,989; Manheim, 1,868; Newport, 2,113; Norway, 1,105; Ohio, 1,135; Russia, 2,389; Salisbury, 2,325; Schuyler, 1,715; Stark, 1,543; Warren, 1,812; Wilmurt, 260; and Winfield, 1,480.

A concise sketch of Herkimer County during this period is provided by Fisher's 1858 *Gazetteer of the United States*.[2] Fisher's report reads:

> "Soil on the Mohawk is very rich. In the North are extensive forests and the best of grazing, the county being noted for its fine cattle and large dairies. It is well timbered, and the North abounds in pine and hemlock. It also has great facilities for manufacturers in West Canada Creek, which falls 23 feet per mile, and the Little Falls of the Mohawk, which descends 42 feet in three-quarters of a mile. The last are celebrated for their beauty, the river bed lying 300 to 400 feet below the banks it has cut through. Minerals of almost every kind are found, iron ore, lead, limestone, and gypsum, being the most useful, and others, noted the world over for the perfection, and beauty of their crystals. Its staples are agricultural, butter, cheese, wool, and cattle. Farms 2,723; manufacturers 277; dwellings 6,664; and population - white 38,062, free colored 182 - total 38,244. Capital: Herkimer. Public Works: Erie Canal; Utica and Schenectady R.R.; Mohawk Valley R.R.; Saratoga and Sackett's Harbor R.R.s."

As best as I can determine from town clerks' records, census reports, regimental and county histories, approximately thirty-five hundred men fought for the Union in the name of Herkimer County. (A more precise accounting of county men in Federal service may not be possible due to incomplete and inaccurate records, and because town clerks often listed out of county men as residents of their towns.)

The Herkimer County men who answered Abraham Lincoln's call to arms were typical of the millions of citizen-soldiers that populated the Union army and navy. The great majority of the Herkimer County boys in blue were in their late teens or early twenties, unmarried and usually from humble backgrounds. For these young men, marching off to war offered the adventure of a lifetime, a chance to "see the elephant." But war soon lost its charms and put on an ugly face as the harsh realities of the struggle became too evident. Yet by and large, the men of Herkimer County did their duty for their country, not as gallant heroes, but as common, private soldiers. As I came to realize, these men were not of a special breed, but simply people like ourselves, removed from us only by time and a different set of values.

To date, I've sadly catalogued (Appendix C) the names of four hundred and forty-four Herkimer County men who went to war, never to return. It is to the memory of these men that this book is devoted.

Many people have contributed to the researching and formation of this book and to them I am truly grateful. My special thanks go to my wife Joan and to my son Jeff for transcribing and re-transcribing my scribbled pages into a readable form and to the librarians at the Little Falls Public Library for often going beyond the call of duty to help me. Extra special thanks go to Hector Allen for his highly valued opinions and ideas and for his inspiration and encouragement.

PROLOGUE

The Presidential election of 1860 was singular in American history for this election would feature not one but two separate races. By this point in time, relations between the slave and free states had deteriorated to such an extent that each region would in truth hold its own presidential election. In the South—where Abraham Lincoln's name would not even appear on the ballot—Southern Democrat, John Breckenridge of Kentucky, opposed the Union Party candidate, John Bell of Tennessee. In the North, the Republican nominee, Lincoln, ran against Northern Democrat and fellow Illini, Stephen Douglas. However, of these two contests, the campaign in the North was the all important struggle, for the free states—the states north of the Mason-Dixon line—held a commanding plurality in Electoral College votes (189) over the slave states (114). The man who could carry the vote of the Northern states would become the next President of the United States.

In Herkimer County, as in the rest of the North, Lincoln and Douglas supporters congregated in well organized militaristic political clubs. The Lincoln men, who called themselves the "Wide Awakes," and the Douglasites, or "Little Giants," formed "companies" in nearly every Herkimer County village and town. Club members donned uniforms, elected officers and travelled throughout the Mohawk Valley, lending support to the rallies of fellow "Wide Awake" or "Little Giant" clubs. In describing a typical rally, *The Herkimer County Journal* reported of a "Wide Awake" meeting in Newport:

> "Saturday [October 6, 1860] was a proud day for Newport. The Republicans of this and the neighboring towns assembled in mass meeting, to the number of about two thousand.
>
> In the forenoon a Lincoln pole was raised and the national colors hoisted. A large white banner was suspended across Main street, on which was printed in large characters, 'Lincoln and Hamlin.' The organized Wide Awakes of Fairfield, Norway and Newport, together with a large number of unorganized Wide Awakes male and female, under the direction of Col. Wm. LaDue, as Marshal, formed in procession at two o'clock p.m. and marched to a field near the village, where a covered stage had been erected and seats arranged.
>
> Hon. Roscoe Conkling, of Utica was introduced, and for two hours held the audience in complete silence, save when a brilliant flight of eloquence or a happy hit called forth the spontaneous shouts of the multitude.
>
> The address was a masterly exposition of the principles of the Republican party. His treatment of the subjects of Slavery, Homestead Exemption, the Tariff, the legislation of the last session of Congress, and the danger of submitting the election of President to the House of Representatives as at present organized, showed a familiarity with details and general principles which places Mr. Conkling high among Republican Statesmen. He handles

the 'Little Giant' [Douglas] and his pet scheme, Squatter Sovereignty, without gloves. Indeed he completely squelched them. The few listening Democrats sensibly withered.

In the evening came off a grand Wide Awake parade and torchlight procession. The village was completely illuminated. Transparencies of various colors were brilliantly lighted. The Wide Awakes of Middleville and Herkimer joined those already mentioned, making in all about five hundred trained Wide Awakes with torches, and in full uniform. The procession, led by Col. LaDue and the Newport Cornet Band, paraded the streets for about three hours. Before the procession broke up, the Wide Awakes were drawn up in front of Hawkin's Hotel, filling the street for a long distance with a dense mass of men and torches. Hon. J.H. Wooster then appeared upon the balcony of the hotel, and made a brief but thrilling and eloquent address. During, and at the conclusion of the address, cheer after cheer rent the air for the speaker and the Republican candidates, while from all parts of the crowd went up rockets, which, altogether, formed the most splendid sight Newport ever witnessed."[1]

Similar "Wide Awake" demonstrations were made in Fairfield, Cedarville, Salisbury, Middleville, Poland and Norway, but the grandest of the meetings took place in Little Falls.

In the late afternoon hours of October 11th, three trains—chartered at half fare prices—from Utica, Fort Plain and Herkimer pulled into Little Falls. From the cars poured over two thousand "Wide Awakes" and their friends, with the Utica train, which consisted of nineteen passenger cars, contributing over one-half of this number. Already at the depot was a vast throng that had come into Little Falls throughout the day by wagon, carriage and on horseback. Adding in the village's own "Wide Awake" delegation and the many spectators, the crowd was estimated at six thousand people.

From this disarray, Grand Marshal Wells Sponable of Little Falls somehow got the various companies of "Wide Awakes" into line and at 9 p.m. the parade of twenty-three hundred uniformed men stepped off. Thirty-one companies, representing twenty-four villages and towns, marched through the principal "north-side" and "south-side" streets of Little Falls. The going was messy for the dirt streets had been churned to a thick mud by an all day icy cold rain. In the column that stretched nearly one mile long were delegations from each of the Herkimer County towns plus "Wide Awake" clubs from Utica, New Hartford, Oneida, Washington Mills, Richfield, Fort Plain, St. Johnsville, Canajoharie and Palatine Bridge. Among the Captains of the Herkimer County groups were John Spofford of Brockett's Bridge, Francis Spinner of Mohawk, W.W. Reals of Little Falls and R. Wilson of Herkimer.

Each of the "Wide Awakes" carried a blazing torch and every company displayed a banner with slogans such as: "Free Speech, Free Press, Free Kansas: No Extension of Slavery," "Honest old Abe is our choice," "No more chains for American Soil" and "Freedom's Sentinels never sleep on their Posts." The Frankfort club was the most inventive, displaying an "automaton" woodchopper hard at work. Interspersed among the black caped "companies" were four brass bands and fourteen "martial" bands.

All along the line of march the citizens of Little Falls displayed their own decorations. From homes, businesses, or from convenient trees hung banners, Chinese lanterns, wreaths and transparencies. Of this display a reporter from *The Utica Herald* noted:

> "Some of the dwellings in the vicinity of the square [Western] were one blaze of many colored lights. Along the line of the houses visible from the railroad, there was one succession of lanterns, and as one caught a glimpse of the streets at right angles, the eye lost itself in the glare and wealth of colors." [2]

The procession finally arrived at Western Square, and after the various companies had encircled the park, one thousand Roman candles were simultaneously launched. The *Utica Herald* reporter commented:

> "Besides the illumination of the streets, the inhabitants had provided handsomely for fireworks. From many of the houses frequent discharges of Roman candles were made. The grand climax of the evening was the halting of the procession about the public square and the discharge of numberless Roman candles from all quarters at the same moment, till the sky was full of them, as if the stars were holding a tournament." [3]

Afterwards the "Wide Awake" clubs marched back to the Little Falls depot and mounted the cars for home. It was notable that on their return to Utica, the Oneida County clubs marched up Genesee Street to City Hall and offered "several rounds of real Wide Awake cheers" before dispersing.

The supporters of Douglas, the "Little Giants," also held rallies throughout Herkimer County. As a rule their meetings would typically draw fewer "torches" than the "Wide Awakes" would muster and half of the "Giants" would not be uniformed. The "Little Giants" held their mass meeting in Little Falls one week after the "Wide Awakes" giant rally.

All that week the Douglasites had boasted that with Douglas' running mate, Herschel V. Johnson of Georgia, scheduled to speak, the "Little Giants" rally would outdo or "beat" that of the Lincoln men. In a report of the "Little Giants" rally, the pro-Lincoln *Herkimer County Journal* congratulated the efforts of the "Giants" but gloated over the fact that the "Wide Awake" rally was much better attended and organized. The *Journal* article read:

> "The Democrats made a very fair display here on the afternoon and evening of the 19th inst. Quite a crowd was here to hear the distinguished candidate for the Vice Presidency, and a goodly number took part in the Little Giant Demonstration of the evening. On the whole, it was a very creditable affair. We are desirous to give them full justice in our notice of the day's proceedings and speak thus highly of their attempt as a frank acknowledgement of a successful effort to get up a good show, but, as a "beat," that had been confidently promised us for the last few weeks, we must in justice pronounce it a miserable failure. In many respects, it was so. After a day of sunshine and beauty as fine as any the sun of Heaven ever shone upon: with the name of Herschel V. Johnson, the great southern

statesman, advertised through the length and breadth of a dozen counties; with the superhuman efforts that have been put forth and the impressing of small democracy into the ranks of the unterrified; after trips to New York for uniforms by Ex-Sheriff's and Post Office officials; after portentous brags and ostentatious prophecies of what the day was to bring forth—it came and brought what?—the said Herschel V. with Col. Clinton, of Miss., but none other of the advertized speakers; it brought Little Giants of which the following is very near a correct table.

In Uniform

Salisbury	84
Fairfield, (partly uniformed)	105
Little Falls, (partly uniformed)	160
" " , Young America	45
Canajoharie	103
St. Johnsville	87
Fonda & Fultonville	110

Without Uniforms

Norway and Newport	20
Mohawk	75
Herkimer	80
Frankfort	85
East Schuyler	40

Making the uniforms, including the clubs a part of whose members were not uniformed, 694—and the ununiformed citizens, 300—in all 994. We know that this is more than many were able to count, but we have made allowances for some scattering ones out of the procession. With 694 uniforms then it is claimed a show was made equal to ours with 2300.

The illuminations were fine, yet merely a display of chinese lanterns, there being very little vanity. In fact, we think this too much a feature in all these parades. In the afternoon there were perhaps on the ground 3,000 persons, an estimate by a democrat. How many were Republicans of course we cannot tell, but should say, at least one-third. We repeat as a show, the affair was very good, better than we expected—as a 'beat' it was a fizzle, just what we expected." [4]

The *Journal* believed that Herschel Johnson's speech was so damaging to his own party that it sarcastically offered to pay any Democrat $25 to deliver a similar speech.

As election day neared and the prospects of Abraham Lincoln being elected became better and better, the Democrats resorted to a desperate "betting" scheme. In warning fellow Republicans to be wary of unscrupulous Democrats, editor J.R. Stebbins wrote in the *Journal*:

"Money is placed in the hands of one or two Democrats in each town, with instructions to make small bets with as many Republicans as possible. The object is to keep Republicans from voting. If Republicans must bet, let each man, before he stakes anything, talk the matter over in the Club Room, so that no more than one shall bet with one Democrat. Then the loss will be even. But be sure and do not let one Democrat bet with a dozen Republicans, and by concealing himself on election day, keep them all from voting."[5]

As was expected, Abraham Lincoln was elected as the 16th President of the United States. Lincoln was only able to garner forty percent of the popular vote, but by carrying seventeen of the free states, he amassed enough Electoral College votes to be elected.

In Herkimer County, from the eighty-seven hundred votes cast, Lincoln finished with a plurality of almost two thousand votes over Douglas. In the hill towns Lincoln's victory was most dramatic as townships such as Newport, Russia and Wilmurt favored Lincoln four to one over Douglas. Only in German Flatts, Little Falls and Herkimer were the Democrats victorious and in each case by only a slim margin. In addition to Lincoln's victory in New York—which he carried by fifty thousand votes—the Republicans triumphed in most of the state races, including the governorship to which Edwin Morgan was elected.[6]

With Lincoln elected President, eleven southern states made good on their threats to secede from the Union. South Carolina withdrew in December; Mississippi, Florida, Alabama, Georgia and Louisiana followed in January, and Texas, Virginia, Arkansas, North Carolina and Tennessee seceded soon after. With this pall hanging over the country, Abraham Lincoln began the trip from his home in Springfield, Illinois, to Washington. En route, Lincoln's train made brief stops at cities and towns along the way. One such stop was made in Little Falls on February 18th, 1861.

Beginning very early on that Monday morning, people from throughout the Mohawk Valley countryside began descending on Little Falls in the hopes of catching a glimpse of "Honest Abe." Just past noon Lincoln's special train was sighted on the eastbound track. The village cannon fired to signal the train's approach and its boom echoed across the valley. Church bells began to ring and as the train slowed at the depot, the newly formed Little Falls Citizen's Brass Band began to play "Hail Columbia." Ladies on the depot's veranda waved their handkerchiefs in unison with the music as the train came to a halt. Abraham Lincoln appeared at the door of his car and waved, causing the crowd to let out a mighty roar. Little Falls village President Seth Richmond stepped forward and announced Mr. Lincoln, who responded to the crowd's call with a much used speech, stating:

> "Ladies and gentlemen, I appear before you merely for the purpose of greeting you, saying a few words and bidding you farewell. I can only say, as I have often said before, that I have no speech to make and no time to make one if I had, neither have I the strength to repeat a speech at all the places at which I stop, even though the circumstances were favorable. I am thankful for this opportunity of seeing you, and of allowing you to see me [Applause]. And in this so far as regards the ladies I think I have the best of the bargain [Applause]. I don't make the acknowledgement however, to the gentlemen [Laughter]. And now I believe that I have really made my speech and am ready to bid you farewell when the train moves."[7]

With that Lincoln re-entered his car amidst the cheering of the crowd. As the train began to pull away from the station, the band played, the church bells chimed, and the village cannon thundered.

In the *Journal's* account of that day, editor J.R. Stebbins reported:

> "Those who saw the smile upon his countenance, wondered that, that face could be called homely, those who heard his manly voice felt intuitively that it was the voice of an 'honest man', while all united in hope, that under his benign administration, the affairs of a prosperous nation might be so conducted as to insure the return of harmony and national confidence." [8]

"Harmony and national confidence" were not forthcoming, for Abraham Lincoln would not be able to heal the wound of secession. On April 12, 1861, the guns of the new Confederate States of America opened fire on Fort Sumter in Charleston Harbor and the War of the Rebellion had begun.

CHAPTER I

"We are in fighting condition"

Spring/Summer 1861 - War Fever
Formation of the 34th N.Y. - Picket Duty on the Potomac

The bombardment of Fort Sumter by the Confederate States of America, which signalled war between the North and the South, was not wholly unexpected.

In early January 1861, South Carolina militia had fired on and driven off the "Star of the West," a Union supply ship that was bringing needed provisions to Fort Sumter's beleaguered garrison. To many people of the North this hostile act was the opening salvo of civil war. In reporting on this incident the *Herkimer County Journal* had framed its article with the headlines, "The First Guns of Treason!," "The Stars and Stripes Assailed!" and "War Declared by South Carolina!" [1] When Confederate cannon opened up on Fort Sumter itself on April 12th, the feared but anticipated rendering of the Union was realized.

On April 15th, two days after the surrender of Fort Sumter, President Lincoln issued a call for the Northern states to supply seventy-five thousand men to suppress the rebellion. As evidenced by a *Journal* article of April 18th, reaction in Herkimer County to Lincoln's call was immediate.

Freemen!! Patriots!!
"It is proposed to initiate proceedings to organize a military company in Little Falls. The citizens are alive to the demands of their country upon them for defense of the government from the hands of Rebels and Traitors. We know our people will rally, and to this end it is needful that systematic organization be made. Let freemen of stout hearts and willing arms, combine to do duty in this hour of national struggles. The act of the Legislature

passed this week provides for volunteers to the number of 30,000 in this state, with an appropriation of $3,000,000 to put the Empire State in a situation to render that military aid needed by the perils of the nation.

Plans are being made to organize a company without delay in Little Falls and a call will be circulated for a public meeting.

Patriots, your country calls for your aid! Be ready to muster into service for the defence of our glorious ship of state, the honor of our national Flag, the protection of Federal property, the perpetuity of our rights, and the preservation of our Constitutional liberty." [2]

Union sentiment was ablaze in the Mohawk Valley. Grand recruiting rallies, complete with bonfires, brass bands and orators, were held in Herkimer, Salisbury, and Brockett's Bridge. Train cars loaded with volunteers from Utica were already passing through the valley on their way to mustering centers in Albany. In Jordanville a large flag erected on "two lofty poles" was saluted by thirty-four guns signifying the thirty-four states of the former Union. At Fairfield Academy a number of students put away their books and enlisted, while others began to drill in hopes of forming their own company. In Mohawk the Union meeting had to be held outdoors because no building in town could accommodate the large crowd that gathered.

The largest of the Union rallies in Herkimer County was held in Little Falls on the afternoon of April 20th. Organized by Little Falls militia officers, P.C. Petrie and Dr. John Sharer, a large number of citizens formed behind the Citizen's Brass Band and marched to the Railroad Depot. There the column was joined by a contingent from Herkimer headed by that village's militia leaders James Suiter and Byron Laflin. The parade continued but a short distance before stopping in front of the home of Zenas Priest, a prominent businessman and a Major in the Herkimer County militia. Major Priest appeared on his balcony and read the latest war news hot off the telegraph wires, "Renegades were burning buildings in Maryland," and "the 7th New York Regiment was nearing Washington." The crowd gave three cheers for the gallant 7th New York and three more for the Union. The procession stepped off again and marched through the principal streets of the village, gathering up onlookers along the way, before dispersing to meet later that evening.

By nine p.m. over one thousand people had gathered in Western Square. Under the illumination of a large bonfire and innumerable torches, Major Priest was elected to conduct the rally. Major Priest's primary duty was the introduction of the evening's speakers who took turns in rousing the crowd. Judge Arphaxed Loomis of Little Falls stated, "I admit the necessity of the contest, I submit to it, and we must meet it. It is ours to stand up to the event at any hazard, at all hazards." Reverend B.F. McLaughlin, pastor of the Little Falls Catholic Church, added, "Herkimer County will as she ever does nobly respond to the call of the country's peril and shall protect the Stars and Stripes from insult and being trampled upon." While Rev. J.D. Adams, rector of the village's Methodist-Episcopal Church, harangued, "Shame upon those who will carry partisan preferences into the present crisis. The guns of Sumter blowed all the such issues into atoms. When our homes, our firesides, our churches, our all is assailed let us fight, fight to defend them."[3] Judges A.H. Laflin of Herkimer and George Hardin of Little Falls also spoke and, like their predecessors, the loud cheering of the crowd frequently drowned out their words. As was expected, at the conclusion of the speech-making a large number of men enlisted on the spot. The meeting concluded with the appointment of a committee to obtain funds for the support and relief of the families of volunteers. Reporting on the show of patriotic spirit at the Little Falls rally the *Journal* would note:

> "Our citizens have at length become aroused to the importance of immediate, determined action. On Saturday such an impromptu meeting was held, as for the unity of sentiment and intensity of feeling [it] was never witnessed here before - a meeting that gladdened the heart of a patriot, and augured well for the perpetuity of our government and institutions. It is refreshing to behold, when dangers threaten the Republic how nobly party issues and animosities are forgotten, how partisan preferences give way to long-slumbering but at last thoroughly aroused patriotism." [4]

Enlistment offices were opened in Herkimer by James Suiter and Byron Laflin, in Little Falls by Wells Sponable and Nathan Easterbrooks Jr., and in Brockett's Bridge by John Beverly. In Graysville, William Ladew, a colonel in the state militia, and Thomas Corcoran "headed the roll."

Throughout the county, relief funds were being raised through subscription of the wealthier citizens. With the promise that Herkimer County would attempt to raise the necessary funds through taxes, a number of prominent businessmen signed their names to indemnity bonds. Holding these notes payable in one year, the banks of the Mohawk Valley advanced the money. In Little Falls $5,000 was secured, which was to be distributed as $5 bounties to each village enlistee and as support for his family. The allotment for family relief was set at $2 a week for the volunteer's wife and $.50 for each of his children, with the total not to exceed $4 per week.

Manheim also raised $5,000, but the fund committee neglected to resolve how the funds should be allocated. In consequence, John Beverly's volunteers were quartered at his house and boarding expenses came out of his pocket.

Ladies aid groups began to meet nightly, preparing bandages "for the sad, fearful, probable necessities of war", scraping lint and making banners for their hometown companies. From the pulpit, sermons took on a patriotic tone and in the *Journal* an anonymous "Old Soldier" gave advice to the young volunteers. The veteran advised:

"How to Prepare for the Campaign - To Young Soldiers"
1. Remember that in a campaign more men die from sickness than the bullet.
2. Line your blankets with one thickness of brown drilling. This adds but four ounces in weight and doubles the warmth.
3. Buy a small India rubber blanket (only $1.50) to lie on the ground or to throw over your shoulders while on guard duty during a rainstorm. Most of the eastern troops are provided with these.
4. The best military hat in use is the light colored soft felt, the crown being sufficiently high to allow space for air over the brim. You can fasten it up as a continental in fair weather or turn it down when it is hot or very sunny.

5. Let your beard grow, as to protect your throat and lungs.
6. Keep your entire person clean; this prevents fevers and bowel complaints in warm climates. Wash your body each day if possible. Avoid strong coffee and oily meats. Gen. Scott said that the too free use of those (together with neglect in keeping the skin clean) cost many a soldier his life in Mexico.
7. A sudden check of perspiration by chilly or night air often causes fever and death. When thus exposed, do not forget your blankets.[5]

In less than three weeks after the President's call six militia-size companies, numbering about forty men each, had formed in Herkimer County. During the first week in May these units began departing for Albany. At rail depots throughout the county great crowds of well-wishers gathered to see off the village companies. Louis Chapin described the scene in Little Falls:

> "They who had to stay at home hung on to their boys at last, and every man wanted to shake the hand of his friend and give him some parting injunction." [6]

At the sendoffs gifts were given to many of the officers and men. Among the favored presents were bibles, shiny new revolvers, money, permission to draw on a benefactor for the cost of a uniform, and from employers, promises that the volunteer's job would be held for him.

The *Journal's* parting words to the volunteers were:

> "Should any of them fall in battle, let the memory of their brave patriotism abide forever in the hearts of their townsmen. Should they return, let it be the return of victors-of conquerors-to whose pride it may be said that they never turned their backs upon the flag of their country. May the God of battles ever attend them." [7]

With the boys gone, life in Herkimer County went on. In Little Falls, H.L. Hurlbut, "the Reformed Drunkard," lectured on Temperance and M.J. Prescott spoke on "Popularity and how to obtain it" at Concert Hall. William Miller's barn on Furnace Street caught fire, No. 3 Fire Company arrived first, but Fire Company No. 1 had first steam. A cow owned by Joseph Lewis gave birth to four calves all of the "male persuasion." The new brass band gave their first concert and John Gilliland reopened his combination barbershop and saloon.

The young ladies of Miss Wright's Select School presented a flag of their making to John Bell, the principal of Little Falls Academy. Zenas Priest donated a flagpole topped by an American Eagle, and the flag was raised over the Academy after appropriate speeches.

In Mohawk a company of Zouaves was being formed and in Herkimer the village ladies prepared a box of "eatables," which included a ten pound cheese, pickles, eggs and cakes, for delivery to their boys in Albany.

The *Journal* sent along the newspaper's best wishes to their three volunteers, George Waterhouse, Louis Chapin, and Henry Stowell. Waterhouse had promised to be the paper's "camp correspondent."

In Albany, during their first months stay, the Herkimer County boys were quartered at the run-down Adams House and in vacant lots. The food served the men was termed "swill" and twice led to near food riots. Correspondent Waterhouse would write:

> "A horrible rumor has gained evidence among some of the friends of volunteers, to the effect that Rats, Mice, Snakes, Lizards, and all manner of reptiles that crawl are hashed up and served out to our county Companies now in Albany. To bring the matter down fine, it would seem that on Sunday, on the passage of a strange dish of provisions from the kitchen to the table of the Syracuse Zouaves, some members of another company either for the fun of the thing, or for the purpose of instigating a row, threw a well grown quadruped upon the tray of one of the waiters. The consequence was that, by reason of the lot of steam of the vegetables, the company very soon began to smell a rat. His ratship, vegetables, tray and all were soon deposited in the street and thus the matter ended." [8]

> "In good spirits were most of them, and complaints as to board and provisions were not so frequent as hitherto. It was intimated, however, that finding of a "thousand legger" in the bean soup of one of the members of Captain Beverly's company, was made occasion of a general rebellion at the dinner table on Friday. Tables, dishes, and eatables were piled promiscuously upon the floor and waiters found rapid exit through windows and doors. Upon being denied their supper, in consequence, the company formed into line, and led by Capt. B, would have stormed the larder, had not the cooks capitulated. The Captain is proud to say, that his men acquitted themselves in this their first engagement, with great coolness, bravery and honor." [9]

After the second disturbance, the food improved and at the end of May the companies were moved to the much more suitable Industrial School Barracks.

The Herkimer County volunteers were under the assumption that their companies would be assembled into a regiment and that the men would be able to elect their own officers. Unfortunately, New York State law required each regiment to be composed of ten companies of at least seventy-seven men; therefore, the Herkimer County units were in danger of being separated and dispersed to other regiments. If that were to occur the men would lose their Herkimer County identity and would be officered by "partizan favorites of Albany relatives." At one point the Herkimer County companies threatened to offer their services directly to the U.S. Government instead of to New York if the county units were divided.

To surmount the problem of inadequate unit size, Captain Easterbrooks disbanded his Little Falls company and distributed the men to the other five county units. In addition, unattached companies from Crown Point, Addison, Champlain, Hammondsport, and West Troy were persuaded to join the Mohawk Valley companies in the formation of a regiment. The New York quota under Lincoln's call was rapidly being filled and failure to join a regiment could mean that a unit might miss the chance to enter Federal service. The unattached companies, with the exception of West Troy, promised to unconditionally vote the "Herkimer County ticket" for regimental officers. Captain Oswald of West Troy had to be assured that his company would be designated company "A" and therefore would have the honored "Right of the Line" regimental parade position. This arrangement would later cause dire problems for Oswald and his men.

The New York State Military Board mustered the regiment into state service on May 24, 1861, as a two year unit and designated it as the Thirty-Fourth Regiment, New York State Volunteers. Due to the preponderance of Herkimer County men and officers, the 34th New York acquired the unofficial title, "The Herkimer County Regiment." At the time of muster the 34th numbered seven hundred and eighty-six officers and men.

The first regimental slate of officers was:

Colonel - William Ladew, Graysville
Lieutenant Colonel - James Suiter, Herkimer
Major-Byron Laflin, Herkimer
Adjutant - George Thompson, Albany
Quartermaster - Nathan Easterbrooks, Little Falls
Surgeon - Socrates Sherman, Ogdensburg
Chaplain - J.B. Van Petten, Fairfield

Company Designations and their commanders were:
A - West Troy, Capt. William Oswald
B - Little Falls, Capt. Wells Sponable
C - Graysville, Capt. Thomas Corcoran
D - Champlain, Capt. Davis Rich
E - Addison, Capt. Henry Baldwin
F - Herkimer, Capt. Charles Riley
G - Herkimer, Capt. Charles Brown
H - Crown Point, Capt. Leland Doolittle
I - Hammondsport, Capt. William King
K - Salisbury, Capt. John Beverly

While in Albany the 34th New York drilled for at least four hours each day. As no military equipment had yet arrived, the men went through their maneuvers without uniforms and except for the officers' side arms, without guns. One of the 34th's favorite drill fields was in front of Miss Schoonhoven's Select School for Girls. Under the watchful eyes of the school's female student body the young soldiers stood a little straighter, stuck out their chests a little farther and went through their drills with a crisper step. The girls were so appreciative of the boys attention that they presented each member of Company K with handmade needle books. But the drill field was not always so enjoyable as evidenced by three cases of severe sunstroke suffered one day by the boys of Company B.

The Federal mustering-in service on June 15th produced a few surprises. During the ceremony five men had refused to take the oath of allegiance to the United States and after rejecting a chance to reconsider, were drummed out of the 34th in disgrace.

George Waterhouse wrote:

> ". . . . Their heads were then shaved, their hands tied behind them and a white string with two white feathers attached, was fastened to the head of each man, by their own company, when they were marched, at the head of the Company—the musicians playing the "Rogue's March" through the streets to their room in these Barracks, where they were made to stand upon a table and go through with the "facing," &c. just the same as though they were in the ranks. When they were marching through the street they were hooted and groaned at by a large crowd of people." [10]

During their stay in Albany the men of the 34th New York were witness to the return of the body of Mechanicsville native and recently martyred national hero, Col. Elmer Ellsworth. Colonel Ellsworth, a close friend of Abraham Lincoln and the commander of the celebrated 11th New York Fire Zouaves*, was shot and killed by a Confederate sympathizer while tearing down a rebel flag in Alexandria, Virginia, on May 23rd. Ellsworth's death added fuel to Northern war sentiment and brought the country face to face with the grim "glory" of war. The 34th's correspondent George Waterhouse wrote of the Herkimer County boys experience:

> "The mortal remains of the late Col. Ellsworth arrived here yesterday morning . . . accompanied by the Fire Zouave who killed the assassin. The Zouave had in his possession the bayonet that he ran through the body of the assassin and also the secession flag that the Colonel hauled down at Alexandria. The flag and bayonet were both stained with blood . . ." [11]

In honor of Colonel Ellsworth, the men of Captain Beverly's Salisbury company (Co. K) changed their name from "Northern Rangers" to the "Ellsworth's Guards."

The 34th's time in Albany was not all spent on drilling and military duties. The boys in their free time played baseball, formed temperance societies, or simply sat on the grass and related "stories of love and adventure during the past and boast of the daring deeds they will accomplish in the future." On one occasion the regiment was called upon to help the Albany firemen put out a blaze at Burt's Brewery. Short furloughs were granted and many men visited home. From the ladies of Herkimer County came boxes for favored companies, filled with cheese, butter, tart-pies and all kinds of cakes. To Captain Sponable's Company B, the Little Falls ladies sent havelocks and from friends in Fairfield, Orderly Sgt. William Walton received shirts, socks and a revolver.

On one Saturday afternoon the 34th, under the command of Major Laflin, had their first dress-parade. A large crowd of Albany's citizens gathered to watch and the men proudly went through their evolutions to the music of the Brigade Band.

One member of the 34th caused a sensation among the volunteers and Albany society by marrying the niece of a wealthy Albany businessman. Sgt. Lewis Clark of Company B, nicknamed the "Little Falls Musician," deceived the Albany belle into believing that he was the captain of his company and owned a lot of land in Herkimer County. Through the covert exchange of love letters, his being dropped from the barracks window, the couple planned their marriage. After a courtship that

---

* Styled after French Zouaves, the 11th New York was composed of New York City firemen.

lasted all of four days the lovebirds were wed. Obviously distracted from his military duties by newfound connubial bliss, Clark was demoted to corporal within a week.

During the last week in June, uniforms, antique Springfield smooth-bore muskets, blankets—"small and shoddy"—and all sorts of other military equipment was distributed to the men. Horace Burch of Little Falls, representing the ladies of that village, came to Albany and presented a stand of colors to the regiment "made of silk and emblazoned with a beautiful emblem." But of premier importance to the boys, they were finally paid. Louis Chapin related:

> " . . . they have not seen a quarter of a dollar in such a long time that if they were shown one now they could not tell whether it was money or an old musket." [12]

After enviously watching the 14th and 18th New York Volunteers leave Albany for Washington in mid-June, in early July the 34th New York got the call. On the morning of July 3rd the men of the "Herkimer County Regiment" boarded the river steamer "Western World" and began the trip down the Hudson to Washington and the "seat of war."

___

The 34th spend July 4, 1861 in New York City, and on the morning of the 5th the regiment boarded a train for Washington, which was reached on the 6th. *The Washington Intelligencer* noted their arrival:

> "The Thirty-Fourth New York Regiment, Col. Ladue, arrived in this city last night about nine o'clock. They are from Herkimer County and number nearly one thousand. They seem to be a hearty body of men." [13]

On Sunday, July 7th, the 34th marched to Kalorama Heights in the Washington suburbs and encamped there for the better part of three weeks. At Kalorama the regiment suffered it's first casualty, George Waterhouse, the former *Journal* employee and the paper's "34th correspondent." While he was bending over to fill a canteen from a nearby stream, Waterhouse's loaded and capped pistol fell from his pocket, discharged when it struck a rock, and sent a ball through his heart. No suitable casket for shipment of the body to Little Falls could be obtained, so Waterhouse was buried at Kalorama with full military honors.

With the death of Waterhouse, Fairfield's Lt. William Walton became the new *Journal* correspondent. In describing the 34th's morale while at Kalorama Walton wrote:

> "As to the regiment, we are in 'fighting condition' and only fear that we shall have no opportunity of invading 'the sacred soil of Virginia.' To be sure we may at any moment be disappointed as we are under orders to be ready to march at twenty minutes notice. As a consequence, we are kept in 'durance vile' like a lot of naughty school boys, being unable to get permission to go out into the city for love or money. Had we not one of the finest camps around Washington, if not in the world, this confinement would be unendurable. As it is with plenty of room and food and water and shade &c. we make out to live and grow fat." [14]

Not all the men agreed with Walton as attested to by a number of desertions —eight alone from Company C—that occurred in the 34th.

At Kalorama the 34th was able to discard their outmoded converted flintlock, smoothbore muskets. Through the intercession of New York Gov. Edwin Morgan, Washington Dep. Comdr. Gen. Joseph Mansfield and Gen. Francis Spinner, Treasurer of the U.S. and a resident of Mohawk, the regiment received new .58 caliber Enfield rifles.

The 34th New York did not take part in the war's first large engagement, the July 21st Battle of Bull Run. The regiment had been ordered to be ready to march, but at the last minute the order had been countermanded. From their camp on the Heights of Kalorama they listened to the sounds of the battle, and as that day was a Sunday, reflected on a "Sabbath sermon of a different kind." Lieutenant Walton related:

> "The fact is, myself and indeed all the rest of the Regiment are 'decidedly excited.' Many of us are now gathered at a point of our encampment overlooking the Potomac and the celebrated 'Arlington Heights' eagerly gazing towards the 'sacred soil,' and intently, if not intensely, listening to the distant boom of cannon which continually reaches our ears and tells us that Northerner and Southerner are engaged in deadly strife at Manassas Junction, you may perhaps think it is very foolish to get excited at such a distance from the scene of action, but come you, and listen as we have, one, two, three and six hours to a constant cannonading (and by the word constant, I mean incessant, for at times there is hardly a second between the discharges) knowing at the same time it is your friends and relatives that are in peril and danger, that many must fall, that many may be thousands, as naught but desperate valor and headlong courage can overcome a foe eighty thousand strong,* entrenched behind massive fortifications, forgetting not the many deeds of bravery, there to be performed - the gallant charge, the brave stand, and think we say of these things as we do now and your hand too, will tremble and your heart beat faster than it is wont . . . ." [15]

The Federal forces under the command of Gen. Irwin McDowell enjoyed initial success at Bull Run, but as the day wore on the exhausted Union boys were struck by fresh Confederate troops and routed. The Federal casualty count, which numbered nearly three thousand, shocked the people of the North. Among the Union dead was Little Falls resident William Watches, a private in the 3rd New York Fire Zouaves.

After the Federal defeat at Bull Run, Abraham Lincoln's first priority was the defense of his capital. A cordon of pickets and forts was established around Washington with the 34th New York joining the chain. On July 28th the regiment broke camp at Kalorama and seven of the companies marched to Camp Jackson near Seneca Mills. The remaining three companies, B, C and I, trudged to Great Falls. Spread along seventeen miles of the Potomac riverfront in Maryland, the 34th took custody of the defensive perimeter from two miles east of Great Falls to eight miles west of Seneca Mills.

* Confederate forces at Bull Run were less than half this number.

The three day march to their posts, although uneventful, was still a rich experience for the country boys. *Journal* correspondent Walton wrote:

> "Leaving the city we took the Potomac river road, which for a long ways, leads through a most fertile and beautiful country. Indeed, while passing along and noting the large and stately residences of the chivalry, with the darkies little and big, yellow and brown and black, surrounding and hanging on the gate posts, staring and gabbering while 'Massa' and 'Missus' and the young ladies stood back on the porch. . . . Several times during the day we stopped for refreshments at cool and shady spots and as night drew nigh picked out our camp in a fine wood near the road-side, where after eating our supper of bread and cold meat and stationing our guards, we lay down with our blankets around us and the blue sky over us and slept as soundly as when leaving the hard mattress of old Fairfield Seminary. . . .
>
> The next morning aroused betimes by the reveille, we arose, drew in the guards, packed away our knapsacks and after an immense sight of going without getting gone we started and traveled on a brisk pace. . . . This night we 'pitched our moving tents' in a mild, romantic spot called Bells Mills. Our nights' experience was the same as before with this exception, that about three o'clock in the morning we were awakened by a heavy rain, but thanks to the kind folks of Fairfield we drew our rubber blankets over us and resumed our slumbers and our dreams. Arising at five o'clock we made an early start, and we assure you the forenoon's experience was most charming. Imagine seven or eight hundred men trudging through the mud, the rain pouring in torrents, clothes, flags, everything wet through, and add to this the fording of a stream twenty to thirty feet wide and from two and one-half to three feet deep and you have one page from 'the eventful Life of a Soldier' . . . " [16]

Camp Jackson was in the wilderness in comparison to Kalorama. Twice a day mail service was reduced to once a week, and all provisions for the men and the horses (one hundred ninety horses had been needed to haul the regiments' train of forty-eight wagons) had to be purchased in Washington and transported to camp.

Runaway slaves soon overran the camp and were largely unclothed, unfed and without shelter. The "contraband of war" policy had yet to be formulated by the Federal Government; therefore, there was no plan for dealing with the refugees. Many were returned to their owners, but a few were secretly shipped north or employed by the officers as servants.

Also occupying the camp were a number of officers' wives. The favorite of the men was Mrs. Lewis Clark, the product of the whirlwind Albany courtship. Lieutenant Walton wrote:

> "The Daughter of the Regiment however is with us always and seems to enjoy the privations and hardships of camp life." [17]

Unfortunately army life didn't seem to agree with her husband. Sgt. Lewis Clark was discharged, for medical reasons, from the service in September.

Besides trading shots with the enemy pickets on the Virginia side and occasionally directing artillery for the 1st Rhode Island Artillery, camp life was easy. Correspondent Walton informed the *Journal's* readers:

"To be sure the enemy are frequently seen on the other side and now and then fire across, but what does that amount to as long as they are so careful or so careless as to hit no one.

The Regiment is abundantly supplied with all the necessities of life and with many of its luxuries. The government is very liberal, and your old friend and neighbor Nathan Easterbrooks, the Quartermaster, is very kind and generous. . . . We are in the midst of a fertile country. Excellent hay and oats are abundant and there is no lack of fresh beef and butter, eggs, &c. Grumblers and falsifiers may talk on, but be sure, Mr. Editor, that none of the Thirty-Fourth have occasion for fault finding. None suffer but those who shamefully waste their rations. [18]

The Thirty-Fourth have two large camp ovens, in which six hundred two pound loaves, of super excellent bread are baked daily, besides pies, that rival the pastry of the Astor or Metropolitan, and biscuits. One of the chief bakers of the Thirty-Fourth, was formerly the baker of Lord Lyons. He makes his yeast from hops and water alone and no better, sweeter or lighter bread was ever tasted." [19]

Three incidents were notable in the 34th's stay at Camp Jackson. Later in the war these events would hardly bear mention, but at this point, they were important and singular to the glory seeking men.

The first was the expedition to capture "the notorious desperado," Jack Cross. Cross was a "violent Secesh" alleged to have murdered a Union colonel and lynched two other Union men, one of whom was his brother-in-law. For three weeks parties from the 34th scoured the countryside looking for Cross, but the "tough old sinner" eluded them. When the chase was abandoned, all that could be shown for the boys' efforts were two prisoners, Cross' brother and a friend, and a supply of corn and potatoes appropriated from his orchard and fields. Finally in mid-October the fugitive was apprehended. William Walton wrote:

"It seems that, a negro woman having told some of our men, that he was in his house, a party was formed and on search he was found stowed away in a small hole off from the garret. It is rumored that he has here been hid for some three weeks and moreover that some of the officers of the Thirty-Fourth were knowing to it. We trust that this is not so, though among the men it is almost universally believed. He is a fine looking fellow and, by the way, has one of the handsomest sisters in all the region round about, which fact throws light perhaps on a certain disputed point. He will probably soon be sent to Washington for trial. The result we know not, but trust he will have justice done him for he has caused us a world of trouble." [20]

The second incident had a more military aspect. On the Virginia side of the Potomac, opposite the 34th were three or four houses that sheltered rebels taking "pot-shots" at the Union pickets. To remedy the situation, James Faville of Salisbury and Johnny Johnson from Little Falls, nicknamed the "infants" because they stood well over six feet tall and the McLaughlin brothers, Robert and John from Salisbury, boated across the river one night and set fire to the houses. The enemy sharpshooters fled and the quartet from the 34th started back across the river barely escaping a band of angry rebels. No shots were fired until trigger happy Federal pickets fired at the Herkimer County boys. Fortunately their aim wasn't very good and the men made it back safely.

The first battle casualties suffered by the 34th New York were realized in the third incident. Captain Sponable, with or without orders, reports varied, led a squad of eleven men across the river under the cover of darkness to reconnoiter a reported rebel buildup four miles away. The men stumbled through woods and fields for a few miles before blundering into an ambush by three rebel companies, who unleashed "a perfect volley."

The sound of gunfire roused the camp of the 34th and in a short time the men lined the riverbank scanning the water for signs of Sponable's squad. Eventually a boat was sighted and as it approached the bank the men forlornly noted that there was only one man on board. On landing, Pvt. William Graves of Champlain told a sad story, he was the only survivor as all the rest of the party had been killed outright or else mortally wounded. Throughout the rest of the night and into the next day eight more survivors from Sponable's scouting party swam the Potomac and staggered back to camp. Only two of the men were actually wounded, but all of them were thoroughly soaked and furious at Private Graves for taking their only boat. Wells Sponable, minus a boot, his hat and his revolver, had floated across in a swamped rowboat. Henry Bramley and Christian Zaugg of Company D were the two wounded men, the former slightly and the latter seriously, a ball having passed through his cheek. Zaugg, who received a medal from the Pope and had participated in the charge of the Light Brigade, or so he said, had escaped capture by lying in a pond all night with just his mouth and nostrils above the water's surface.

Of the three men who had not returned, Oliver Darling of Salisbury had been killed and Robert Gracey and Cyrus Kellogg of Crown Point had been taken prisoner. Gracey, who was also seriously wounded, would recover and escape back to the 34th within a month. Of his hospitalization and escape Gracey would write:

> "I couldn't have been treated better by my father than I was treated there, I think that my treatment in the hospital was better than that of their own men. They appeared to have plenty of everything but coffee-of which they substituted whiskey and with, the majority of the men this is far preferable. . . . I feigned weakness and restlessness. Why, I was so weak that it required two men to help me walk and I was restless that enormous quantities of opium were necessary to make me sleep nights. This weakness and restlessness continued until I had saved quite a quantity of opium and as it is customary with the 'secesh' to take a drink of coffee at night, I slipped some of the opium in and waited for the effect and it come along anon. I bid adieu to my friends and started." [21]

While encamped at Fort Jackson, disease was a far greater threat to the men of the 34th than were rebel bullets. "Intermittent Fever" (malaria), typhus, dysentery and other maladies visited the regiment. Since leaving camp at Kalorama Heights five men had died of diseases, including Lt. James R. Carr of Tuscarora and former

Journal apprentice, Homer Wraught, who succumbed to "dumb ague." Boxes of hospital supplies, pillows, blankets, dressing gowns and slippers, were sent to the regiment by the ladies of Poland, Cold Brook and Little Falls. Considering the poor hygiene and general lack of sanitation in most camps the 34th's health was better than that of most regiments. Much of the credit could be given to the Regimental Surgeon, Dr. Socrates Sherman.

On the morning of October 21st, the 34th broke camp at Seneca Mills and began an eight-mile march to Poolesville. Awaiting them was a part in the disastrous Battle of Ball's Bluff.

CHAPTER II

"The enemy and victory before us"

Fall/ Winter 1862, Spring 1862 - Formation of the 97th N.Y.
Ball's Bluff - The Peninsula Campaign - The 97th Heads South

On July 22, 1861, one day after the Federal defeat at Bull Run, Congress autho-rized President Lincoln to accept the services of volunteers for three years, in num-bers not exceeding one million. Although no formal call was issued and no formal quota was set, New York was "requested" to furnish its "fair share" of men. Charles Wheelock, a prominent Boonville produce dealer, was appointed by Gover-nor Morgan to organize a regiment in the Mohawk Valley region. Wheelock was also empowered to establish a camp for this new regiment in his area of recruitment. Since this unit was to be drawn from Oneida and Herkimer counties, Wheelock cen-trally located his camp in Boonville. John Spofford of Brockett's Bridge (Dolgeville after 1881) and J.P. Leslie of Little Falls were selected to head the recruiting drive in Herkimer County.

To encourage enlistments, Federal, state and county bounties, to the sum of two hundred dollars, were offered along with the possibility of a land grant. As was done in April, many of the Mohawk Valley communities staged Union rallies complete with brass bands, bonfires and patriotic orations. The pro-war *Journal* gave its ratio-nale for volunteering.

> "The inducements for enlisting in the army of the Government were never so strong as now. In the first place, the pay of the American soldier [thir-teen dollars a month to a Private] exceeds that of any other.
> 2nd. He is rationed, clothed and paid from the time of enlistment.
> 3rd. He is provided with competent medical attendants and receives his

pay as usual if sick.

4th. He is placed under careful and experienced officers who are obliged to pass a rigid examination before commissions are given them.

5th. He may secure a part of his wages to be paid to his family or friends.

6th. His family is, in almost every locality, furnished with proper care and provision during his absence.

7th. He is earning, in most instances more than he could do if he should remain at home and is sure of his pay.

8th. He is promised a Bounty of one hundred dollars on discharge from the service.

9th. He will also, without doubt, receive a land warrant for one hundred sixty acres of land in addition to the Bounty of one hundred dollars.

10th. He will, if disabled or wounded, or his widow will, if he be killed, be liberally pensioned by the Government.

11th. Business at home is exceedingly dull and the prospect is not encouraging to the laborer for months to come.

12th. The country calls upon him. She needs his services. The demands of patriotism, the perils of Liberty, and the endangered blessings of a free and treasured Government, the threatened ties of the very home circle, urge him forward to the path of duty and honor. All that a patriot or a freeman would hold most dear is at stake. Government, religious tolerance, free institution, a free press and a free speech, A COUNTRY is periled in a wicked rebellion.

Yes, no such inducements were ever before offered to the soldier and no such honors were ever given as will be vouchsafed to those who now nobly bare the breast and raise the arm in response to a nations cry." [1]

By the 15th of October, nine companies of men from Oneida and Herkimer Counties had been organized in the new regiment. The Boonville campsite chosen by Wheelock was in a converted canal warehouse and was dubbed Camp Rathbone. About one-quarter of the over nine hundred officers and men were from Herkimer County, with a majority of these men being from Salisbury, Brockett's Bridge and the north country towns. While awaiting official numerical designation, the regiment adopted the titles "Conkling Rifles," in honor of a popular congressman from that district, and "Third Oneida," the 14th and 26th New York from Oneida County having preceded it.

With the war in the South having come to a standstill, the new regiment was permitted to remain in Boonville to complete its training. Drill and the occasional parade for the benefit of the residents of the village constituted the greatest part of the men's martial duties. A grand dress parade, at which the ladies of Boonville presented the regiment with a stand of colors, was held two days before Christmas. The flags had been purchased with the proceeds from a four day long "Ladies Fair."

In the close quarters of the canal warehouse barracks, disease spread quickly. A measles epidemic laid low sixty men, killing three of them, and cases of diphtheria, scarlet fever and typhoid were not uncommon. The people of Boonville, Alder Creek, Forestport and other north country communities lent a hand in caring for the sick and sent hospital supplies.

Finally, on February 15th, 1862, Wheelock's regiment was mustered into U.S. service as the 97th Regiment, New York State Volunteers. The Herkimer County companies were D and F from Salisbury, commanded by Captains Rouse Egelston and Stephen Hutchinson and Company I from Little Falls, under Capt. James Leslie. Companies C, E and H also contained a number of Herkimer County boys. The chief regimental officers were: Col. Charles Wheelock; Lt. Col. John Spofford; Maj. Charles Northrup and Adj. Charles Buck.

At about the time that the "Third Oneida" was moving into Camp Rathbone in Boonville, the 34th New York was pulling up stakes at Camp Jackson near Seneca Mills and was preparing to venture into Virginia. On the morning of October twenty-first, the 34th started off up the Potomac River in the direction of Poolesville, but two miles en route their destination was changed to Edward's Ferry.

Across the Potomac from Edward's Ferry were situated four regiments of the Confederate infantry in the vicinity of a small village called Leesburg. The Union commander in this zone, Gen. Charles Stone, was being prodded by the army's dashing new leader, George McClellan, to make a demonstration of force somewhere along this line. Stone, after surveying the front, targeted the rebel force at Leesburg and developed a foolproof plan to crush it. Since the better part of the enemy's strength was near Edward's Ferry, Stone would send Gen. Willis Gorman's brigade across the Potomac at that point to hold the rebels in place. In the meantime, Col. Edward Baker would cross the river at Harrison's Island, a few miles to the north and would swing back south, hitting the Confederates in front of Gorman on the left flank and in the rear. Unfortunately, the Confederate commander, Gen. N.G. Evans, had gotten wind of Stone's plan and had a substantial part of his force poised and ready to greet Baker's men when they crossed at Harrison's Island. Down at Edward's Ferry, Gorman's brigade was slow in crossing the river and those units that did cross were pinned down by one regiment of Mississippians.[2]

The 34th New York, now attached to Gorman's brigade, reached Edward's Ferry at about noon and waited in line to cross the Potomac. As with the Federal units that preceded them, when the 34th reached the Virginia shore they were of little use to Colonel Baker's already overwhelmed troops. Louis Chapin of the 34th would write:

> "The means of transportation to the western bank of the river were nothing to brag of. Two old scows had been conscripted from the adjacent Chesapeake and Ohio Canal, and were poled back and forth in primitive fashion. During the afternoon our turn came, and for the first time the regiment squatted on the sacred soil of old Virginia. Pickets were thrown out, and the scant forces, thus quite isolated, awaited events. Toward midnight, most unsavory rumors began flying about. These were to the effect that Colonel Baker's forces, which had crossed at Harrison's Island, above, had been badly cut up; that Colonel Baker himself, had been killed; and that the victorious enemy were now on their way to give us a dose of the same medicine. Immediately began a hurried retreat back across the river."[3]

Colonel Baker's men had crossed the Potomac and climbed a steep hill, called

Ball's Bluff, only to be trapped with their backs to the cliff by three of the Confederate regiments from Edward's Ferry. Initially the Federals held their ground, but with the death of Colonel Baker, the battle turned into a rout. Without a sufficient number of boats to remove the troops, many a frantic Federal soldier slid down the cliff face into the river, only to be shot or drowned. The regiments downstream, which included the 34th New York, in their failure to break the enemy line at Edward's Ferry, had freed up rebel reinforcements to aid in the attack on Colonel Baker's command.

Horace Greeley in describing the stalemate at Edward's Ferry noted:

> "Meanwhile General Stone had directed General Gorman to throw across the river at Edward's Ferry, a small force, which made a cautious reconnaissance for about three miles, on the road to Leesburg, when, coming suddenly upon a Mississippi regiment, it exchanged volleys and returned. General Gorman's entire brigade was thrown over at this point during the day; but, as it did not advance, its mere presence on the Virginia side of the Potomac, so far from the scene of the actual combat, subserved no purpose." [4]

For his part in the debacle at Ball's Bluff, in which the Federals would take almost one thousand casualties with nothing to show for it, General Stone would be arrested and without the benefit of a trial would spend six months in a military prison.

After retreating to the Maryland side the 34th New York, along with the rest of their brigade, re-crossed to the Virginia shore and spent two days under fire. On October 23rd the Federals pulled back to Maryland once more. As Lieutenant Walton wrote, the men of the 34th believed they had done their duty:

> "A word as to our Virginia expedition. We see that the papers have sadly confounded it with the affair at Conrads Ferry [Ball's Bluff] with which we had nothing to do. All that we were ordered we accomplished and were not repulsed as many of the papers intimate. We seized the Ferry-advanced inland four or five miles, drove back the enemy with heavy loss, held our position for two days, in the face of a heavy force and then successfully recrossed the river. . . ." [5]

After leaving Edward's Ferry, the 34th New York continued on its march to Poolesville, Maryland. At Poolesville, winter quarters were established alongside the 15th Massachusetts, 1st Minnesota, and 82nd New York. At this camp, dubbed Camp McClellan, the 34th New York would remain until spring.

The winter of 1861-62 announced itself in the Mohawk Valley late in November with a snow storm that dropped over eighteen inches on the hills. Farmers broke out their sleighs and "good sledding" became the password.

The beginning of winter marked the start of the indoors entertainment season. Moving through the Mohawk Valley this winter were the Barker Family Singers, comedian Ossian Dodge, and Minnie Crawford the celebrated blind vocalist. At Concert Hall in Little Falls the crowd favorites were Fox's Minstrels and Ben

Blood's lectures on Napoleon.

The winter season also was the time for lady's church groups in Herkimer County to hold their annual bazaars, typical of which was the "Fair and Festival" of the Ladies Sewing Society of the Methodist Church of Little Falls. Held at the Benton House, the ladies sold baked goods, displayed their arts and crafts and served up ice cream and various other treats. Afterwards there was music and dancing, the latter being rather lively as all three Little Falls Fire Companies were in attendance.

With Christmas drawing near, advertisements for gift ideas crowded the pages of the *Journal*. Bennett Bros. of Little Falls warned shoppers that unless they hurried they would miss the store's sale on Dr. J. Bovee Dad's "celebrated, all curing, Wine Bitters."

As to military happenings in the Mohawk Valley . . . Captains Sponable and Corcoran, accompanied by Sgt. George Morse, were home on furlough trying to recruit fifty men for the 34th New York. Competition was coming from Captain Leslie and Lts. Romeyn Roof and George Skinner recruiting for the 97th New York in Little Falls and Newport. Rev. D.B. White with the help of the Remingtons (Philo, Samuel and Eliphalet), who were offering ten dollars and a new revolver (probably the Remington 1858 .44 Cal. "New Model Army") to each enlistee, was aiding Wheelock's officers in the Ilion area. In the towns of Russia and Ohio, officers of the Second New York Artillery were enlisting men for Company M, Morgan's Artillery.

Mohawk Valley men were also joining the elite 44th New York, better known as "The People's Ellsworth's." The 44th drew men from throughout New York State, initially accepting only one man from each village or ward. New recruits also had to meet rather high physical standards and were required to buy their own equipment, but after awhile these standards were relaxed. Nearly fifty men from Herkimer County would be drawn into the "Ellsworth's."

The 97th remained in Boonville at Camp Rathbone. Since the paymaster had yet to make an appearance, and wouldn't until spring, Colonel Wheelock was called upon to loan thousands of dollars to his men to help them support their families.

For the most part the soldiers of the 97th were well behaved during their stay in Boonville. The only exception came when a group of men ventured out one night in February and wrecked Adams bowling alley and billiard saloon and destroyed casks of liquor at Warren Hunt's store. A temperance motive was suggested, and because the culprits couldn't be identified, Oneida County was made libel for the damages.[6]

Down in Maryland the 34th New York was snug in its winter quarters situated among forty thousand other Federal troops encamped within a four mile radius. Just across the Potomac River sat the rebel army also bedded down for the season. The Union army was not stagnant in their winter quarters. Under the leadership of General McClellan discipline tightened and drilling seemed almost constant. Company, regimental and brigade drills, complete with regimental bands and the occasional grand review helped the men gain confidence in their commander and themselves. William Walton of the 34th New York wrote:

"To drill-if not the chief end of man seems to be the only end of a soldier. In the word drill you have the sum and substance of our experience for it is nothing but squad, company, regimental, battalion and brigade drills from morn to night. But of this we will not complain for it is just what is making soldiers of us and just what will render the thirty-fourth more 'terrible to the enemy than an army with banners' for our General will tell you that we had better be without banners than without drill or discipline as he calls it."[7]

To add pride to the regiment and to bring civility to their camp the men of the 34th organized a band and built a chapel for the chaplain, Rev. Van Petten. Lieutenant Walton related:

"Among the 'new things under the sun' we must not forget to mention our band. We will call it our band because we are not ashamed to own it, regarding it as a grand success, showing what can be accomplished under difficulties. . . . The subject was laid before the boys and it required but very little blowing to raise the needful and the instruments were ordered. No sooner did they arrive than they were seized upon by old blowers, who having deserted the Home Guards to serve their country, were by no means loth to return to their former avocation. They are fast attaining proficiency and woe be to him who dares a word against our band."[8]

"Through the exertions of our Chaplain, there has recently been erected a large and commodious Chapel, which of course is a great addition to our camp. In it we have preaching each Sabbath, and on Sabbath, Tuesday and Thursday evenings we have a prayer meeting: on Monday evening Bible class and Wednesday evening Lyceum."[9]

The first shelters used by the 34th at Camp McClellan were simple army tents. The Northern boys, believing winters in the "Sunny South" would be mild, were unprepared. William McLean of Fairfield reported:

"Winter has come at last, in right good earnest. Thermometer below 'Temperate,' two inches of snow on the ground and the river and canal frozen over, force us to the conclusion that our 'warm, Sunny South' has emphatically 'played out' for the present at least. Mittens, overcoats and fires are greatly to be desired during the day, and at night we long for the dear old homes far away. . . . The night being the coldest of the season we had to lie close to each other to keep warm, and were rather uncomfortable with all our blankets and straw which we spread on the bottom of our tents. The tents are just large enough for four or five to sleep in and when they lie down they cover its whole area."[10]

Having learned that the winter weather of Maryland was far from being "tropical" the men laid out a more permanent camp and constructed better quarters. Of the 34th's camp William Walton boasted:

"A description of the Barracks may perhaps interest your readers. Imagine, then, three sides of a square surrounded by cabins, with a front of some ten or twelve feet, constructed of logs and either thatched or roofed with shingles or boards. The appearance of the interior, of course, depends somewhat on the occupants, though in all there is plenty of light and, may be, if required, an abundance of warmth. In fact, considering everything, we have cause to feel proud of them, for not only do they answer the purpose, but some of them, especially the Hospital, Commissary Building and the quarters of the field and line officers, present evidences of architectural ability by no means to be despised."[11]

Interchange with the rebels across the river was common and normally quite friendly. Although contact with the enemy was against orders, many meetings were made in mid-stream to exchange coffee, tobacco and newspapers. But of this interchange, the men most of all just enjoyed talking with the enemy. The 34th's Lieutenant Walton noted:

"... they have become quite bold now and come down to the water's edge and talk with us hours at a time. These tetes a tetes, though conducted at the top of the voice are of great interest to both parties, many questions on various subjects being readily answered."[12]

When the river froze, the Northern boys sat on the river bank wishing they had brought their ice skates, as they watched the rebels cutting figures on the ice. However, dealings with the enemy were not always friendly and at times turned into a deadly sport. Walton informed the *Journal's* readers:

"The perpetual skirmishing of our outpost pickets is one source of excitement. The Mississippi Tigers, owing probably to the exhilaratory news-querry, to them or us?—from Roanoke and Forts Henry and Donelson, have become emphatically saucy of late, and vent their spleen by firing on us at every opportunity. . . . It is indeed not very pleasant to go to the river for water and know that you are offering a splendid mark to half a dozen rebels who are sure to fire on you, or, to be sitting with your comrades around a fire and have a ball go whizzing through your midst, or be walking along and suddenly having a dozen balls flying past you some cutting off the branches just above your head and others ploughing up the ground in all directions around you. Nothing however could please the boys more . . . for men used to hunting in the North woods are just in their element while shooting wild beasts of any kind, even though they be Mississippi Tigers. They have been several times to bear off wounded or dead men, and it is a veritable fact, beyond dispute, that Snyder of Co. C late of Norway, did actually kill, the other day their Field Officer of the Day."[13]

Christmas 1861 brought presents from home to the boys along the Potomac Line. Ladies Aid Societies that had sprung up in Herkimer County sent boxes packed with mittens, scarves, quilts, jams, cakes and brandies to their townsmen or favored companies. Any leftovers were distributed to members of the 34th from other counties, who in turn shared their gifts with the Mohawk Valley boys.

Christmas Day was celebrated with comical dress parades and with the exchange of positions for the day by the officers and men. Later on the boys dined on turkey and fried oysters.

Overall however, the stay in winter quarters was marked by sheer tedium. Moses

Bliss, a member of the 44th New York and a resident of Salisbury, described a typical day in winter camp writing:

"Perhaps I can best illustrate the manner in which we manage to 'kill time,' by giving you some memoranda of a couple of days duty. We get up in the morning, look out of the door of the tent, see a couple of inches of snow on the ground and find it raining. We console ourselves with the thought that we shan't have to drill to-day and that it isn't our turn to stand guard. We venture out in the mud to get our breakfast, cold bacon and coffee, and then seat ourselves in our tent to read a book, (for occasionally we find a book) or write to our friends, congratulating ourselves that we are free from duty for the day. Pretty soon we hear the Sergeant Major at the head of the street calling out 'Sergeant Allen detail three men out of Company B, to report with axes at the Adjutant's tent.' A cold shiver runs through our veins, for just as likely as any way we shall be the unlucky ones. We listen anxiously till we hear the footsteps of the Sergeant going down the street, when we turn to our book or paper with a feeling of thankfulness in our heart. About ten minutes pass, when the voice of the Sergeant Major is again heard. 'Sergeant Allen, detail four men to report to Corporal Harris at the head of the street, to cut wood for the guard house.' We groan in spirit for we feel a premonition that we shall catch it this time. In a minute or two the well known phiz of our Sergeant is thrust into the tent and, 'report yourself at the head of the street,' seals our doom. Sadly and disconsolately we put up our things hunt up an axe, 'report at the head of the street' and are marched off to the woods. We select as good a tree as we can find and commence haggling. I say haggling, for such axes as, Uncle Sam furnishes can't be found outside the army. We work and sweat till we get a couple loads of wood short enough to burn when we start for camp. We arrive there about the middle of the afternoon eat our dinner, 'old horse,' and make a pass for our tents. About the time we get comfortably warm and dry, the 'assembly' beats and we have to go out on dress parade. This over, we get our supper, coffee, and den up in our tents again, thankful that we shall not have to get out again till tattoo. At tattoo, we learn that we are detailed for guard duty on the morrow, and then with many misgivings, wet, cold and tired we turn in for the night." [14]

As an avenue of escape from boredom many men turned to alcohol. Although the enlisted men were forbidden to have hard liquor—officers on the other hand could purchase it openly at the commissary—somehow the men could find a supply. William Walton informed the *Journal's* readers:

"I am sorry to state, yet I am fearful it is too true, that drunkeness is on the increase in the army of the Potomac. . . . During cold, wet weather when men have been on duty, it is considered by both officers and men, especially by the former, necessary that they should have some whiskey. . . . It is not an uncommon thing to see a private tight, and even sometimes when on guard: but this is not surprising when so many Commissioned officers are frequently in the same condition." [15]

Horace Hurlbut from the town of Norway, "the Reformed Drunkard" who had lectured on temperance throughout the Mohawk Valley, travelled south and gave a timely talk on the evils of alcohol at the 34th's chapel.

Among other diversions enjoyed by the men in winter quarters were, the occasional patrol, foraging about the countryside for hay and corn and the appearance of Professor Lowe's hot air balloon. Of the Professor's balloon, which was being employed by McClellan to monitor rebel troop movements, Lieut. Walton wrote:

> "Considerable stir was occasioned last Saturday morning by the report that Prof. Lowe of balloon notoriety, had come up from Washington the day before and was, that evening going to make an ascension to reconnoitre the enemy's position. True enough, about two o'clock his monster gas-bag, which he has christened 'The Intrepid', was seen slowly rising above the trees, a short distance off and presenting, when the sun shone on it, an object of exceedingly great beauty. At first we felt a lively interest in his ballonship, but now that repeated ascensions have satiated our curiosity, we treat him with chilling indifference, hardly deigning a moment's notice." [16]

Never far from the men was the disease, sickness and death associated with the winter camps. Typhoid and dysentery were constant companions and the spring and summer scourge, malaria, was replaced by "pleuro-pneumonia." During their time at Camp McClellan, four men from the 34th New York died and over twenty were discharged due to illness. Among the dead was Jason Bennett of the town of Ohio and George Saterlee of Salisbury. Dr. Socrates Sherman, the regiment's surgeon, did such an admirable job tending the sick, that the men of the 34th presented him with a bright new sword complete with a sash and a belt.

The strength of the 34th was further reduced when twenty men volunteered to join the Western Gunboat Flotilla.* In addition, during the stay at Camp McClellan the 34th realized eleven desertions. The most notable of the deserters was Louis Chapin the *Journal* printer. Chapin was put in the guardhouse for sleeping on sentry duty, but fearing that he would be given the death penalty made his escape. A number of days later he returned to camp on his own volition and all charges were dropped.

On February 26th, 1862, the 34th left Camp McClellan and started for Harper's Ferry. Crossing the Potomac to the Virginia shore, the regiment marched to Adamstown where they loaded on box cars for the rest of the trip. One week was spent at Harper's Ferry and three days at nearby Bolivar Heights before orders were received on March 7th to proceed to Charlestown.

Two of the towns visited by the 34th, Harper's Ferry and Charlestown, had played prominent parts three years earlier in the ill-fated raid of Abolitionist John Brown. On October 16, 1859 Brown led a band of fellow fanatics on an attack against the U.S. Arsenal at Harper's Ferry in hopes of securing enough firearms to support an expected slave uprising. The raiders were soon driven into a nearby Engine House and after a brief shootout with Federal troops under the command of Col. Robert E. Lee, Brown was taken into custody. Imprisoned in Charlestown, Brown

---

* These men would be involved in fights along the Mississippi River.

was tried and convicted of treason and on December 2nd he was hung. To many people of the North, John Brown became a martyr and in this vein the sightseeing boys of the 34th toured Harper's Ferry in awe. Lt. William Walton related:

> "The place [Harper's Ferry] presents a most desolate appearance. War is to be seen everywhere. . . . One of the most interesting sights is the engine house where John Brown made his brave and desperate stand. The pictures of it in the papers were perfect, and therefore it was readily recognized by us. The holes in the wall through which the devoted band fired, the iron doors burst open by the U.S. Marines, are all to be seen and you may feel assured that we gazed upon them with deep interest. We shall tomorrow be at Charlestown, where the Virginia cowards under brave Wise consummated the John Brown tragedy by the drop scene." [17]

After a short stay in Charlestown, the 34th marched on through Berryville almost reaching Winchester before turning about and heading back to Bolivar Heights. During this excursion two important events in the regiment's history occurred, the resignation of Colonel Ladew and the incorporation of the 34th New York into the 2nd Army Corps.

In General McClellan's reorganization of the army the 2nd Corps was formed and placed under the command of Gen. Edwin Sumner. The 34th New York was assigned to the 1st Brigade of the 2nd Division, a position they would retain throughout their tenure in the service.

On March 20th, Col. William Ladew, who had been absent from the regiment much of the last five months due to illness, resigned his command of the 34th New York. James Suiter of Herkimer was promoted to colonel and given command of the regiment and in turn Byron Laflin moved up to lieutenant colonel and Charles Brown to major.

Back in the Mohawk Valley, an ice storm in late March bent trees a foot in diameter over to the ground, but the weather was quickly warming and all signs pointed to the coming of an early and prosperous spring. The price of cheese was on the rise, two new canal boats - each capable of carrying seven thousand bushels of grain - had been built by the Little Falls Transportation Co. and the state senate had approved the building of a new road from Mohawk to Richfield Springs.

At Concert Hall in Little Falls the young ladies of Miss Wright's Select School held an Exhibition. The Alleghanies, "well known singers and bell-ringers," entertained, and for fifteen cents one could view a large Panorama of the War and listen to "the wonderful powers of a youth on a wooden whistle."

Readers of the *Journal* regularly followed the activities of the 34th New York and 97th New York, but were also treated to correspondence from Mohawk Valley boys in the 44th New York, Berdan's Sharpshooters and even from Lt. Lester Beardslee aboard the War Steamer "Saratoga" off the coast of Africa.

On the war front, Gen. Ulysses Grant won glorious victories at Forts Henry and Donelson and fought Gen. Albert Johnson to a draw at the bloody battle of Shiloh in Tennessee. In far off Arkansas, Gen. Samuel Curtis defeated Confederate Gen. Earl

Van Dorn at Pea Ridge, securing Missouri to the Union, and off of Hampton Roads, Virginia, the "Monitor" and "Merrimac" neutralized each other in the first clash of ironclad ships. This latter battle caused a "tongue in cheek" sigh of relief from Jordanville. In a letter to the *Journal* "Bird O' Freedom" wrote:

> "Nothing can depict the consternation of the inhabitants of this quiet village upon the arrival of the news that the Merrimac had attacked and destroyed our fleet at the mouth of the Chesapeake. You remember this town is situated on the Susquehannah and everybody knows that the Susquehannah empties into the Chesapeake Bay and that it is but a short distance from that place to Fortress Monroe. So you can see at once the great danger in which we were placed, (thanks to the little Monitor we are safe now) for had she succeeded in annihilating our fleet what could hinder her from steaming up the Susquehannah and bombarding our town or plowing us up with her iron horn. The excitement rose to about one hundred seventy five pounds to the square inch.
>
> The officers of the village immediately assembled and, after a long and earnest consultation it was decided that 'Something must be done.' In pursuance to this resolution Lyman's dam and saw mill situated about one mile below the village, was selected as the first strategic point to be defended. If defeated there our brave boys were to retreat to Fort Beavertown where the last man was to die in the last ditch.
>
> Upon taking an inventory of our arms, we found we could muster only one iron fifty-six and one twenty-four; our long one pounder, having become disgusted, burst a short time previous. With these it was resolved to do or die. All this time it was gravely reported that General C____ had determined to board her if she attacked us and two horse pistols were shown as evidence of his desperate intentions. A committee was about starting for Washington to represent our defenceless condition and ask an appropriation for our security when the news arrived that the little Monitor had attacked the monster and driven her back to Norfolk. We immediately freighted the plucky little thing with our hopes and subsided." [18]

Since the beginning of the war the primary strategic objective of the Lincoln government was the capture of the Confederate capital, Richmond. The harsh lesson of Bull Run and reports of an even stronger rebel defensive line along the Rappahannock River ruled out a direct overland approach from Washington to Richmond. The Union army's commander in chief, George McClellan, suggested an alternate route that, after much debate, was approved by President Lincoln. McClellan proposed moving his Army of the Potomac by water down to Union held Fortress Monroe located at the tip of a peninsula that jutted between the mouths of the James and York Rivers. From that point, McClellan's force would march up the peninsula and strike Richmond from the southeast. With a little luck and a timely march the rebels would be caught unawares and Richmond would fall, essentially ending the war.

The 2nd Corps was to be an arm of McClellan's strike force and in consequence the 34th New York was put into motion. On March 23rd the 34th traveled by train from Harper's Ferry to Washington and encamped in front of the Capitol building.

While in Washington the men visited Congress and attended church services in the House of Representatives. In the front row seats sat President Lincoln and his Cabinet. After resting a few days in Washington, on March 29th the 34th New York boarded the steamer "R. Williams" and headed south. On nearing Fortress Monroe, two days later, the men rushed to the rail to catch a glimpse of the heroic little "Monitor." William Walton related:

> " . . . in the harbor near Fortress Monroe, it gratified my curiosity as it also did that of many others on board the boat, to behold, a short distance from the landing the famous Monitor, that little cheese box affair that so neatly whipped the rebel Merrimac and sent her growling to Norfolk." [19]

Landing at Hampton, Virginia, the 34th New York, along with the rest of Sumner's 2nd Corps, began the march up "the Peninsula" reaching Big Bethel on April 4th and Yorktown the next day. As a part of General McClellan's massive army of one hundred thousand strong, the men of the 34th were confident that this great campaign would mark the end of rebeldom. Lieutenant Walton informed the people of Herkimer County:

> "Know then that Friday morning last we were gratified with the intelligence that we were to immediately make an advance. Soon we were on our way and for two days, were on the march and never have we enjoyed one more. The day was clear and warm, the roads in excellent order, the enemy and victory before us and hearts happy and light within us." [20]

All along the route the Union columns passed by deserted homes, the inhabitants having fled in front of McClellan's approaching army. The boys in blue thought little of plundering these dwellings, justifying their actions in the name of "confiscating Secesh property." William Walton commented:

> "It was laughable to see our boys after ransacking a lately deserted house. One would have his arms full of bread, another hugging a crock of butter, one with a bonnet and cape on, another sporting a dress with crinoline of amazing proportions, some enjoying the luxury of sitting in a rocking chair, others staring in wonder at their own face in a looking glass. Some of the literary turn would appropriate some work that suited their tastes, while the wits would be ransacking desks and bureaus for Secesh love letters over which they could make themselves and others merry. " [21]

During a break in the march General McClellan rode up to the 34th's place in line and paused in front of the overawed troops. In forming the disjointed regiments of civilian soldiers into the grand Army of the Potomac, McClellan had instilled pride in his men and they in turn showered "Little Mac" with affection and confidence. Lieutenant Walton described McClellan's charisma to the *Journal's* readers writing:

> "While waiting here to let some regulars pass, Gen. McClellan and staff accompanied by his body guard passed us. It was here that we had our first good view of our young and gallant commander-in-chief. He is not handsome, he is not noble as we in general regard a handsome or noble man; but

yet there is an intellect, a fire of genius as it were, that flashes from his eye, makes you feel that he was born to will and command. As for a few moments he reined in his steed near us and, almost at a glance, surveyed the enemy's works, we realized what might be meant by the expression 'a man with an eagle eye,' and we did not wonder that the army of the Potomac had such faith in their chieftain. Politicians may grumble and his enemies may demand his removal, but let the Government do it at its peril, for it would be more than ten victories to the cause of the rebels. For the present he is the man for the time and place. He has now the opportunity to prove it to the world and if he fail, if he prove recreant, let him be accursed. But he will not fail, for with his genius, with his army equipped and armed as no army ever was before and composed of soldiers brave and true as steel and ready to do or die for their noble cause and gallant leader, there is no such word as fail." [22]

On reaching Yorktown the Army of the Potomac stalled in front of a string of Confederate earthworks. Although the fortifications were manned by only ten thousand rebels, a fraction of the size of the Federal army, McClellan convinced himself that the enemy force was equal to or larger than his own. "Little Mac," noted for his overly cautious and downright lethargic moves, settled in for a siege. In doing so the element of surprise was lost, giving Gen. Joseph Johnston time to pull his troops from the Rappahannock line and re-establish them at the gates of Richmond. For the next month, in an almost constant rain, the men of both sides improved their defenses, sent out pickets and exchanged artillery fire. Of the continual threat of sharpshooters the 34th's Lieutenant Walton wrote:

"Our loss is small so far, principally among the sharpshooters. These are terrible fellows, we assure you, using telescopic rifles and picking a man at a miles' distance every time. They have approached as near as possible to the fortifications and scarce a man shows himself who does not receive his death wound." [23]

Of their own sharpshooter, the 34th was quite proud as Walton would note:

"We must not neglect, however, making mention of the exploits of our sharpshooter, Serg't Morse, who has probably thus far caused the enemy more injury than all the rest of the regiment combined. Several times he has visited the 'fronties' and with the aid of his telescopic rifle made many a Secesh bite the dust. Last Wednesday afternoon, while on a fray of this kind, it is said by others that he laid low at least seventeen, though he modestly put it at eight or ten." [24]

On the night of May 3rd the rebels secretly abandoned their works at Yorktown. The next morning the 34th entered the deserted forts. Lieutenant Walton described the scene:

"All that we had heard, thought, or imagined came far short of the world of pits, ditches, ramparts, batteries, forts within forts, &c., that now presented themselves to our view. . . . Everything indicated that they had left in a hurry, for clothing was scattered around in all directions as were provisions of all kinds and in their ovens was found half-baked bread still warm. On the part of the boys there was a great desire to secure curiosities or Secesh relics such as bullets, papers, letters, &c. . . . . Their hatred to the Yankees or rather their fanaticisms were exhibited in many ways. To a telegraph post was a large figure in effigy which was intended to represent 'Old Abe.' On the tents and boards and sandbags were written many insulting phrases, of which the following is a good example, 'Come on you d___n Yankees - we can whip double our number of you at any time.' For wit commend us to this sentence written by some lukewarm Alabamian on the side of his tent 'Liberty or a slight flesh wound.' " [25]

Wary of underground torpedoes planted by rebels, the soldiers took advantage of the spoils left in the hasty rebel retreat. Walton continued:

" . . . here we found some two hundred barrels of flour and some corn meal, sugar, dried peaches, apples, salerains and some other articles. We helped ourselves to sugar and other articles despite the hint that it might be poisoned. We made pancakes out of secesh 'timber,' baked them in secesh spiders, ate them off secesh plates with secesh knives and forks, sweetened them with secesh sugar, stewed some secesh peaches in a secesh pot, made some secesh tea and in fact filled ourselves with secesh victuals, but that did not make us secesh by any means." [26]

Yorktown had well served its purpose for Joseph Johnston. Surprised and disorganized by McClellan's landing on the Peninsula, stalemating the Army of the Potomac had given Johnston time to consolidate his forces and strengthen Richmond's defenses. The evacuation of the Yorktown garrison was accomplished just one day before McClellan planned to unleash his huge siege mortars on the works.

Critics of McClellan were outspoken at the snail-like pace and ineptitude that had so far characterized the General's campaign. Yet the men of the Army of the Potomac retained confidence in their leader. William Walton defended McClellan writing:

"'Little Mac' I see is blamed by many grumblers for not advancing immediately on his arrival to the assault of the place, and in confirmation of their views, they point complacently to the fact now disclosed, that at that time there were only eight thousand troops there garrisoned. It is a pity that our leader was not aware of this at the time, but it is fated that even commanders-in-chief cannot know everything." [27]

The morning of May 7th the 34th New York boarded the "Daniel S. Webster" and steamed to West Point, Virginia, thirty miles up the York River, arriving late in the afternoon. In the distance the closing shots from a clash between the rebel rear guard and Union cavalry near Williamsburg were heard. A few days later some of the Herkimer County boys toured the battlefield. Louis Chapin of Little Falls related:

" . . . the sights they saw were bloody. The woods were thickly strewn with the dead and wounded, and the buildings in town were filled with the same. The rebels had fled so precipitately that they have been compelled to leave their wounded behind, and their dead unburied." [28]

The 34th moved on to Kent Court House where on the second day of their five day stay an incident occurred that almost destroyed and certainly shamed the regiment.

One year earlier in Albany the West Troy company, captained by William Oswald, was induced to join the 34th by being promised the honored "right of the line" position as Company A. Although this was against regulations—the "A" designation belonged to the company whose captain had the most seniority—the arrangement had gone unnoticed by military officials and except for some grumbling had caused no problems in the regiment. Somehow General Gorman, the brigade commander, learned of this breach of regulations and ordered the 34th into conformance with military law.

The next day at dress parade Captain Oswald led his company to its usual position in line, and when ordered out of it by Colonel Suiter the West Troy boys advanced twenty paces and stacked their arms. Such an act was tantamount to mutiny and in response Suiter ordered three armed companies to guard the insurgents. That night the mutineers were marched off to the stockade by the provost marshal.

The following afternoon the prisoners were paraded back to camp and each in turn promised to do his duty and obey his superiors. Arms were returned and the men were permitted to return to their quarters.

Captain Oswald and his friend and co-conspirator, Capt. Davis Rich of Company D, remained under arrest. At a subsequent trial by a Military Tribunal Oswald and Rich were sentenced to death, but General McClellan stepped in and commuted the sentences. Both men were dishonorably discharged and Oswald was sentenced to one year in prison. Davis Rich would later become a captain in the 153rd New York, a Montgomery County regiment.

From New Kent Court House, the 34th New York marched through Austin's Church and Cumberland before finally stopping near Bottom's Bridge on May 21st. Of the march that day William Walton related:

> "Wednesday, the 21st of May, was a day long to be held in ungrateful rememberance by every member of this division, for on that day we were marched at quick time under a broiling sun, a distance of fourteen miles. All suffered and many dreadfully for, in addition to the great heat, we had to trudge much of the way through deep sand, loaded down with gun, knapsack and haversack and carrying three days rations and forty rounds of cartridges. More than all, we were tormented with fierce thirst, for as a general thing water was as scarce and precious as molten gold, while the little that could be obtained, after a rush and push and a general squabble, was so foul and muddy that the most thirsty horse or cow at home would have refused it with loathing and disdain. The men were continually becoming exhausted and falling out by the wayside and, by the time we reached our destination, we were minus numbers of both officers and privates. Many were so worn out as to be unable to join their regiments before the next morning, while three poor fellows died from heat and extreme weariness."[29]

After the grueling May 21st march the 34th went into bivouack, now only fourteen miles from Richmond.

At about the time the 34th began its move to the Peninsula, the 97th New York arrived at Little Falls on their way to Albany and the war. *Journal* editor J.R. Stebbins noted:

> "On Wednesday afternoon, the NY Ninety-seventh Regiment known in this quarter as the Boonville Regiment passed east by Rail Road. A large concourse of people assembled at our depot to say farewell to the men who belong in this section. A large number of these Volunteers are citizens of Little Falls and vicinity, and warm greetings were exchanged here between friends and relatives, with many a hearty farewell and parting blessing upon the soldiers. Amid cheers, the waving of handkerchiefs and national flags, the train passed towards the seat of war and its scenes of carnage." [30]

From Albany the 97th travelled by train to New York City where the regiment detrained and marched to the Park Barracks. There the men received their first arms, .577 caliber Enfield rifles and "A" pattern tents. Leaving the city that same evening the 97th journeyed by steamboat and rail through Philadelphia and on to Washington. A night was spent at the Soldiers Rest in Washington and the next day the boys marched to barracks on Kalorama Heights. Scarcely had they arrived when they were shifted to another encampment in the Washington suburbs, Fort Corcoran.

During their three week stay at Fort Corcoran the 97th New York was assigned to the Military District of Washington and brigaded with the 104th and 105th New York, the 88th and 107th Pennsylvania and the 12th Virginia (from pro-Union Western Virginia) under the command of General Abram Duryea. The General had been the commander of the elite 7th New York and was raised in New York City. The two Pennsylvania regiments were soon transferred and the remaining regiments would constitute "Duryea's Brigade" until year end.

In mid-April, the 97th moved nine miles to Clouds Mills, Virginia, and spent the better part of a month at an instruction camp, Camp Reliance. Along with normal drill, the men were taught outpost and picket duties, and offensive and defensive tactics.

On the 11th of May, the 97th left Camp Reliance and entrained to Catlett's Station. Duryea's Brigade now became attached to Gen. Nathaniel Banks' Department of the Rappahannock which had the assignment of ridding the Shenandoah Valley of Stonewall Jackson.

For the next several weeks the 97th New York was kept in motion as three Union armies tried to bring the wily Jackson to bay. In every instance the hard-marching rebels either eluded the Federals or turned and stung Union detachments at places like McDowell, Cross Keys and Port Republic. At Front Royal, Jackson got behind Banks' army and destroyed a huge Union supply depot forcing Banks to withdraw towards Winchester. Fortunately for the Federals, in early June Jackson's force was recalled to Richmond to help take on McClellan.

The 97th returned to Catlett's Station and spent the balance of June encamped there. At month's end, the regiment was assigned to the First Brigade, Second Division of the Third Corps (Army of Virginia) commanded by Gen. John Pope.

CHAPTER III

"Our boys behaved like veterans"

Summer 1862 - Fair Oaks - The Seven Days

After being deadlocked at Yorktown, McClellan maneuvered his huge army to the very gates of Richmond. Now, on the morning of May 31, 1862, the Army of the Potomac was divided, with the rain swollen Chickahominy River separating the two sections. North of the river sat the 2nd, 5th and 6th Corps while on the southern bank were the 3rd and 4th Corps. Only two bridges had been constructed to provide mutual support and the now raging river had rendered one impassable and the other, held together by grapevines, was floating atop the water. Confederate general Joseph Johnston, aware of the isolated and vulnerable position of the two Union corps south of the river, attacked them on the afternoon of that last day in May with twenty-three brigades. The brunt of the attack fell near Seven Pines on General Keyes' 4th Corps, which retreated against heavy odds.

On the north side of the river, General Sumner received Keyes' call for help and sent General Sedgwick's Division of the 2nd Corps, which included the 34th New York, across the swaying "grapevine bridge." Lt. William Walton noted:

> "Hurrying forward over an awful road, we crossed the Chickahominy
> on a rude bridge just constructed, and pressed forward through woods and
> fields, sometimes wading through water two and three feet deep, and after
> making some five miles, approached the battle-field." [1]

Meeting with the fleeing remnants of the broken right wing of the 3rd Corps, Sedgwick's Division reached the vicinity of Fair Oaks Station and formed into battleline. Sedgwick arrayed his troops into two lines that met at right angles. Eight

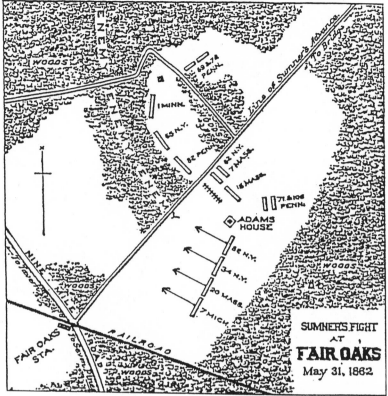

History of the Second Army Corps - Walker

regiments faced to the southwest on the longer of the two lines, while four regiments made up the shorter, northwesterly facing front. At the pivot point of his formation, Sedgwick sited Lt. Edmund Kirby's battery of regular army artillerists alongside the Adams House. The 34th New York was placed on the lesser line between the 82nd New York and the 20th Massachusetts.

Less than ten minutes after having formed, rebels pursuing the 3rd Corps men poured from the woods and struck the longer part of the line trying to get at Kirby's Battery. Volley after volley of musketry, coupled with cannister from the battery, stopped the Confederate charge in its tracks. General Sumner, who had just arrived on the scene, ordered the 34th New York and the other regiments that formed the short section of the line to fix bayonets and charge. Lieutenant Walton wrote of the 34th's baptism of fire:

> "As soon as we were in position we received the command to fire and instantly the whole front was one blaze of flame or as the rebels afterwards said 'a wall of fire.' Our boys behaved like veterans, and though our comrades were continually falling under the wasting fire of the enemy, we pressed forward at the command, halting every few yards to pour in our rapid volleys and then again advancing until we were half way across the field, when Gen. Sumner rode up and, with his hat waving above his head cried out 'Charg'em boys, charge' and with loud cheers we rushed forward, driving those of the enemy who had advanced back again into the woods,

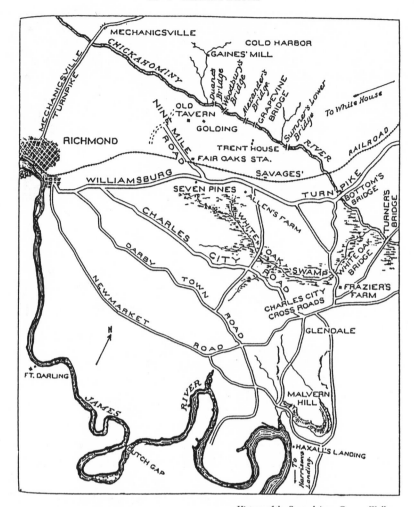

History of the Second Army Corps - Walker

The 34th New York in front of Richmond, 1862

and after halting at the edge to pour in a volley, we entered, still driving them and soon compelled them to flee leaving large numbers of wounded behind and the ground strewed with dead. . . . Gen. Sumner, an old veteran —having entered the army at fourteen—assured us that better fighting he had never seen, and he told our Brigadier General [Gorman] that he could hardly be convinced that this was our first engagement."[2]

The charge had struck the enemy on the right flank, routing the advance and, as night was falling, ended the day's fighting. Sedgwick's timely arrival had saved the 3rd Corps.

The fight at Seven Pines (Confederate name for the battle) or Fair Oaks had been a draw with the relative positions of the two armies remaining virtually unchanged. The casualty count would put Union losses at nearly 5,000 and Confederate losses at over 6,000. [3] Among the rebel wounded was Gen. Joseph Johnston who was wounded by shell fragments while surveying the field at Fair Oaks. With the loss of

Johnston the command of the Army of Northern Virginia passed to Gen. Robert E. Lee.

The second highest casualty count in Sedgwick's Division belonged to the 34th New York. The 34th, in its first real fight, had acted recklessly. Ranging far ahead of the other regiments in line, it had exposed its flanks and in consequence it had realized ninety-seven casualties, including twenty-nine killed and three missing and presumed dead, in the two-hour Fair Oaks fight. [4] Of the 34th's impetuous charge Louis Chapin wrote:

> "A regiment in its first fight, knows not the sentiment of fear. The dangers are all present, but the men are unconscious of them. The psychic life of a man, so to speak has never traversed this ordeal before. Next time the men will be afraid; but not this time. And so it was." [5]

The people of Herkimer County did not learn of the bloody part played by the 34th New York in the fight at Fair Oaks until nearly two weeks after the battle. The major New York and Washington newspapers made no mention of Sedgwick's Division being in the fight and as no member of the 34th New York appeared on the preliminary official casualty lists it was assumed that the "Herkimer County Regiment" was not at all engaged. Finally in the second week in June mail from the boys in the 34th began to make its way to Herkimer County. A letter written by Lt. Col. Byron Laflin to his wife in Herkimer was among the first received. Laflin wrote:

> "My Dear: I wrote you hurriedly yesterday that the day before we had a battle, in which we lost, killed and wounded, ninety-eight. The regiment covered itself all over with glory. It is said their brilliant bayonet charge drove and routed the entire enemy.
>
> Our men walked up to it with a good line as though they were on dress parade - keeping up a perfect wall of fire as they advanced. Gen. Sumner said that he never saw or heard of a charge made by a 'wall of fire;' and when told that they had never previously been under a strong fire, said he could not believe it. Our Division General - Gen. Sedgwick - told an officer in the Minnesota regiment [1st Minnesota] that he never saw such a charge - never saw it so cooly done, and that he should see we had a nice flag, with the words 'Fair Oaks' on it. This is very gratifying, but when we look upon the dead and wounded, it seems dearly purchased. Where our regiment fired and charged, lay any number of dead, a wounded General, and two dead Colonels. While I write, I am wearing the spurs of Col. Champ Davis, 16th North Carolina regiment, whom we killed.
>
> One rebel, whom Capt. King came across, and, seeing wounded, asked if he was badly hurt, but like the villain he was, pulling his revolver he fired upon King, just grazing his (King's) neck. In a second after, the sword of our brave King ran him through his heart." [6]

At last, full reports of the battle of Fair Oaks, including complete casualty lists, were published by the *New York Times* and the *New York Herald*. Armed with this information and with a packet of letters received from men in the 34th, the *Journal* headlined its June 12th edition with:

The Thirty-Fourth in the Battle at Fair Oaks
Their Great Bravery
A Splendid Bayonet Charge[7]

And in the article that followed all praise was given to the hometown boys:

"Our own county regiment has at last been tried under fire and nobly
have they redeemed the pledges they had given us. We knew they would.
God bless the brave fellows!"[8]

In the *Journal's* casualty list were the names of sixteen Herkimer County men
slain or mortally wounded at Fair Oaks. The men were: Sgt. Allan Middlebrooks,
Pvts. John Loomis and Stephen Ballard of Little Falls; Pvt. Clinton Lamb from Man-
heim; Sgt. Robert Kirk and Pvt. Enoch Norris of Mohawk; Pvt. John Myers of
Herkimer; Pvt. William Thrasher of Ohio, and Pvt. Hayden Petrie from Graysville.
Hardest hit of the Herkimer County towns was Salisbury which lost Pvts. Nicholas
Sixby, William Peck, Jesse Van Hagen and John Williams, Cpl. Robert McLaughlin
and the Terry brothers, nineteen year old Albert and seventeen year old Victor.
Notable among the wounded were Capt. Wells Sponable, with a bullet wound in
the thigh, and the *Journal's* correspondent, Lieut. William Walton, wounded in the
chest.
Of the personal tragedies in the 34th many stories were related. Louis Chapin
wrote of the Terry brothers:

"There were in our Company, three brothers, Joseph, Victor and Albert
Terry. Victor and Albert were both wounded in the leg at the battle. Amputation was necessary, after which they were placed in separate ambulances
and started for the General Hospital, in the rear. On the way to the Hospital,
both young men died. They were placed in one ambulance, and returned
to the battlefield. Early the next morning, June 1st, during a continuation of
the battle, while the regiment was standing as support to the troops fighting
in our front, Joseph Terry, the older brother, was excused from the ranks to
bury his two brothers, whose remains he had placed side by side under a
tree, a short distance behind our line. Setting his Enfield rifle against a tree,
he began digging that grave. When the battle raged too near, and the spent
balls were falling about us, he would put his spade aside, take his rifle and
resume his place in the company. When the roar of musketry and the
Union cheers would show the enemy were being driven, he again would
take up his spade. When the battle would again sway toward our line, he
would return to the ranks, thus alternating between the ranks and the grave,
until the sad task was done. Think you Joseph Terry did not also wonder
what the folks at home would think when they heard that those two young
brothers were dead?"[9]

William Walton who was not seriously wounded eulogized Cpl. Robert Mc-
Laughlin, writing:

"If there was one, however, who shared . . . the honor of being first and foremost in the hearts of his comrades it was our noble 'Bob,' given in the list of the killed as Corporal Robert McLaughlin. Large in stature and of determined spirit, always cool, always reliable, he was looked on as one of the standbys, one of the pillars of the company. . . . He too, in the engagement of Saturday, fought nobly, in the front rank, as cool as ever, not throwing away a shot, until he fell pierced by two balls and was carried from the field. As he entered the Hospital he asked of those bearing him 'How is it going' and, on being told that we were driving the enemy, he said, 'that's good, I'm glad'. He lingered until the next day, but in the mean time had been placed in an ambulance to be conveyed to more comfortable quarters, but died on the journey. His grave was made on the banks of the Chickahominy, in a fair and beautiful spot where may he peacefully sleep until the great and final day of the Lord!" [10]

And to the family and friends of William Thrasher, Lieutenant Walton wrote:

"We fought for two hours desperately, and then made our gallant charge, and the rebels broke ranks and ran. It was almost dark. We followed them into the woods; when but a few rods in, a bombshell burst right in front of our company. A large piece of the shell struck your son, William D. Thrasher, and killed him instantly. I ran up to where he was, and he could not speak. He was dead in less than one minute. We buried him under a peach tree, and I put a pine board at his head, with his name and the company and regiment he belongs to on it.'" [11]

The *Journal* even published a letter of condolence written to E. A. Middlebrook by Capt. John Beverly reporting the death of Middlebrook's son Allan. Beverly wrote:

"Dear Sir: I have to convey to you the sad tidings that Serg. A. G. Middlebrook, your son, is no more. He was killed in the battle fought here yesterday while gallantly leading the right of his company. He was buried here today. I offered $150 to have him sent home but it could not be done.

I write this on the battlefield, I will write again soon. We all sympathize with you and your friends in this your bereavement." [12]

Those men of the 34th that were killed on the battlefield of Fair Oaks or that died shortly after, were buried near the field. Later when the remains were moved to a more suitable burying ground all identity of the men was lost. The dead of the 34th New York would forever lie in unknown graves at Fair Oaks.

The Journal also published an extract of a letter from the 34th's regimental Surgeon, Dr. Socrates Sherman, to the *Utica Herald*. In the aftermath of the Fair Oaks fight, Sherman, aided by Dr. Benjamin Bushnell who had hurried down from Little Falls, spent the better part of a week treating the wounded. The surgeon's work for the most part entailed performing simple amputations. The large caliber, soft lead "minnie balls" thrown by the muskets of both armies, pulverized large sections of bone on impact making reconstruction of an injured limb impossible. The surgeon and his assistant, the aptly titled Surgeon Carpenter, usually had no recourse but to saw off the damaged appendage. Of his grisly work Dr. Sherman related:

"The enemy's dead, and all his wounded that could not take themselves off, fell into our hands. From them we learned that the rebels opposed to us were their choicest troops, 'the Hampton Legion', the 'Richmond Guards' &c.

I have cut off in great numbers the arms and legs of rebels from Virginia, North Carolina, South Carolina, Georgia, Alabama, Mississippi, Louisiana and Tennessee and I recollect my political opponents, when I left home, admitted that I would be likely to do my country some service if I got a chance to practice professionally on her enemies.

Well, after the battle of Saturday, I labored Sunday, Monday and Tuesday, harder than I ever did before in my life, and after the first day, exclusively at amputations." [13]

During a break in his work, Dr. Sherman toured the battlefield and made note of the relative effectiveness of the various weapons used. In describing his findings Dr. Sherman wrote:

"The execution of our men in battle was almost incomprehensible, and their firing as evinced by marks left on the trees where the enemy lay, was of wonderful accuracy. We killed more than double the number of rebels kill of us, which they ascribed to our having artillery and their wont of it, but among the results of the Saturday night and Sunday's fight, I found among all the dead and wounded on both sides by artillery, only two of the former and three of the latter, and the two killed were our men killed by our own guns. The slaughter was by the deadly Minie musket ball, and with all the talk by newspaper correspondents about the deadly havoc of the bayonet, I failed to find among the dead or wounded of either side, any evidence that it had been used at all. The fact is that when a bayonet charge is made, in my opinion, it is very seldom that weapons are crossed, one party or the other giving way before they come in contact." [14]

After awhile tangible evidence of the terrible battle of Fair Oaks and the true price of war began arriving in Herkimer County. Wells Sponable returned to Little Falls with a bullet in his thigh (a souvenir that would be with him the rest of his life), John Van Etten came home and displayed holes in his side and back showing where a ball had passed through his body, and the corpse of Matthew Kennedy, who had died in a Philadelphia hospital from his Fair Oaks' wounds, was brought home to Little Falls. The *Journal* report of Kennedy's funeral read:

"On Saturday last the body of Matthew Kennedy, a private in Co. B, 34th Regiment, arrived here and on Sunday hundreds of our citizens hurried to express their sorrow and sympathy with his friends at the funeral. The procession was formed at the house of the deceased and was led by the Citizens Brass Band, whose softened dirges spread deep solemnity over the village. The firemen followed, company No. 3 of which he was a respected member acting as body guard. The hearse was appropriately decorated with the national flag in whose defence the youthful hero had offered his life and was followed to the Catholic church by a very large number of citizens, not more than a third of whom were able to gain admittance. It is estimated that there were more than three thousand persons in attendance." [15]

For three weeks after the battle of Fair Oaks the Army of the Potomac sat on its haunches waiting for something to happen. The army's commander, George McClellan, had no plans to storm the city. His expertise, or so he believed, was in siege warfare and therefore his strategy lay in a bloodless blockade of the rebel capital. However, the Army of Northern Virginia's new leader, Robert E. Lee, was not about to let McClellan have his way. Lee realized that to remain on the defensive and try to endure a siege would inevitably lead to the loss of Richmond. One month after taking command from Joseph Johnston, who was still laid up from his Fair Oaks wound, Lee went on the offensive.

On June 26, 1862 cannon fire to the north of the 34th New York, still encamped at Fair Oaks, signaled the start of what would be called the Seven Day's Battles. The initial clashes at Gaines Mills, Mechanicsville and Golding's Farm were fought with the 34th unengaged but standing at the ready. Pvt. William McLean of Fairfield wrote of the regiment's wait:

> "During these three days our cartridge boxes and belts had not been taken off, nor had we slept in our camp, but were held behind our breast works in readiness at a moment's warning, to fight or to move. Our knapsacks were kept packed, and our haversacks stored with three days rations of 'hard tack' and salt beef. At sunset orders were given to sling knapsacks and be ready to move instantly. This was obeyed, but again we lay down behind our protection, and slept poorly, as our baggage trains and artillery were moving all night and we expecting at every breath to be called away to some other field of action. At last the day dawned, and a thick fog favored us, as by its covering we could leave our camp, unobserved by the watchful foe." [16]

On June 29th the 34th received orders to break camp and begin moving south. To better secure his supply line, McClellan was withdrawing his army from in front of Richmond and shifting his base of operations from the Pamunkey to the James River. While on the march from Fair Oaks the 34th was shelled near Savage Station, but fortunately took no casualties.

The next day the 34th and its brigade were shuttled to the support of Israel Richardson's Division at White Oak Station and then to bolster Sedgwick's Brigade at Nelson's Farm before being sent to the aid of Philip Kearny's Brigade at Glendale at dusk. Since early in the day the rebels had been hammering General Kearny's position in the hopes of dividing the retreating Union column. A Confederate breakthrough seemed imminent, but the 34th's brigade arrived just in time to plug the gap. In a brief firefight the 34th lost six men killed and eleven wounded, but the rebel threat was stymied. Among the 34th's dead were Eugene Kibbie of Salisbury, Henry Martin of Herkimer and John Nichols and John Sixby of Devereaux. The mortal wound received by John Sixby, a musket ball to the center of the forehead, was identical to the death wound that had taken his brother Nicholas one month earlier at Fair Oaks. Among the wounded were Capt. Thomas Corcoran of Graysville, Sgt. William Burns of Salisbury, whose left arm was amputated, and Lts. Emerson Northrup from Salisbury and, for the second time in a month, *Journal* correspondent William Walton. Walton was taken prisoner soon after when the Confederates overran the brigade hospital.

Although the Army of the Potomac parried each of Lee's thrusts and still remained the larger and stronger of the two armies, on July 1st McClellan withdrew his forces to the heights of Malvern Hill and entrenched. The 34th New York took its position on the ridge in support of the hundreds of cannon that were parked nearly hub to hub. Even though the Union's position appeared impregnable, the Confederates repeatedly attacked it and each time were driven back with heavy losses. In an article entitled "Whisky", the *Journal* recounted Capt. John Beverly's thoughts as to why the rebels had made their suicidal charges at Malvern Hill. The article stated:

> "The fact that all the canteens of captured rebels contained the miserable fiery whisky of the South is vouched for by Capt. Beverly, and accounts for the utter recklessness with which they threw themselves upon our forces. Many of them were found drunk and the slaughter made among them by our artillery was terrible indeed." [17]

The coming of night ended the killing on Malvern Hill. The battle had been a decided Union victory, yet McClellan immediately ordered the retreat to continue.

The 34th New York had suffered only two casualties, but the men, Maj. Charles Brown (killed) and Sgt. George Morse (severely wounded), were singular members of the regiment. Louis Chapin related the grisly details of Major Brown's death, writing:

> ". . . I stood alongside of him [Major Brown]. He lay upon his right side, leaning on his elbow, the bridle of his horse in his left hand, as it lay upon his hip. His ankles were crossed. The shell came bounding over the stacked arms, falling directly on his ankles, and going on its way. He fell over on his back, but raising himself in a sitting position, took his leg in his hands, and lifted it up and his foot hung by the piece of boot-leg, not entirely cut off. Both feet were the same.
>
> I have seen the expression on his pale face hundreds of times, in memory since he lifted that foot and saw his condition. . . . " [18]

George Morse, the 34th's famed sharpshooter, died of his Malvern Hill wounds on July 8th. The *Herkimer County Journal* reprinted an excerpt from the *Albany Journal* that paid tribute to Morse. The Albany newspaper's article read:

> "We are deeply pained to hear that George Morse, the well known North Woods Guide, was killed [Morse was only severely wound at the time] in the terrible battle of Monday, June 30, near the James River. Born in the woods he was never contented out of them....He was lost in towns, while he knew every river, and mountain and lake of the vast forest reaching from the Mohawk to the St. Lawrence. . . . His habits of life rendered him invaluable as a scout, and he was employed as such whenever unusual skill was necessary to accomplish the result desired. His adventures, while thus employed, would fill a volume. Scores of rebels were made to bite the dust by his trusty rifle. . . . With the best intentions in the world, he could never tie himself down to camp life or to the soldiers' drill. Colonel knew this, and making him a Sergeant, allowed him to do as he pleased.
>
> Those who knew him can fancy his efficiency in battle. He never fought

in the ranks. He was his own Captain and General. He never wasted powder or ball: and every other man in the army may have been fatigued but he
was not.

He leaves a wife and five children, in his wilderness home, far back on
the Sacandaga, to mourn his death." [19]

Herkimer County boys in the 44th New York could also be found on the casualty
rolls from the march up the Peninsula and the Seven Day's Battles.

Among the losses in the "Ellsworth's" were: Sgt. Henry Howell of German Flatts
struck by lightning and killed at Gaines Mills; Eleazor Stoddard of Salisbury and
Floyd Young of Columbia, killed at Hanover Court House; William Borden of Fairfield and Jerome Saterlee of Salisbury, taken prisoner at Gaines Mills; Luke Jones
of Fairfield and Sgt. Henry Galpin of Little Falls, wounded at Gaines Mills and Guy
DeLong of Little Falls mortally wounded at Gaines Mills. Henry Galpin described
his and DeLong's ordeal, writing:

"Tuesday [June 27th] we had some hard fighting. Our regiment was
under the fire of the enemy's batteries nearly all day, but fortunately only
one man was wounded. About 6 o'clock we formed in line of battle and
advanced against the rebels who were attempting to charge upon our batteries. Without wavering our regiment marched up and opened upon the
rebels. They broke and ran. We advanced and another regiment came out.
We fought in advance of our other forces until ordered to fall back. Then I
was struck in the back of the head and about the same time Guy was shot
through the breast. We fell back and as he turned around he was struck by
another bullet on the right side of his forehead. We both went back to the
Doctor's and had our heads bandaged and Guy was told to go back to the
general hospital. I was not much injured and should have gone back to the
regiment but Guy needed assistance. So with the help of another comrade,
I got him to the hospital. It was then dark. The house was full of the
wounded and the yard under the trees was rapidly filled up. I procured a
place for him and covered him with a blanket. Then Capt. Larabee came up
and asked me if I could march, 'Yes' said I 'as long as I can stand'. He told
me to come right on as the brigade was ready and on the move and so I
bade Guy good-bye and hurried on with a sad heart." [20]

Soon after Galpin left the enemy took possession of the hospital. Guy DeLong
succumbed to his wounds on July 6th.

Exhausted from a week of constant marching and fighting and weakened by
disease, the frustrated Army of the Potomac trudged to Harrison's Landing in a driving rainstorm. At Harrison's Landing McClellan's battered army would find safety
under the guns of Union gunboats cruising the James River. Although the boys in
blue had fought to at least a draw in each of the previous week's battles, Robert E.
Lee's inferior force had unceremoniously pushed the Army of the Potomac back to
its starting point. In seven days the Union army had travelled from the brink of victory at Richmond's doorstep to the depths of defeat, cowering on the muddy banks
of the James. Surprisingly, much of the army still had faith in George McClellan.
Captain Beverly of the 34th related:

" . . . the men, though tired beyond description, are as yet full of pluck, spirit and enthusiasm as ever. Every confidence is had in Gen. McClellan by his soldiers and by all military men in the army, it is thought that this recent movement in the face of the enemy has proved one of the greatest successes ever known. It will hardly do to throw out anything against 'Little Mac' to the returning soldiers." [21]

While Captain Beverly's view of the army's condition may have been overly optimistic, Pvt. Louis Chapin, who slogged through the mud with the other enlisted men, analyzed the situation with a more realistic eye. Chapin wrote:

" . . . and so it happened that the march from Malvern Hill to Harrison's Landing on the James was not much of a show in the way of a nicely executed military movement. It wasn't a rout, but it looked like it. The road was narrow, and under the falling rains it was deep: and what with the passage of countless teams hauling the army wagons, the passage of the artillery and the cavalry, and 90,000 men on foot, it could hardly be expected that the road would be in prime condition.

. . . However, the most of the army eventually reached Harrison's Landing. The army by this time had lost all pretense of being an organized body. It was little better in appearance than a mob. No enemy could have more completely demoralized it: there were scarcely a dozen men of any one regiment together." [22]

The Army of the Potomac spent the rest of July and well into August encamped at Harrison's Landing. Except for a brief reconnaissance back to now rebel-held Malvern Hill, the time was spent in refitting and reorganizing the army. New clothes and equipment arrived and, most importantly to the men, the paymaster made a visit. Broken up units were rebuilt, inefficient officers were cashiered, and recruiting drives were made back home to fill up weakened regiments. Lt. Emerson Northrup, recovering from his Glendale wound, and Maj. John Beverly, trying to get over a bout of scurvy, were in Herkimer County trying to enlist men for the 34th whose roster had fallen to four hundred and forty-two men. Beverly had recently been promoted to major with the death of Charles Brown.

In the mud and heat of Harrison's Landing the diseases of midsummer, in combination with general exhaustion and inadequate rations, caused great suffering in the Army of the Potomac. Typhoid fever, malaria, scurvy, "rheumatism" and sunstroke plagued the men. The pall of death hung over every camp, including that of the 34th New York where nineteen men perished in July and August. Counted among the 34th's death toll were, Wilford Wilcott of Herkimer, Edwin Harris of Fairfield, John Crewell from Columbia, Norway's Chauncey Bullock, and Charles Coloney and Charles Rider from Little Falls. Lt. William Walton, who had recently been set free by his rebel captors, described a visit to a hospital ship writing:

"While at the Landing several deaths occurred, but we can only recall that of Charles Rider, a member of Co. K. He was enlisted . . . by Capt. Easterbrooks, and faithfully discharged his duties until taken ill with that

terrible disease, Typhoid Fever. We call it terrible, as many a poor fellow
has found it to be his sorrow, and this day hundreds and thousands are
enriching the soil of Virginia, victims to its power. On being taken on board
the Hospital boat, Euterpe, at Fortress Monroe, we found many patients
sick with it, who were to be removed to Northern cities. A more wretched,
pitiable looking lot of human beings we have seldom seen. Members of our
Regiment, whom we left in the full enjoyment of health, stout and robust,
we here found hovering on the verge of the grave, looking far worse than
death in the pictures with their sunken, ghastly eyes, hollow cheeks and
fleshless limbs." [23]

Both regimental surgeons, Drs. Sherman and Walker, were also ill. Sherman's
sickness was serious enough to cause him to return home to Ogdensburg.

But the diseases of Harrison's Landing seemed to run their course. The weak
were weeded out and, as the plague passed, the enthusiasm of the survivors returned.
William McLean of Fairfield noted:

"During the first two weeks of our stay in this camp there were many
sick, and almost every hour of the day could be heard the fife and drums
sounding the death march as the last tribute of respect to some departed
soldier of this corps. Now these dark and gloomy sounds have ceased in a
great measure, and the men are in fine spirits, and as eager as ever for an
advance movement upon the rebel capital." [24]

Perturbed with the apparent stagnation of the army and frustrated with the apparent lack of fight in its commander, Abraham Lincoln came down to Harrison's Landing in July to confer with McClellan. In order to view the condition of the troops
firsthand, Lincoln made a tour of the camps. William McLean related the President's
visit to the 34th's campsite, writing:

"On the 9th inst. [July 9th] we had the honor and happiness of seeing
the President, who rode through our camps with Generals McClellan, Sumner and Sedgwick and their staff officers. The usual salute of twenty-one
guns was fired by the artillery belonging to each division as they passed,
and the bands played lively national airs, while each regiment was receiving its special review, and giving three deep-felt cheers which attracted the
attention and caused a smile to gather up the honest countenance of Old
Abe, - smiles that bespoke his unmistakable satisfaction and confidence in
the army of the Potomac." [25]

Eventually the Army of the Potomac was becoming whole again. The sick and
wounded were returning from Northern hospitals, men captured during the Peninsu-
lar Campaign were rejoining their regiments—thanks to the prisoner exchange program—and the living conditions in the camps were improving somewhat. But most
importantly, the inexperienced volunteers of 1861 had, through the trials in front of
Richmond, become hard-bitten soldiers. For these men the glory of the reckless
charge, the stand-up fight and the parade ground advance, would be gone. They had
learned that war simply meant suffering, hardship and death, and nothing more. The
34th's Pvt. William McLean expressed this best, writing:

"Those troops that have been in the warmest battles are coolest and most satisfied, and can never be heard saying that they want another engagement, or are anxious to shed blood."[26]

History of the 34th Regiment

Camp of the 34th New York at Poolesville, Maryland

Maj. Wells Sponable   *Col. Byron Laflin*   *Lt. L. N. Chapin*

Capt. William Walton, 34th New York, 1862 and 1900

History of the 34th Regiment

Rev. John B. Van Petten, 34th New York

History of the 34th Regiment

History of the 34th Regiment

The 34th New York's Fair Oaks Battleground. In the lower photo, the 34th charged from the fields on the left, across the road, into the woods on the right.

The 34th New York in Camp at Falmouth, winter of 1862-63. Seated, left to right, Captain Warford, Major Sponable, Captain Scott, Lieutenant Colonel Beverly, Captain Riley. Standing left, to right, Captain Northrup, Colonel Laflin.

Colonel Laflin's headquarters at Falmouth. Left to right, Lafayette Cook, J. Reineur, Colonel Laflin (seated), Captain Riley, Quartermaster Easterbrook.

CHAPTER IV

"The balls flew like hail stones"

Fall 1862 - Formation of the 121st N.Y. - 2nd Manassas

McClellan's failed campaign on Richmond had cost the Army of the Potomac sixteen thousand men (Lee suffered twenty thousand casualties) and during its stay at Harrison's Landing thousands more were lost to disease and desertion. As a consequence, early in July Abraham Lincoln issued a call for three hundred thousand volunteers, and one month later he would ask for three hundred thousand more militia to serve for a term of nine months.

From the July levy of three hundred thousand men, New York State was requested to supply almost sixty thousand recruits. The Provost Marshal of New York State in turn, using a formula of one recruit for each sixty-five residents, determined that the quota for Herkimer County, with a population of roughly forty thousand, be set at six hundred and twenty-four. The Herkimer County Volunteer Committee using the same formula as the provost marshal further subdivided the quota to the township level. The breakdown for each town, showing the town's population and quota, was published by the *Herkimer County Journal*:

"According to the figures of the [Albany] *Evening Journal*, the quota of this state under the new levy is 59,705, and that of this county is 624. This will give the following figures as quotas for the towns of the county respectively:

Columbia	1,893	30
Danube	1,711	27
Fairfield	1,712	27

Frankfort	3,247	50
German Flats	3,940	60
Herkimer	2,804	43
Litchfield	1,520	24
Little Falls	5,989	92
Manheim	1,868	29
Newport	2,113	33
Norway	1,105	17
Ohio	1,135	17
Russia	2,389	36
Salisbury	2,325	35
Schuyler	1,715	26
Stark	1,543	24
Warren	1,812	28
Wilmurt	260	4
Winfield	1,480	22
Total	40,561	624

"We believe that some plan will be adopted by the state authorities to whom the draft has been committed which will credit to each town and county the number of volunteers already sent, so that the deficiencies of one locality shall not be asked to be supplied from another which has already sent more than its proportion. We hardly feel like asking Salisbury or Ohio to submit to a draft to raise the men which should have come from Warren or Stark, and it is probable that the militia roll, now on file, will be revised and an account opened with each town and county."[1]

Although it was threatened that failure to fulfill a quota would result in conscription, the threat was idle, for at this point in time the Federal government did not have the mandate to draft citizens. But to many the possibility of a draft was very real and no town or county wanted to bear the disgrace of having its residents serving only through compulsion.

To entice volunteers, Herkimer County and each of the townships offered enlistment bounties that were in addition to the Federal and New York State premiums. Each volunteer was paid a standard $50 by the county and typically about twice this amount by his town. After the first call in July, the numbers of men volunteering lessened and many towns upped their bounties in the hopes of outbidding their neighbors for enlistees. As noted by the *Journal* this "bounty war" caused bad feelings among the Herkimer County towns. The newspaper's editor, J.R. Stebbins, wrote:

"We have all long objected to the system of Town Bounties, as it has been conducted in this county. The want of uniformity in the amounts offered to be paid volunteers has already produced much confusion and, now that some localities are carrying the matter to such unwarranted extremes, we may expect more trouble flowing from it than ever. For instance, the town of Fairfield offers a bounty of $500. She has only about a score of men to raise and we believe she could have that number just as readily with a bounty half as large. On the other hand, adjoining towns which, equally as patriotic, as the lists of men furnished by them show, are yet unable to reach so high a figure - we simply ask, then, whether the town of Fairfield, in her efforts to supply her own men, is not, unintentionally of course, working great injury to the general cause and the interests of the county? It is perhaps too late to cure the matter. We look upon the proceedings as a mistake of policy which will seriously effect the business of recruiting throughout the county." [2]

The money for town bounties was raised by soliciting contributions from prominent citizens of the community. Large rallies, complete with brass bands, parades and speeches—often made by hometown war veterans—were held throughout Herkimer County. Notable among the contributors were the Remington brothers who pledged $1,000 and an additional $100 per month to the Ilion bounty fund.

The total bounty incentive, about $300 in July and as much as $1,000 in August, coupled with the fear of being drafted, spurred many men to enlist. Recruiting offices were opened in Little Falls by Sgt. Henry Galpin of the 44th; in Brockett's Bridge by Jonathan Burrell and David King; in Fairfield by Angus Cameron, in Danube by George Davis; in Herkimer by Clinton Moon, and in Mohawk by John Ramsey. Before the end of July over four hundred men had enlisted in the name of Herkimer County.

Herkimer and Otsego counties were each requested by the state to form their volunteers into five companies and to cooperate in combining these units into a regiment. Officials of the two counties met and agreed that a plot of land alongside the Mohawk River between Mohawk and Herkimer would make the best site for a camp. The land was leased from H.J. Schuyler, campgrounds were laid out, tents were erected and the place was fittingly dubbed Camp Schuyler. By mid-August, almost a full regiment of men from the two counties were encamped there. The contract for feeding the troops was give to Messrs. Lowell, Prescott and Shull of Mohawk, for thirty cents per day per soldier.

The citizens of Herkimer and Otsego Counties were encouraged to visit Camp Schuyler. Due to its proximity to the volunteers' homes many civilians toured the grounds to get an up close look at "soldiering" and to see how their boys were making out. Of his trip to the camp J.R. Stebbins informed the *Journal's* readers:

> "Yesterday morning we had the pleasure of breakfasting with the soldiers of the new regiment in camp near Herkimer. To say that we were pleased with the general appearance of order, neatness and discipline of the camp would poorly express the truth of the matter. Everything seemed adapted to the wants of the officers and men and everyone appeared determined to acquire the habits and appearance of military life as quickly as possible. . . . The fare furnished the men by the contractors is excellent and every arrangement of kitchen and dining hall has been made on a grand scale combining neatness with convenience." [3]

On August 13, 1862, the regiment was mustered into Federal service for three years and was designated as the 121st Regiment, New York State Volunteers.

The staff officers at muster-in were: Col. Richard Franchot, a congressman from the Otsego District; Lt. Col. Charles Clark, formerly a captain in the 43rd New

York; Maj. Egbert Olcott, son of the president of the Cherry Valley Bank; Adj. Alonzo Ferguson; Q.M. Albert Story, son of the cashier of the Herkimer County Bank; Surgeon William Bassett; and Chaplain Rev. J. R. Sage of the Little Falls Universalist Church. Rev. Sage had originally enrolled as a private and had refused any bounty money.

The Herkimer County companies were designated as A, B, C, D and H, and were commanded by Capts. Henry Galpin (formerly of the 44th New York), Irving Holcomb, Clinton Moon, John Fish and John Ramsey, respectively.

On August 25th the 121st was ordered to break camp but, for want of uniforms, equipment and transportation, it did not leave for Washington until the 30th.

On the homefront, the Ladies Aid Societies of Herkimer County were now requested to send their work directly to the Sanitary Commission, a private soldiers relief organization, rather than to favored regiments. Too often, regiments or companies from affluent neighborhoods luxuriated on plentiful supplies from home while their counterparts from poorer areas suffered from want of even the most basic necessities. With the Sanitary Commission acting as a clearinghouse, hospital supplies, food, clothing and other aid was more equitably directed to the most needy. In Herkimer County the Ladies Aid groups raised money for the raw materials necessary for their work by holding festivals and bazaars. At weekly sewing circles and meetings the women then turned out the goods most requested by the Sanitary Commission. The *Journal* was happy to help the ladies with plugs such as:

> "The ladies of Mohawk announce a Festival to be given at Odd Fellow's Hall, in that village to-morrow evening. The Mohawk Valley Brass Band will be in attendance; also Hewes and Bradley's Harp Band for dancing. The entire proceeds will be devoted to their relief of sick and wounded soldiers."[4]

and . . .

> "To answer the recent demand made for hospital clothing, the Aid Society intend to prepare another box to be sent to the Sanitary Commission, as it is the most reliable source by which the sufferings of the sick and wounded are reached. Those wishing to assist in any way need have no fears lest the effort will reach the end for which it was designed. . . . "[5]

But all was not related to the war, life in the valley went on much as usual. In Fairfield, the Seminary held its Anniversary Week highlighted by the Aethenian Society's "Public." Soon after, the Seminary and the Little Falls Academy began enrollment for their fall terms.

In Brockett's Bridge, free blacks from Herkimer and adjoining counties joined in a week long camp meeting. White folks who "behaved themselves" were granted admittance.

At Concert Hall in Little Falls performances were given by Blitz the great magician and ventriloquist who displayed his "birds, rabbits and wonders" and by the "Great Dramatic-Equestro" troupe. The latter show was censured by the *Journal* for its acts of, "low rowdyism and obscenity which render them eminently disgusting." Also travelling through the Mohawk Valley was the fabulously named Hippo-zoonomodon and Lent's great circus.

In Little Falls, Maungwudaus, an Indian medicine man, set up his tent near Casler's Store on Main Street offering his healing powers, and the Baptist Sabbath School of the village held their annual picnic near "the Falls" at East Creek.

The *Journal* noted that a new state law limiting the taking of fish and game had been enacted. One week later the newspaper proudly announced that a group of local "sportsmen" had returned from Jock's Lake with five hundred pounds of trout.

During the summer of 1862 the economy of Herkimer County was excellent. Four hundred thousand pounds of cheese was leaving the depot in Little Falls each week and canal tolls, notwithstanding a break in Fultonville, were up almost 40 percent. The sale of lots in Little Falls brought higher than expected prices and even Moss Island was purchased as a potential factory site. The cotton factory of Chrysler and Morgan hired an efficient new superintendent and production was on the rise.

Of tragic note in Little Falls, the four-year-old son of John Hurley drowned in the canal basin and the young daughter of William Gray, a member of the 97th New York, died after being severely burned while playing with matches.

The *Journal* also reported on a "disgraceful row" in Little Falls. It seems that a band of rowdies from Herkimer got "beastly drunk" on the south side of the river and headed for the saloons on the north side. On their way the toughs met a Little Falls boy, Jack Day, and for no apparent reason threw him into a gutter and beat him senseless. The Herkimer men were soon arrested and taken before Judge Uhle, with a hooting crowd following them every step of the way.

Uhle fined the men $2 each and directed them to get out of town. On their way to the train depot, under the escort of Constables Barber and Conant, the miscreants were attacked by the friends of Day. A regular riot ensued and the police officers backed off, letting the prisoners "shirk for themselves." A running fight continued all the way to the rail station with several "knockdowns" registered and sticks and stones freely hurled. At the depot Major Priest and a number of other prominent citizens intervened and somehow got the Herkimer boys on the train and safely on their way home. Of this incident the *Journal* noted:

> "We have no words to express proper rebuke to the actors in this affair. It was the most disgraceful occurrence we have had to record in many months, and speaks volumes against the efficiency of the police regulations of the village. We believe prompt and determined measures should be immediately taken for the punishment of the offenders that we may, at least, be saved a repetition of an affair so disreputable."[6]

July 4th came but no Independence Day celebrations were held in most Herkimer County communities. So much money had been obligated to the relief of sick and wounded soldiers and their families, that none was left for such festivities.

In northern Virginia a newly formed Federal army began its own drive on Richmond. In an attempt to ease the pressure on McClellan and to protect Washington,

Abraham Lincoln had consolidated the three independent Shenandoah Valley detachments into one force and gave command of this army to John Pope, a blustering general from the Western army. In mid-July Pope left the environs of Washington and started his "Army of Virginia" marching in a southwesterly line towards the rebel capital. Pope planned to trap Lee between himself and McClellan and bragged to his men that there would be no turning back. Among the troops that marched along with Pope was the 97th New York.

On the morning of July 22nd the 97th New York broke camp near Catlett's Station and marched through Warrenton before turning south to Waterloo. Outside of Waterloo the 97th encamped along the banks of the Rappahannock River at Hart's Ford. At dawn on August 5th, the "Third Oneida" took their place in line and began to march south once again, for Pope had learned that Stonewall Jackson was sitting forty miles away in Gordonsville. Describing the march Isaac Hall of the 97th wrote:

> "The day was hot and many men fell out of the ranks, some from fatigue and exhaustion and others in order to 'gather' from the farms and houses along the way a refreshing drink of cool buttermilk, or roasting ears of sweet corn, and appropriating pigs, turkeys or such other articles of food as the premises might afford. After marching eleven miles the brigade [Duryea's] encamped, at night in a fine open grove near Hazel River. At an early hour the march resumed and continued through a rich agricultural country, abounding in fine farms, which had not hitherto suffered by the devastations of warfare. The day's march extended to a point within two miles of Culpeper Court House. . . . "[7]

Unbeknownst to Pope, Stonewall Jackson was also headed to Culpeper.

Now that McClellan was safely out of the way at Harrison's Landing, Robert E. Lee ordered General Jackson to head off Pope's northern threat. In response, Jackson moved his division, along with those of A.P. Hill and Ewell to Gordonsville. Fearing that Pope would soon be reinforced, Jackson headed north, crossed the Rapidan River and on August 8th struck and routed a Union cavalry detachment. Reacting to this challenge, John Pope sent his army out looking for Jackson and unfortunately his smallest corps, Banks, found him. Without waiting for reinforcements, General Banks' force of about eight thousand men attacked the rebel position at Cedar Mountain on August 9th. Although Banks was initially successful, he was counterattacked by the full might of Jackson's army, three full divisions backed by Jeb Stuart's cavalry—sixteen thousand men in all—and driven back with the loss of nearly one-third of his corps.

Late in the afternoon, after listening for many hours to firing in the distance, the 97th New York, along with its division (Rickett's), headed towards the battle. As related by Isaac Hall, the 3rd Corps boys were too late to help Bank's men:

> "Finally at 5 p.m. the order came to march, and Rickett's division marched with alacrity in the direction of the battle field, leaving its knapsacks piled in charge of a guard. Every man seemed to realize the importance and seriousness of the occasion. There was but little straggling and shrinking from duty.
> General Pope and his staff overtook the division soon after this march

began and was duly cheered as he passed on the front, and as Ricketts's division advanced in that direction it became more and more evident that the relief it was bringing had been altogether too tardy.

The ambulances met were packed with wounded men and officers, and some were walking with bandaged arms and legs covered with fresh blood and gore of the field. Others were mounted, unable to walk and occasionally two upon one horse. All were covered with smoke and begrimed with the late encounter. Trying as these scenes were to the nerves of our raw troops, none faltered, but all pressed on in silence towards the front."[8]

Reaching the edge of the Cedar Mountain battlefield, the 97th made camp. Within an hour of building campfires, which proved a beacon to Confederate gunners, an artillery barrage hit the regiment. Hall related,

"At this juncture the gallantry, good judgement and presence of mind of Lieutenant Colonel Spofford, commanding the 97th at the time, was conspicuous and important, and served to prevent panic in the regiment, and had its influence with other troops, many of whom, as well as the 97th, had never before been under fire."[9]

Only one man was wounded, and counter-battery fire soon quieted the enemy guns.

Reinforcements were now rushing to both armies. Longstreet was heading to Jackson and divisions detached from McClellan were on their way to Pope.

Leaving their camp near Cedar Mountain on the night of August 18th, the 97th built up their campfires as a diversion, and silently began to march back north towards the Rappahannock. The twenty-two mile journey was completed the next night as the regiment crossed the river.

On the 23rd, while encamped along the Rappahannock, the 97th was again subjected to artillery fire and again Spofford calmed the men. Isaac Hall wrote:

"As he sat upon his horse beside his adjutant, in front of his command, a solid shot, nearly spent, passed between them, and tumbling down carried away the arm of one of the men of the regiment and wounding also Sergeant J.H. Smith. Of course those who saw it were not slow in getting out of the way of this missile. A wag of the regiment cried out: 'Boys, what are you dodging for? the colonel don't dodge.' 'No,' said another, 'he is too lazy to dodge.' "[10]

For most of the next week the 97th marched aimlessly over the countryside looking for Jackson, through Warrenton, past Hart's Ford, back to Warrenton, to New Baltimore, on to Gainesville before finally stopping at Bristow. The troops now began questioning the ability of their commander, General Pope. The 97th's Hall noted:

"For the last twenty-four hours there seemed to hang over the brigade, division and corps commanders, an uncertainty which was depressing and was felt by the troops. The entire command seemed in a condition of a ship at sea without a rudder."[11]

By this time, Stonewall Jackson had maneuvered behind Pope's army and had destroyed his supplies at Manassas Junction. The Federal units, either chasing or retreating from the Confederates, no one was quite sure which case it was, had to rely on the land for food. Isaac Hall would write:

> "The 97th was destitute of provisions, but a plentiful supply of green corn was found, which with meat obtained by foraging supplied present wants. Forage from well-filled barns was obtained, and lovers of the weed did not fail to appropriate from tobacco-houses along the route a plentiful supply of that luxury." [12]

On August 29th the 97th left Bristow and passed by the ruins of Pope's destroyed supply depot at Manassas Junction. Duryea's Brigade had been ordered to march to Sudley Church on the Warrenton Turnpike and to remain in reserve on the right of the Union line. As the men trudged along, the sound of cannon fire off to the west could be clearly heard.

That morning Pope had found Stonewall Jackson's twenty thousand men firmly entrenched in a railroad cut near Groveton and was attacking the rebel position with the bulk of his force, now swollen to sixty thousand men. Despite the Federal's preponderance in numbers, the rebel line held firm as Pope sent in his troops piecemeal with little coordination of assaults. Sitting undetected on Pope's left flank, watching and waiting for the most opportune moment to strike, were thirty thousand men in gray under the command of James Longstreet.

The 97th New York did not participate in the day's action and spent that night bivouacked near the famous stone house of the Bull Run battlefield.

The next morning, August 30th, the 97th took up position astride Sudley Lane between Sudley Church and Groveton and waited. The line formed by the regiment was angled with seven companies facing west and three south. Late in the day, Longstreet finally committed his troops. The rebel blow struck Pope's left flank end-on, rolling up the Union line before hitting the 97th on its southern flank. Isaac Hall described the rebel assault:

> "About 6 p.m., from the west, General Featherstone's brigade, of Longstreet's corps, consisting of four regiments, two abreast in front and two to the rear, emerged from the main woods directly in front of our batteries on the hill and of that part of Duryea's brigade fronting south. As it struck into the field the distance of the left flank of the Confederate column from our front could not have exceeded 200 yards. This force presented a perfect phalanx of disciplined, veteran troops. They marched with arms at a right-shoulder shift while their guidons and colors just to the front kept line. Their General rode a dark horse in front of the space between the preceding regiments. So soon as they appeared in our front, Lieut. Colonel Spofford—in command of the 97th—standing in rear of Company G, said: 'Boys I think they are rebs, fire on them.' Companies K, G and B began to fire, and some of the 105th N.Y., catching the impulse, began firing at the same time. Some of our shots took effect, others raised a dust in close proximity to their lines. A momentary pause—not a halt—was observed and then the Confederates continued at a quick march. Their commanding officer, at a glance had probably taken in the situation, and noticed that our line

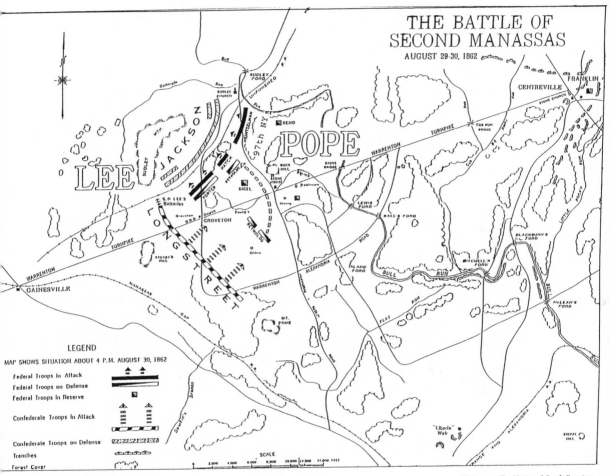

THE BATTLE OF SECOND MANASSAS
AUGUST 29-30, 1862

LEGEND

MAP SHOWS SITUATION ABOUT 4 P.M. AUGUST 30, 1862

Federal Troops In Attack

Federal Troops on Defense

Federal Troops In Reserve

Confederate Troops In Attack

Confederate Troops on Defense

Trenches

Forest Cover

SCALE

"Manassas" - *National Park Service*

was composed of raw troops, for the colonel in command of the 105th, so soon as the firing began, cried out: 'Cease firing, cease firing, you are firing on our own men.' This checked the firing, both in his regiment and in that of the 97th. As the Confederates advanced, fragments of their men struck by solid shot and shell from our guns on the hill, could be seen flying to their rear and they left a trail of dead and wounded, but kept on closing up their ranks as they were rent. At this juncture an overwhelming Confederate force, enveloped by clouds of smoke in the woods, attacked our brigade, taking the regiments fronting the south in flank. The brigade now understood that the enemy, in dead earnest, was upon them, and made a determined resistance, fighting gallantly. The Confederate line was checked, and a rapid firing on both sides began. But the troops which had passed our front were soon bearing down upon our left and rear, when the order to fall back in the direction of Bull Run creek: and this order came none too soon." [13]

Longstreet's flank attack had routed the Union army and if not for a stand on Henry Hill and the coming of night, Pope's army would have been obliterated. As it was the Federals suffered sixteen thousand casualties to the Confederates' nine thousand at this second battle of Bull Run.[14] On this day the 97th New York would lose one hundred and ten men. Of this total, ten men were slain on the field, forty-one were wounded and fifty-nine were taken prisoner.[15] The 97th's dead from Herkimer County were; James Haar of Salisbury, Edward Wheeler from Russia, Walter Rourke of Danube and Lt. Dwight Faville from Brockett's Bridge. In addition, James McIntosh of Norway, Monroe Haur from Manheim, and Salisbury men Nicholas Burton and Dennis McCuen (a forty-three-year-old drummer boy), would die from their Second Bull Run wounds in the coming months.

In a letter home, Frank Faville of Brockett's Bridge related his version of the 97th's fight and detailed the death of his cousin, Dwight, writing:

"Last Saturday, Aug. 30, was an awful day for the defenders of the Union. Our regiment had been in several engagements but had escaped with small losses: but Saturday morning at daylight, we were ordered to the front and held it during the day. Our part of the fight was in the woods, mostly. Among those who fell Dwight is numbered. He had often told me that he had no plans for the future, but he never expected to go home and the like: but he was never low in spirits and went into action cheerful and with a will.

We had been ordered to hold a position, and were lying behind a fence watching for the rebels to come out so we could surprise them: But before we were aware of it, and before we received any order to fall back, they had turned our left flank, and also attacked us in front, making bad work among us. Just as we received the order 'fall back', Dwight was shot, a ball passing through both lungs from right to left. He was about ten feet in advance of me and said, 'Frank, I am hit' placing his hands on his side and staggering towards me. I asked him where. He said, 'through the heart'. I asked him if he could run, he did not answer, but ran some six or eight rods and fell. I helped him up and he staggered a little further and fell on his face. I turned him over, raised his head and held my canteen to his lips. By that time some of the rebels had climbed the fence. I said 'Dwight, they are on us!' He tried to get up and I put my right arm under his left and raised him and loosened his belt and jacket. Just then another ball struck him, passing through his head and killing him instantly. As I let him down upon the ground, he groaned 'Oh God' and then was still in death.

I dodged the rebels who supposed they had me and overtook our captain and some of the boys near Centerville. We were under fire for over one mile of our retreat . . . .

On Monday a flag of truce was granted our surgeons to gather the wounded, and Chaplain Ferguson and Willard Judd went back to look for missing friends. The chaplain found Dwight and had him buried by an oak tree." [16]

In describing the fate of the 97th's prisoners of war, William Burberry of Cold Brook wrote:

"We have been in one of the sharpest battles known to history, and it was my luck to be taken prisoner with about seventeen hundred more. We are now, however, on parole among friends, waiting to be exchanged. Our regiment went into the fight a week ago to-day and came out at night with only two hundred and fifty sound men. I was taken on the field by cavalry. We were surrounded and I tell you the balls flew like hail stones, but it pleased God that they should all miss me. I am at present at Annapolis, Md, and there are thirty two boys from our regiment with me. . . . " [17]

After retreating over Bull Run the 97th stopped at Centerville and spent the night. The next day much needed rations were drawn and the men rested behind the fortifications at Centerville. On September 1st the 97th was on the move again as Duryea's Brigade, along with a force under Irwin McDowell, was ordered out to stymie a Confederate attempt to get between Washington and Pope's battered army. At Chantilly the blue and gray columns met, and amid flashes of lightning and booms of thunder fought a standoff, an indecisive battle. Placed at the far right of the Union line, the 97th New York was not engaged that day.

With Lee stopped for the moment, Pope's retreat continued unmolested to the defenses of Washington. The 97th and the rest of Duryea's Brigade stopped at Hall's Hill on September 2nd. To the soldiers' delight, Pope was removed from command and George McClellan came north to lead the beaten army. Isaac Hall succinctly put the campaign under Pope in perspective, writing:

"There is nothing so dreadful and demoralizing to a veteran army as to feel that its commanding general does not know what he is about." [18]

CHAPTER V

"The fury of a hurricane storm"

Fall 1862 - The 121st Enters the War - Antietam

The 34th New York was one of the last regiments to leave the Peninsula and did not take part in the 2nd Bull Run battle. Leaving Harrison's Landing on August 16th, the 34th crossed the Chickahominy River and headed north on a long and tiring march through Williamsburg, Yorktown and Big Bethel. As described by Louis Chapin, the mid-summer trek through Virginia was no picnic:

> "No rain had fallen for some time, and the great army, marching over the narrow roads, made the dust unspeakably annoying. It was so deep it rolled over into the tops of the men's army shoes. The subtle irritant penetrated everywhere, even through the woolen clothing. The men were badly chafed, and suffered intensely under the burning sun, and under their heavy loads." [1]

Arriving at Newport News, the sun beaten men of the 34th stripped off their clothing and enjoyed a plunge into Chesapeake Bay. Afterwards, the boys waded the shallows of the James River feeling for the oysters that abounded on the river bottom, with their bare feet. A plentiful supply of the delicious bivalves was gathered and the soldiers dined on this delicacy to their hearts' content.

On August 25th, the 34th boarded the steamer "Mississippi" and three days later landed at Alexandria, on the outskirts of Washington. After spending the better part of the next two days in the Washington area, the 34th marched to Centerville. Meeting up with the remnants of Pope's retreating army, the 34th took up position as a rear guard unit and headed back to Washington on September 1st. On this return trip an eerie event occurred that Louis Chapin would title, "The Midnight Attack of the Phantom Cavalry." Chapin wrote:

> "What with all the hard marching we had been doing since we arrived from the Peninsula, we were probably the tiredest lot of men that ever lived. The incident . . . occurred in the middle of the night. We had halted for a moment. Immediately every man sank down in his tracks, utterly beat out, and went to sleep. Officers and men alike yielded to the pleading voice of tired nature for a rest. In the roadway itself, and all along its sides, the ground was covered with the sleeping men. It was in a dense woods, and the moonlight, filtering through the trees, made the place look very beautiful, and very ghostly. How long we had been sleeping it is impossible to state. But suddenly, as if roused by some supernatural power, every man sprang to his feet, every man excitedly exclaiming 'What is it?' But nobody could tell, for nobody knew. We all had some idea that we had suddenly been charged upon by the enemy's cavalry; but there was no enemy in sight. Even after regaining their feet, the men were half asleep and utterly bewildered. The writer had some idea, as he opened his eyes, of seeing a dash of men in gray on horseback. But one thing is certain, no men on horseback could ever have ridden along that road without trampling on a thousand sleeping men. But nobody had been hurt; and to this day the mystery of that sudden awakening has never been cleared up."[2]

After routing Pope, Robert E. Lee now became the aggressor and turned his army northward. Lee's prime objective was the mammoth railroad bridge at Harrisburg, Pennsylvania, which served as a main link in the Union's east-west supply artery. But more importantly, Lee sought to move the war from Southern soil to the homes of his enemy. On September 6th and 7th, Lee crossed the Potomac at Muddy Branch into Maryland with forty thousand men.

The Army of the Potomac, now whole again with McClellan in command, immediately began shadowing the Confederate column. McClellan, keeping in mind both offensive and defensive strategies, was careful to keep his army between the rebels and Washington. Joining in the maneuver were the 34th New York, the 97th New York and the new Herkimer County regiment, the 121st New York. Herkimer County was now represented in the Army of the Potomac by three regiments.

On August 30th, the same day that the 97th New York would get their first taste of battle outside of Groveton, the 121st New York left Camp Schuyler, mounted railcars at the Herkimer Depot and started for Albany. The regiment's first stop was at Little Falls where the Herkimer County boys bid goodbye to the home folk. J.R. Stebbins described the scene:

> "They occupied twenty-three cars and were greeted at this depot by an immense concourse of citizens and friends. The sad parting word was spoken by many a trembling lip and tears of affection, and yet of earnest self-sacrificing patriotism, were shed at the sundering of so many family and friendly ties. The train moved away followed by the hopes and confidences of the county and well do they merit both, for a finer body of men never

offered themselves to the cause of Liberty."[3]

The 121st travelled on to Albany where they were treated to a supper by the ladies of the capitol city. That night the regiment boarded a river steamer and continued their trip. Lt. Frederick Ford of Fairfield, who had agreed to be the *Journal's* 121st correspondent, related the 121st's adventures in Albany and the particulars of the journey on to Washington, writing:

> "At Albany we were treated very handsomely by the citizens. The food was good and we were waited upon by those who looked clean. After we had marched out into the street from the eating saloon, every one appeared anxious that we should have dessert. Company C, at least, went away satisfied. We had peaches and muskmelons passed up and down the lines, and finally we were totally routed by a couple of ladies who kept shelling us with apples from a commanding position in an upper story window, as long as we were in easy range.
>
> About dark the regiment marched aboard the New World, and at 10 o'clock she began heaving and surging down the North [Hudson] river. At daylight we were among the highlands but I failed to observe anything very striking about them-probably because I had somehow lost a haversack with a chicken in it. The restoration of the lost article, however, caused me to enjoy the palisades-and chicken immensely. About noon we marched up to the Park barracks and pushed out one of the new regiments: I believe the 126th. The food there was not very good, and rather dirty. If the secessionism of cities is to be measured by the amount of dirt which they feed to soldiers, New York will stand shoulder to shoulder with Baltimore.
>
> . . . During the day a couple of Jersey engines hauled us through the Jersey marshes, and by night had run us into Philadelphia, and a rain-storm. We were marched to the Cooper eating-saloon and halted in the street about half an hour. Of course, we had a refreshing shower-bath while the next two tables full were eating.
>
> Morning saw us in Baltimore, and night too, for that matter. We slept, or tried to sleep, on board the cars another night. At daylight we were dragging slowly over the rivers and arms of the Chesapeake, and finally we came past a group of soldiers,—Zouaves, New York, Wide Awakes, &c.— washing in the muddy rivers about Washington."[4]

Soon after arriving in Washington, the 121st was placed in the 2nd Brigade, 1st Division of Gen. William Franklin's 6th Corps. On September 7th, the 121st left their camp at Fort Lincoln and joined the rest of the Army of the Potomac in the march across Maryland. In a letter to his friends, Sgt. George Snell of Little Falls, detailed the 121st march into Maryland, writing:

> "We were ordered last Saturday, to strike our tents for a march; but just as the boys were ready, the order was countermanded. Sunday I took paper and pencil and went under a tree to write home, but was hardly seated when orders came to march and leave everything behind but guns, powder and haversack. I dealt out rations for two days, and about one o'clock Sunday afternoon we started. We marched until eleven o'clock at night, and camped on the ground: but had no more than lain down before the order

came to march again, and so we all started and traveled till Monday afternoon at 4 o'clock, when we camped for supper.

We lay there till eight o'clock and then started again and marched till eleven at night. We then rested over night and have marched ever since till to-day.

I am in command of the baggage train and ride horseback most of the time. We are all well in the advance and after Stonewall Jackson. Our advance is in a dangerous position. The boys sleep on their arms every night. Our brigade is first and we are 'backed up' by artillery. The advance boys in our brigade captured twelve rebels yesterday afternoon, among them a Major.

I stopped at a house yesterday and saw a rebel just dying. He had three sword cuts in the head and looked horrible enough. The rebels are not more than one day ahead of us and our cavalry are skirmishing with them most of the time. You ought to see the baggage trains from ten to fifteen miles long - all four-horse teams.

We are in tip-top health, but awfully dirty. We eat pork with a relish and don't think of getting more than two meals a day. Of course we have no bread-nothing but hard crackers which we soak in coffee or water before eating.

We passed the 34th regiment on Tuesday. I saw Easterbrooks and all of our boys. They were glad enough to see us and were apparently in good spirits.

The dust is about two feet deep and the boys are awfully dirty."[5]

Also on the move was the 97th, which had spent four days in the defenses of Washington after its retreat from Manassas. At dusk on September 6th it left the city and marched north to Rockville. Travelling through friendly Maryland brought a renewed enthusiasm to the men. Louis Chapin remarked:

"The home-like appearance of the dwellings, and large capacious and well-filled barns and enclosed fields were in striking contrast to those of Virginia, and did not fail to produce an exhilarating effect upon the spirits of the army. From many a housetop was unfurled the flag of our Union and tiny flags appeared in juvenile hands along the way while fair ladies gracefully waved the star spangled banner to welcome and cheer us on.

. . . There was another source from which this army of ragged soldiers drew inspiration, and one not to be mistaken. There had been a change in department and corps commanders and McClellan was again at the helm. However prejudice may detract the capacity and character of McClellan, the army, which was the best judge of his worth, always emphasized its appreciation of him, and its gratitude, at his restoration to command was felt and manifested throughout this eventful campaign."[6]

The 97th marched on through Mechanicsville, Brookville, Cooksville and Frederick, climbed over the Catoctin Hills and reached the base of South Mountain on September 14th. Awaiting the 97th were the 121st and the 6th Corps and on the way were the 34th and the 2nd Corps.

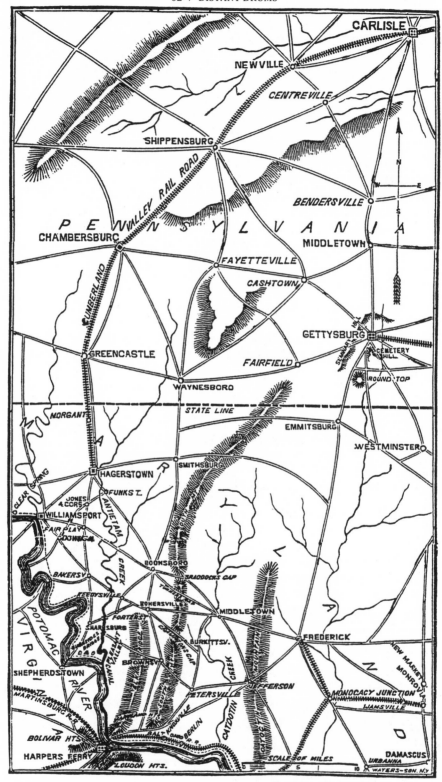

The History of the Civil War, Schmucker

The Maryland/Pennsylvania Theater

McClellan did not have to guess at the rebels' next moves for he had come into possession of a copy of Lee's detailed plans. These important papers, Special Order No. 191, were dropped by a Confederate officer and found wrapped around some cigars by Union infantrymen near Frederick. McClellan now knew that Lee had divided his army, sending Longstreet to Hagerstown and Jackson to invest the Union garrison at Harper's Ferry. Lee, having learned of McClellan's discovery through a spy in the Federal camp, was frantically trying to reassemble his army near Sharpsburg, Maryland. The two gaps at South Mountain, Crampton's and Turner's, were all that now stood between Lee's twenty thousand men and eighty thousand Federals. To buy time, Lee ordered D.H. Hill to fight a delaying action at the gaps until Longstreet and Jackson could return.

Of the three Mohawk Valley regiments, only the 97th New York actively participated in the battles of South Mountain. The 121st New York, having been in the service but one month, was judged too green to be of combat use and the 34th New York had not yet come up. The 97th, with Duryea's Brigade, arrived just in time to help repulse a final Confederate countercharge. Isaac Hall described the action:

> "Our arrival was most opportune, for at that critical moment the enemy had put forth all its strength in that part of the field, in a final assault: and the Union line with ammunition nearly expended, and bleeding with previous encounter, was being forced back over the ground from which they had driven the enemy.
>
> Our general at once ordered a charge, and with bayonets fixed and a tremendous cheer the brigade advanced to the encounter and up the mountain—with the Ninety-seventh on the right—following with cold steel the Confederate hosts.
>
> Occasionally the Confederates would 'about face', and fire a few shots: but the declivity was so steep that they passed harmlessly over our heads. About sixty of the enemy were overtaken among the rocks and trees on the mountain slope and captured in our rapid ascent. At the summit they made a stand, but by a well directed fire of our line the Confederates were soon dispersed and disappeared in the darkness down the other slope." [7]

In the fight at South Mountain the 97th New York suffered two men killed and three wounded.[8] The two men slain were Sgt. Charles Starin of St. Johnsville and Pvt. Christian Ropeter of Ephratah.

On the morning of September 15th, with the gaps now open, the Union forces began to pour through. The 97th passed over the summit near Turner's Gap, the 34th followed through the gap that afternoon and the 121st came through at Crampton's Gap. For the 121st, the first views of a battlefield were shocking. A soldier from the 121st, who chose to remain anonymous, wrote to the *Journal*:

> "Early next morning we were on the road: we passed over part of the battle-field and Oh God! what a ghastly spectacle. The Union dead had been collected by their comrades, and arranged in rows. The face and form of each covered with his blanket and a board with the name and regiment of the deceased, laid on each man's breast. A trench was being dug, for the reception of the bodies, along the whole line. I had not time to count the

number, but they were many. I could not help a thing and doffing my cap 'nod' with a tear to the memory of the gallant dead. I passed on. Soon the rebel dead made their appearance not in ones nor twos, nor dozens, but in hundreds. They had been dragged to the right and left to clear the way for our artillery and there they lay, two and three deep, some on their faces, some on their backs, heads up or feet up, their glassy eyes and mouths open and their faces blackened in the sun. I rode off the road, along a stone fence a little ways, and it was all the same as far as the eye could reach-one vast charnel house of blackened corpses. The sight nearly sickened me. Putrefaction had already commenced and the odor was offensive. I had seen enough. I retraced my steps to the road, urged my horse to a trot, and without looking to the right or left, passed through the remainder of the field. Such is the pomp and circumstance of war." [9]

While the 34th and the 97th continued on to near Keedysville, the 121st encamped at Pleasant Valley and were ordered to round up straggling rebels and help bury the dead. Clinton Beckwith of Herkimer provided a grisly account of the burial detail, writing:

"I went over the line and position occupied by the Rebels for a considerable distance and saw many of them lying on the field dead. Those I saw had not changed much from life, but they lay in all shapes and positions. Many were shot through the head. I came along to a burial detail. They had dug a long trench on the mountain side. The dead Rebels were carried to it and laid side by side until one tier was made, when another was piled on top until all the dead in the vicinity were gathered up, when the earth was put back over the mound." [10]

Lee had arranged his army on a north-south line between the village of Sharpsburg and a small creek, called Antietam. The line, about three miles long, extended from a stone bridge below the town, to an area of open fields and rocky ledges a mile north of Sharpsburg. On Monday, September 15th, Lee had less than twenty-thousand men, now on Tuesday, with Jackson returning from his victory at Harper's Ferry, the Confederate ranks were swelling towards forty thousand. Lee immediately posted Jackson and the bulk of the army at the left of the line. This position along the Hagerstown Turnpike encompassed three groves (to be forever known as the North, East and West Woods), a large cornfield, a few farm buildings and an austere little white church of the Dunker sect. Besides the "lower" stone bridge, two other stone bridges, the "middle" and the "upper" spanned the creek. These latter two bridges were a distance from Lee's lines, and appeared indefensible. Lee correctly surmised that McClellan would cross these two bridges and direct his main attack on Jackson's men.

The Union army, with twice the number as Lee's army, was poised on the opposite side of the Antietam. On the afternoon of the 16th, regiments from the Federal right wing crossed over the upper stone bridge, and after some resistance from Jackson's pickets in the East Woods, positioned themselves to the east and north of the Confederate left. Among these Union regiments was the 97th New York.

The Battle of Antietam, fought on Wednesday, September 17, 1862, would be composed of three separate actions. On the Federal right, the fight started at dawn with attacks and counterattacks surging back and forth across the cornfield and through the woods near the Dunker church. Towards noon the action would move to the center where head-on Federal charges against men in gray, entrenched in a sunken wagon road, would turn the lane into an open grave. At the southern end of the field the battle would rage from afternoon till evening as General Burnside's divisions would fight their way across the lower stone bridge only to be repulsed outside of Sharpsburg by Confederate reinforcements rejoining Lee from Harper's Ferry. The Mohawk Valley regiments that were engaged that day, the 34th New York and the 97th New York, were only involved in the fighting to the north. The 121st New York did not participate in the battle, but remained in reserve, guarding prisoners and supporting artillery. The 97th was the first to go into action.

At 6 a.m. on that fateful September morning the 97th, under the command of Maj. Charles Northrup (Colonel Wheelock and Lieutenant Colonel Spofford were away on sick leave), formed into battleline with the rest of Duryea's Brigade and began marching due south. Emerging from out of the North Woods the "Third Oneida" fell in step with other elements of Gen. Joseph Hooker's 1st Corps and headed towards Stonewall Jackson's line less that eight hundred yards away. Reaching the edge of a cornfield the order to halt was given and the men of the 97th lay down in the shadow of D.R. Miller's farmhouse. A few minutes passed as the blue columns were aligned before the order to rise and advance into the corn was given. Isaac Hall described what happened next:

> "The enemy were throwing a few shells over our heads. After a few discharges of canister shot by our batteries, over us, the brigade was deployed and the march continued through the field of corn, skirted by a row of broom corn which the men began to poke to the right and left to discover what was in their front, when the Confederate line was discovered—drawn up in [the] rear of a low rail fence—about 220 yards distant, and the firing on both sides simultaneously began. In from thirty to forty minutes nearly one-half of the regiment, composed then of 203 men and officers, were killed and wounded.
>
> Longstreet's [Jackson's] and Hooker's men had met,—and without advancing — there they stood and shot one another till the lines melted away like wax. No attention by either line was paid to the low rail fence in front, but each stood and fired upon the other. The row of broom-corn in front of our brigade was soon shot and broken down.
>
> After forty minutes time had passed there were but few to advance. The hour had come when each had been relieved from doing the other harm. Yet none had left our line, but those ordered to the rear to carry off the wounded. A few here and there remained like lonely saplings left amid a forest leveled by the fury of a hurricane storm.
>
> As a fresh Confederate division approached from beyond the Dunker chapel, a captain [Rouse Egelston] of the 97th looked to the left where first our line had rested, but now only the dead remained; and stepping to the right to where the 107th Pennsylvania had stood—till he could look over a

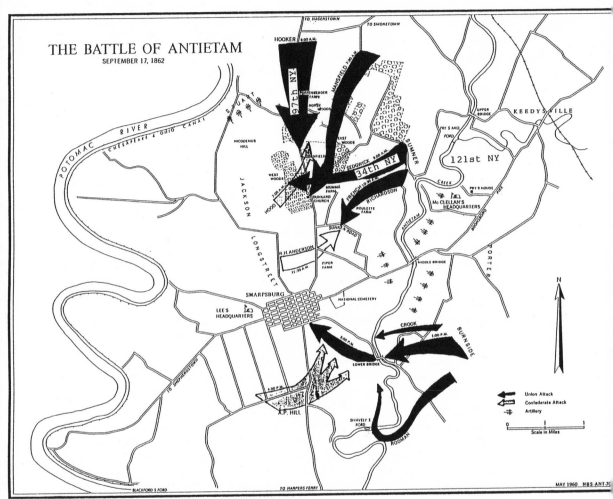

THE BATTLE OF ANTIETAM
SEPTEMBER 17, 1862

"Antietam" - *National Park Service*

roll in the field, to the turnpike, he said to his lieutenant: 'None remain on our right'; and bidding the remnants of various companies—now of less than twenty men —to close up into two ranks, he in good order left the field." [11]

Withdrawing from the cornfield, Duryea's cut up brigade made its way back to Miller's farmhouse and spent the rest of the day in support of artillery batteries there. The 97th at this point could only muster seventy men.

At about the time that the 97th was quitting the field, the 34th New York was preparing for its own try at Jackson's position.

On the eastern bank of Antietam Creek, Gen. John Sedgwick formed his division of the 2nd Corps into three great sweeping brigade lines, five hundred yards long and fifty yards apart. On the extreme left of the front line (Gorman's Brigade) was the 34th New York. At 7:30 a.m. the columns stepped off towards the sounds of cannon fire to the west, splashing across the Antietam, before marching on through the East Woods. At the edge of the woods the lines were permitted to reform and then the order to double-quick across the cornfield was given. The time was a little after 9 a.m.

Running across the field, now littered with the dead and wounded of both sides, the 34th New York somehow became separated—by over four hundred yards—from the rest of the brigade. Veering to the south, the wayward 34th reached the far edge of the field and entered the West Woods just a few rods to the north of the little Dunker church. At this point the enemy was met. Col. James Suiter described the ensuing firefight, writing:

"The order to go into line of battle was given and at double quick the men got into line. Over fences, stone walls and ditches we were rushed into the woods not an enemy in sight until I had gained a point twenty yards in rear of an old stone church. At this point I discovered them coming up the hill in strong force, when I ordered my men to fire, which they did pouring in a deadly and tremendous fire upon the Rebels, which they returned with equal force. I had, for some reason, been detached from my brigade and placed upon the extreme left of the line, without any support in my rear or on my left. On my right was the 125th Regiment Penn. volunteers, a new regiment which went to the rear at the first fire, which left my right unsupported. I now discovered that the enemy were moving a strong force to my left in columns ten or twelve deep." [12]

The rebel columns noted by Col. Suiter were Lafayette McLaw's Division of South Carolinians just up from Harper's Ferry. Positioned squarely on the 34th's left flank, the rebels poured an enfilading fire into the regiment. A Georgian reported:

"You could hear laughing, cursing, yelling and the groans of the wounded and dying, while the awful roar of musketry was appalling. . . . Where the line stood the ground was covered in blue, and I believe I could have walked on them without putting my feet on the ground." [13]

William McLean of Fairfield gave his version of the fight, writing:

"We fired two or three tremendous volleys, which thinned their ranks:

but we in turn received quite as warm a fire as we were able to give, and being flanked and cross-fired upon, were obliged to fall back. We did so at first, in good order, loading and firing as we could: but the advancing of the rebels and their deadly fire was at last too much for the famed 34th, as well as for many other regiments, and we broke for a time and ran about thirty rods: then we rallied and turned upon the foe, who gave way before us.

The action was short, not exceeding fifteen minutes, and our loss in killed, was 32 and wounded, 108. All this was the fault of some one who led us into the face of the foe unsupported on the left. We were within ten rods of the enemy when the first fire was opened, and before we fell back far, they came so close as to take ten prisoners, and others were wounded with gun-stocks, &c. This we could call nothing better than outright slaughter, and the time and number of victims show it was nothing else." [14]

Unable to withstand the fire in their front and flanks, Colonel Suiter received permission from General Sedgwick for the 34th to retire. Chased back across the field, the men halted behind a battery which stopped the pursuing rebels. Of this action Lt. William Walton noted:

"Their triumph, however, was short, for no sooner had our unit formed behind the guns than they opened with grape and cannister at less than field pistol range and the scene that followed beggars description. The enemy fell by scores and hundreds and though they madly tried to advance against the terrific and murderous fire, the attempt was vain and at last they gave way and rushed back even faster than they advanced." [15]

The 34th New York which had marched across the blood soaked cornfield with over five hundred men, in less than thirty minutes had left almost one-third of them lying dead and wounded in the West Woods and around the Dunker church.

The fighting on this part of the battlefield sputtered out by mid-morning and moved on to the contests at the sunken lane and the lower stone bridge.

The casualties of September 17, 1862 would mark it as the bloodiest day in the history of the United States. Twenty-three thousand men were struck down at Antietam, over five thousand of them dead. Another three thousand men would be listed as "missing." [16] Of the twelve thousand Union casualties, the 97th New York contributed thirty-nine killed and fifty-nine wounded [17] and the 34th New York counted forty-eight killed and ninety-six wounded. [18] From these two regiments, twenty-three Herkimer County men were slain on the field or mortally wounded and over three times that number were wounded, many quite severely. Among the dead from the 97th were, Cpl. William Gray, Sgt. Roswell Clark and Pvt. Daniel Horton of Little Falls, Pvt. William Snyder from Norway, Pvts. Patrick Finnegan and Edward Torrey of Newport, Pvt. Ephraim Pullman from Cold Brook, Cpl. Clinton Ackerman of Newville, Pvts. David Maxfield and Benjamin Wandour from Russia and Pvt. Patrick McConnell of Salisbury. The Herkimer County men killed in the 34th were, Pvts. John Beardsley, John Dixon and William Rubbins from Herkimer, Sgt. Garland Mead of Litchfield, Pvt. William Salisbury of Norway, Sgt. Aaron Helmer of Fairfield, Cpl. David Crouch of Columbia, Pvts. Warren LaDew, Stephen Cool and Ralph Walby from Little Falls, Pvt. William Lewis of Brockett's Bridge and Sgt.

Jacob Ashley from Graysville. The lists of dead and wounded from the 34th and the 97th would fill many columns in the *Journal*.

Quite notable among the wounded was Color Sergeant Charles Barton of Graysville. After the rest of the color guard were all killed, Barton kept the 34th's flag from enemy hands although he was seriously wounded. Lieutenant Walton wrote of the heroic Barton:

> "The color-sergeant, brave Charles Barton we are happy to state was not killed, though severely wounded receiving three balls in different parts of the body. Nobly he did his duty and when at last he fell brave hands eagerly seized the colors and safely carried them through the fight, . . . in every part [of the flag] small holes appear made by balls. It was [flown] from a broken staff, cut in two in the thickest of the fight. The ladies of Little Falls we learn are making for us a new and costly one, for which we shall be very grateful and thankful, but they must pardon us if first and foremost in our hearts we prize and cherish the black and tattered thing which we are proud to call our flag, our colors." [19]

Regarding the deaths of two members of the 97th, Isaac Hall would write:

> "Two German brothers by the name of Gleasman from Lewis County, were standing together, when one of them was killed by the unerring aim of a Confederate marksman who had steadied his rifle against a tree. The other, aware of the position of the man who had fired the fatal shot, said: 'There is the man who killed my brother, and he is taking aim now against that tree.' An elbow was seen to protrude from a solitary oak in the enemy's line and the next moment he lay dead beside his brother, shot by the same hand which had slain the other." [20]

It was later learned that the two Gleasman brothers were well beyond the maximum age, forty-five years old, for military service. Godfrey Gleasman was fifty-six years old and his brother George was sixty-two.

The next day the two armies, in about the same positions that they had been in before the battle, agreed to a truce and collected their wounded. Although McClellan had a fresh reserve force, in itself equal in number to all of Lee's battle weary army, he failed to renew the struggle.

The bloodied 34th and 97th regiments, spent the day caring for their wounded, standing picket and trying to reassemble their shattered units. That night Lee's army silently withdrew from Sharpsburg leaving McClellan with a hollow victory. With the enemy gone, the men in blue surveyed the field, looking for missing friends and burying the dead. From these men came a vivid description of the carnage of battle. William McLean wrote:

> "The enemy were in possession of a part of the battle-field for twenty-four hours during which time they robbed our dead; turning every pocket inside out, and taking the shoes off their feet, and occasionally other articles of clothing. We need say nothing of the horrible sight the battle-field

presents. It is three miles long and two miles wide, and every rod of its surface was dotted by a dead or wounded body." [21]

Isaac Hall added:

"On the morning of the 18th, in front of where Duryea's brigade had stood was strewn promiscuously—like sheaves of grain tossed together by a reaper—a line of Confederate dead. They had fallen in their tracks where they had stood, and marked plainly the course of the enemy's line." [22]

And Louis Chapin related:

"Milford N. Bullock [of Stratford], of Company K, was found dead on the field after the battle. The position in which he was lying indicated the painful circumstances of his death. He was lying on his back, his rifle by his side. The ramrod of his gun was in his hand, the lower end against the trigger of the gun, and the muzzle of the gun at his head. It appeared at the time that the wound he had received had not been sufficient to cause instant death; but, being in mortal agony, he had contrived to end his suffering by taking his own life. He had placed the gun by his side, the muzzle at his head, and by means of the ramrod had succeeded in discharging it." [23]

But it was Clinton Beckwith of the 121st New York that penned the ghastliest but most candid account of the scene at Antietam. Beckwith wrote:

"That the enemy suffered terribly from our fire may be gathered from the fact that for more than a mile I could have walked on their dead bodies, while in some places they lay in groups, and in others as many as fifteen lying in close line together. Mounted officers lay under their horses both dead. A great many dead horses were on the field. Near the church in the edge of the woods, by the sunken road and the edge of the cornfield, the conflict by its results seemed to have been the fiercest. All the dead presented a horrible spectacle, and it would have been impossible to recognize a brother, they were so changed from life. The weather is extremely hot, the men heated with passion, immediately after death decomposed rapidly, gases formed and the bodies swelled up to enormous proportions. For instance, the eyes would bulge out from their sockets and look more like small bladders. Many had burst, so great was the pressure upon their tissues. The remains of the horses looked even worse than those of the men, and for such carrion decent burial was impossible: and so rude cremation was resorted to, and in many cases the ashes of heroic men, dumb brutes and fence rails mingled in one heap.

Every thing seemed quite different to me from what it did when hearing the war speeches, and the deeds of valor enacted, at home; and as I thought of the vast number of dead I had seen lying unburied on the field, and the myriads of wounded men, I felt the awful horror of war upon me, and I again felt thankful that we had been permitted to see and know what we were coming to. The abandoning of the dead seemed horrible to me, and I hoped if it should be my fate to perish in battle, my comrades would give me a decent burial.

Away over on the right in the woods, I came across a body lying near a tree and partially supported by it. In the right hand was a daguerreotype of a woman and a child, and this rebel soldier, his duty done, shot to death, had made his way to this spot, taken out the picture of his wife and child, and with his thoughts upon them in their far Southern home, alone, the pangs of death clouding his sight, giving them in his terrible anguish, the unfathomable love of a dying soldier. I did not take the daguerreotype, but some one did; for passing back that way I saw it was gone. Afterward I was sorry that I did not take it, because some day it might have gotten to the wife and child. Perhaps it did. I hope so." [24]

Not until the 22nd of September did the burial details complete their work. Most of the corpses were buried with their identity only known to God. Later when the bodies were gathered and interred in the Sharpsburg National Cemetery most of the 34th's and 97th's dead were consigned to "unknown" graves.

Although the Mohawk Valley regiments were battered and bloody their morale was surprisingly high. The fight at the Antietam had been pretty much a standoff with neither side winning the field. Yet in the end, Lee's invasion of the North had been turned back and of this the defenders of the Union were justly proud. Lt. Lewis Carpenter of Little Falls, a member of the 97th who had been wounded at Antietam, described the men's spirit to the readers of the *Journal*, writing:

"I thought I would write you a short letter to let you know that some of the 97th are left: yet they are so few that we can hardly say we are a regiment: but those who are left are fighting men, and are ready and willing, but are not 'spoiling for a fight', as they were at Cloud's Mill. Should the necessity, however, show that our little band was wanted, we could show a hundred and sixty men that have been tried, and have heard the fearless whizzing of shell and the friendless zipping of the rifle. Old Herkimer county can well be proud of her representatives in this war. Let her look at the remnants left of the two regiments, the 34th and the 97th. There are not men enough left in both to make one half of a regiment. You can go to the hospitals and to the grave, and there you will find the balance of our brave boys. It is sad, but I suppose, it is honest. We enlisted to fight, and have done so: but it looks hard to see the brave men slaughtered in this cruel war. We enlisted to help put down this rebellion, and we will do it." [25]

Each of the Mohawk Valley regiments left Sharpsburg within a week of the battle and marched to other Maryland encampments. The 97th took up picket duty near Mercersville, the 121st was sent to guard Dam No. 4 along the Potomac at Bakersville and the 34th returned to their spring campgrounds on Bolivar Heights above Harper's Ferry. The regiments would remain at these locations until the latter part of October.

The two veteran regiments were in sorry shape, the 97th numbering less than two hundred men and the 34th about three hundred. But the men of the 121st, unengaged at the Antietam, were having a fine time. Lt. John Smith of Mohawk and Little Falls boys, Sgt. Joe Heath and Cpl. George Snell, cooperated to pen a letter to the *Journal*, in which they let the readers know how much fun "soldiering" was. Lieutenant Smith started off:

"Here we are drawn up in line of battle, waiting for further orders. We are after Jackson and we are going to get him. That's what's the matter. If they will only let Gen. McC. alone, he will wind up the war in double-quick time. We have travelled from Fort Lincoln to here since two weeks ago yesterday. It was quite a jaunt for green troops: but the boys don't grumble, and are as happy as clams. Pete Emmel and L.H. Greenman are now cooking dinner and they sweat like the old Harry. George Snell just came in camp with his dog that he 'jayhawked', and a rabbit which his dog caught. We are going to have the latter for supper. I wish that you could come in and see us devour the animale. Night before last we came by the last Wednesday's battle-field [Antietam] and such a sight you can't imagine. The rebels lay in piles for miles around. Geo. Snell says that he counted twenty-six rows, with from three to four hundred in a pile. It was dreadful. The rebels were so deep that our men could not make a charge. You can well imagine what a battle it was. I should like to finish this, but I have got to attend to the rations to the company."

George Snell continued the letter:

"We are stationed now in a small hollow, just east of a wood where the rebels were day before yesterday. It is quite a pleasant place, but I am afraid we will have to leave tonight or in the morning. We have good living here as a general thing. I pity the goose, chicken or pig Company A gets a sight at. You would laugh to see Charley Hammond and Bill Judd cut up the fresh meat and sail in on the provender. Snell, Redway and Frank Burt are lying down here so lazy they can't move, and big Joe Heath is putting some hard crackers down that big mouth of his."

And "Big Joe" Heath ended the letter:

"We started from Camp Lincoln, and moved from there beyond Georgetown and encamped for the night,—and the dew fell thick enough that night, you may believe, for in the morning, when I aroused the boys for a march, our blankets were nearly wet through: but that is what makes us healthy and tough. But, Stebb [Stebbins], what pulls on the boys are those long marches. After marching from seven to twelve hours they begin to "loll" and when we retire to our respective places we drop away into the land of nod in no time.

We are now in the enemy's country and don't know when we may be called on to battle for our rights: but bully for our side and down with rebellion, and hoop de doodle do for Company A and Capt. Galpin for he is the finest captain in the 121st regiment. You may think I am bragging, but if you don't believe me, come and see. We have lots of fun and are getting as fat as bucks: feel like bull dogs, fat, ragged and saucy."[26]

While the fight at Sharpsburg had been only a draw tactically, strategically it had been a decided Union victory. The Army of the Potomac had thwarted Lee's invasion and had sent the Army of Northern Virginia limping back to Richmond. Unfortunately, McClellan had failed to pursue Lee and had missed a chance to end the war. Disregarding Lincoln's orders, McClellan fumbled around Sharpsburg long enough to let Lee slip away and then settled his army in Maryland.

Five days after Antietam, President Lincoln issued the Emancipation Proclamation. The decree, which was to take effect on January 1, 1863, paradoxically only freed slaves in those parts of the nation that were outside the reach of Federal control. Slaves in the nonseceded border slave states of Missouri, Kentucky, Maryland and Delaware, and in Union-held areas of Louisiana and Virginia were not declared free. Not until the passage of the Thirteenth Amendment in December 1865 would slavery be completely abolished in the United States.

CHAPTER VI

"It was naught but murder"

Fall/Winter 1862 - Formation of the 152nd N.Y. - Fredericksburg

Even before the quota for Lincoln's call in July was filled, a second call for an additional three hundred thousand men was made on August 4th. New York Governor Edwin Morgan chose to disregard the Federal government's requested quota, instead he asked Herkimer and Otsego counties to again cooperate in the formation of a regiment. To provide the requisite five companies, the levy on Herkimer County was set at a voluntary quota of four hundred and sixty-two men.

Under the first call, a surplus of volunteers had been realized. This group, which totalled about a company, was composed mainly of men unwanted by the 121st, who were left behind at Camp Schuyler when the regiment went south. These "rejects" from the 121st, who were older men and men of questionable health, would constitute the core of the new regiment.

Alonzo Ferguson from Cobleskill, who had acted as adjutant in organizing the 121st, was requested by the governor to act in this capacity again. Ferguson designated Mohawk as the official organizing site and sanctioned recruiting in Little Falls by Timothy O'Brien and Daniel West, in Herkimer by Peleg Thomas, in Salisbury Center by A.C. Bartlett and in Norway by William Burt.

Recruiting moved slowly at first. In Little Falls, village president M.W. Priest asked the businesses of that community to help out. In an article carried by the *Journal,* Priest's petition read:

> "In accordance with the expressed wish of many citizens and the Town
> Military Committee, I earnestly recommend that, till the 3rd of September

and commencing this day, the stores and principal places of business in the village be closed at 4 1/2 o'clock of each afternoon, and that our citizens unite in the work of securing volunteers for the purpose of avoiding, a draft in the town." [1]

But with increased town bounties, war meetings and the specter of a draft, town quotas were being approached and met. Quite conspicuous was the enlistment of a dozen students and two professors from Fairfield Seminary. By the first week in September, over one half of the regiment was filled and by the second week, companies were forming and officers were being elected. Although not yet officially mustered, the regiment was designated as the 152nd New York State Volunteers.

Governor Morgan chose Leonard Boyer of Little Falls to command the new regiment. Salisbury's Lorenzo Carryl had been the governor's first choice, but he had turned down the commission due to business commitments. Assisting Boyer as lieutenant colonel was Alonzo Ferguson.

Camp Schuyler, outside of Mohawk, was again used as the assembly and training center, and contractors Prescott, Shull and Lowell of Mohawk remained to board the men. By September 18th, the Herkimer County quota was nearly filled and seven hundred men were in camp.

Due to the fear of desertion of these "high bounty men" (on average each man received $300-$500 in bounty money) and to prevent "wandering," two hundred men from the regiment were assigned as camp guard. Even with this level of security, many men did manage to elude the sentries. Routine visits were made to a nearby canal grocery, where "a canteen of corn juice" could be obtained to keep away the chills.

Unlike the previous county regiments, the men of the 152nd were issued uniforms and equipment during their early days in camp. However, the problem of obtaining modern weapons remained. Pvt. Henry Roback of Danube noted:

> "We were armed with an old fashioned state musket, but upon our departure they were mostly all rendered worthless, by the constant use they were put to in stirring the campfires." [2]

Numbering eight hundred and fifty-seven men, the 152nd New York was officially mustered into Federal service for three years, on October 15, 1862.

The slate of staff officers was,

Colonel - Leonard Boyer
Lieutenant Colonel - Alonzo Ferguson
Major - George Spalding
Adjutant - Cleaveland Campbell
Quartermaster - George Ernest
Surgeon - Silas Ingham
Chaplain - Hiram Talbot

Companies A, B, C, E, F and K, commanded respectively by Capts. Timothy O'Brien, William Burt, James Curtiss, Simon Coe, Daniel West and Lambert Hensler, were composed chiefly of Herkimer County boys.

On the morning of October 21st, the 152nd New York began the long, circuitous trip to Washington and the war. Led by a brass band, the new regiment marched from Camp Schuyler to the Herkimer train depot and were met by friends and relatives from throughout Herkimer and Otsego counties. At the station, the boys said their goodbyes, some for the final time, and filed on board the train for Albany. Arriving in Albany at about 6 p.m., the men were treated to sandwiches and coffee by ladies of the city. After the meal, the 152nd was ferried across the Hudson River and the troops boarded a "soldier train" bound for New York City. The Herkimer and Otsego county regiment reached New York late the next morning and proudly strutted down Broadway to temporary lodgings at the Park Barracks. All along the route the regiment was welcomed by hearty cheers from the city's inhabitants. At sunup the next day, the men were herded onto a river steamer which carried them to Perth Amboy, New Jersey. There the men climbed aboard "second class emigrant cars" and entrained to Philadelphia. Frequent stops along the route gave the boys a chance to sample the local "refreshments." Henry Roback related:

> "The train stopped at several stations, giving the boys an opportunity to sample an historic fluid commonly called Jersey lightning, containing more electricity than a fully charged galvanic battery."[3]

In Philadelphia the 152nd were guests at the Cooper Union—a popular soldiers' rest stop—where the men enjoyed their first meal of the day. The Upstate New York boys were so taken with the hospitality of their hostesses, that many of the men declared that when the war was over they would go to Philadelphia "to pick out a wife."

From Philadelphia the 152nd travelled by train to Baltimore. En route the 152nd suffered its first casualty when Sergeant Seymour Smith, a Fairfield Seminary student, somehow fell between the railcars and was horribly mangled. The Regimental Surgeon, Dr. Silas Ingham, tried his best to keep Smith alive, but the boy died before his father could arrive from Fairfield.

The 152nd spent two days at the depot in Baltimore, sleeping on "corporation sofas"—cobblestone mattresses and curbstone pillows—and dining on oysters before travelling on to Washington. After quartering for two days at a Washington freight house, on the first day of November, the 152nd marched over the Chain Bridge and out into the Virginia countryside. At the edge of a pine woods, about seven miles out from Washington, a tract of ground was cleared and small shanties were built. For the next three months this camp, christened Marcy, would be their home. In less than two weeks after leaving Camp Schuyler, the 152nd New York had become a link in the cordon of defenses around Washington.

In their camps near Sharpsburg, Maryland, the 34th New York and 97th New York were getting healthy. A number of the Antietam wounded were released from hospitals and with the weather cooling off, the diseases of summer were waning and the sick were getting well. New recruits were coming in (Wells Sponable alone brought six Brockett's Bridge men to the 34th), and fresh clothing, better rations and the paymaster, with four months back pay, arrived.

The story was much different in the 121st. As a general rule, the first few months of a regiment's existence were the most trying on the men's health. Country boys, living in crowded unsanitary camps, subsisting on unhealthy and unaccustomed diets, and left to their own devices, were especially prone to disease. Their bodies, and more importantly, their minds were not attuned to the hardships of a soldier's existence and could not cope with the maladies of the field camps. The health of the men of the 121st did not prove an exception to this rule. The hardy regiment of one thousand men that had marched through the streets of Washington early in September, at month's end could muster only five hundred for dress parade.

The men blamed their infirmities on spoiled rations, an ignorance of proper food preparation and on the fatigue of marching. The 121st's Lieut. Ford noted:

> "The fare that we get is rather rough: in fact so poor that when the regiment returns once more to civilization, there will be very little complaint about food. There will be quite an appreciation, too, of 'women's work.' The most of us have already found out that cooking isn't funny at all. Marching is very severe work, severer than any of the men have ever been accustomed to. The largest and fleshiest men fail first."[4]

But Chaplain J.R. Sage's explanation of the 121st's health problems was probably closer to the mark. Sage wrote:

> "We are now passing the critical time. The men have not learned to take care of themselves as old soldiers do, and they eat too much trash - the main troubles being appleplexy and pie eaty! There are very many of the most villainous pies hawked around the camp by the inhabitants nearby. But we shall learn one of these days. . . . Our real troubles commenced when we stopped in this camp. But putting this and that together I judge that moderate marching is better for an army than perfect quiet in camp."[5]

Only the most critically ill were removed to hospitals in Philadelphia, Washington or New York. The majority of the sick were expected to get well in the field "hospitals." Frederick Ford voiced his disgust with the handling of the 121st's sick:

> "The sick were all left on the ground with no better accommodations than the well, until day before yesterday, when the worst cases were taken into a barn. I do not know how long they would have remained unsheltered if there had not been a tremendous rain-storm threatening. It would have been no better than wilful murder to have left some of the sick out in our cornstalk wigwam, so they were ordered in. There has been a great deal of complaint among the men about the treatment which the sick have received, and in many cases the complaint was not uncalled for. Yet with regards to such things there is as much in having a strong will to back one up as in any case which the sick soldier can receive here. Lieut. Cameron is lying in a 'poor white's' house nearby sick with fever. Lieut. Davis in about the same condition. Wilbur F. Lamberson is lying in a barn (barn lodging here is equivalent to feather beds at home) very much discouraged by an attack of fever."[6]

George Davis of Little Falls and Wilbur Lamberson and Angus Cameron of

Fairfield would succumb to their illnesses. The regiment's acting physician, Assistant Surgeon Steven Valentine, was discharged three months later for gross incompetence.

Besides disease taking its toll, the green troops' unfamiliarity with their firearms posed a constant hazard to themselves and others. Of such incidents in the 121st, Reverend Sage wrote:

> "One of Co. A, named Jacob Prame, accidentally discharged his gun while his left hand was resting over the muzzle, tearing it frightfully and rendering amputation necessary. He is getting along well however. Such accidents are common in new Regiments. I came very near to a whizzing bullet about two weeks ago, which some careless fellow had fired off, while I was riding along by a cornfield. It came near enough to enable me to get the key, and I am frank to say I did not quite like the pitch. I mention this to show the great number of accidents liable to occur in such a raw lot of men." [7]

But for those men in the 121st with strong dispositions who had learned to care for themselves, the war was as yet a lark. Building their own shanties, cooking their own meals and playing soldier, the young men were simply on a giant campout with their friends. One happy soldier in the 121st, who went by the pen name "Hardtack," informed the *Journal's* readers:

> "I wish you could come in our cornstalk house just now to see what a ranch we have got. It is a gay mansion. It is about 15 feet square, with a window and a front door in it. We are going to enlarge it to-morrow with our new tents, which we are going to put on the rear of this one and use as a sleeping apartment and use this as a sitting room and dining hall. We have got a dining table just large enough for our family to sit around. Joe Heath, Bill Judd and I sit on one side and George Snell, Charley Hammond and Frank Burt on the other and Pete Emmel on the end. Oh! we live gay here you can bet! We had a 'bully' dinner to-day. I wish some of our friends could have been here to help us eat it. It was composed of fresh beef-steak, potatoes, and good bread." [8]

The views on camp life from the veterans in the old 34th and the 97th differed markedly with those of the rookies. To the men of the old regiments, away from home over a year now, day to day existence was not quite as cheerful as that in the 121st. The 34th's William Walton moaned:

> "While at home, even surrounded with friends, we always did hate the rainy days of early winter. But a rainy day in camp! It's enough to give one an ague fit in August to think of it. We have had some such lately - dark, lowering days, when the clouds looked cold and cheerless, when the landscape looks drear and a general gloom pervades the camp. And then the slow, ceaseless patter of the rain! How it chills through and through the poor sentry, while it sends his scarcely less fortunate comrades huddling about the fires or shivering to their comfortless tents. When the soldier at such times, draws a contrast between home life and camp life, the balance is largely in favor of the former." [9]

Another point of disagreement between the old and new troops centered on the leadership abilities of George McClellan. Veteran troops affectionately viewed "Little Mac" as the man that had taken the raw recruits of 1861, and through his superior generalship, turned them into the proud and powerful Army of the Potomac. The new regiments, on the other hand, saw George McClellan as an arrogant, ego-centric leader that had no stomach for a fight. Three frequent correspondents, Frederick Ford of the 121st, Julius Townsend of the 152nd and William Walton of the 34th, debated McClellan's worth in the pages of the *Journal.* Lieutenant Ford wrote:

> "(Napoleon Bonaparte) McClellan marched an army of brave, earnest, eager men right up a steep: over a hill down into the 'Valley of Humiliation,' where they are now resting and are likely to remain until they are frozen into winter quarters. The whole army, or at least all of that part lying about here, has moved. McClellan seems to stir us about for exercise, just as an owner would his horse, but when night comes its the same old horse in the same old stall and that horse is getting to be only a spavined hack and the stall is only a stall anyway. It seems that the 'army of the Potomac' would no longer be an army unless it should be disgracefully picketing along the river whose name it bears. The regiment went in there last Thursday and came out Saturday. Opposite us there was one rebel post with one solitary, but terrible rebel in it, all day confronting our three or four Companies put there to keep him from attacking us. Quite evidently quaker guns work well still in this one sided war." [10]

Private Townsend, who probably best expressed the views of the common citizen since he had been in the army only a short time, echoed Ford's comments about McClellan, writing:

> "On the eve of his departure he, Napoleon like, issued a proclamation to his soldiers, promising them long marches, arduous and fatiguing duties, but ultimately the overthrow of our traitorous enemies. How well he has fulfilled the first part of this double pledge, the bleaching bones of thousands of our brave volunteers, which now lie scattered along the shores of the Potomac, amply testify how well he has fulfilled the latter, the disgraceful surrender of Harper's Ferry, the seven days fight before Richmond and the ill-planned and even worse executed battle of Antietam afford abundant proof. Failure after failure, blunder after blunder, and defeat after defeat were palliated with excuses of the most frivolous character, until finally, mistakes so gross, errors so palpable, could no longer be concealed. As a fond mother endeavors to conceal the follies of her wayward offspring, even so the North sought to keep the weakness and inability of their National idol unrevealed. But it was of no avail, for facts, stern, stubborn, irrefutable, removed the veil of delusion from the eyes of the North, and instead of an American Napoleon, they found at the head of their armies, a general, who possessed neither the ability to plan a campaign nor the energy to execute it." [11]

It was up to Lieutenant Walton of the 34th to defend McClellan on behalf of the old guard. Walton replied to the criticisms of "Little Mac," writing:

"It is very easy to criticize and find fault and talk sarcasm, but how foolish and useless to pass judgement on our generals, knowing as little as we do of the plans and motives that influence them. We have been induced to do this, but with one or two exceptions have refrained, for, first of all, it is a soldiers' duty not to find fault but to take things as he finds them, not to question, but to obey, and we must confess that in ofttimes it angers old campaigners of eighteen months service to hear new comers tell how this General erred or that one went astray at some period of the bloody past. True, every one has a right to his opinions, but there are some things we should keep to ourselves and soldiers should wait until they are again citizens before they arraign, try and execute their leaders and commanders." [12]

One thing that many of the Mohawk Valley men did agree upon was their disappointment with the election of anti-war Democrat, Horatio Seymour of Utica, to the governorship of New York State. The men had no complaint with the voters of Herkimer County, for the county had given Seymour's rival, Union party candidate James Wadsworth, a decided plurality of over one thousand votes from the six thousand votes cast.

Only in Herkimer and Little Falls did Seymour carry the vote. However, Seymour's thirty thousand vote margin in New York City was enough to offset Wadsworth's ten thousand vote mandate in the rest of the state. To the men at the front, Horatio Seymour's victory showed a lack in faith by the homefolk for the abilities of their soldier boys. William Walton of the 34th related:

"Those of us not in sympathy with the Seymourites feel as though New York has sent forth her sons to the battlefield to brave death in every form and then betrayed them at the ballot box. She told us she was sending us forth to aid in the subjugation (how we love that word!) of the rebels, that her sympathies and her prayers would follow us, but when we are fairly down here she elects a governor who is an unprincipled compromising Democrat, who is in favor of ending the war, regardless of the manner, in the quickest possible time. We are one of those who believe that it is a matter of interest and consequence to all that this war should end soon: but in comparison to the importance of how it shall end, the when sinks into all significance." [13]

On September 25th, Col. Richard Franchot, commander of the 121st, resigned his commission. Franchot, a politician and not a military man, realized from the start that his lack of military training would be detrimental to the regiment. During the 121st's stay in Washington Franchot asked his friend, Gen. Henry Slocum, to find a replacement for him. The man chosen by Slocum was twenty-three-year-old Emory Upton, a West Point graduate and a captain in the 5th U.S. Artillery. On October 23rd, Upton was promoted to a colonel and placed in command of the 121st. The new colonel was a stern taskmaster and a no nonsense military man, but he was also a friend to the private soldier. Under Upton's leadership the 121st New York would be whipped into a model unit that would earn the nickname, "Upton's Regulars." In his letters to the *Journal*, the 121st's Lieutenant Ford, let the people of Herkimer County know that their boys were in good hands. Ford wrote:

"October 26th . . . Yesterday, our new Colonel took command of the Regiment. Several things have happened since which, if they were the result of his orders, as is said to be the case, will not injure his reputation among the men. In the first place, the sick are all to be removed to a brick church. He is reported to have said that 'his men should not lie in uncomfortable out-houses.' Again, the guard have been provided with guard's tents for shelter. Before this we may have been compelled to lay unsheltered when on guard duty. And to-day, as it is raining hard, the guard have all been drawn in except three or four actually necessary. A mess of straw has been distributed to each tent, what we had before either bought or stolen. Whoever acted, it was a good days work." [14]

"November 2nd . . . Our new Colonel has taken wonderfully well with the men. If he only wears as well as he takes, in six months we shall be one of the finest regiments in the service. The secret of success in an officer, is to give no unnecessary orders, [and] to have necessary ones obeyed. He has the secret." [15]

"November 27th . . . Our present Colonel is all I represented him to be, brave and gentlemanly. He seems to consider that although we are now slaves through necessity we were once freemen by right. You may believe any good of him. The people may be assured that their sons will be dealt justly so long as Upton commands." [16]

In the autumn months of 1862, with the war in the East at a standstill and President Lincoln's calls for volunteers filled, life in Herkimer County returned to almost normal. Although fighting still raged out west at places like Perryville, Kentucky, and Iuka, Mississippi, the Army of the Potomac was bedded down in Maryland and the hometown boys were safely in camp. The pages of the *Journal*, for the time being, were filled with news of a peacetime flavor.

At Concert Hall in Little Falls the fall and winter lecture season began with Dr. A. O'Leary speaking on the subject of "Health and Beauty," Professor H.A. DeMunn giving a discourse on "The Preservation of Hair" and with "Dr." Maungwaudaus expounding on natural health cures. Chief Maungwaudaus was assisted by a number of his brother Oneida Indians. Also performing at Concert Hall were the Tremaine Family Singers accompanied by Miss Louise Bennett, Dan Rice's Great Circus— which the *Journal* was pleased to announce was free from any vulgarity—and Yankee Robinson's "Great Moral Exhibit" of the three great epochs in American history. Robinson's exhibition was originally intended to be an outdoors affair, but during his opening performance a violent thunderstorm came up and leveled his "Water Proof Pavillion." The collapsing tent scattered the audience, knocked down Robinson's scenery, wrecked his "clockwork historical figures" and set free his ferocious wild bear. The bewildered bruin ran amok through the terrified crowd, doing little damage except causing a few ladies to faint, before he was recaptured by his handlers. The balance of Yankee Robinson's shows were transferred to the safe confines of Concert Hall.

Autumn was also the time for the Farmers Club Herkimer County Fair. The fair was held at the county fairgrounds on the river flats to the south of Herkimer and as usual was highlighted by the horse races. This year, "O. Bort" won the race for four year old colts, but "Lady Franklin," the "spike-tail canal horse," stole the show with her four heat victory in the trot. "The Lady" ran the last mile heat in the flashy time of two minutes and forty-six seconds.

In other news carried by the *Journal*:

. . . Dr. A.E. Varney was appointed as the physician at the Herkimer County Poor House. Varney's salary was set at $150 a year.

. . . The students of Fairfield Seminary held a meeting to celebrate and endorse President Lincoln's "Proclamation of Emancipation."

. . .The village of Little Falls sought bids for replanking and rebuilding the sidewalks on Main Street.

. . . The body of a man was found floating in the Mohawk River near Waite's Dam in Little Falls. Papers in the dead man's pockets identified him as forty-four-year-old James Gordan, but did not give a clue to his hometown. Military discharge papers on the corpse showed him to have been a member of the 43rd New York, who had been discharged due to "old age." With no idea of how Gordan had ended up in the river, a coroner's jury gave the official cause of death as "Found Drowned."

Winter came early to Herkimer County in 1862. Severe frosts in September damaged many garden and field crops, and in early November, a snowstorm of unprecedented proportions blanketed the Mohawk Valley countryside. Later that month, heavy rainfall, caused the Mohawk to flood its banks and Spruce Creek to surge. The Spruce Creek "freshet" did its worst damage in Salisbury, destroying the Mike Miller Bridge, wrecking Ives' Mill and most tragically, taking one life. Of the incident the *Journal* reported:

> "At the 'Tuttle Bridge' [in Salisbury], occurred the fatal accident. A family named Murphy were 'moving' across the bridge. The team with furniture, &c. barely reached the shore and Mrs. Murphy and her daughter were upon it driving a calf when it broke asunder, carrying all into the current several feet below. The lady was immediately swept away from all succor and her body was recovered some half mile distant. The little girl clung to a plank and struggled to save herself when Mr. Alexander Traver—all praise to the brave man who did so noble a deed—rushed into the surging flood and with difficulty succeeded in reaching and in saving her." [17]

Down south, the Army of the Potomac finally stirred in late October and began another move on Richmond. Since the battle of Antietam, Abraham Lincoln had been pressuring George McClellan to do "something" and now "Little Mac" believed he saw an opportunity. In consulting his map, McClellan came to realize that the Army of Northern Virginia, encamped in the Shenandoah Valley, was actually farther from Richmond than was his own army. Accepting the belief that the capture of the Confederate capital was the key to ending the rebellion, McClellan set his soldiers in motion for Richmond.

On October 25th the head of the Federal column turned south and began crossing the Potomac River at Harper's Ferry. Unfortunately, unforeseen delays bogged down the Union troops and eight more days would transpire before all of the army was across the river. In the meantime, Robert E. Lee got wind of McClellan's designs and pushed his army ahead of the Federals, effectively blocking the Union thrust. Abraham Lincoln had finally seen enough. On November 7th McClellan was deposed as commander of the Army of the Potomac and Ambrose Burnside was given command. Burnside had his limitations as a leader, but to his credit, upon taking the mantle of a command that he didn't want he acted quickly and decisively. Organizing the army into three "Grand Divisions," the Right, Left and Center, he sidestepped Lee and rapidly moved the Union columns again south. By November 20th, seven Union corps were assembled on the heights opposite Fredericksburg, Virginia, less than fifty miles from Richmond.

From their Maryland encampments, the 34th, 97th and 121st New York regiments had trudged along with the rest of the Army of the Potomac. The long and fatiguing march, under McClellan and now with Burnside, brought the Mohawk Valley boys through Snicker's Gap, Rectortown, Warrenton and on to Fredericksburg. Aside from frequent harassment by rebel skirmishers, the march had been rather uneventful save for one strange incident that would remain with the men of the 34th. Stopping one night after a grueling march, the tired men stacked their guns and, still in their ranks, literally sank to the ground. During the night four inches of snow fell atop the slumbering men. The next morning, early risers were treated to an eerie scene that seemed to portend the future. Lt. Louis Chapin related:

> "The sleeping men were all under snow; and as they had lain down in rows, same as they marched, the appearance was that of a cemetery, the graves all in rows, according to the fashion we are all familiar with. The sight was weird enough." [18]

Burnside's end around maneuver had surprised Lee and now all that lay between the Union army and the road to Richmond was the Rappahannock River. However, despite Burnside's request that pontoon bridges be at Fredericksburg on his arrival, no pontoons were ready and none would arrive for almost a month. Across the river in Fredericksburg, the rebel force was building as reinforcements were arriving daily. Burnside encamped his army and gazed across the Rappahannock watching his advantage slipping away. The 34th New York, near Falmouth and the 97th and 121st New York, at Belle Plain, had an excellent view of the city that they could have easily taken a few days earlier, but that now appeared quite formidable. Lt. William Walton of the 34th commented:

> "Fredericksburg, seen from the heights on this side of the Rappahannock, appears to be a 'mazing nice sort of a place.' Large churches with most portentous heaven aspiring spires, large mills and factories of vast dimensions and handsome private residences fit for a prince, are scattered around with no sharing hand. The river at this point is very narrow (no wider that the West Canada) and one feels almost like being shut out of Paradise to see it so near and not be permitted to enter. So far there has been

no attempt to take it and as the darkies say it is 'mighty uncertain' whether it will be occupied by us at all. It may be that it is not wanted for it is allowed on all sides [that] during the first four and twenty hours it could have been taken with little or no loss. Not so now. The enemy have made the most of their time and now large forces occupy and numerous batteries frown down upon it from the heights just beyond the city, and [if] we enter without first driving them from their position the place would be untenable." [19]

Not knowing how long their stay would be and with the winter weather having turned downright wretched, the men quickly erected shelter tents and built crude log huts. Thanksgiving Day was spent in the cold, wet, dirty camps, and as noted by Lieutenant Walton, provided little joy for the men:

"Thanksgiving day passed all very quietly, there being no feasting or hilarity for the very good reason that we had nothing to make merry with. We are living, in fact, in a wilderness as far as eatables are concerned. No eggs, no butter, no chickens, no anything of the kind can be obtained at any price." [20]

The pontoons finally arrived during the second week in December and the engineers began bridging the Rappahannock. Rebel sharpshooters, concealed in riverfront buildings, caused the construction to proceed very slowly. As soon as the engineers ventured out on the span, deadly rifle fire would kill or wound a few and the rest would scurry back to safety. To put an end to this menace, Burnside had Fredericksburg shelled. William Walton wrote of the bombardment:

"Our men were fired upon by the concealed sharpshooters of the enemy, and many a brave fellow there met his untimely fate. The firing of the first gun, however, was the signal for our batteries to open. Shot and shell were poured upon the ill fated place from one hundred and fifty pieces of artillery, with a noise almost deafening and with an effect terrific and terrible in the extreme. Years and years will pass away, but scores will be numbered ere that city ceases to wear its scars and recovers from that one days' bombardment. Many of the buildings were burned, and there is scarcely a habitation that was not pierced through and through with the cruel missiles.
     The city is one wreck and ruin. Desolation dwells in its streets and despair in the hearts of its inhabitants." [21]

To completely secure the bridgehead, the 7th Michigan, supported by the 19th and 20th Massachusetts regiments crossed the Rappahannock by boat and cleared the waterfront of the remaining rebels. Late on the afternoon of December 11th, the bridges were completed and Federal units entered the city. Vicious street fighting with a small Confederate force went on into the night, but by morning the city was safely in Union hands. The rest of that day was spent in bringing over the bulk of the troops and in positioning them for the next morning's planned attack. The troops, waiting for the bloody struggle that they knew was coming on the morrow, rampaged through the abandoned city. Fairfield's Lieutenant Walton wrote of this scene:

"The houses were deserted and at least, partly destroyed, and yet so
hastily were they abandoned that they were filled with everything that
wealth could procure or luxury desire. The wearied soldiers rested their
tired frames on feather beds, eat their fat pork on costly china or silver
plate, or if disposed dined on jellies and pickled fruits, and for recreation
read from the Poets bound in 'blue and gold.' Hundreds of thousands of
dollars worth of property were destroyed daily, and what was a short time
since a wealthy city, is now nothing but a poverty stricken place. Do our
friends cry out against this? So do we—it is wrong, essentially wrong, but
it is War." [22]

On the heights beyond Fredericksburg, Lee arrayed his army of eighty thousand
men along a seven-mile line. On the left, behind the city, he placed Longstreet and
on the right, Jackson. The position, heavily fortified by rifle pits, breastworks and
scores of cannon, bore at its center a stone wall near Mr. Marye's house. The boys in
blue knew that to even reach this line they would have to cross a thirty-foot-wide
mill race and almost one-half mile of open ground. They also grimly noted that the
rebel artillery was situated in such a way as to take every inch of this ground into
their field of fire.

After a month of inactivity and constant pressure from Washington, Burnside
chose the morning of December 13th for his head-on attack. The plan devised by the
Union high command called for General Sumner's Grand Division to strike the Confederate left, General Hooker's to attack the center and for General Franklin's men
south of Fredericksburg, to go against Jackson. Burnside believed that Sumner's men
could forge a breakthrough against Longstreet's troops and then move southward
along the crest of Marye's heights folding up the rebel line as they went. Hooker's
and Franklin's soldiers would serve to hold the rebels in place while Sumner carried
out his mission.

At dawn on the 13th, the 97th New York, with Franklin's Grand Division, was
in position and ready to advance on Jackson on the Confederate right. But sunrise
revealed a thick fog enveloping the countryside, so the men lay on their arms waiting
for the mist to clear. Two hours later, at 9 a.m., the haze lifted and Franklin's regiments, brigades and divisions rose, aligned and began their march across an open
field. Their target was a set of woods a half mile to the front. Half way across the
field, enemy batteries concealed in the woods, opened on the men with grape and
cannister. Receiving the order to halt, the 97th dropped to the ground, where they lay
protected by a slight rise in field. The rebel barrage continued for three hours, until
Union batteries from across the river silenced the Confederate guns. At noon the
order to move forward was once again given and the 97th joined the rest of
Franklin's Grand Division in a battleline a mile long, and three ranks deep. Reaching
a point 150 yards from the woods, rebel infantry sent a volley at the troops and down
again went the men. After thirty minutes of hugging the ground the order to charge
was given. Sgt. Henry Way of Little Falls described the action:

" . . . we received orders to fix bayonets. We did so, and the next moment we got the order to charge, and charge we did with a will, making the
woods ring with our shouts, as the rebels broke and fled, some for the

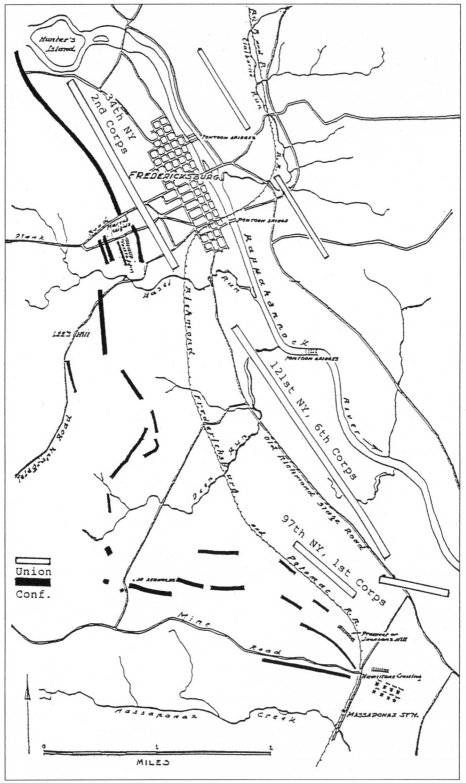

Fredericksburg, December 13, 1862

woods, some for our ranks to give themselves up. The advantage did not last long, for the enemy had a masked battery in the woods and a heavy reinforcement of infantry. We stood within ten rods of them, giving and taking volley after volley of rifle balls and grape and cannister. At last Tower's brigade [also in the 1st Corps] began to waver and then fell back and left the field, leaving the 97th and part of the 88th [Penn.] alone: but the 97th getting out of ammunition fell back to the railroad and rallied again, firing now and then a shot as the men could get cartridges. The enemy seeing us fall back, came charging down on us with an overwhelming force. The regiment then fell back about twenty-five yards and again rallied and came to a front. Not five men in the regiment had any ammunition."[23]

The 97th had expended over nine thousand rounds of ammunition and at this point was searching through the cartridge boxes of the dead and wounded. Although the 97th's situation was desperate, Colonel Wheelock would not leave the field without orders, so Captain Parsons was sent back to headquarters to ask permission for the regiment to retire. Fortunately, Parsons returned quickly with the orders to withdraw and the 97th marched back to the morning's jump off point.

The 97th's losses during the one hour and forty minutes that they were actually engaged were comparatively light. Four men had been killed, thirty-four wounded (four mortally) and four men were missing.[24] Two of the dead, John Young of Salisbury and Anson Robinson of Newport, were Herkimer County men.

At about the time that the 97th New York arose, and began marching with its mile long column, the 34th New York, acting as a reserve regiment, moved out from Fredericksburg and out onto the battlefield. Ordered to take up a position in front of a rebel battery, the 34th huddled behind a bluff out of reach of the battery's guns. Concentrating on the cannon straight ahead, the men failed to notice enemy artillery on their flank. In describing the carnage that followed, William Walton wrote:

"Off to our right on an eminence was a battery that completely commanded our position, as we soon learned to our sorrow. It was not far off and we looked meaningly at each other as we saw the cannoniers step to their places, load and - it cannot be told. The blue smoke would rise and then with the rapidity and force of lightning the sure messenger of death would strike in our midst and so Sully's Brigade [1st Brigade, 2nd Division, 2nd Corps] numbered so many more in killed and wounded. It was fearful, it was horrible. Brave men turned pale and strong men held their breath in suspense. Think of it, picture it: but you cannot think, you cannot picture the fearful scene, one must see it to know it. But as best you can imagine the hollow shell, itself death and filled with death, striking in the midst of a large body of men, crashing through the body of one, severing the limbs from another, scattering far and wide the brains of a third and then, as it bursts, bruising and mangling many more and you have a faint but true idea of the power of one of these terrible visitants. Never in all our experience as a Regiment-at Fair Oaks, Seven Days Fight, Antietam, never were we placed in so trying a place. It was looking grim death in the face and daring it to do its worst. We were powerless. Advance we could not and retreat we would not. We lay there and waited our fate. . . .

But it may be asked why we did not charge and take the battery. Gladly would we have done so, hardly a man but would have hailed with delight the order to advance, but the order came not. As we now know it, it was well that we did not, for had we attempted it, there would not have been enough left to tell the tale. But enough of this slaughter—this murder, for it was naught but murder, cold-blooded murder."[25]

The Union artillery across the river soon got the range of the rebel battery that was enfilading the men and silenced it. The 34th moved a short distance to their right where they lay till midnight amid the sights and sounds of the day's carnage. Walton related:

"Around were the dead—some headless, some armless—the torn, the mangled, the dead and the wounded—thousands passed the long weary hours moaning in their pain, groaning in agony or, as the sharp winds 'like javelins of steel' pierced their tender wounds telling in piercing shrieks their fearful tortures."[26]

Ordered to move back to Fredericksburg, the 34th spent the night and all of the next day in the city, fortuitously avoiding the fate that befell the regiment that replaced them. Lieut. Walton wrote of the narrow escape:

"Soon after midnight we were relieved by a regiment of regulars [4th U.S. Regt., 1st Corps], and drawing in our pickets, we retired into the city to seek a little rest. Here we would mention that of the two companies of regulars that relieved our men on picket, but one escaped. As soon as it was light the rebel sharp-shooters opened upon them and killed or wounded all save one."[27]

The 34th suffered three killed and twelve wounded (four mortally) and eighteen men missing.[28] Among the regiment's dead were Andrew Smith of Devereaux, whose last words were reported as "Tell my mother that I die like a man," and Adam Moyer, one of the six new recruits from Brockett's Bridge that had followed Captain Wells Sponable south in September. Orlando Fosket of Columbia and Alexander Comins from Manheim would soon after die of their wounds. Notable among the 34th's wounded was frequent Journal correspondent, William McLean of Fairfield.

The 121st New York's part in the Fredericksburg fight involved a daylong trial of picket duty along the banks of Deep Run Creek at the left center of the Union line. At daylight on the morning of December 13th, the 121st was ordered out to relieve the picket line of the 15th New Jersey in an unsheltered portion of the field. Double-quicking across the shot strewn plain, "Upton's Regulars" were surprised to see the 15th New Jersey boys turn and hightail it to the rear at the approach of the 121st. Now began the 121st's first combat lessons. Sixteen-year-old Herkimer native, Clinton Beckwith, gave a firsthand account of the regiment's fight. Beckwith wrote:

"Nothing had been said to us, no orders had been given, and I doubt very much if our officers knew what was expected of them, or us. I stood where the Jersey men had left me for a little time. I looked in front of me. Along a sort of meadow ran a rail fence separating it from a piece of woods. From this fence sprang out puffs of smoke, and the instant hiss of a missile in our vicinity told us that we were the object of the rifleman's attention. Almost instantly I saw two on my right, [Levi] Doxtater and [Ashabel] Davis, tumble down shot, and on my left heard Delos Doxtater cry 'I am shot'. I felt a fierce tug and numbness run along my left arm and side and felt I had been struck myself. Benny West sang out 'lie down,' and seeing I had been hit, I dropped down on my face and hands. In the brief time I had been standing there I saw that we were in a bare, unsheltered place, and several men of the regiment that we had relieved were lying in our front. I examined my arm and side, but found to my great relief that excepting a numbness, they were all right, and I immediately turned my attention to the fellows in our front who were seeking to assist us in shuffling off this mortal coil. We fired at them several times, but they returned our compliments with accuracy and earnestness. I got my tin plate out of my haversack for a starter and soon scooped out a hole which afforded some shelter from the sharpshooters in our front.

. . . Benny West and I fired at the puffs of smoke many times in turn , but only succeeded in getting the dust spattered about us where the balls struck from the return fire, and the ping, pang, spoch, sounds made by the bullets were not pleasant to the ear. A little way off, one of our men, breathing through the blood that was choking him to death, made an awful sound.

. . . First we wondered how long this thing would last, whether we would have to get up and charge those cusses in front, whether the rest of the fellows were in as bad a place as we were, and whether the battle would be fought about us. Then our attention was attracted by the terrific firing of all arms, both on our right [Marye's Heights] and left—the terrific crash of musketry, the yelling and cheering of thousands of men, and the heavy thunder of artillery. The hours dragged terribly slow. After noon the firing in our front slackened and finally stopped, and after a time we hung up a handkerchief in answer to one from their side; and we gathered and carried back our dead. . . . Of course as soon as the firing ceased the strain under which we had been so many hours was off, and the future and its concerns occupied our minds. I looked about me and got something to eat from my haversack and talked with the other fellows. Of course we lay low, for the reputation of the gentlemen in our front was of such a character as to prevent us from giving them too much of an opportunity to kill us, and we all agreed that we did not want any more picket or skirmish line work, especially where the enemy was under shelter and we were lying exposed on a bare field. We were too much in the position of the chicken at a chicken shoot.

. . . When night came, and the moon came up and the fog rose from the marshy ground in our front and along the creek bottom, I had none too many clothes on to protect me from the penetrating chill of the damp, cold air and fog. We took turns watching the front. I do not think a sound escaped our ears, and I was very much vexed at one of our fellows who was off duty snoring for a time. . . . It was moonlight when relief came, the 77th N.Y., I think."[29]

At Fredericksburg, four men of the 121st New York were killed and twelve wounded.[30] Slain from Herkimer County were Ashabel Davis and Oscar Spicer of

Winfield, and Levi Doxtater from German Flatts. Among the 121st's casualties were four men that suffered accidentally self-inflicted gunshot wounds.

Burnside's assaults had failed miserably. His head-on attacks against the impregnable Confederate fortifications were simply slaughter. Wave after blue wave moved up the hills behind the city, only to be dashed in turn. Most notable was the carnage wrought in front of Mr. Marye's stone wall. Almost thirteen thousand Federals had fallen, against less than half that number of the enemy, without any gain.[31] No man in blue had even reached the gray line.

On the night of December 15th, Burnside withdrew his beaten army back across the Rappahannock.

Returning to their camps at Belle Plain and Falmouth, the 34th, 97th and 121st constructed winter quarters. The little huts with tent roofs and small fireplaces kept the men comfortable, but the uncommonly severe weather of this Virginia winter made any outside activity miserable. Christmas Day, like Thanksgiving Day, passed without much notice by the weary, disheartened troops.

At Camp Marcy, about fifty miles to the north of Fredericksburg, the 152nd New York, snug in its Washington fort, viewed the war much differently. As with most new regiments, the men of the 152nd longed for the glory of battle; after all, they had enlisted to fight. In their present occupation, strengthening the defenses around the capital, the troops believed that rather than learning the necessary "arts of war," the regiment was stagnant in its military training. Edward Townsend wrote to the *Journal's* J.R. Stebbins:

> "No doubt it would interest many of your readers to know what is our chief occupation. Probably they indulge in the idea that we drill most of the time. Well, we do drilling, build roads, dig ditches, rifle pits and construct bridges and most everything relating to the mud line. Once in a while we are called out to form ranks and indulge in a little military recreation: after that we fall back into our old occupation and how! how natural it seems! Why, I believe, were the 'long roll' beat at dead of night to summon us to immediate action against the Rebs, every man would jump for his pickaxe or shovel and defiantly march to digging roads or building bridges, instead of seizing his musket and cartridge box and preparing for action. We certainly are in no condition to fight, as a regiment: though take us individually we might do very well and perhaps work to more advantage than if we were drawn up in line of battle." [32]

From their location near Washington, the 152nd saw the war in a much broader light than could their brother regiments at the front. The troops along the Rappahannock only saw the effect of the debacle at Fredericksburg on the army; the men of the 152nd could see its effect on the people. Fairfield's Edward Townsend wrote:

> "The sudden failure of Burnside is agitating the public mind around here. The Capital is in a high fever, though the recrossing of the Rappahannock by the Federal army has not been substantially considered a defeat, merely a reverse. But to-day the facts have been slowly developing them-

selves, and truth reveals that we are awfully whipped. Also, to-day rumor says that Little Mac is to be re-appointed to his old position, as commander of the Army of the Potomac." [33]

Although the 152nd's men chafed to go into action, their spirit was excellent. Sickness and disease had yet to show its face and the regiment still could count only one casualty, Sergeant Smith, killed in a train accident.

Christmas Day 1862 was observed by the 152nd in a much different fashion than it was by the other county regiments. Julius Townsend informed the *Journal's* readers:

"Christmas was celebrated by some regiments in a manner peculiar to soldiers. An adjacent regiment performed most of the ceremonies with which soldiers are known to celebrate the day. Climbing a 'greased pole,' catching a 'greased pig,' 'sack races,' 'sack vaulting,' 'mock guard mounting,' and 'burlesque dress parades,' were among the amusements of the day. Discipline for the time being was relaxed and each man was, for a day, his own king." [34]

The year 1862, which had begun with such promise melted away in failure as 1863 arrived. On the heights opposite Fredericksburg, the shivering, demoralized troops of Burnside bore little optimism for the future. Lt. Frederick Ford of the 121st related:

"The good spirits and confidence of the men, and indeed of the army so far as I have had chances for observing, have been steadily ebbing ever since the fight and butchery at Fredericksburg. I hope that the dejection of feeling has about touched bottom." [35]

CHAPTER VII

"Uncle Abraham looked very much worn out"

Winter/Spring 1863 - Winter Camp - Conscription
The 152nd in Washington

In Herkimer County, Christmas 1862 was celebrated in the traditional manner. At twilight on Christmas Eve people flocked to their brightly lit churches for a round of caroling, yuletide sermons and appropriate refreshments. At the end of the festivities, most congregations presented their pastor with a monetary gift, and their Sunday school and singing teachers with small presents. After the services, knots of people passed from church to church admiring and comparing the decorative wreaths, inscriptions, and most of all, the Christmas trees.

On Christmas Day, after gifts were exchanged, Herkimer County families sat down to dinners of roast turkey or goose, topped off by mince, apple and pumpkin pies. In the afternoon, calls were made on friends or relatives, where cookies, cakes and jams were served along with a spot of brandy to chase away the chill.

For those people looking for other entertainment, Concert Hall in Little Falls offered a matinee performance by the famed acrobat, Albertini Charisky. Of Charisky's act the *Journal* reported:

> "His exhibition of strength and endurance in standing on the small slack wire for an hour at a time, swaying himself to and fro to the tune of Yankee Doodle, is truly astonishing." [1]

As the year turned to 1863, a cold front moved through the valley, turning the Mohawk River and village ponds into skating rinks. The boys donned skates and practiced their figures under the admiring gaze of prettily attired young women, who "left their embroidery and pianos" for the parks.

In mid-January temperatures rose bringing unseasonably warm weather. All except the lumbermen welcomed the rather balmy conditions. The woodsmen were having a difficult time trying to skid their logs through the mud of the mid-winter thaw.

The warm, pleasant weather did lead to one fatality. A Mr. Higby of Little Falls, while ice fishing for "trout salmon" for his fish pond, fell through the ice on "Pasico Lake" and was drowned.

In Virginia, the 34th at Falmouth, the 97th at Belle Plain and the 121st at White Oak began the new year bundled in their winter quarters. Although still quite despondent after the defeat at Fredericksburg, the mood of the soldiers began to slowly improve. The weather moderated as temperatures rose, short furloughs were granted to a few men from each regiment and visitors from home came to the camps. Most notable of the visitors were Seth Richmond, Oliver Ladue, William Dorr, James Weatherwax and John Feeter from Little Falls. On a protracted visit to the 34th was D.A. Northrup of Salisbury, who had come to see his son, Capt. Emerson Northrup. For many of the boys, belated Christmas presents arrived. Louis Chapin of the 34th reported:

> "January 10, 1863, was a good day. On that day the men received a lot
> of express packages, containing goodies from the friends at home. For a
> long time fresh butter, from the home churnings, sweetened many a hard
> biscuit." [2]

The men had hoped to put the war behind them until spring, but General Burnside had other ideas. Early in the third week of January, two of the Grand Divisions, the Left and the Center, dismantled their shanties and sent their sick and wounded to the rear. Burnside's plan was to hold the Confederates at Fredericksburg with the Right Grand Division, while the remainder of his army marched north five miles along the Rappahannock and crossed the river at Banks Ford. If this maneuver could be successfully executed, the Army of the Potomac would be able to interpose itself between Lee's army and Richmond.

January 20th, the first day of the march, was dry and pleasant and the troops, which included the 97th New York and the 121st New York, moved easily. But, just after sundown, it began to rain and the wind picked up. Isaac Hall of the 97th related:

> "The morning dawned upon as miserable a host as could be imagined,
> and as the ground was soft, the guns and most of the wagons sank to the
> axles, and could be moved only with the greatest effort. Each passing vehi-
> cle left the road still worse, and it became necessary to double teams to pass
> the more difficult places, and sometimes twenty horses would be harnessed
> to one cannon, and even then fail to move the ponderous weapon. On
> every side were witnessed scenes of hardship-of which the 97th came in for
> its full share-and the country for miles around presented the miserable
> spectacle of a vast sea of mud, in which the army was stuck." [3]

The 121st, in the Center Division, also slogged through the mud, while the 34th remained with the Right Division at Falmouth opposite Fredericksburg.

The storm continued for the next three days. The roadways, churned by wagons, artillery, horses and thousands of men, were impassable. To add to the misery, all along the route, the bedraggled Federals had a mocking audience. Across the river, the rebels jeered at the unfortunate Yanks, ridiculing Burnside's "Mud March," with sign posts such as "This way to Richmond."

Finally, on January 23rd, Burnside abandoned the undertaking and turned his columns back toward their camps. The return trip was equally as harsh. Regiments dissolved as exhausted men, cold, wet and hungry collapsed by the wayside. The Grand Divisions disintegrated into a mass of straggling men that would take weeks to reorganize.

The morale of the army had reached its lowest point of the war and the men were not afraid to express their opinion directly to their commander. The 34th's William Walton described one such episode:

> "You may say that the rank and file are foolish, prejudiced and unreasonable, still it remains that they will have to do with no man save McClellan, if they but have their way. Never was this feeling more openly manifested than at the last review of the right Grand Division by the Commander-in-Chief. The men looked well, the evolutions were perfect and the field presented an animated and brilliant appearance. But it was easy to be seen that something was wanting. There was no feeling, no enthusiasm. When cheers were called for Gen. Burnside there was no response save from a few regiments of new troops. The sentiment expressed on all parts was, 'give us McClellan and then we'll cheer for you,' 'bring us Little Mac and the ground shall tremble with our cheers.' "[4]

On January 26th President Lincoln replaced Burnside with Gen. Joseph Hooker. The men of the 97th and the 121st re-built their huts and returned to the routine of their first winter quarters in the field. The 34th, undisturbed during the fiasco in the mud, continued their second and last winter encampment.

Hooker was much more of a soldier's general than the dour Burnside. "Fighting Joe," as his men knew him, promptly had brigade bakeries built, adding soft bread to the standard rations, and he ordered fresh and desiccated vegetables to be regularly doled out by the commissary to regimental quartermasters. New clothes, blankets and other camp equipage arrived and along with supplements of hospital supplies provided by the Sanitary Commission, the men lived in reasonable comfort.

The Mohawk Valley Ladies Aid Societies sent boxes of socks, pillows, sewing kits and "eatables" to their hometown favorites. All of the parcels arrived safely except for a box of mittens sent to the 121st which was lost in transit and didn't arrive until spring.

Hooker also issued orders abolishing the Grand Division scheme and, as a means of readily identifying a regiment's corps and division, he ordered that color-coded insignias be put on each soldier's cap. Members of the 34th's division would wear a white clover leaf, boys from the 97th's division would be distinguished by a white sphere, and the men of the 121st's division would sport a red St. Andrew's Cross. But most importantly to the men, General Hooker instituted a program of ten day furloughs allowing them to visit home. A prerequisite for obtaining this privilege required each regiment to pass a camp inspection, and to show a high level of discipline. Among the few regiments that failed to meet the requirements was the 34th New York.

The 34th's commander, Col. James Suiter of Herkimer, was not a strict disciplinarian and it showed in the appearance of his men and their camp. Late in January, Suiter resigned for "personal reasons" and another Herkimer man, Bryon Laflin, was promoted to colonel of the regiment. With the aid of John Beverly from Salisbury, now the lieutenant colonel, and Wells Sponable of Little Falls, promoted to major, Laflin brought the 34th back into military order. William Walton remarked:

> "Our late Colonel [Suiter] was faultless and faulty. Brave as bravery itself, he was ever at his post in the hour of danger, but in camp failed to enforce that strict discipline which is so necessary to the well being of every Regiment. This will account for the 34th being included among the regiments which recently incurred the displeasure of the Commander-in-Chief. But there has been a change. Our new Colonel [Laflin] has assumed command and everything so far goes to prove that he is worthy of the position. We are ready now and willing to challenge criticism on every particular. Our camp is well laid out, neat and tidy. The men are well-dressed and manifest much interest in their personal appearance and in the performance of their various duties. All this has come to the knowledge of Gen. Hooker and as a consequence, the privileges of which we were deprived for a short time have been restored to us."[5]

Among the other staff changes that occurred in the valley regiments were: the resignation of the 34th's chaplain, John Van Petten, to assume the position of lieutenant colonel in the 160th New York, and the naming of Sylvester Schoonmaker to take his place; the transfer of the 34th's adjutant, George Thompson, to a lieutenant colonel in the 152nd New York, with Albert Doty promoted to adjutant; the resignation of the 121st's Lt. Col. Charles Clark and the promotion of Egbert Olcott to fill that position. A number of junior grade officers, disgusted with army life, also resigned. Unlike enlisted men who were locked into the service for the duration of their terms, commissioned officers could tender their resignations without qualification.

In the 121st, seemingly biased promotions and the transfer of outsiders to staff positions caused dissension. The regiment, which was made up equally of Herkimer and Otsego County men, was becoming unbalanced in favor of officers from Otsego and other counties. Equal representation in the staff by Herkimer County men was not being maintained. An anonymous writer from the 121st reported to the *Journal's* readers:

> "Is the 121st Regiment to be the recipient of every ruined proligate, who may have a friend in the field? If a vacancy occurs in the field must it be filled by an outsider who is a 'boon companion'? If a vacancy occurs in the staff, must it be filled by a youth from West Point who has left that

institution on account of sore eyes? . . . I do not wish to be personal in this letter, but the regiment has been grossly insulted by the introduction of officers who were strangers to the Regiment, when there are men in it far superior to them in every respect. Now such things demoralize a regiment beyond measure. Will you look over and see where the officers are from, who have command in a Regiment gotten up by Herkimer and Otsego counties?

Of the commandants of companies four are from Herkimer County, five from Otsego, and one from Albany: of the 1st Lieutenants three are from Herkimer and four from Otsego: of the 2d Lieutenants two are from Herkimer and six from Otsego; of all the Field and Staff officers two are from Herkimer County."[6]

The troubles in the 121st went far beyond an unequal distribution of officers. The Army of the Potomac during this period was realizing a desertion rate of two hundred men per day and the 121st was contributing its share. In the latter part of January and the first few weeks of February, nearly one hundred men deserted from the regiment.

One of the prime causes for desertion was simple homesickness. This "disease," most prevalent in new regiments such as the 121st, often would be triggered by disheartening letters from home. The chaplain of the 121st, Rev. J.R. Sage, wrote:

"This home-sickness is one of the most baffling and subtle diseases the army surgeon has to contend with. It is of the mind, and no tonic or alternative can reach it-only the tonic of cheering and brave words from home. It is caused in most cases by the desponding tenor of home letters. . . . No man can fight well or toil manfully, if there is a timid and cringing and heartbroken wife or mother holding to his skirts with the grasp of despair."[7]

Each week lists of deserters from the 121st were sent to the *Journal* for publication. Typical of these was a letter from the 121st's adjutant, Francis Morse, which read:

"Sir: I forward you the following list of Deserters from this Regiment, men who received nearly two hundred dollars to enlist and serve their country, and then disgracefully and cowardly deserted their comrades and the service of their Government. They are fit subjects to be published to the world and ought to be scorned by every honorable person. They have defrauded their friends at home, and cheated the Government of their services."[8]

Adjutant Morses's list, which contained ninety names, was published by the *Journal*.

Surprisingly the men of the 121st held little contempt for deserters. Lt. Fred Ford of Fairfield remarked:

"You have probably received a list of deserters from the regiment . . . . The facts in the case are that one half of them are the best soldiers in the regiment, or so accounted formerly. A still more significant fact than this is that these deserters had the good wishes of the whole regiment, almost without exception. Men here attach no disgrace to desertion."[9]

To put a stop to the desertions, sentries were posted around the camp of the 121st. Of this ignominy, Sgt. Reuben Holmes of Little Falls reported:

> "The 121st regiment, by the way, is becoming somewhat renowned, not for the heroic deeds displayed upon the battlefield. . . . But its great renown is a result of the numerous desertions, a fact I am sorry to acknowledge, but which is too true. Yet I hope and pray there will be less in the future, for it is not only bringing disgrace upon their own heads, but causing their friends to look back and blush for them. . . . Our City, is governed by Martial Law, and surrounded by twenty or more guards who make it their business to keep the rest of the Regiment from running away." [10]

Most of the deserters were never caught, but nine men from the 121st that were seized, were court martialed and sentenced to "unrenumerated hard labor" at the "Rip Raps" prison near Norfolk, Virginia.

The health of the valley regiments was relatively good during the winter months of 1863. The 34th and 97th each lost four or five men to disease. The 121st, after its dreadful tally of the previous autumn and early winter, when twenty-seven of its sick died, now counted about the same number. The men who died of disease in camp were buried with little fanfare. Isaac Darling of the 121st related:

> "When one of our boys dies here there is a hole scratched in the dirt and the body is then borne to the tomb. I have but once seen the comrades or company turn out, no drums are beat, no vollies are fired over the grave of the departed. On all occasions however our worthy Chaplain is present." [11]

One thing that had improved during the winter quarters of 1863, was the spiritual health of the men. In the winter camps of the year before, whiskey flowed freely and drunkenness among officers and men was common. In 1862, the homefolk had real cause for concern regarding the moral health of their boys. The field camps of 1863 saw very little of this behavior. The 121st's Rev. J.R. Sage stated:

> "There is much said in the religious papers and from the pulpits at the North, of the demoralizing influence of army life upon our young men, and of the dreadful vices which prevail. . . . It is true, we have not here the gentle restraints of home and female society to keep young men from evil habits. It may be true also, that some are led into profanity and kindred vices of speech here who were very correct in this respect while at home. But there are counter-balancing advantages in our situation, and the army is comparatively free from some of the worst evils which infest your villages and cities at the north. There is not a hundreth part of the amount of liquor drank here that there is by the same number of men in your large towns. And the very good reason is, the men cannot get it. . . . The officers can obtain the ardent more easily than the men under them, but they are generally too careful of their shoulder-straps to over-indulge often, even if they are addicted to the beast by nature." [12]

Army life was even a tonic for such moral corruption as cursing. Reverend Sage continued:

> "Profanity is the worst vice we have to contend against, and that I am

happy to believe, has decreased more than fifty percent in this Regiment. The discipline of the army is a very excellent training to the young men of a nation which has come largely to confound liberty with license. Let us hope and believe that all the seeming evils of the present will be over-ruled for good." [13]

The correspondents to the *Journal*, with little more to write about than the tedium of camp life, filled their letters with their political and philosophical views of the war. Innocently enough, in expounding on these subjects, a nerve was touched and a war of words between the writers from the 34th, 121st and 152nd was fought in the *Journal's* columns. While the points attacked were specific to these regiments, the arguments were a reflection of feelings throughout the army. The animosity between old and new regiments, and between those in the field and those in the rear, was manifested in the exchange.

The dispute started with a *Journal* column by Lt. Frederick Ford of the 121st:

"When taking leave of the army the other day, he (McClellan) was loudly cheered by the old ones. The why that the old regiments from our own state are so fond, is probably in the fact that they are two years men and will, of course, win their discharge in about six months. Under McClellan, they might reasonably hope to spend these last days in ruinous ease, making a big mud-puddle of the suburbs of Washington." [14]

Capt. William Walton of the 34th, taking offense at Lieutenant Ford's remarks regarding the veteran regiments, responded:

"We regret that your correspondent allowed himself to write as he did for he is an old and valued friend of ours and with surprise and pain we see his name attached to what is so evidently an injustice. As it is, we do not wonder at the indignation of our comrades and though painful the task, we cannot overlook the wrong done them and all the two years troops. . . .
We trust our friend did it not intentionally, but was rather hurried away by the ardor of the moment, for, if penned designedly it shows extreme hardiness on his part thus to slur those who have so long been in the service of their country. These are not they who hung back and said to others 'you go, we will wait awhile and see how matters work.' To them no golden inducements in the shape of two, three or five hundred dollar bounties were held out, but 'without money and without price they came forth and if we mistake not have borne the heat and burden of the day,' for which they will not receive the amount that many obtained before leaving the state. Mercenary motives, therefore, cannot be laid to their charge: the appellation 'boughten men' in no way applies." [15]

After another letter denigrating the 121st was published in the *Little Falls Courier*, this time written by Louis Chapin of the 34th, Lieutenant Ford lashed back at that regiment:

"I have been twice called a fool on the account of these 'two years' men—once before by Capt. Walton, and now again. . . . As for the latter part of the occupation, did it ever strike you, Louis, that one who hires out to butcher his fellow for 'eleven dollars per month [Privates' pay] and no other reward,' is infinitely meaner than he whom a larger sum induces to do the same thing." [16]

A letter unrelated to the quarrel between the 34th and 121st was written to the *Journal* by an "Observer" in Co. B of the 152nd. The writer, not intending any harm, was simply describing a speech by Lt. Col. Ferguson, of that regiment:

"In conclusion he told us to be content with the place we now occupied, to be careful of our health and try to do the duty enjoined upon us with cheerfulness. He said that the cause of the 121st's having so much to undergo was on account of the ambition of some of its leaders to take them into the field before they were thoroughly drilled." [17]

Lieutenant Ford, feeling the 121st, and particularly Colonel Upton, was being attacked, replied to the remarks of Colonel Ferguson:

"I see that Col. Ferguson of the 152d, thinks that the '121st suffered so much on account of the ambition of its commanding officers!' Col. Ferguson knows, or at least ought to know, that the field officers of a regiment are put at its head to make it as perfect a human machine as possible, and in no case have anything to do with its moving. The General-in-Chief ordered such troops against Jackson and Lee in Maryland as he had most confidence in, knowing of course their respective leaders. Our regiment has been ordered into active service and the 152d is grubbing away in the sand hills at Washington." [18]

Julius Townsend of the 152nd answered Lieutenant Ford's letter:

"We notice a 'slash' at a favorite officer in the 152d, from your correspondent in the 121st. We should think his propensity to torture the motives and actions of others into wrong channels would expend itself on regiments without meddling with the private character of individuals . . . the commanding officer, whose business it is 'to make as perfect a human machine of it as possible and in no case to have anything to do with its moving', instead of going where he was ordered, succeeded in getting his regiment attached to Gen. Slocum's division [6th Corps]. Then the General-in-Chief [McClellan] at the battle of Antietam, placed this regiment 'which he had the most confidence in, knowing of course, its respective leader,' in the rear." [19]

Mercifully, "A. Calliope" of the 97th stepped in and mediated a peace:

". . . there is something in its [*Journal*] columns, of camp correspondence, that grieves us sadly. It is this. The controversy that has arisen between schoolmates, chums and members of an old and honorable Society. Why is it that they wrangle at such petty things when so much is at stake? This is no harmless debate, but it concerns every man from Herkimer County. We are all companies in arms. We see no difference between volunteers with or without bounty, for no man will expose himself for the paltry sum of a bounty. We know it is hard to have the word 'bounty' thrown in your face by older regiments, but it is no less hard to be called 'scum of the land': yet we can afford to pay no attention to these things. If we were from another state, we would have some reason: but from one's own county, it looks bad. If the 34th has gained an eminence in military fame far be it from us (the 97th) to drag it down from its position: or, if the 121st is more efficient in tactics than we are, we will not run it down, but rather pride ourselves that we came from the same county. It is for our own good that we should do so, because by honoring them we shall honor ourselves." [20]

And so ended the war of words in the *Journal's* pages.

On March 3rd, 1863, the Conscription Act was passed by Congress, giving President Lincoln the power to forcibly draft all able-bodied male citizens between the ages of twenty and forty-five. Written into the law were clauses that allowed a draftee ten days to provide a suitable substitute or to pay a $300 commutation fee. Satisfaction of either of these two conditions would exempt the man from that draft.

Prior to the passage of the act, Lincoln had no real legal authority to compel state governors to comply with his calls and no backing behind the threat of a draft. But now, Lincoln had in his pocket an authorization to conscript at almost anytime he desired.

The passage of the Conscription Act was hailed by the men in the field, who could also foresee the reaction of the draftable men back home. Reverend Sage of the 121st, opined:

> "The conscription is immensely popular with us. We regard it as a saving ordinance, and we're going to see that it is thoroughly enforced. We hear some mutterings of discontent, and threats of resistance from some quarters, but let anything like active or organised resistance attempted by any set of men and they'll have an avalanche of soldiers upon them." [21]

And Edward Townsend of the 152nd, added:

> "The 'Conscription Act' has finally passed, though proceeded by much tumult and debate. How it will fall upon the sensitive and superstitious, time will quickly reveal. Evidently the nation will speedily be converted into an Asylum for cripples. Twenty-fives and forties, will immediately fall below eighteen, or be surprised to find themselves upon the verge of fifty. Exemption will be the universal cry, and strong men will mysteriously become disciples of the cane and crutch." [22]

In March, the Virginia weather turned mild and as the sun warmed the land, the soldiers emerged from their huts and shanties. In their native northern clime, the Herkimer County men would still be shivering in the blasts of winter, but at this southerly latitude it was springtime. The troops of the blue and the gray revelled in the sunshine and for awhile became boys again. The 34th's Louis Chapin related:

> "Occasionally, we get a peep at the sun. It's genial warmth steals along that

densely-peopled height [Falmouth], bringing joy and gladness. No friend was ever more welcome. Homesickness vanished beneath that gentle touch, and lots of other troubles. Every sort of thing is resorted to by the men, when they have an idle hour, to keep themselves in spirits. Strangely enough, baseball with the men of the fifteenth Massachusetts, was one of the popular pastimes. . . . The ball was a soft one, and you plugged a man with it to put him out.

The pickets on the opposite sides of the river also relaxed their awful severity, although it was strictly 'against orders.' Little cornstalk boats would be floated with messages of friendly interest. There is no mistake about it, 'visiting' of this kind is the most delicious diversion in the world.

. . .Here, as on the Potomac a year before, there was the swapping of commodities, coffee, tobacco, newspapers, &c." [23]

The disconsolate mob that straggled back to their camps after three days in the mud with Burnside, was transformed back into an army by General Hooker. Better rations, new uniforms and strict military discipline instilled pride and confidence once again into the Army of the Potomac.

Early in March, Hooker held a grand review of his army that was reminiscent of its former commander, George McClellan. The pageant, complete with dignitaries from Washington, was staged as a dress rehearsal for an expected visit by the President.

On April 5th, Abraham Lincoln, accompanied by his family, arrived at Falmouth to inspect Hooker's one hundred and thirty thousand men. For three days, the President toured the camps and reviewed the troops. The first day of review was devoted to the cavalry, the second to the artillery and the third day to the infantry. The 34th, 97th and 121st New York's were among the infantry regiments that proudly paraded past Abraham Lincoln. Isaac Darling, a member of the 121st from Salisbury, reported:

"On Wednesday last, we were called upon to be reviewed by the President, Abraham Lincoln, Esq., as were all the rest of the army of the Potomac. It was a grand spectacle—some 60,000 men all armed with burnished bayonets gleaming in the sunbeams. Uncle Abraham looked very much worn out, and well he may, for a man with such awful responsibilities resting on him, must be care-worn." [24]

Never lost in the months after Fredericksburg was the Herkimer County boys' faith in their President and the Union cause. Although confidence in their commanders waxed and waned, and the support of even the home folks was questioned, the men were always with "Old Abe" and he with them. And, no matter how harsh the trials had been the boys retained their humor. Frequent *Journal* contributor, Isaac Darling, stated:

"The words usually offered by the soldiers here on retiring, run something after this wise - Our Father which art in Washington, Uncle Abraham is thy name, thy victory won, thy will be done at the South as at the North. Give us this day our daily rations of crackers and pork and forgive us our shortcomings as we forgive our Quartermasters, for these are the prayers of the soldiers and negroes for the space of three years unless sooner discharged." [25]

_____

At Camp Marcy, on the outskirts of Washington, the 152nd New York was occupied in maintaining the fortifications of the Capital's defense perimeter. Living in small shelter tents or crudely built huts, the troops spent the early part of 1863 in relative ease and comfort compared to the soldiers in the field. Their rations were the usual army fare, hard-tack, salt pork, beans, rice and coffee, but there were extras. Henry Roback of Danube, noted:

> "The cows which were in the habit of loafing around 'our quarters' in
> the silent hours of the night were rather scant with their mornings milk." [26]

Occasionally the commissary even issued a one-ounce whiskey ration to each man. For those men that required more than this allotment, the needed liquid could be obtained in Washington and smuggled back to camp by wading the Potomac or by "running" the guard on the Chain Bridge. If a man was confined to camp, "colored ladies with full skirts" who frequented the area could produce a bottle of "firewater" for a price. When an enlisted man had imbibed too freely, a unique cure was available to sober him up. Henry Roback described the treatment, writing:

> "When a soldier became very full he was taken to the central guard
> house and given a room, the floor being overflowed with two inches of
> water, a foot-bath being deemed essential to draw the 'spirits fermenti'
> downward, to prevent brain fever." [27]

Free time in Camp Marcy was spent reading editions of the *Washington Chronicle* supplied by the Regimental Surgeon's son, Steven Ingham, or in writing letters. At night the men enjoyed sitting around the campfire listening to the music of two of the 152nd's tunesmiths, Lyman Snell of Manheim and Duane Wiswell of Little Falls. Quite often the men would get the urge to dance. Henry Roback related:

> "The ball-room was located on the platform of mother earth, and danc-
> ing was enjoyed, the 'partner' turning their cap fronts around to represent
> the gentle sex, and all would trip the light fantastic toe, and all promenade
> on the broad bottoms of the army shoe." [28]

But, the event most looked forward to was the arrival of the mailman. Newport's Julius Townsend reported:

> "The letters arrive about noon. They are then separated by the Regi-
> ment Post Master into different piles according to the several companies to
> which they are addressed. Each captain then takes charge of those belong-
> ing to his company. He calls his men together and proceeds to distribute the
> letters, reading aloud the name on each. All is still as midnight. Not a whis-
> per, not a breath can be heard, nothing save the voice of the Captain and the
> beating of anxious hearts. Finally the ceremony is over, and as the Com-
> pany returns to their quarters, an observer can, by scanning each counte-
> nance, readily perceive who are the fortunate and who the unfortunate.

Here you will hear an exclamation of joy, there one of sorrow. Here you will see a look of triumph, there one of disappointment. Here you will hear an outspoken blessing, there a muttered curse. The soldier is not famous for keeping his thoughts to himself, and numerous are the anathemas pronounced against friends at home because they neglect to answer promptly his letters. We have seen many before now so chagrined and disappointed at not receiving letters long since due them, that, had we immediately gone into battle they would have been reckless to desperation."[29]

Among the personalities in the 152nd were Thomas Maguire of Danube, a Fairfield Academy professor of languages, who conducted Latin classes in the regiment and Henry Lewis and Smith Foster, who respectively stood seven-foot one-inch and six-foot seven inches. Nicknamed "baby" and "infant" or the "U.S. ramrods," uniforms for the two giants had to be specially ordered from Philadelphia.

On January 10th, Col. Leonard Boyer resigned and Alonzo Ferguson was promoted to command the 152nd. George Thompson, formerly adjutant of the 34th, replaced Ferguson as lieutenant colonel.

The 152nd finally got their marching orders in mid-February, but the move was not in the direction that they had hoped. Instead of marching south to "the seat of war," the regiment plodded the seven miles back to Washington. The tedium of building breastworks was replaced by the boredom of provost duty, guarding hospitals, bridges, government buildings and prisoners in the city.

Shelter tents were stowed and the men took up residence in barns. Edward Townsend informed the Herkimer County folk:

"Our regiment is encamped on 'Caroll Hill,' quartered in diminutive barns, a short distance from the Capitol. I will not go into an extensive description of our lodgings, but will simply remark, that we think the sheds in which we tarry were originally intended for comfortable, summer, sheep-pens, being very airy and admitting considerable light."[30]

In the enclosed quarters an epidemic of measles broke out in the 152nd that reminded one of the fate that befell the 97th in Boonville the year before. Scores of men were prostrated by the disease and several men died, including Alonzo Wright of Winfield and Tim Donovan from Little Falls.

In their position as guards, the country boys had ample opportunities to witness the workings of the government and to see many important people. On March 31st, the men of the 152nd were privileged to attend a joint session of Congress. Edward Townsend described the visit to the *Journal's* readers, writing:

"Last Tuesday evening there was the grandest assembly of people at the National Capitol, ever before known in this city. The House of Representatives, and also the Senate Chamber were literally packed with the living masses and to affirm that the occasion was an interesting one, is but a moderate way of getting at the truth. We had the pleasure of being present, and acknowledge it to be the most exciting and impressive political demonstration we ever witnessed. In the House of Representatives the meeting was honored by the presence of President Lincoln and the members of his cabinet, besides many distinguished Military characters. The speakers were men celebrated for eloquence and wit, but added to those elements of their oratory, was the fervency, the zeal and the high souled patriotism which flashed forth in every sentence they uttered. Democrats and Republicans forgot their political differences, buried party opinions, and stepping forward upon one common platform joined hands in true and loyal devotion to the Government, the Constitution and the Laws. The gem of the entire evening was the speech of ex-Governor Andrew Johnson of Tennessee. His address was an hour and a half in length, and evidently it was one of the best, if not the happiest effort of his life. . . . He advocates the most stringent measures for suppressing the Rebellion and scorned the terms Compromise and Peace."[31]

In mid-April, Gen. Francis Spinner again interceded on the behalf of a Mohawk Valley regiment. Spinner, a native of Mohawk, used his influence as Treasurer of the United States to procure the 152nd's pay, (the men not having seen the paymaster in six months) and he obtained modern Enfield rifles for the regiment. The Austrian rifles that the men carried were "consigned to oblivion."

On April 21st, the regiment packed up and boarded the steamer "John A. Warner." The next morning, the boat pulled away from the dock and headed south on the Potomac. The 152nd was finally going to join in the war.

CHAPTER VIII

"It was a bloody and sorrowful baptism"

Spring 1863 - The 152nd Enters the War Zone
Chancellorsville - Salem Church

After the January thaw, the winter of 1863 returned in full force and lingered in Herkimer County. In March the sun barely appeared and the valley people shivered as the average temperature remained a winter-like 25 degrees. On a Friday night, in the middle of that month, snow began falling and continued without letup all weekend. By Monday morning, high winds had driven the snow into drifts ten to twenty-five feet high. The main thoroughfares were impassable and country lanes were filled to the fence tops. The stage lines were shut down for four days and even rail traffic for a time came to a halt.

The advent of April brought no relief. Early in the month another storm struck the valley, leaving "bad roads, big drifts, lean cattle and empty graneries."

But, irresistibly, springtime arrived. The warmth of the sun returned, the snow melted and by the second week in April the sap of the maple trees was being tapped. A.N. Haile of Eatonville proudly presented the season's first maple sugar to the *Journal* on April 16th.

No matter how harsh the winter, the hardy people of Herkimer County had long ago learned to cope and indeed to thrive in it. The snow clogged roads might hinder travel between the villages, but in the communities social activities always peaked during the winter season. On almost every weekend throughout Herkimer County, entertainment of one form or another was available.

In Little Falls, Miss Wright's Select School for girls gave an exhibition of readings and recitations, the Citizens Brass Band held a concert for the benefit of the

Ladies Aid Society and the scholars of the Northside Public Elementary School sang at Concert Hall. The students cleared $26 towards the purchase of a new Melodeon for their "Intermediate Department." At Odd Fellow's Hall in Mohawk, the village's Union Free School held their annual exhibition, and in the Brockett's Bridge Methodist Church, Mr. G.W. Howard's music classes put on a two-day "Musical Convention."

For entertainment of a more professional nature, Professor Whitney, the "necromancer" and LeGrand B. Cushman with his show of "Music, Personation and Recitation," were at Concert Hall in Little Falls.

For those persons inclined to dancing, Washburn's Hotel in Herkimer offered an "Old and Young Folks" party, and the General Herkimer Fire Co. 3 of Little Falls held their annual Firemen's Ball at Joe Vosburg's hotel in "Finks."

The bad weather did not adversely affect the more mundane workaday aspects of life in Herkimer County either. The business sector and the economy in general prospered during this second winter of the war.

On the New York Central Railroad, the level of freight travelling through the valley on its way to the war front was unparalleled in the road's history. Most important to the Mohawk Valley people, the cars were also stopping at the village depots to load locally produced goods. Among the cargo shipped from Herkimer County were revolvers and rifles from the Remingtons' factory in Ilion, cloth for army uniforms from the Mohawk Mill in Little Falls, hay and maple sugar from area farms, and of course butter and cheese. The commodity items were now commanding premium prices compared to what they had brought barely six months prior. A ton of hay had risen from $7 to almost $20, cheese prices were up from eight cents a pound to twelve cents and, with a scarcity in cane sugar, a healthy market for maple sugar was forecast.

In the towns themselves new businesses from the large to the small were opening. In Herkimer, Harvey Farrington was building a new cheese factory, of which he crowed, was capable of producing three hundred thousand pounds of cheese per year. In Little Falls, Nicholas Gerhart started manufacture of lager and "strong beer" at his Monroe Street "factory," and at the "Brick School," Miss Addie Cressy began a new singing school, charging a tuition of 50 cents per term. Also in that village Samuel Woolverton, recently discharged from the 121st, opened a dry good store. The *Journal* willingly gave a "plug" to the new shopkeeper:

> "S. Woolverton advertises a new stock of flour, feed, groceries &c. at his store opposite the Baptist Church. One of the first of the volunteers in the 121st regiment, he narrowly escaped death by sun-stroke and although but partially recovered as yet, he is still able to sell goods at very low prices and to please his customers always. He deserves and will receive general patronage and support."[1]

For those unable to raise the capital for new ventures, the county treasurer had $1,300 of surplus county money that he was willing to loan to persons with good security. Coincidentally, $1,311 had been collected in license fees by the treasurer from the county "dog tax."

For the time being the war was not on center stage in Herkimer County. The boys from the Mohawk Valley were in winter quarters and only a bloody battle in far off Murfreesboro, Tennessee, early in January caught the people's attention.

Ladies Aid Societies were still at work making quilts, pillow cases, hospital gowns, bandages and the like for shipment to the Sanitary Commission. The work progressed at a leisurely pace, for there was no immediate need for these supplies. However, with the expected spring and summer campaigns nearing, a stockpile of hospital essentials had to be built up. The ladies had sufficient quantities of all the necessary raw materials for their work save one. The Society made an appeal to area farmers to donate or to sell, "at a reasonable price," chicken feathers needed for pillow stuffing.

Early in April recruiting in Herkimer County took on a new twist. With the Emancipation Proclamation becoming law on January 1, 1863, the Negroes of the North gained a new status. For the already free black man doors began to open, including the opportunity to enlist in the Federal Armies. Since many white soldiers vehemently protested serving in the same unit as a Negro, separate "colored" regiments officered by whites were authorized by President Lincoln.

Among these new "colored" regiments was the 54th Massachusetts, under the command of Boston socialite, Robert Gould Shaw. Early in April, Enoch Moore and N. Gibbs travelled through Herkimer and Montgomery counties enlisting blacks for the 54th Massachusetts. Within a week they had collected a number of recruits from the black population of the Mohawk Valley and headed back to Massachusetts. *The Albany Statesman* noted their passage through that city:

> "A squad of forty-five colored men recruited in Little Falls and else-where by Messrs. E. Moore and N. Gibbs, left this city to-day for the camp of the 54th Massachusetts (colored) Regiment at Readville near Boston. The men are mostly canallers, and will make brave and hardy soldiers. Previous to their departure, they were each furnished with a copy of the New Testament by the Albany Young Men's Christian Association which slight token of regard was fully appreciated and thankfully received." [2]

Down in Virginia, the Federal camps were abuzz as the army began preparing for the inevitable spring campaign. The 152nd was the first of the Mohawk Valley regiments to go on the move.

The 152nd New York left Washington aboard a river steamer on April 21st and arrived at Norfolk near midnight on the following day. Although the rain was coming down in torrents, the shivering men on the open deck of the boat were not allowed to go ashore to find shelter. By late afternoon when the regiment disembarked the men were thoroughly soaked. The 152nd boarded a gravel train in Norfolk, and after a trip of twenty-two miles in open cars, arrived in Suffolk, Virginia, eighty miles southeast of Richmond.

Early the next morning, the 152nd was ordered from its quarters at a Suffolk church to the support of an artillery battery on the outskirts of the city. Skirmishing went on in front of the 152nd, but the regiment itself was not engaged. From this assignment the inexperienced men gained their first impression of front line duty. Pvt. Henry Roback opined:

> ". . . it is far more preferable to support a wife and six children than a six gun battery at thirteen dollars per month."[3]

At Suffolk the 152nd New York was assigned to the 1st Brigade, 1st Division of the 7th Corps, a force of twenty thousand men under the command of Gen. John Peck. The situation that the 152nd came into was a prime example of a military stalemate. Confronting and nearly surrounding the Federals were a like number of Confederates led by Gen. James Longstreet. Longstreet who, unable to attack because of the presence of Union gunboats on the nearby Nansemond River, laid siege to Suffolk. Inside the city, General Peck was also unwilling to go on the offensive for he believed that the rebels outnumbered him three to one. To keep Longstreet on guard, Peck was content to conduct a number of "reconnaissances in force." These forays were designed to probe the enemies defenses and to demonstrate to the rebs that the besieged army still had some sting left. In each of these minor engagements the 152nd took part, but being untested, was always kept in the background. No action was seen and no casualties were taken by the regiment, yet the men were quite proud of the fact that for once they had actively shared in the war. Julius Townsend proudly remarked:

> "On Friday we were ordered to 'fall in' for a short march. We were then marched out on the Edenton road. Some fifteen thousand were there drawn up in 'battle array' and immediately put in motion, under the command of Gen. Corcoran [commander 1st Division, 7th Corps]. They marched about two miles, when they came in contact with some of the enemy. A short skirmish ensued, which resulted in our driving the enemy from the road, and forcing him to seek shelter behind his entrenchments. Our troops returned towards evening, having captured some eight or nine prisoners, several cows, pigs and turkeys.
>
> All is quiet here. The guns of our pickets are not now heard from morning until night, neither is our sleep disturbed by the heavy roar of artillery, neither are we called out, one night at eleven o'clock, another at two and still another at three to wait with strong arm and steady nerve the approach of some real or fancied danger. We tasted the experience of some ten days before the enemy, but now we have become tame again."[4]

On the night of May 3rd, the 152nd was ordered to prepare one day's rations and to double check their guns and equipment. In the morning the regiment was to go on a "scouting expedition." As Julius Townsend related, the men were anxious to get in on the glory of war:

> "We slept soundly that night, but in our dreams fancied ourselves bringing in to camp some Rebel prisoner of infamous notoriety, such as Gen. Lee, Longstreet or Hill. The morrow finally came. At the first call all sprang into line. We were soon moving through town marching to the time of the fife and drum. All was joy, interest and excitement. 'What regiment is this?' asked many of the bystanders. 'The 152nd New York,' was the reply. 'Bully for New York,' says the spectator, 'Where are you going?'

'Don't know, but guess we are going over the river to see what we can find.' "[5]

Townsend described the men's disappointment when they realized the true nature of their mission:

> "After we crossed the river an observing person might have seen three wagons each drawn by four horses, following the regiment. Indeed most of us were observing enough to notice them. 'What can these wagons be for?' asked one. 'Why to convey to Suffolk whatever we may capture or find that will be of use to the government' answered another. This opinion under the circumstances, seemed to be a reasonable one and was readily adopted. We marched through fields and along roads where but four days before we would have been greeted with a shower of shot and shell. We had marched some three miles when we were ordered to halt. Immediately in front of us was a Rebel rifle pit, and an embankment on which large guns had once been mounted. The teams, which had been in our rear, were now ordered to the front. What could we be going to do? . . . Three or four men were ordered on to the wagons to throw out their contents, when out came one after the other, spades, pick-axes and shovels . . . we were to level the Rebel rifle pits! What memories, which had been buried during the exciting time of the previous ten days, did the sight of those agricultural implements recall? A shade of disgust mingled with disappointment and anger passed like a cloud, along the rank and file of the regiment. Oh you ghosts of Camp Marcy! What has the 152nd done that they should again be tormented by your unseemly presence! Tell us wherein we have erred, wherein we failed to do our duty, and we will try to amend for the past by a full atonement in the future, but in mercy's name haunt us not with your unsightly appearance again."[6]

Longstreet and his men were gone. General Lee, taking note of major troop movements in the Army of the Potomac, had ordered Longstreet to break his siege of Suffolk and march north. The Federal spring campaign of 1863 had begun.

In northern Virginia, "Fighting Joe" Hooker's army was moving along the same route that Burnside had followed during his ignominious "Mud March." Hooker's plan, like Burnside's, was to hold the Confederates at Fredericksburg with a portion of his army, while the bulk of his forces marched north along the Rappahannock, crossed at the upstream fords, and fell on the rebel's left flank and rear.

Troop movements started on April 28th, as the 3rd, 5th, 11th and 12th Corps and two divisions of the 2nd Corps went into motion. These units under Hooker's command, which numbered ninety-thousand men, comprised the flanking force. Gen. John Sedgwick, with twenty-five thousand troops of his Sixth Corps, and one division of the 2nd Corps, was to once again attack the heights beyond Fredericksburg. Ten thousand men of the 1st Corps would be positioned to go to the aid of either command. Across the river at Fredericksburg, Lee's sixty thousand men would be caught between the jaws of the two Union forces and crushed.

Of the Mohawk Valley regiments, the 34th New York and 121st New York remained near Falmouth under Sedgwick's command and the 97th New York, with the 1st Corps, marched north to act as either Hooker's or Sedgwick's reserve.

Looking across the Rappahannock at the Confederate fortifications, and most especially at the stone wall at Mr. Marye's house, the men of the 34th questioned their part in the bloody fighting that was soon to come. The 34th regiment had been mustered into New York State service for two years on May 1, 1861, and many of the men had actually signed the enlistment rolls on April 15th of that year. Whichever date was used, the men believed that they were entitled to go home and should not be forced to climb that awful hill again. The 34th had been fortunate back in December, suffering relatively few casualties, and the men didn't want to press their luck.

Unfortunately, the U.S. Army saw things differently. According to the War Department, the 34th New York was mustered into Federal service on June 15, 1861, and only at that point had the two year clock begun ticking. Officially, the men of the 34th still owed the government a month and a half of Federal service.

As May 1st came without the hoped for discharge, many of the men in the 34th "stood out" (refusing to do duty), claiming that their service time was expired. The regiment was quickly confined to camp and surrounded by a detail of guards from the 15th Massachusetts. The affair ended rather abruptly when Gen. John Gibbon, who commanded the 34th's division in the 2nd Corps, visited the camp and threatened to give the order for the guard to open fire if the mutineers did not return to their duty. Grudgingly, the men took up their arms and returned to camp duties, resigned to the fact that home was still six weeks away.

The only real victim of the affair was the 34th's Brigadier, General Sully. The 34th's Louis Chapin reported:

> "But this little incident proved a bothersome thing to General Alfred Sully, who had returned, and was in command of the brigade. He reported to General Gibbon, very foolishly, that 'it was not in his [Gibbon's] power to enforce discipline in his [Sully's] command.' Whereupon General Gibbon immediately relieved him. . . . General Sully did not return; but was sent west to fight the Indians." [7]

With the removal of General Sully, the 34th's colonel, Byron Laflin of Herkimer, was temporarily put in command of the brigade (1st Brigade, 2nd Division, 2nd Corps) and Lt. Col. John Beverly took command of the 34th.

On the morning of May 2nd, the 97th New York, with the rest of the 1st Corps, was encamped at U.S. Ford, ten miles north of Fredericksburg and about five miles east of Hooker's army at Chancellorsville.

Hooker's forces crossed the Rappahannock and the Rapidan rivers and on May 1st marched into a densely wooded tract called the Wilderness. Full of confidence, the troops advanced through the jungle on two narrow roads, the Gordonsville Plank Road and the Orange Turnpike. Joe Hooker, believing he had "stolen a march" on Lee and would soon have the rebels trapped between his army and that of Sedgwick, was stunned when the head of his column was attacked by an enemy that should not have been there.

Lee, after judging Hooker's motives, was not about to be out-generaled. Leaving a token force at Fredericksburg, he threw his army at the head and flank of the thin Union columns moving down the Wilderness roads. Like a turtle, Hooker retracted his lead troops against his generals' wishes, and formed a defensive line centering on the Chancellor House.

The next morning furious rebel assaults on the Federal lines caused a now over-cautious Hooker to summon his reserve, the 1st Corps, commanded by Gen. John Reynolds.

Of the march to Chancellorsville, Isaac Hall of the 97th wrote:

> " . . . about 9 o'clock Saturday morning, May the 2nd, . . . Reynolds marched rapidly towards Chancellorsville. Crossing the Rappahannock at U.S. Ford, and upon approaching a wood, a halt was made. But while the men were cooking coffee and preparing for a repast an orderly dashed up to General Reynolds and the order came quick and sharp to pack up. It was then twilight, and the men had but partly unpacked, so that in fifteen minutes the whole corps was again on the march. It had scarcely entered the woods when a sound like the distant thunder of Niagara struck upon our ears. As we proceeded the sound became more distinct; the earth jarred, and a roar 'like the tread of a mighty host' filled the woods in our front." [8]

The "tread of a mighty host" that the men of the 97th heard, was in fact the stampede of Hooker's right wing. Undetected, Lee had divided his army, and had sent Stonewall Jackson on a march across Hooker's front. Late in the afternoon, Jackson's twenty-six thousand men, screaming the rebel yell, stormed out of the woods directly on the flank and rear of Gen. O.O. Howard's 11th Corps at the extreme right of the Union line. The 11th Corps, composed primarily of Germans and Dutch, quickly dissolved in a rout. The 97th came up in time to witness the debacle and to help stem the tide of crazed men. Isaac Hall related:

> "Presently the rattle of supply trains, the shouting of teamsters, the lowing of cattle and the yelling of herdsmen were plainly heard; and then numerous stragglers, in greatest confusion and disorder, without arms, ammunition or knapsacks, appeared. An order came from the commanding general to deploy on each side of the road and stop every man. The moon was shining brightly, and but few escaped being picked up by the advancing force. Nothing but the stern point of the bayonet turned some of them." [9]

Fortunately darkness fell and the savage rebel charge came to a halt. The 97th continued its march, picking up stragglers as it went, before finally halting on the Union right, which was now pushed back to the Rapidan River. The regiment immediately went to work building breastworks and even Colonel Wheelock stripped off his coat and helped roll logs. Ahead in the darkness, within earshot of the axemen, Stonewall Jackson was scouting for a way to cut off the Union retreat. Jackson stumbled into a picket line of North Carolinians, and in the ensuing gunfire was severely wounded by his own troops. Eight days later, Stonewall Jackson would die of com-

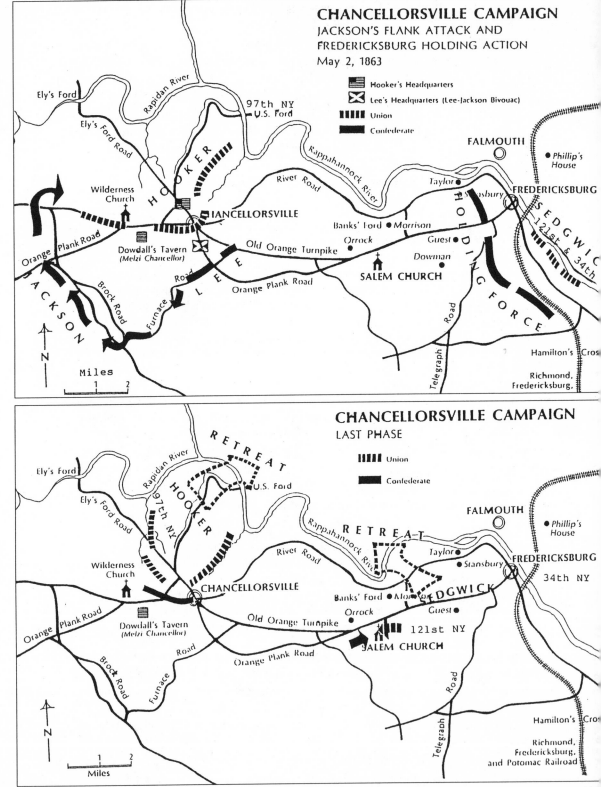

CHANCELLORSVILLE CAMPAIGN
JACKSON'S FLANK ATTACK AND
FREDERICKSBURG HOLDING ACTION
May 2, 1863

🏴 Hooker's Headquarters
⚔ Lee's Headquarters (Lee-Jackson Bivouac)
▌▌▌▌ Union
▬▬▬ Confederate

CHANCELLORSVILLE CAMPAIGN
LAST PHASE

▌▌▌▌ Union
▬▬▬ Confederate

Salem Church Embattled, H

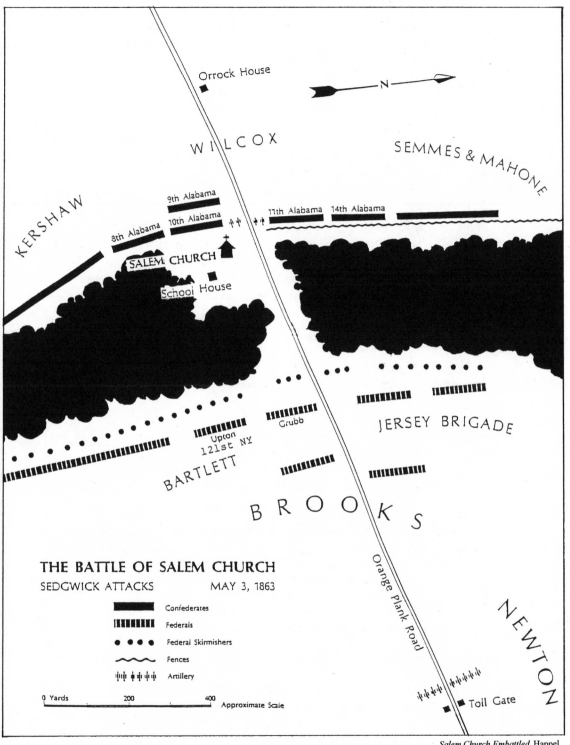

Orrock House

N

WILCOX

SEMMES & MAHONE

KERSHAW

9th Alabama

8th Alabama   10th Alabama

11th Alabama   14th Alabama

SALEM CHURCH

School House

Upton
121st NY

Grubb

BARTLETT

JERSEY BRIGADE

B R O O K S

THE BATTLE OF SALEM CHURCH

SEDGWICK ATTACKS   MAY 3, 1863

Confederates

Federals

Federal Skirmishers

Fences

Artillery

0 Yards   200   400

Approximate Scale

Orange Plank Road

NEWTON

Toll Gate

Salem Church Embattled, Happel

plications from his Chancellorsville wounds.

The 97th guarded their position all the next day but no attack came. In fact, the enemy was strangely quiet. Lee had again divided his army. Leaving a small force in front of Hooker, he sent four brigades of his infantry to counter a new Union thrust at Fredericksburg.

The 121st New York broke camp at White Oak, near Fredericksburg, on April 30th and marched four miles to the high bluffs overlooking the Rappahannock to the south of the city. To mask their position from enemy pickets across the river, the men were kept silent and were not permitted to light campfires. At midnight the regiment divided into groups of forty-five men and marched down to the riverbank to await the arrival of boats. Three hours later the boats arrived and the 121st, preceded by General Russell's brigade, embarked across the Rappahannock. On landing the men fanned out, drove off a handful of enemy pickets and established a beachhead. Pontoons were quickly laid and the rest of the 6th Corps began crossing. All of that day, May 1st, the fording continued as General Sedgwick formed his corps into battle positions.

The next day a courier brought news of the fighting at Chancellorsville, along with Hooker's orders requesting Sedgwick to put pressure on the Confederate right. To bring his army to maximum strength, Sedgwick ordered the 2nd Division of the 2nd Corps, which included the 34th New York, to effect a crossing at Fredericksburg as quickly as possible.

Pontoon bridges were laid across the Rappahannock at Fredericksburg without enemy interference, but the threat of rebel sharpshooters made it necessary to secure the city before large numbers of men could cross safely. To accomplish this task, each of the regiments in the 34th's brigade (the 1st Minnesota, 15th Massachusetts and 82nd New York) was requested to provide twenty-five volunteers and one officer to drive the enemy from the city. Lt. Louis Chapin remarked:

> "Along in the middle of the night there comes a call for a lieutenant and twenty-five men, to go to the river for a storming party. Now almost any man with an able imagination can understand what kind of duty is expected of men under such circumstances. Such a call means business. And yet it did not take five minutes to obtain all the men wanted. . . . Of the 25 volunteers of the Thirty-fourth Regiment, 18 were among the number reported as unwilling to serve longer than the first of May." [10]

Nicknamed the "Light Brigade," the advance patrols met no opposition either in crossing on the pontoons or in the city. Outside of Fredericksburg the detail was confronted by enemy pickets and a short firefight developed. Deploying as skirmishers, the "Light Brigade" drove the thin rebel line two and one half miles before halting near a large Confederate force.

At sunrise on May 3rd the rest of the 34th New York crossed the Rappahannock and entered Fredericksburg. After remaining in the city a short time, the regiment was ordered to move opposite the left of the rebel line so as to draw forces from the enemy's center. With the center weakened, General Sedgwick planned to focus his attack on that point. Chapin described the 34th's maneuver:

> "Our movement was along the river, with a wide plain between us and the rebel lines. Across this meadow from where it tapped the river [was] a wide hydraulic canal. As our movement was perceived, a column of rebel infantry moved westward from its side, the column keeping parallel with ours. The canal flowed between. It was a strange sight, those men in gray, and those men in blue, in parallel moving columns; and only a little distance apart. Not a shot was fired on either side. But over us, and all around us, screamed and burst the rebel shells. Between those two lines, eyeing each other like cats, each ready for a spring, was the grave of Washington's mother.
> . . . Slowly the lines creep forward, each still watching every movement of the other. Not a gun is fired; only the artillery being too far away to feel the suppression of the painful suspense, keeps on with its booming; and the men behind us, in other regiments, are falling; for every shot finds a place where it can break through the ranks. Then the thin lines creep back again, back, into the city, and the movement is over." [11]

Only two men from the 34th were wounded in the action. Surprisingly, the regiment immediately behind the 34th suffered over thirty casualties.

General Sedgwick's diversionary tactic worked. Units of the 6th Corps broke through the thinned Confederate center and the Stars and Stripes finally waved on the heights above Fredericksburg.

Passing again through the city the 34th marched up to the heights and continued on for two miles. Louis Chapin related:

> "Through avenues of the dead and dying we pass. Here are a lot of cannon that could not get away in time. Our men were too quick for them. And here are a lot of prisoners. On close acquaintance, a rebel looks much like any other man. Out on the far heights we go, till the view north and south of the river is most noble and commanding." [12]

After stopping to eat, the 34th turned and marched back to Fredericksburg. Along the way the 121st New York was met heading in the opposite direction. Of this encounter, the 34th's William Walton wrote:

> "When coming down from the heights, we met the 121st going up. Great was our delight at this unexpected encounter. Hands were shaken with vigor, congratulations passed, and with a 'God bless and keep you,' on each side we parted to meet, some of us--never more." [13]

That morning, May 3rd, the 121st New York arose at 1 a.m., formed ranks, and with the rest of their brigade, moved a short distance forward in a battle line. At sunrise a rebel battery sighted in on the men and sprayed cannister and grape on the brigade until Union batteries silenced the enemy's guns. The 5th Maine regiment adjacent to the 121st suffered a number of men killed but "Upton's Regulars" counted only five or six wounded.

Just after noon the 121st, with its brigade, marched through Fredericksburg and up the recently secured heights. It was at this point that the 34th New York was passed. The 121st's column was on its way to relieve the pressure on Hooker's embattled army, ten miles to the northwest, at Chancellorsville. Unbeknownst to the Federals, four Confederate brigades were marching down to meet them at a crossroads called Salem Church. Capt. Henry Galpin of Little Falls, described the 121st's arrival at Salem Church:

> "We passed through Fredericksburg and took the plank road. When we had gone nearly four miles, a rebel battery opened on our advance. Our batteries got in position and silenced them. We filed on off the road and our brigade advanced cautiously in line of battle through the woods and fields. After advancing over a mile in this manner, it was ascertained by our pickets thrown out in front that the rebels had made a stand in rear of a narrow strip of woods directly in our front. Now comes the most sad and eventful hour the 121st ever witnessed, now were we to receive our baptismal fire.
>
> We were ordered to advance. Steadily we entered the woods, the underbrush somewhat impeding our progress; but not a man faltered. As we reached the edge of the woods towards the rebels, the firing commenced. There was a brick house about a rod to the front and right of our regiment, and two log out-houses along the line of the regiment, and they were filled with rebels." [14]

In front of the 121st lay a strong rebel line astride the Orange Plank Road. Anchoring this position, which effectively blocked the path to Chancellorsville, were Salem Church (Galpin's "brick house") and two wooden sheds. By the time the 121st arrived at Salem Church, a full brigade of graycoats from Alabama had manned the buildings with riflemen and were dug in behind a small embankment. Gen. Cadmus Wilcox, a former West Point instructor who ironically had taught the 121st's Emory Upton at the Academy, was in command of the Alabamians.

Lying between the Federals in the woods and the Confederate line was a small patch of open ground that made for a perfect killing zone. Although attacking Wilcox's position seemed suicidal, the order for the 121st's brigade to advance was given. Clinton Beckwith of Herkimer provided a private's view of the fighting that followed. Beckwith wrote:

> "I can remember now a strange sort of quiet in the ranks. I had no idea, nor do I think any one near me had any premonition of any impending calamity. I was the extreme left man in the ranks of the regiment. Joe Rounds, I think, was the sergeant on the left of the company. We moved at an ordinary step forward into the woods perhaps seventy yards, with no sound except a growl from Eli Casler because some one had held a bush as he passed and let it fly back into his face.
>
> The firing seemed to be coming to us, and reaching the distance I have named we came nearly up to our skirmish line and they commanded and received our admiration, for the plucky and persistent way in which they did their work. The officer commanding just in front of us was a brave man and understood his business thoroughly. He shouted to his men to move up and push forward on the right, and fired his revolver at something in front that I could not see. At that instant there was a yell of pain, and Arthur

Proctor, a young man from Mohawk, a little way up the line cried out that he was shot, and Herringshaw took hold of him and began to help him. A little farther off another was hit and we were immediately ordered to 'fix bayonets and forward, double quick, charge,' and we went forward on the run. What became of those skirmishers I could not see. I suppose they pushed their opponents as far as they could, and then lay down and let us charge over them. We moved forward on a run a distance of not more than one hundred yards until we could see the clearing beyond the woods, when suddenly as if by magic, a line of men rose up and delivered their fire almost in our faces. The crash seemed terrific. I was paralyzed for an instant but continued to move on. Benny West who was next to me gave a terrible bound and pitched against me, shot dead. Hank King stuck his gun up against the side of my head, as I thought, and fired, and I pointed my gun at the men in front of me and fired, all the time moving forward and over a little ditch into the road. The men who were in the ditch and behind the brush fence through the gap which I passed, jumped up and ran, some to their rear and some to ours. I loaded and fired up the road twice. Joe Rounds stood beside me doing the same. The fire from the enemy seemed to come from that direction, but it was so smoky that I could not see much. . . . Just then John Dain said he was hit. He mistook the water running from his canteen, which was pierced, for blood. I remember I laughed at the expression on his face at the time. I kept looking and firing in the direction from which the bullets seemed to come, and our fellows kept crowding down among our company to get away from the fire. After a time the smoke cleared a little and I could see some buildings, and from a brick building . . . came the fire which was so destructive to us. There seemed to be men in the church who were firing from the windows, and our men were crowding away from it toward us to escape being hit. In front of us and to the left there were no Rebels that I could see. How long we would have stayed there I do not know, I suppose until we were attacked and driven away. I realized how useless it was for us to stay, but did not know enough to run, and it was well that Captain Wilson of General Bartlett's staff rode up and ordered us back, accompanying the order with the inquiry, 'D__n you, don't you know enough to fall back?' I started to go back rather slowly. A lot of our fellows were lying down. I remember Joe Rounds shouting, 'Come on, we're ordered back,' and then seeing Sile Goodrich and Benny West who had been shot dead, and having the thought come to me, 'Why, these are all shot and dead.' " [15]

Under a hail of bullets the Federal attack dissolved. The veteran regiments of Bartlett's Brigade, the 27th New York, 5th Maine and 96th Pennsylvania, quit the field leaving the 121st New York as the last unit to off. Of the horrendous damage done to the 121st, Capt. Marcus Casler of Little Falls reported:

"After firing two rounds our Regiment advanced into the road, when the Rebs in the pits poured a volley into us, mowing us down like grass. We held the road about fifteen minutes, when having fired nearly all our cartridges, we were ordered to fall-back, which we did in good order. But on getting our Regiment in line again and looking, we found it only half as large as it was before the fight.

Lieut. Doubleday fell, shot through the head, while bravely encouraging his men: Capt. Arnold was first wounded in the arm, but continued to cheer his men when he received another ball in his breast and fell: Lieut. Ford was mortally wounded: Capt. Mather was wounded in the shoulder: Lieut. Bates killed: Capt. Wendell, killed or taken prisoner. A great many of the Little Falls boys were wounded and all came from the field. Poor Wash. Babcock received a wound in the abdomen, near the hip the ball passing out near the spine. . . . I did not get a scratch, but the balls flew about my head as thick, that there would have been no use of dodging, if I had been so inclined. One passed through my blanket, that is the nearest I came to being hit. Our killed, wounded and missing amount to 273—half of our number. It was a bloody and sorrowful baptism for us, but the Regiment did what was required of it honorably, and has the praises of the corps. The Colonel's horse was shot from under him, when he took the ground and fought like a perfect demon. He don't know what fear is. Out of perhaps forty or fifty thousand bullets fired at us, only 273 took effect." [16]

Gen. Cadmus Wilcox would later write of the 121st's charge:

"I knew the troops attacking us were unused to battle by the way they hung on. They ran over our line and took fifty or sixty prisoners on the right of the 16th Alabama, and then stood and let us shoot them down like sheep." [17]

Night fell on Sedgwick's men, who were now cut off from a retreat to Fredericksburg. During the battle at Salem Church, Confederate forces had retaken the heights behind the city, driving off the Union troops in the area. The 34th New York and its brigade, caught between the advancing rebel forces and the river, evacuated Fredericksburg at dusk and recrossed the Rappahannock. The shattered 121st New York and the rest of the 6th Corps were in danger of being encircled.

Lt. Adam Clarke Rice of Fairfield related:

"Everything was in chaos. Fragments of fifty regiments were drifting around in wild confusion. Broad fields were covered with wounded, and stragglers running, they knew not whither.

By nine o'clock something of order was restored; regiments reorganized, and most were ready to rest from their weary toils. The night passed off as do all nights after a day of terrible battle. The next morning dawned and the storm opened again with all its fury. We began to realize the peril of our situation. Our Corps was surrounded except by a narrow passage to the river at Banks Ford, three miles above Fredericksburg." [18]

Fortunately, no major Confederate attack was made early in the day and the 6th Corps was given the opportunity to fortify its line. Late in the day the rebels furiously attacked the beleaguered corps. Of the rebel assault, the 121st's Lieutenant Rice noted:

"Five o'clock came and with it the most terribly sublime scene I ever saw. The enemy advanced upon us, from every side, and opened a fire that made the earth tremble beneath our feet. We were surrounded by a wall of fire; the black clouds of smoke hung like a pall around the dying day; the deafening roar of artillery sounded like death howling through the wilderness, and all the angry war fiends seemed to be conspiring against us." [19]

The coming of night put an end to the enemy assaults and under the cover of darkness, Sedgwick got his columns moving toward Banks Ford. Winning the race to the Rappahannock, the 6th Corps escaped the closing rebel trap and crossed to the safety of the opposite shore. Adam Clarke Rice remarked:

> "We moved down to the river and the whole Corps was massed upon three acres of land. We remained there until eleven o'clock, when the 121st was taken out about half a mile to the front, to guard against any advance of the enemy, while the army was crossing. About four o'clock we moved down to the river as quietly as possible, and were the last regiment to cross." [20]

At Chancellorsville, Hooker's army began withdrawing on May 5th. Formed into a defensive "V," it had resisted a major attack on May 3rd and constant pressure the next two days from a rebel force not one quarter its size. As the beaten army began crossing the Rappahannock at U.S. Ford, a detachment from the 97th did rear guard duty as the 121st had done some five miles to the east. Capt. Isaac Hall of Leyden wrote:

> "To accomplish a safe retreat to the other side it was necessary to mislead the enemy, hence a large detail was made of men and officers, with pioneer tools for falling timber and intrenching, and under the command of the captain of Company A, 97th N.Y. [Hall]; it was led to the east and north of the Chancellorsville House by Hooker's chief of engineers, who caused the trees to be blazed as he led the way to the left and rear—toward the river." [21]

The men of the 97th crossed the river early on the morning of May 6th and marched back to Falmouth.

The Chancellorsville campaign had been a galling Union defeat. Lee, with half the force of Hooker, had bloodied the Federal columns in the Wilderness and then audaciously had divided his force and routed Sedgwick at Salem Church. The Union offensive was repulsed on all fronts and the invaders were again thrown back across the Rappahannock.

The cost had been dear on both sides. The Army of the Potomac suffered over seventeen thousand casualties and the Confederates thirteen thousand. [22] Of the Mohawk Valley regiments, the 34th New York, with two wounded [23] and the 97th New York, reporting no casualties, [24] were virtually unscathed. The 121st New York, on the other hand, had been terribly mauled. Of the five hundred and eighty-three men of the 121st that answered roll call on the morning of May 3rd, two hundred and seventy-six would end up on the casualty rolls. In less than thirty minutes in front of Salem Church and in the next day's fighting, the 121st would realize eighty men killed in action, one hundred and seventy-three wounded (sixteen mortally) and twenty-three men missing.[25] The death toll in the 121st in two days of action would exceed the 34th New York's battlefield deaths in that regiment's two years of service. Although Herkimer and Otsego Counties shared equally in the makeup of the 121st, the number of casualties among Otsego County companies (157) far outweighed the count in Herkimer County companies (119). This discrepancy was attributable to Company D, raised primarily in Frankfort and Schuyler, being detached on skirmish duty elsewhere and therefore not on the field at Salem Church.

The Herkimer County men slain on the battlegrounds of Salem Church or that would die soon after from wounds received in the fight were: Warren Spencer, Alonzo Casler, Abner Huntley and O.C. Gransbury of Salisbury; Millington Harter from Herkimer; Charles Williams and frequent *Journal* correspondent, Lt. Frederick Ford of Fairfield; Capt. Nelson Wendell of Winfield; Isaac Backus and George Westcott from Russia; Richard Matthews of Litchfield; George Hewitson of Danube: Robert Fox from Columbia; Fred Starring, John Maguire, Washington Babcock, Orlando Casler, John Brazamber, Mike Fagan, U.H.B. Harrington and Adjutant Thomas Arnold of Little Falls, and Silas Goodrich, Henry Crittenden, Jacob Cristman and Clinton Beckwith's fifteen-year-old buddy, Benton (Benny) West, from German Flatts.

At Salem Church the 121st fell prey to the same dubious sense of honor and courage that so dearly cost the 34th New York at Fair Oaks and the 97th New York at Antietam. All too often, new, unbloodied regiments saw the "glory" of war as a willingness to go toe to toe with a rival or to buck the odds and attack a strongly defended position. Unfortunately, as was the case of the 121st at Salem Church, the grim realities of battle did not become evident until the baptismal fire.

Soon after "2nd Fredericksburg," Adj. Francis Morse of the 121st sent to the *Journal* the official list of casualties suffered by the regiment. The *Journal* published the list on its front page in a column fully thirty inches long. Prominent in the listing were Capt. Thomas Arnold and Lt. Frederick Ford. Ford was shot in the thigh and bled to death on the field. Prisoners from the 121st later saw his naked body thrown into a communal grave near Salem Church. Captain Arnold, wounded in the arm and chest, lingered two weeks in Potomac Creek Hospital, finally succumbing to his wounds with his father by his side.

After receiving a telegram announcing Arnold's death, the *Journal* eulogized the two officers:

> "And thus from the same neighborhood are taken two officers, brilliant, virtuous, and beloved by large circles of friends and relatives—Capt. Arnold and Lieut. Ford—both falling as became true men to fall! No man ever fell a victim to a worthier cause: no man has written a brighter, nobler example upon the page of Freedom's history. Tablets of honor are reared in the hearts of community and tears are shed in memory of two whose virtues will ever remain as incentive and inspiration for the generous and good. Alas! how fearfully near is this terrible war bringing tears and sorrow and death to our every hearthstone."[26]

CHAPTER IX

"Brave Defenders, Home Again!"

Summer 1863 - The Blackwater Expedition - The 34th Comes Home

After the Chancellorsville defeat, General Hooker once more settled his army on the heights opposite Fredericksburg, Virginia. The 34th at Falmouth and the 97th and 121st near White Oak Church pitched their tents and relaxed in the warm spring-time weather.

Of the Mohawk Valley regiments, only the 121st had been severely tested in the battles of early May 1863. The stand-up fight that the 121st had endured at Salem Church had cost the regiment almost one-half its number. To offset these losses, the 121st was the recipient of over two hundred men transferred from the 16th, 18th and 32nd New York regiments.

Like the 34th, these regiments had been formed in the spring of 1861 as two-year units and now were being mustered out. In each of the regiments there were men who had enlisted after the regiment's formation and were under the impression that they had signed on for two years, not three. These were the men transferring to the 121st and needless to say they were unhappy with their lot. Separated from their comrades and thrust into a foreign regiment, the transfers had lost their unit identity and had seemingly gained one year of service time. Although they performed their duties in the 121st, their discontentment was evident. Many months would pass before any camaraderie would exist between the new men and the original members of the 121st.

Trickling back to the 121st were paroled men from the regiment taken prisoner at Salem Church. Many of these men were wounded and required hospitalization.

But, even if they had been healthy, they were not useful to the 121st until exchanged.

At this point in the war neither side wanted nor could cope with the burden of prisoners. An exchange system, similar to that used between warring European nations, had been agreed upon by the North and the South since early in the war. This system allowed each side to "trade" prisoners without actually physically retaining the captives. In essence, captured men below the grade of commissioned officers would be released by the captor upon taking an oath which specified, that the parolee would not serve in any military capacity until formally released from this obligation. Wounded men and non-combat personnel often would be returned to the nearest enemy force, while healthy soldiers would be marched off to a "parole camp" in friendly territory. Releases from parole could be obtained by the exchange of paroled men for each other or for commissioned officers. Using a private as the lowest common denominator, a general could be exchanged for forty privates, a colonel for fifteen and so on.

The paroled men from the 121st were waiting to be exchanged and although not of service to the regiment were heartily welcomed back by the other men. Since each of the former prisoners of war had been in the enemy lines they were eagerly sought out to relate the conditions in the rebel camps.

Two members of the 121st's medical staff captured at a field hospital near Salem Church, provided such an account to the *Journal*. The newspaper's editor, J.R. Stebbins, paraphrased the story, writing:

> "Surgeon Holt and Hospital Steward Phelps of the 121st, were on the field of battle near Fredericksburg when the Union forces were withdrawn and were taken prisoners by the enemy. They were detained ten days at Salem Church and were busied in caring for the wounded. They saw the burial of our dead soldiers by the rebels and estimate the enemy's loss as large in that part of the field, if not larger than our own. Our dead were all buried together in one deep pit and these prisoners recognized among them many of their old comrades, of whom were Lieut. Ford, Capt. Wendell, Private West and others. Their account of the rebel situation is most interesting. For the first four days they had scarcely anything to eat, but the rebel soldiers fared no better. They were well treated and suffered to depart without molestation.
>
> They give the prices of provisions and other articles in the rebel lines as follows: Potatoes, $15 per bushel: Tea, $6 per pound: Coffee, not to be had: The doctor paid $1.50 for half a pound of candles: Ham, $1.35 per pound: Eggs, $2 per doz.: Flour, to the Government, $24 per barrel: Butter, $3 per pound: Whiskey, $20 per quart or $1 per drink (a positive fact!): Calico, $4 per yard: Army boots, $60 per pair: Pork and Beef, not to be had: and so on through the entire market catalogue." [1]

Isaac Darling of Salisbury, a frequent *Journal* correspondent who wrote under the name "Ding," related his personal rendition of being captured at Salem Church and of the treatment of wounded prisoners by the rebels. "Ding" wrote:

> "I was one of the unfortunate ones and was wounded as well as taken prisoner. I did not hear the order to fall back, and upon gazing around, I

saw no one near me and upon turning to see where they were I was hit in the center of the back of the neck. The ball came out just in front of my left ear. After I fell, as the force of the ball knocked me down, I suddenly recovered and found I was in a very dangerous place, as the balls and pieces of shell were falling all around me. I got up on my knees and, upon looking in front of me, I saw Lt. Ford. I looked at him a few moments, but from some cause could not speak; so I crawled on a little further and then got upon my feet. When looking around I saw several of our boys lying dead and dying upon the ground from where our Regiment had retreated. I was going up to speak with some of them when a rebel came up and said I had better go with him. I told him, if he would give me some water and lead me I would go, for I had bled so much I was quite faint and the blood dried upon my face and I could scarcely see, so he unclasped my cartridge belt for me and relieved me of my knapsack. It was but a short distance to where the rebs had established a hospital. To this place they took me, where I lay until about 8 o'clock when the prisoners who were not wounded began to come in. I remained there until morning when I was removed with others to their General Hospital about three miles from the battlefield. I stayed there two days, when I was removed to what is called Salem Church. It rained the day I went to the Church, and the next day, but the 3rd day after I went out to look after the dead as they had not yet been buried. Among the dead I found Warren D. Spencer, U.H. Harrington, Oliver C. Gransbury, Frederick Starring and John Bramsby all of Co. A. I also recognized Lt. F.E. Ford your correspondent and upon further search, found Capt. N.O. Wendell, Co. F. There were many others, but I did not know their names. On Thursday, the rebs buried all of our dead. Serg. Geo. Huertson died in the Church. On Thursday we were all paroled. Our treatment while over in the rebel lines was of the best-that is they did all they could for us, after we were in the Hospital, but they took everything most of the boys had, not leaving them their clothes."[2]

While at White Oak, details from the 121st routinely drew two or three day picket duty in the Virginia countryside. The regiment's area of responsibility was on a line extending from the Rappahannock River to the Potomac, in the vicinity of King George Court House. While on picket duty the men had an opportunity to see for themselves the war's effect on southern citizens.

An anonymous writer from the 121st related a typical experience:

"We generally enjoy ourselves better on picket duty than in any other part of our warfare. We occasionally come in contact with citizens and servants (principally the weaker sex) and if we can engage in conversation with them it is quite interesting to us soldiers. I visited two or three plantations in the vicinity of our lines. The first was owned by an old man named Randall. His family consists of a wife and two daughters, apparently 23 and 25 years old. Also five grown contrabands and two litters or groups of small ones of 5 or 6 in each group and of nearly the same age. This old gentleman and family once enjoyed the pleasures of quite a large estate. But how changed! All seem depressed with sadness and gloom brought on by this wicked rebellion. No steps seem to be taken even to cultivate a few vegetables. For the old man has given up in despair and can be seen wandering, crying, 'I am a ruined man' as all advocates of treason eventually will exclaim."[3]

The soldiers sympathized with the plight of many of the families that they met, yet they believed their suffering was a just punishment for years of oppression of not only the negroes but also of the poor whites.

Regarding these views, the unsigned soldier of the 121st went on to say:

"Previous to my enlistment, I was neutral in regard to slavery, but my short experience here, I confess, has made me an abolitionist, (if you may term it so). In the first place, slavery is morally unjust. It has been the great hindrance to civilization and cultivation of a great portion of the fertile soil of the south, held so by the ruling or slave power. The poorer class of whites, who are the majority in the country, are inferior in capabilities to the blacks."[4]

No sympathy was shown for the active Southern partisan. The soldiers of the 121st advocated a program of retribution not unlike the approach that would be taken by Gen. William Tecumseh Sherman one year later in his march through the deep south.

The 121st's anonymous correspondent added:

" . . . I do say too much lenity is shown to traitors when passing by the property about to engage them face to face. I believe in shelling every place of shelter, whether house or barn and shatter it to ruins, where so many secret and pour volleys of shot into us as we advance. Take a man's dairy of cows away and he has to look out for another and perhaps loses the avail of his farm for one year. So if we destroy the property of traitors and deprive their families of shelter, they will soon come to their relief and the rebellion is ended and many lives saved on both sides."[5]

Relieved from picket duty, the 121st broke camp on June 5th and marched with the rest of the 6th Corps to the high bluffs overlooking the Rappahannock south of Fredericksburg. Batteries of artillery moved to the river's edge as engineers began laying pontoons. As had happened previously, enemy sharpshooters began picking off the bridge layers, but on this occasion Union cannon fire forced the rebels to cower in their rifle pits. For the third time, the 121st was ordered to cross the Rappahannock to the Fredericksburg shore.

Lt. Adam Rice of the 121st described the encounter:

"Under the protection of this fire our men lowered their boats into the water, and rowed across to the other side. This artillery fire was kept up until three or four regiments had crossed over, and formed in line of battle on the other side. Then all at once a signal was sounded, and the firing ceased, and this line of battle made one of the finest charges upon those rifle pits, known in the history of war. The rebels had not time to recover from the shock which they had received from our cannonading, and being in a perfect state of confusion and chaos, were unable to make the feeblest resistance. Some throwing down their arms rushed over the works, and gave themselves up. Others essayed to fly, and were shot down. But the majority lay down behind the embankments, and like helpless suppliants, cried for mercy and protection. Thus once more our great army gained a foot-hold, a firm foot-hold upon the hostile bank, where twice it had stood before, and twice had been beaten back."[6]

The 121st New York, with the rest of the 1st Division of the 6th Corps, established a picket line over a mile long. For two days the men traded shots with the enemy but only minor casualties were taken. On June 7th the division was relieved and the 121st recrossed the Rappahannock.

The whole movement was a mystery to the men. After achieving a beachhead with an entire division, no move was made to carry the heights beyond. In fact, the rest of the Army of the Potomac had already begun to move away from the Fredericksburg arena.

Along the Blackwater River in southeastern Virginia, the 152nd New York, with other units of the 7th Corps, spent the latter half of May tearing up the railroad tracks in that district.

Marching from Suffolk on May 13th, the 152nd travelled due west ten miles to Carrsville, a small village sixty miles south of Richmond. After deploying skirmishers, the men went to work with pry bars lifting rails from the track of the Roanoke & Seaboard Railroad. The loosened rails, instead of being heated and deformed, were hoisted on to wagons for transport back to Suffolk. For two weeks the 152nd was employed along this rail line and that of the Norfolk & Petersburg Railroad. The destruction continued north to Windsor, Virginia before the 152nd was recalled to Suffolk. The mission along the Blackwater resulted in the confiscation of twenty miles of rail iron worth over one million dollars.

Travelling closely with the 152nd was the 1st New York Mounted Rifles, a cavalry unit recruited not only from the Empire State, but from throughout the Union. Among the officers of the Mounted Rifles were the son of prominent abolitionist Henry Ward Beecher, and Capt. Edward Z.C. Judson, better known by his pen name, Ned Buntline. Judson was no stranger to the Mohawk Valley, having passed through there in the Fall of 1862 recruiting for the 1st New York. No one from Herkimer County signed up with Judson, but a number of boys from Oneida and Onondaga counties did.

The Mounted Rifles were famous for, among other things, their foraging prowess. On the Blackwater expedition the horsemen had little trouble procuring food from area farms, but keeping it from the hungry mouths of the infantry was quite another thing. Henry Roback of the 152nd related:

"One night a detail as silent as the sons of Momus left the camp of the Mounted Rifles, and with muffled spurs proceeded to the outskirts of a large plantation a few miles from camp. Entering a lonesome and dismal forest, they unearthed a smokehouse which was hidden in the dense foliage. Dismounting, they proceeded to transfer the ham and bacon across the pommels of their saddles. Arriving in camp they disposed of the booty in a careless manner. The camp guard of the 99th and the 152nd N.Y., scenting the smoked pork with natural instinct, crawled on their hands and knees, and, seizing the plunder, they conveyed it to their quarters and buried it out of sight, leaving the Rifles one ham for breakfast."[7]

On May 18th, two regiments in the 152nd's brigade, the 10th New Jersey and the 170th New York, mistakenly fired into each other, resulting in a number of casualties. Initial reports erroneously identified one of the units in this incident as the 152nd New York. The story, which was carried by New York City and Washington newspapers, made its way to Herkimer County. Needless to say, the report caused a great deal of hand wringing among the families and friends of the men in the 152nd. Nearly two weeks passed before an article in the *Journal* dispelled the story:

> "Much excitement was caused last week by a telegraphic dispatch in the daily papers to the effect that an unfortunate mistake had occurred near Suffolk: that two Union regiments opened fire on each other, each supposing the other to be a rebel force: that considerable loss was suffered, and that the 152nd N.Y.V. was one of the regiments.
> From later dispatches, however, we are led to believe either that the whole story was a hoax or that it was some other regiment and not the 152nd that was engaged in it."[8]

One week later, Edward Townsend of the 152nd fully explained the accident:

> "No doubt many of our friends saw a notice in the New York Herald and also in several other papers that the 152nd had been in a fight with the 11th Rhode Island in the night, all through mistake. We wish to inform our friends that it is a base falsehood. We have been engaged in no such disgraceful affair. The sad mishap occurred between the 170th N.Y.V. and the 10th New Jersey. The damage however was slight. Both of these regiments belong to our Brigade, and in forming in line, it being early in the morning, they mistook each other for the enemy's consequently the fatal blunder."[9]

During their march along the Blackwater, the men of the 152nd ate quite well. The arduous labor of marching and tearing up the rails gave the men hearty appetites which were satisfied by forage from the countryside. Sheep, chickens, pigs and cattle disappeared from their pens and coops, and reappeared in the soldiers' cooking pots. Although fresh meat and vegetables were available for every meal, a great many of the men fell seriously ill for want of another essential, potable water.

The soldiers' dilemma on the march was described by Fairfield's Edward Townsend:

> "Many of the soldiers were taken sick, owing to the quantity of impure water which they drank, and quite a large number were brought back to the hospital. The habit of drinking a large quantity of water, is the most common while upon the march. Water is the soldier's friend and stand by, and frequently it proves his destroyer, for often is the volunteer necessitated by extreme thirst to drink muddy and filthy water. Drink he must, and drink he will. He can get nothing but the most miserable apology for water, nevertheless thirst blinds reason, and all he wants is water, water. We are aware

that many of our friends extend to us good advice upon this subject, and kindly tell us to 'get along without drinking so much.' Now it is well enough to tender such counsel, and we receive it in the same spirit with which it is given, but when we come to make a practical thing of the theory, it utterly fails. A soldier on the march, with eyes and mouthful of dust, with a hot sun pouring its melting rays upon him and wringing the streams of perspiration from his scorching brow, is in a poor condition to keep temperate. His being is on the flames, and all he wants all he asks for at the time is water. Counsel is forgotten-the advice of mothers and fathers in regard to drinking too much, is left behind among the cooler moments. He thinks of something that will alleviate his thirst, and leaping to the first mud-hole that he sees, he pours the stale element in, to mingle with and corrupt his life's blood." [10]

Eighty-five men from the 152nd fell out on the Blackwater marches because of sickness and were sent back to the hospital at Hampton, Virginia. A few of the boys died and were buried on the hospital grounds overlooking the waters where the "Monitor" and "Merrimac" had dueled a year before.

Returning to Suffolk on May 29th, the 152nd remained in camp until June 3rd when they were again ordered out. On this occasion, their mission was to seek out and engage enemy units in the Blackwater region. No sizable rebel force was discovered and only minor skirmishing ensued, yet the 152nd and the other Federal units suffered under the broiling Virginia sun.

Edward Townsend of Fairfield described the expedition and questioned its worth:

"We were ordered to the Blackwater and for six days, we marched over a distance of one hundred and thirty miles. The object of our leader was to draw the enemy into a fight but all we could do, was simply to skirmish with them a little, while on our own part the loss was the heaviest - not that we suffered severely from the enemy's bullets, but scores and hundreds sank down in the road, exhausted or sunstruck. We do not wish to be understood as manifesting a spirit of complaint, especially when the object to be gained is worthy of such sacrifice, yet we object to useless and wholesale slaughter. Our tramp to the Blackwater may have been called for, but the inhumanity which characterized some portions of our march will ever be remembered and spoken of only with the bitterest curses. There certainly was no necessity for the cruelty displayed. Many a volunteer, has lost forever his energy both physical and mental just from the effects of that march." [11]

After resting for almost two weeks in Suffolk, on June 19th the 152nd received orders to report to Yorktown. Word had it that the regiment was to be involved in a move on Richmond.

In Herkimer County the townspeople began preparing for the 34th's return in mid-May. The village of Herkimer offered to host the regiment's reception, but Little Falls argued that since it was the largest community in the county it should be chosen for such an honor. The County Reception Committee, chaired by Judge Ezra

Graves of Russia, unanimously accepted Little Falls' offer. With a reception site selected, the reception committee appointed fifty-five men to oversee the arrangements. Care was taken that each of the Herkimer County towns had at least one representative on this "Executive Committee." In the latter part of May, Chairman Graves sent a letter to Colonel Laflin of the 34th, announcing the reception and inquiring as to a convenient date.

In Little Falls a special committee was named to oversee the construction of picnic tables, decorations and the orators' platform. Also sworn in were twelve special policemen to help the regular officers maintain order among the crowds expected to descend upon Little Falls.

The county committee was also hard at work arranging the day's program, procuring orators and organizing units for a parade through Little Falls. To surmount the problem of obtaining refreshments for the anticipated throng of people, the committee requested contributions from each town. The *Journal* carried the notice:

> "So far as refreshments are concerned the plan is to provide one large
> table for the regiment for which donations should be sent in from all sec-
> tions of this county. Besides this, there will be prepared a table for each
> town, where all those who desire may partake of such refreshments as they
> may provide, thus joining in one grand picnic." [12]

On the morning of June 9, the 34th New York, escorted by the other regiments of the brigade, marched to the Falmouth train depot. Amid music from the regimental bands of the 1st Minnesota, 15th Massachusetts and the 82nd New York, the men of the 34th New York mounted the cars to the cheering of their comrades. With shouts of "good-bye" and "god-speed," the troop train started on its journey north. Col. George Ward, commanding the 15th Massachusetts, noted in his diary:

> "This morning the New York Thirty-fourth left for home, their term of
> service having expired. It seemed like losing a friend, for they had been
> with us over twenty months." [13]

The train took the 34th to Washington and then on to Philadelphia where the men were treated to dinner at the Cooper Union. New York City was the next stop and Albany was reached on June 12th.

The *Albany Journal* announced the 34th's arrival:

> "The Thirty-fourth Regiment reached this city early this morning. After
> breakfast at the Delavan House, it formed and took up a line of march
> through some of the principal streets for the Capitol, where they were wel-
> comed by the Governor [Horatio Seymour], in an appropriate speech, com-
> plimenting them for their distinguished services in the field. Lieut. Col.
> Beverly responded in a few brief and appropriate remarks. The Regiment
> then proceeded to the Barracks.
> A committee, consisting of Senator Hardin, Canal Commissioner Skin-
> ner, Hon. H.P. Alexander and Oliver Ladue, are here to escort the Regi-
> ment to Little Falls where a reception awaits the gallant veterans equalling
> even that with which Utica recently honored her brave sons. The reception
> takes place Saturday. In the evening the Regiment will return to this city to
> be mustered out of service." [14]

Saturday, June 13th, was the day set for the 34th's welcoming home party. With this date only being learned on June 9th (when the 34th started north from Falmouth), Little Falls was in a frenzy preparing the final arrangements. Although it rained almost constantly, by Friday night, June 12th, everything was ready. In Ward's Square (the village's eastern park), long picnic tables were set up, store fronts and homes were decorated with banners and wreaths, and on Ann Street a large wooden monument had been erected in memory of the 34th's dead.

The memorial, which was contributed by the Village of Little Falls, featured a twenty-foot-high shaft, topped by a large eagle grasping an American flag in each talon. The column itself was wreathed with cedar boughs and white flowers and bore the names of the regiment's battles: Fair Oaks, Glendale, Antietam, Yorktown, Fredericksburg, South Mountain, Malvern Hill, Edward's Ferry, Nelson's Farm, Savage's Station and Peach Orchard Station.

Friday evening the monument survived an encounter with a drunken wagoneer. The *Journal* reported the incident in an article entitled, "A Good One—Too good to be lost":

> "The night before the reception a burly farmer, who had been imbibing rather freely and had so been belated till after dark, took his way up Ann Street, behind a team permitted to keep the road about as they pleased. As they reached the large monument, prepared in honor of the gallant heroes of the 34th who will never more return, the horses ran the wagon against it, nearly tipping the toper overboard. It was some minutes before he found his reckoning and then, with the look of a drunken man, he profanely asked, as if to himself 'who in (hic) h__l is buried here?' and jogged along homeward." [15]

By sunup on Saturday morning, the roads leading into Little Falls were jammed with people. Delegations from throughout Herkimer County came into town, aboard heavy farm wagons, in elegant carriages, on horseback and on foot. Well-wishers from communities east and west of the village crammed special trains stopping at the depot. Every stable and hitching post in town was appropriated as the crowd swelled to an estimated ten thousand people.

The 34th New York and a contingent of escorts from Herkimer County left Albany for Little Falls aboard an early train. Arriving in Little Falls at 11 a.m., the regiment was greeted by a deafening roar from the huge crowd that had gathered at the depot. Cheer after cheer rent the air as the soldiers emerged from their cars. The 34th's officers tried their best to get their men into line, but the surge of the crowd made any formation impossible. After a semblance of order was restored, Little Falls village president, M.W. Priest, formally welcomed the troops:

> "Gentlemen of the 34th Regiment, upon me, as President of this village, devolves the duty and the pleasure of welcoming those of you, the officers and soldiers of the 34th Regiment of New York State Volunteers, who belong to this county on their return home. In behalf of my fellow citizens I thank those of you who belong to other parts of the state for your presence on this occasion, and I hope that nothing may occur here that may cause any but kind recollections towards us when you shall be faraway. To the

relatives and friends of those brave men who, alas! do not return I can only say that you have the sincere and heartfelt sympathy of this entire community.

Hon. Amos H. Prescott will address you in a more appropriate manner than I am able to do: and again I bid the heroes of the 34th Regiment, a warm and cordial welcome to the village of Little Falls." [16]

Following Priest's address, a procession, headed by a squad of Little Falls police, formed on John Street. The parade's first division consisted of Zenas Priest, the "Marshal of the Day," the Mohawk Valley Band, the County Reception Committee, and other prominent citizens mounted on horseback. In the second division were, the Frankfort band, the President and Trustees of Little Falls, the "Orators of the Day," clergymen, factory owners and any other citizen that wished to march. The third division was led by the Fire Chiefs of Herkimer County, followed by fire companies from Herkimer, Mohawk, Ilion and Little Falls, the Little Falls Citizen's Brass Band, the Mohawk Valley Drum Corps and finally the 34th regiment. Bringing up the rear of the parade marched disabled and discharged soldiers from throughout the county.

After everyone was in line, Rev. S.B. Gregory of the Little Falls Baptist Church delivered an invocation and Judge Amos H. Prescott of Mohawk greeted the 34th on behalf of Herkimer County.

The procession then proceeded east along John Streeet, up William Street and back westerly along Main Street. Along the parade route, wreaths, banners and other decorations were hung on every storefront and residence.

The *Courier* office displayed the banner, "Soldiers of the 34th Regiment, grateful people welcome you" and at the corner of William and Main Streets a large pencilled likeness of "Little Mac," surrounded by cedar wreaths, was mounted on a pole wrapped with red, white and blue cambric. The Benton House on Main Street showed off a forty foot long flag and above its doorway was the banner "Brave Defenders, Home Again!" Opposite the *Journal* office, two arches sheathed in cedar boughs intoned, "To Valor and Constancy" and "Brave as the Bravest." At Kibbe's saloon were hung portraits of Washington and McClellan, accompanied by the phrases, "How are you boys?" and "Happy to greet you." A bronze eagle topped the awning of William Taylor's store and a statue of Washington surrounded by a cluster of American flags stood in the storefront.

As the parade turned up Ann Street, the procession reached the monument dedicated to fallen men of the 34th. The *Journal* reported:

"As the procession passed this point heads were reverently uncovered, steps were measured to the solemn music of the bands, silence came over the crowds of people and many a tear was shed in memory of those who would never return. The effect upon the brave fellows of the regiment, as they looked anew upon their thinned ranks, was too deep for utterance. It was indeed a beautiful tribute to departed patriotism—a tribute too often forgotten in the glad times of welcoming those whose lives, though not less freely offered have not been taken." [17]

Continuing up Ann Street the line of march turned east on Gansevoort Street, passing banners at the residences of George Ashley, H.M. Burch, Albert G. Story,

James Aldrich and Jerome Petrie.

Describing the various decorations along the parade route the *Journal* reported:

> "Upon the whole these decorations were most beautiful and are said to have surpassed even those of our neighbors of Utica at their recent reception: and although there would seem to be a sameness which no effort of ours can avoid in a brief description of them, yet the styles of lettering and the variety of tastes displayed in ornamenting were so different that the effect, in almost every instance, was good." [18]

Reaching Wards Square, the procession divided, forming ranks on both sides of the park, with only the men of the 34th being admitted to the center.

On an elevated platform in the middle of the green, thirty-four young ladies dressed in white were arranged in a "pyramid of beauty." The crowd quieted as the girls, students of Miss Wright's school, recited their welcoming tribute to the boys of the 34th:

> "Soldiers, we welcome you! Gladly we hail this day that returns to home and friends those who went forth to battle for a nation's honor. You left us amid rejoicing, tears and benedictions, your return is greeted by the same. Rejoicing that, protected by an invisible hand, you have returned, scarred perhaps by many a conflict, but returned to home once more.
>
> Tears we drop for the fallen brave, tears for the unmarked grave. Hallowed be the spot where the bones of our bold repose! And benedictions, aye, let them rest unnumbered upon the heads of those who have fought our battles.
>
> We know the war cry still resounds, the angel of peace sits afar off with folded wings, and who can know when his blessed pinions shall again hover over this free 'Land of the West?' God in his mercy has chastised us deeply, and while we bow in humility to His will, we would not forget those who, thus far, have so nobly done the nation's bidding. We welcome you proudly, no stigma of cowardice has ever coupled with the name of our gallant 34th.
>
> When the tale of Fair Oaks gleams upon history's page, it will picture a true, warrior band, eagerly responding to the noble Sumner's command. Even now we hear that order—'Charge 34th'—and your thinned ranks tell, alas, too well, how there you met the traitor.
>
> Of memory's immortal tablets we know there is one for the heroes of Malvern Hill, Antietam and Fredericksburg. Kindly we welcome you to the rest so nobly won." [19]

As the speech concluded each girl came forward and threw a bouquet of fresh spring flowers to the men of the 34th.

The main orator of the day, Judge Ezra Graves, stepped to the dais and delivered an hour long speech detailing the regiment's history.

At the end of the Judge's oration, Colonel Laflin of the 34th called for three cheers from the regiment, which the men heartily responded to, throwing their caps high into the air on the third cheer.

Afterwards the soldiers were conducted to a thousand-foot-long table, heaped with food. The "eatables" spread before them included; eight hundred pounds of meat, two hundred loaves of bread, one hundred and fifty pies, two hundred cakes, one hundred pounds of sugar, one hundred pounds of cheese, forty pounds of butter, pork and beans, pickles, radishes, oranges and tarts. Over one hundred ladies waited on the soldiers, making sure that none of the men left the table hungry.

When the regiment finished eating, the crowd of onlookers was allowed to join the feast. The *Journal* reported the near riot that ensued:

> "After the soldiers had left the tables the hungry crowd rushed forward and scenes were enacted both shameful and ridiculous. People who, we presume to say, have enough to eat when at home, acted as though they expected never again to have such a chance and a general stampede for the tables began. But, by the efforts of the committee some show of order was finally secured and we believe everybody ate to his heart's content-and there was plenty to spare which, it is a pleasure to announce, has been distributed among the needy widows of families of deceased soldiers." [20]

Wandering through the park after their meal, the men of the 34th were the objects of the crowd's adoration. Men vigorously shook the soldiers' hands, women kissed them and on many a cheek flowed tears of affection.

At five o'clock those members of the regiment that had not drawn furloughs marched back to the train depot and loaded onto cars bound for Albany. As the train departed, the crowd gave the men one last loud cheer.

As reported by the *Journal*, the day had been a grand success:

> "Not an unhappy or disgraceful scene occurred during all the day. Everything was in good taste and in good order, and everybody was happy and proud of his participation in the festivities." [21]

Three days after the 34th's reception, the men that had remained behind on furlough attempted to take the train to Albany without the benefit of tickets. The regiment had been transported for free on Reception Day, but now that offer no longer stood. The *Journal* reported the comeuppance that these soldiers received from a stubborn train conductor:

> "On Tuesday morning a number of the soldiers of the 34th regiment who, instead of returning to Albany on the special train provided for them Saturday evening, had remained to see friends, took the train here supposing they would be taken through without charge. They therefore refused to pay their fare and threatened trouble if the attempt should be made to put them off. But the conductor knew a trick worth two of that. The soldiers being alone in the hind car, he backed up on the switch, uncoupled the car and left them quietly behind. Most of them went down on subsequent trains and of course paid their fares." [22]

Back in Albany, the 34th New York was quartered in the same Industrial School Barracks that they had occupied as new recruits in the Spring of 1861. A number of the men, trying to eschew army life as quickly as possible, moved into boarding houses and purchased civilian clothes. Photographic galleries in Albany were overworked for a few days, as the men had a last picture taken of themselves in uniform.

During their stay in Albany the men did very little duty, although three companies were called out on June 17th to help keep the peace at a labor strike. As a final gesture to Governor Seymour, the 34th New York offered its services, if deemed necessary, for the defense of the country.

On June 30th, 1863 the 34th regiment New York State Volunteers was officially released from Federal service. Immediately after mustering out, the men dispersed and headed back to their home towns.

The records of the 34th New York showed:

Mustered in on June 15, 1861 or later recruited 1110
Mustered out on June 30, 1863 496
Killed or mortally wounded 94
Died of Illness or other causes 68
Total casualties of war 355

The casualty rate in the 34th New York was roughly one in three men, while the mortality rate was approximately one in seven men. Combat wounds claimed the lives of over eight percent of the 34th's men.[23]

The staff officers at muster out were:

Colonel - Byron Laflin of Herkimer
Lieut. Colonel - John Beverly of Salisbury
Major - Wells Sponable of Little Falls
Adjutant - John Kirk of West Troy
Quartermaster - Nathan Easterbrooks of Little Falls

No matter how severely the 34th had suffered, the spirit of its men was never broken. Before the war would end, ninety men mustered out of the 34th would rejoin the service. Favored regiments would include the 14th and 16th New York. Heavy Artillery and the 2nd and 18th New York Cavalry. While these men apparently had not lost their enthusiasm for the cause of the North, they had certainly lost their ardor for the life of a footsore infantryman.

CHAPTER X

"What a glorious day for us was the 3d day of July"

Summer 1863 - Lee Invades the North - Gettysburg
The 97th on Seminary Ridge

Early in June of 1863, the columns of Robert E. Lee set out on a second invasion of the North. The previous summer, after defeating Pope's army at 2nd Manassas, the gray legions had invaded the border state of Maryland. Outside of Sharpsburg the rebels were stopped by McClellan after a titanic battle along Antietam Creek. Now, after whipping Hooker at Chancellorsville, Lee was again headed north.

Strategically, a victory on Northern soil by the South could achieve two goals. First, the three major European powers, England, France and Russia, were as yet undecided about their intervention in the American conflict. The Confederate government believed a rebel triumph in the North would encourage the Europeans to intervene. Secondly, the North was realizing a growing peace movement and surely another defeat of the Union forces and an invasion on Federal ground would only bolster an inclination to peace.

Tactically, there were also two aims for a northward invasion. Out in Vicksburg, Mississippi, Gen. Ulysses Grant had that city, which controlled Mississippi River traffic, invested and was slowly starving out the defenders. An incursion into the North might draw Grant's forces away from Vicksburg, allowing the defenders to break the siege. The second tactical goal had a more material aspect. With much of the Virginia farmland ravaged by two years of war, Confederate troops were running out of food. The rich granaries of Pennsylvania, untouched by the war, held abundant supplies that could be swept up the advancing rebel columns.

By mid-June Lee's men were on the march, gobbling up Federal garrisons as they moved through the Shenandoah Valley and crossed the Potomac into Maryland. Traversing that state virtually unopposed, the gray line paraded into the Cumberland Valley of southern Pennsylvania, passing along the way the battlefield of Antietam.

Gen. Joseph Hooker did not sit idly by watching the Confederate intrusion into the North. Soon after Lee's movement began, Hooker consolidated his forces and put the Army of the Potomac on the rebel's track, all the while keeping his troops between those of the enemy and Washington.

In an attempt to slow the rebel advance, a plan was formulated by the Federal high command aimed at drawing units from Lee's forces. Two Union infantry corps were directed to what was believed to be a now uncovered Confederate capital. Ten thousand men of the 7th Corps, commanded by Gen. John Dix, was to move along the Pamunkey River, severing the rail lines north of Richmond. From the south Gen. Erasmus Keyes, with six thousand men of the 4th Corps, was to march up the Peninsula and menace the rebel capital, diverting attention from General Dix's forces. On temporary assignment to the 4th Corps was the 152nd New York Regiment.

Travelling by steamer from Norfolk, the 152nd arrived at Yorktown on June 20th. The regiment set up camp in a beautiful glade overlooking the York River, expecting to remain there for several days. But two days later came the order to pack up and be ready to march.

The first day's march brought the 152nd to Williamsburg, Virginia, where the night was spent. The next day the regiment advanced ten miles to a desolate crossroads called Ordinary, which the men thought to be appropriately named.

From the direction of the march and their proximity to Richmond, the rank and file believed that they were to invade the rebel capital. The soldiers had no idea that their mission was only as a diversionary force for General Dix and ultimately for General Hooker. Edward Townsend of the 152nd related the men's expectations:

"Our troops are commanded by Gen. Keyes and we trust that this Peninsula Campaign will leave a worthy and brilliant record for the world to read. We are about forty-five miles from the Confederate Capital and expect in a very few days to be warmly engaged in its front. Our prayer is that we may have the honor and the name to be among the first Regiments which shall enter that doomed city. Time alone can tell, we anxiously await a propitious future."[1]

The 152nd's adjutant, Alfred Quaiffe of Little Falls spoke of the soldiers' confidence:

"We have a very large force about twelve miles ahead, four brigades here in sight, and new troops constantly coming in. Gen. Keyes commands the expedition, and from all accounts has a good chance of success. Gen. Lee's army is occupied elsewhere, and bushwackers captured on the way say that the only force protecting Richmond is Wise [Gen. Henry Wise] with about twelve hundred men."[2]

The march continued on to the community of White House, where the 152nd rested for three days, and then moved on to Bottom's Bridge, about ten miles south of Richmond. The regiment bivouacked there for a week, occasionally trading shots with rebel pickets. On July 2nd orders came for the 152nd to return to Yorktown.

The two pronged Union feint on Richmond was a failure. The diversion had not drawn troops from Lee's army in Pennsylvania and no more than a mere dent had been made in the defenses of Richmond. The 7th corps of General Dix had succeeded in damaging rail lines at Hanover, north of the rebel capital, and along the South Anna River, but the breaks were quickly repaired. Before the Federals could do further mischief, Confederate cavalry under General Wise, drove off the 7th Corps.

To the south, the columns of the 4th Corps were blocked by two brigades under Gen. D.H. Hill. Rather than engaging the rebel force, General Keyes turned his army around and began a withdrawal to Yorktown. A rear guard action, in which the 152nd New York was not involved, was fought near Baltimore Cross Roads, Virginia, on July 2nd.

For two days the disillusioned men of the 152nd, marching in a constant rainstorm, slogged through water that at times filled the narrow roads knee deep. Halting near New Kent Court House, the troops were read a telegraphic dispatch just off the wires; Vicksburg had fallen to Grant.

Julius Townsend described the scene:

> "Just before we reached New Kent Court House, and while we were standing in a field, in—we think—the severest rain storm we ever saw, the news came that Vicksburg had surrendered. Caps, coats and blankets were thrown into the air, not withstanding the rain storm, in wild confusion. Cheer after cheer went up, and told in language more emphatic than we can describe, that no Copperheads* existed among us."[3]

The 152nd New York reached Yorktown on July 8th. The last fourteen miles were made without a halt and the men's feet were "boiled, blistered and sore."

The exhilaration and confidence exhibited on the march to Richmond was replaced by a sense of bewilderment at the army's retreat.

Julius Townsend of the 152nd questioned the mission's intent:

> "Our Peninsular Campaign was a 'bogus' one: at least, as far as we know. Whether it was a real, bonafide movement to take Richmond or merely a feint is more than we can at present say. That we did not take the Rebel Sodom we well know, and that we made no very strenuous effort to take it is a fact equally well established, but whether it was the real intention of our military authorities to attempt the capture of the Rebel Capital and they were prevented from so doing by the pressure of circumstances elsewhere, or the whole movement was merely a 'scare' to weaken the force of the enemy in some particular quarter by forcing the withdrawal of troops to the protection of their Capital is more than we can conjecture."[4]

Before the 152nd had started on its Richmond expedition or the 34th had paraded through the streets of Little Falls, the other two Mohawk Valley regiments, the

---

* Copperheads were Northern Democrats who opposed the war and favored a negotiated peace.

97th and 121st had left their camps near Falmouth. Marching with the Army of the Potomac, the 97th was at the head of the column and the 121st at the rear.

On June 11th, the 97th New York received orders to break camp at White Oak Church, Virginia, and make ready to march at a moment's notice. As the men began striking their tents, the order was countermanded and the regiment returned to their quarters. The next morning the marching orders were repeated and the camp was quickly dismantled and packed away. The order to fall-in did not come until three hours later and in the interim the boys of the 97th passed the time "horsing around."

Isaac Hall recorded the scene:

> "The men were fresh and vigorous from their long repose, and could not resist the temptation for a frolic, which this irksome leisure offered. Around their late camp, now in ruins lay the usual quantities of rubbish; of broken canteens, and cups, bottles, oyster cans and cast off articles. Some one began tossing these at his comrades and the fun soon became general, the men dividing into opposing lines, and fighting a mock battle in the best of spirits and without serious accidents. From this they proceeded to the amusement of tossing in a blanket which was duly performed and with entire success. These favors were dispensed freely, and without respect to shoulder straps: to the satisfaction of all (except perhaps a lieutenant who demurred and was jeered and hooted), without malice and simply because they had nothing else to do."[5]

The 97th's march northward with the left wing of Hooker's army, (composed of the 1st, 3rd and 11th Corps) began on June 12th. During the next five days, the 97th marched sixty miles, passing through Rappahannock Station, Manassas Junction, Centreville and Leesburg. Halting outside of Leesburg, the 97th set up camp on the banks of Goose Creek and remained one week. As usual, to relieve the boredom of camp life, the boys were quick to manufacture their own entertainment. One such diversion was described by Isaac Hall:

> "During our encampment at this place [Goose Creek] an amusing incident occurred which occasioned some merriment at the expense of one of the favorite officers. There chanced to stand on the right bank a tall oak which leaned over the stream and from which hung a grape vine nearly to the opposite bank-having swung away from the body of the tree as it leaned. The vine reached nearly to the surface of the water. Several men and officers as a trial of agility, climbed the tree and sliding down the vine, near to the water, sprang upon the other shore. The officer alluded to had been several days excused from duty on account of rheumatism, and being a spectator was challenged to try his strength. He finally accepted a wager of two dollars that he could not spring from the vine where others let go, to the bank from which they started to climb the tree. Seizing a hatchet and reaching out over the water he cut the vine in two, and taking hold of the hanging part where others made their final leap, and giving himself a swinging motion which was increased at each vibration till he acquired sufficient momentum, he landed safely upon the other side amid the shouts of the spectators, and to the no small merriment of all save the one who had lost the wager. The next morning was when the laugh came in on the afore-

named officer; he found himself reported for duty by the adjutant." [6]

Resuming the march on June 25th, the 97th crossed the Potomac at Edward's Ferry and bivouacked for the night at Poolesville, Maryland. The next day the regiment entered Pennsylvania near Barnsville and travelled past Greenfield, Adamstown and over the Blue Ridge Mountains to Hamburg, which was reached on June 28th.

The 121st New York was two full days behind the 97th. The 1st Division of the 6th Corps, of which the 121st was a member, had drawn the assignment of guarding Hooker's huge baggage train at the tail of the Union line.

Leaving White Oak Church on June 14th, the 121st met the wagon train and marched all night reaching Stafford Court House on Acquia Creek at sunrise. After halting for an hour, the column re-formed and started on a fifteen mile march to Dumfries. The day being extremely hot, the exhausted men soon began collapsing along the roadside. Adam Clarke Rice of Fairfield described the agony of the march:

> "Onward we pushed, without rest, without water, without shade, without a single cool breath of air, with nothing but burning dust, and scorching sun, and heated air, and hot sandy plains, and barren hills, and deep, wide channels, without any murmuring streams, till at last, blindness fell upon the poor, weary, foot-sore soldiers, and one by one, yet thick and fast, they dropped by the way-sides." [7]

The pace of the march slowed after reaching Dumfries. On June 20th, the 121st marched into Manassas, where the regiment rested for a few days, before continuing northward. Maryland was entered on June 28th at Edward's Ferry. While at the crossing, the news of General Hooker's resignation and the promotion of Gen. George Meade to the command of the Army of the Potomac was read to the men.

"Fighting Joe" Hooker was doing a good job keeping Lee shielded from Washington, but the Northern leaders were seeking much more from the army's commander. With the rebels rampaging through Pennsylvania, Philadelphia and Baltimore appeared to be at their mercy, and all Hooker seemed to be doing was acting as Lee's shadow. Instead of remaining on the defensive, the powers of Washington wanted Hooker to attack Lee and drive the raiders from Northern soil as quickly as possible. Hooker, still smarting from the beating Lee had given him at Chancellorsville, was not ready for another confrontation. Unable to withstand the constant pressure from Lincoln and his cabinet, he resigned on June 27th. His resignation was accepted, and General Meade was handed the reins of the Army of the Potomac.

Although George Meade had very little time to formulate an offensive strategy, he quickly took the initiative to bring on a fight. Meade's plan called for his army to move through Frederick, Maryland, and assume a position that would menace the rebel supply line and force Lee to turn and do battle. Meade kept the Union army moving northward, intending to fortify a line along Pipe Creek, near the Maryland and Pennsylvania border. General Lee, learning of Meade's designs through his spy network, immediately ordered his commanders, spread from York to Chambersburg, to consolidate near Gettysburg, Pennsylvania.

Moving with the 1st Corps, the 97th New York passed through Gregertown on June 29th and continued on to Emmettsburg the next day. On the approach to the village the men, sensing that a fight was in the offing, broke out in song. Isaac Hall of the 97th recorded the scene:

> "At this moment some one at the head of the column struck the John Brown chorus, which was quickly taken up along the whole line, and presently every man fell into a step in time with the cadence of this simple yet soul stirring hymn. Full many a brave man in that long column, never looked upon another setting sun, yet with that buoyant hope which ever lightens the burden of the soldier, and never deserts him, even in battle, each one gave expression to the emotions of the occasion, and none heeded the destinies of the morrow."[8]

That night the 97th encamped outside of Emmettsburg along the banks of Marsh Run.

Early the next morning, July 1, 1863, the 97th received orders to hasten to Gettysburg, Pennsylvania, ten miles up the Emmettsburg road. Nearing the town, cannon fire was heard and the pace quickened. From the head of the column came a rider shouting the word that McClellan was back in command. The rumor, which was false, served its purpose. The quick-step of march turned into a trot, and throughout the trials of that day, many of the men were "wholly sustained" on the idea that "Little Mac" was back in charge and everything would be all right.

The Battle of Gettysburg was a confrontation that neither Meade nor Lee as yet wanted and at a location that neither general would have chosen. The conflict started accidentally as Gen. James Pettigrew's brigade of barefoot rebels, seeking shoes rumored to be stored in town, brushed with Gen. John Buford's Union cavalry division on the outskirts of Gettysburg. The heavy skirmish quickly escalated as each side called in reinforcements from the numerous units hovering in the area. The little college town in southern Pennsylvania quickly became the focus of both armies.

The 97th New York was among the first regiments to reach Gettysburg. Marching up the Emmettsburg road, the 97th turned northwest and mounted a ridge overlooking the city. Halting near the theological seminary that gave the ridge its name, the 97th waited in reserve. A short distance to their front Buford's dismounted cavalry were being slowly pushed back.

The 97th New York, with the 11th Pennsylvania on its left, was soon ordered to form a skirmish line astride a field of timothy grass near the crest of Seminary Ridge. The two regiments slowly advanced for two hundred yards through the field towards a high rail fence. A few hundred yards to the front, on a hill skirted by some woods, the colors and men of a Confederate line were clearly visible. Reaching the rail fence, the 12th Massachusetts came up on the right of the 97th, and the whole Union line marched to a position behind a decaying stone wall. The rebel line ahead soon moved into musket range and a firefight ensued. Isaac Hall described the 97th's initial action at Gettysburg:

> "The 97th suffered from this Confederate skirmish line in the field and road to the right [Mummasburg Road], and covered itself as skirmishers as

best it could in the rear of the wall, several men springing up in concert and firing as closely as possible whence the smoke from the Confederate fire arose. In this manner Reese Lloyd [from Boonville], of Company A was killed—from whose cartridge box a young lad (J.R. Manchester) who had belonged to the instrumental band supplied himself with cartridges—and many others were wounded by the enfilading fire of this line." [9]

The fire soon slackened and except for a few desultory shots, this portion of the field quieted. Many of the tired "Third Oneida" men left their positions at the wall and lay on the ground trying to catch their breath. At about three o'clock, a sudden and thunderous volley fired by the 11th Pennsylvania, on the 97th's left, was followed by the chilling sound of the rebel yell. Three North Carolina regiments, the 5th, 20th and 23rd, under command of Gen. Alfred Iverson, assaulted the Union line. The men of the 97th sprang to arms behind their stone wall and poured a withering fire into the front and left flank of the charging rebels. The gray line recoiled, but re-formed and charged again. This time the rebel soldiers were shot at almost point blank range. The rebel charge melted and the survivors scurried to the shelter of a ravine fifty yards from the stone wall. In front of the 97th New York and the 11th Pennsylvania lay over three hundred of the Tar Heel State boys, one hundred of them dead.

White flags soon began appearing from the gully. Lieutenant Colonel Spofford, without waiting for orders, called to his men "Boys of the 97th, let us go for them and capture them." With that, the men leapt over the stone wall and started for the ravine, under the cover of the rifles of the 11th Pennsylvania. Sporadic fire on each flank harassed the 97th, but the gully was reached and two hundred and thirteen of the enemy plus the flag of the 20th North Carolina were captured. Returning to the stone wall, the men again ran a gauntlet of fire which wounded a number of the prisoners. Of the surrender, General Iverson (not among the captured) wrote:

> "When I saw white handkerchiefs raised, and my line of battle still lying down in position, I characterized the surrender as disgraceful: but when I found afterward that 300 of my men were left lying dead and wounded on a line as straight as a dress parade, I exonerated (with one or two disgraceful individual exceptions) the survivors, and claim for the brigade that they nobly fought and died without a man running to the rear. No greater gallantry and heroism has been displayed during the war." [10]

Soon afterwards, Colonel Wheelock espied another Confederate line approaching from the northwest. Directing that the prisoners be brought to the rear, he ordered the 97th back over the wall. With the support of the 11th Pennsylvania and the 12th Massachusetts, the "Third Oneida" charged across the meadow at the rest of Iverson's Brigade and that of Gen. Stephen Ramseur's. The Confederates broke and ran, and eighty more prisoners were taken. Before the Federals could return to their lines a large rebel force appeared on their right flank.

To the north of the 97th New York, the 11th Corps of Gen. O.O. Howard, which was protecting the Union right flank, collapsed under the pressure of Gen. Richard Ewell's attack. As they had done at Chancellorsville in May, Howard's men aban-

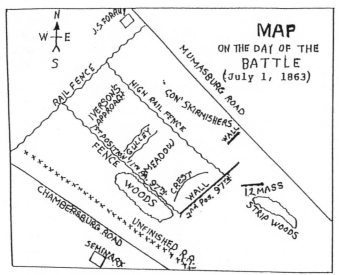

History of the Ninety-Seventh Regiment, Hall

The 97th New York on Seminary Ridge

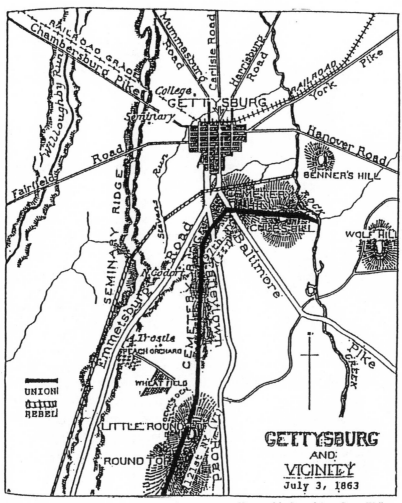

History of the Second Army Corps, Walker

doned their position and retreated in wild confusion. With the Union right now un-covered, Ewell's Corps advanced along Seminary Ridge, taking the 97th and the rest of the 1st Corps on the flank and in the rear. Seventy men from the 97th were quickly surrounded and captured. Included among the captives were Colonel Wheelock, Lieutenant Colonel Spofford, Captains Egelston and Chamberlain, and Lieutenants Murphy and Rockwell.

Carrie Sheads, a resident of the young ladies seminary at the foot of the ridge, gave an account of Colonel Wheelock's surrender to a Washington newspaper reporter. The reporter's story read:

> "Among the last to leave the field were the 97th New York infantry, commanded by Colonel Charles Wheelock, who, after fighting hand to hand as long as there was a shadow of hope, undertook to lead his broken column through the only opening in the enemy's lines, which were fast closing around him. Standing in a vortex of fire, from front, rear and both flanks [Wheelock] encouraged his men to fight with naked bayonet, hoping to force a passage through the walls of steel which surrounded him. Finding all his efforts vain, he ascended the steps of the seminary, and waved a white pocket handkerchief in token of a surrender. The Rebels not seeing it, or taking no notice of it, continued to pour their murderous volleys into the helpless ranks. The colonel then opened the door, and called for a large white cloth. Carrie Sheads stood there, and readily supplied him with one. When the Rebels saw his token of surrender, they ceased firing, and the colonel went into the basement to rest himself, for he was thoroughly ex-hausted." [11]

To save themselves from the humiliation of surrendering their swords, Colonel Wheelock secreted his saber with Miss Sheads, and Lieutenant Colonel Spofford threw his sidearm into a thicket. (Wheelock later retrieved his sword from Miss Sheads after his escape, and Spofford's sword was found by a Confederate soldier and returned thirty years later.)

The men of the 97th who were not caught in the rebel snare, retreated down the slope of the ridge and tried to make a stand at a railroad cut. As described by Lt. Willard Judd of Brockett's Bridge, the enemy fire was murderous:

> "The bullets were flying from each side as a perfect shower. The air seemed so filled that it seemed almost impossible to breathe without inhal-ing them. Some one fell beside me almost every step. It was here that Serg. Fred Munson fell mortally wounded, and Lieut. James Stiles was killed. Our Inspector General, of General Baxter's Staff, had his head shot entirely off by a cannon shot." [12]

Overwhelmed by the rebel force coming over the crest of the ridge, the 97th broke to the rear and ran through Gettysburg before climbing a hill south of town.

By five o'clock p.m., the 97th was off the field of battle and safely within Fed-eral lines on Cemetery Hill. After lying with their arms all night, the regiment was relieved by a brigade of the 2nd Corps. During the next two days of the Gettysburg fight, the battered 97th New York acted as a reserve unit in support of artillery.

In the four hour back and forth fight on Seminary Ridge, the 97th New York, which counted two hundred and eighty-six muskets at the start of the day, lost one hundred and twenty-six men. Of this total, fourteen men were killed outright, thirty-two men were wounded (four mortally) and seventy-six men were captured or missing.[13] Among those slain were Lt. James Stiles, Sgt. Fred Munson and Pvt. Francis Darling from Salisbury.

The Confederate brigades of Iverson and Ramseur that opposed the 97th New York and its two sister regiments, the 11th Pennsylvania and the 12th Massachusetts, lost almost eight hundred men.

The 121st New York didn't reach Gettysburg until the afternoon of July 2nd, the second day of fighting. Leaving Germantown, Pennsylvania, the night before, "Upton's Regulars" marched thirty-three miles in nineteen hours and were in no condition to fight. Consequently, the 121st was posted as a reserve regiment and was not actively engaged in the Gettysburg battles. The 121st was placed in support of a battery atop the crest of a hill called Little Round Top, at the extreme left of the Union line. Protected by a strip of woods, the regiment would only suffer two slightly wounded men. From the top of the mountain the 121st had an excellent vantage point from which they could watch the third day of the struggle unfold.

The Federal line of eighty-five thousand men stretched on a north-south axis from Little Round Top to Culp's Hill. Connecting these two elevations was a spine of land called Cemetery Ridge. Robert E. Lee, with seventy-five thousand men, had attacked both Union flanks on July 2nd. Fierce rebel onslaughts on each end of this line had been repulsed, but the blue defenders had suffered severely.

Failing on the flanks, Lee decided that his next attempt to break the Union line would be made at its mid-point. Preparatory to the rebel attack, the Confederate artillery opened a mass barrage on the Union center.

From his position on Little Round Top, the 121st's Captain Marcus Casler related:

> "I cannot describe the awful thunder of the 160 guns on the part of the rebels and about 30 on our side. One would have thought the heavens were about to burst with the tremendous peals. How lucky that the 6th Corps was not in this battle. Still the artillery of our brigade did the enemy the most damage. The enemy threw shells and solid shot among us (that is our regiment) but thank God, no one was injured." [14]

On Cemetery Ridge, Lt. Willard Judd of the 97th reported:

> "Our line of battle was in the shape of a horseshoe, the toe or center on the cemetery above the town. About 1 p.m. the enemy opened on that hill from all directions and such a terrific cannonading as followed it is impossible to describe. One hundred and fifty pieces all centered on that hill; but nobly did our boys respond. For two hours it seemed impossible for man or beast to live." [15]

Fortunately the rebel artillery aimed too high and most of the cannon shells passed over the men on Cemetery Ridge and fell in the rear of the Union lines.

Nearly out of ammunition, the Confederate cannon stopped firing at about three p.m.

General Lee, believing that the Union center was now weakened by his artillery, ordered ten brigades under the command of Gen. George Pickett to advance against Cemetery Ridge. Pickett's target would be a clump of trees, one-half mile away. Advancing through an open field, the slow marching gray mass made for an easy target, and the Federal gunners began tearing great gaps in Pickett's ranks. By the time Pickett's men reached the Federal line their force was spent, and although a fierce fight did develop at an angle in the blue line, the rebel charge was over.

From Little Round Top, Marcus Casler of Little Falls reported:

> "Whole divisions of them were put to rout by our artillery and infantry —every time our batteries sent a shell among them they would leave a vacant place in their ranks. They fought with desperation, but freemen can hold their own against these myriads of liberty-tramplers, and their defeat was certain and they retreated in confusion. Such cheers as we sent forth when they retreated and were pursued you can imagine better than I can describe. A whole brigade numbering 6000 threw down their arms and surrendered. What a glorious day for us was the 3d day of July!" [16]

From his vantage point on Cemetery Ridge, Lt. Willard Judd of Brockett's Bridge described the rebel repulse:

> "We opened a heavy fire of grape and cannister and broke their ranks, and then our lines charged back upon them and took the whole division (except killed and wounded) prisoners and three stands of colors. Over two thousand prisoners were taken at this charge. A more cheering or thrilling sight I never saw, but from that time until dark I assure you it was quiet. Brig. Gen. Hayes [William Hays, 2nd Corps] rode up and down the lines, trailing one of the captured flags under the feet of his horse, and such a deafening roar of cheers as went up you never heard." [17]

Pickett's charge had failed. Of the fifteen thousand gray soldiers that started across the field, barely one half made it back to their lines.* The Confederate army experienced the same slaughter that the Federals had suffered at Fredericksburg.

Isaac Hall of the 97th related the sights of the now quiet battleground:

> "As the division took position in front of the guns of Haye's command, on the slope southwest of town, an indescribable scene of confusion and disorder presented itself. The havoc upon the field in our front was appalling; the dead lay at intervals one upon another, torn and mangled; and were strewn over the field in every conceivable condition. From among the slain arose the wounded, who struggled to reach our line; some in their vain endeavor, fell to rise no more; others who could not rise cried for help and for water." [18]

July 4th, 1863 passed quietly on the fields and ridges of Gettysburg. The three-day fight had claimed over fifty thousand casualties, including seven thousand dead. With neither side in condition to resume the struggle, the battle was over.

---

* Pickett's force included divisions led by Gen. Isaac Trimble and Gen. James Pettigrew.

Using the cover of a heavy rain to his advantage, Lee began to withdraw his forces late in the day. At this point, Lee's primary goal was to get his battered army safely across the Potomac before the Federals could cut him off. Meade's army did follow Lee, but much too slowly to hinder the rebel columns.

The 97th New York and the 121st New York were both put on the enemy's blood trail, but no active contact was made with the rebels by the Mohawk Valley boys. All along the route were strewn the pieces of Lee's broken army. Marcus Casler of the 121st described the magnitude of the Confederates' suffering:

> "The barns and buildings near the Pennsylvania line, are completely filled with their wounded and dying. I saw this with my own eyes. The barns and houses for 5 miles around their rear, are filled with them. We found in our chase after them, 5000 wounded in one place—in barns and houses and large hospital tents. And such a sight I never want to witness again. Wounded men, imploring death to relieve them from their sufferings —praying for the care of nurses and physicians and surgeons whom the rebel Generals, in their inhumanity, neglected to leave them, wounded in every part of the body. We took a great many prisoners in our chase and came upon them at Fairfield, Pennsylvania, firing shells among them and making them skedaddle at double quick." [19]

Lee's army did escape, crossing the rain swollen Potomac at Williamsport, Maryland on July 13th. Lincoln initially reprimanded Meade for permitting the enemy to slip away, but after Meade offered to resign, the President officially congratulated the general and his army for repelling the rebel invasion.

July 4th, 1863, was observed rather quietly in Herkimer County notwithstanding telegraphic reports of a glorious Union victory in Pennsylvania. The hopes of the people of Herkimer County had been dashed too many times before by false reports of Lee's defeat or Richmond's fall for them to openly celebrate the unconfirmed news. Not surprisingly, the July 9th edition of the *Journal* reported, "comparative quiet pervaded throughout this usually noisy anniversary." [20]

But three days later, the news of the fall of Vicksburg to Grant set off countywide celebrations. The *Journal* described the scene in Little Falls:

> "On Tuesday evening upon the receipt of the glorious news of the capture of Vicksburg, the enthusiasm of our citizens could no longer be restrained. The bells of the village were rung, and a salute of an indefinite number of guns was given. A promiscuous but jubilant impromptu procession was led through many of the streets by the C. B. Band and was greeted by the ladies at every hand by waving flags and handkerchiefs. Capt. Dan Snell, marshaled forth his company of light 'infantry' [local militia or "Home Guards"], a band of doughty warriors, whose stately tread and majestic mien gave dignity and a proper esprit de corps to the parade, and the utmost good feeling and joy prevailed, if we were to except some half dozen or more Copperheads whose faces are not wonted to light up at news which gladdens the patriot heart. Cheers were given for Gen. Grant, Gen.

Meade, the Union Army, the Old Flag, Vicksburg, &c., &c. No doubt could be entertained of the truth of the glad news which came, not from Philadelphia, but from Admiral Porter, of the Mississippi squadron and the entire village went off in an uncontrollable convulsion of happy delight." [21]

As reported by the *Journal*, one painful but not serious accident occurred during the Little Falls celebration:

"On Tuesday evening, as Chauncey Petrie was firing a cannon on the Eastern Square [Ward's Park], in honor of the fall of Vicksburg, the piece, not having been properly 'swabbed out,' was accidentally discharged, severely burning his chest and bowels. He was able to walk home and the injury is not thought to be very serious. He has had some experience in gun shot wounds before, having been wounded on the Peninsula while a member of Capt. Sponable's company of the 34th." [22]

Tempering the festivities in the Mohawk Valley was the arrival of the 97th's casualty list from Gettysburg. Among those listed as missing and most probably dead were, Col. Charles Wheelock of Boonville, Lt. John Norton from Norway and Lt. Henry Chamberlain of Fairfield. Lt. Col. John Spofford and Capt. Rouse Egelston of Brockett's Bridge were also reported as missing, but were not thought to be mortally wounded. The wives of Spofford and Egelston set out for Washington in hopes of finding and caring for their husbands.

The distraught friends and relatives of the missing officers of the 97th, were relieved when the *Journal* published a letter from Rouse Egelston. Egelston, a captain in the 97th, had been captured with the others but had recently escaped. The captain's long letter not only vouched for the safety of the 97th's officers, but also touched on the rebel treatment of the prisoners and the system of parole. Egelston wrote:

"I was taken at 4 p.m. July 1st. Col. Spofford was with me. We were taken to the rear where we made a short halt, when who should be brought in but Col. Wheelock. We were marched around about two miles, when we came back nearly to the spot where we fought, and here met another party of prisoners among whom was Frank [Lieut. Frank Murphy, Herkimer] and two more of my company. After being counted we marched a mile or so and encamped for the night. There were about three thousand of us.

The next morning the commissioned officers were called out and their names taken-in all one hundred and thirty. After moving a mile or so to a small creek, the names of the men were taken with the intention of paroling them. Each company officer was asked to give in a list of the names of his men and sign it: but I did nothing of the kind, as I doubted the right of the men to accept the parole under an order against paroling prisoners on the field. The officers and men were not permitted to see each other after the names were taken, as I suppose the rebels feared we would advise the men not to take their parole as we certainly should have done.

The officers were called out into line and offered their parole, with a provision that, if our Government would not accept the parole, we should deliver ourselves up again and go to Richmond. The offer was refused by most all the officers myself among them. We thought that, if they wanted to take us to Richmond they must send us under guard. We told them our folks would recapture us before they could get to Virginia. We then marched about two miles and encamped separate from the men on the banks of a fine stream. I took off my shirt and washed it, going without while it was drying. About 11 a.m. they gave us some flour, mutton and salt, the first rations we had received. Some had good appetites, but many had been so long without eating that they were not hungry. We mixed the flour with salt and water and baked it on barrel-heads or anything else we could find. I got a rebel cook, for fifty cents, to bake up the flour for our officers. There were five of us: Col. Wheelock, Col. Spofford, Lieuts. Chamberlain and Murphy and myself.

On the morning of the 4th they moved us back from the road where we could not see their wagons skedaddle. After marching from one place to another we went back some ways towards Gettysburg in a heavy shower and encamped for the night. It rained most of the night and I slept some of the time on two rails without a pillow.

In the forenoon of the 5th we marched to Fairfield and left there at 4 p.m., crossing over the hills to the pike running from Emmettsburg to Hagerstown. Over this pike the rebels were on grand skedaddle. They had about three thousand prisoners, the officers marching in front of the column. The rebels could not stop till night and I made up my mind to leave them as soon as it was dark and I did so. In my next I will give some particulars of my escape. Suffice it to say now that, in company with a New Jersey man, I took one rebel soldier, a waiter, a good horse and a saddle.

I am out of danger for the present and shall join the regiment as soon as I can. Have no fears for me. If I fall it shall be while doing my duty. I would like to go to Richmond but didn't just like the style of being taken there.

I have learned that our boys were paroled and am sorry to hear it." [23]

Egelston never explained the particulars of his escape, but fellow Brockett's Bridge native John Ingraham, a private in the 121st New York, did. In a letter home, Ingraham wrote:

"Capt Egelston got away from the Rebs. I suppose come right down to the point of it, our division freed him. We were marching close to the Rebs. After we arose up the hill we saw them. We got our batteries in position and gave them grape and cannister. You ought to see them skedaddle. Well they had a lot of our men prisoners, all that they had taken at Gettysburg the day before our Corps arrived there. They was then in the village of Fairfield. They then rushed them right through. They got up in the mountains and it was very dark and they were scattered pretty bad on account of our shelling them. Capt & Lieutenant slipped through the guard and laid up in the mountain two days. They found a house on the mountain and went to get something to eat and went in and found 8 Rebs in the house eating. Part of them had arms when Capt saw them. He saw he was caught and to turn it off he said you're my prisoners. They said I don't know about it. Well, Capt says if you won't come I will call the Cavalry and they will take care of you, and then they gave up themselves, so they brought in 8 Rebs and Capt did not have any arms. *Big Thing.*" [24]

With the exception of Colonel Wheelock, who also escaped, the commissioned officers of the 97th New York were moved on to Richmond. The fifty-one-year-old, two-hundred-pound-plus Boonville produce dealer, had eluded his captors by rolling down a steep, briar-filled hill. In a letter home, Wheelock related his experiences in making it back to the Union lines:

"After passing picket lines and being fired on, I narrowly missed being recaptured, but succeeded in getting into the mountains. I travelled two days, at least one thousand feet above C_____. The rebels were on each side of me, and I had no chance but to travel one way, while they were getting away as fast as possible the other.

I can assure you my reflections were not very pleasant, two days and two nights without food or water, except berries, and water from the heavens, which was plenty, as it rained constantly. While making my escape from the guard I fell down a ledge of rocks, about eight feet, and perhaps that saved me from going to Richmond, as I was contented to remain there through the night for the reason that I could not well help myself. I am yet sore from the effects of that fall. I killed a rattle snake which I dislike almost as bad as I do a rebel.

On the third day I ventured down the mountain to a small house, but found a good Union man and boy. Giving him money he went out and got provisions enough to last his family and myself while I remained with him, which was not a very small amount I can assure you, for I had been fasting for some nine days from the time I was first taken prisoner. I shall always remember that family with kindness."[25]

Colonel Wheelock rejoined the 97th New York on July 14th.

Col. Charles Wheelock, 97th New York

Boys in Blue, Thomas

Capt. Isaac Hall, 97th New York

Boys in Blue, Thomas

Lt. Col. Rouse Egelston, 97th New York

History of the 97th Regiment

Capt. Frank Faville, 97th New York

History of the 97th Regiment

Col. John P. Spofford

Courtesy of the Spofford Families

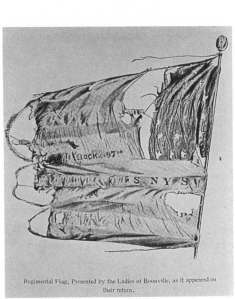

Regimental Flag, Presented by the Ladies of Boonville, as it appeared on their return.

History of the 97th Regiment

Flag of the 97th New York, 1865

Courtesy of the Spofford Families

Regimental Band of the 97th New York

CHAPTER XI

"We live on the fat of the land now"

Summer 1863 - Herkimer County Summer - The Draft
The 152nd in New York City - The 121st in New Baltimore

In Herkimer County the ideal weather of the Summer of 1863 was in direct contrast to the cold, snowy, and overcast spring. Warm, sunny days, combined with just the right amount of rain at exactly the right time, furnished growing conditions that every farmer and gardener could have only dreamt of. Huge strawberries were gathered by the bushel, new potatoes were dug before June was out and the fields of green corn were chest-high by the 4th of July. After sampling the delicious giant muskmelons from the Van Valkenburg patch in Manheim, the editor of the *Journal* remarked:

> "We regard it peculiarly fortunate for him, for ourselves and for his patch, that he lives so far from town. We would not like to have our morality put to a test some of the moon-light nights, having our 'longing eyes' exposed to such golden temptations."[1]

Dairy cattle fattened in lush pastures and consequently milk production increased dramatically. With so much excess milk available cheese makers worked overtime. On July 27th, the train depot in Little Falls was inundated with a record two hundred and sixty thousand pounds of cheese. From before sunrise to well after dark on that day, the streets leading to the depot and freight house were jammed with teams and wagons trying to unload their wheels of cheese. A few wagoneers were obliged to spend the night in Little Falls, closely guarding their cheese until it could be unloaded the next day.

As the glut of cheese continued, the per pound bid price dropped from an unprecedented high of thirteen cents down to eight cents. In response to this collapse in the market, most farmers chose to withhold their cheese until bid prices again turned favorable.

Also prospering in the fields and pastures during this most perfect of summers, were the horses of Herkimer County. Surplus animals attracted Captain Fuller, an agent of the Quartermaster Department, who was looking to procure horseflesh for the U.S. Army. Scouring the countryside, Fuller purchased almost seven hundred horses during July and August and shipped them to Washington via the Little Falls train depot.

The fine summer weather was a boon to the overall economy of Herkimer County and quite justly, most of the rewards were realized by those rightly entitled to them, the farmers. To this end, the *Journal* remarked:

> "At the present high prices of produce farmers are likely soon to become the millionaires of the community—no class more deserves prosperity and none may more fittingly wear the honors which wealth brings than they who have so industriously toiled and so richly earned the rewards now vouchsafed to them."[2]

Also sharing in the farmers' good fortune were the bounty-depleted coffers of the Herkimer County Treasury. Alonzo Greene, the Deputy County Clerk, reminded the taxpayers that their annual income tax returns were due by August 12th. All persons neglecting or refusing to file returns would have their income estimated by Greene, who was authorized to add a fifty percent surcharge to their tax.

As with any other summer there were outdoor activities much less strenuous and much more enjoyable than the toil of a farmer's field.

For the fisherman, Herkimer County's streams, ponds, lakes and Mohawk River abounded with pike, perch, bass and the favorite of the sportsmen, brook trout. Most renowned among the anglers was John Simons of Little Falls, of whom the *Journal* noted:

> "John must have some art or arts by which the speckled tribe are controlled, for he never returns empty-handed."[3]

For the bird hunter, a quarry much easier to catch and much more profitable than the elusive brook trout arrived. Beginning in late May, immense flocks of passenger pigeons descended on ancestral nesting sites in the woods around Salisbury and Stratford and farther to the east along the Sacandaga River. Almost before the birds could alight, teams of pigeon hunters armed with poles and large snare nets went to work collecting the birds. Within a day, an experienced "hunter" could easily fill many bushels with the carcasses of these rather docile birds. Packed in barrels of ice, at thirty dozen birds per barrel, this delicacy would bring $1.50 per dozen in New York City markets. In June alone, over fifty barrels of passenger pigeons were shipped from the Little Falls Depot.

In Little Falls a most unusual sort of hunt took place during the summer of 1863. On a Sunday afternoon in early July, a purportedly rabid dog ran through the village, biting a number of its brethren before the police dispatched it on Furnace Street. Within twenty-four hours the Little Falls Board of Trustees passed an ordinance that established a fifty cent bounty for shooting and disposing of any stray canine. As reported by the *Journal* the bounty had to be increased after the village "hunters" displayed their lack of marksmanship:

> "The village 'Dog Ordinance' was amended last Monday evening by the Board of Trustees so as to offer one dollar, instead of fifty cents, as before, for killing and burying every unmuzzled dog. Doubtless the ten rounds of powder and ball discharged at a large black 'pup' the other night by several distinguished sharpshooters, showed the unprofitableness of the job under the former rates." [4]

Even with the higher bounty the stray dogs had the run of Little Falls. Finally in early autumn the village constable and his deputies took charge of the matter and entered the "Little Falls dog war." In an article entitled "Police versus Pup," the *Journal* described the confrontation:

> "Our 'Chief of Police' with a squad of assistants, armed to the teeth, have been patrolling this village for the past few days, waging a war of extermination upon unlucky curs found at large without muzzles. Nearly fifty have already been shot and the work will continue to be prosecuted until our streets are as clear of dogs as they have been of Copperheads for a week past." [5]

The readers of the *Journal* were treated that summer to another type of chase, the quarry in this case was a husband.

Two Little Falls women seeking mates placed an advertisement in the *Utica Herald* intended to attract potential spouses. The *Journal* reprinted the ad, and as a matter of course added their own comments:

> "Matrimonial: Two young ladies of education and refinement, excelling more particularly in musical attainments, are desirous of corresponding with two young gentlemen about the age of twenty-five, with a view to matrimony. Money not essential as she has sufficient for both. Enclosing Carte de Vistes, address.
>
> Louise Mortimer, Box 194, Little Falls, N.Y.
>
> *In the name of gallantry and christian benevolence, we call attention of our young men to the above advertisement of 'suffering humanity,' taken from the Utica Herald of Monday. That ladies of such 'education and refinement,' and with such 'a view to matrimony,' should be compelled to send abroad for 'gentlemen' is an instance of destitution as scandalous to the fair fame of the village as it has been hitherto unheard of in its history. The crisis is one which young men are called upon to meet. Little Falls Light Guards! To Arms! To Arms!"* [6]

Miss Mortimer's notice did bring one response which she foolishly passed along to the *Journal*. In the letter, her suitor recited amorous prose and included some disparaging remarks about the *Journal's* editor, J.R. Stebbins. Taking offense at these remarks, the *Journal* published extracts from the intimate letter and Stebbins added some rather harsh retorts:

"'Louise' has found a booby at last. He turns up at Mohawk and addresses her as 'Dear Louise' for, he says 'I feel you are dear to me already.' He had just been reading the Journal and 'came acrost' her advertisement, whereupon he thinks the 'Editor is devoid of all principles of honor as well as education, or he would have passed so innocent an article by, without making such ungentlemanly remarks concerning it,' and adds 'I'll bet he's an old bachelor.' He has a strong 'view to matrimony,' and thinks he is 'just the article' and boasts a 'Lieutenancy in the regular Navy.' He trusts she will 'bestow upon him a little corner of her delicate little heart' and thinks his carte de viste will suit the taste of the most fastidious.

For shame, 'Louise Mortimer, Box 194 &c!' How could you send such a 'confidential' letter in the hope that it would be published! You deserve to live and die as beauless as you evidently are heartless." [7]

Although many of the *Journal's* readers may have hoped for a romantic ending to the story, no liaison between "Louise" and her Navy beau appeared in the paper's "Matrimonial" columns.

In the summer of 1863, President Lincoln, empowered by the Enrollment Act, issued the first licit draft call in United States history. With volunteering at a mere trickle, conscription was necessary to maintain the Federal armies depleted by the discharge of two year regiments and by losses sustained at Gettysburg. Instead of forming new regiments, as calls in the past had done, conscripts would be directed to existing regiments.

Dissatisfaction with a draft had always been voiced by the Democrats and now, with Lincoln's call an actuality, those liable to be drafted were stirring. Of major contention was a clause in the Enrollment Act that allowed a draftee to escape conscription by furnishing a substitute or by paying a three hundred dollar commutation fee. To the lower class this clause reinforced their opinion that this was "a rich man's war and a poor man's fight."

Early in July draft wheels began to turn in many of the North's larger cities. Outside of draft offices the crowd's agitation built as each unlucky man's name was announced. In cities such as Rutland, Vermont; Portsmouth, New Hampshire and Wooster, Ohio, gatherings degenerated into angry mobs and police had to be called in to quell near riots. In New York City, the mood was much uglier. For three days in July a full blown riot raged out of control, resulting in over one thousand dead and wounded and the destruction of millions of dollars worth of property. The riot was finally brought under control by the intervention of field-hardened Federal troops.

No draft was ordered for Herkimer County's senatorial district in July. However, because of the civil unrest noted at draft offices in nearby Albany and Troy, county officials began to formulate contingency plans to head off trouble. In this vein, Seth Richmond, the Sheriff of Herkimer County, issued a proclamation calling for citizen involvement in the event of draft disturbances. Richmond's Proclamation read:

"To the good People of the County of Herkimer: I, Seth M. Richmond, Sheriff of said County, hereby give public notice and call upon all loyal citizens, especially those in the larger villages in the county, to make all necessary preparations to defend your homes and to hold yourselves in readiness to assist each other promptly in resisting any mob or rioters who may get together for the purpose of murder, robbery and the destruction of property, under the pretense of resistance to the draft.

I also call upon all military organizations in the county to be ready to report for duty, if called upon by the proper authorities, for the purpose of putting down any riot that may spring up in our midst.

All tax payers are interested in saving life and property, for the county is justly liable to pay for all property or personal damage destroyed or sustained by a riot.

Delay not one moment to arrest any one who breaks the peace and violates the law and order, for no person is safe unless the laws are obeyed.

Dated Little Falls July 20, 1863 Seth M. Richmond, Sheriff"[8]

The proclamation was printed in area newspapers including the *Journal*. In that paper, J.R. Stebbins editorialized:

"We trust that the proclamation above inserted may, in the event, be proved unnecessary. And while we endorse its suggestions and heartily recommend their adoption, we can but feel a confidence in our citizens which refuses the indulgence of fear as to the result.

Yet a perusal of descriptions of the terrible scenes that have been enacted in some of our cities proves the importance of a readiness on the part of all true citizens to meet promptly the first appearance of an outbreak. Men of parties, who will be called upon by the tax-collector to help reimburse any loss that may be sustained by a riot, have a direct interest in the preservation of peace and order, and it may as well be stated here that losses so sustained may be recovered of the County and become part of the taxation of the County. Where so much is at stake it is well that measures should be quietly taken to meet any emergency which may arise."[9]

In response to Sheriff Richmond's call, most of the county villages and towns either reactivated their militia or formed new National Guard units. In Little Falls, two National Guard companies, each with about thirty men, were assembled under the commands of Eli Morse and Sandy Casler. Already existing in the village was a company of local militia called the "Little Falls Light Guards," headed by John Gilliland.

While Herkimer County was mobilizing to head off potential draft problems in the Mohawk Valley, the men of the 152nd New York were already on the job helping to repress the draft riot in New York City.

The 152nd left Yorktown on July 11th with orders to join the Army of the Potomac in the pursuit of Lee's army. Travelling on two steamers, that part of the regiment commanded by Maj. Timothy O'Brien reached Washington hours before the vessel that carried the acting regimental commander, Lt. Col. George Thompson. A member of Meade's staff waiting at the dock ordered O'Brien to get his men in line and begin marching at once. Major O'Brien refused to move without Thompson and the rest of the 152nd, and ordered his men to stack arms and await their arrival. Although Meade's aide threatened O'Brien with court martial, the soldiers from the 152nd sat tight. By the time Thompson's steamer pulled to the dock, a sudden and violent rainstorm had hit the Washington area. Surging flood waters on the Potomac River washed out a key railroad bridge, effectively severing all travel to Meade's army. Unable to proceed, the 152nd bivouacked on the outskirt's of Washington.

Two days later new orders came that thoroughly astonished the men. Instead of heading into the war zone, the 152nd was now to proceed to New York City with all possible haste. Breaking camp and packing up at record speed, the 152nd boarded a train and headed for Baltimore. In Baltimore the men were met by Colonel Ferguson, who had been gone for over a month on sick leave.

The 152nd reached New York City on July 16th, the third day of the draft riots. Confronted by an angry mob, the Mohawk Valley men affixed bayonets and marched unimpeded down Broadway to quarters in a Negro church on Mulberry Street.

That night, New York City military commander, Gen. Harvey Brown, ordered the 152nd out in search of a cache of weapons and ammunition stolen from the U.S. Armory. Several rioters menaced the regiment but a few well-thrown, lit "hand grenades" dispersed the mob. The 152nd searched six buildings near the armory, recovering eighty muskets and capturing nine of the perpetrators.

The regiment's next few days in New York passed without any major troubles as the might of the military began to take control of the city. Much of the rioters' anger was directed at the city's black population (this being the reason that the 152nd was lodged in a black church). Over a dozen black men were lynched, scores more were beaten and a black orphanage was burnt.

The boys of the 152nd were firsthand witnesses to one such incident. The black servant of Capt. David Hill—one of twelve "contrabands" in the 152nd—one day ventured too far from the 152nd's quarters and was viciously attacked by two white men. The servant broke free and raced back to the regiment's quarters, with his assailants hot on his heels. At this point Captain Hill appeared, drew his sword and hacked an ear off of one of the pursuers. Both "insurgents" were summarily arrested and carted off to the nearest jail.

With the rioting at an end, companies from the 152nd were moved to different points around New York City. Companies A and H went to David's Island, companies G and I to Riker's Island and the remainder of the regiment was sent to Fort Schuyler at the mouth of the East River. From these locations the men were in position to extinguish any riotous flare ups.

On August 8th, two hundred men from the 152nd were ordered to report to, of all places, Schenectady, New York. That city's draft was about to take place and it was thought that troops might be needed to maintain order. As the men boarded a steamer for the trip up the Hudson, the grins that creased their faces were impossible to hide. Arriving the next day, the men were quartered at the Eagle Hotel. Edward Townsend of Fairfield described the accommodations:

"Didn't exactly get a suite of rooms, but the authorities exhibited their

broad philanthropy by allowing us free access to the barn-yard, which was
neatly attached to the Hotel. We had free use of the horse shed, that is when
the dear animals were on duty. Otherwise we depended on their hospitality." [10]

Believing that they deserved better quarters, the men staged a minor riot of their
own. The town of Danube's Henry Roback reported on the uprising:

"Through some blunder or misunderstanding we were quartered in a
hotel yard, surrounded by a high fence. The dinner hour having arrived
rations of boiled potatoes were served, and brought in the yard in washtubs.
We at once entered a violent protest by pelting the people on the street with
the boiled Murphies, and proceeded to tear down the fence. The Provost
Marshal sensibly conferred with the Mayor of the city, when we were at
once marched to a first-class hotel and treated like men with all the rights
of citizenship." [11]

The draft was held in Schenectady on August 10th and to the relief of the men
"perfect order and civility reigned."

Rumors abounded that the next stop for the 152nd was Utica, where the soldiers
were again to be used as a deterrent to draft-day troubles. But hopes for a stopover
in Herkimer County and a trip to Utica were dashed when orders came for the 152nd
to return to New York City.

Reaching New York on August 13th, the majority of the 152nd's men were quartered in a large building at 44 Worth Street in the middle of the "plug ugly" neigh-
borhood. When the residents of stylish Stuyvesant Park asked for protection from
bands of hooligans that still roamed the streets, the regiment was more than happy
to change quarters.

During their stay in Stuyvesant Park the unscrupulous contractors, Messrs.
Walker & Co., provided rations for the 152nd. The food served to the men was in
most cases unfit to eat and the boys had to rely on packages from home or handouts
from sympathetic citizens to keep from starving. Unable to get the situation resolved
through military channels, Colonel Ferguson invited reporters from the *New York
Tribune* to dine with the regiment. The newspapermen, taken aback by the "garbage"
that was being passed off as food and always on the lookout for a good story, were
more than happy to report on the 152nd's plight. In a lengthy and detailed account
the *New York Tribune* article stated:

"The treatment of the 152nd Regiment New York Volunteers, now encamped in Stuyvesant Square, has been such as to call forth from the men
the most severe complaints, and to secure from them the entire and substantial sympathy of the citizens living in the immediate vicinity, who have
visited the camp, and have on various occasions found the rations so utterly
filthy, and otherwise objectionable, as to call forth from them the most in-
dignant remonstrances, and also to claim their more substantial exertions
for the comfort of the men.
The contractors for the rations were Walker & Co., who also supply
many other regiments with cooked rations, and who have their headquarters at the Park Barracks. The food furnished by them, according to the

universal testimony of the men, from the commandant (Lieut. Col. Geo. W. Thompson) to the drummer boys, has been of the most uneatable description, with the exception of one or two articles, which even contractors could not spoil, such as hard bread &c. The stuff sent up as soup has been swill, as the men say: and the Captains informed our reporter that the men had a number of times skimmed off maggots from the top of the soup with spoons and brought them to the Officer of the Day for exhibition. In a number of cases, too, the salt meat served out was alive with maggots, and, of course uneatable.

A few days ago a treat was sent to the men, in the shape of some 'apple-sauce.' It was made from the sort of apples the farmers call 'wind falls,' which were stewed up, cores, stems, skins, worms, dirt, rottenness, and all, and sent to these soldiers as a 'treat'; to the country boys at that. Other articles were served up after the same fashion. Messrs. Walker & Co. seeming to think that the dirtier and wormier everything is the more fit it is for the soldiers who have been fighting for their country, while such men as this Walker & Co. stay at home to swindle at the same operation both the Government and the men.

A portion of the maggoty meat having been sent to Gen. Canby, [Edward Canby, NYC troop commander] that officer went to the camp on Sunday, turned out Walker & Co. and had things set right. On that day the food was good and tolerably clean, and the trouble, so far as this one regiment is concerned, is doubtless remedied. But does it not behoove those who have such matters in charge to deal summarily with such men as Walker & Co. or turn them over to be fed one—only one—meal a day for a week on their own food, and let the soldiers have charge of the feeding, and see that they eat their rations? This regiment has done a year's good service, and has been reduced by the casualties of war from 900 to 400. They came here to protect this city from ruin and destruction by rioters, and they certainly deserve that the citizens of New York see to it that they are fed on something different from rotten apples and wormy pork, and also that Messrs. Walker & Co. get their desserts." [12]

In the middle of September the 152nd's headquarters were moved to Castle Garden and its companies were detailed to the provost marshal offices in New York City and Brooklyn. The primary duty given the 152nd was the "escorting" of reluctant conscripts to transport steamers bound for Alexandria, Virginia. Since the guards received a bounty of thirty dollars for the return of each deserter, very few of the draftees escaped.

While in New York the officers and occasionally the private soldiers of the 152nd, frequented famous "watering-holes," such as Niblo's Gardens, the Bowery, Wallack's and Tony Pastor's. Restaurants, including the Revere House and Delmonico's, were dined at and on occasion the men attended plays and were entertained by such actors as Edwin Forrest, the famous tragedian.

The 152nd remained in New York City throughout most of the Autumn of 1863.

In northern Virginia the 97th New York and the 121st New York remained on the trail of Lee's army. Travelling in tandem with the rest of the Army of the Potomac, the two Mohawk Valley regiments passed into Maryland and marched through Hagerstown, Williamsport and over South Mountain before crossing into Virginia near Waterford. To this point the men had marched only fifty miles but the journey had been grueling. With much of the route passing through hilly terrain and with each day's trek being made either in the heat of the mid-July sun or in the mud of a driving rainstorms, the poor infantrymen were spent. John Ingraham of Brockett's Bridge, described the 121st's ordeal in travelling over South Mountain:

> "We commenced climbing the mountain about sundown and it com-
> menced raining soon after (it had rained most of the day before) and about
> dark it came right down and it began to grow dark and it was so dark you
> could not see your hand before your face and we traveled up that mountain,
> mud knee deep and rocks & stones in the road. We traveled until twelve
> o'clock midnight and only just got to the top of the mountain (it was called
> three miles over). It was so steep we would fall down on our knees when
> we would stop. We had not 25 men when we stopped. In the Regiment they
> all fell out and lay by the road.
>   . . . It rained so hard the water ran in streams all over the mount. The
> Col. told us to lay down, what there was left, and rest till morning. Hank
> Brown, Co. C, and I laid down our rubber blanket and tent cloth, took off
> our coats and boots, and laid down in the rain wet through & through. Put
> a blanket over us and covered our heads up, went to sleep in about two
> minutes. Woke up in the morning, it was raining just the same. Ordered to
> fall in, first thing we done, poured the water out of our boots, wrung our
> socks, raised up from where we laid and I will swear that there was an inch
> of water under us. My back was wet through and breeches from top to
> bottom just as if I had dipped them in water. Picked up my coat (I had put
> it under my head for a pillow) and the water dripped a perfect stream off
> from it, and had to put it right on and start. A great many men did not come
> up till next day. Now you can form an idea of soldiering." [13]

Continuing southward through Virginia, the Army of the Potomac passed through New Wheatlands, Middleburg, White Plains, Bealton and Warrenton. Near Warrenton, the 121st New York, with the rest of the 6th Corps, split off from the main column and headed to New Baltimore, about ninety miles northwest of Richmond. The 97th New York, with the 1st Corps, continued south for almost thirty miles, before finally stopping along the Rapidan River at Raccoon Ford.

Lee's army had escaped from Meade and now rested safely on the outskirts of Richmond. The people of the North, believing that the rebel army was near its end after being bloodied so badly on the third day at Gettysburg, were once again frustrated by the ineptitude of the Union army commanders. But no one was more disappointed than the common soldier. Capt. Marcus Casler of the 121st, characterized the men's feelings:

> ". . . instead of such a glorious result we submitted to his [Lee's] almost
> unmolested crossing of the Potomac, he taking his course down south on
> one side of the Blue Ridge and our 'Victorious' Army on the other, like the

race between the dog and the wolf, 'it was nip and tuck' but in this case the wolf was 'about a leetle ahead', and we are now snapping and snarling and showing our teeth at each other, 'one-afraid-and-the-other-dare-not' aspect on both sides, satisfied with picking what few 'sheep' stray from either fold. Thus it has been with the Army of the Potomac ever since the war began. The Rebels know very well we cannot subdue nor drive them out of Virginia with an equal number of men. Why, a good and strong position for defence may be laid every five miles in the State of Virginia. If we succeed in forcing them, as we sometimes have done, from one position, all they have to do is to fall back to a stronger one. . . . I don't want this war to last two or three years longer, and it need not, if that earnestness so necessary to the accomplishment of all great undertakings, be at this time and henceforth displayed and brought to bear with all the terror of annihilation, against these hell-doomed traitors." [14]

For the remainder of the summer, the 97th's picket duty along the Rapidan was rather uneventful. The only action seen was in sporadic exchanges of fire with the rebel pickets across the river.

To the north of the 97th, the 121st was encamped at New Baltimore protecting the right wing of the army. New Baltimore, situated at the base of the Blue Ridge Mountains, was strategically sited a few miles from both Ashby's and Snicker's Gaps. The rebels held the gaps and the Shenandoah Valley beyond and the 121st with its brigade were positioned as sentinels against a quick enemy thrust through the gaps.

New Baltimore's Fauquier County and neighboring Loudon County, constituted the stomping grounds of the infamous gray guerrilla, Col. John Mosby. Mosby commanded a quasi-military troop of mounted partisan rangers that posed a constant distraction to the Federals in this part of Virginia. Farmers and shopkeepers by day and raiders by night, Mosby's men were well known by their signature lightning raids and subsequent vanishing acts. The men of the 121st were well aware of Mosby's tactics and were constantly on the alert, yet the guerrillas still managed to get the drop on the Union boys. The 121st's James Cox of Newport, described one of these attacks:

"On Friday night last, a portion of Moseby's Cavalry attempted to make a raid through our camp. Fortunately Gen. Bartlett had not yet retired, and consequently heard the first discharge of guns by our pickets. The enemy succeeded, however, in drawing our pickets and proceeded to Gen. Bartlett's Head Quarters, where they fired into the vacant tents usually occupied by the band. The assault resulted in the wounding of a bass drum and canteen. They drove immediately in front of Head Quarters and fired a volley through Gen. Bartlett's and Capt. Wilson's tents. The only thing injured in the tents, so far as I can learn, were the General's trunk which took the full force of one bullet. Gen. Bartlett, I am told was very near there, using his revolver to the best advantage. In the meantime, the battery got in position, and the 95th PA and the 121st were on their way to the scene of action, expecting to have a brush with the intruders who had dared thus boldly to enter our camp, and interrupt our quiet slumber and pleasant dreams. But the villains no doubt came to the conclusion that the noise in our camp and the rattling of bayonets boded no good to them: so they made good their escape." [15]

Provoked by Mosby's harassing raids, Colonel Upton was given permission to take the 121st out into the countryside in an attempt to entrap the guerrillas. The regiment marched out of New Baltimore on the morning of August 8th and reached White Plains at noon. Resting there until sunset, the march was again taken up, and after an all night trek Middleburg was reached at sunrise. Francis Lowe detailed the 121st's "capture" of Middleburg:

> ". . . reaching there just at daylight: the place was immediately surrounded by a line of skirmishers. The remainder of the troops then commenced to search the town for arms, prisoners, horses, &c. All able bodied men who could not give a good account of themselves were taken prisoners and brought to camp. Among those taken was one of Mosby's men with his horse and trappings and all who were taken were very much frightened and expected nothing less than hanging or shooting. After searching to our satisfaction, our troops were withdrawn from the place, and divided into three Divisions, each taking a different route for camp so as much as possible to search the country. Some very good horses were taken in all 55 in number. Of prisoners we had 20, dressed in as many different styles. Many others were taken but finally released after a good scare." [16]

During the return trip to New Baltimore, four horsemen were seen on the road between Middleburg and Salem headed in the direction of the 121st. When the riders caught sight of the boys in blue they suddenly veered off the road and disappeared near a stone house. A detail from the 121st was sent to investigate, but were unable to find the horsemen or to get any information from the white inhabitants of the house. Finally, after questioning a slave woman, the men found out that Mosby was one of the riders. Fairfield's, Adam Clarke Rice related:

> "There were several negro women around, all very intelligent and true to our cause as they are free by the Law of God. One of them followed us to the milkhouse, and while giving us some milk, assured us that the horsemen of whom I had spoken, were Mosby himself and some of his men: that he had been around there several days, and that she hoped we might capture him and bring upon his unholy head the doom which he had executed upon many of our poor soldiers." [17]

During their stay at New Baltimore, camp duties in the 121st were light. Drill lasted only one to three hours each day and dress parade was held only two or three times a week. For the officers, who lived in comfortable quarters built by the men and had the services of an enlisted man as a personal cook, life was quite relaxed and easy.

And for once, food was plentiful. With southern farms no longer off limits and with abundant supplies of wild fruits and game, the men gladly put aside their regular army fare and ate heartily. Capt. Marcus Casler described the "eatables" that made their way to 121st's cook pots and dinner tables:

"I have just eaten a hearty dinner of Quail, Stewed Apples, Quail Soup and Hard-Tack. We live on the fat of the land now. Quails come right in front of our tents, like chickens around a barn, and with my little pistol I can soon have a mess. They don't fly more than two or three rods after one shoots at them, and we can approach to within 10 feet of them. We get plenty of apples to stew, in the orchards in this vicinity. Our cracker-box table, with a newspaper for a table-cloth and four sticks driven perpendicularly in the ground for legs to support, holds a good large dish of sweetened blackberries at breakfast, dinner and supper.

What sheep are found belong to us by right of discovery, and whole families of swine are killed, so that they will 'stop squealing and not keep us awake at night.' It wont answer to leave those bee-hives for some one else might go too near them and get badly stung! So to prevent future harm, we take care of them for the present." [18]

In regard to the treatment of Southern citizens and confiscation of their property, the boys in blue no longer felt any remorse. Captain Casler, like many of the men, bore little sympathy for Confederate sympathizers and partisan families and believed that the harsh treatment of these civilians was what the Union war effort needed. Casler remarked:

"I tell you that this time through Virginia we will show them no leniency. Their sheep and swine, and whatever would give them aid, should we move in another direction, are seized and consumed, or put in such a shape that they will be of no use to any person, after we have done with them. But there is one thing more we should do. We should force their women and children to go to their friends in the South, that they might the sooner consume the scanty amount of provisions they have on hand. Then let them all beg for mercy together and if they should still be obstinate, let them all starve together." [19]

While at New Baltimore, the 121st's division was ordered out to witness a military execution. The soldiers looked on as Thomas Jewitt of the 5th Maine was executed by a firing squad for desertion. In a letter to his father in Brockett's Bridge, John Ingraham of the 121st described the execution:

"The deserter rode in an army wagon without a cover on. He sat upon his coffin. All the way there the Chaplain was with him. When we arrived there we formed the whole Division into a square of three sides leaving one end open where he was to be shot. When we were formed they drove all around the square inside. He sat on his coffin and did not seem to mind it a great deal. He had a scrap of some kind of reading I think. But the worst of all was to hear our Brigade Boys Band play the mournful dirge as he passed us. And as they came around to Jersey Band they played a burial dirge. That is what sounded solemn. It did not seem to make any difference with him there too. When they got around to the other end they halted the wagon. He got up off from his coffin, jumped out of the back end of the wagon pretty spry. They then took the coffin, placed [it] on the ground in position. He then shook hands with the men that were to shoot him and the Chaplain and had his hands tied behind him and kneeled on the coffin and then got up and sat on it facing to the front and the men that were to shoot him were in front of him about two Rods. The Chaplain made a prayer and then shook hands with him again and bid him goodbye and left him. Then there was an officer rode by and read his Court Martial to the whole Division and rode away. The officer then that was in Command of the men that were to shoot him stepped up and blindfolded him. Commanded his men to shoulder arms. Ready. Aim. Fire and it threw him right over his coffin. His head struck the ground before his feet. He never knew what hurt him. His head & breast was shot through & through. They were ten men out of the 96th P.V. Regt. done it. 10 shots, 8 balls & two blanks."[20]

The 121st remained in New Baltimore for seven weeks. In mid-September the 121st received orders to break camp and join Meade's columns in another march south.

CHAPTER XII

"Some of you may fall,
but you will all go to heaven"

Summer/Fall 1863 - The Draft in Herkimer County
The 152nd Takes the Field - Rappahannock Station

The draft in New York's 20th Senatorial District, which encompassed Herkimer, Lewis and Jefferson counties, was ordered by Provost Marshal, Gen.James Fry to commence on August 25, 1863. By virtue of the Enrollment Act of March 1863, all male citizens between the ages of twenty and forty-five, with the exception of judges, governors and a few other government officials, were ordered to participate in the draft and to be liable for military duty.

Watertown, being the seat of the 20th District, was selected as the drawing site, and the district's Provost Marshal, Capt. Frederick Emerson, was directed to oversee the process.

Although the actual day of the draft was not announced by General Fry until a week before it was to take place, the people of Herkimer County had been preparing for the event since early in July. At that time, twenty-six men, representing the county's nineteen villages and towns, were charged by Provost Marshal Emerson with compiling draft eligibility lists for their communities. These men, now considered as representatives of the Enrollment Board, were able to quite easily and accurately construct rosters from information on their township's militia rolls. Presaging the need for such rosters, the government of New York State had passed the State Militia Law of 1862 which required each male citizen between the ages of eighteen and forty-five to enroll at least once every two years with the commander of their local militia.

With these militia rolls in hand, Herkimer County enrollment officials prepared lists of the qualified men in their community and categorized these men as either of first class or second class status. First class men included all draft-eligible unmarried men and married men between the ages of twenty and thirty-five. Second class men were married men between the ages of thirty-five and forty-five. The "pool" of second class men would not be drawn from until the first class pool was depleted.

To further prepare themselves for the impending draft a number of the Herkimer County enrollment officials attended the draft ceremonies of their next door neighbors, the 18th Senatorial District. The 18th District, which included Schenectady, Saratoga, Montgomery, Fulton and Hamilton counties held their draft in Schenectady on August 6th through August 10th. The Herkimer County men not only gained practical experience in conducting a draft, but also got a chance to visit with their townsmen from the 152nd Regiment, who were in Schenectady keeping order.

Tuesday, August 25th finally arrived and a draft "ticket" for each qualified man of first class status was placed in a rotating hopper. The draft "tickets," which were prepared by the provost marshal's office from the township enrollment rosters, listed the individual's name, county, town and first or second class status. The draft, which spanned three days, began with Jefferson County, drew from Lewis County on the second day and on the last day from Herkimer County.

J.R. Stebbins, one of three newsmen invited to report on the draft, described the drafting process in the *Journal*:

> "The morning train brought hundreds of visitors from Herkimer and Lewis County and from the southern part of Jefferson, who came to witness the ceremony of the Draft. The town [Watertown] was quiet. The tables occupy the centre of the office, upon of which is the wheel, a small, clean and unstained rotary churn; with an opening and lid on one side. It was turned by an iron crank in the presence of Inspectors chosen by the Provost Marshal.
>
> At five minutes to ten precisely, Provost Marshal Emerson, Commissioner Pond and Surgeon Walker [Edward Walker, former Surgeon of the 34th and 121st N.Y.], made their appearance at the old County Clerk's Office on Court St. followed by the Committee of principal citizens who had been designated to examine into the fairness and conduct of the drawing. At this time but a very small crowd had assembled and there was no appearance of any undue excitement. After making some preliminary arrangements the Provost Marshal read the order of the President and the Provost Marshal General. To Mr. P. Munday was given the list of names enrolled in order that they might be properly checked as drawn, and after being carefully counted, were placed within the wheel.
>
> The oath was then administered by the Marshal to Mr. Wilbur Hough, of Watertown, the blind man who had been chosen to draw the names, who was also carefully blindfolded.
>
> Only two soldiers were in sight and these sat near the door with fixed bayonets, evidently not suspecting any serious work for the day.
>
> Mr. Pond now announced that the draft would commence and the wheel was turned by the Marshal. Amid the deepest silence the first card was drawn and contained the name of Wm. Pearson. Three cheers were immediately given with a will, and when the name was announced as that of Geo.

P. Clark, much laughter and merriment was manifested and cheers given.

Throughout the entire drawing the labors of the Provost Marshal and Commissioner were most severe, every opportunity was afforded by them for the most careful investigation and the complete readiness in which everything was found greatly facilitated operations. In our acquaintance we have seen no two men who could have performed their duties more satisfactorily."[1]

All that Tuesday and Wednesday the wheel turned and names of men from Jefferson and Lewis County were drawn. On Thursday, August 27th, Herkimer County "tickets" were put into the drum and the names of Mohawk Valley men were pulled out. Due to the lateness of the draw, the regular edition of the *Journal* was only able to publish a partial list of the draftees. A special second edition, which was published on Friday, August 28th, carried a complete listing of all the Herkimer County men drawn. The listings, which were broken down by town, revealed a total enrollment of 4,352 men, of which 1,185 names were drawn. There were some inequalities to be sure, such as Newport having one name drawn for every three enrollees, while the town of Warren's ratio was one in ten, but as a whole, most of the Herkimer County towns and villages realized a draft rate of about one in four.[2]

Along with the names of the unlucky men drawn, the *Journal* published quirks of the draft, although the recent draftees probably didn't appreciate the humor. The *Journal* noted:

"Lawyers, ministers, teachers, merchants, mechanics, and almost all other trades and professions are represented in the ranks of the 'newly elect,' except the editorial fraternity. But one editor in the district is drawn —Phillips, a right good fellow too, of the Lowville Republican.

A majority of the enrolling officers will serve notices on themselves.

Several of those turning the wheel were 'caught in the act,' and the excitement and nervous hilarity of the crowd inside the office was intense.

In the list will be found the names of George Washington, John Q. Adams, Lorenzo Dow, and other well known celebrities who evidently mean to take a hand in the terrible game of war the nation is now playing in."[3]

With the "drawing" phase of the draft completed, the thankless task of serving notices on the drafted men was begun by the township enrollment officials. By law, written notification had to be served on the draftee within ten days of the draw. On an average, each of the Herkimer County enrollment officials was required to make almost fifty of these unwelcome visits within the allotted ten days.

Upon receipt of the draft notification, the burden of action now switched to the draftee. Within ten days of notification, the draftee either had to report to Watertown for duty or could pursue one of the options for avoiding conscription; physical or "family" exemption, payment of a $300 commutation fee or provision of a substitute. Men claiming physical exemptions could only be released from conscription after being examined by Surgeon Walker in Watertown. Physical exemption claims based on an examination by a village physician were not accepted.

For "family" exemptions a number of alternatives were available. The *Journal* published the various options:

> ". . . The only son liable to military duty, of a widow dependent upon his labor for support; The only son of aged or infirm parent or parents dependent upon his labor for support; Where there are two or more sons of aged and infirm parents subject to draft, the father, or, if he be dead, the mother may elect which son may be exempt; The only brother of children not twelve years old, having neither father nor mother, dependent upon his support; The father of motherless children under twelve years of age, dependent upon his labor for support; Where there is a father and son in the same family and household, and two of them are in the militia service of the United States, as non-commissioned officers, musicians or privates, the residue of the family and household, not exceeding two shall be exempt."[4]

Men requesting either physical or "family" exemptions could only issue their claims after the completion of the draft. All "family" exemptions required submission of the appropriate forms (#20-25), which could be obtained from the provost marshal's office in Watertown, Attorney John Graves' office in Herkimer, or could be clipped from the pages of the *Journal*. Each of the forms required the signature of the claimant and in most instances the endorsements of two respected community leaders. The claimant had to appear before the Enrollment Board in Watertown to have his case judged. Travel to and from Watertown and "subsistence" during the claimant's stay in that village were at the government's expense.

For those men denied exemptions or that chose not to pursue this route, Section 13 of the Enrollment Act provided yet another way to escape the draft. Section 13 stated:

> "And be it further enacted, That any person drafted, and not found to appear as aforesaid, may on or before the day fixed for his appearance, furnish an acceptable substitute to take his place in the draft: or he may pay to such person as the Secretary of War may authorize to receive it, such sum, not exceeding $300, as the Secretary may determine, for the procuration of such substitute, which sum shall be fixed at a uniform rate by a General Order made at the time of ordering a draft for any State or Territory; and thereupon such person so furnishing a substitute, or paying the money, shall be discharged from further liability under that draft."[5]

Payment of the $300 commutation fee had to be made within the requisite ten days after a draftee's notification. Either cash or a draft drawn on an approved bank was accepted. Remittance of the fee could be made to either G.A. Bagley at the provost marshal's office in Watertown or to L.L. Merry, the Herkimer County Commissioner of Internal Revenue, at his office in Ilion.

The second avenue for escaping conscription opened by Section 13 of the Enrollment Act, the "hiring" of substitutes, was made wider in Herkimer County by the timely arrival of military recruiters and on a small scale, by substitute "brokers."

Representing the 16th New York Heavy Artillery, Frank Burt and Orrin Beach of Little Falls and Cassius Caswell from Otsego County opened a recruiting office in Little Falls. Burt and Caswell were formerly with the 2nd New York Artillery and

Beach had been a 1st lieutenant in the 34th New York. Attracted by the relatively easy duty of a heavy artillerist in the forts around Washington, over one hundred Herkimer County men joined the 16th New York (also known as Foster's Artillery). Among the new recruits were twenty-three former members of the 34th New York. Also recruiting in the area was the "Corning Cavalry" which was more formally known as the 18th New York Cavalry. The 18th's representative in the Mohawk Valley was Parley Eaton of German Flatts, a former member of the 44th New York. About twenty five Herkimer County men enlisted with Eaton, almost one half of whom were former 34th New York men.

No matter what unit the men enlisted in, payable to them were: the Federal bounty, $102; the New York State bounty, $75; and most probably a sum approaching $300 that could be collected from one of the recent draftees who was in need of a substitute. No Herkimer County bounty or township bounty was offered during this phase of the war.

On the fringes of the draftee-substitute configuration were men who acted as go-betweens, substitute "brokers." In sparsely populated rural areas such as Herkimer County, the need for these "matchmakers" was not as great as it was in larger metropolitan areas. For a fee, typically five to ten percent of the transaction, the go-between would match a willing substitute with a draftee looking to buy his way out of the service for a lesser sum than the $300 commutation fee. On occasion, the substituted man may not have been a willing participant in the deal. It was not unheard of for an inebriated individual to sober to the realization that he had been "shanghaied" into the role of a substitute by an unscrupulous broker. In this first draft Herkimer County didn't play scene to such acts.

On the other side of the coin, there were many dishonest substitutes who would collect their substitution fee upon enlistment and desert from the army at the first opportunity. By repeatedly playing this role of substitution-desertion, a man could collect a tidy sum of money.

In Herkimer County, although there may have been a number of active "brokers," only Horace Greene, a Little Falls tax assessor, chose to advertise his services. Greene's advertisement, which was carried in the classified section of the *Journal*, read:

Substitutes Wanted
"A few 'sons of poor but honest parents' can get the highest cash price
to go as substitutes for conscripts who cannot leave home."[6]

With so many options available for avoiding conscription, it was not surprising that of the men drafted from Herkimer County in August of 1863, very few if any actually were compelled to serve. The *Journal*, in an early October edition, proudly noted that all of the Little Falls men had avoided the draft and that many of the other villages and towns in the county would soon be able to report the same.

The low conscription rate in Herkimer County was much the same as was realized across New York State and for the rest of the Union. The statistics for the July/August draft in New York State revealed that of the men drawn, only two percent were forced to do military service. Of the men that "dodged" the draft, seven percent found substitutes, seventeen percent paid the commutation fee, twenty-one percent were exempted for physical or mental disabilities and the remaining fifty-three percent were exempted for other reasons.[7]

On the surface, the summer draft of 1863 appeared to be an abysmal failure. But the Enrollment Act was never intended to force men to serve, but was meant as a tool of coercion to stimulate volunteering. To this end, it was highly successful. This draft, in combination with another draft in the fall of 1863, would bring over three hundred thousand "volunteers" into the Union Army.

The draft in Herkimer County had proceeded peacefully with none of the riotous behavior noted in many other locales. Unfortunately, an incident motivated by racial prejudice, that led to the death of a black man, marred the county's image throughout the state.

In early September, a gang of drunken deckhands from the canal boat "A.S. Carpenter," many of whom were conscripts, attacked a black man, Moses Bliss, outside of his shop near Frankfort. Bliss, a barber, part-time lock attendant and the father of two children, was chased by the rowdies to the Mohawk River, where in desperation he plunged in. The next day his bruised and beaten body was found on the shoreline a short distance from where he was last seen. Twenty-six year old Lamon Widenick, who gave his residence as "The United States," was arrested and charged with the murder of Moses Bliss. The story gained statewide notoriety when it was picked up and published by the *New York Commercial Advertiser*.

Widenick, and another member of his gang were brought before a judge in Utica, who released them for lack of evidence. Public outcry, especially from citizens of Utica who had known Bliss, had little effect and the alleged murderers quickly left the area.

As the summer of 1863 began to draw to a close, events in southeastern Tennessee began to influence the armies of Meade and Lee in Virginia.

In early September, Gen. William Rosecrans, commanding the Army of the Cumberland, flanked Gen. Braxton Bragg's Confederate Army of the Tennessee out of Chattanooga and took up a pursuit of the rebels through northern Georgia. Bragg telegraphed Richmond for reinforcements and in response Robert E. Lee detached two divisions of his army under Gen. James Longstreet and sent them to the aid of Bragg.

General Meade, learning of Longstreet's departure and now realizing a two-to-one numerical advantage over Lee, began an advance towards the Confederate army encamped in the vicinity of Culpeper, Virginia. The 121st New York, with the rest of the 6th Corps, was ordered to join in on the move.

Leaving their camp at New Baltimore, Virginia on September 15th, the 121st marched due south to Warrenton. The regiment stopped there for the night and most of the next day, doing guard duty on the railroad junction and depot. Taking up the march at sunset on the 16th, the 121st advanced seven miles to Sulphur Springs, where after a brief rest, they crossed the Rappahannock. The march continued southeast through Brandy Station, finally reaching Culpeper on September 19th. Unfortunately the enemy was already gone. Lee, knowing that his army was substantially outnumbered, had retreated across the Rapidan. Meade halted his columns, and the 121st New York, with the rest of the 6th Corps, encamped about three miles east of Culpeper.

The 121st set up their tents in a fine chestnut grove and relaxed in the cool weather of early fall. With the paymaster arriving and the quartermaster supplying fresh food, morale was high. Lieut. Francis Lowe reported:

> "As for our Regiment for the past week we have had the easiest time since leaving home, have nothing to do but a little camp duty and to make ourselves comfortable. We have but very little sickness in camp at present and the boys are in fine spirits, ready for anything that wears a grey coat.
>
> Since we have been here we have had soft bread, meat and vegetables —all we wanted. We are now supplied with eight day's rations, good clothes and plenty of money." [8]

Although Francis Lowe described "very little sickness" in the 121st, there was one death. On September 20th, Lt. Adam Clarke Rice succumbed to Typhoid Fever. Rice, a resident of Fairfield, was one of the brightest scholars at the village's academy and a promising young officer in the 121st. Rice's brother, Elfazer, accompanied the body back to Fairfield.

As the 121st was setting up their camps near Culpeper, Virginia, Rosecran's pursuit of Bragg, in northern Georgia, took a decided turn in favor of the Confederates. Now reinforced by Longstreet, Bragg stopped his retreat and set a trap for Rosecrans, which the overconfident Union general marched his army right into. Attacked along Chickamauga Creek, the Federals held their own on the first day, but a misunderstood order left a gap in the blue line on the second day and the opportunistic rebels broke through and routed Rosecran's men. Chased back into Chattanooga, the Union army was quickly besieged by the advancing rebels who took up commanding positions atop the surrounding hills.

Reacting to Rosecran's call for help, Gen. Meade dispatched the 11th and 12th Corps from his army, under the command of Gen. Hooker. With Meade's numerical superiority now diminished, Lee went on the offensive. In early October, the Confederate columns began a move that would result in the Federals being pushed forty miles back across the state of Virginia.

Driven eastward, the 121st broke camp at its chestnut grove near Culpeper and marched to Raccoon Ford on the Rapidan River about ten miles distant. Bivouacking along the river's banks, the men of the 121st were happy to learn that the camp of the 97th New York was only a mile away.

The 97th New York had spent all of the month of September on picket duty along the northern banks of the Rapidan. Across the river the rebels had made no threatening moves and the Union boys, eyeing the formidable enemy works, were content to stay on their side. John Ingraham of the 121st, described the Confederate fortifications that confronted Colonel Wheelock's 97th:

"The Rebs have got an awful strong position here, as much stronger than they had at Fredericksburg as you can think. They are on a great high bluff as high as Brockett's Big hill and it is all level where we are. They have the hills all fortified, entrenchments all along, and they are digging every night throwing up Rifle pits and strong works." [9]

Except for some desultory firing between pickets, the 97th's stay at Raccoon Ford had been rather uneventful. Although the enemy in their front was their prime consideration, an event back home garnered much of the men's attention.

On August 20th the regiment received word that their commander, Colonel Wheelock, who was at the time in Elmira taking charge of some conscripts, had been dishonorably dismissed from the service. The charges against Wheelock specified that he had knowingly approved fraudulent vouchers.

After a three week investigation, the War Department dropped the charges against Wheelock and restored him to rank. In a letter to Colonel Wheelock, Judge Advocate L.C. Turner revealed the details of the investigation. Turner wrote:

"Sir: Enclosed is the order restoring you to command, and pay from date of dismissal.

It is due to you to state your dismissal was a mistake, inadvertence— and wrongful.

An account was presented for payment of $650.90 for subsisting recruits. This account was referred by the War Department to H.S. Olcott, Special Commissioner, New York, for investigation and report.

Mr. Olcott investigated, and reported the account false and fraudulent, save perhaps about $150, and endorsing that Henry Root was the special contractor; J.P. Leslie, captain, certifying officer; and C. Wheelock, Col., the approving officer of the false and fraudulent account.

Whereas, the fact is you did not approve of the bill, but only approved of the transportation charge of $10.45, in duplicate, and this charge was right.

Upon the discovery of this mistake you were at once ordered restored, and the order of dismissal revoked.

I make this statement to relieve you from the slightest imputation, in this regard, upon your character as a man and an officer." [10]

It was notable that Capt. James Leslie of Little Falls resigned in July 1862, soon after the incident supposedly was to have occurred.

Wheelock returned to the 97th, but not until the first week of December.

The 97th New York broke camp along the Rapidan at 2 a.m. on the morning of October 10th and joined the rest of the Army of the Potomac in the retreat from Lee's forces. Moving north through Stevensburg and Brandy Station, the regiment crossed the Rappahannock at Kelly's Ford on the 11th. A few hours after the 97th passed through Brandy Station, Gen. Alfred Pleasanton's rear guard cavalry units were attacked near that village by Jeb Stuart's gray horsemen. In one of the largest cavalry fights of the war, the Union boys drove the Confederate cavalry from the field.

Before daybreak on the 12th, the 97th was back on the road, continuing northeast through Bealton. On the night of the 13th, the regiment reached Manassas Junction, where they bivouacked on the old Bull Run battlefield. After resting for a few days, the march was resumed but now the direction was westward. Moving on October 19th, the 97th passed by Gainesville, Haymarket, through Thoroughfare Gap and on to Bristow, Virginia. At Bristow, about twenty-five miles southeast of Washington, the 97th set up camp, remaining there for almost two weeks.

The 121st New York, with the 6th Corps, had taken much the same route as the 97th. Moving in concert with the 1st Corps, the 6th Corps boys had made up the left flank of Meade's columns. Marching through Manassas Junction, and then north to Chantilly, the 121st about faced and headed south to Warrenton, Virginia, forty miles southeast of Washington. While pitching their tents, the men of the 121st were surprised to discover that the 152nd New York was encamped nearby.

The 152nd New York, which had rightfully earned the nickname, "the wandering regiment," received orders on October 13th in New York City to pack up and be ready to move at a moment's notice. The next morning the men took a steamer across Raritan Bay and boarded a troop train at Amboy, New Jersey. Travelling sixty-five miles to Camden, the 152nd stopped to eat at a soldier's refreshment saloon and reboarded a train bound for Washington. Henry Roback described the regiment's travel accommodations:

> "We arrived at the depot and boarded a cattle train. Our condition was nearly the same as the former occupants. They were sent to the front to be killed whenever the necessity of the occasion required it. Sleeping on our soft and ammoniac berths, we rolled along the endless rail." [11]

The train travelled on through Washington finally stopping at Fairfax Station, eighteen miles south of Alexandria, Virginia. In preparation for the march out into the Virginia countryside, the men of the 152nd were outfitted for the first time with equipment and rations typically given to the field soldier. As Henry Roback described it, the men were proud of their "soldier's gear," but were not very satisfied with the food:

> "The Quartermaster furnished a knapsack containing two suits of clothes and underwear; one large overcoat and blanket extra heavy; one rubber blanket, one shelter tent, one canteen holding three pints, a cartridge box and belt with cap box. The Ordnance Department issued forty rounds of ammunition. . . . The Commissary . . . issued eight days' rations, which carried in the haversack; the tin pans, spider, quart cup and hatchet were hung on the outside. This was a full-fledged soldier, who presented a formidable appearance.
>
> . . . [The] eight days' rations were issued, and we hurriedly packed a part of the viands in our haversacks, throwing away the pork, which contrasted fearfully with the dishes we had partaken at Delmonico's, the Revere House and other noted restaurants [in New York City]." [12]

The 152nd marched to Manassas, and after moving back and forth across the old Bull Run battlefields for a few days, the regiment headed to Bristow where they

VIRGINIA & WEST VIRGINIA

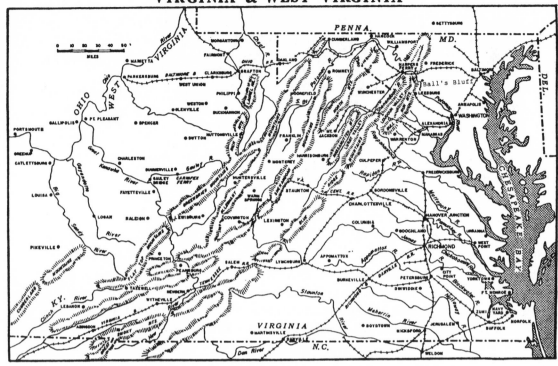

RAPPAHANNOCK & RAPIDAN BASIN

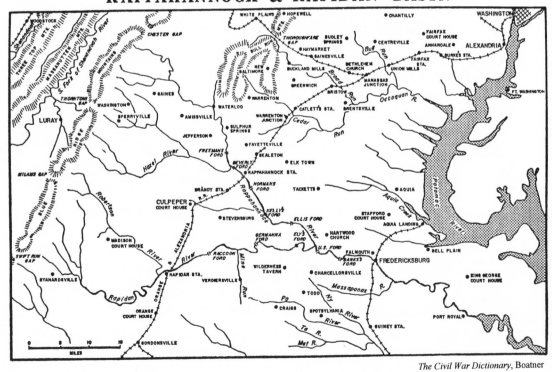

The Civil War Dictionary, Boatner

arrived on October 20th. Soon after reaching Bristow, the men learned that the 152nd New York had been assigned to the 1st Brigade, 2nd Division of the 2nd Corps. Coincidentally, the "old 34th New York" had held the same position.

Moving on the 23rd with their new corps, the 152nd reached Warrenton and encamped. Two days later the 121st New York arrived.

Although the men of the 152nd had been in the service for over a year, when it came to field soldiering they were raw recruits. John Ingraham of the 121st, after visiting the 152nd's camp, commented on the inexperience of its men:

> "I went over to see the 152nd Regiment yesterday. I tell you they are green enough. Some of them curse the war. All sorts they don't know how to cook and ain't got anything to cook with. They make their coffee in their drinking cups and they don't like it. It don't taste good [to] them. I tell you it is fun to hear these green horses talk & grumble & hear them tell what hardships they have seen. They ain't seen nothing compared to us. They have never done any fighting or marching, only from Fairfax out here." [13]

Unused to the rough army fare and not very well versed in cooking their own meals, many of the men of the 152nd either learned how to cook on their own or turned to the veterans for help. Henry Roback described a "recipe" that must have been taught the men by a field-hardened trooper:

> ". . . we moved [into] a deserted rebel camp, where we found a physician's mortar and pestle. We proceeded to pound hardtack for the purpose of making pancakes and puddings. No musical instrument had a sweeter sound than that mortar and pestle. All day long and until 'lights out' was sounded, could be incessantly heard, this grinding mill. The hardtack when soaked in water was often very tough, and about as easy to masticate as a vulcanized rubber boot, doubtless owing to the contract system. The breakfast generally consisted of hardtack soaked in water, and then fried in pork fat. For dinner we would reverse the order, frying them in grease, then soaking them in water, making two distinct dishes. Ten tacks per day was a regular daily allowance, weighing a short pound, and if there was any left, they were worked up in a light repast for supper." [14]

Roback related a novel approach that was taken by those men still unable to curb their hunger:

> "Rations were growing small and appetites large. To supply the deficiency, we ate green persimmons, which had the effect to shrink the stomach, and make it fit the issue. Each persimmon, when eaten green, equaled an ounce of alum. . . . " [15]

On November 7th, the 152nd broke camp at Warrenton and joined the 97th New York, newly arrived from Bristow, and the 121st New York, as the Army of the Potomac started south yet again in the back and forth struggle across northern Virginia.

Unable to get between the fast retreating Federals and Washington, and with his own supply line grown tenuous, Lee decided to end the pursuit of Meade and with-draw his troops. To cover his crossing of the Rappahannock, Lee posted Gen. Jubal Early and a brigade of Louisiana boys to guard a bridgehead at Rappahannock Station on the north bank of the river.

Taking the initiative, George Meade moved the 3rd, 5th and 6th Corps toward Rappahannock Station in an attempt to cut off Lee. At about noon on November 7th, the 5th and 6th Corps, under Gen. John Sedgwick, came within cannon range of Early's men. Federal batteries were quickly wheeled into position and began bom-barding the Confederates' hastily constructed breastworks. The first brigade to arrive on the scene was the 2nd Brigade, 1st Division of the 6th Corps, with Col. Emory Upton of the 121st New York temporarily in command. Upton's brigade was com-posed of the 5th and 6th Maine, the 5th Wisconsin and the 121st New York.

The 121st New York had broken camp at Warrenton very early that morning and with the rest of its brigade marched ten miles to Rappahannock Station. Shortly after halting, two companies from each regiment in the brigade were ordered out as skir-mishers. From the 121st, Companies B and D, numbering about forty men, were selected and sent out under the command of Capt. John Fish.

At about 1:30 p.m., the skirmishers were ordered to advance and take the en-emy's outer works. Charging through a hail of musketry and cannon fire, the boys in blue drove the rebels from their rifle pits and took one hundred and twenty-seven of them prisoner. Of this opening attack at Rappahannock Station, Clinton Beckwith related:

> "We moved forward briskly and soon discovered the Rebel skirmish line. They waited a good while, an age I thought, before they fired on us, and I knew somebody would get hit. Finally they let go and we started on a run after them, and they skedaddled. One fellow waited until Jack Mar-den, one of our boys, got close to him, and then fired and hit Jack. But the ball, striking something in Jack's pocket, glanced off. The Rebel shouted, 'I surrender', but Jack shot and wounded him badly. He said that he belonged to the 6th Louisiana, Hay's Brigade, Early's Division, Ewell's Corps, and his name was Slidell. The artillery in the fort was now firing rapidly and the cannon shots flew over us and went after our fellows who were coming up behind. The Reb skirmishers kept falling back, but kept up a sharp fire. We connected on our left with the 6th Maine, and in half an hour after starting we drove in their skirmishers, they jumped over the breastworks and we busied ourselves firing at them. Just at sunset the reserves came up, the 95th and 96th Pennsylvania, and joined the line of battle behind us. As they started to advance Captain Fish ordered us skirmishers to charge, and going forward on a run, with a yell, we came to the rifle pits, and jumping on them the Rebels in them began to run." [16]

For two hours the Union skirmishers huddled in the captured trenches under fire from the main Confederate force and from enemy batteries on the other side of the Rappahannock. At 4:00 p.m., the rest of the 2nd Brigade, which had been sheltered in some woods, were ordered to advance across an open field and join the skirmish-ers. Lt. John Gray, of Little Falls, described the brigade's advance:

"We advanced under a heavy fire from the enemy's artillery. The shells were flying over and around us and bursting: in fact it was no comfortable place. We moved forward until we came under cover of a little hill and there we stacked our guns and rested for a short time, when orders came for us to move forward again. All the while there was heavy firing on the skirmish line." [17]

The heavy firing heard by Lieutenant Gray was a bayonet charge by the 6th Maine and the 5th Wisconsin. Twice repulsed, these two regiments finally forced a lodgement in the enemy's line and now it was the 121st's turn to attack. Lieutenant Gray continued with his narrative:

"It was just about dusk and we moved forward the last time, and it was at a double-quick. In this manner we moved until we were a few rods from our skirmish line. There we halted under fire of the rebels. We lay down for a few moments, then got up and took off our traps, such as knapsacks, haversacks &c. for a 'charge.' Our Colonel [Upton] came up to us (he is commanding our brigade at present, Gen. Bartlett having command of a division) and said 'Boys, or rather Old 121st, I am with you again. We are going to make a charge, and some of you may fall, but you will all go to heaven. And I am going with you over the works.' Then he ordered us to march by the right flank, then forward, 'Charge Bayonets.' We did forward and went clean over the works, driving the Johnnys before us and jumping over the rest. Then we started at a double-quick up the works and sent some of our men down to the river to keep them from crossing on their Pontoon Bridge." [18]

The charge of the 121st New York and 5th Maine so surprised the rebels that very few shots were even fired. With their backs to the river and cutoff from their pontoon bridge, the Confederates surrendered in droves.

Lieutenant Gray completed his story by relating his personal role in the surrender:

"After going a short distance the prisoners began to come in, there being no way for them to get away, only by swimming the river which a great many did, and in the attempt I do not doubt that a number were drowned. As I was going to say, the prisoners came in very fast, and I moved forward and came up to a squad of rebels. There were at least a half dozen in it. I ordered every 'd____d one of them to surrender or I would run them through.' They said they surrendered. One fellow jumped out of the pit and said, 'I surrender, I surrender,' and at the same time offered me every thing he had. One splendid Repeating Rifle he gave me and some cartridges. I tell you he was awfully scared. Well, it was a ticklish position to be in. One of the squad was a Lieutenant. He said to me, 'Lieutenant, I surrender,' and at the same time handed me his sword which he prized very highly, saying, 'that blade I took last summer at Winchester from one of your officers and the scabbard from one at Gettysburg,' so of course it is a very nice prize for that if nothing more. It is not very handsome, but a common one: the rifle I have with me also. It can be fired seven times without loading: so you see it is a pretty nice thing, and I can say that both the sword and the rifle were surrendered to me by their owners." [19]

The charge was over in a matter of minutes and the final tally for 2nd Brigade was astounding. With a little over six hundred men, the four regiments of the brigade had captured over fifteen hundred prisoners, including forty-eight commissioned officers. It had also confiscated six pieces of artillery, almost two thousand muskets and eight battle flags.

The loss to the Federals was less than one hundred and fifty men killed and wounded. In the 121st New York, four men had been killed outright and twenty-one were wounded (three mortally).[20] Among the men killed were; Pvt. William Watson of Frankfort, Cpl. Delos Platt from Manheim and Pvt. William Eastwood of Warren. All three men were members of the Co. D skirmishers. Another Co. D boy, Robert Johnston from Frankfort, would succumb shortly after from his wounds. Included in the wounded was frequent *Journal* correspondent Capt. Marcus Casler of Little Falls. Casler was shot through the forearm, but no bones were broken and amputation was unnecessary.

Notable among the 121st's heroes that day was Lt. H. Seymour Hall from Barkersville, Saratoga County. For his gallant action in reforming his company after the initial charge at Rappahannock Station, Hall was awarded the Medal of Honor. Amazingly, this was not Lieutenant Hall's first Medal of Honor. While a member of the 27th New York, Hall had been cited for valor in the June 1862 battle of Gaines's Mill.

After burying the dead and removing the wounded, the 2nd Brigade bivouacked near the battlefield and waited for the rest of the army to arrive.

Four days after their brilliant charge at Rappahannock Station, Emory Upton assembled the 2nd Brigade and paraded to General Meade's headquarters. On behalf of the 5th and 6th Maine, 5th Wisconsin and the 121st New York, Upton presented Meade with the eight rebel flags captured at the Station. Taken aback by this unexpected tribute, Meade replied to this gesture with an impromptu speech:

> "I receive with great satisfaction the flags, evidences of the good conduct and gallantry you displayed on the 7th inst., in the assault upon the enemy's position at Rappahannock Station, entrenched with redoubts and rifle pits, and defended by artillery and infantry. Carried as it was by the point of the bayonet, it was a work which could only be executed by the best of soldiers, and the result of which you may justly be proud, gives me great confidence that in future operations I can rely on the men under my command doing when called on, all that men can do. . . .
>
> I shall transmit these flags to the War Department. I have already reported your good conduct and received and transmitted to your commanders the approval of the President."[21]

The mood was much different in Lee's camp. Although the bulk of the Confederate army had safely made its way across the Rappahannock, the one-sided defeat of the rear-guard caused indignation throughout the rebel army. Never before had the Army of Northern Virginia been dealt such a bitter blow by the Army of the Potomac.

The 97th and 152nd New York had departed Warrenton too late in the day to witness the action at Rappahannock Station. Both regiments did march by the scene of the battle the next day, but continued south four miles, crossing the river at Kelly's Ford. With Lee's army on the run, General Meade had the Army of the Potomac in pursuit.

CHAPTER XIII

"We waited in suspense to start for the next world"

Fall/Winter 1863 - Herkimer County Autumn - Mine Run

The 1863 edition of the Herkimer County Agricultural Society's fair was held on September 23rd, 24th and 25th at its customary site in Alfred Gray's fields, between Mohawk and Herkimer. Since 1841 Gray had donated the use of the grounds and dirt race track, which were bounded by the Mohawk River on the south, Turnpike Road on the west and Upper Bridge Road on the east.

This year's fair boasted five hundred and thirty-three exhibits, with exhibitors from as far away as Syracuse. Record crowds were in attendance for the fair's first two days, but heavy downpours on the third day kept many people away.

As usual, on display there was something for everyone. For those interested in livestock there were twenty-two classes of horses, twenty-two classes of cattle and oxen, plus assorted breeds of chickens, ducks, pigs and sheep. For the gardener there were prize winning cucumbers, cabbages, peppers, popcorn, beans, onions, cranberries, peas, potatoes, tomatoes and pumpkins. The giant of the vegetable exhibit was a one hundred and fifty pound squash grown by R.D. Browne. In the fruit section were Bill Feeter's forty varieties of apples, J.G. Snell's twenty-six types of pears and J.J. Gilbert's eleven varieties of grapes. The handiwork exhibits included assorted blankets, mittens, stockings, wax flowers, oil paintings, crayon drawings, cut flowers and even a display of embroidered drawers. For the farmer, manufacturers of farm implements presented two-horsepower threshing and sawing machines, patented pumps, water elevators, cultivators, farm wagons and ploughs for all types of soil.

Probably the most interesting displays were in the "miscellaneous" categories. Besides the ordinary items such as cheese, honey, butter, maple syrup and of course jellies, one could also view the extraordinary—trained bees, caskets, sea shells, Chinese tea plants and several live northern pike.

Those exhibits judged best in their category were awarded cash prizes ranging from ten dollars to fifty cents, but every exhibitor received a diploma of appreciation from the County Agricultural Society.

Special events at the fair included, the fireman's tournament, which was won that year by Hose Co. 3 of Little Falls (the Canajoharie contingent felt that the contest was rigged) and, of course, the horse races.

Normally held on the fair's last day, the races that year had to be postponed to the following Tuesday because of inclement weather. The featured race of the 1863 fair was a trot for two year olds and under, which was won in four heats by M.R. Bellinger's yearling Ethan Allen over R. Helmer's sorrel chestnut. Ethan Allen "blazed" the mile long race in an average time for the four heats of two minutes and fifty-two seconds and won forty dollars for his owner.

In spite of the bad weather on the last day, the 1863 Herkimer County fair was highly successful and realized gate receipts of over $1300. The *Journal* reported the fair to be "the best ever held in the county," and "twice as good as the year before."

With the weather remaining mild in the Mohawk Valley those activities typical to early autumn continued. In Little Falls the ladies of the African Society and the Zion Church held Ice Cream Festivals. The Zionists owed their pastor $75 for his services and the proceeds from their festival were devoted to pay off the debt.

Sunday school picnics were still being held and, as usual, the Universalist Society's Sabbath School of Little Falls conducted the most ambitious of these events. An excursion packet boat was rented by the society and all were invited to travel the Erie Canal to "below" Fort Plain, for a picnic. To insure a good time, the boys of the Citizen's Brass Band were on hand with their instruments.

As the weather cooled and the days grew shorter in November the indoor entertainment season began. In Brockett's Bridge a "musical convention," under the direction of S.U. Cookinham was held at the Brick Church. The Morris Minstrels performed at Concert Hall in Little Falls, and at Maine's Hotel in Herkimer the Ladies Aid Society of that village offered an oyster supper and dancing to the music of Crumwell's band. The proceeds from the oyster supper were to be used to purchase comforts and delicacies for the soldiers, "most particularly those from Herkimer County."

But the rage of the indoor entertainment circuit this fall was an exhibition of the properties of Laughing Gas [nitrous oxide], by the celebrated Dr. Colton and his assistant, Mr. Collins. In noting their forthcoming appearance at Concert Hall, the *Journal* included an excerpt from the *Boston Daily Advertiser* that remarked:

> "Those who have not seen 'Laughing Gas' entertainment can form little idea of it. It is a compound of all the entertainments ever placed before the public. The subjects of the Gas, who are many and willing, give specimens of dramatic and forensic eloquence innumerable; they sing, declaim, dance, laugh in all the most extravagant degree, and according as their unre-

strained inclinations lead them." [1]

After a free matinee exhibition, which was open only to the ladies, the first performance for the general public was described by the *Journal*:

> "Concert Hall was crowded last evening by one of the largest and most intelligent audience of ladies and gentlemen that we have seen out on any occasion and the exhibition in every way was a perfect success. Those who have never witnessed one of these Laughing Gas entertainments can form little idea of it from a brief description. The whole affair almost uncontrollable to an ordinary man was managed most adroitly by Mr. Collins who seems to have a peculiar faculty for treating his subjects. While the audience were now excited by some thrilling manifestation of character, they were next convulsed by the novel antics of some merry subject. Altogether it was one of the most amusing entertainments ever given in this place. Mr. C's Lecture upon Laughter contained many admirable hits and was well received." [2]

Unfortunately life in the Mohawk Valley was not all county fairs, oyster suppers and laughing gas exhibitions. During the late summer and early fall of 1863, the people of Herkimer County witnessed an abnormal number of tragic accidents.

The tracks of the New York Central Railroad, notoriously a dangerous place, claimed its share of victims. Nicholas Miller, of Little Falls, was struck by a train while crossing the tracks near Furnace St. and suffered a severed left arm; young John Gainer, a railroad employee of the Central Railroad, was run over and killed by a locomotive two miles east of Little Falls; and an unknown resident of the County Poor House was caught between two rail cars in Herkimer and horribly mangled. Besides accidents to local men, the rail line also claimed the life of a soldier passing through the Mohawk Valley on his way home. The *Journal* reported:

> "A middle aged man by the name of Nichols was found dead last Saturday morning on the Railroad at East Creek. He was a member of the 43d Mass. Regiment on his way home from Port Hudson with his Regiment. On the evening before he complained of considerable indisposition caused as was supposed by over-eating at Utica. He left his companions on the car to go out on the platform as he said to vomit and it is supposed he fell causing his death. His body was taken in charge by his brother-in-law who returned in search of him. He leaves a wife and child." [3]

An unusual accident occurred in broad daylight on Ann Street in Little Falls. Two men, who were target shooting behind Sheperd's store on Main Street, fired a stray ball that struck a Miss Ramsey in the face as she was walking on Ann Street. Fortunately the wound did not prove fatal, and since no laws had been broken the men were not charged with any wrongdoing.

But the most tragic occurrence took place on the southside of Little Falls. Frances Harris, a young woman who "worked" at a "house of bad reputation" owned by a Mrs. Miller on the village's southside, accidentally brushed against an oil lamp and caught her clothes on fire. Aroused by Miss Harris's screams, a gentleman from Lockport and the girl he had "gone upstairs" with, rushed from the house instead of going to the aid of the burning girl. Mrs. Miller tried to douse the flames but caught herself on fire and ran from the house screaming. The house itself was now ablaze, and Miss Harris was left to perish in the flames. Fortunately, an unidentified good samaritan braved the inferno and dragged the girl to safety. Neighbors who had gathered at the scene, refused to take the suffering girl in and let her lie in agony on the cold street. Early the next afternoon, Frances Harris died from her burns. The man from Lockport and his mistress were arrested in a nearby tavern and led away in handcuffs, and Mrs. Miller, to whom no charges were brought, lay at a friend's house severely burned.

The *Journal* described the incident as "the most horrible, shameful affair we have had to record in our local column for many a year" and characterized the neighbors who only looked on while Miss Harris suffered as "acting more like barbarians than human beings."

But, no matter what the local news was, either good or bad, war news outweighed all else. As the autumn of 1863 wore on, the full attention of the people of Herkimer County was once again drawn south, as their hometown boys began to advance in Virginia.

After routing the rebel rear guard at Rappahannock Station early in November, the Army of the Potomac went into bivouack for two weeks. Blocking the Federals from a direct route to Richmond, General Lee had posted his forty-eight thousand troops along a thirty mile front on the southern bank of the Rapidan River. Hidden behind strong fortifications, the gray line stretched from Liberty Mills to the northwest to Mine Run to the southeast. General Meade, under pressure from Washington to act, decided on one more attempt at the rebel capital before winter set in. Although Meade outnumbered Lee almost two to one, he discarded any notions of a straight on frontal attack and searched for a way around the enemy. After reconnoitering the Confederate line, Meade selected Mine Run as his target. Meade reasoned, that if the Army of the Potomac moved expeditiously, it could interpose itself between Richmond and the Army of Northern Virginia before Lee's scattered forces could react.

Early on the morning of the nation's first Thanksgiving Day, November 26th, the Union army went into motion as units of the 3rd Corps began splashing over the lower Rapidan at Germanna Ford. But from the start Meade's Mine Run maneuver was doomed to failure.

The 97th New York, with the 1st Corps and the 152nd New York, with the 2nd Corps, both stepped off for Mine Run on the morning of November 26th, but neither regiment made it very far. As if on schedule, just as the Union columns stepped off, a fierce rainstorm drenched the area and quickly turned the roads into a sticky mess. With the roads partially blocked by floundering wagon and artillery trains, and with an inexplicable delay by the 3rd Corps up ahead, the 1st and 2nd Corps were brought to an abrupt halt. The 97th was able to cross the Rapidan at Culpeper Ford before going into bivouack, but the boys of the 152nd were ordered to backtrack to their camp.

The 121st, which was detailed to guard its 6th Corps wagon train, did not leave its camp at Rappahannock Station until after nightfall and missed the brunt of the storm, but with the roadways churned into a paste by the trains of other corps, the 121st's march was miserable. George Eaton of Little Falls remarked:

> "We departed on the evening of the 26th, which was very cold, and it soon appeared that our brigade was rear guard. We were close behind the wagon train and such a time as we had I shall never forget. There were a good many wagons got stuck in the mud and we had to pull them out. We got in camp about twelve o'clock that night." [4]

As the morning of November 27th dawned the Union army was up and moving again, but the delays of the day before would prove costly. General Meade, knowing that speed was the essential element in his campaign, was furious that in the last twenty-four hours his army had barely moved. Although the heavy rains of yesterday had contributed to the ponderous movement of his columns, Meade was laying the blame squarely on the 3rd Corps and its commander Gen. William French. The 3rd Corps had been given the task of spearheading the Union advance and setting a rapid pace for the other corps to follow. Instead, French's men had taken the wrong road and in backtracking had piled up traffic at the Rapidan crossings. It was due to this traffic jam that the 97th New York had to bivouack after crossing the river and that the 152nd New York was stopped in its tracks and forced to return to camp.

Now alerted to the Federal troop movements on his right flank, Lee began to shift the weight of his forces towards Mine Run. By daylight on the 27th, Lee had moved most of Gen. Jubal Early's command into the woods at Locust Grove, between the Rapidan and Mine Run. Lee realized that Early's almost twenty thousand men were no match for Meade's five corps, but with more troops arriving by the hour, he was hoping that Early could slow down the Federal advance until the Mine Run position could be made secure.

On the morning of the 27th, the three Mohawk Valley regiments once more joined in the Union advance. The 97th New York left its bivouack at Culpeper Ford and fell in with the rest of the 1st Corps. The 152nd New York broke camp once again and joined the 2nd Corps in crossing the Rapidan at Germanna Ford. The 121st New York, after a brief rest from their night time march, crossed the river at Thomas Ford.

With the 3rd Corps in the lead, the Union column struck the Orange Plank Road and marched southwest along the western fringe of the Wilderness. Meade's primary objective was to reach Orange Court House which he believed would put his army in Lee's rear.

As the 3rd Corps approached Locust Grove, its lead units, which were expecting only token enemy resistance, were attacked by Jubal Early's gray backs. The brief fight, which cost each side about five hundred men, put another crimp in Meade's timetable. With the Federal advance momentarily stopped, Lee had the time he needed to complete his troop concentration at Mine Run. Having accomplished their task, Early's men withdrew to the defenses at Mine Run. The Federal army spent the night bedded down in the vicinity of Locust Grove.

The next morning the Union advance slowly slogged forward, caught once again in a terrible downpour. At mid-morning the Union march came to a halt as lead elements of the 3rd Corps came within sight of Confederate breastworks across Mine Run.

Confronted by a rebel battleline seven miles long and as formidable as the works Burnside faced at Fredericksburg, Meade sat down to ponder his next move. In the meantime, Meade deployed his troops in a line parallel to the enemy breastworks. The 6th Corps took up position on the right flank, the 2nd Corps on the left and French's 3rd Corps stood at the center. The 1st and 5th Corps were held in reserve behind the main line.

Just before sundown the rain finally stopped only to be replaced by bone-chilling cold. Under orders not to build fires, the men of both armies shivered as water in their canteens froze. George Eaton of the 121st described his regiment's suffering:

> "We were almost frozen, and when they told us we were to stay there till morning there was many a sorry looking face. For about six hours we had to walk to keep warm, and when the sun appeared above the trees, it looked warm, I tell you." [5]

During the night the men received a cheering bit of news, Grant had broken the siege at Chattanooga and routed Bragg's Confederates.

All the next day, November 29th, the standoff continued, with neither side choosing to attack the other. For the common soldier the wait meant another day in the bitter cold. Herkimer's Clinton Beckwith commented:

> "As soon as daylight came several shots in our front and bullets flying close to us, gave warning that our foes were alert and knew our exact position. So without fire, all through that cold winter day, watching for an advance, and dreading an order to drive their skirmishers, we lay there and suffered, and hailed with joy the friendly darkness of night, which permitted us to rise up and stretch and pound ourselves to restore our chilled circulation. Finally at midnight orders came to march silently, and assemble on our left. We were so benumbed that we could scarcely move. At last we reached the road and began moving toward the river. I kept along with the column until we came to what appeared to be a tannery which had been burned and was still a great mass of embers. Seeing it I made a bee-line for it, and the way I soaked up the heat was a caution. Lying down on some bark I got a good nap before a cavalry man woke me up and said, 'Get out of here, the Johnnies are coming and will gobble you up.' " [6]

That night, General Meade formulated as unimaginative a plan as any of his predecessors. His "strategy" called for Sedgwick's 6th Corps on the right and Warren's 2nd Corps on the left, to make headlong charges on the rebel entrenchments. The attack was planned for the next morning at 8 a.m., and was to commence at the firing of a signal cannon.

As the sun came up the next day, the men of the 2nd and 6th Corps readied themselves for what they knew would be nothing short of a suicidal charge. Henry

Roback of the 152nd related the mood of the men of his regiment:

> "On the morning of the 30th of November we found ourselves in line
> with the whole army, and confronting a most formidable breastworks of the
> enemy. The trees had been felled, with the limbs sharpened forming an
> impenetrable abatis. The order was given to charge at 8 a.m. Unslinging
> knapsacks we made all preparations. Many turned all private effects over
> to Chaplain Talbot, with the parting injunction to have them sent to mother
> or wife 'if I fall.' We waited in suspense to start for the next world, for all
> believed it would be an utter impossibility to cross that apparent river of
> death." [7]

Five minutes before eight, General Warren rode up to the 152nd's line. Dismounting, he surveyed the rebel fortifications one more time, and decided that he would not order his corps forward even if it cost him his commission. After ordering his division commanders to maintain their positions, Warren rode off to see Meade. As the men of the 152nd relaxed, the signal gun was fired and sporadic musket fire was audible to their right.

At the urging of Warren and the other corps commanders, Meade called off the attack. Unfortunately, skirmishers from the 6th Corps on the right wing had not received word to break off the attack and had begun to advance across Mine Run. After firing a few volleys, the skirmishers were ordered to withdraw.

Isaac Hall of the 97th described the aborted attack:

> "Our skirmish line charged across the creek and drove in the Confeder-
> ate skirmishers, but it was glad to get back. The water was nearly four feet
> deep, and it was ten feet across and freezing, consequently when our men
> attempted to return they became benumbed and their clothing so frozen that
> it was necessary to employ stretcher-bearers to bring some of them off." [8]

For the rest of the day and throughout the night the men at the front stood at ready, again shivering in the freezing temperatures without the benefit of a fire. The men in the rear were permitted to build bonfires and huddled closely around them trying to stay warm.

The next morning, the first day of December, General Meade ordered a withdrawal. Unable to advance and with winter fast approaching, Meade decided to pull back north of the Rapidan and put his army into winter quarters.

The 97th New York from its reserve position began marching northward soon after dawn. The 121st New York and the 152nd New York, being in the front lines, were among the last troops to leave Mine Run, not stepping off until after nightfall.

A general withdrawal in the face of the enemy was always a risky venture, and to conceal their movements, Henry Roback of Danube described the precautions taken:

> "We marched at quick-step, as no one wished a room at Hotel Libby
> [Libby prison in Richmond]. The long, dried wild grass was set on fire,
> burning the under brush and hiding our movements under cover of the
> dense black clouds of smoke which rolled heavenward. Woe unto the strag-
> gler who fell out; if the guerrillas did not gobble him the fire might con-
> sume and destroy him." [9]

After an all night march, the Army of the Potomac completed their recrossing of the Rapidan on December 2nd. Continuing northward, most of the units halted on December 4th and began surveying the vicinity for suitable winter quarters. With their corps, the 152nd stopped at Stevensburg, Virginia, the 121st at Brandy Station and the 97th near Kelly's Ford. Without undue haste, the men of the Mohawk Valley regiments, like the rest of the army, constructed crude but comfortable huts and settled in for a winter's rest.

In the movements of late November 1863, which would be known as the Mine Run Campaign, the Mohawk Valley units' losses were minimal. The 152nd reported two slightly wounded men,[10] the 97th's loss was four missing[11] —who were most likely deserters—and the 121st realized no casualties.[12]

The Northern press had a field day criticizing Meade for not attacking Lee at Mine Run. But most of the private soldiers who had been there, stood by their commanding general. Julius Townsend, of the 152nd, came to Meade's and the army's defense, remarking:

> "He [Meade] is blamed by certain Northern demagogues for not charging the enemy's works on Monday, Nov. 30th, yet the confidence of every officer and Private in this army in his ability to command and lead them, is immeasurably increased by the wisdom he manifested in not attempting to take these strongholds which could not have resulted other-wise than in ignominious defeat and irreparable disaster. . . .
>
> This army is not made up of cowardly stuff, neither are its Generals. When the 2d Corps, together with the 3d Division of the 6th, were drawn up in line of battle at Mine Run, they were told by their officers the danger before them. The frowning battlements, the embrasures through which the enemy's glittering brass pieces were seen, were pointed out to them. They were told that they would see their officers fall by scores, their comrades by hundreds, but that they must and would succeed: yet not a cheek blanched, not a muscle quivered. There they stood with their knapsacks unslung and their belts tightened ready for the command 'Forward!' but the command came not, and for this reason Gen. Meade and this army have been censured."[13]

Moses Bliss, a Fairfield Academy classmate of *Journal* editor, J.R. Stebbins and a member of the elite 44th New York, questioned Meade's strategy in the Mine Run campaign. Bliss began his letter to Stebbins by criticizing his commander, but as the letter continued on, the indomitable spirit of the common soldier emerged. Bliss wrote:

> "Our last grand movement over the Rapidan and back is a thing of mystery to me. If it was made simply to attract Lee's attention and prevent re-enforcements from being sent to the Southwest [Chattanooga] it may have been a success. If it was to fight the enemy wherever he could find him, it was a failure. True we found the enemy but we did not attack him. With a slight alteration, Gen. Meade might have adopted the laconic dispatch of an ancient General. Thus amended it would read, veni, vidi, refugi. Gen. Meade's seven day's campaign across the Rapidan will hardly become as notorious as Gen. Hooker's nine day's [Chancellorsville]. Both resulted in

finding the army on its old ground again. In the one case we lost thousands, in the other hundreds. In the one we dared fight, in the other, not. Still the most zealous can hardly regret the failure to fight. It is cosy sitting around a warm fire, to imagine and say what ought to have been done, but let one lie on the frozen ground for hours while on picket or in bivouac as we did, and he will not much regret the loss of a chance of lying wounded on the field of battle. Winter is not the time to fight; Summer is the time. Give us the men the President has just called for and we will show you a campaign next summer worth the telling about." [14]

Bliss wrote the letter while recuperating from a gunshot wound to his right hand, taken while on picket at Mine Run.

As President Lincoln's day of thanksgiving passed and autumn turned to winter, the attention of the people of Herkimer County was drawn from their local boys, now safely in their winter camps, to the possibility of another draft.

Back in October, President Lincoln had issued a call for three hundred thousand men to fill gaps in the regiments already in the field. As with the mid-summer call, the Federal government didn't assign official state quotas, but made it clear that if the requisite number of men did not volunteer, a draft would transpire.

Learning from mistakes made in the summer draft, new rules were formulated for this and future drafts. The most notable and most logical of the rule changes permitted men to file for both "physical" and "family" exemptions prior to a draft. The pointless action of drafting men who would immediately request and receive exemptions, was remedied by this change.

Two other proposals: drafting from the "second class" pool of men, made by the *Washington Chronicle*, and exemptions for men with prior service, made by Provost Marshal, Gen. James Fry, were not acted upon.

In mid-December, the *Journal* obtained a list of the approximate New York State mandated quotas for each of Herkimer County's villages and towns from county Enrollment Board member, F.S. Wilcox of Mohawk. Wilcox's information, which was supplied by District Provost Marshal Emerson, gave the total quota for Herkimer County as six hundred and twelve men.

To avoid the ignominy of a draft, an effort to raise volunteers, that was reminiscent of the recruiting days of the fall of 1862, was begun. The system of township bounties was revived, with each of the communities offering, on the average, $300 to volunteers. As in 1862, the *Journal* expounded on the advantages of volunteering. In speaking of Little Falls, a *Journal* article stated:

> "The proper action has been taken by the Town Officers, the notes have been signed by our most responsible citizens and, we believe, the money is now ready for the prompt payment of a bounty of $300 from the town of Little Falls to every resident who may enlist under the recent call and be accepted. A respectable and united effort will raise our town quota and free us from the coming draft. . . . There is every inducement now to volunteer that men can ask—extravagantly large bounties, the prospect of an increase

in pay by act of Congress to $25 per month for privates [pay did not increase, remaining at $13 per month] the moral certainty that but one more triumphant effort is needed to crush out the rebellion, and the hardships of the draft. The volunteer receives his large bounty*, has the privilege to select his branch of service and his regiment, and a better opinion of himself than the conscript who gets nothing but his monthly pay [conscripts could still collect Federal and State bounties], and is taken to whatever position and service the authorities may prefer." [15]

The offer of township bounties, combined with the efforts of recruiters from the 16th New York Heavy Artillery and the 1st New York Light Artillery, led to enlistments in numbers that would soon satisfy the quotas. Although the second draft in Herkimer County had not yet formally been announced, all those men that volunteered now would be deducted from the quotas when the draft became official.

As the Christmas season passed and 1863 came to an end, the people of Herkimer County looked optimistically toward 1864. The defeats at Chancellorsville and Chickamauga had been more than balanced by the fall of Vicksburg and Chattanooga and by Lee's repulse at Gettysburg. The 34th was back home, the 97th (at Gettysburg) and the 121st (at Rappahannock Station) had won Herkimer County men great honors, and the 152nd was now ready to show its worth. With the entire length of the Mississippi now in Union hands and the shrinking Confederacy split asunder, 1864 would surely see the end of the rebellion.

* $102 Federal bounty, $75 New York State bounty.

CHAPTER XIV

"I have staked my all
in favor of Union and Freedom"

*Winter 1863/1864 - Winter Quarters - Herkimer County Winter
Letters to the Journal*

After their withdrawal from Mine Run, the 152nd New York halted midway between Brandy Station and Stevensburg, Virginia, and established their winter quarters. The camp, dubbed Cold Hill, was situated in a large oak grove atop a gentle slope. At the base of the hill ran a small stream called Mountain Run, which although almost a mile distant from the camp, served as the regiment's chief water supply.

Even though the oak trees held the lumber necessary to build huts, for want of axes, hatchets and nails, the 152nd spent their first few weeks at Camp Cold Hill in shelter tents. Fortunately, the regimental sutler was able to obtain the needed tools and nails, and before cold weather set in, the oak grove vanished and crude huts sprang up. Patterned after the design of the veteran regiments encamped nearby, the typical shanty built by the men of the 152nd was six feet by ten feet with a fireplace and door at one end and bunks at the other. Shelter tents were used as roofs to complete the structures which were intended to accommodate four men.

With the oak grove gone, firewood was obtained from a forest one mile from camp. Each day three men from Co. B were detailed to chop wood for the regiment, hauling it back to camp with the aid of the trusty army mule.

The 121st New York set up their winter quarters a few miles east of Brandy Station on a fork of land between the Hazel and Rappahannock Rivers. Located in a hickory and white oak grove that covered fifteen acres, the camp of the 121st was about three miles north of that of the 152nd.

After building their requisite huts, the men further improved their camp by constructing a corduroy sidewalk that fronted their homes. Visitors to the camp of the 121st remarked that it was the prettiest and best laid out encampment in the Army of the Potomac.

While confined to their winter camp the men of the 121st managed quite well. Isaac Best related:

> "Soon after our return from Mine Run, we got nicely and comfortably fixed in camp, and whenever the weather permitted, some duty or drill was the order of the day to keep the men occupied and fit. Our mails came regularly, and sutlers had an abundant supply of all sorts of good things. An amusement hall was built and an amateur troop gave interesting entertainments. Checkers, chess and cards were favorite amusements in camp, and the festive and alluring game of poker, though forbidden, was extensively engaged in, the stakes being small on account of the scarcity of money. Many of our wounded and sick were returned to the regiment and it began to look like the old time solid battalion of the preceding winter. Boxes of good things from home made life pleasant and cheerful, and camp life in winter quarters was voted by all the best thing yet in army life."[1]

Adjacent to the camps of the 121st and the 152nd, sat Brandy Station, which during the winter of 1863/1864 served as the distribution center for the Army Corps encamped in the vicinity. Situated at the terminus of the Federal supply line, the small once quiet village was transformed into a bustling community of sutler's shacks and warehouses. Being in such close proximity to thousands of soldiers, it attracted the bored men like a magnet. George Eaton of Little Falls described a visit to the "Station":

> "It is quite a sight to see Brandy Station, the depot of the supplies of the Army of the Potomac. Persons of almost any trade are improving the time by making money from the soldiers. There you will see a sign over the door of a little board shanty 'Oysters,' 'Fresh Fish,' 'Condensed Milk,' 'Beer,' and numerous other signs which tempt the pocket book of the soldier, and out it comes and away goes his money—careless how he spends it, but enjoys it nevertheless. At all times there are a great many army wagons traveling up with forage and commissary stores, express boxes and clothing, which creates quite a lively appearance, as they go in and out. It is quite interesting to persons who have never been in the army to see the heaps of hardtack and salt pork piled up ready to be conveyed to the regiments. It makes a soldier think of the time to come when soft bread is out of the question, of the weary march when a hard-tack is a very delicious morsel to a hungry soldier. About 3 o'clock p.m., the news boy comes along crying, 'New York Herald, Washington Chronicle, Baltimore American', and so on, which please all in hearing, who are generally very anxious to hear the news: 5 cents per paper is the price."[2]

The third Mohawk Valley regiment, the 97th New York, crossed the Rappahannock at Kelly's Ford on December 4th and went into camp about one mile north of the ford. Log huts were built as winter quarters and the next two weeks were spent on picket duty along the river. Orders were received on December 22nd for the 97th to move their camp one mile to the east. Working on their new quarters that day and spending the night at their old camp, the men had almost completed their new shanties when orders came for the regiment to move to Brandy Station.

The 97th reached Brandy Station on Christmas Eve, and the tired soldiers quickly set up their tents on a piece of low level ground. A rainstorm that night turned the bivouack area into a small lake and the men spent Christmas Day trying to stay dry on small islands of land. Colonel Wheelock scouted the countryside for a more suitable site and on December 28th the regiment moved once more. Almost before the shelter tents were erected, orders came to leave and on New Years Eve the 97th marched to Cedar Mountain. Thinking that this location must finally be their site for winter quarters, trees were felled and shanties began to go up. But before the huts were completed, the dreaded orders to move came once more and the 97th marched to Culpeper, about seven miles west of Brandy Station. Thankfully, the exhausted and frustrated men of the 97th were finally allowed to settle into their quarters for the remainder of the winter. The "Third Oneida" left three vacant sets of winter camps strewn along the serpentine twenty mile path from Kelly's Ford to Culpeper.

Unlike the wandering 97th, the 121st and 152nd were able to enjoy Christmas and New Year's Day snugly in their camps. For the benefit of the people back home in Herkimer County, Sgt. Lester Baum of the 121st and Pvt. Charles Decker of the 152nd described the boy's holidays. Danube's Sergeant Baum wrote:

> "Our Merry Christmas is enjoyed in various ways, according to the tastes and habits of men. Today seems to be a day of recreation of the privates, for I believe the officers had theirs yesterday and day before, an example not to be followed by us, partly because our rations of Commissary [whiskey] are missing and mostly because a private is arrested and often strung up to a tree if found drunk. But it is a blessing that as a body we are not allowed free access to that which intoxicates and makes men appear so silly. And would that our superiors might set us an example that would shield us from all punishment.
>
> Night before last we were visited by Gen. Bartlett and Staff, who made a speech upon our conduct under him, also congratulating the officers and men upon the Brigadiership of which he recently received his commission. And today the men have had dealt to them a barrel of Ale, given to each regiment in the Brigade, as a Christmas present by him, which is very much appreciated by us, although a small allowance.
>
> The men are all cheerful and are being entertained in different ways. Our Brigade Band is now playing between our Company and Headquarters while some of the boys have created quite a crowd and laughter by sparring with the boxing gloves, owned in Co. A." [3]

While Private Decker of Little Falls reported:

> "Perhaps you would like to know how we passed what you call at home 'Merry Christmas.' Well, I will tell you. As I said before, we moved in our shanty on Christmas and the same morning Wilson received a box from

home, containing everything in the shape of eatables that a body could wish. For breakfast we had beefsteak coffee, bread and butter, fried cakes, cheese, apple-sauce, and a few hardtacks by way of variety. At dinner we ate lightly on frosted and fruit cake and peach preserves. Next came supper. Bill of fare, please read: Tea, bread and butter, beefsteak, sausage, fried eggs, frosted fruit, jellied and fried cakes, peach, cherry and plum preserves and cheese." [4]

But not all of the men of the army were able to enjoy the holidays as did the boys of the 121st and 152nd. For those men on picket duty or like the 97th on the march, the Christmas season brought little cheer. Moses Bliss of Salisbury, a member of the 44th New York, related the sentiments of those men unable to participate in the holiday festivities. Bliss, in a letter to the *Journal*, wrote:

"Holidays are like Sabbaths, we have none in the army. One day is like another and different not in duty. We remember that the day is being kept somewhere, but to us it only serves as a period to mark off the time we have been or still are to remain soldiers. We sit down to our meal of hardtack and coffee, and think of the feasts at home, of the circle around the family hearth stone, of the friends we have left behind us: and all idea or desire of pleasure or hilarity fades from our mind. So it becomes a day of sorrow instead of joy." [5]

As winter wore on, the drudgery of standing guard and picket duty, cutting wood, building corduroy roads and drilling caused the men to seek other diversions. Debating societies and glee clubs formed, band concerts were held and with the weather remaining mild, baseball games between regiments were played. But in this Winter of 1864, overshadowing all else, a great religious revival was sweeping the camps of both the blue and the gray.

The Christian Commission, an association of Northern clergymen concerned with the men's spiritual health, had been ever present in the camps, handing out religious tracts, preaching and helping out in the hospitals. This winter the commission increased its involvement with the men by detailing clergymen to the camps. Chapels were built, nightly prayer meetings were held, and regular Sunday services were conducted.

Among the "missionaries" sent to the camps was Rev. W.L. Tisdale, pastor of the Methodist-Episcopal Church of Little Falls. Reverend Tisdale, who preached in the camps from Bristow to Brandy Station, visited the camps of the 97th and the 121st and wrote home of the well-being of the hometown boys. Stopping at Warrenton Junction, Reverend Tisdale, with the help of two assistants, set up a large chapel tent capable of holding almost three hundred men. Overjoyed by the number of men that attended his services and their enthusiasm, Tisdale wrote:

"From the very first service to the present time, our chapel has been crowded at nearly every meeting. We have been received most cordially by both officers and men. We have preaching twice on the Sabbath and two or three evenings during the week: the other evenings we hold prayer meetings. Religiously, this is a most interesting field. I never saw men so attentive to preaching. Scores, if not hundreds, at this station are seeking the

Savior, and many are rejoicing in the great salvation. We find the greatest
encouragement in our work."[6]

The two great armies facing each other did not remain wholly static in their
winter quarters. Although the unpredictable weather and poor road conditions dis-
couraged active campaigning, each of the armies sent out frequent reconnaissance
expeditions. Ranging in size from a regiment to a whole corps, detachments were
ordered out to find the enemy and to "develop" his troop strength and position.

Typically upon reaching the enemy's line, skirmishers would be sent out to engage the enemy's pickets. By observing the pickets' reactions—did they hold their
position or did they fall back—the commander of the reconnaissance force could
gauge the troop strength behind the picket line. With this information, headquarters
could better estimate the enemy's troop movements and if necessary move its own
men to counter an enemy threat. Usually, after a brief firefight, the reconnoitering
force would withdraw back to its camp.

In the Winter of 1864, the 97th New York and the 152nd New York would each
take part in just this sort of expedition.

On February 2nd, the 97th, with the rest of its brigade, was ordered out to Raccoon Ford on the Rapidan River. A rebel probe had penetrated the Union picket line
and the 1st Corps boys were hustled forward to halt the enemy advance. Taking up
position behind artillery and cavalry units, the men watched as cannon fire and repeated cavalry charges stopped the Confederate incursion. The 97th bivouacked at
the ford for a few days afterwards to make certain that the enemy did not repeat their
raid. On February 6th, the 97th returned to their winter quarters. No men were lost
to the "Third Oneida" on this mission.

On the same day that the 97th returned to camp, the 152nd New York left their
quarters at Cold Hill and moved out on a Federal "scouting" expedition. Two divisions of the 2nd Corps and General Kilpatrick's cavalry were detailed to the reconnaissance. After crossing the Rapidan at Ely's and Morton's Fords, the Union
columns were confronted by a large rebel force a short distance from the river. Light
skirmishing quickly developed into a full fledged fight. The outnumbered Federals
held their own on the first day, but as additional rebel troops came up, the 2nd Corps
retreated back across the Rapidan. Edward Townsend of the 152nd described the two
day expedition:

> "It was last Saturday morning, at half past four, that the inharmonious
> and unwelcome notes of early 'reveille' broke upon our slumbering senses,
> and directly after this serenade around came our quarter-master and
> sergeant-major, politely informing us that our regiment was to be in line at
> half past six, and that extra baggage must be packed up and left in our tents,
> ready to move at a moment's notice.
>
> Breakfast being hastily swallowed, knapsacks packed, and with three
> day's rations of 'hard tack' and salt pork, the regiment fell into line and soon
> was on its way to someplace. The morning was cloudy and everything por-
> tended rain, a fact which filled many a soldier's heart with a vain hope that
> the order might be countermanded.
>
> Soon the whole corps was under way, and straight the troops started for

the historical Rapidan. The river was speedily reached and there being no bridge across the ford and the pontoons not having arrived, the 3d division of our corps crossed, wading up to their waists in the cold 'damp' water. Skirmishers were immediately deployed and promptly charged upon a stone fence behind which were a number of the 'Johnnies' and our boys succeeded in capturing a small number of them. It appears they were a 'picket guard' and had only a few moments previous relieved the old sentries.

After the 3d Division had successfully gained the opposite bank, a small bridge made of poles was thrown across, and later in the day, our Division, which is the 2nd, started to reinforce the gallant 3d, as the enemy were making very hostile demonstrations. Although the skirmishing had been very spirited and well contested on both sides, yet at this juncture the firing became very heavy: and the minie-balls and shells went whistling by, as though they were in something of a hurry. Although our troops could not use their 'big guns' with much effect, still the fire-arms came well in play, and the result was, the Union lads forced their way across the roaring Rapidan: then the fight became quite fierce and sanguinary;-both parties trying for signal triumph-the Rebs endeavoring to gain the ford and cut off the retreat of the 3d Division, while our Division was striving to defeat their purpose. They were obliged to fall back, and get behind their entrenchments. But most, and we may say all of this scene was enacted after sunset, and darkness soon coming on, the men could not well see their foes, and had to be guided by the flashes of their muskets.

As we stated the Union troops held their own, and the enemy's also: but the Rebs receiving reinforcements, our boys in the eloquent language of soldiers, had to hastily 'dig out' and recross the river about two o'clock in the morning.

Daylight speedily broke forth, and instead of skirmishing with the Rebs, as on the day previous, our troops lay still until night; then the orders came, to return to camp, which the Regiment reached about nine that same night, tired and worn with heavy fatigue, though only two days out. The weather during that time was very disagreeable: raining constantly.

Of course, what sleep or rest the men did obtain, we had upon the damp ground, and that with wet clothes as a covering. But even under these difficulties and discomforts, there was much cheerfulness and good feeling throughout the entire ranks. The casualties upon our side, were, according to official report, two hundred and four wounded, and ten or twelve killed. It is reasonably estimated that the loss of the enemy was not so severe as our own."[7]

The 152nd suffered no casualties on the "Rapidan Expedition."

Throughout January and February, the weather of the Virginia "winter" rivaled that of an upstate New York summer. During an extended period in February, afternoon temperatures ranged from a comfortable sixty degrees to a downright sultry one hundred and six degrees. Except for two cold snaps and some intermittent rain and snow showers, the weather remained relatively dry and quite mild throughout most of the season.

The temperate weather, along with experience gained from past winter quarters in the field, resulted in a comparatively sickness-free winter for the veterans of the 97th and the 121st. Two men from the 121st did succumb to illness, but at most of the morning roll calls no men answered the sick call.

The situation was much different in the 152nd. Unattuned to the rigors of the field, disease took hold of many men in the regiment and rapidly spread in the close quarters of the little winter huts. Typhoid, dysentery, pneumonia, and other diseases visited the relative rookies of the 152nd and put them through a trial most of the other regiments had already faced.

John Ingraham of the 121st, after a visit to the camp of the 152nd, wrote:

> "There is a good many of the 152nd boys sick. They have lost six by
> disease and their hospital is crammed full now and a great many of them
> are not expected to survive." [8]

Those men in the 152nd that died at Camp Cold Hill were rolled up in blankets and buried in shallow graves at the foot of the slope.

During their stay in winter quarters, the 152nd underwent two organizational changes. Col. Alonzo Ferguson, who had been in poor health for many months, resigned his commission. George Thompson was promoted to colonel, and command of the regiment passed to him.

The 152nd also was moved from the 1st Brigade of the 2nd Division of the 2nd Corps to the 2nd Brigade of the same division. The 152nd New York was now brigaded with the 69th, 71st, 72nd and 106th Pennsylvania and the 1st California.

The winter of 1864 was marked by a significant infusion of new men into the thinned ranks of the field regiments. Unlike the past when replacements came south in the form of entire new regiments, now the new recruits were being fitted into existing units. Placing the raw men under the tutelage of battle-hardened veterans and experienced officers prepared the rookie soldiers for the hardships of the field much better than any training camp could.

Each of the Mohawk Valley regiments was the recipient of hundreds of these new men. The 121st and 152nd each gained almost three hundred men, while the 97th acquired over five hundred new members. In each case the majority of the conscripts and substitutes were supplied by New York State's larger cities—particularly Buffalo and New York City—while the volunteers came from Herkimer, Otsego and Oneida counties. The efforts of Captain Fish and Sergeant Timmerman of the 121st and Major Curtis of the 152nd—who operated out of recruiting offices in the Benton House in Little Falls—resulted in most of the volunteers that enlisted in the Mohawk Valley regiments.

Although most of the conscripts and substitutes would faithfully serve their country until war's end, each regiment received men either unwilling or unfit for service. From this class of men, the 97th was the recipient of one of the more obvious versions. The 97th's new soldier was quite unhappy with his lot and was seemingly afflicted with every bodily disorder known to man. Hoping to be released from duty, the forlorn soldier wrote a letter to Secretary of War Stanton requesting a discharge. Somehow the *Journal* came into possession of the soldier's letter and published it under the title, "Oh Dear! Oh Dear!" The letter, with numerous grammatical and spelling corrections made to make it more readable, read:

> "dear sir. I now take this oppurtunity to inform you of the facks of my
> condition to see if I can find one man that will do justus by me. Last fall I
> was drafted and when I was notifide I had not been able to do any thing and
> had not in three months on the count of rumittism and for the last three
> wekks I have not been able to dress my feet on the count of bloating and
> swelling. I swell all over my body and my legs swell so that they busted by
> drawers all to pieces and get cold. I am the same I have not been able to do
> duty more than one third of the time since I have been in the servis and on
> about every march they have to carry me and the time we come hear I had
> to come in my sock foot and when I got to Culpeper their I stade all nite and
> the next day the dockter put me in the wagon and carried me the rest of the
> way and he said that he did not know that the cramping rennits were so bad
> before when I first got to the regament. They [would] have thrown me out
> on the count of my rite arm being stiff so that I could not sling my knapsack
> or open my cateridge box and still I am here. When I am in good health I
> way 185 and all I way now is 100 and 15 pounds and my apitite is so poor
> that it takes the most of my wages to buy a piece of bacon. I cant eat army
> rations. When my family needs it. These facks can be found out by the hole
> company or dr. Little or dr. Chambers. Now I hope that you will look into
> this and do justis.
> To Mr Stanton 97 Reg Co I new york volunteers in the care of Cornel
> Wheelock. Please rite as soon as you recieve." [9]

For obvious reasons the *Journal* did not disclose the poor soldier's name but noted; "Our readers in pitying his sad condition, will not fail to shed a tear over the wretched fate of his 'drawers.' "

In January and February the 97th Regiment realized an extra boost when almost two hundred of its veterans opted to re-enlist for "three years or the war." Although most of the "old guard" of the 97th still had one year to serve on their original enlistment, the army offered a thirty-five day furlough as an incentive for the men to "re-up" now. With the prospect of a visit home dangled in front of them and the certainty that the war could not possibly last much longer, it was not surprising that many of the veterans re-enlisted.

As winter headed toward spring, the manpower strength of the Mohawk Valley regiments was greater than it had been in a long time. In addition, the morale of the troops was high, due to the mildness of the winter and most importantly because of the prospect of serving under the army's dynamic new leader, Ulysses S. Grant. On March 9th, Grant, the conqueror of Fort Donelson and Vicksburg, and the savior of the trapped Union Army at Chattanooga, was promoted to a position last held by George Washington, lieutenant general. Three days later on March 12th, he was named General in Chief of the Armies of the United States and given the responsibility for the strategic direction of the war.

In Herkimer County the Winter of 1864, although not as harsh as the previous winter, was by no means temperate. Subfreezing temperatures struck the county well before Christmas and massive snowstorms after the first of the year delayed trains and clogged roadways. Ironically, the northern part of the county saw very little snow while the southern half was often buried under huge drifts.

As temperatures fell below zero, ponds, lakes, and the canal were transformed into ice skating rinks. On the icy surfaces young gentlemen "cut their figures" as pretty misses coyly looked on. In Utica, large crowds of skaters were attracted to the well-manicured rink at Excelsior Park, but this winter they were all white. Early in the skating season the park's managers issued a notice that Excelsior Park was designated for whites only and was "off limits" for Blacks. As to this ordinance the *Utica Herald* opined:

> "So colored folks are henceforth expected to understand that the 'Excelsior Park' is a white folks' park and keep away from it. We believe Utica takes the lead in this new reform." [10]

Taking an opposite view of this law, the *Journal's* editor, J.R. Stebbins, responded:

> "We are ashamed for our Utica neighbor. The managers of the Park are gentlemanly and attentive to their patrons and visitors, . . . but in this matter they have made a mistake, which, although perhaps satisfactory to 'certain respectable patrons' is opposed to the good sense and doubtless to the wishes of the great masses of those who skate." [11]

With the cold weather overworking fireplaces, stoves and furnaces, the danger of fires increased. The *Journal* reminded their readers to use caution when disposing of ashes and to inspect their stove and chimney pipes. Nevertheless, numerous fires flared in Herkimer County overworking the hose companies. Fortunately none of the conflagrations were major and no lives were lost.

On New Year's Day, 1864, the *Herkimer County Journal* announced that it had bought out its crosstown rival, the *Mohawk Courier*, and henceforth the masthead of the paper would read, the *Herkimer County Journal and Courier*. Owner and editor, J.R. Stebbins, asked his seventeen hundred subscribers to help enroll three hundred additional subscribers so that the paper could put on a "new face" through the purchase of new type, "rules" and press machinery.

Among the items carried that winter, the *Journal*, (as it was still most familiarly known), were:

. . . Mr. Louis Ransom of Salisbury had invented a new process of propelling street cars by means of "condensed air." Ransom's "air car" input fifteen thousand pounds of compressed air to the vehicle's crankshaft which translated five thousand pounds of force to the wheels. Ransom, who was well known in the area for his painting of the "John Brown Picture," was seeking investors to put up the capital for further developmental work.

. . . The semi-annual dividend of the Herkimer County Bank was announced as being 4%.

. . . A project was afoot to build a "horse railroad" between Mohawk and Ilion. The enterprise was being highly touted as a favorable method of public transportation and looked to be a profitable investment.

. . . A new telegraph line was being strung along the "central thoroughfare." Reductions in telegram rates and prompter transmission of messages were expected. In addition, a branch line was planned to be run from Herkimer up through Middleville, Newport, Fairfield and Poland.

. . . The New York State Board of Regents announced grants of $613.70 to Little Falls Academy and $237.50 to Fairfield Academy. The annual grants were derived from revenues realized from the Regent's Literature Fund.

. . . "Dr. Maungwadaus" was back in Little Falls dispensing his line of health potions made from herbs and roots. The Indian medicine man had taken up residence at the home of Charles Scott on Gibraltar Street on the village's southside. The Chief's medicines purportedly could cure all manner of diseases and maladies, and now, for the first time, written instructions came with every bottle.

. . . A proposal to create the new township of Ilion was in front of the Herkimer County Board of Supervisors. Portions of German Flatts, Herkimer, Litchfield, Schuyler and Columbia would be used to form the town.

. . . DeWitt C. Pickett, of Mohawk, was arrested by Officer E.W. Partridge, of that village, for aiding deserters. Pickett was accused of harboring two deserters from the 152nd New York, Jacob and DeWitt Shoemaker of Mohawk. Of the Shoemaker brothers, the *Journal* noted:

> "It appeared that they were desperate fellows, and that DeWitt had deserted some four or five times. They were both arrested by officer Partridge about the last of December last, and were taken to Governor's Island, New York, by U.S. Agent Hubbard, of this city. They told officer Partridge they would escape again within three weeks, and threatened him with dire vengeance. It seems they did escape within nearly the time promised, at least Jacob did." [12]

The Shoemaker boys would be recaptured—DeWitt returning to the 152nd and Jacob being dishonorably discharged. DeWitt Pickett was brought before Commissioner Boyce in Utica, and was held on $500 bail for the May term of the U.S. Court in Rochester.

In early February the *Journal* published a human interest story that touched many of its readers. Under the title "A Child Abandoned by its Mother," the article read:

> "The family of Mr. A.C. Richlmyer, of Paine's Hollow, were startled by the cry of an infant on Sunday night last, and proceeding to the door they found a young child about ten days old on the door step. It was nearly frozen and would undoubtedly have perished had its discovery been long delayed. With it were several articles of clothing, a small bottle of milk, but no clue to its identity. Even beasts will cherish and protect their young, and a mother who will abandon her infant to the chances of death or accidental charity must not only be inhuman but even worse than beastly." [13]

The child's mother could not be found and the Richlmyers continued to care for the infant.

Valentine's Day came and the *Journal* noted, "the young people exchanged cards with pictures and verses on them, which did sad havoc among the hearts of lads and misses."

The newspaper also reported on the area's first bounty jumper:

> "A young man of this village [Little Falls] named Henry Keller has it is said absconded after enlisting in two or three localities and obtaining several hundred dollars in bounties. Taking with him, as partner pro tempore, 'Rosa' a woman of loose reputation, he leaves home and friends for the life of an outlaw and a deserter." [14]

One week later, after learning that Keller was actually serving with an unnamed regiment and wasn't a deserter, the *Journal* printed a retraction. The *Journal* article, which neglected to apologize to the young man, read:

> "We are informed that the notice given of Henry Keller in last week's number was incorrect, and that he is now with his company at Elmira and has neither enlisted in two or three localities nor 'run away with any woman.'
>
> We published the report as it had been given 'on the street' uncontradicted, for several days and are glad to hear that it is not true." [15]

During the Winter of 1864, the readers of the *Journal* were treated not only to the usual correspondence from the Mohawk Valley boys quartered in Virginia, but also could follow the exploits of Herkimer County men removed from the war's mainstream.

In December, the 97th's Lt. Col. John Spofford, captured six months before at Gettysburg, wrote to J.R. Stebbins from his cell in Richmond's Libby Prison. Spofford's letter read:

> "I send you this to give you a little insight in regard to our manner of living in and around Richmond. In this, the 'Libby,' are nine hundred officers: across the street in another 'Hotel' are eighteen hundred of our men: three rods from that is another with twelve hundred more: still beyond that are others of like description, prisons for our men. Castle Thunder is on the opposite side, containing about fifteen hundred, chiefly political prisoners and deserters. In this building we occupy six rooms: forty-five by one hundred feet, and one hundred and fifty prisoners to each room. We sleep on the floor and sit on the floor, except when we have received boxes and barrels to make temporary seats. We have now two blankets each, one furnished by the U.S. Sanitary Commission and the other by the Rebs, which comprise our bed and bedding. For rations we get about twelve ounces of corn bread (flour is $100 to $125 per barrel and not to be had in quantity sufficient to feed us) two thirds of a gill of rice, no meat (the Rebs told us yesterday that they could not get meat for us) in lieu thereof to-day they gave us one or two sweet potatoes, according to size. Most of the officers have received boxes from home and manage to get along. But with our men it is very different, especially those on 'Belle Isle' [a Confederate prison for

enlisted men in the James River at Richmond], many of whom are without coats, shirts, shoes, stockings, blankets or even shelter, and hundreds of them die from starvation and exposure. It is but a few nights since fifteen were brought from the Island to the hospital, in the room below us, and the next morning nine of them were carried out in coffins: one of them actually died while trying to eat a crust of bread. Our Government has sent on clothing and blankets (which are not being distributed) and I think is doing everything it can to make them comfortable. Many of the men express a willingness to remain here as long as it is for the interest of the government that they should. We are surrounded by a very strong guard which has been doubled within a few days past. They seem to be aware that their liberty is at the price of eternal vigilance, still if our folks make a demonstration, as we expect, they may wake up some fine morning and find themselves without city.

We are allowed to purchase from the city markets and our purchases amount to over $1000 per day, at the following prices: Butter $9 to $10 per lb; sugar $8 to $10 per lb; tea $14 to $20 per lb; flour $1 per lb; bacon $2 1/2 to $3 per lb; corn meal $1 per qt; potatoes $1 per qt; molasses $4 per qt; apples 5 to 10 for $1; very inferior letter paper 2 sheets and 4 envelopes for $1, and all other things in proportion. We hear that our surgeons have been exchanged and are to leave here in a day or two. We are in hopes it will be our turn soon. One reason for articles costing us so much is because there are two speculators between us and the market." [16]

On February 9th, Spofford and one hundred and eight of his fellow inmates escaped from Libby Prison by way of a tunnel built by Col. Thomas Rose and his cohorts. Over one half of the escapees eventually made their way to freedom but Spofford was among the forty-eight men recaptured and returned to Libby.

The *Journal* also received two letters from "Fred Mason," a man unfamiliar to most residents of Herkimer County. Preceding the second letter, the *Journal* provided a background on Mason:

"We were given extracts from two letters written by this colored gentlemen [Fred Mason] to Mr. Palmer Vincent, of this town [Little Falls]. About two years ago he escaped from slavery and hired to Mr. V. to work on the farm. He could not read, much less write, knew nothing of the value of figures and was in fact, one of the most ignorant of his race and class. But he had that within him which would not and did not permit him long to remain in this condition. With a little help from the family, he mastered the alphabet and soon was able to read rapidly and well. In a short time he had mastered a complete file of the National Era which he brought down from the garret, devouring with avidity every item relating to the early history of his race and of the nation. After a few months residence with Mr. Vincent and a short stay in Massachusetts he enlisted in the Union Navy and has done noble service in the cause of Freedom. To-day finds him a scholar, a clear thinker, a ready writer. Few young men who have spent their lives at school can boast a more easy style or wield a more vigorous or powerful pen. The following letter is taken almost verbatim from his manuscript which he could not read and scarcely understand two short years ago. Who shall say that the black man may not occupy a higher place among the people of the earth!" [17]

Fred Mason was doing duty as a deckhand on the "USS Seminole," an armed steam sloop in the Western Squadron blockading Sabine Pass, Texas. In his letters to Palmer Vincent, addressed to "My True Friends," Mason described the life of a seamen and gave the people of Herkimer County a glimpse of the war through a black man's eyes. In Mason's first letter he wrote:

> "I have staked my all in favor of Union and Freedom, and I cannot turn back until they are above the reach of their enemies, for us from the grave of old John Brown, up from the graves of the thousands that have fallen, up from the grave of the gallant and noble Fred Ford [a member of the 121st, from Fairfield, killed at Salem Church], comes the cry to me, fight for your country and your race until the end. As soon as my time expires I shall ship again, and will stand by the country until every inch of her soil is taken from the rebels—until that old flag that fills your hearts with memories sweet and endless, is honored and respected by those who dishonor it now: until our evening bugles play our national tunes in every port from the Rio Grande to the Sunrise State [Florida].
>
> You do not know the hardships we are passing through, and the trials we have to encounter: with the rebels to watch upon one hand, with blockade runners to chase, the storms of the ocean to contend with, and no friendly port to run into—prepared for a fight night or day—I tell you it comes hard, but mind you, I do not speak of it because I am sorry to be here, no,—no,—it is the price of Liberty, and I accept it willingly, thanking God for the opportunity." [18]

Mason's second letter was written from New Orleans, where the "Seminole" had been ordered to participate in a show of force while a vote for Louisiana's re-admission to the Union was taken. Under President Lincoln's "Ten Percent Plan," a seceding state would be considered for re-admission if ten percent of that state's voters affirmed their loyalty to the Union and its laws. The requisite number of loyal votes was garnered in Louisiana, and the state was re-admitted to the Union in the early part of 1865.

Granted shore leave, Mason, who had last entered New Orleans as a slave, described the scene:

> "We reached, not the city of slave owners and man stealers of 1860, but this city of free men of 1864. Sabbath afternoon the Commander of the flag-ship Pensacola visited us. We were all mustered before him. He paid us a high compliment for our fidelity to our Commander and the Union. We all have a little vanity you know, and when men feel that they have done, and are still ready to do their whole duty, it is rather pleasant to hear the words, well done, fall from the lips of these old sons of the ocean. Monday morning, Feb. 22d, bright and early, we trimmed our ship with flags. At sunrise the reports of our guns told the inhabitants of this city that the true defenders of the Union were honoring the day that gave birth to him who laid its foundation [George Washington].
>
> At nine o'clock the order came for all to dress and spend the day on

shore. After six months afloat we were not long in obeying that order I can assure you. . . .

It was at 10 o'clock Monday when 112 of us left the ship for the shore, where we were separated into different parcels, each bent upon pleasure. With five of my companies, four white and one colored, all natives of the old State and noble fellows too, I started for the 8th ward where the solid business men of New Orleans were throwing their votes to Freedom. Last Monday was the greatest day that the men of Louisiana have ever seen. When Farragut came here with the old flag flying at his mast head, it was then that he struck the blow that brought this day and secured the State for the Union: and upon the evening of Washington's birth day, as the Sun was twinkling and playing in the western sky, the shout went up that Louisiana was redeemed and regenerated.

What I saw and heard that day proved to me that God had decreed that slavery shall end, and it is not in the power of living man to change that decree. As I stood upon the side walk among my companions, within fifty feet of one of those slave-pens, where in other days my people were bought and sold, and saw the same men that have bought and sold men, women and children, marching boldly up to the ballot-box to vote for freedom and Union, the thoughts that flew through my brain, the feeling of joy that played around my heart, I must leave you to define, for I cannot wield a pen powerful enough to describe them to you. All that I can say is in the language of old Horace Greely, 'the world does move.' " [19]

The people of Herkimer County were also able to follow the achievements of Wells Sponable, the former major of the old 34th New York. Sponable had not mustered out with the regiment, but transferred to the 15th U.S. Infantry Regiment of the Veteran Reserve Corps. Appointed Inspector General of Prisons, Sponable was assigned to Camp Douglas on the southside of Chicago. Camp Douglas, a former training center, now served as one of the larger Federal prisoner of war camps.

An article, complimentary of Sponable's supervision of Camp Douglas, was published in the *Chicago Journal* and reprinted in the *Herkimer County Journal*. The article stated:

"The post of honor occupied by Capt. Sponable in charge of the police in the prison square, is one of eternal vigilance. The 2nd Kentucky regiment, Morgan's men [members of Gen. John Hunt Morgan's Confederate cavalry raiders captured in July 1863], is composed of doctors, lawyers and students who felt exceedingly restive under their seclusion from the delight's of modern society. This squad keeps the Captain and his assistants constantly on the look out to prevent their taking long walks beyond the precincts of the camp. The Captain has an eye like a hawk, and is not easily caught napping. Last week he had a suspicion amounting to conviction that 'digging out' was underway somewhere. He passed several sleepless nights in watching, but failed to discern the leaks. At last, however, a few nights since, a prisoner ran suddenly, about one o'clock, from the kitchen to his barracks, and it was discovered that the ashes in the fireplace had just been disturbed. Here was something surely. On removing the ashes, the Captain discovered a board, and under the board some one had been digging down, preparatory to a new tunnel to the fence, about fifteen feet which would have soon poured out scores of these chevaliers d'industrie, much to the sorrow of their Uncle Samuel, who is willing to board the nephews, while they are completing their education in loyalty at his college: filled up especially for them, without regard to expense.

Another mode was tried by a wealthy prisoner—and one which really seemed quite plausible—to effect his escape with nine of his Confederates. It was in the offer of a check on New York for ten thousand dollars, if the Captain would wink at their escape. The gentleman thought it was hard that those who owned so much property in the South should be confined here so long. But he had mistaken his man. Captain Sponable gave him a rebuke he will not soon forget. He was assured that there was not money enough in the Confederacy to effect that yet, and that if he tried to escape he would find his brains pretty well scattered." [20]

As usual, Herkimer County itself was the scene of war related activity. Col. Hiram Berdan, commander of the 1st Regiment, U.S. Sharpshooters, better known as Berdan's Sharpshooters, spent the early part of winter with his family at Osgood's Hotel in Ilion. The purpose of Berdan's visit was to superintend construction of three breech loading guns of his own design, a carbine, musket and rifle, at the Remington's arms factory.

Ladies Aid societies continued to knit clothes and quilts, make lint and can fruits and vegetables in their local groups. Supervision of the Herkimer County township societies was now centralized under the direction of Mrs. Seth Richmond of Little Falls. Mrs. Richmond, whose husband was the county sheriff and the owner of a paper mill, had been president of the Little Falls Ladies Aid Society since the war's inception. Appointed by the Sanitary Commission to act as a mediator between the commission and the Herkimer County aid groups, Mrs. Richmond transmitted the commission's needs to the local ladies and directed the shipments of goods to the Sanitary Commission's New York City headquarters. To Mrs. Richmond's query as to the commission's requirements this winter, Laura Ormieux, Secretary of the Sanitary Commission, wrote from New York City:

> "In answer to the inquiry as to what is most needed, I might almost say everything: for the very thing of which we had so much that we thought we ought to sell it, and put the money in shirts and drawers, namely old cotton, and linen rags, has been so much asked for at the West, that we have sent 90 barrels of it out to Louisville. I send you, however, our new list of supplies needed. Things come in now a little more plentiful, and we hope much from more distribution of printed matter." [21]

In response to Miss Ormieux's request, Mrs. Richmond forwarded a box of "delicacies" from Miss Southworth's Bible Class of Little Falls, a quantity of dried apples from Mr. Simms of Newville, plus a keg of pickles, second hand clothing, lint and bandages collected from the area Ladies Aid Societies.

On February 1st, President Lincoln upped his October call from three hundred thousand to five hundred thousand men and set a draft for deficiencies to be held on

March 10th. By mid-February most of the Herkimer County towns had already either filled their quotas or were very close to doing so and by draft day the county had supplied the requisite six hundred and twelve men.The task had been accomplished through the offering of town bounties, by vigorous recruiting from officers of the 121st and 152nd, and by the threat of the draft itself. March 10th came and once again the draft wheel turned in Watertown, but no Herkimer County tickets were in the drum.

However, four days later President Lincoln issued another call for two hundred thousand men and set the draft date for April 15th. After an all too brief rest Herkimer County's recruiting machine cranked up once more. The quota set for the county under this call was for six hundred and seventy-nine men.

Although the whole draft process was becoming tiresome, the people of Herkimer County believed the one last push needed to crack the Confederacy was in the offing. No nonsense, hard-driving, "Unconditional Surrender" Grant was now leading the boys and with the massive army that he had to work with, the war should be over this summer.

CHAPTER XV

"With a cheer and a yell, like fiends incarnate, we rush forward"

Spring 1864 - Grant Takes Command
The Wilderness - Spotsylvania

The plan formulated by Ulysses S. Grant to end the rebellion was directed at a target quite different than that of the Union army's former commanders. Whereas McDowell, McClellan, Burnside, Hooker and Meade all were caught up in the "On to Richmond" obsession of the government and the people of the North, Grant focused his attention on the destruction of the rebel armies. Grant reasoned that the Confederate States would remain viable no matter where their political capital was located but that the heart of the rebellion would be cut out with the loss of the rebel's armed strength. To this purpose he directed his top two generals, William T. Sherman in the West, and George Meade in the East, to engage the forces opposing them in a struggle to the death. With a two to one manpower advantage on both fronts, Grant was more than prepared to fight a war of attrition and as circumstances developed, the contest evolved into just that. Before too long the Northern press would be changing Grant's nickname from "Unconditional Surrender Grant" to "the Butcher."

Leaving the details of dealing with Joe Johnston's army in Georgia to Sherman, Grant directed his energies on the key rebel force, Robert E. Lee's Army of Northern Virginia. Although Meade was retained as titular head of the Army of the Potomac, and supervised its day to day activities, Grant took hands on control of its movements. To add further weight to his thrust against Lee, Grant ordered Ben Butler's Army of the James, at City Point, to menace Richmond from the south and Franz Sigel's Army of West Virginia to march through the Shenandoah Valley. All of these movements, including that of Sherman in the west, were to be coordinated to com-

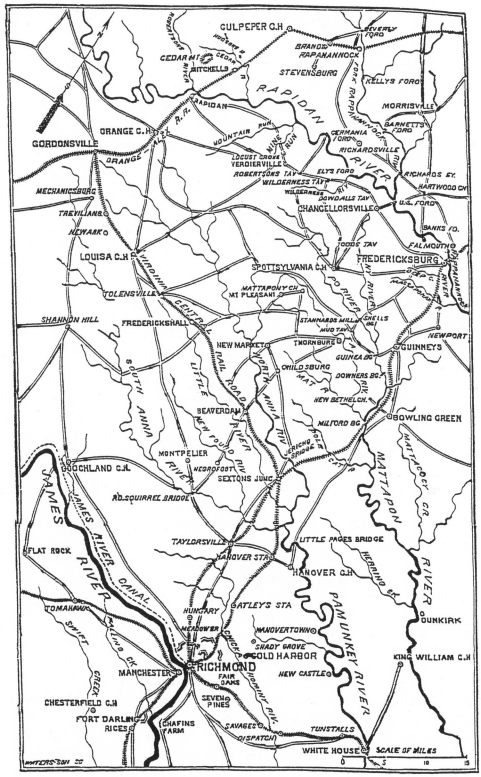

The History of the Civil War, Schmucker

Grant's Drive South, Spring 1864

mence during the first week of May.

Prior to the start of the campaign Grant made a major change in the organization of the Army of the Potomac. Two of the five corps, the 1st and 3rd, were broken up and their men were redistributed to the remaining corps, the 2nd, 5th, and 6th. Designed to meet a double purpose, the reorganization tightened the chain of command and rid the army of a number of incompetent general officers. The 97th New York was the only Mohawk Valley regiment directly affected by the realignment. With the disbanding of its 1st Corps, the 97th and its entire 2nd Division was transferred to the 5th Corps.

The primary tactical problems faced by Grant centered on a way to get Lee out from behind his fortifications at Mine Run and out into the open where the Federals' man-power advantage and superiority in heavy guns would have a telling effect.

A head-on attack was out of the question. Since November, when Meade had contemplated such an attack, the twenty mile line of Confederate breastworks and gun emplacements had been further strengthened. To charge these works now would be suicidal. A move around Lee's left or western flank had its advantages; open country and a ready made supply line in the Orange & Alexandria Railroad, but such a move would leave Washington uncovered.

Therefore, all that was left to Grant was a move around Lee's eastern flank. This route would keep Washington covered, make for a shorter march, and with its numerous navigable streams, access to supply depots in the rear would present fewer problems. However, one major hurdle stood in the army's path if it moved in this direction. Just across the Rapidan River in eastern Virginia lay the one hundred square mile tangled jungle of stunted oak and pine thickets called the Wilderness. Just one year ago, Joe Hooker's massive army had been caught by Lee in this forbidding forest and given a whipping at Chancellorsville that many of the men who now marched with Grant remembered all too well.

In hope of "stealing a march" on Lee and not being attacked in the maze of the Wilderness, Grant would rely on speed and deception, two commodities the Army of the Potomac had never before shown. Grant planned on moving across the Rapidan and into the Wilderness at night, relying on the cover of darkness to screen the march. If he could get his army through the Wilderness in forty-eight hours and gain the open area beyond, he would have plenty of room to maneuver before Lee could interfere.

After consulting with General Meade and his corps commanders, Grant set his eastern campaign to begin at midnight on May 4th.

The private soldiers were not privy to the plans of the high command, but the experienced men had long ago learned the telltale signs that usually preceded a major campaign. The sick and wounded were transported to the rear as field hospitals emptied to make room for the campaign's inevitable casualties, regimental quartermasters drew abnormal amounts of rations from their brigade commissaries, wagon trains assembled, sutlers were ordered to the rear, and couriers and officers scampered back and forth. It was apparent to the men that Grant's spring offensive was in the offing and from what they had learned of the man, his hard-driving, relentless style of warfare meant that long and bloody days were ahead for the common soldier.

On the 1st day of May, new uniforms, canteens, caps and cartridge boxes were issued to the men. The new gear was cryptically labeled with the initials "I.C." which the boys quickly translated to stand for, "I'm Condemned."

Eight days rations and forty rounds of ammunition were drawn by each man on the afternoon of May 3rd, and strict orders were given to have every canteen filled with water. At 11 p.m. that night the troops were ordered to fall in and at midnight, May 4th, the Army of the Potomac went into motion.

By mid-morning the 2nd and 5th Corps were across the Rapidan, with the 2nd Corps, the army's largest, in the lead. Of the Mohawk Valley regiments, the 97th New York with Warren's 5th Corps crossed at Germanna Ford and the 152nd New York with Hancock's 2nd Corps crossed a few miles to the east at Ely's Ford.

The Union columns rapidly penetrated into the Wilderness, but around noon the men halted and went into bivouack. This halt was necessary to permit the 6th Corps and the army's huge wagon train time to catch up. The 97th encamped at the Lacy House about five miles from Germanna Ford and the 152nd set up camp at Chancellorsville, about three miles further to the east.

The wagon train, which would have stretched sixty miles if each wagon were placed end to end, took all of the afternoon to cross the Rapidan. The 121st New York, with Sedgwick's 6th Corps, finally crossed the river at Germanna Ford just before dark and marched a few miles into the Wilderness. The 121st and the rest of Wright's Division (1st), bivouacked at Spotswood.

Well before sunrise the next morning, May 5th, the men were given time to grab a quick breakfast of cold pork and hardtack, before the march continued south along the Germanna Plank and Brock roads. The 2nd Corps was still in the lead, followed by the 5th and 6th Corps. Burnside's 9th Corps, which Grant had ordered to join his columns, was still north of the Rapidan, but was preparing to cross at Germanna Ford.

Shortly after 7 a.m., Warren, whose 5th Corps was astride the intersection of the Germanna Plank Road and the Orange Turnpike near Wilderness Tavern, informed headquarters that a sizable enemy force had been spotted three miles to the west, along the turnpike. The whole Union column ground to a halt and Warren was given orders to engage the enemy.

The rebel troops that Warren saw that morning on the Orange Turnpike were members of Gen. Richard Ewell's 2nd Corps of the Army of Northern Virginia. Robert E. Lee had not sat idly by while Grant's army splashed across the Rapidan fords and, in fact, had predicted just such a crossing. After ascertaining that the Federal move was real and not just a mere feint, Lee had his army in motion well before Sedgwick's 6th Corps was across the river. Thinking along with Grant, Lee knew that if the Union army was permitted to get through the Wilderness unmolested, the Federal's preponderance in numbers, (one hundred and twenty thousand men) would surely prevail over Lee's smaller force (sixty-five thousand men). Lee's aim, as it had been with Hooker, was to intercept Grant in the rugged terrain of the Wilderness and

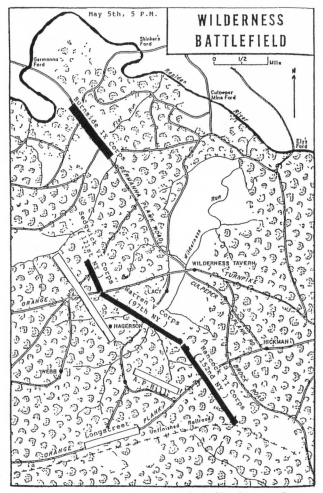

The Civil War Dictionary, Boatner

hopefully divide the Federal columns. To accomplish this goal, Ewell's Corps and that of A.P. Hill, had filtered through the western fringes of the forest and encamped within three miles of the Union bivouacks. On the morning of May 5th, in anticipation of the arrival of General Longstreet's corps, Lee ordered Ewell and Hill to strike the Federals.

Towards mid-morning, Griffin's 1st Division of the 5th Corps, in response to Grant's order to engage the enemy, began to advance westerly along the Orange Turnpike. Coming from the opposite direction were two brigades of Ewell's men. About two miles down the road the two forces met, touching off the battle of the Wilderness. In the fighting that ensued, Griffin's division routed one of the Confederate brigades but in turn was struck on the right flank by the other and driven back. The 97th New York, with the 2nd Division of the 5th Corps, came to the support of Griffin's retreating men and simply by their appearance halted the rebel advance.

Breastworks were hastily thrown up by the men of both sides and for the time being the firing quieted. At around 3 p.m., the 121st New York, with Wright's divi-

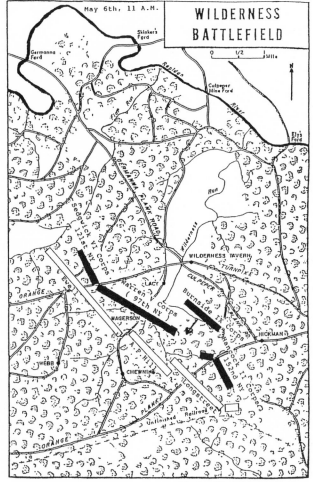

The Civil War Dictionary, Boatner

sion of the the 6th Corps, arrived on the scene and took up positions to the right of the 5th Corps. At this juncture the 97th stood behind their breastworks in the woods on the south side of the Orange Turnpike and the 121st was posted on the north side of the road.

Along the Orange Plank Road, a few miles south of the 5th and 6th Corps, the situation was much the same. Hancock's 2nd Corps had stepped off at first light, but had halted when an enemy force was detected on the Orange Plank Road.

Like Ewell to the north, A.P. Hill had hoped to strike the Federal army strung out on the Brock Road and split off the 2nd Corps from the rest of the Union line. Fortunately, the rebel thrust was discovered in time and Hancock's counter-marching troops were able to form a junction with the 5th Corp's left flank, thwarting Hill's plans.

The 152nd New York, which was in the vanguard of Hancock's column, had already reached the intersection of the Brock and Cartharpin Roads near Todd's Tavern, when the order to countermarch was received. Now acting as the 2nd Corp's rear guard, the 152nd was detained near Todd's Tavern, fighting off stabs by rebel cavalry. Lt. Dwight Smith of the 152nd described the action:

> "Our regiment was on the right of the 2d Brigade, on the right of the Division and Corps, which placed us in the extreme advance. Soon after passing the celebrated field of Chancellorsville we came to Todd's Tavern when a halt was made, while the 152d was advanced about a mile further down the road, formed line cross wise of it, and advanced our skirmishers, and exchanged shots with the skirmishers of Stewart's [Jeb Stuart] Cavalry, which made us the first infantry engaged. After some six or eight hours work here, we were suddenly withdrawn and moved rapidly back 3 or 4 miles, where the fight proper had now commenced." [1]

Upon reaching the intersection of the Orange Plank and Brock Roads, where the rest of the 2nd Corps was drawn up in line of battle, the 152nd was ordered to form up in the rear of the main line. As reported by Henry Roback, the mood of the heretofore untested men of the 152nd, (known as the "One hundred and fifty toothless" by the rest of its brigade), was quite somber:

> "We formed into line by companies, obtaining position in a tangled undergrowth of shrub oaks. Dazed with the terrible and incessant peals of musketry, all joking and merriment ceased in expectancy of the next scene on the programme. The sun sinks in the west. The shade of the dense forest spreads its gloom over the land. The firing has ceased; quiet reigns along the front." [2]

Just after dark the 152nd's brigade commander, Gen. Joshua Owens, received orders to send a regiment into the woods to "feel the enemy." Owens selected the yet unbloodied 152nd New York for the duty. Henry Roback of Danube and Lt. Dwight Smith of Richfield Springs provided accounts of what was to be the 152nd's baptismal fire. Roback wrote:

> "We leave our position among the snarled oaks and cross the breastworks; the occupants gave us words of courage. We entered the woods, passing over the bodies of those who had fallen before. We forced a passage through the thick undergrowth, becoming separated and considerably mixed up.
>
> The enlignment [alignment] was perfect as we press forward. A sharp crackling of musketry and the whizzing of many bullets cause the men to stagger and fall. The attack was so sudden that it caused the line to waver. It was supposed our picket line was advanced farther in the woods, and we were seeking a position to strengthen and support it. Col. Thompson drew his sword and rallied the men with encouraging shouts, supported in a like manner by the staff and line officers. Instantly recovering, we began to fire at will, and poured volley after volley in the darkness of the night. We fell back a few paces and formed the picket line." [3]

Smith reported:

> "We were quickly formed and ordered to load but not prime, and as we advanced immediately, supposed, as we had no skirmishers out, that there

was another line of battle in our front. Suddenly we were opened upon by a perfect earthquake of musketry, at such short range that the powder from their guns absolutely peppered our faces. Coming so unexpected, our line wavered and at some points broke, but quickly rallied. Before any other battalion of the line formed we had already given a cheer and poured in a stunning fire, which was followed up so quickly by another and another. ... It soon became so dark that the firing ceased, except an occasional rattle at random."[4]

Among the many casualties suffered by the 152nd—an accurate count was not readily possible because so many men were missing—was the regiment's first battle fatality, Capt. Washington W. Husler of Litchfield. In a letter of condolence to Husler's widow, Cpl. H.R. Matteson of Litchfield described the captain's last hours:

"I was the nearest person to him at the time he fell, and the only one knowing of his fall for some moments. The regiment was advancing through a piece of woods in line of battle and was not expecting the enemy to be so near us, when all at once we received a volley which caused us to retreat for a short distance, but I saw my beloved Captain fall before I turned. The regiment, however, soon rallied, and drove the enemy from the ground where your husband lay, and then myself, with three comrades went out in face of the enemy and carried our Captain off the field, and something over a mile to a hospital. He retained his senses while life remained, and told me he had got to die. I asked him if he had any word for you. His answer was, 'Tell her how I died.' He was wounded on the 5th about 5 p.m., and died I believe the same evening."[5]

At about the same time as the 152nd New York marched into the woods along the Orange Plank Road, the 97th New York was ordered into the thick underbrush to the south of the Orange Turnpike. Cautiously advancing alongside two other regiments from its brigade, the 12th Massachusetts, and the 11th Pennsylvania, the 97th New York soon ran into a Confederate skirmish line. A brisk and deadly fight developed and slowly the rebels were pushed back until darkness ended the struggle. In the brief engagement that lasted less than an hour, the 97th New York suffered sixty casualties, many of whom were recent conscripts in their first fight. The rebel fire had been so heavy that not only was the color bearer struck several times, but his flag staff was also reduced to splinters.

During the 97th's skirmish, the 121st New York remained in reserve behind their breastworks on the north side of the turnpike.

Night brought a close to the day's fight, and the exhausted soldiers from both sides lay on their arms in lines so close that the antagonists drew water from the same streams.

As reported by Lt. Dwight Smith of the 152nd, sleep not only served to restore the men's vigor but more importantly helped them block out the scenes of carnage that lay all around. Smith wrote:

"As soon as night set in Capt. Burt deployed his company so as to cover our line, and remained as pickets during the night, while the line of battle sunk in their tracks for a much needed sleep. What a blessing it was to be tired, very tired, then. Else who could picture the horrors of that night among the dead, the suffering and mangled wounded of both armies, scattered so thickly and promiscuously in that dismal wilderness!" [6]

The day's fight had been pretty much a standoff with both armies in relatively the same positions as they had been in that morning. Neither commander was at full strength yet, Grant was waiting for Burnside and Lee for Longstreet, and therefore neither took the initiative for a full scale offensive. Spirits were high on both sides. The boys in gray were expecting a second Chancellorsville, and as described by the 152nd's Henry Roback, the boys in blue believed in the invincibility of U.S. Grant.

> "We lay on our arms all night listening to an innumerable choir of whip-poor wills. The boys along the line changed the sound to 'Grant will whip, Grant will whip.' " [7]

That night, with the arrival of Burnside's 9th Corps and the absence of Longstreet, Grant ordered an attack all along the line to begin at dawn.

Before daybreak on May 6th, the Union boys crawled from underneath their blankets, gulped down a few mouthfuls of food, and formed ranks. At 4:30 a.m. the signal to advance was given and the twelve mile long Federal line lurched forward. Irresistibly, the blue wave drove in the surprised rebel pickets before smashing into the main body of Lee's troops. All along the front the Confederate line was steadily forced back.

On the Federal left flank the 152nd New York, with the 2nd Corps, was driving A.P. Hill's men, and on the right flank the 97th New York, with the 5th Corps, and the 121st New York, with the 6th Corps, were pushing back Ewell's Corps. Henry Roback and Lt. Dwight Smith provided accounts of the 152nd's advance.

Roback wrote:

> "By eleven o'clock we had advanced with such vigor that we had gained a mile of ground by persistent, hand to hand conflict. The enemy could be felt but not seen, nor could they see our force as we drove them onward. The forest was so dense and covered with a thick undergrowth of scrub oak, laurel and sassafras, that the aim was taken only at flashes and lines of smoke. The storm of leaden hail cut the young trees and tore them into shreds. The ground is covered with killed and wounded of both armies, lying side by side. We cross a small stream, and a comrade stops to obtain water. A member of his own company receives a cup of water from his hand. He drinks it with one draught and passes up the bank. A bullet strikes him and the blood gushes in a torrent from his mouth. The dry leaves take fire, and the flames spread over the ground. The wounded cry for help; some are saved; for others there is no help, and the charred and blackened remains lie on the ground. Neither General of the armies can tell with any degree of certainty, the exact movements they have met with." [8]

Lieutenant Smith reported:

> "Long before day we were ready for the enemy, nor had we long to
> wait for his coming, for at the first grey of the morning they briskly at-
> tacked our skirmishers who spitefully held their ground until our line of
> battle, steadily and determinedly pressing forward, poured in volley after
> volley so rapidly and with such deadly effect that with all their stubborn-
> ness they were forced to fall back a few yards at a time. Each time they
> rallied our fellows would give a cheer and a dash at them, most invariably
> setting them going. Thus, we drove them, the intervals of the ceasing of
> firing being signalized by hundreds of frightened 'rebs' throwing down
> their arms and running wildly into our lines as prisoners."[9]

Along the Orange Turnpike the 5th and 6th Corps were also meeting with great
success. Isaac Hall of the 97th New York described the action on this front:

> "The Confederates were surprised while cooking their corn-bread, and
> driven a mile or more. Some of their deserted Johnny cakes were grabbed
> smoking from the fire by the boys in blue, and eagerly devoured as they
> passed along. As the Confederates were followed on a southerly course, the
> effects of the death-dealing struggle of the preceding day became manifest.
> In the rear of old logs, which evidently had been hastily thrown together,
> occasionally not more than forty yards apart, the alternate lines of Union
> and Confederate dead lay with their accoutrements and side arms on—men
> and officers—as they had fallen, undisturbed, save by the bold army
> 'bummer,' whose presence is ever revealed by the inevitably reversed
> pocket. Pressing the enemy rapidly over these lines of moldering clay, to
> the plank road, a wheel to the right was made, and the Confederates were
> followed to their fortifications, when their line opened with artillery, and a
> halt was ordered to reform. This was a fatal mistake."[10]

In the dense woods the Union regiments and brigades had become considerably
mixed up, and in the time taken to reassemble the line, the momentum of the Federal
thrust was lost. Making use of this hiatus in the blue advance, Confederate officers
reformed their panic stricken troops, and with Longstreet's reinforcements having
just come up, the rebels turned and went on the offensive.

The left flank of the 5th Corps, which had become disassociated from the right
flank of the 2nd Corps, was set upon by elements of Longstreet's newly arrived
corps. Two Union brigades were demolished and when the 97th New York's brigade
came up, it was also driven back with considerable loss. All of the ground gained in
the morning was quickly lost as the tide of battle turned.

On the extreme right flank of the Union line the situation was much the same.
Ewell, discovering that this part of the Union line was unsupported, outflanked and
routed a division of the 6th Corps. Ewell's advance rolled up one mile of the Federal
line before it was stopped by the 121st New York's division of the 6th Corps. In
describing the 121st's part in this action, Clinton Beckwith of Herkimer wrote:

> "Just before dark heavy firing to our right indicated trouble . . . and in
> a very short time, Colonel Duffy [of the Division staff] rode up and ordered
> us to move to the right and restore our lines, which had been broken. The

firing in that direction was pretty well maintained, showing that the enemy was meeting with steady resistance. Colonel Olcott was at the head of the regiment and we hurried along moving by the right flank in column of fours. I do not know how far we went, but it was not a great distance when we came in contact with the enemy. They seemed to be coming from the direction in which we were going. I thought there were some of our troops in front of us, but instead we ran slam bang into the enemy. They ran over some of our fellows, and I fired into them. A bunch of them ordered us to surrender and fired a volley into us, which hit a number among whom were Dennis A Dewey, John H. Reynolds and Wm. MacElroy. They immediately advanced and ordered us to surrender and go to the rear. There was a general scattering. Some of our fellows stopped to take care of the wounded, and it seemed to me that some more of our fellows were coming up behind. The Rebels seemed to be in a hurry to get back and hurried us up. It was now quite dusky and you could not tell a man's uniform a little ways off. I ran a short distance in the direction the Rebs wanted me to go, expecting every instant a volley from one of our regiments. Finally some one, a Rebel officer I suppose, said, 'Throw down that gun.' I had it in my hands and dropped it. I went only a little distance farther and threw myself down on my face. I expected to be punched every instant, but the balls were flying pretty thick, and it being near dark I was unnoticed. As soon as I thought it safe, I jumped up, went and picked up my gun, and started right back the way I came, until I saw some of our men going to the rear. . . . As I came out of the woods a little way, I saw a line of battle was formed and the men as they came up joined it. I loaded my gun which I had fired only once during the affair. . . . It was found that something like a hundred of our regiment were missing, and one-half of them were dead or wounded." [11]

At the 5th and 6th Corps field hospitals the surgeons, orderlies and the wounded knew they were in the path of the rebel onslaught and resigned themselves to being taken prisoner. John Ingraham of Brockett's Bridge, who was assigned as an orderly in the 121st's Divisional Hospital, described the scene and related his avenue of escape. Ingraham wrote:

"Our Division Hospital was in the rear of our corps and our corps was on the extreme right. About 10 p.m., our Division Surgeon received orders to load the wounded that could not walk and have those walk that could. (We had about four or five thousand wounded) they got all the wounded off but about eight or ten hundred and we heard picket firing in the rear of our Hospital. The Doctors began to dig out. The head Surgeon made a detail of two to stay, and also all of the Hospital attendants to stay with the two Surgeons to take care of the wounded when we fell into the enemy's hands. Of these I was one. There were some darkies on picket in the rear of our Hospital who kept firing all night and in the morning fell back to the main army. That left us between the two armies. I made up my mind to see Richmond then sure. I considered the thing all over in my own mind, got everything arranged for the worst, took what articles I wanted the most out of my knapsack and put in my pockets. After daybreak we were momentarily expecting them but as luck would have it they did not come until about 4 p.m., and just as they were advancing out of the woods behind the Hospital one of the Doctors picked out one man to stay with him and told the rest of us to escape, if we could. I thought I would run my chance in getting away. You can bet the shell and little bullets flew some. I started and kept under the cover of the house until I struck a wood then I made good time until I came to our out posts and arrived in our lines safe and sound." [12]

On the left flank of Grant's line the fate that befell the 5th and 6th Corps also visited the 2nd Corps. With the arrival of Longstreet's Corps, Hancock's surge on the Confederate right was stopped. Longstreet, looking to go on the offensive, learned of an unfinished railroad cut that would serve as a covered approach to the 2nd Corps's exposed left flank. Just before noon, four Confederate brigades came seemingly out of nowhere and exploded upon Hancock's southern flank, overwhelming it. The rebel surge shattered the Federal line until it reached a series of breastworks that Hancock had ordered built just that morning. Among the units already behind these fortifications was the 152nd New York, which had fortuitously left the field earlier in the day to replenish their ammunition. Reinforced by Burnside's 9th Corps which had finally shown up, the pieces of the broken 2nd Corps slowed the rebel tide. Lt. Dwight Smith of the 152nd, described the regiments's fight behind the log barricade. Smith wrote:

"Down on our left was a certain road the 'Johnnies' wanted badly. We had a battery planted here, one section being directly in the road and the other two sections, a little to the left of it, with a line of breastworks of dry logs and brush about 300 yards in front. A second work on either flank of the centre and left section, and a third line still in the rear. Here the wily Longstreet massed his corps and ordered a charge, which they executed with a desperate determination to win. Those in front could only press ahead for the thick mass of yelling 'greybacks' crowded all before them as they drove our skirmishers into the first line. Our men opened a terrific fire of musketry, but soon the combustible material of the breastworks took fire, and the place becoming too warm the first line broke to the right and left, and our guns, doubled shotted with cannister, sent their loads of iron hail howling and tearing great gaps through their dense columns. Still on they came to the point where Longstreet's corps flag is planted, near our second line. For nearly an hour they contested the ground.

The hissing shower of Minnies and cannister had done its work, and their forces are withdrawn, leaving their heaps of dead and wounded." [13]

The stiff Federal defense and the coming on of night checked the Confederate advance, but the accidental wounding of Lee's "War Horse," General Longstreet, contributed most heavily to the loss of the rebel initiative. Eerily reminiscent of Stonewall Jackson's mortal wounding one year ago and just five miles away at Chancellorsville, Longstreet and his entourage were mistaken for Union cavalry and shot by their own men. Although Longstreet unlike Jackson would recover, once again the main impetus behind a complete rebel victory was lost.

The morning of May 7th did not see a renewal of the struggle. Huddling behind their breastworks the exhausted men of each side were content to maintain their positions and, except for the occasional crack of the sharpshooter's rifle, all was quiet. For the time being both armies rested and began to realize the slaughter they had wrought.

In the two day fight Grant's army had suffered over seventeen thousand casualties while Lee had lost less than eight thousand men.[14] In comparison with last year's Chancellorsville fight, in which Hooker had also lost seventeen thousand men and Lee had realized twelve thousand casualties, Grant's first encounter with Lee had ended in a decided and terrible Union defeat.

To the Union casualty total, the three Mohawk Valley regiments contributed their bloody share. The 97th New York had lost ninety-nine men, twenty-eight of whom were killed outright or mortally wounded.[15] The 121st New York, which entered the fight with four hundred and twenty men, counted twenty-one killed out of their total of seventy-three casualties.[16] The 152nd New York, in their first major engagement lost fifty-one men, seventeen of whom were killed.[17]

On the night of May 7th Grant began withdrawing his troops. The 97th New York, with Warren's 5th Corps, took the lead, preceded by Sheridan's Cavalry and were followed in order by the 2nd, 6th and 9th Corps. After such an ignominious defeat the soldiers expected, as in the past, that their columns would limp back north to safety. To the men's surprise the line of march was headed down the Brock Road, towards the south and not the north. Grant had been whipped, but had not turned tail and run like McClellan and Hooker. To the men's elation, the Army of the Potomac was not giving up, but was continuing onward towards a final confrontation with the enemy. Above all else this was just what the Union boys wanted, a chance, no matter how bloody, to end the rebellion and go home.

Grant's objective now was to get out of the tangle of the Wilderness and beat Lee to Spotsylvania. Winning the race to this vital crossroads would put the Federal Army beyond the Confederate right flank. As Warren's 5th Corps stepped off, Lee, with his gift of foresight, was already ordering Jeb Stuart's Cavalry and Longstreet's Corps (now commanded by Gen. Richard Anderson), on the road to Spotsylvania.

The rebel horsemen won the race to the crossroads and when Sheridan's Cavalry arrived on the morning of May 8th its path was blocked by Stuart's dismounted troopers. Unable to dislodge the rebels, Sheridan called for help from the 5th Corps. Warren's men had been on the road all night and the march had not been an easy one. Much of the route had been obstructed by trees felled by Confederate cavalry and by the time the 5th Corps men reached Spotsylvania they were exhausted. Nevertheless, General Warren ordered his 2nd Division (which included the 97th New York) to charge the rebel works, which he believed were only lightly held by Stuart's Cavalry.

Advancing up a ridge behind the Alsop House, the Federals easily pushed aside Stuart's skirmish line and continued on. Reaching the crest of the hill, the blue line was staggered by a tremendous volley of musket and artillery fire from Rebel infantry that was not supposed to have been there. Warren's 2nd Division had blundered into a division of Longstreet's fast-marching corps.

In a wild retreat the 97th and the rest of its division ran back down the hill and only the appearance of a sword waving Warren stopped the stampede. Two other divisions of the 5th Corps tried the hill but both were repulsed. For the remainder of the day the Federals entrenched at the base of the slope waiting for the rest of the army to come up.

In defending the 2nd Division's retreat, its commander, Gen. Richard Coulter, wrote:

> "I may here remark that the division from date of leaving Culpeper had been labored to its utmost ability, either marching, engaged with the enemy, or employed in the erection of defensive works. It had also marched the entire night previous to and went into this action without having had either rest or refreshment. . . . One of the men advancing having obtained through the thick undergrowth, a view of the enemy's skirmishers, remarked: 'Pretty dismounted cavalry, carrying knapsacks.' " [18]

Through the rest of that day and on into the next, the full complements of both armies arrived and after jockeying for position, established their lines. The 152nd New York fought off an attack on three batteries that they were supporting, and settled in with the 2nd Corps as Grant's right flank. The 97th New York, with the 5th Corps, remained just west of the Alsop house in the Union center and the 121st New York's 6th Corps, after fighting their way across the Ny River, formed the left flank. Burnside's 9th Corps had moved far to the left of the 6th Corps and at this point was not contiguous with the rest of the Union line.

On both sides the soldiers were hard at work improving their entrenchments as their officers cautiously scanned the enemy's position. A constant threat to both the common soldier and the "shoulder-straps," be they in blue or gray uniforms, was the dreaded sharpshooter. Most of the marksmen used telescopic sights and anyone showing themselves even at one thousand yards distance was fair game. On the morning of May 9th, the 6th Corp's commander, John Sedgwick, ridiculed his men for flinching from these long range missiles. Seconds later, Sedgwick was struck in the head and killed by a sharpshooter's bullet.

Lt. Dwight Smith wrote of the 152nd's contest with the rebel marksmen:

> "Towards night we were advanced to a position in the woods upon a hill south east of Spotsylvania, as a sort of advanced guard. Here we lay all the next day engaged with rebel sharpshooters, who occupied a strong position, many of them stationed on tops of trees mostly out of sight to us, and picked off our brave fellows at their leisure: but some of these rascals came down from their elevated positions quicker than they could possibly have gone up, and learned to light upon the ground in a very decided manner." [19]

With the death of General Sedgwick, command of the 6th Corps passed to Gen. Horatio Wright.

On May 10th with his army in proper alignment and their defensive fortifications completed, Grant ordered a major attack on the Confederate works. Warren's 5th Corps, supported by elements of the 2nd Corps, was chosen to lead the offensive which was to be directed at Anderson's Corps on the rebel left flank. The attack started at 4 p.m. but quickly bogged down as the first Union line became entangled in brush, slashings and trees piled in front of the rebel breastworks. As Warren's men tried to cut their way through the obstacles the enemy poured a withering fire into

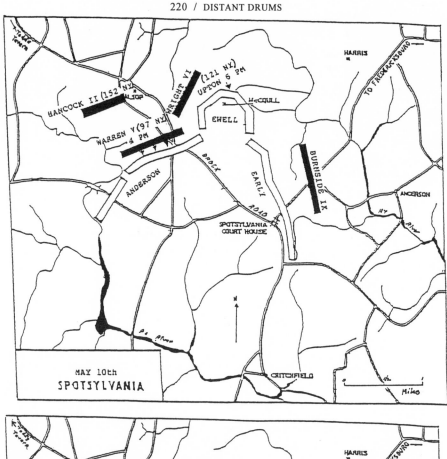

MAY 10th
SPOTSYLVANIA

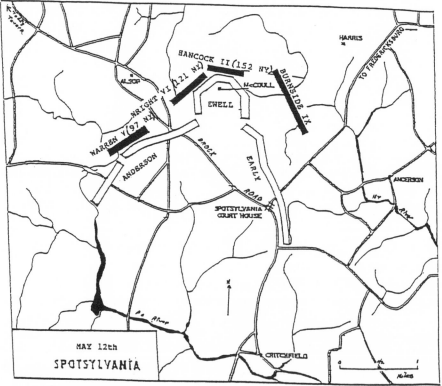

MAY 12th
SPOTSYLVANIA

The Civil War Dictionary, Boatner

them. Unable to withstand this fire, the front line turned to retreat only to pile into the next line coming up. In a matter of minutes the confused columns of the 5th Corps were in full retreat. Isaac Hall, whose 97th New York was in the rear of the attacking force, described the repulse:

"At this juncture one of those singular phases occurred which in an unguarded moment overcomes veteran troops and the best organized plans, turning a victory sometimes into a defeat.

This force when in readiness to move was not far from three hundred yards from our fortified position and about the same from that of the enemy. It stood in a wood on a gentle slope which was more precipitate as it descended towards our works. Not more than seventy five yards to the front was the edge of the woods, skirted by thick bushes, and beyond an open field sloping towards the enemy's works. Our skirmish line [the 97th's] as afore indicated had been absorbed into this force, the lines of which were about two yards apart, and it now moved but a short distance towards the edge of the woods, when it was halted and all but the front line ordered to lie down; this had advanced but a short distance—to reconnoiter—when a line of Confederates, springing suddenly to their feet, fired into their faces. As a natural consequence the advancing column did what almost any other line would have done under similar circumstances, it precipitated itself upon the second, striking it just as it was springing up and with such force as to carry this upon the next in like attitude in which the second was caught; and this accumulating mass struck the fourth line with the power of an avalanche and the whole was borne down the slope with the rush and roar of a cataract; yet, there was no panic, but a temporary one by the first line; and the others were borne back by the force of circumstances over which they had no control. But before our works were reached the mass had become somewhat separated and their speed began to slacken, and the officers had regained their breath, which at the onset was knocked out of them. These now began to be heard from in loud tones of authority, commanding a halt, which was obeyed by most of the men when they had gained their fortifications. A few went beyond but were soon returned by mounted officers and orderlies."[20]

Undaunted by the failure of Warren's men, Grant ordered Hancock to have his 2nd Corps ready to attack at 6:30 p.m.

After watching Warren's 5th Corps uselessly smashed against the rebel works, Col. Emory Upton of the 121st New York formulated his own strategy to pierce the Confederate line. Upton's approach, which was contrary to traditional military tactics, called for a concentrated attack force, rather than a spread out battleline, to strike a distinct point on the enemy line. In addition, Upton's compact phalanx would rush across the field without firing a shot until the rebel breastworks were reached. Once inside, the lead regiments would fan out to the left and right, securing the breach for a supporting force to come up and make the breakthrough complete.

Upton, who was acting as the brigade's commander, brought his plan to his superior, Gen. David Russell, who in turn reported the idea to the 6th Corp's new leader, Gen. Horatio Wright. Wright liked the scheme so well that he gave Upton twelve regiments, including the 121st New York, with which to attempt it. In the meantime Wright convinced Grant to cancel the order for the 2nd Corp's attack.

Upton formed his force into four rows, each three regiments wide. At 6 p.m. the signal to charge was given and without firing a shot—the men had loaded but not capped their rifles—the blue spear flew at the rebel line. Clinton Beckwith of Herkimer described the enlisted man's side of the assault, writing:

"It was nearly sundown when we were ready to go forward. The day had been bright and it was warm, but the air felt damp, indicating rain. The racket and smoke made by the skirmishers and batteries, made it look hazy about us, and we had to raise our voices to be heard. We waited in suspense for some time. Dorr I. Davenport with whom I tented, said to me, 'I feel as though I was going to get hit. If I do, you get my things and send them home.' I said, 'I will, and you do the same for me in case I am shot, but keep a stiff upper lip. We may get through all right.' He said, 'I dread the first volley, they have so good a shot at us.' Shortly after this the batteries stopped firing, and in a few minutes an officer rode along toward the right as fast as he could, and a moment afterward word was passed along to get ready, then 'Fall in,' and then 'Forward.' I felt my gorge rise, and my stomach and intestines shrink together in a knot, and a thousand things rushed through my mind. I fully realized the terrible peril I was to encounter (gained from previous experience). I looked about in the faces of the boys around me, and they told the tale of expected death. Pulling my cap down over my eyes, I stepped out, the extreme man on the left of the regiment, except Sergeant Edwards and Adjutant Morse who was on foot. In a few seconds we passed the skirmish line and moved more rapidly, the officers shouting 'Forward' and breaking into a run immediately after we got into the field a short distance. As soon as we began to run the men, unmindful of, or forgetting orders, commenced to yell, and in a few steps farther the rifle pits were dotted with puffs of smoke, and men began to fall rapidly and some began to fire at the works thus losing the chance they had to do something, when they reached the works to protect themselves. I got along all right and there were a number of us in the grass-grown unused road, and several were shot, but I could not tell who, because I was intent upon reaching the works. We were broken up some getting through the slashing and the abatis. By this time the Rebels were beginning to fire the second time, and a rapid but scattering fire ran along the works which we reached in another instant. One of our officers in front of us jumped on the top log and shouted, 'Come on, men,' and pitched forward and disappeared, shot. I followed an instant after and the men swarmed upon, and over the works on each side of me. As I got on top some Rebs jumped up from their side and began to run back. Some were lunging at our men with their bayonets and a few had their guns clubbed. . . . One squad, an officer with them, were backing away from us, the officer firing his revolver at our men. I fired into them, jumped down into the pits and moved out toward them. Just at this time, our second line came up and we received another volley from the line in front of us and the battery fired one charge of cannister. Colonel Upton shouted 'Forward' and we all ran towards the battery, passing another line of works. . . . While moving as ordered, some Rebel troops came up and fired a volley into us. We got on the other side of the rifle pits and began firing at them and checked their advance. It was now duskish and it seemed as though the firing on our front and to our right became heavier, and the whistle of balls seemed to come from all directions and was incessant. . . We could now see the flashes of the guns and knew they were coming in on us. A great many of our men were shot in this locality, but I thought the wounded would all have a chance to get back. I knew that we could not stay there. The wounded between us and the Rebs were in a terrible plight, and must all have been shot to pieces by the fire from both sides.

Colonel Upton asked for volunteers to make a rush on the Rebel battery, but did not get any. The undertaking looked too desperate. He asked for men from the 121st New York, saying, 'Are there none of my old regiment here?' But there were only a few of us there and our cartridges were running low. I do not know how long we remained there firing. It seemed like an hour, but I don't suppose it was. Finally word was passed along to fall back quietly to our skirmish line and back we started."[21]

Upton's plan had worked perfectly. The fast moving Union column had punched a hole in the Confederate works, and although the first line had suffered severely, the succeeding waves had overwhelmed the defenders and driven them back two hundred yards. Spreading out on either side of the breech, Upton's men held their ground, but their supporting division never came (one rumor had it that the general in charge of the division was drunk). Under a murderous fire from rebel reinforcements that hurried to the break, the Federal boys had to retreat.

Official reports listed the 121st's casualty count for the May 10th charge as forty-six killed and over seventy wounded.[22] Among the wounded were the two top ranking officers in the regiment, Colonel Upton and Major Galpin. Both sustained slight wounds that would for a short time put them out of action.

Ulysses Grant was so impressed with Emory Upton that he submitted his name for promotion to brigadier general. In addition, Grant liked Upton's strategy so much that he directed General Hancock to ready the 2nd Corps for an "Upton Style" assault. Hancock's target would be a salient in the center of the Confederate line and jump-off time was scheduled for the morning of May 12th.

May 11th was spent in maneuvering the 2nd Corps into attack position. While the exhausted 121st New York and the 97th New York held their places in line as reserve units, the 152nd New York moved with the rest of Hancock's Corps.

Much of the 152nd's march was made after dark in a cold rainstorm that turned the roads into a heavy mud. Slogging along through the muck, the 2nd Corps passed to the left of the 6th Corps and halted near the Landron farm. Opposite the men was their objective, a heavily fortified angle in General Ewell's section of the rebel line, near the McCool house. Lt. Dwight Smith described the rebel fortifications that confronted the 2nd Corps:

"In our front was, first, 3 lines of rifle pits, and in the rear of them 2 lines of regular shaped log forts, very formidable, constructed upon scientific military principles, arranged so each successive line commanded those in front, about 5 feet thick at the base, 6 feet high, with spaces for the infantry to fire through below the upper logs and not be exposed to the fire of the attacking party. There were heavy abbatis as an outer protection and batteries on the flanks in every position that could be worked advantageously."[23]

At 4:30 a.m., May 12th, the order to charge was given and twenty thousand men in blue surged forward. Henry Roback and Lieutenant Smith of the 152nd gave detailed and graphic reports of the attack that would prove to be unsurpassed in the war for its sustained savagery. Roback wrote:

"A funeral silence pervades the assembly, and like spectres the men in blue await the order to attack. At daylight the fog is heavy. Objects can only be seen four or five rods.

All being in readiness and no prospect of the fog lifting the voice of Gen. Owen was heard: Attention! Second Brigade, Fix Bayonets! Forward! Guide! Centre! Charge!

On through the open field dotted here and there with overhanging shrubbery, moving swiftly and in silence one-half the distance, one-quarter of a mile. Suddenly the cannon opens fire, and with a cheer and yell, like fiends incarnate, we rush forward, all three divisions, mingling in one solid line. A heavy picket line opens fire upon us as we sweep forward up the slope. The dim outlines of the embankment appear in view, and with one grand rebound, we are over the works, fighting and struggling hand to hand for mastery. The bayonet is the most effective weapon, as it strikes terror to the hearts of man. The slaughter of the rebels was fearful as we swept them from the field, and force them into our lines. They madly rush into their dugout shanty pits, piling upon each other and through the intense excitement are shot, and writhe in mortal agony. Three thousand five hundred prisoners are sent to the rear, forty-two cannon are captured with Brig. Gen. George H. Stuart, and Gen. Fitzhugh Lee. The men captured were members of Stonewall Jackson's old corps. Our success was followed by a heavy cannonade along the whole line to which the enemy replied with great vigor."[24]

Lieutenant Smith related Company H's part in the assault:

"As soon as it was light enough to see, the signal to charge was given and the whole corps flew forward. Had the men been able to restrain their enthusiasm we would have doubtless 'caught them napping' but as they dashed over the first and 2d line of rifle pits and gobbled the swarms of 'Greybacks' manning them their feelings burst forth in a wild yell of triumph, which was almost instantly countered by a withering fire of Cannister and musketry. Still undaunted as they pushed [on], Sergt. Hurlburt Norton was in advance a little with the colors, and our line surged ahead to keep pace with them. Norton's fingers were shot away from his right hand that grasped the staff, but he quickly raised them with his left and pushed on: the next instant a shell pierced his brain. The whole color guard being killed or wounded, the staff of the State flag cut in two, the men hesitated at the 3d line. Capt. David Hill caught up the old flag and with a shout bounded into a section of the pit in front and alone sent thirty bewildered Confed's to the rear. In an instant the line was pouring on and over the works the colors carried still by Capt. Hill who was soon obliged to drop

them, as he received a painful wound. The State flag was caught up by the
1st Serg. David B. Fitch, Co. H, and turned over to some one who carried
them throughout the balance of the fight. Fitch also took care of the old
battle-flag until Serg. Barnes of the same Co. volunteered to act as color
Sergeant. This gallant soldier Fitch was hit in the head and shoulders in
scaling the inner works at the head of his Company. As our corps were
called upon to retake the position lost by the 6th Corps, his successor, Serg.
Bloodgood received a shot through the arm—the last remaining non-
commissioned officers with that Co. above the grade of Corporal.

I very much doubt if ever before during the war, there has been such
hand to hand fighting as took place here. Muskets were clubbed, and bayonets used freely. The works were carried and with them were captured
some 6,000 prisoners, 42 guns, horses, stores, &c. &c. The 152d alone took
3 stands of colors. Private John Weeks,* Co. H, captured one battle flag,
and Gen. Owens sent his name with it to Head Quarters. The first gun that
our regiment came up to and captured they quickly wheeled so as to bear
upon the Rebs and ramming in the cannister, sent their compliments to the
'Johnnys' with what was a moment before their gun. As they didn't understand the friction lanyard, they primed it with powder from musket cartridges and touched it off with a coal of fire." [25]

The Federal charge had taken the Confederates completely by surprise and for
the better part of an hour Hancock's men punished those of Ewell. But rebel reinforcements soon arrived and the situation stabilized. For the rest of the day, separated only by the log breastworks, the two armies clawed at each other in a ferocious
death struggle. Bayonets were thrust through the log chinks, men maniacally leaped
on top of the works and fired in the masses below, only to be shot down in turn and
arriving troops trampled to death many of their own wounded.

Henry Roback continued with his narrative of this hellish fight. Roback wrote:

"We had safely ensconced ourselves behind the works when the enemy
appeared in force, with a heavy skirmish line, with the apparent intention
of driving us off the field. All that day we held the works against repeated
assaults. Five times they charged to the very parapets, and with hand to
hand conflict were mowed down.

During the day a large force, bearing a flag of truce, advanced at trail
arms. Rejoiced to see so many coming over on the Lord's side, we mounted
the works cheering them on. When they arrived quite close they dropped
their flag and commenced firing. Several dropped from off the works killed
and wounded.

Recovering our surprise we gave them a volley, which sent them reel-
ing back. Later on they repeated the same trick. On they came with the
white flag above their heads. We had double shotted every musket along
the line and were prepared to receive our erring brethren with cold and
cruel lead. They came so close we could see the gray spots in their eyes.
Every man arose as one and gave them a concentrated fire, filling them
with lead enough to build a monument in honor and remembrance of the
Second Division, Second A.C.

* Weeks, of Hartwick in Otsego County, was awarded the Medal of Honor.

Through the day the contest goes on, keeping up a steady fire for the purpose of keeping the muskets dry, a drizzling rain descending. The 14th New York, Brooklyn boys, who wore red breeches, lay off to our right in four lines of battle. They cover a position where there are no works. A gap in the line. They keep up an incessant fire on that part of the line all day, loading while lying on their backs, rolling over and firing. The continuous peals of musketry and cannonading all along the line, arouses the union and confederate alike to maintain their positions to the bitter end. The dead, dying and wounded are lying literally in heaps, hideous to look at. The writhing of the wounded and dying who lay beneath the dead bodies, moved the whole mass at times. The storm of leaden hail sweeps through the woods and over the entrenchments, cutting and rending the branches into shreds. It was here where the oak tree was cut down by the continual stream of lead. The stump measured two feet across and was preserved. It is long past midnight before the firing has ceased in front of the Second Corps."[26]

Although the 2nd Corps have borne the brunt of the fighting, units from the other corps were drawn into the battle. In the May 12th fight along the rebel salient the 97th New York suffered two killed and ten wounded[27] and the already thin 121st New York lost sixteen killed and over twenty wounded.[28] The 152nd New York which was in the forefront of the day's struggle, tallied a surprisingly low figure of nine killed and forty-five wounded.[29]

In assessing the damage done to the 121st so far in Grant's campaign, Sgt. Joe Heath wrote to his father in Little Falls:

"I am still sound yet, after eight days hard fighting. We have lost heavily. Our gallant old leader, Gen. John Sedgwick, of the 'bloody sixth corps,' is killed, and our noble Colonel Olcott is also no more.* Maj. Galpin is wounded in the eye and is at Fredericksburg hospital. We went into the fight with 440 men and 15 officers, and came out to-day with 4 officers and not a hundred men. I have just taken the 'census' and find we have just 94 men.

Corp. W.H. Barnes is wounded through the shoulder. Burnham is all right and so is Redway. Johnny Gardinier is wounded in the foot with a piece of shell. Out of 56 men in Co. A, there are 7 left."[30]

The attack on the angle in the Confederate center, forever afterward to be known as "the Bloody Angle," ended the major fighting at Spotsylvania. The next five days, from May 13th to the 17th would be comparatively quiet although frequent cannon duels, brief skirmishes and sharpshooters exacted a number of casualties.

The ten days at Spotsylvania, starting on May 8th, had taken a great toll on the manpower from both armies. In the fighting, Grant had lost almost eighteen thousand men and Lee about ten thousand.[31] In describing the carnage of the fight at Spotsylvania, Henry Roback of the 152nd wrote:

---

* Although seriously wounded, Olcott survived and was taken prisoner.

"We passed a row of dead men who had been stripped of their clothing, showing conclusively they were our men. They had turned as black as night and were unrecognizable. While passing over the deserted lines, we saw several men dead and standing upright. They had been caught in the forks and crotches of the abatis. Nearing the enemy we came to a clearing, and passed over the space on a double quick, and occupied a trench where the enemy had buried their dead. The bodies lay several deep, having a light covering of dirt, many exposed to view. All was still in the woods on the left and front, and as silent as the mortal remains lying beneath our feet."[32]

In combining the Spotsylvania and Wilderness casualties, the Union army's running count was thirty-five thousand killed, wounded and missing, while the Confederates tabulation was about half this number. But Grant could replace his lost numbers, while Lee could not. On May 16th a telegram was read to the Federal troops announcing that twenty-two thousand reinforcements were on their way from Washington. The bulk of these reserves were men from heavy artillery regiments drawn from the forts around Washington who had been ordered by Grant to leave their cannons and shoulder their muskets. The infantrymen questioned the fighting ability of these "heavies" who had, they believed, lived a life of leisure in Washington and had never smelled the gunpowder of battle. In truth many of the artillerists were former foot soldiers who had re-enlisted after their infantry regiments were mustered out and were well acquainted with the arts of war.

During the struggle of May 12th, Lee had constructed a second line of breastworks one mile back from the original line. Once again confronted by formidable fortifications, Grant choose not to attack head-on, but to sidle once again around the Confederate right flank. Leap-frogging his corps, Grant began a slow crab-like march to the southeast.

To verify this Federal movement, Lee had Ewell lead his meager corps of six thousand men against Grant's right flank. Attacking on the afternoon of May 19th, Ewell's men ran into a superior force composed mainly of Grant's reinforcements, the former Heavy Artillery regiments. Among these "heavies" was the 2nd New York, also known as Morgan's Artillery, which included in their number over one hundred Herkimer County boys. In the fight, which was known as the Battle of the Harris Farm, Ewell's men were severely repulsed and the artillery men gained a measure of respect from the infantrymen. In the fight the 2nd New York H.A. lost twenty-six killed and eighty-nine wounded.[33] Among the dead were Philip Evans of Schuyler, Laverne Staring of Manheim, Albert Firl from Stark, and Samuel Tubbs from Little Falls.

For the remainder of the month of May, the armies of Grant and Lee continued their jousting through Virginia as the Federal army kept on its slide to the southeast. No major battles were fought, but as the two opposing forces headed for a road junction, at a place called Cold Harbor, all signs began to point to another significant confrontation.

CHAPTER XVI

"Many believed their hour was nigh"

Summer 1864 - The North Anna - Cold Harbor - Petersburg

In Herkimer County, during the first few weeks of May 1864, the telegraphers' keys chattered out a seemingly endless list of casualties suffered by the three Mohawk Valley regiments. The five hundred and twenty-three men lost to the 97th, 121st and 152nd New York regiments at the bloody clashes in the Wilderness and at Spotsylvania approached in ten days the number of men killed, wounded and missing, that had been suffered by these units in all their past battles combined. Of this total, Herkimer County-raised companies contributed two hundred and seventy-six casualties, including thirty-eight men killed.

The full impact of the losses sustained by the three regiments was best realized by the *Journal's* publication of the official casualty lists. In three lengthy columns, the newspaper detailed the reports of the 97th's adjutant, Willard Judd, the 152nd's adjutant, Alfred Quaiffe, and the 121st's acting adjutant, Sgt. Joe Heath. Each adjutant provided listings by company of the killed and wounded, often adding a description of the wound and its severity. Sergeant Heath also added a section headed "Straggled from Company and in No Battles."

Among the men from Herkimer County who were slain or mortally wounded in the Wilderness and Spotsylvania battles were: from Manheim - Germaine Fox (97th), Sgt. Thomas McClone (152nd), James Brown (121st) and Fred Dingler (121st); from Schuyler - Benedict Burdict (97th), James Friz (152nd), Frank Stack (152nd), George Parkhurst (121st), Malcolm Graham (121st) and Boselle Clemons (24th N.Y. Cav.); from Newport - John Jedets (152nd) and Hurlbut Norton (152nd);

from Salisbury - Lt. William Drescher (97th), Clother Whitford (97th) and Swift Roback (152nd); from Litchfield - Capt. Washington Hulser (152nd) and Aaron Millan (152nd); from Stark - Felix Bronner (152nd), Horatio Bronner (152nd), Alfred Shaul (152nd) and Josiah Wormett (121st); from Wilmurt - Francis Clough (152nd); from Ohio - Josephus Onderkirk (152nd); from Mohawk - Nicholas Cassens (152nd); from Danube - Norman Eckler (152nd), William Hale (152nd), Andrew Lanz (152nd) and Sgt. Lester Baum (121st); from Warren - John Conklin (152nd); from Frankfort - John Hyer (152nd), Darrin Brown (121st), John Eitelby (152nd) and Capt. John Fish (121st); from Little Falls - James Monk (152nd), and Levi Sherry (121st); from Russia - Lt. Edward Johnson (121st), George Collins (121st) and John Barkley (121st); from Winfield - Samuel Button (121st) and from German Flatts - eighteen-year-old James Judge and his sixteen-year-old brother Daniel, from the 121st.

On occasion, the adjutants made woeful mistakes in reporting a man dead who was only missing. On the other hand, in a few instances men who were reported as only slightly wounded had already succumbed to their injuries by the time the lists were published.

For the benefit of relatives and friends who wished to correspond with or travel to the bedsides of their wounded boys, the *Journal* printed listings of the hospitals that the men had been taken to.

The readers of the *Journal* were also treated to the story of the capture and escape of Moses Bliss of the 44th New York, who was taken prisoner in his regiment's ill-fated charge on the supposed Rebel cavalry at Spotsylvania. Bliss, a resident of Salisbury and a former Fairfield Academy student, wrote:

> "Instead of a few cavalry we charged on a brigade of South Carolina Infantry. Their line was much longer than our two Regiments and as soon as we reached the works they swarmed out and flanked us. I cannot describe the scene at this moment. To say that it rained bullets would convey but a faint idea. The left of the 44th had to pass through a mass of fallen pines and did not see that they were flanked till they were surrounded. The result was twenty-five of us found ourselves prisoners, Sylvester Delong, Wm. Haver and myself from Herkimer County were among the number. We were hurried back to the rear about a mile, where we remained till next morning. After we were turned over to the Provost General we were treated well. Before that whatever a soldier saw that he fancied, he took. Hats, canteens, haversacks, &c. were taken without a word. Wait a moment. I did hear a Major of artillery apologize for taking a canteen from one of our men, but he said he must have it.
>
> Sunday night quite a number from the 6th Corps were brought in. Monday morning we started for Beaver Dam Station some twenty-two miles distant. Some thirty guards under the charge of a Lieut. escorted us. We could not have been treated better by our own men. We marched slow and were allowed plenty of opportunities to get water. We had nothing to eat, but the guards were as poorly off as we. We had just turned a corner in the road within a quarter mile of the Station, when I heard a shot (fired in the rear) and some one cry 'the Yanks are coming.' I turned and saw a

squadron of cavalry coming round the turn at full speed. Such lusty cheers as went up from three hundred and fifty throats are not very often heard.

The guards put spurs to their horses and left, but not quickly enough for all to escape, some were taken prisoners and the Lieut. killed. We were sorry for this for he was a man if he was an enemy. Three wagon loads of arms, some ambulances and a large amount of rations were the results of this forage. The men helped themselves to what they wanted and the remainder was destroyed. Here we stayed all night and in the morning started on with the 'raiders.' " [1]

The horsemen that liberated Bliss and his comrades were members of Gen. David Gregg's 2nd Division Cavalry, who themselves were running from Jeb Stuart's Cavalry. Often running to keep up with the mounted troops, Bliss and many of the men narrowly avoided being recaptured and safely made it back to their lines.

As the hospitals quickly became overwhelmed with casualties and supplies were rapidly depleted, the Sanitary Commission sent out emergency appeals through its Ladies Aid Society network. In Herkimer County, the request for clothing, bandages, lint and "delicacies" was forwarded through Mrs. Seth Richmond of Little Falls. In having been recently appointed as an Associate Manager of the Women's Central Association of Relief, Mrs. Richmond was officially given the responsibility of unifying the actions of the Herkimer County township Ladies Aid groups. The Herkimer County women were quite willing to produce the needed items but they were sorely lacking in the necessary raw materials. To this end, the Sanitary Commission promised to send a box of cloth, rags etc. for each box of finished hospital supplies sent to them.

The Christian Commission also appealed to the Mohawk Valley folk for donations to their soldiers' relief fund, which was earmarked to provide for the aid and comfort of the hospitalized men. The most notable contribution came from the workers at the Mohawk Woolen Mill in Little Falls, who donated $153 to the fund. The owner of the mill, J.W. Stitt, added an additional $50 from his own pocket.

In Virginia, after twice being frustrated by Lee's blocking tactics in the Wilderness and at Spotsylvania, Grant once again began moving his army in hopes of slipping around Lee's southern flank.

At midnight on May 20th, Hancock's 2nd Corps, preceded by a large force of cavalry, broke camp near Spotsylvania and moved out in a southeasterly direction. Hancock's tentative objective was Hanover Junction, to the north of Richmond. The 152nd New York, marching with Hancock's columns, travelled past Massaponax Church, Guiney Station, Bowling Green and crossed the Mattaponi River five miles south of Milford's Bridge. On May 23rd, the 152nd waded across the North Anna River, just north of Hanover Junction and less than twenty miles from Richmond. Confronted by a sizable rebel force, Hancock halted the 2nd Corps and waited for the rest of the army.

Following close behind the 2nd Corps, the 5th and 6th Corps crossed the North Anna the next morning and took up positions a few miles to the west of Hancock's men. The 121st New York, with Wright's 6th Corps, had marched in the tracks of the 2nd Corps, while the 97th New York, with Warren's 5th Corps, had followed a more westerly route. The "Third Oneida" had crossed the Po River, and marched through Mt. Carmel and Jericho Ford before reaching the North Anna.

At this point the 2nd, 5th and 6th Corps were all on the southern side of the North Anna but were precariously separated by entrenched Confederate units at a bulge in the river. Burnside's 9th Corps attempted to cross the North Anna and fill in the gap, but were repulsed by enemy troops posted on steep, rocky shelves at the bulge's center.

Lee, now reinforced by Gen. John Breckinridge's Brigade fresh from their defeat of Sigel in the Shenandoah Valley, and well aware of the vulnerable Union alignment, attacked Grant's right wing at 6 p.m. on the 23rd.

The 97th New York, which had just arrived at the front and had halted to rest, was hit by artillery fire at the onset of the action. During the cannonade the men got their first look at their new division commander, Gen. Samuel Crawford, and formed an instant dislike. Isaac Hall wrote of the encounter:

> "The 97th occupied the third line in the formation and shortly after the men were relieved of their pieces General Crawford—commanding Third Division—and staff rode up and took position to the right of the regiment on a depression in the field, near the river, which formed a bow northerly to his rear. This was the first sight the 97th had obtained of its new division commander since the Second Division was united or identified with the Third in command. Shortly after arms had been stacked and before the pontoon bridge had been completed, a Confederate battery upon our left having an enfilading fire upon our column, opened with shells upon our position. General Crawford and his staff, clapping spurs to their horses, were off without a parting adieu; not an order was left for the action of our division.
> No demoralization occurred in the brigade. Some broke from the ranks and took shelter under the bank of the river, but the boys of the 97th, taking their arms, stood firm under the cheer of their officers till General Warren had crossed his artillery and silenced the enemy's guns."[2]

In the shelling the 97th lost one man killed and six wounded. The battle, which would be known as Jericho Mills, produced about six hundred casualties on each side and resulted in a stalemate with neither army gaining any ground.

Realizing the predicament his army was in, astraddle the river, Grant began withdrawing his men back across the North Anna on May 25th. The 152nd New York with its 2nd Corps acted as the Union rear guard and didn't wade to the north side of the river until the night of May 26th.

After escaping Lee's trap at the North Anna, Grant repeated his move by the left flank, and with the 5th Corps in the lead, began a slide to the east of Richmond. Crossing the Pamunkey River, the Union army occupied Hanovertown and halted to consolidate their strung out columns. The 97th New York reached Hanovertown at noon on May 27th, the 152nd New York arrived the next day and on the 29th, the 121st New York marched in.

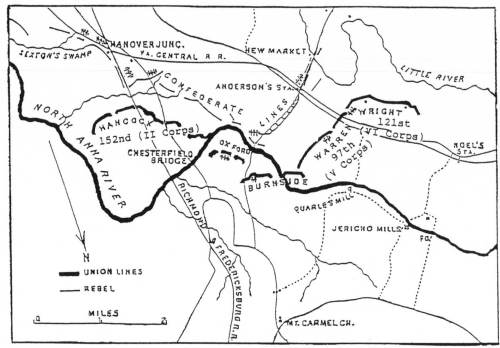

The History of the Civil War, Schmucker

North Anna River, Virginia, May 25, 1864

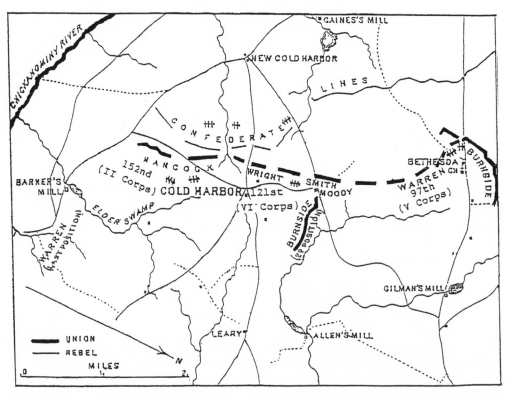

The History of the Civil War, Schmucker

Cold Harbor, Virginia, June 3, 1864

With the Union column now whole again, Grant's advance continued towards an important road juncture at a village called Cold Harbor.

Robert E. Lee had shadowed Grant's army all the way from Spotsylvania, and with his foresight and interior lines of travel, he had been able to block Grant at every turn. Missing his opportunity to destroy the Union army at the North Anna, Lee sent his nephew, Gen. Fitzhugh Lee, with a force of cavalry to secure the crossroads at Cold Harbor. On the morning of May 31st, Fitzhugh Lee's men were attacked by Union cavalry and driven out of Cold Harbor. Robert E. Lee, learning that the Union 18th Corps had been detached from General Butler at Bermuda Hundred and were on their way to Cold Harbor, sent General Anderson's corps and part of another to the aid of his nephew.

On the morning of June 1st, Anderson's men attacked the newly arrived 18th Corps but were repulsed when reinforcements from the 5th Corps came up. The 6th Corps arrived that afternoon and in concert with the 18th Corps attacked the rebel line. After initial success the Union drive stalled and both sides went to work improving their defenses.

The 121st New York did not participate in the 6th Corps' attack having been ordered out on a skirmish detail. Maj. Henry Galpin, who had just returned to the regiment after recuperating from the Spotsylvania wound that had cost him the sight in one eye, described the detail that the 121st's men had been given. Galpin wrote:

> "Came to Cold Harbor and were sent as skirmishers. About twenty of
> our men were ordered by Gen. Rupel to charge and take a house which we
> did. The bullets whistled very lively. We had none wounded at first but
> while holding the position the following were wounded: Lieut. F. Lowe, in
> right side; Priv. M.F. Irish, Co. F left arm; Serg. A.N. Armstrong Co. D left
> leg, very slight, Priv. S. Foote, Co. I right arm; R. Bennet, Co. I right leg
> shot off by shell, mortal; Joseph Edson, Co. I leg not serious."[3]

The 121st held the house and surrounding grounds throughout the night and retired the next morning to the rear lines after being relieved by a regiment from the 2nd Corps.

By the evening of June 1st both armies were at full strength, Grant with one hundred and ten thousand men and Lee with sixty thousand. As the morning of June 2nd dawned the battle lines were set. On the Federal left, Hancock's 2nd Corps faced A.P. Hill; Warren's 5th Corps on the right confronted Jubal Early, and Wright's 6th Corps in the center was opposite Richard Anderson. The Union 9th and 18th Corps were held in reserve.

Grant had originally planned to assault the rebel lines early in the morning, but the attack was postponed to 5 p.m. Just after noon a heavy rain, complete with thunder and lightning, began to fall. The attack was once more called off and was rescheduled for 4:30 a.m. the next morning. Given a temporary reprieve, the Union boys huddled behind their breastworks trying to stay dry as the rain continued all night.

On June 3rd the attack force, composed of the 2nd, 6th and 18th Corps, moved out precisely at 4:30 a.m. The 152nd New York, in the second wave of the 2nd

Corp's advance, was the only Mohawk Valley regiment to take part in the charge at Cold Harbor. Henry Roback described the 152nd's effort:

"Before daylight Capt. Burt passed through the camp with sword drawn, and awoke the men from their slumbers. Placed upon the extreme left, the Second Corps was about to repeat the battle of Spotsylvania C.H. Our brigade, commanded by Gen. Owen, was massed in eight lines of battle and faced Watt's Hill, which, if gained, would command the whole rebel line, enfilading it at that point. At a given signal the whole army moved at once. We passed over the broken ground on the double-quick, the First Division leading.

Arriving on the ridge, the brigade being massed in a solid square by order of Gen. Owen, rushed parallel with the enemy's works through the cleared field, which was swept by shot and shell. A shell bursts in the ranks of the regiment as we rush on, the smoke lifts, and N. O'Brien, of Co. E, and Thos. Evans, of Co. F, lay crosswise of each other, dead. We turn and rush toward the front, crossing the sunken road and swamp. Ascending the hill, we madly charge across the level space, and are met with a cyclone of bullets. A windrow of the First division lie cold in death. Our solid square presses on, the 184th Pa. leading, with the 152nd N.Y. We scale the enemy's works and capture three cannon, holding the breach made, five minutes. Gen. Finnegan [Gen. Joseph Finnegan, CSA] at once rallied his reserves and drove us out, capturing the helpless wounded."[4]

All along the line the Union charge was repulsed with devastating losses. In less than twenty minutes seven thousand boys in blue fell, while the rebel loss was less than two thousand men.[5] A number of small scale attacks and counterattacks continued, but the main Union thrust was over.

The 152nd New York, like many of the other broken Federal units, dropped back only a short distance before digging in. Retreat at the moment was out of the question, for Confederate artillery fire commanded the field and trying to run the gauntlet back to the main line was suicidal.

The men of the 152nd quickly threw up fortifications, and maintained a fire to their front, but Union artillery fire from their rear posed a bigger problem. Henry Roback wrote:

"We fell back to the ridge, an average distance of 100 ft. from the rebels' works, and began to throw up breast-works, using case knives and tin plates. Recovering from their surprise the enemy rashly exposed themselves and sought to drive us from the saucy position we had taken, by jumping upon their breastworks and taking deadly aim at the men lying upon the ground. We maintained our position until the shovels and new muskets arrived, when all was made secure. The side hill below the line in front was filled with men who were engaged in loading and passing the muskets to those in front, who were keeping up an incessant fire.

While the battle was raging, a battery which was located at the rear, in the woods, opened fire, apparently with the intention of knocking down a brick house, situated within the enemy's works, the roof being apparently three feet above the top of the works. For the purpose of getting the exact range, the cannon was depressed to such a degree that the solid shot and shell fell short and buried in the side hill, exploding among the men, causing great consternation, as there was no remedy but to lay still and receive the death dealing missiles.

J.J. Nau, Co. F, Capt. Hale, Division Inspector General, and many others were wounded. D.H. Lewis, Co. C, was struck in the head with the brass plug from a shell. Many others were shot, unnoticed by their comrades who lay by their side. A fence rail was raised above the breastworks for the battery to get the range. A private soldier walked back with orders to cease firing."[6]

General Meade cancelled all further Union attacks shortly after 1 p.m., and for the rest of the day both sides worked on improving their fortifications. The 152nd New York, which had suffered seven killed and twenty wounded in the charge, dug in on the Union left.[7] The 121st New York and 97th New York were posted, respectively, in the center and on the right. Not having been in on the attack, neither of these two regiments had realized any casualties on this bloody day.

With the lines less than one hundred yards apart, the men hunkered down in their trenches and dared not expose themselves to the enemy's sharpshooters. The fighting was left up to the artillery, who rather than dueling with their counterparts on the other side, chose to drop their shells on the poor infantrymen. Henry Roback of the 152nd wrote:

"A mortar battery was erected and brought to bear on the enemy. The shots seemed to do some execution, causing merriment among the boys. After the first day the compliments were returned with their respects. Then the laugh came from the other side. The noise and whistle of the mortar shell is very peculiar and not in any way charming. The boys undertook to build bomb proofs, but abandoned the work, the sand caving in, burying several."[8]

In the no-man's land between the two lines the helpless wounded, lying amidst innumerable corpses, baked in the Virginia sun. Each day fewer and fewer of them cried out for water, some having crawled to safety but the majority having perished on the field.

On June 7th Grant finally swallowed his pride and requested a truce—Lee had no reason to do so because most of the casualties were Federals. For two hours that evening burial details gleaned the field.

The soldiers from both armies emerged from their trenches and in no time the blue and the gray intermingled in a mass of bantering and bartering men. An anonymous writer from the 152nd New York described the camaraderie that truly underlay the feelings of the two antagonists. The soldier wrote:

"The truce of two hours night before last from 6 to 8 to bury the numerous dead that had lain between the lines five days, was one of the finest things I ever witnessed. As soon as a few pocket handkerchiefs were seen in front, hundreds of officers and men with hands and faces begrimed with powder from firing at each other a few moments before, threw aside their guns and belts, swarmed over their respective works and mingled and conversed like 'brothers tried.' Strange to say, the night passed without any picket firing, but the most romantic scene came off yesterday morning. At dawn (the time for the ball invariably to open) all was quiet and men from each side, began to squint over to see if the other was going to fire, but no one opened, both parties seemingly anxious to pair off and look at each other again, and until 10 a.m. the two hostile armies were up on their works and walking about in plain view. At a point on our left, where the opposing works are not more than 20 yards apart, a squad of Johnny's were tossing tobacco to our boys, and they in return, throwing back case knives and little bags of coffee. It was strange and romantic in the extreme, and seemed more like dreamland than reality, carried on as it was, without any regular arrangement whatever. About ten o'clock a Rebel officer hailed our fellows to 'get down out of sight' and in a short time if a head showed itself on either side, a hostile bullet would go for it." [9]

Living in the filth and dirt of their trenches the men in blue and gray were attacked by an enemy that didn't discriminate against either side. In the hot humid weather of Virginia, the sand chigger population of Cold Harbor exploded. Henry Roback wrote of the soldiers' losing battle with this indomitable insect:

"The peddaculles'es' began to appear in great numbers Doubtless they crossed over from the other side, as it was generally believed they had an overproduction. The Western boys called them sand bugs, as they were supposed to generate from grains of sand and sweat, the soldier being the incubator. Prior to this we had a few, but now it was very evident the peds had us. They were no respecter of persons, but treated us all alike. From the General commanding to the eight corporal and private, all were attacked, the mule only escaping. The average amount allotted to each man, officer and private alike, was nine hundred ninety and nine to the square inch. The souls of the murdered ones entered into the new crop, and after three days of maturity, they with redoubled energy and vigor, worked without ceasing.

Why were they made with that terrible claw, and born with that terrific maw? To suck a soldier's blood in cruel war, crawling and biting, creeping and fighting, through each and every hour. The cannons' roar they heeded not, not feared the whizzing blistering shot, the explosion of the mortar shell, the fiendish, exulting rebel yell. Beneath each garment of shoddy blue, in armies great they did not wait, but climb and clamor, fight and chew." [10]

Included among the Union dead at Cold Harbor were: from the 152nd, Nicholas O'Brien of Danube, Thomas Evans from Fairfield and Elisha Smith of Norway; from the 121st, Aaron Miller of Frankfort; from the 2nd New York H.A., John Farrington of Frankfort and Joseph Downer from Russia; from the 81st New York, (organized primarily in Oneida and Oswego Counties), William Smart of Russia, James Pruyn from Wilmurt and Allen Smith of Gravesville.

While at Cold Harbor the 97th New York was the recipient of five hundred and fifty-eight men transferred from the 83rd New York. The term of service of the 83rd had expired and those men that still owed the government duty time joined the

"Third Oneida." Among the transfers from the 83rd New York were a number of men who originally belonged to the 26th New York (the "Second Oneida"), and were being transferred for the second time.

Grant, blocked yet again by Lee, once more swung his army toward the southeast aiming it at Petersburg, a vital rail center twenty-five miles due south of Richmond.

On the afternoon of June 11th, with the music of massed brass bands masking the sounds of the marching troops, the 121st New York with the 6th Corps headed towards the James River. Throughout the next two days the 97th New York and the 152nd New York with their Corps, used the same ruse to silently retire before the enemy.

The Union columns crossed the Chickahominy River and between June 14th and 16th, forded the James. Of the Mohawk Valley regiments, the 97th boated across on the steamers "James Brooks" and "Joseph Powell" from Charles City Court House, while the 152nd and 121st, marched across on a two thousand-foot-long pontoon bridge constructed by the Engineer Corps at Wilcox's Landing. Describing the experience of crossing on the bobbing bridge, John Ingraham of Brockett's Bridge wrote:

> "We crossed the river on the night of the 16th about 9 o'clock. It took 104 boats to lay the Pontoon bridge at the narrowest place. At this point you can imagine it took some time to walk over. It would make a man walk as though he was about three sheets in the wind."[11]

Grant, it seemed, had finally stolen a march on Robert E. Lee. The silent withdrawal from the Cold Harbor lines and the rapidity with which the James was bridged and crossed had put Grant's army less than twenty miles south of Petersburg with almost nothing in its way. In addition, General Butler's army, which had been bottled up at Bermuda Hundred since early May, was also advancing on Petersburg with General Smith's 18th Corps in tow. On June 15th all that stood between a Union force of over sixteen thousand men and the capture of Petersburg were fifty-four hundred Confederates under General Beauregard. With the fall of Petersburg, the fall of Richmond would be inevitable, for all of the rail lines and many of the roads that serviced the Confederate capital ran through Petersburg.

Early on the morning of the 15th Gen. August Kautz's cavalry, supported by a raw division of black soldiers from the 18th Corps, struck the outer trenches and rifle pits of the Petersburg line near Baylor's farm. The rebel defenders, made up mostly of homeguard troops and dismounted cavalry, quickly broke and ran, and the black troops took possession of the works. Gen. Baldy Smith, after delaying the advance of the remainder of his 18th Corps in hopes that Hancock's 2nd Corps would arrive, attacked the rebel line at 7 p.m. Again rebel resistance crumbled and the Union boys gained part of the enemy's main works near Harrison's Creek.

The 152nd New York with the 2nd Corps finally arrived on the outskirts of

Petersburg just after midnight. Hancock's column had been delayed at Windmill Point, awaiting rations that they didn't need, by bad maps, and simply because no word was received that Smith's 18th Corps planned to attack.

Although exhausted after their twenty mile march, units from the 2nd Corps, including the 152nd New York, were advanced to the front to relieve General Smith's black troops.

No Union attack materialized the next morning or afternoon as Hancock and Smith awaited the arrival of Burnside's 9th Corps. In the meantime reinforcements from Lee's army were flooding into Petersburg and taking up positions on the breastworks. At 6 p.m. the 2nd Corps and the 9th Corps attacked and, in the three hours before nightfall, captured four redans along the rebel line, but suffered considerable loss in doing so.

The 97th New York with Warren's 5th Corps arrived on the field early on the morning of June 17th. Taking up position on the Federal left, Warren's men held their line as the 9th Corps attacked the rebel works and were repelled. The rest of the day was spent in arranging the Union battle line, which, arrayed north to south, read; 18th Corps, 2nd Corps, 9th Corps and 5th Corps. That evening the reins of the 2nd Corps passed to Gen. David Birney, when General Hancock's old Gettysburg wounds flared-up, incapacitating him.

At 4 a.m. on June 18th, the 2nd, 9th and 5th Corps, coming from due east of Petersburg, charged the rebel line. Although some initial inroads were made in the enemies works, the Federal advance was eventually blunted. Henry Roback described the 152nd New York's action near the Hare House. Roback wrote:

> "We moved promptly up to the works but were met with a murderous fire enfilading the left. We struggled desperately through the ordeal, and approached the works, but recoiled, leaving the dead and wounded on the field."[12]

Grant, undeterred by the reverse, ordered another general attack, and with their ranks reorganized, the Federals charged at 5 p.m. The Confederate defenses again proved to be too strong and for a second time the Union assault was stopped. Henry Roback once more reported on the 152nd's part, writing:

> "The order came, and with one grand sweep the front line advanced towards the enemy's works. Ten paces were taken, when from behind the enemy's works there poured forth a most murderous fire, resembling a violent tornado or rushing wind, the minnies [minie bullets], passing over our heads. The minnies, striking the trees, glanced and wounded several. The front line recoiled, leaving one half their number dead and wounded on the field. Success being hopeless, the order to charge the rest of the troops were countermanded, and we lay under the incessant volleys fired by the enemy, until night."[13]

Fortunately for the 152nd, they were in the fourth line of the charge and escaped relatively unscathed.

The 97th New York, which had not participated in the earlier attack, charged the rebel fortifications from its position with the 5th Corps on the Union left flank.

Placed in the front line of its division's advance, the 97th performed like the seasoned troops that they were. Isaac Hall wrote:

> "At the word of command the column moved briskly forward across a piece of interval land, and crossing a brook ascended the timbered bluff, but as they emerged from the strip of timber skirting its summit, upon an open plowed field, they were struck by a destructive fire in front and on their right flank. The preceding regiment dropped down upon the rear of a gentle slope which shielded them from the enemy's fire. The 97th, following this example, also got down so soon as closed up to the 104th [N.Y]. For half an hour or more these regiments thus lay; the men and officers knowing the utter impracticability of carrying, unsupported on its flanks, a line of works strongly fortified and manned by an extended line on either hand, hesitated to go forward. But the order to charge upon the enemy's works had been given, and being veteran troops they felt the responsibility of its execution.
>
> While to the rear of the 97th, the officer in command and the adjutant were urging the regiment to go forward, a captain [Isaac Hall himself] on the right sprang to his feet and swinging his sword said: 'Boys of the 97th, follow me!' One man [Evan Evans] of his company followed close to his heels, and as he looked over his shoulder he saw most of his regiment and part of the 104th coming in broken lines over the field made dusty by the enemy's bullets. As he neared a low rail fence, about 100 yards from the enemy's fortification, he halted in the rear of a pile of rails and awaited the closing up of his regiment. In three minutes the color bearer of the 97th was by his side, and his regiment had arrived at the fence and kept the Confederates down by its well directed fire.
>
> The shades of evening now closed in, when these regiments were withdrawn, suffering some loss in retiring." [14]

That evening General Grant suspended further assaults on the main rebel works and abandoned his attempts at taking Petersburg by frontal assaults.

During the actions of June 15th through June 18th, the Union army had suffered over eleven thousand casualties; rebel losses were unknown.[15] Losses in the 97th New York were ten killed and forty-two wounded[16] and in the 152nd New York, one killed and seven wounded.[17] The 121st New York, with the 6th Corps along the Bermuda Hundred line to the northeast of Petersburg, suffered eight wounded.[18] Among those killed at the initial assaults on Petersburg were: from the 97th, David Theobald of Russia, Albert Von Garner from Manheim and John Bailey of Norway; from the 81st New York, Henry Rich of Russia; from the 2nd New York H.A., Sgt. Abel Rust of Russia.

Once again Grant had smashed his army against Lee's fortified line and once more had been repulsed with bloody consequences. Now began the slow, tedious process of enveloping the city and cutting the supply lines to the rebel army inside it. The siege of Petersburg had begun.

Since May 4th, the Union army had either been engaged with the enemy or on the move to yet another battleground. Hospitals were filled and the men were exhausted, but sitting now at Richmond's doorstep, the Union boys were resolved to see this thing to the end. Henry Roback of the 152nd, after visiting some of his comrades at a field hospital, described the horrors of war and spoke of the resigned spirit of the men. Roback wrote:

> "Upwards of one hundred graves were filled at the farm house occupied by our Division, many dying on their way to Washington. The dooryard presented a horrible spectacle on the morning of the 19th. The mutilated remains of the heroes were piled in heaps and scattered around; the wounded lying on stretchers awaiting for death to relieve their agony.
>
> The final results of a battle can only be seen at the hospital. The amputating tables containing the wounded, the dead and the dying, and parts of bodies lying upon the ground, will give a clear idea of the scenes enacted on the field.
>
> The time had arrived when a spirit of demoralization came slowly creeping upon all who were exhausted from want of sleep, and forced marches. The chances of life were unfavorable; many believed their hour was nigh, if not by the bullet or shell, then by sheer fatigue. Yet there was none who would willingly give up the fight and trust to his Satanic Majesty, Jefferson Davis. Newspapers were scarce, but one arrived giving an account of Andersonville prison and was generally believed by all intelligent men." [19]

In just a few weeks Gen. Ulysses S. Grant had irrevocably changed the whole complexion of the war. Gone were the one or two day battles after which the blue and gray armies would rest and regroup for months before having at each other again. From now on the blood would flow continually.

CHAPTER XVII

"The President had an opportunity to witness something of the terrible reality of war"

Summer 1864 - Lincoln's Call - Summer in Herkimer County
The Weldon Railroad - The 121st in the Shenandoah Valley

The cumulative quota for Herkimer County under Abraham Lincoln's calls in the winter of 1863-1864 was set at twelve hundred and ninety-one men. Lincoln's March 14th call, General Order No. 100, specified that if the quotas were not met by April 15th a draft for deficiencies would, "if practicable," be held on that date. Fortunately for Herkimer County and its 20th Senatorial District, as the draft day came and went and May passed toward June, no draft was ordered.

Using the advantage of this grace period the Herkimer County Enrollment Committee, headed by Little Falls Supervisor, Zenas Priest, and the township recruiting boards, continued their work of encouraging enlistments. Aiding in the endeavor was the 121st's Capt. John Fish (killed at Spotsylvania on May 12th), who opened a recruiting office in Herkimer, and the enticement of bounty monies.

The Federal $100 bounty and $75 New York State bounty remained. To maintain the state bounty fund, a state tax of two and one-eighth mills on each dollar valuation of real property had to be imposed. The township bounties in Herkimer County were standardized by mutual agreement at $300 to prevent in-fighting for recruits among the county municipalities.

By the first week in June, eleven hundred and fifty-three credits were given to Herkimer County. The composition of these credits were; four hundred and thirty-five men who paid commutation fees, sixty-six men already in the service that re-enlisted, twenty-three credits were gained from the excess of the previous draft and six hundred and forty-four men enlisted or provided substitutes.

District Provost Marshal Emerson finally announced that the draft for deficiencies in Herkimer County would be held in Watertown on June 8th. Since Herkimer County had not met its quota, on that date one hundred and thirty-eight names of county men were drawn from the drum for "personal service" to the Federal government. Transposing statewide statistics for this draft to the number of men drawn in Herkimer County, of the one hundred and thirty-eight names drawn; eighty-five men were exempted for physical or mental disabilities, twenty-four men provided substitutes, twenty-seven paid the commutation fee and only two men were actually inducted. Notable among the draftees were Assistant Assessors Addison Lamberson of Brockett's Bridge and Matthew Dygert of Mohawk. Adding a touch of irony to the draft, the town of Russia's enrolling officer, Dr. S.R. Millington, had his ticket pulled from the drum at Watertown.

Many of the valley towns had met their quotas and in fact a few had even realized excesses which would be credited to them if another call was made. These excesses, fifteen in all, were the property of the towns that realized them and were not debited from the county's quota. Of the towns that were deficient only German Flats with fifty-six deficiencies, Manheim with seventeen, Russia with twenty-four and Salisbury with eleven, had missed their quotas by sizable margins. A number of the towns felt that they had not been duly credited with the correct number of recruits. Of the situation the *Journal* noted:

> "Very many re-enlisted veterans who have been paid large bounties by their respective towns have not yet been credited on the town quotas. For instance: the town of Salisbury paid bounties to quite a number in the 97th regiment, but has not received credit for a single man in the regiment. So with Little Falls, Manheim and some other towns. Whether the fault lies with the officers of the regiment or with the officials at Albany or Watertown, it is difficult to say. It is no wonder that those drafted should feel impatient over the delays in this matter-delays which, to them, are all-important, for as soon as the proper credits are given many of them will be 'stricken from the rolls' of conscripts."[1]

With this draft just completed, the *Journal* informed its readers that yet another draft was imminent. The June 23rd edition of the *Journal* reported:

> "The Troy Whig is of the opinion that there is a mortal certainty that there will be a draft for '300,000 more' early in July. The government, when the call is made, will not wait for localities to fill up their quotas, as it has hitherto done, but it will on very short notice proceed to make a draft. There are now indications that the $300 commutation clause will be repealed. The government and the generals in the field want men and not money, and the War Department therefore seems disposed to take the readiest means within its power to fill up the depleted ranks of the army. With the commutation clause repealed, no one subject to draft when drafted can get off without furnishing a substitute, and we have reason to believe that not much time will be allowed for this purpose."[2]

Taking this intelligence as fact, the supervisors of Herkimer County met in Herkimer to develop a countywide plan to help meet the expected new call. A

Herkimer County recruitment committee, composed of Zenas Priest, Ezra Graves, John Barry, Robert Etheridge and John Treadway, was appointed and a number of resolutions were passed. These resolutions were: 1) The committee was authorized to select agents to recruit, on the county's behalf, throughout the North and even into the rebellious states; 2) A $300 bounty, drawn on the taxable property of the county, would be offered to each volunteer; 3) All travel, lodging and other expenses realized by the agents would be reimbursed by the county; 4) The volunteers recruited by the agents were to be apportioned to each town in proportion to the number of enlistments the town raised on its own.

In addition to actually procuring volunteers for the townships, the supervisors also passed a resolution whereby bounties up to $300 paid by a town to a volunteer could be charged upon the county. To prevent competition among the Herkimer County towns, the supervisors also resolved that any town that offered bounties exceeding $300 would be excluded from any financial assistance from the county.

As would be expected, at town meetings throughout Herkimer County, referendums to continue township bounties at the $300 level passed nearly unanimously. In Little Falls the vote was two hundred and fifty "for" and two "against." Of the two nay votes the *Journal* remarked:

> ". . . at least one of these was but the habitual expression of a chronic hostility on the part of the voter to all measures of public good or general interest."[3]

In many of the county's towns and villages resolutions also passed to pay a $300 bounty to any man who procured a substitute for himself.[4] These enactments provided an extra incentive for those men liable to be drafted to find a substitute on their own without incurring any great personal expense.

On July 4th both Houses of Congress passed the expected new Enrollment Bill. This bill empowered the President of the United States to call, at his discretion, any number of men as volunteers he deemed necessary, for terms of one, two or three years. It also specified that if quotas were not filled within fifty days of the President's call, a draft would be immediately ordered to fill the vacancies with one year conscripts.[5]

Among the other provisions of the bill, which amended or added to the February 1864 Enrollment Act, were:

> - Federal bounty payments of $100 for one year, $200 for two years and $300 for three years of enlistment. Bounties would be paid in installments of one-third upon mustering, one-third at the mid-point of service and one-third upon discharge. In the event of death in the service any residual bounty would be paid to the man's widow, children or mother (if she was a widow).
> - The $300 commutation escape clause was repealed.
> - Volunteers, substitutes or draftees would be placed in a unit from their own state of enlistment or when practicable could select their own unit.
> - Recruiting agents were permitted to recruit in any rebellious state

with the exception of the states of Arkansas, Tennessee and Louisiana.

- Substitutes must be either aliens, veterans with at least two years of prior service or men between eighteen and twenty years old. In other words, substitutes had to be non-draftable men.

- If a draft was ordered in a district, the Provost-Marshal General, at his own discretion, could double the number of men to be drafted to fill the deficiency.

In expectation of a call by President Lincoln, the 20th Senatorial District's Provost Marshal, Capt. Frederick Emerson, issued new guidelines based upon the policy changes caused by the Enrollment Bill for those men seeking exemptions or presenting substitutes. In a set of resolutions Emerson's dictum read:

> "I. Resolved, That Persons enrolled not liable to military duty on the account of 1st Permanent Physical Disability, 2nd Unsuitableness of Age, 3d Alienage; May appear before the Board of Enrollment [at Watertown] each day, Sundays excepted, between the hours of 10 and 11 a.m. to be excluded for the purpose of having their names stricken from the enrollment.
> II. Resolved, That the hours of each day, between 2 1/2 and 3 1/2 o'clock p.m., Sundays excepted, be devoted to the examination of Substitutes and Volunteers.
> III. Resolved, That representative recruits presented by persons not liable to draft shall have the preference in examinations.
> IV. Every person wishing to present a substitute or a representative recruit, will be required to give notice to the Board in writing, setting forth as follows: 1st The home of the person presenting such substitute or recruit and his place of residence. 2nd When he wishes to make such presentation, 3d The name of such substitute, 4th his age, 5th his occupation, 6th his nationality, 7th his present residence, 8th Whether he be liable to do military service under draft or not."[6]

On July 18th President Lincoln's awaited call for volunteers was made, but instead of asking for three hundred thousand men as had been speculated, Lincoln requested five hundred thousand. In compliance with the Enrollment Bill, September 5th, being fifty days from the date of call, was ordered as draft day for deficiencies.

Having expected a quota based on a call for only three hundred thousand men, the enrollment officials in Herkimer County learned to their disappointment, that even with the nearly one thousand credits gained since the last call, as of August 1st the county was still short of their quota by almost eight hundred men. With draft day fast approaching and with surrounding counties luring men away with large bounties, the towns of Herkimer County began taking drastic steps to enlist recruits. German Flatts and Little Falls, each still deficient by over one hundred men, were the first townships in the county that passed resolutions to increase their bounty money to $800 per volunteer. Disregarding the county's suggested $300 maximum bounty, many of the other Herkimer County towns followed suit and the $800 bounty became the norm. In an editorial in the *Journal*, J.R. Stebbins described the draft scene in Little Falls and questioned the merit of the bounty system. Stebbins wrote:

"For several days the town has been greatly excited by the offers of large bounties and the enlistments of many of our young men. Several of them made arrangements last week to go to Utica to enlist, and on Monday morning were preparing to do so, when a meeting of our town Board was called and a resolution adopted to pay volunteers for either one, two or three years, the sum of $800. In a very short time forty names had been enrolled and there is a present probability that not more than twenty-five or thirty names will be drafted from this town.

On Monday a procession of wagons, headed by the Band, paraded the streets with banners and on Tuesday quite a number left for New York to be mustered into the Navy for one year. Several of them however, were not more than fifteen or sixteen years of age and will probably be rejected.

We have always believed that the best manner to recruit our armies was by the draft, and the more we see of this large bounty system the more are we satisfied of the correctness of our early-formed impressions. It is a question of some importance as to how much real service men who enlist merely to obtain large sums of money are likely to be in the great work of putting down the rebellion: and it is a question, too, of the moment, as to how long the county can afford to pay these enormous sums for recruits. To test the matter in this town, suppose the whole amount of bounties necessary to relieve us from the present draft (say one hundred thousand dollars) be put into an assessment roll for immediate collection. Would it not be well to try the experiment?" [7]

With the total of the township, state and Federal bounty money exceeding one thousand dollars per enlistee, Herkimer County's credits toward the July call increased rapidly. Township agents continued to travel throughout New York State garnering "volunteers" for their villages. German Flatts, which had been deficient in the June draft and had been so far behind on this quota, reached its manpower goal when a group of thirty to forty men enlisted in the Navy under that town's credit.

When draft day arrived on September 5th, no names were drawn from Herkimer County. Through the hard work of enrollment committees and by the expenditure of large amounts of money, each town had met or surpassed its quota.

It would seem by outward appearances that the drafts, the campaigns in Virginia and Georgia, and the war in general, fully occupied the attention of the Herkimer County people, but as evidenced in the pages of the *Journal* the flow of everyday life went on in the Mohawk Valley.

In an agriculturally-based society such as that of Herkimer County, the weather was of major concern, and in the early summer of 1864 it was downright terrible. During the first two weeks in June, a period most critical to the establishment of new crops, killing frosts struck the Mohawk Valley severely retarding plant development. The weather then reversed itself turning very hot and dry, and a subsequent drought in early July caused further damage to the already late corn and hay crops. With the yields of these important dairy cattle feeds down, milk production dropped and consequently cheese manufacture suffered. The scarcity of cheese brought bid prices to an unprecedented high of twenty cents per pound. Unfortunately, most of the farmers couldn't benefit from these premium prices simply because they had no cheese to sell.

In a bit of good economic news, Erie Canal Auditor Nathaniel Benton of Little Falls revised the canal's navigational rules in permitting canal boats to now draw six feet of water. This simple revision allowed the boats to carry an additional twenty tons of freight. Benton also reminded the canallers that the use of grappling hooks, irons or anchors to fasten their boats to the tow paths or to bridges would result in a $25 fine.

To the delight of the schoolchildren, public schools and academies in the county closed in late June and early July. For those pupils who hoped to advance a grade, most schools required an exhausting two-day session of examinations and recitations. To add to the anxiety of the students, the public was cordially invited to witness the testing.

The *Journal* also contained items on typical summertime diversions.

On schedule, two circus groups, Spalding & Rogers Great Circus and Robinson & Howes Champion Circus, made their annual tours through the Mohawk Valley, stopping for a day or two at most of the larger towns.

Keller Hall in Little Falls featured George Christy's famous Minstrel troupe and the legerdemain of Professor Bardnard, the American "Fakinostrator." The professor not only performed feats of magic, but also presented valuable gifts of bedroom furniture, silver tea sets, and cutlery to members of the audience. A seat at one of Barnard's performances and a chance at winning one of his prizes could be had for the price of twenty-five cents. Travelling with Barnard was Harry McDonough, the great Chinese juggler, who performed his unrivalled "Double Drum Solo" act.

For entertainment with more of a homegrown flavor there was the long awaited match race between Alexander Fox's gelding "Little Mac" and Edward Simms' bay mare "Lady Lincoln." For weeks prior to the race the merits of each horse were "debated" throughout Herkimer County's saloons and by race day the "Lady" was the slight betting favorite. The best two out of three heat race for a $50 purse was held on a Saturday afternoon in mid-July at "Petrie's" one-half mile track on the east side of Little Falls. A huge crowd watched as "Little Mac" took the first heat and "Lady Lincoln" took the second. After the second heat, Mr. Fox, claiming that the "Lady" had fouled by running part of the race on the infield, appealed to the judges to award the heat and therefore the race to his horse. When the judges disagreed, Fox withdrew "Little Mac" from the third heat. "Lady Lincoln" pranced the last heat unopposed and took the $50 purse. Mr. Fox and the bettors who had backed his horse left the track threatening to file a lawsuit to recover their money.

Once again the Fourth of July passed rather quietly in Herkimer County as many people travelled to Utica or St. Johnsville to celebrate. In Little Falls there was the usual amount of "small firing" and rather more than the usual "drunkenness and rowdyism." Of the Independence Day activities in St. Johnsville the *Journal* reported:

"The celebration at St. Johnsville drew quite a large concourse of people and we never saw more loafers and drunkards, more street brawls and rowdyism in one day than ran riot there. The established reputation of that village was fully sustained. The oration of Judge Smith of Utica, was a brilliant production and received the highest praises from all who had the pleasure of listening to it. The greased pole was too slippery for climbing and the chasing of the pig amounted to little more than the tramping down of a fine patch of corn." [8]

On a romantic note, two veteran soldiers of the 81st New York, William Leland and George Anderson, ran a personal ad in the *Journal* seeking correspondence with the "Fair Ladies" of Herkimer County. The boys hoped that an exchange of letters would result in "mutual improvement" with "views towards matrimony." Photographs of the ladies were desired but not necessary.

Up and down the valley, village law enforcement officers were busy looking for two counterfeiters. A "sharp" looking gentlemen had been passing counterfeit ten dollar bills from the West Winfield Bank, that, although well-executed, bore a number of subtle distinguishing marks. At the same time another counterfeiter was spreading five dollar bogus notes from the Bellinger Bank in Herkimer. These bills were easily discernible because that bank had never issued bills in that denomination.

Among the other police work reported by the *Journal* were, the arrest of Stephan Adams at his "Four Mile Grocery" in Ilion for selling "moonshine" without a license and the breakup of a near riot in Little Falls, between a group of Germans and the family of a Mr. Kana. The "Dutchmen" it seems were picnicking without permission on Kana's land and their horses were damaging his fields. When Kana asked the picnickers to leave, words ensued and blows soon followed. Just before police arrived Kana's son was considerably injured when he was hit on the head by a stone.

In Little Falls a tragic accident shook the village when a rowboat carrying five people was swept over the upper mill dam, drowning all on board. The victims were Jerry Vaughn and his son, John Casler and the sons of a Mr. McHenry and a Mr. Carr. It was rumored that the two adults were trying to frighten the children by sailing close to the dam when the boat became caught in the current, pulling all of them to their death.

In Virginia, Ulysses S. Grant waited only three days after his unsuccessful June 18th frontal assaults before once more having a go at Petersburg's defenses. Grant's objective now was to cut the Weldon Railroad, one of two principal rail lines that supplied Lee's army. The track, which entered the city from the south, linked Petersburg with the port city of Wilmington, North Carolina.

Grant's move began on June 21st as Union cavalry units under the command of Gen. James Wilson and Gen. August Kautz struck the Weldon at a point about ten miles south of Petersburg. The cavalrymen were only able to rip up a small portion of the track before being attacked and driven away by advance units of A.P. Hill's Corps. Backing up the cavalry, the 2nd, 5th and 6th Corps began a westerly advance, entrenching along a north-south line just east of the Jerusalem Plank Road, which paralleled the Weldon Rairoad.

Early on the morning of June 22nd, with the 6th Corps on the left flank and the 2nd Corps on the right, the Union advance continued. Grant's complicated plan of attack called for the two corps to swing in concert to the northwest while maintaining an unbroken front. This "swinging door" maneuver was aimed at enveloping the Weldon rail line and extending Grant's line westward.

Unfortunately, with a longer route and more difficult terrain to traverse, the 6th Corps moved much more slowly than the 2nd Corps resulting in a huge gap forming in the Federal battleline. Gen. A.P. Hill quickly discovered the opening in the Union line and exploited it fully. Sending one division to hold the western facing 6th Corps in place, Hill slipped two divisions through the Federal gap and sent his men onto the left flank and into the rear of the northward facing 2nd Corps.

The 152nd New York with Mott's Division was on the left flank of the 2nd Corps' line and was among the first regiments struck by the rebel charge. Henry Roback of the 152nd described the regiment's part in that day's action. Roback wrote:

"Gen. F.C. Barlow commanded the Second Corps in the absence of Hancock. About noon Barlow advanced the First Division, breaking connection with the Sixth Army Corps and covered the railroad, leaving the Sixth Corps far to the left and rear, with an immense swamp intervening. He was about to intrench, when Mahone's Brigade [of A.P. Hill's Corps] came driving through the dry swamp, sheltered from view by the tall and overhanging alder and whortleberry bushes. Mahone at once attacked the left and rear of the First Division, sending a portion of a regiment to keep back the Sixth Corps. In the meantime the enemy in front of Gen. Mott and our division moved out of their works and advanced in line of battle, firing heavy volleys. Capt. Hensler, Capt. Gilbert and Lieut. Lewis Campbell occupied the skirmish line with a detail from the regiment and brigade. There being no salvation for them in that position they were gobbled up. Emboldened by their success the troops in our front advanced and retreated, firing and receiving ours with a good grace. The noise and confusion in our front drowned the music on the left, where Mahone was slowly rolling up the two divisions preparatory to sending them to Andersonville.

At last the wave struck the left of the 152nd, the enemy pressing through the woods. Sergeant Cornell, Co. H, took direct aim and fired at the rebel color bearer. Major Timothy O'Brien, commanding the brigade, ordered Capt. Burt to fall back; but the confusion was so great, with the shots and shell, and the rebel horde closing around, with furious and exultant yells, that few heard the order. Every one acted independently, and using their own judgement and legs in getting away, a few running into the ranks of the enemy amid the blinding smoke, and were captured."[9]

Thirty men from the 152nd were taken prisoner in the rebel surge, two men were killed (Sgt. William Cornell of Little Falls and J.W. White from Otsego County) and seven men were wounded.[10] The remainder of the regiment found its way to the rear and reformed near the entrenchments that they had left that morning.

Roback continued with his narrative:

"Capt. Burt with 20 men formed around the colors, and fought their way back to the plank road where they planted the flag, and awaited for the men to rally. We were then ordered across the road and joined on the Corcoran Legion [the 155th, 164th, 170th and 182nd New York]. We moved up the gentle slope in line of battle, and halted on the ridge. The enemy at once opened a battery upon us, charged with grape and canister. We lay in that position one hour, with the leaden hail showering over and around us.

When we recrossed the road, the enemy sent solid shot and shell bounding down the plank, rolling like balls on a ten pin alley, using the Yanks for pins. One ball struck Capt. Burt's feet rolling him in the dust. One struck Wm. Watts, of Co. A, in the heel, spinning him around like a top. At 8 p.m., we charged with the line, the works we had lost, and held them until morning, at the point of the bayonet. On the 23d we fell back to the plank road and occupied a low breastwork of logs."[11]

In the June 22nd assault on the Weldon Railroad the 2nd Corps lost nearly twenty-four hundred men, of which over seventeen hundred were captured. The 6th Corps, which never became fully engaged, suffered only one hundred and fifty casualties.[12] This disparity in numbers also held true for the two Mohawk Valley regiments involved in the movement. While the 152nd lost thirty-nine men, the 121st showed only one man killed.[13]

Grant had failed to break the Weldon Railroad but had achieved an important extension of his lines below Petersburg. The Union army now went to work building forts and breastworks in a consolidation of the newly gained ground. John Ingraham of Brockett's Bridge, in a letter to his sister, described the fort on Spring Hill occupied by the 121st. Ingraham wrote:

"First there is wire strung along the outside. The first wire will take a man just about the feet, next above the knees & next a little higher & if a man runs against that on a horse he ain't agoin to know anything until he strikes the ground. If he lives over that and attempts to charge on he will run into a line of sharp pointed sticks which would check him I think, but if not as soon as he went through them he would find himself into a twenty foot deep trench if he found himself at all, but I doubt his ever finding himself after going into that. No man can climb from that upon the fort. Five thousand men could hold 25 thousand from taking it. Cavalry could never charge it. 32 pounders [cannon] is the heaviest they have mounted in them now. They have had heavier ones but have moved them somewhere else."[14]

The other two Mohawk Valley regiments were also positioned south of Petersburg. The 152nd New York set up camp at the headwaters of the Blackwater River, while the 97th New York bivouacked at yet unfinished Fort Prescott. For the rest of June and well into July, the 97th and the 152nd remained at these camps doing picket duty and further strengthening their fortifications. The 121st New York on the other hand would only spend a short time at Spring Hill before being ordered back to, of all places, Washington.

Robert E. Lee knew that unless he could break the siege of Petersburg, the might of Grant's army would eventually encircle the city and strangle his army inside of it. In late June, Lee ordered Gen. Jubal Early and his force of ten thousand men in the Shenandoah Valley to go on the offensive and invade Maryland and Pennsylvania. If the opportunity presented itself, Early was to threaten Washington. Lee hoped that Early's raid would result in the capture of needed supplies, and most importantly, might divert Grant's troops from the Petersburg front and relieve the pressure of the siege.

Early did his work well. Pushing aside Federal units in the Shenandoah Valley, he drove through Maryland—levying Hagerstown for $20,000 and Frederick for $200,000—before entering Pennsylvania. Marching his army through southern Pennsylvania, Early arrived at Washington's doorstep on July 11th. Suspecting that the city was only lightly defended, Early planned an assault for July 12th.

The politicians in Washington had followed Early's advance with more than trepidation. Grant, in calling out the Heavy Artillery regiments, had stripped the capital of most of its manpower, leaving the city defended by a handful of home guard and government office workers. With Early's raiders fast approaching, an appeal went out to Grant to send troops.

On July 10th, the 121st New York, with the 6th Corps, was ordered to report to Washington. Rumors of a move north had been circulating through the camps for a few days and as John Ingraham remarked to his sister, the boys were all for it. Ingraham wrote:

> "I heard today the 3d Div of our Corps had been ordered to go to Harpers Ferry. I heard in fact the whole of our Corps were agoing & only one Div to be sent at one time. I hope it is true. I should like to serve another Campaign in Md. We served two. I think if we should go there we would not be apt to come back here again. It is too good to be true." [15]

The 121st New York, numbering less than one hundred and fifty men, left their fort on Spring Hill and marched to City Point. There they boarded the river steamer "Tappahannock," and travelled in company with the 96th Pennsylvania down the James River to Newport News where they anchored for the night. Early the next morning, the "Tappahannock" started up the coast, reaching the Washington Naval Yards on July 12th. Disembarking, the 121st New York formed ranks and hurriedly marched up 7th Street, before halting five miles outside of the city.

Jubal Early, upon learning that the veterans of the 6th Corps now manned the Washington fortifications, called off his planned assault and began withdrawing his troops. Before Early could pull back all of his troops a sharp skirmish developed between the rebel rear guard and units from the 6th Corps. From their perch on the parapets of Fort Stevens the men of the 121st New York stood alongside Abraham Lincoln and watched their 6th Corps comrades drive the rebels from the gates of the capital. Herkimer's Clinton Beckwith wrote:

> "The day was exceedingly hot and that made the marching in the thick dust very hard after we had left the pavements of the city. When the sound of musketry reached us just before reaching Brightwood, we saw General

Wright stopping by the roadside with a gentleman whom we immediately recognized as President Lincoln. He answered our greeting and cheers by raising his hat. Instantly afterward we heard the sing of a bullet and we knew that the President was under fire. Moving up to the fort and deploying to the left in rear of our works, we found them swarming to suffocation with all sorts of people, invalids, reserves, convalescents, clerks, citizens, marines, any and everybody who could or would be able to fire a gun. . . As soon as we were deployed, before in fact, General Bidwell rushed forward with the 7th Maine, the 61st Pennsylvania, 43d, 45th, 77th and 122d New York regiments, and swept back the troops of Rodes' division of Ewell's corps, then under Early, and pushed them down across Rock Creek and beyond Montgomery Blair's residence at Silver Spring, losing quite heavily at the outset, but inflicting a greater loss upon the enemy. Under the eyes of President Lincoln, Secretary Stanton and a vast multitude of soldiers and civilians standing upon the works, where they had for many hours fearfully awaited the advance of Lee's choicest troops, the superb veterans of Bidwell rushed upon the old time foes and pushed them from our front, under a devouring fire of musketry, but stimulated by the cheering of the spectators. We were proud of our comrades and glad that the President had an opportunity to witness something of the terrible reality of war." [16]

In subsequent action that day, the already thinned out 121st lost five men killed and nineteen wounded.[17]

With Early on the retreat, General Wright and the 6th Corps took up the pursuit. The 121st New York, moving with its division, passed through Maryland, forded the Potomac at Edward's Ferry and crossed into Virginia. Continuing the chase, the 6th Corps marched over the Blue Ridge Mountains and linked up with Gen. David Hunter's Army of Western Virginia on July 18th.

Unable to catch Early and believing that the rebels were on their way to Petersburg anyways, Wright about-faced the 6th Corps on the 19th and began a forced march back to Washington. The capital was reached on July 23rd and preparations were made, much to the men's dissatisfaction, to return to Petersburg.

Early's raid hundreds of miles to the south posed little threat to the Mohawk Valley but did cause considerable consternation to the Herkimer County militia men. In answer to the rebel incursion on Northern soil, on July 5th, President Lincoln ordered New York's Governor, Horatio Seymour, to have twelve thousand of the state's militia ready to move. Provost Marshal, General Fry informed Seymour that under the president's emergency call these men were liable to be drafted for one hundred days.

As a reminder to the Herkimer County men of their obligations under New York State's Militia Enrollment law, the *Journal* published a summary of the rules:

"The law requires the enrollment for service in the State militia of all white male inhabitants of the State between the ages of eighteen and thirty-five excepting:

1. Persons in the army and navy.

2. Persons who have been honorably discharged from the army or navy, in consequence of the performance of military duty, and such firemen as are now exempt by law.
3. Persons who have served as commissioned officers in the militia for the period of seven years.
4. Persons who have performed military service in independent companies for the period of seven years.

Non-residents and those physically or mentally disabled, are also exempt. The notice of enrollment is required to be delivered to the person enrolled, or at his place of residence, and if he claims exemption under either of the classes of exemption by the law, he must file a written statement thereof 'verified by affidavit, in the office of the town or city clerk, to be designated in said notice' before the 15th of August. In case no statement is filed as required, the person must appear for 'training' on the first Monday of September 'and equipped as the law directs' or pay one dollar commutation on or before the first day of December. In case neither of these conditions be complied with, the assessor is required to assess taxes upon the delinquent, and issue his warrant for the collection of the same.

The names of persons who commute appearance at parade by paying one dollar are kept on file by the military authorities and in case a call is made upon the State militia for actual service, a draft is made from such names."[18]

Militia groups began to assemble in the towns of Herkimer County. In Little Falls, Capt. John Gilliland issued a call for his company, Co. E, 38th Regiment New York State Militia, to meet at the No. 2 Engine House in that village.

Fortunately for the men of Herkimer County, the 6th Corps arrived behind the defenses of Washington and drove back Early's raiders. With the danger passed, the militia alert was called off.

History of the 121st Regiment

Officers of the 121st New York. Top, Col. Emory Upton; Left, Col. Egbert Olcott; Right, Maj. Henry Galpin

History of the 121st Regiment

Corp. Clinton Beckwith, 121st New York

Pvt. John Ingraham, 121st New York

Courtesy of Mr. Edward Ingraham

Lieut. Adam Clarke Rice, 121st New York

Letters of Adam Clarke Rice

CHAPTER XVIII

"They arose like demons from the bowels of the earth"

Summer 1864 - Deep Bottom - The Crater - Strawberry Plains
Globe Tavern - Reams Station

On the Petersburg front the Federal war machine ground to a halt. After having smashed his army against the city's defenses in mid-June, Ulysses Grant eschewed any further thoughts of taking Petersburg by direct assault and began the slow, laborious process of extending his lines to cut off Lee's supply routes.

With the prospects for a quick end to the war looking bleaker and bleaker, Lt. Col. Henry Pleasants of the 48th Pennsylvania Volunteers presented a novel way to broach the Confederate line. Pleasants, who in civilian life had been a mining engineer and who commanded a regiment largely populated by coal miners, proposed to dig a shaft under the rebel works, fill its gallery with gunpowder and literally blow open the enemy line. Pleasants' plan made its way up the command chain before being approved by Burnside and half-heartedly by Grant. In the last week in June, the miners from the 48th Pennsylvania began digging. Given virtually no support by the Corps of Engineers, the excavation proceeded slowly, but as the end of July neared, a five hundred-foot shaft, capped by an eighty foot long lateral gallery, lay beneath a rebel salient named Fort Elliot.

In conjunction with the mine's detonation, Burnside readied the 9th Corps for a rush through the expected breech. To help draw attention and Confederate troops from Petersburg, Grant ordered Hancock's 2nd Corps and Sheridan's Cavalry to make a demonstration at Deep Bottom, situated mid-way between Petersburg and Richmond.

As part of Hancock's diversionary force the 152nd New York broke camp on the

Blackwater on the afternoon of July 26th and joined the 2nd Corps column in its northward march. The Appomattox River was crossed at Point of Rocks and early the next morning a pontoon bridge was laid across the James River. After crossing the James, the line of march swung westward and Hancock's men approached the rebel position near Deep Bottom. Wasting little time, the 152nd's division formed into battleline and assaulted the enemy's outer works, driving in the rebel pickets. Ordered to continue the advance, the 152nd passed through a set of woods before emerging into an open field. Confederate artillery fire immediately began to pound the field but the men of the 152nd were ordered to dig in and weather the shelling. One casualty was realized in the bombardment, Pvt. William Syllbach of Herkimer, who was mortally wounded by a cannon ball.

Holding this position throughout that night and well into the next day, the 152nd was ordered late on the afternoon of July 28th to withdraw and rejoin the brigade. Cautiously advancing westward, the 152nd was detached from the brigade and ordered to throw up breastworks in a cornfield. Once more the men of the 152nd spent the night in an open field behind their slim fortifications.

Having drawn a division of Lee's men away from Petersburg, on the evening of July 29th the 2nd Corps was ordered back to Petersburg. The James was crossed that night, and by the early morning hours of the 30th, the 2nd Corps was back at Petersburg positioned behind the 9th Corps.

The detonation of Pleasant's mine was scheduled for 3:30 a.m. on the morning of July 31st, but due to faulty fuses, the eight tons of gunpowder in the mine's gallery were not touched off until 4:30. Henry Roback of the 152nd, from his position opposite Fort Elliot, described the spectacle that followed:

> "At 4:40 a.m. a heaving and trembling of the earth was followed by a terrific explosion. The fort with all its contents, six cannon and two hundred and eleven men, were immediately raised high in the air. The mighty column poised for a moment, resembling a great fountain, when it descended with a resounding thud. A yawning crater one hundred feet in length by fifty broad and twenty feet in depth, was all that was left. Instantly upon the explosion one hundred heavy guns broke out and joined in a fire which exceeded in intensity that of Gettysburg." [1]

The 97th New York at this time was posted on the southern end of the Union line, acting with the rest of the 5th Corps as a reserve unit. The men of the "Third Oneida" had been roused by Adjutant Judd at 1:30 a.m. that morning and were notified to be ready to march by 2 a.m. Two o'clock came and went and no orders to move were received. Many of the men had dozed off to sleep when the mine explosion and the subsequent artillery barrage jarred them awake. Isaac Hall of the 97th wrote:

> "Just after the break of day, when the men had become weary in waiting, and some had fallen asleep, all at once a jar and rumbling sound, similar to that of an earthquake, was heard, and the artillery all along our line thundered forth their fire. The heavy guns and mortars to our right, were particularly active, and news soon passed along our line that a fort in front

of the Ninth Corps had been blown up by a mine, and that our lines there had gone forward into Petersburg, or had taken the enemy's works in close proximity to the city. Our brigade and division expected momentarily to advance upon the enemy's fortifications, but the distance was so great, and success on our right so uncertain, that no order came to go forward." [2]

The first Federal unit to reach the mine's crater was the 14th New York Heavy Artillery Regiment. The 14th, which recruited principally in the western part of the state, included a handful of men from Herkimer County including nine former members of the old 34th New York. The artillerists turned infantrymen had already suffered over six hundred casualties since Grant had pulled them from their cozy Washington forts in May, and this day would add another bloody page to the 14th's history. "C.H.B." wrote of the 14th's charge at the crater:

"Hardly had the rubbish reached earth . . . when was sung out in a voice that never wavered, 'Forward 14th!.' Away we went yelling like fiends. The rebels, thunderstruck by the explosion, took to their heels, and we carried their first line at the point of the bayonet. Now they brought their artillery to bear, and swept us with shell, grape and canister: to stay, we could not, and again we went forward on the charge—a sharp volley of musketry, a yell that would send the blood boiling in a man's veins, and the second line of works were ours. Now it was thought best to relieve the division, and accordingly a brigade of darkies were ordered up, we going back to the first line." [3]

After having spearheaded the charge, the 14th New York Heavy Artillery was released to the rear to escort back prisoners and wounded. In leading the assault the 14th New York Heavy Artillery added one hundred and thirty-two casualties to their total. [4] The rest of the brigade—commanded by Col. Elisha Marshall of the 14th New York Heavy Artillery—fanned out to the left and right of the crater, holding the gap open for the support troops that were supposed to come up.

The rest of the division did come forward, but instead of advancing to the support of Marshall's brigade, the men stopped and gawked at the devastation wrought by the mine explosion. Some of the more adventurous men climbed into the pit, but lacking the foresight to bring ladders were now having a hard time getting out. To add to the confusion, this key element of Burnside's attack was without a leader. The division's commander, Utica native Gen. James Ledlie, was safely back in his bombproof and was reported to be quite drunk.

Without proper direction from the front, two more 9th Corps divisions piled into Ledlie's milling men. One of these divisions also advanced leaderless as its commander, Gen. Edward Ferrero, stayed behind and joined Ledlie in the bombproof. What had started out as a well coordinated assault now quickly deteriorated into a shambles.

Given a reprieve, the rebel defenders regrouped, pushed back Marshall's advance brigade and herded the Federals into the crater. Gaining the rim of the pit, Lee's men poured musket and artillery fire into the panic stricken Federals below. Into this slaughter, General Burnside advanced his fourth division which was composed chiefly of black troopers.

One of the regiments in this division, the 23rd U.S. Colored Troops, was officered by two men, Lt. Col. Cleaveland Campbell and Capt. Edward Townsend, who were quite familiar to the Mohawk Valley folk. Campbell, from Otsego County, had been an officer in both the 121st New York and the 152nd New York, before taking command of the 23rd U.S. Colored Troops. In the crater struggle Campbell would be severely wounded and would die within the year. Townsend, a Fairfield student, was also a former member of the 152nd New York and while with that regiment had been a frequent correspondent to the *Journal*. Just two weeks prior to the crater battle, Townsend had written to the *Journal* about the quality and traits of the black soldier. Townsend wrote:

" . . . the colored soldier is easily initiated into [the] broken manner of traveling throughout life, and one of the chief beauties in his character is, that he learns to conform himself without grumbling to [the] multiplied changes in his condition, and the continual interruption of necessary rest. He feels that he is a soldier of Uncle Sam, and proud of that edict which has clothed him in a blue uniform, and raised him to the position of a national vindicator, he endures night marches and the heat of a southern sun, conscious that privation and fatigue are necessary auxiliaries to his personal liberty and the full freedom of his posterity.

It is quite amusing and entertaining to hear our colored boys sing, and many of their songs are full of melody and sweetness.

They will collect around a fire at night and soon one of their number 'strikes up' a song, a few others join in, and quickly a loud chorus of voices are pouring forth their peculiar characteristics of verse and song. Whole regiments catch the inspiring notes making the fields and woods alive with the echoes of music. I tell you what, no one can easily get the blues if silence alone engenders them, for we are surrounded by music, wit and fun: for the negro is naturally full of life and vivacity, ever ready to talk, sing or dance.

Please inform any of the colored population at Little Falls and vicinity, that if they desire to fight for the liberty of their brethren in the south, a fine opportunity is offered them in the ranks of the 23d United States, now at the front. Let them come, for this war is for the emancipation of slaves, and they should not remain idle while duty calls them to shoulder the musket and meet the oppressors of their race."[5]

Unfortunately for the 23rd U.S. Colored Troops, their "oppressors" in this fight had a distinct advantage. With the appearance of the black soldiers at the crater, the rebel's savagery intensified. Moving down into the pit, the gray soldiers began to use clubbed muskets and the bayonet, giving little quarter to the black Federals or their white officers.

Finally, just after noon, Burnside issued orders for a withdrawal. Running a gauntlet of musket and artillery fire, the battered divisions of the 9th Corps made it back to the safety of their lines leaving over four thousand of their number at the crater. Neither the 97th New York or the 152nd New York suffered any casualties, for neither had been engaged in the fiasco that Grant would term "the saddest affair I have ever witnessed in the war."

Generals Burnside, Ledlie and Ferrero, among others, were officially censured by the War Department for their parts in the crater disaster. Burnside and Ledlie requested leaves of absence from the army from which they never would return.

L. Bartlett Barker, the principal of Fairfield Academy who was assigned to the Petersburg area as an agent for the Christian Commission, offered his thoughts on the reason for the mine failure. In a letter to the *Journal* Barker wrote:

> "The plan was well conceived, and the springing of the mine success-
> ful, but the ultimate object was not reached. The time fixed for the spring-
> ing of the mine and the whole plan of attack were known the night before
> all along the lines, and yet one and a half hours elapsed after the fort was
> blown up, before the commanders had their men ready for the contem-
> plated charge. The men attributed this to a want of friendly feeling between
> Generals in command. An altercation the night previous to the assault, is
> reported and believed by the soldiers to have taken place between two of
> our first Generals: respect for these officers and an unwillingness to believe
> this of them forbid the mention of their names in this connection. Whether
> the report be true or false the belief of it has a most damaging effect on the
> men under their command. Had the execution of the plans been as good or
> honorable as its conception, your humble correspondent . . . would have
> had the exquisite satisfaction of getting into Petersburg-whereas he now
> had only the privilege of looking into it, a privilege which he did not fail to
> improve. A wicked contempt of the negro soldier had not a little to do with
> the failure of the undertaking, and for this wickedness we have been, and
> are still in danger of being sorely punished. That God is 'no respector of
> persons' is a truth which, as a people, we seem unwilling to heed."[6]

While the action at Petersburg slowed, the fighting in northern Virginia was just heating up as Jubal Early returned to the Shenandoah Valley. Almost as quickly as Wright's 6th Corps began their counter-march to Washington, Early's raiders started advancing once again down the valley. Pushing aside Gen. George Crook's 8th Corps at Kernstown, the rebel columns moved into Pennsylvania and burned Chambersburg. In response to this incursion, in early August Grant ordered Phil Sheridan to take command of the Union forces in the Washington and Shenandoah theaters.

Through his intelligence network, Grant learned that Confederate troops were preparing to leave Petersburg and reinforce Early. Robert E. Lee's intent was to escalate the war in the Shenandoah Valley, moving the focus of action away from the Petersburg-Richmond area. Grant, after working so hard to put pressure on Lee's army, was not about to see it relieved. In hopes of holding the rebel forces in place, thereby depriving Early of reinforcements, Grant ordered a demonstration to be made on the Confederate left. The Union troops selected for the job were Hancock's 2nd Corps and Gen. David Birney's 10th Corps and the area targeted was once more Deep Bottom.

On the afternoon of August 13th, the 152nd New York broke camp at the Blackwater and marched to the James River where the regiment, along with the rest of the 2nd Corps, loaded onto transports. At sundown, the troop flotilla embarked downstream on the James in a ruse to divert attention from the intended objective to the north. Dropping down ten miles, the ships anchored until 11 p.m., at which time they about-faced and began steaming upstream. Deep Bottom was reached at 4:30 a.m. the next morning and the troops disembarked without incident.

At around 7:00 a.m., under an already blistering sun, the 152nd began to advance inland from the James. Although the march was relatively short, the heat of Virginia's summer sun and the exhaustion of two months of almost constant fighting made for an agonizing trek. Henry Roback of the 152nd related:

> "On Sunday morning, the 14th, when the good people of the North were quietly wending their way to the several houses of worship, we were advancing on the road to death, destruction and eternity. We advanced two miles from the river, and came to a deep woods, where we halted. The heat was intense, the foliage was withered, and the air was suffocating. A comrade of Company E started in quest of water, carrying seven canteens. The order came to forward, quick step march. The 152nd was the last in line. The men began to drop with sunstroke, the froth foaming from the mouth, many dying in convulsions. Lieut. D.B. Fitch excused the comrade who carried the double load [Roback], his own and the water-bearer's, and just in time to save his life. After resting a few moments, he arose to proceed, when he was called back by Leonard Baldwin, the hospital steward, and assisted him in prying open the jaws of a comrade of the 20th Mass., forcing a potion of medicine down his throat. The comrade coming up with the water, we straightened up our patient and proceeded, counting seven men who had died with the intense heat."[7]

Approaching the enemy's works, the 152nd New York formed with the rest of its brigade into two lines of battle and were ordered to charge. Ascending a slope, the men became entangled in "wait-a-bit" vines and were struck by deadly volleys from an enemy armed with six-shooting repeater rifles.* Continuing his narrative of the day's events, Roback reported:

> "Those who succeeded in pressing forward up to and within the enemy's breastworks were shot down or taken prisoners. The distance to the enemy being so close, their shots were more effective, and the loss was greater for the number engaged than on any other occasion. Our position among the shrubs and undergrowth was scarcely tenable. We could neither advance nor retreat, the enemy keeping a steady fire upon all who were exposed. Capt. J.E. Curtiss, A.A. Gen. had his horse shot under him, and was wounded. John F. Harter fell wounded and lay helpless upon the field, the enemy keeping up a steady fire until he was killed. Sergt. Theo. Doubleday, while being carried from the field, received another wound. John Dorsey lay upon the field groaning with pain, his comrades not daring to assist him. Albert Hall received a wound in his leg, resulting in amputation. Jimmy Morton, of Company A, joined the regiment at City Point. He was a new recruit, and at once began preparations to receive the mysteries and miseries of war, by taking all the different degrees at once. He advanced to the parapets of the enemy's works, side by side with the old vets.

---

* Not standard issue in the Confederate army. Probably taken from dead or captured Union cavalry.

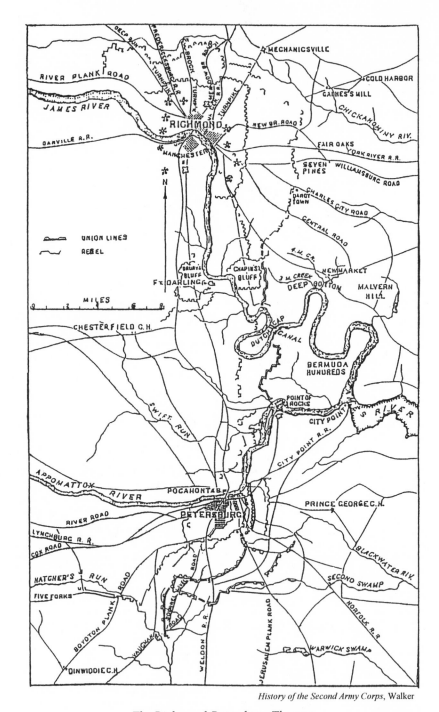

History of the Second Army Corps, Walker

The Richmond-Petersburg Theater

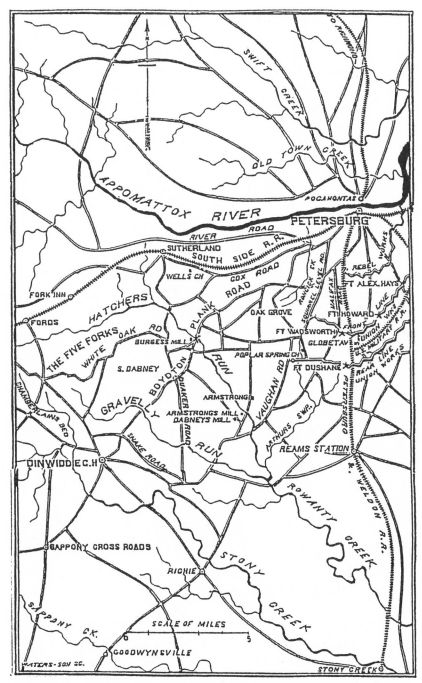

The History of the Civil War, Schmucker

The Richmond-Petersburg Theater

A cruel bullet hit him, and he fell within the rebel works; the surgeon of the Confederacy sawing off his arm several days later."[8]

In the assault—which was known as the battle of Strawberry Plains—the 152nd lost twenty-seven men, including three killed.[9] Of the men mentioned by Roback; John Harter of Herkimer had been slain, but Jimmy Morton and John Dorsey of Little Falls, Albert Hall of Herkimer and Sergeant Doubleday of Fly Creek, survived their wounds. Captain Curtiss, although for a time trapped under his horse on the field, was only slightly wounded.

Under the cover of darkness, the 152nd withdrew from its hillside position. For the next five days the regiment served as a reserve unit while the 10th Corps unsuccessfully probed for a weak spot in the Confederate defenses. On August 20th the 152nd and the rest of the 2nd Corps marched to the James River, climbed onto troop transports, and steamed back down to City Point.

The rebel troops that Grant believed were on their way to Early had in truth remained posted at Deep Bottom. In addition, rebel troops were also shifted from the southern side of the Petersburg line to help block the Federal move. In doing so, Lee had thinned his forces along the Weldon Railroad and had presented Grant with the opportunity to once again seek this prize. Given this opening, Grant ordered Warren's 5th Corps to advance against the rail line.

The 97th New York broke camp at Fort Prescott on the morning of August 18th and with its division of the 5th Corps began a march for the Weldon. The weather was extremely hot and not long into the march men began to fall by the wayside, victims of sunstroke. Early in the afternoon the column struck the railroad near Globe Tavern where it halted. The weary men fell out, fires were quickly kindled and meals were being prepared, when an enemy skirmish line appeared. After exchanging a few shots, the 97th was ordered to fall in with its brigade and the march continued along the east side of the track, north towards Petersburg. Advancing slowly, the brigade easily drove back a small rebel force and halted after moving about a mile from Globe Tavern. Once again the men broke ranks to rest, cook their bacon and boil their coffee.

Towards sundown the brigade re-formed and continued their advance, cautiously keeping the skirmish line only a short distance from the main column. In the gathering dusk the skirmishers stumbled into a rebel force that, at point blank range, unleashed a few deadly volleys into the Federal line before retiring. In this brief encounter, the 97th New York lost two men killed; John Sheldiner, a draftee from Utica and William Hart from Morehouseville, and a number of wounded, most notably Capt. George Alexander from Rome and Capt. John Grimmer from Lowville. Four other officers were taken prisoner: Capt. Henry Chamberlin of Fairfield, Lt. Frank Faville of Brockett's Bridge, Lt. Thomas Burke of Harrisburg (in Lewis County) and Lt. Archibald Snow of Boonville.

With darkness having fallen, the brigade stopped for the night and entrenched. After trees were dropped to form a thirty yard wide abatis across their front and a low line of breastworks were constructed, the men were allowed to retire for the night. But there would be no rest for the members of Companies A and I of the 97th who were detailed out on picket duty.

Early the next morning, August 19th, a rebel skirmish line struck the two unfortunate companies from the 97th and drove in the pickets. The brigade quickly formed behind their works and the enemy assault was speedily repulsed. Company A of the 97th lost in the attack three wounded and two captured, including Lt. Aaron Yerdon of Boonville.

In marching north from Globe Tavern, the 97th's brigade had become the extreme right flank of the 5th Corps. To the right of the 97th was the left wing of the 9th Corps, but to the consternation of Colonel Wheelock, a three hundred yard gap existed between the two forces. Wheelock, who was the acting brigade commander, complained to division headquarters about this break in the line, but to no avail. The enemy quickly discovered this soft spot and late in the afternoon attacked it, driving a wedge between the 5th Corps' right flank and the 9th Corps' left. General Warren, unaware that the 97th's brigade still held its position, ordered his artillery to open on the charging rebels, not realizing that he was killing friend and foe alike. Of this confused and tragic action, Isaac Hall of the 97th wrote:

> "The position occupied by our brigade was in dense second-growth woods, but to the right of it, consisting of the gap, it was sparsely timbered; much of the woods having been cut away. In front of this space, a little before 5 p.m., Mahone's brigade or more of his division, in solid column, attacked the picket line, and following it up rapidly was soon in our rear, and deploying was about to sweep down towards our left, when General Warren opened upon it with grape and canister.
>
> Wheelock's command, all unconscious of this change in the programme, was astonished only at the direction and emphatic manner in which the attack was made. Several of the 97th were killed and wounded, Lieutenant Henry Fitzpatrick among the former.
>
> Col. Wheelock immediately dispatched his Adjutant to report to General Crawford [Division commander] that he was killing his own men. That officer of course rode into the Confederate column, his horse and equipments were taken from him and he was ordered to their rear. This brought him to his own brigade with the first intelligence that the enemy was in our rear." [10]

Nearly encircled and being hit by their own artillery fire, the 97th found a gap in the rebel line and barely escaped capture. Isaac Hall continued his narrative of the engagement:

> "Moving in good order, at a quick step to the left, along the rear of the line, troops who considered themselves already taken were found lying down with their arms on the ground awaiting escort to the enemy's rear. [These] men advised the 97th to throw down their arms and surrender or they would be shot down. But a prompt command from the commandant of the regiment was in time to prevent this demoralization; the men being told to keep their arms and use them if necessary, and our circuitous route saved the 97th from coming in contact with the enemy.

The regiment had nearly reached a point to the rear of the position it had occupied at the front, when a rapid firing of infantry was heard from the position occupied by the brigade, and soon after Colonel Wheelock emerged from the woods with the balance of his command. At Wheelock's appearance a shout of triumph arose from all the troops in sight, which was borne along our lines to the right and left."[11]

The 9th Corps finally formed a junction with the right of the 5th Corps and the enemy attack was driven back. The 97th with its brigade marched back to its former position.

After spending a miserable night in a constant downpour, the next morning the 97th was ordered back to the vicinity of Globe Tavern, where it formed behind General Wainwright's massed artillery. The rain continued the rest of that day, August 20th, and well into the night.

With the 5th Corps now in possession of a section of the Weldon track, A.P. Hill's Corps furiously counterattacked on the 21st, trying to dislodge it. An assault at 10:00 a.m. was repulsed although the 97th was flanked and was forced to jump to the other side of their works for protection. In the early afternoon the rebels moved on the center of Warren's line, only to run into the concentrated fire of Wainwright's artillery. Isaac Hall described the slaughter:

"From the woods off the left flank of Warren's front line came Mahone's heavy and compact columns in grand array. Time was given them to swing clear of the woods and open out on the plain towards the left of our main, front line. It was a grand sight; with their steady, firm tread now just begun, and their colors floating in the breeze agitated by this steady moving phalanx.

A change comes suddenly over these moving battalions; Warren's batteries open and this living mass of humanity becomes a mass of mangled flesh and bones; and the living drop with the dead and dying. No infantry fire touches their ranks, yet they go down like wheat before a reaper. White emblems of a surrender arise and our batteries cease firing."[12]

With this bloody defeat, the Confederate attempts to drive the 5th Corps from astride the Weldon were ended.

In the battles of August 17th to the 21st, Federal losses of four thousand men were compared to only sixteen hundred for the enemy,[13] but Grant had gained the prize he wanted, a foothold on the Weldon supply line. In the fighting of those four days, the 97th New York lost one hundred and eleven men. Of this total, ninety-two men (mostly draftees and substitutes) were taken prisoner, seven men were killed and twelve wounded.[14] The 97th's Herkimer County boys who were killed were Lt. Henry Fitzpatrick of Salisbury and Pvt. William Whitman of Newport.

Even though the Federals had gained a hold on the Weldon Railroad, much needed supplies for Lee's army in Petersburg still flowed along this artery. Trains laden with food, forage, munitions and other war material, from the ports of Wilmington, North Carolina, and other supply points, still chugged north as far as Reams

Station, five miles south of the 5th Corps' block at Globe Tavern. At Reams or at more southerly stations, the freight was off loaded and carried by wagon around the Federal lines to Petersburg. In an effort to make this rebel supply line even more tenuous, Grant ordered a ten mile stretch of the Weldon from Globe Tavern to Rowanty Creek, five miles below Reams Station, to be demolished. Hancock's 2nd Corps was recalled from the stalemate at Deep Bottom and given the task of tearing up the Weldon's rails.

The 152nd New York, with its division of the 2nd Corps, arrived south of Petersburg on the morning of August 21st. The casualties taken at Deep Bottom and the rigors of the march back to Petersburg had reduced the manpower of the 152nd to such an extent that when the regiment set out for the Weldon Railroad the next morning, only seventy-five men shouldered muskets. Fittingly, with the size of the regiment reduced to that of a company, a captain, William Burt of Mohawk, commanded. All three of the field grade officers, Colonel Thompson, Lieutenant Colonel O'Brien and Major Curtiss, were incapacitated due to battlefield wounds.

Upon arrival at Reams Station, the men of the 152nd New York were immediately put to work, along with the rest of the 2nd Corps, tearing up the Weldon's track. The work of the "trackmen" involved lifting whole sections of track (using a rail as a pry bar), feeding the cross-ties into a huge bonfire and heating the metal rails until they deformed into an unusable shape.

Under the protection of cavalry pickets, the men of the 2nd Corps had destroyed eight miles of the Weldon from Globe Tavern to below Reams Station by the end of the workday on August 24th. Only one more day would be needed to wreck the last two miles of line above Rowanty Creek and the mission would be accomplished.

On their way to work on the morning of August 25th, the small band of men from the 152nd were startled by heavy musket fire to their front. Horsemen galloping to the rear soon appeared, providing a sure sign that the cavalry picket was being driven in. The 152nd was ordered to a sugar cane field where the men laid low while the 1st Maine Cavalry, armed with sixteen-shooters, slowed the enemy advance.

While the cavalry held off the rebel skirmishers, General Hancock assembled his corps behind some low breastworks built by the 6th Corps in June. Hancock's line, which resembled a horseshoe, was situated with the open end facing to the east. The distance from one "leg" of the shoe to the other stretched less than one-half mile.

Heavy rebel assaults struck the Federal line three times between 2 p.m. and 4:30 p.m. and each time the Union boys held solid. During this fighting the 152nd was kept behind the main line, either guarding the rear approaches or hustling from one point of attack to another. No matter where the Union boys were positioned, due to the narrow circumference of the "horseshoe," they always seemed to be under the enemy's fire. Enemy artillery and musket fire directed at the front of one wing of the Federal line often carried into the backs of the men on the other wing. Of this inescapable fire, Henry Roback of the 152nd wrote:

> "We were now the centre of gravitation attracting numberless molecules of lead from three-fourths of the compass." [15]

At 5 p.m. the 152nd was detached from the rest of its brigade and sent to the front lines at the center of the "horseshoe." Just after taking up position, this section of the Union line was struck by the enemy's most concerted attack. Henry Roback described the rebel assault and the resultant Federal rout:

> "Our position overlooked the whole situation. We at once opened fire upon Pegram's Artillery, which had arrived and was sending shot and shell across the centre, which completely paralyzed our men with the deafening roar and terrible shrieking of shells, each shot being aimed at one point—the centre. Meanwhile the Johnnies crawled through the underbrush and lay directly under our works. When the cannon ceased firing they arose like demons from the bowels of the earth, and with one prolonged yell they vaulted over the works and with the bayonet drove the men, capturing many and cutting the line in two parts. Our division not being pressed, was hurried to the centre and began to restore order. Wade Hampton [Gen., CSA] seized the opportunity and crossed the works left vacant. They crowded in on all sides and the driving-in process was continued, the entire front giving away. In vain the men were rallied. The artillery was captured and the guns spiked and the horses shot on the field.
>
> . . . Our regiment viewed the scene, keeping up a sharp fire until the day was lost. We were seen by a party, who advanced toward us, firing rapidly. Our ammunition being exhausted we retired rather hastily toward the rear. Elias McCammon and James Hill fell dead together, before we had taken twenty paces. We kept on the outside of the works and ran the length of the line, the bullets striking the ground before and around us at every step." [16]

Darkness soon put an end to the fighting, and small groups of Hancock's men stumbled and groped their way to the rear in a torrential downpour. Rebel forces did not follow, being content with having driven off the Federals and having taken possession of Reams Station. In the fighting that day, the 2nd Corps lost twenty-seven hundred men, the bulk of which, two thousand, were taken prisoner. Rebel losses amounted to less than eight hundred. [17]

In the 152nd New York, twenty men, including five killed, were lost. [18] Two of the men killed, Lester Huntley of Columbia and Elias McCammon of Manheim, were Herkimer County boys. Notable among the Herkimer County losses was that of Adj. Alfred Quaiffe of Little Falls, who was taken prisoner. Of Quaiffe's capture, Henry Roback related:

> "During the charge he became overcome by the intense heat and fatigue and fell to the ground unconscious, and was left upon the field for dead. The terrific thunder shower, long after we had left the field, restored him to consciousness. Groping his way without guide or compass, through the inky blackness of the night, he arrived at a house where was stationed several Union pickets in charge of a wounded officer. Early the next morning the house was surrounded by the enemy's cavalry. The pickets were captured and sent to Hotel DeLibby [Libby Prison] for refreshments." [19]

Even though Grant had not totally eliminated the Weldon Railroad as a Confederate supply line, Hancock's men had so devastated an eight mile stretch of the track, that its future value would be limited. In addition, the Reams Station and Deep Bottom movements had prevented Lee from sending reinforcements to Early in the Shenandoah and to General Hood fighting Sherman in the West.

After the military operations of July and August the Petersburg lines stabilized as both armies sought to catch their breath and lick their wounds. For the remainder of the summer and well into autumn the front was quiet except for occasional probes, cavalry raids and the desultory fire of the sharpshooters and the cannoneers. The scenes of action now turned to Atlanta, the Shenandoah Valley and most importantly, to the impending Presidential election.

CHAPTER XIX

"It is a big victory
although we suffered severely"

Fall 1864 - On the Home Front - Fisher's Hill - Cedar Creek
The 1864 Presidential Election

In early August the people of Herkimer County received the happy news that two of the area's favorite officers, the 97th's Lt. Col. John Spofford and the 121st's Lt. Col. Egbert Olcott, had been released from rebel hands. Spofford of Brockett's Bridge, who was captured at Gettysburg and Olcott of Cherry Valley, who was taken in the Wilderness, were among fifty officers who were specially exchanged from their imprisonment in Charleston, South Carolina. The Federal officers had been transferred from Libby Prison in Richmond to the waterfront houses of Charleston Harbor for use as a human shield to discourage Union naval bombardments of the city. After a proper show of indignation by Washington and threats of retaliation against Confederate officers in Federal custody, Richmond agreed on an exchange.

While Olcott headed home to Cherry Valley, Spofford journeyed back to Brockett's Bridge. Upon his arrival in New York City on August 10th, Spofford telegraphed his family in Brockett's Bridge that he would be arriving in Little Falls the next day aboard the New York Express. Although there was little time to prepare a proper reception, when Spofford's train pulled into the Little Falls Depot on the afternoon of the 11th, it was met by a large crowd and the Citizen's Brass Band. Word quickly spread that Gen. Joseph Hooker was travelling on the same train, and Spofford was temporarily upstaged when a number of people began calling for "Fighting Joe." Hooker appeared, and as reported by the *Journal*, gave a brief speech:

> "He answered from the platform of the car, saying that while in Washington the citizens got out all the bands in the city and endeavored to get him

to make a speech, but he didn't do it then, and he would not now. He was no speech maker. He was going to Jefferson County to see a couple of sisters he had not seen in fifteen years. He then intended in returning to his post in the army fighting this rebellion, and after the war was over he would come and stay with us until we got tired of him. His little speech was greeted with cheers, and the train moved onward."[1]

With Hooker gone, all attention turned to Colonel Spofford. After a healthy round of hand-clasping, Spofford was welcomed home on Herkimer County's behalf by Henry Link, a prominent Little Falls attorney. The colonel responded to the greeting with "a happy effort," whereupon the Citizen's Band began to play, appropriately enough, "When Johnny Comes Marching Home." The guest of honor mounted a carriage and the band led an impromptu parade up Ann Street to the Benton House, where "refreshments" were waiting. Following the downing of a few "cupfuls of cheer," Colonel Spofford was escorted to Brockett's Bridge by a "committee of gentlemen."

During his stay at home, which would stretch into January, Colonel Spofford rejected a number of requests to speak of his exploits, consenting only to address crowds in Brockett's Bridge and Utica. When asked by the *Journal* to write a series of articles about his prison life, Spofford begged off, but he did write an open letter to the paper dispelling rumors that he had become a Southern sympathizer. In defending himself, Spofford wrote:

> "I would, however, like to set my record right politically. Since my return home a report has been freely circulated that after thirteen months in southern prisons and contact with southern institutions, sentiments and people I have returned and out and out anti-Administration man, a Fernando Wood and Vallandigham democrat. An assertion more false cannot be made, for on the contrary, after my experiences and most serious reflections upon the condition of our country I am more of an Administration man than ever before. And I believe Fernando Wood, Vallandigham, and others of that stripe more dangerous to the country than ever was Aaron Burr or Benedict Arnold. For I have been repeatedly told by well informed southern men that if they (the South) had not received positive assurances of assistance in their designs upon the Constitution and country by men of that stamp, there would have been no rebellion."[2]

During the late summer of 1864, the regular columns of "Camp Correspondence" from boys in the local regiments disappeared from the pages of the *Journal*. No letters "From the 121st" appeared. Of the three Little Falls boys from the 121st that regularly corresponded to the *Journal*: George Eaton was wasting away in a rebel prison camp in Florence, Georgia; Marcus Casler had been discharged due to wounds, and "Big Joe" Heath, recently promoted to a 1st Lieutenant, was occupied on the march with Sheridan in the Shenandoah Valley. The column "From the 152nd" was also missing from the newspaper. Gone from the 152nd were its frequent reporters, Edward Townsend of Fairfield, who had transferred to the 23rd U.S. Colored Infantry as a captain and Julius Townsend from Newport, who was discharged due to illness. No reports came "From the 97th" as Brockett's Bridge boys,

Willard Judd and Rouse Egelston, mired in the Petersburg trenches, found little time to write.

One occasional contributor, Salisbury's Moses Bliss, a member of the 44th New York, wrote his final letter to the *Journal*. The 44th, a three-year regiment, had fulfilled its military service and was about to be mustered out. On the eve of the regiment's departure from the front, Bliss, reflecting on the 44th's service, wrote:

> "Having endured patiently for over three years the privations, toil and fighting incident to service in the field, to-night the 44th starts on its way homeward. That it is not in sorrow we leave the bustle and excitement of military life for the peaceful pursuits of citizenship you may well imagine. Yet there is seen no more of that boisterous enthusiasm or joyous hilarity that characterized our departure from Albany three years since. The day of cheering long since passed with us. Three years in the field, will take the life and spirit out of anyone. We are all happy, not overjoyous. One cannot avoid thinking of the many who came out with us but do not return. Virginia's soil is indeed enriched with the blood of our comrades.
>
> In the company to which I belong (B) seventeen have fallen by the bullets of the enemy, more have been crippled and maimed than this even. Of the original number in the company (101) thirteen are here to return with us, and two remain as veterans.
>
> We are sad too, when we think of the many vacancies we shall find in the home circle. The voices of many who amid tears bid us "Godspeed," at our departure will not be heard in tones of welcome at our return. The great destroyer has been busy at home as well as in the battlefield. We would be better satisfied, too, did we leave the work complete and the rebellion ended. We think, however, that we have done our share and are now entitled to a little rest for a season at least."[3]

In their three years of service, the 44th New York, Ellsworth's Avengers, lost three hundred and thirty-five men.[4]

Letters to the *Journal* from the front now came from wholly new sources. Edward Chapin from Little Falls, a member of the Signal Corps stationed at the Avery House near Petersburg, wrote of the array of Federal forts that encircled the city. Another Little Falls resident, Maj. Orrin Beach, an ex-member of the old 34th and now an officer in the 16th New York Heavy Artillery, detailed the activities of his regiment (attached to the 10th Corps) at Petersburg and provided his views of the Copperheads and of "Old Abe." But the most interesting accounts of life at the Petersburg front came from a non-combatant, L.B. Barker, the Fairfield Academy principal. Barker, in his position as a Christian Commission agent, toured the camps making a special point of his trips to visit the Herkimer County regiments. Describing his call on the 152nd New York just prior to that regiments move on Deep Bottom, Barker wrote:

> "A polite officer with shoulder straps, whose name I did not learn conducted me to the 1st Brigade, passing along in line I asked for the 152d. An innumerable number of men lay rolled up in their blankets before me, on asking for the 152d up sprang Capt. Burt of Norway [Mohawk]. He had

recognized my voice and came from his sandy bed to welcome me to the sleeping place of a soldier on the march.

In every direction, as far as a bright moon light would enable me to see, were camp fires, men sleeping in the open air, or riding, or walking, as inclination, duty or rank might determine. Here were supply wagons, and yonder promiscuously interspersed among the sleepers and tied to stakes driven into the ground, were horses . . . this was my first real knowledge of the inconveniences attending a soldier's life. On inquiry, I found that the boys were not only tired and sleepy, but hungry also. Accompanied by Capt. Burt, I proceeded to the headquarters of the Christian Commission at the Point, and loading myself with pickels and crackers, returned to the camp and distributed my cargo among the boys of Herkimer and Otsego. It was but little that each received but that little was received with gratitude and eaten with zest.

Though it was now past 9 p.m. . . . the Capt. struck a fire and treated me to a cup of army tea. Chaplain Talbot was among the number whose slumbers my coming had broken. Some rest being needed by us all, I bade them good night and returned to my lodgings on the Point. Early the following morning I was on my way to the regiment with a supply the same as before, happy that I was permitted to give so much as a 'cup of cold water' to the brave defenders of the rights of man and of the institutions of liberty. As a recompense for the crackers and pickels, I was this time treated to a cup of coffee by the Chaplain. I learned from the regimental quartermaster that 160 men drew rations that day and that the regiment now numbers in all about 500. The regiment has 'gone up the river.' "[5]

Barker also paid a visit to the 44th New York. While with that regiment he got a close-up look at the Federal trenches and gained first-hand knowledge of what it felt like to be shot at. Of these experiences Barker wrote:

"The amount of digging and fortifying done by our troops in this part of our army is almost incredible. In approaching the front where the 44th New York is stationed, you pass along a covertway or canal, through which supplies are taken up to our outer works. This way is wide enough to admit an army wagon, and sufficiently deep to cover it from the view of the enemy. It is circuitous, and therefore lengthy. To a very great extent the soldiers have built bombproof tents, these resemble outdoor cellars at the north.

. . . Wishing to have a better view of the Johnnies and their works, than could be had in our trenches and behind our embankments, we stepped out upon a hillock whose summit rose gently between us and the rebel pickets. We had been there but a moment when, crack, crack went two muskets, a faint flash of light and a coil of smoke were seen before two rebel picket posts at which we were just looking. Whizz! Whizz! Went two balls, one passing on by, and the other striking a mound of earth just behind us. My soldier friend ducked his head and remarked coolly 'that means us.' As I had not come out 'in a fighting capacity,' I suggested that we take a less conspicuous position at which my friend smiled and acquiesced."[6]

Barker noted that in front of the all-white 5th and 2nd Corps, the pickets were on friendly terms and did not fire at each other. But as he evidenced at the 9th Corps' position, due to the presence of colored troops on that line, the rebel pickets and sharpshooters showed no quarter to an exposed Federal.

The *Journal* carried a number of articles on military news generated in Herkimer County itself. Among these items were:

. . . A company of artillery to be attached to the 70th New York Battery was being raised in Little Falls.* The officers of the company elected by the men were: Capt. Theodore Burnham, 1st Lt.Thomas Dundas, Senior 2nd Lt. George Keller and Junior 2nd Lt. Henry Uhle. As of September 22nd, the company numbered one hundred and seven men and was shortly expecting to receive uniforms and four brass field pieces.

. . . A number of Herkimer County men that had tried to enlist in the Navy were "receiving bad treatment" from the Naval Department's enrolling officers. To this end, letters of complaint from "prominent Union men" in the county, from J.R. Stebbins of the *Journal*, and from the U.S. Treasurer, Mohawk native, Gen. Francis Spinner, were sent to the Secretary of the Navy, Gideon Welles.

In letters to Spinner and Stebbins that were printed in the *Journal*, A.H. Smith, Chief of the Naval Recruiting Bureau, explained the Navy's reasons for rejecting many of the men. Smith wrote that most of the enlistees had no maritime training and therefore, with the exception of the position of Landsmen, were unsuitable for naval use. Since the Navy already had a surplus of Landsmen, the Herkimer County recruits were being directed to the infantry.

J.R. Stebbins, in a *Journal* response to Smith's letters, rejected the Bureau Chief's explanation and claimed corruption at the Naval recruiting office. From reliable sources, Stebbins had learned that only through extortion of a recruiting officer could a man become a Landsmen. In addition, the editor stated that men presented by brokers had a much greater chance of being accepted than did unrepresented men.

. . . The Herkimer County Board of Supervisors met in mid-September and passed a number of resolutions, among which were: 1) All county recruiting agents sent to the South were to be immediately recalled; 2) County bonds, payable on February 1st, 1865, were approved for issue to procure funds to reimburse the county towns for bounties paid under President Lincoln's last call; 3) The county promised to pay the $300 per volunteer reimbursement to each town even if that town offered a bounty higher than $300.

The Board of Supervisors also confirmed and ratified the bounty plan of the township of Herkimer. This plan contained a graduated bounty system—$700 for a one-year recruit, $800 for a two-year recruit and $900 for a three-year recruit. In addition, the Herkimer draft committee authorized payments, based on the graduated bounty, to men who furnished substitutes. Monies to cover these bounties would be procured by the issue of Herkimer township bonds, payable April 1st, 1870.

The board ended their meeting by recognizing Herkimer County recruiting agent E.S. Gillett for the fine work he had performed in procuring recruits towards the county's quota. Gillett had enlisted one hundred men from the Alexandria Bay area

---

* No record was found of this unit being mustered into Federal service.

who were credited to Herkimer County.

. . . The Ladies Aid Society forwarded to the Sanitary Commission a large box containing: 350 handkerchiefs, 15 flannel shirts, 21 drawers, 6 feather pillows, 18 bran pillows, 5 linen coats, 3 cravats, 7 bottles of blackberry brandy, 91 pounds of dried fruit, a cask of pickles and one dollar in cash.

Mrs. Seth Richmond, the Sanitary Commission's liaison in Herkimer County, received a request from the Commission's Chairman, Ellen Collins, for brandy, canned tomatoes and preserved vegetables. Collins' letter of September 3rd read in part:

> "The return to the Blackberry [brandy] appeal has been most liberal, and we are able to fill requisitions almost daily. The past week has been a busy week, and we have sent goods to City Point, Newburn, New Orleans, Baltimore and Washington. We have also supplied to a limited extent, the hospitals of this vicinity [New York City]. The men bring up with them the diseases contracted on the field, and have in several instances proved the efficacy of the use of blackberry brandy. Dr. Douglas mentioned to me to-day that the rates of sickness were reduced very considerably within one week after the Commission began to distribute vegetables to the army in July. There had appeared among the men very marked symptoms of scurvy, and the disease was promptly arrested by the use of fresh and pickled vegetables. So that though our onions have not taken Richmond, they have helped to take Atlanta."[7]

Among the interesting items of a non-military nature carried in the pages of the *Journal* during the late summer of 1864, there appeared:

. . . A tongue-in-cheek advertisement for "Seymour's "patent, back-action rotary, copper bottomed, receiver of dead men's votes. The "Seymour" referred to was, undoubtedly, Democratic Governor of New York State, Horatio Seymour.

. . . With the return of favorable weather in August, after the frosts of June and the drought of July, milk production increased and with it the manufacture of cheese. The quality of the milk was such that the Union Cheese Factory in Danube proudly announced a one day production record of over one thousand pounds of cheese made from only one thousand gallons of milk.

The price of cheese continued to rise, reaching twenty-six cents per pound, but many farmers held back their product, speculating that it would go even higher. Unfortunately for the speculators, near the end of September the cheese market collapsed and prices dropped to thirteen cents a pound.

. . . A "Gift Entertainment" was advertised by Prof. Young at Keller Hall in Little Falls. The Professor promised a night of "Magic, mystery and mirth" and he proposed to present one hundred and fifty beautiful and valuable gifts to his audience.

. . . A Little Falls "Fruit Grower," in a letter to the *Journal*, complained of pilferage from his small orchard and sternly warned off future "Fruit Thieves." The letter read:

> "The raising, in a small way, a little fruit for one's family, is something of an uphill business in our village. Whatever is not purloined by young

pests, who think thus to gratify their heroic ambition by converting to their own use, unknown to the producer, what little he has in his yard, is left to the mercy of those of riper age. For some time past I have missed from my pear trees small drafts at a time. Last week I concluded to put a lock on my gate. Very early on Saturday morning last a young man wearing a cloth cap, lark coat and check pants and a neat little shoe or boot, was seen conveying pears from my trees to his pockets. If this guerrilla warfare is continued a little lead may be a little too summary a way of settling the matter. Yet the act of Saturday morning presented a fine opportunity of thus dealing with the thief, but the fellow owes a debt of gratitude to a lady who interposed and saved him from at least being wounded. For the future no such interposition will be available."[8]

As summer ended and the autumn of 1864 began, the attention of the people of Herkimer County was drawn to the Shenandoah Valley, where the 121st New York, with its 6th Corps, was moving with Phil Sheridan's army.

In August of 1864, Ulysses S. Grant consolidated the heretofore independent Union forces in the Shenandoah Valley into the Middle Department. To command this department, which controlled the military affairs of Maryland, Pennsylvania and the newest state, West Virginia, Grant selected Gen. Philip Sheridan. Given to Sheridan were the dual tasks of driving Jubal Early from the valley and rendering the Shenandoah countryside unfit to ever again sustain a rebel army moving through it.

Sheridan took command on August 6th and his first order of business was to unify the various Federal forces in the Shenandoah and to concentrate them as quickly as possible along the Potomac near Harper's Ferry. Drawn together in the Middle Department were General Averell's Cavalry Division, General Crook's Army of West Virginia (8th Corps), General Wright's 6th Corps, General Emory's 19th Corps and two divisions of cavalry from the Army of the Potomac. When the junction of these troops was completed, Sheridan's force would number over fifty thousand men, more than doubling Early's twenty-three thousand soldiers.

In hopes of keeping Early off balance while his troops concentrated and to test the enemy's strength, Sheridan advanced into Martinsburg, West Virginia, and Williamsport, Maryland, while making feints on the Virginia cities of Front Royal and Winchester. Jubal Early willingly retreated, trying to draw the Federal troops into a trap.

During the middle weeks of August, Sheridan and Early continued their cat and mouse game, with one army occupying a city for a day or two before withdrawing. Sheridan followed this scenario so many times at Harper's Ferry that the southern newspapers nicknamed him "Harper's Weekly," after the popular news magazine of the era. All of this marching and countermarching permitted the generals to show their stuff, but tramping the roads in the mid-summer heat was hard on the men. Moving with Wright's 6th Corps was the 121st New York, which was as of late no stranger to this type of maneuvering. Even before Sheridan arrived the 121st had extensively travelled the Maryland countryside. As described by John Ingraham of the 121st in a letter to his brother "Oll" in Brockett's Bridge, the 6th Corps men suffered. Ingraham wrote:

"We have been nearly marched to death since we left the Army of the Potomac. We have been on the move nearly every night and day since. I don't mean to say we march night & day but we march day and a greater part of the night. We hardly halted any night before nine and some nights until two in the morning. I'm sorry to say it but to tell the truth our Corps is awfully demoralized. They are killing up the men as fast as possible, marching them so. This hot weather, I never experienced warmer weather than we are having now and it is so dusty. We have no rain. We had one shower since we left Petersburg. Every hour in the day you can see men dropping down in the ranks overcome by the heat. Men sun stroke all along the roads. Yesterday our Brigade marched in rear of the Corps and on both sides of the road men were lying very thick, completely played out, some of them hardly alive. What were able bathed the heads of others with water, and in one instance I saw two young ladies carrying water to bathe them. There has a great many men died since we left Petersburg and a great many men never will be fit for the field again. We have lost more than we would if we had stayed there at Petersburg. What there is of us are noted for high cheek bones and are very slim. Flesh isn't more than three or four inches on their ribs." [9]

To this point, Sheridan and Early's tactics had resulted in little more than cavalry skirmishes with no major infantry engagements. But when Col. John Mosby and his partisan rangers destroyed part of Sheridans' wagon train forcing the blue column to fall back, Early saw an opening to attack Sheridan's rear guard. Retreating through Winchester, Sheridan halted the 6th Corps on August 19th at Charlestown, West Virginia, to guard the tail of his column. On the morning of August 21st, Early attacked Wright's Corps and momentarily caught the Federals off guard. In a letter to his parents, John Ingraham related the part the 121st New York took in the action. Ingraham wrote:

"Last Sunday morning, 21st, we were anticipating a day of rest but on the contrary it was a day of labor. Most of the men and officers were at the Brook near our camp washing and putting on clean clothes when at once we heard firing in front of us and but a short distance off. We were not alarmed in hearing firing for the reason the boys had been shooting all the morning, shooting the hogs that had been running through camp and mutton &c. all through the country. Finally the firing came nearer and clearer and finally sharper. We then found out the Johnnies had made us a visit. The whole Corps was alarmed in about ten minutes. Long rolls beat and bugles sounded the pack up call and then we were ordered to fall in under arms immediately. As soon as our little Regt. of about 150 to 160 men fell in they were ordered to march through the cornfield which ran parallel . . . with our camp. As soon as they marched through the field one of our Lieuts was wounded through the thigh, Lieut [Van Scoy].* We were then ordered to deploy as skirmishers by order of Gen Upton and soon checked the Reb

* Lt. Hiram Van Scoy, of Butternuts in Otsego County, recovered from his wounds

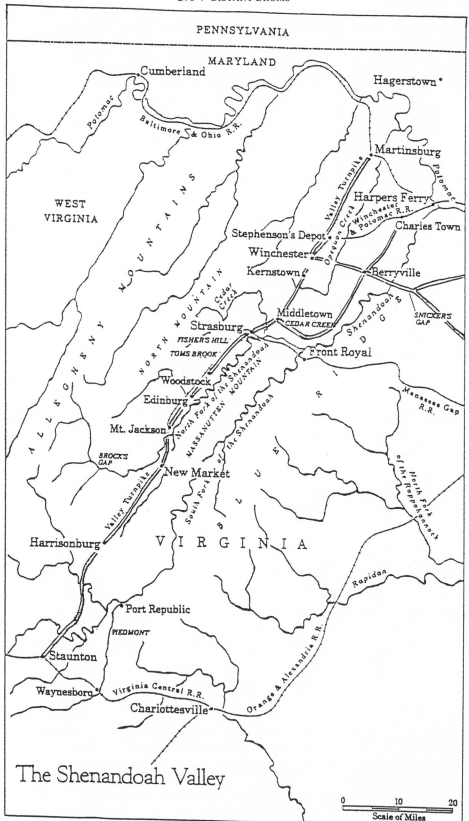

The Shenandoah Valley

The Guns of Cedar Creek, Lewis

skirmishers until the lines of battle were formed. There was no lines of battle engaged that day. . . . Our Regt was firing on the skirmish line all day Sunday and until Monday morning 3 o'clock, then were relieved. We had two men killed, five or six wounded. We had about 2 or 300 killed and wounded in the Corps." [10]

Early's attack was blunted by the 6th Corps which rejoined Sheridan's columns in a withdrawal to Bolivar Heights overlooking Harper's Ferry. Numbered among the 121st's casualties was Wilbur Champany of Litchfield, who was killed on the skirmish line. Of Champany's death wound, Clinton Beckwith wrote:

"We held our ground all day long, firing all the time. Wilbur Champany of our company was instantly killed by a sharpshooter. We had warned him to be cautious, as they had placed several balls close to us, one lodging in the blankets of one of the boys, and another in Hank Cole's gunstock. But Wilbur said, 'I'll have another shot at him any way,' and was in the act of aiming when a ball pierced his head. He was a fine, fearless soldier, and had not been back with us long, having just recovered from wounds in both legs, received at Salem Church. At dark we carried him back and buried him." [11]

For the next several days the two armies lay eyeing each other across the Shenandoah River before Early, running low on supplies, withdrew his men back up the valley. Sheridan, as if tethered to Early, quickly crossed the river and set his columns into motion on the rebel's trail. Advancing to the week-old battlefield at Charlestown, the Federal troops halted and encamped for the next few days. On September 3rd, the Charlestown camp was broken and the line of march continued to Berryville, where after repelling a half-hearted enemy attack, Sheridan's men settled into bivouack for the next two weeks.

Up to this point Grant had forbidden Sheridan from heavily engaging what was thought to be a rebel force equal in size to Sheridan's. Grant feared that if this army of the Middle Department was defeated, nothing would stand in the way between Early's force and Washington. But, as rebel cavalry raids continued in Maryland and Pennsylvania and Early's troops began to menace major rail lines, Grant let go of the reins on Sheridan and ordered "Little Phil" to go on the offensive.

Phil Sheridan wasted little time in moving on Early's army. Within forty-eight hours of being released by Grant from its defensive posture, the columns of the Middle Department were advancing southward, up the Shenandoah Valley, towards Early's force rumored to be lying east of Winchester. Before sunrise on the morning of September 19th, Sheridan's army of forty thousand men struck Early's ten thousand rebels along the bank of Opequon Creek.

The 121st New York, moving with its 6th Corps, hit Gen. Steven Ramseur's Division, forming the Confederate right flank, at 5 a.m. Although the enemy put up a stubborn resistance, the Federal preponderance in manpower irresistibly drove back the rebel line five miles to the outskirts of Winchester. Isaac Best of the 121st described part of the regiment's fight that day. Best wrote:

"General Upton ordered us to fix bayonets and not to fire until he gave the command, and the word was passed along the line. At last the enemy reached to where there could not be any doubt of their identity, and General Upton gave the order, 'Ready, aim, fire,' and crash went that volley of lead, and down tumbled those brave fellows. 'Forward, charge,' rang out Upton's short, incisive command, and away we went. Reaching the point where their line had stood we saw many of them lying there, not all shot however. Some of them had dropped down to escape death and became our prisoners. But those who could get away fled for their lives, not stopping on the order of their going." [12]

Late in the afternoon, Union cavalry attacked and crushed the Confederate left and under the cover of darkness, Early withdrew his men south to Fisher's Hill.

In the daylong fight known as the battle of Winchester, Federal losses amounted to over five thousand men, while Confederate casualties numbered about four thousand.[13] In this action, the 121st New York would have two men killed and thirteen wounded.[14] The two slain men, Sgt. Edgar Jones and Pvt. Julius Jones, were from the town of Russia. In addition, Pvt. Amenzo Stauring of Little Falls would soon die of his Winchester wounds.

Among the most seriously wounded men in the 121st was twenty-year-old Edwin Ford of Fairfield, who had been shot in the left side. Ford, one of Fairfield Academy's brightest students, would linger for two weeks at Taylor Hospital in Winchester before succumbing to his wounds on October 8th. Sarah Beck, a nurse at the hospital who had developed more than a passing interest in young Ford, wrote a touching letter to Edwin's father, William, relating the boy's last days. The letter, which was published in the *Journal*, read:

> "May the Dear Redeemer be very near you and strengthen you, when I tell you that your darling son Edwin has exchanged this world for his glorious and happy home above.
>
> Oh! may our dear Savior support you and your family under the coming blow and comfort you as He only can. He has dealt very tenderly with your dear boy during these past two weeks, giving him great peace, and secure hope of heaven through a Saviour's death and interception. He again and again said to me 'I feel ready to go, I can trust in Him, I am not afraid to die. I have been well taught at home,' and calmly and peacefully he at last passed away.
>
> What a glorious home is he now in, singing the praises of that precious saviour, 'who loved him and gave himself for him' and whose face he now beholds with such adoring gratitude.
>
> The only regret the dear boy expressed in dying, was that he could not see you all again. One evening, as I sat beside him, fanning him, he said 'I have such a happy home. I shall be so happy with them when I get back.' Then he told me about you all, and showed me the photograph he had in his pocket.
>
> Among many wounded in the same way with himself, whom we visited every day here, I felt especially drawn toward this dear boy. I could not help loving him, he was so young and so manly - so gentle, and lovely and patient. It has been a painful trial to me to have him die, and many tears have I wept over him.

His sufferings were not great. His left side often gave him pain, but still it was not very severe. His physicians, who are excellent men and who have done all they could for him, had every hope of his recovery until the past two days, when he began to fail. I had been sitting with him part of this morning, and had returned home, when the nurse came for me, saying he was dying and wished me to come to him. I went, taking the Dr. with me, who administered some stimulant, when he revived to that he left him, thinking he had fallen asleep. I had hardly left the house when he gently breathed his last. That was at 2 p.m. to-day. I send you enclosed a lock of his hair, and shall see that he is properly buried."* [15]

Three days after the Battle of Winchester, Sheridan attacked the rebel position on Fisher's Hill. With the 6th and 19th Corps assaulting the Confederate line from the front, the 8th Corps marched around Early's left flank and just before sunset struck the rebel rear. Early's troops broke and retreated once more to the south. In the September 22nd battle of Fisher's Hill, Federal casualties of about five hundred men were almost tripled by Early's loss of thirteen hundred.[16] The 121st New York, which participated with the 6th Corps in the frontal attack, suffered only five men slightly wounded.[17]

Following the battle of Fisher's Hill, Sheridan's army pursued Early's weakened force for two weeks, but with the exception of sporadic skirmishes with the rebel rear guard, the enemy could not be brought to bay. In early October, after a march of over eighty miles, Sheridan's troops halted in front of Early's heavily fortified position at Browns's Gap, some eight miles southeast of Port Republic. Sheridan, knowing that he could not dislodge Early from this stronghold and with his supply line imperiled by raids from Mosby's partisan guerrilla's, decided he must withdraw back north, down the Shenandoah Valley. Commencing this retrograde movement on October 6th, the Federal column backtracked to Strasburg, fourteen miles south of Winchester, and encamped along the banks of Cedar Creek.

During the return march, Sheridan set his men to work at ravishing the countryside. As described by John Ingraham of the 121st in a letter to his parents, the Union soldiers did their job well. Ingraham wrote:

"The whole Valley lays to waste. It is a horrible sight to hear the women and children begging & crying to save their barn and grain, all they have to live on. All unmovable property of any account is burned to ashes. Everything that could be driven off we're driving, such as cattle, sheep, horses, hogs &c. I should mention niggers & negresses, they are under the same head. And there are a great many refugees coming in all the while. They say they can't live here & they must go north or south (they prefer north.) Every supply Train that goes back is loaded with refugees & contrabands. I think by the time Sheridan gets through with the Shenandoah Valley, it will be of little account. Wherever the Army stops for the night and as soon as the men stack arms and the order is given to go into camp you see them start for the houses. They will go through them in about 15 minutes, take everything they have in the eating line. Apple Butter & preserves of all kinds is the favorite of the soldier. Bee hives don't stand long, or

* Edwin Ford's father arrived a few days later and brought his son's body back to Fairfield.

mutton, fresh pork, sweet potatoes &c. It looks hard but we must stop this
Guerrilla warfare and also end this Rebellion. This Valley is noted for this
kind of warfare and we're going to end it here."[18]

Jubal Early, whose decimated army had been reinforced by twelve thousand
men from Petersburg, came out from behind his works at Brown's Gap and began to
follow the retiring Federals. By October 13th, he was back at Fisher's Hill and although his army was still outnumbered two to one by Sheridan's force, he began to
formulate plans to go on the offensive. On the night of October 18th, under the cover
of a heavy fog, three divisions of Early's men silently positioned themselves on the
flank and in the rear of General Crook's 8th Corps. Just before daylight on October
19th, the Confederates attacked.

Sheridan's army at Cedar Creek was posted on three hills, three miles apart, on
a north-south line. The southernmost rise, which was only four miles from Fisher's
Hill, was occupied by the 8th Corps. One-half mile to the rear of Crook's men was
the 19th Corps and behind them sat the 6th Corps. Being situated in this manner,
when the rebel surge hit the totally off guard 8th Corps at dawn, the resulting panic
of Crook's troops quickly infected the units behind them. The wild retreat of the 8th
Corps smashed into the line of the 19th Corps, carrying it with it, and precipitated a
mad scramble of troops towards the 6th Corps. Fortunately for the Federals, the gunfire to the south had somewhat prepared the 6th Corps for Early's attack, and
Wright's men were able to slow the rebel tide. John Ingraham of the 121st described
the scene that morning. Ingraham wrote:

"On Wednesday morning just about daylight we were awakened by the
noise of cannon and musketry. The Rebs attacked the pickets in our center
along the 8 & 19th Corps. Our Corps was in the extreme right. The Rebs
fired a volley or two on the picket line on the right of our Corps (all this for
a Feint). All this while they were massing their forces on our extreme left.
As soon as our Corps heard the firing the men began to dig out and get their
breakfasts. We began to think of a general fight. Before we could get our
breakfasts we had to pack up and fall in. The Rebs had flanked the 8th &
19th Corps and they were coming back pell mell, lines all broken. They
came in a complete rout, lost part of their artillery, wagon train, tents &
camp equipment & came rushing through the ranks of our Corps like wild
men and the Rebs after them in the same way. The Rebs came on shouting
& pouring in the musketry & grape & canister into the 8 & 19th Corps.
When they came up to the bloody 6th Corps as we're called, they found a
snubbing post. Our Corps poured it into them wicked, which checked them
for a while. Then they came on with heavy force and pressed our Corps
back but not in disorder as did the 8 & 19th Corps. The 8 & 19th ran disgracefully. Their officers could not rally them for a long while. If we could
have had their support we could have held the Rebs in the start or as soon
as our Corps got engaged. For a while our Corps had to confront the whole
Rebel Army and of course we had to retire slowly but in order. We finally
checked them."[19]

Although the 6th Corps slowed the rebels, the promise of rich booty strewn about the Union camps more than anything else, stopped Early's ragged and half-starved men. Ingraham continued with his narrative:

> "The Rebs thought they had us all on a complete rout so they came on too in a rout and a great many stopping to plunder our dead & wounded and to plunder the 8th & 19th Corps camp & trains which they captured. Then is when our officers were robbed. They were wounded and fell in their hands. . . . Capts Burrell & Dow were taken prisoners. They were wounded so bad they could not get off the field. The Rebs took about 100 dollars in green-backs and a gold watch from Capt Burrell, and even the rings off his fingers. Robbed him of everything he had but the clothes he had on. They took a large amount of money from Capt Dow. They robbed all of our boys that fell in their hands wounded. They took 53 dollars in money from Mert Tanner and his photographs. He begged of them to let him have them but they would not." [20]

General Sheridan was not on the field when the rebel attack erupted, having spent the night in Winchester on a return trip from Washington. But, at the sound of distant gunfire from the direction of his Cedar Creek camps, Sheridan rode the dozen miles like a madman, arriving at the battlefield near mid-morning. Using the lull in fighting realized while the enemy was plundering the Union camps, Sheridan rallied and reorganized his broken troops. Forming broken sections of the 8th and 19th Corps around the 6th Corps, Sheridan counter-attacked Early's army late in the afternoon. John Ingraham completed his narrative of the Cedar Creek fight by relating a description of "Little Phil's" arrival and the subsequent Union charge. Ingraham wrote:

> "When he [Sheridan] was coming up the road he met a good many of the 8th and 19th Corps skedaddlers bound [for] Winchester. I tell you he was awful mad when he saw them. The 3rd Bri [gade] of our Corps & of our Div were doing provost duty at Winchester and have been since the battle of Winchester, arrested and put under guard between 2 & 3 thousand skedaddlers from the 8th and 19th Corps by order of Gen Sheridan. Our Corps was in line of battle about ready to make a charge and what men they could get together belonging to the other two Corps. As soon as he arrived he rode along the line of the 6th Corps to let us know of his presence. Such long and loud cheers as we gave him. Just as he came in front of our Brigade, says he give'em hell boys. I heard him say it, and in about 1/2 hour they did give them h___(as he said). Our whole Corps charged & cavalry charged with them and drove them like sheep, got them in a perfect panic. They got their artillery and what they captured from us all jammed together and could not get away with it. There wasn't but one bridge across Cedar Run and they couldn't get over fast enough. We took 2200 prisoners cavalry and infantry together, took 61 pieces of artillery & their wounded and all of ours & the 19 & 8 Corps trains that they captured in the morning. The cavalry are in pursuit, when last heard from were at Woodstock. It is a big victory although we suffered severely." [21]

Ingraham was correct in calling Cedar Creek a "big victory," but he overestimated the numbers of rebel soldiers and artillery pieces taken. Early's army had lost just under three thousand men, of which one thousand were taken prisoner and twenty-five cannons were captured. But of more importance to the Federals, almost all of the Confederate wagon train was seized. Without provisions and with the loss of most of his big guns, Early had to retreat back down the valley.

Federal losses of October 19th amounted to over fifty-six hundred men, verifying the severe suffering related by Ingraham.[22] From the 121st New York, ten men had been killed on the field, forty-two men were wounded (five mortally) and five men were missing.[23] The casualty count of the 121st would represent almost one quarter of the regiment's two-hundred and twenty-nine men that had reported for duty that morning. Maj. Henry Galpin of Little Falls, who himself had been shot through both thighs, detailed the casualties taken by the 121st's officers. Galpin wrote:

> "In the room where I am is Capt. Burrell, wounded in the right knee, Capt. Douw wounded in the leg and will probably have to be amputated, Lieut. Jas. Johnson badly wounded in the hip, Lieut. Howland flesh wound in the leg. I had my horse killed, Olcott's was also killed and the Adjutant had his wounded. Lieut. Col. Olcott is the only field officer in our Division. Capt. Jackson and Lieut. Weaver acting adjutant are the only officers in our regiment. Lieut. Tucker was killed."[24]

Of the officers named by Galpin: Capt. Jonathan Burrell of Salisbury would die after having his leg amputated above the knee, Capt. John Douw of Mohawk died in November of complications from his leg wound, Lts. James Johnson and Ten Eyck Howland would recover from their wounds, and Lt. William Tucker of Roseboom was slain. Galpin recovered from his injuries but would be discharged for disability in December.

Among the enlisted men killed were: William Cary of Little Falls, John Rowland of Frankfort and William Reynolds of Salisbury.

Notable among the wounded was frequent *Journal* correspondent, Lt. Joe Heath of Little Falls. The official description of Heath's ugly wound read:

> "He received a Gun Shot wound, the ball going in his mouth as he had his mouth open on a charge on the enemy. Hollering as loud as he could, the ball passing through his mouth & right cheek, coming out of the right cheek, breaking his jaw & taking out his molar teeth & lodging itself in his right shoulder."[25]

Heath would recover from his wound and would rejoin the 121st in November.

After Cedar Creek, except for occasional cavalry skirmishes and guerrilla raids, the fighting in the Shenandoah Valley was essentially finished. Neither Early's army nor any other Confederate force would ever again use the Shenandoah to raid the North and threaten Washington.

The 121st New York would remain in the valley with the Middle Department six more weeks before being transferred in December with the rest of the 6th Corps to the Petersburg front.

The focus of the war now turned even further north. The fight to save the Union would shift from the fields of the South to the ballot boxes of the North.

Notwithstanding civil war, 1864 was an election year and the democratic process of electing a president was to be carried out. On the surface, the campaign of 1864 pitted Abraham Lincoln against the Army of the Potomac's erstwhile commander George McClellan; however, the true choice before the voting public was the momentous question of whether the war should be continued.

George McClellan ran on the ticket of the Peace Democrats, whose platform, which incredulously was not supported by their candidate, sought a cessation of hostilities and peace with the South. In the other camp was the Union party, a coalition of Republicans and War Democrats who for want of a better candidate, offered Lincoln. The design of the Unionists was for a continuation of the struggle until the South was subjugated and the peace was won.

As the summer of 1864 progressed and the Union drives stalled in front of Petersburg and Atlanta, the Peace party began to gain momentum and Abraham Lincoln's prospects of being re-elected faded. The northern populace that had sent its sons south in bright uniforms only to see them returned in wooden boxes, was becoming ever-increasingly war weary. Back in the spring of 1861, this rebellion was to have been crushed in three months; now three years later the Confederate States were still holding firm and no end to the conflict was in sight. The campaigns of Grant in the east and Sherman in the west had exacted an enormous toll in human lives and the monetary cost of conducting this war was amounting to millions of dollars each day. The unthinkable began to be spoken, maybe this war could not be won after all. Many of the hard-core pro-war faction now began to concede that a change in leadership and a re-direction of the war effort might be needed. Although the prospect of a compromise settlement with the South and therefore disunion was unsettling, the prospect of peace was very inviting. As August drew to a close, all signs pointed to a victory by McClellan and the Peace Democrats. The fortunes of the Unionists looked so bleak that even Lincoln believed his defeat was a foregone conclusion.

Into this time of despair came just the tonic that the Union Party desperately needed. On September 3rd, General Sherman telegraphed the joyous news to Washington, "Atlanta is ours, and fairly won." The North had finally earned the major victory it needed to get the Federal engine of war back on track and moving. Throughout the North, the announcement of Sherman's achievement set off spontaneous celebrations. In Herkimer County, the news was received, for the most part, with jubilation. Of the scene in Little Falls the *Journal* reported:

> "On Monday at 12 o'clock the church bells in this village were rung and thirty-two guns were fired in honor of the capture of Atlanta. The streets were alive with joyous Union men and Union flags were everywhere flying. We say 'Union' flags, for of those owned by Copperheads we believe not one was thrown to the breeze! It is well that these men have boldly announced that they can no longer rejoice over Union victories, inasmuch as such triumphs hurt the prospect of 'Little Mac.' " [26]

Sherman's success at Atlanta had definitely turned the tide in the Unionist's favor, yet in Herkimer County the struggle between the war and the anti-war factions was just heating up. Herkimer County, which geographically lay near the center of New York State, was also politically situated at the dividing line between the Peace Democrats to the east and south and the Lincolnites to the west and north. Within the county itself, the lines of political sentiments were even more distinct. In the more heavily populated townships of Little Falls, Herkimer and Manheim in the southern part of Herkimer County, the Democrats held sway, while in the rest of the county, and especially in the north country, the Republicans were in power.

Fortunately for the Unionists, the county's most circulated newspaper, *The Herkimer County Journal & Courier*, was a decidedly Republican sheet. The *Journal*, far from being apolitical, unabashedly trumpeted the Unionist viewpoint and at every turn denigrated the Copperheads and McClellan. J.R. Stebbins, owner and editor of the *Journal*, was a staunch Republican and his editorials appealed, not only to the Unionists, but also to fence sitting Democrats, to "do the right thing" and support Lincoln. In an early September issue of the *Journal* Stebbins wrote:

Work! Work!

"Union man, do you love your Country? Do you wish to see the Union cause—the cause of God and right—succeed in the coming election? Do you wish to see your liberties and those of your children, preserved? If you do, go to work for the Union cause! It is in danger from the apathy of its friends—and from that alone. The very fact that success is so apparent, lulls us into a false security! A wary enemy is opposed to us—an unscrupulous enemy—one who will not scruple to resort to force, violence, BLOOD-SHED, and even WAR at our own doors, if necessary to gain their triumph! It is hightime then, to awake and go to Work—but not with threat or violence—WORK with argument—with fact—with appeal, and work as becomes freemen, who love their country. Our soldiers in the field are fighting our battles against the traitors and rebels of the South—let us fight theirs and ours against rebels and traitors at the North, and both will conquer." [27]

Will They Do It?

"There are many Democrats in Herkimer county (and many prominent ones in the town of Little Falls) who have been among the foremost in voting money, encouraging enlistments, and advising active prosecution of the war. They have done these things as men and not as politicians. They rank high among the people as men who desire that the rebellion shall be put down. Their sons and brothers are now upon the battlefield. But they are now called to forget country and kindred for the sake of party. They are asked to vote for McClellan on a distinctive peace platform; they are asked to vote for an 'immediate cessation of hostilities,' although they know it could only strengthen our enemies and weaken ourselves; they are asked to support a code of principles which contains no word of rebuke to traitors for whose overthrow they have given of their money and their kindred; and they are asked to elect a man for Vice President [George Pendleton] who 'thanks God that he never voted a dollar for the support of the war.' Will they do it?" [28]

In early September, from each party's state convention came the slates of candidates for state positions:

	Democrats	Unionists
Governor	Horatio Seymour	Reuben Fenton
Lieut. Governor	David Jones	Thomas Alvord
Canal Commissioner	Jarvis Lord	Franklin Alberger
Inspector of Prisons	David McNeil	David Forrest

During mid-September, internal party caucusing began at the township level. At these meetings, the electors from each town selected three delegates to represent them at their respective Assembly District Conventions. In Herkimer County, there were two Assembly Districts, the 1st, which encompassed the eastern part of the county, and the 2nd, which entailed the western portion.

At the Assembly District meetings, the township delegates nominated their party's candidate for the office of Assemblyman. In addition, five members were chosen from their number to attend the 20th Congressional District's Convention, where the party's choice to run for Congressman would be selected.

On the county level, the delegates from each town met in late September at the Court House in Herkimer to nominate their party's slate of candidates for county offices. Chosen at that time were the men to run for Sheriff, County Clerk, District Attorney, Justice of Sessions, and the two County Coroner positions.

Emerging from these meetings and conventions were the rosters of candidates:

Democrats

1st Dist. Assemblyman	Zenas Priest, Little Falls
2nd Dist. Assemblyman	Col. Harter, Warren
U.S. Congressman	Fred Hubbard, Lewis Co.
Sheriff	L.L. Lowell, German Flatts
County Clerk	Jarius Mather, Fairfield
District Attorney	Henry Link, Little Falls
Justice	Charles Spinner, Mohawk
Coroner	George Smith, Russia
Coroner	Gaylord Campbell, Frankfort

Union Party

1st Dist. Assemblyman	Henry Tillinghast, Norway
2nd Dist. Assemblyman	Bradley Lee, Winfield
U.S. Congressman	Addison Laflin, Herkimer
Sheriff	George Cleland, Warren
County Clerk	Zenas Green, Herkimer
District Attorney	Sewell Morgan, Winfield
Justice	Reuben Wood, Ohio
Coroner	Ben Bushnell, Little Falls
Coroner	Isaac Piper, Frankfort

With the slates of candidates set, campaigning began in earnest. Almost daily at one village or another, either the Democrats or Unionists held a rally. These meetings, complete with brass bands, bonfires, distinguished speakers and of course refreshments, typically drew large audiences. Of one such Union meeting the *Journal* reported:

> "On Friday evening of last week one of the most enthusiastic political meetings ever held in Herkimer County came off at Odd Fellow's Hall, Mohawk. The large and commodious hall was comfortably well filled at an early hour to hear the eloquent young Irish orator, Patrick Corbett, but when the Loyal Avalanche from Ilion charged into the Hall with their brass howitzer in advance, there was no room to spare—the Hall was literally packed. The meeting was organized with R.H. Pomeroy as President and opened with prayer by Col. Broadie, the Norwegian fighting clergyman of the 61st N.Y. Volunteers, after which Mr. Corbett was introduced and for two hours and a half poured forth the most convincing arguments in favor of the National and State Union candidates. The best evidence of the appreciation of the Speaker's remarks was the deafening applause which greeted nearly every sentence. While in the midst of the speech the audience discovered that something was up, for A.H. Laflin was considerably excited and everybody was on tip toe to know what it was. As soon as the speaker reached a stopping place, for which Mr. Laflin could scarcely wait, the President announced the glorious news of Sheridan's victory at Fisher's Hill, and such a shout as greeted the news never before went up from Old Herkimer. The audience rising to their feet, swinging handkerchiefs and tossing hats in to the air, gave cheer in the wildest enthusiasm, and in such a manner as would send joy to the hearts of our brave soldiers, but terror to the hearts of traitors as it did to some of the canine tribe that were present." [29]

As a culmination to the township rallies, each party held grand county-wide mass meetings at the river flat fairgrounds between Mohawk and Herkimer. The Democrats held their rally on October 5th, advertising New York City Mayor Fernando Wood, and John Van Buren, the son of former President Martin Van Buren and currently the Attorney General of New York State, as main speakers. In an article entitled, "A Big Swindle," because neither Wood nor Van Buren appeared, the *Journal* reported on the Democrats rally:

> "The sham Democracy in the county has been busily at work for the last two weeks preparing for a 'Grand Mass Meeting' which was to come off yesterday.
>
> So far as numbers are concerned the meeting was very respectable, the number present being, in our judgement about five thousand. Very few, comparatively, however, went from this direction and most of the crowd came from the southern towns who turned out largely of both parties from curiosity to hear Fernando Wood, in much the same way as they would to see Jeff. Davis. The procession from the northern towns numbered just 49 single, 41 double and 4 four-horse wagons.
>
> But as to enthusiasm and speakers the meeting was a failure, a fizzle and a swindle. It may be all very well to put the names of such men as

Fernando Wood and John Van Buren upon the bills for the purpose of drawing a crowd, but we imagine the Democracy will find it don't pay to so disappoint the people.

The . . . banners on the ground were made up of a lot of trash like the following: 'Clear the track, Sambo, let the white man rule'; 'The stamp act our grandfathers opposed'; 'No more arbitrary arrests'; 'Down with the Bastile'; 'We want no one but white men at the helm'; 'We will obey laws, not proclamations'; 'We want the Constitution strictly construed' &c., &c.

We left the grounds at half past three o'clock and up to that hour not one of the speakers advertised had appeared. We heard however that Mr. Church and Judge Parker made their appearance just as the crowd was going home. The orators were 'granny' Benedict of Utica, a Mr. Weaver, a Mr. Smith (John, we presume) whom nobody ever heard of before or cares to again and Mr. Starbuck of Watertown. Everybody knows just what the talking was as we can tell them. Ridicule of Uncle Abe, attacks on the Government, professions of Unionism, cries of 'peace,' 'no draft,' 'taxation,' 'niggers' &c., made up the addresses. Not a word of rebels or traitors! No rebuke to the enemies of the country! It is no wonder there was so little enthusiasm at a meeting of which the majority held a most hearty contempt for the principles uttered; for even had Jeff. Davis and his southern hordes been present they could have found no word of fault with the disloyal tone of the wishy washy speeches."[30]

The Unionist rally was held on the same grounds on October 15th. All the previous week the weather had been rainy and dark, and even on that Saturday morning heavy showers were falling, yet an estimated fifteen thousand people showed up at the rally. J.R. Stebbins of the *Journal* tabulated that there were eleven hundred wagons parked at the fairgrounds. As further proof of the rally's popularity, the Union committee proudly announced that it had paid for over one thousand tolls at the Middleville and Mohawk toll gates. This figure the Unionists boastfully compared with the fewer than five hundred toll fees the Democrats had realized at their rally the week before. The toll keepers tally for the Union gathering also did not include the innumerable Little Falls and Danube people that took the train from the Little Falls depot or the Frankfort and Schuyler delegation that chartered a steam packetboat.

The various delegations assembled at the Herkimer train station and paraded to the fairgrounds in a column which took well over two hours to pass. The procession was led by the Mohawk band, which was followed by three hundred and fifty young men on horseback, forty-eight mounted firemen from Newport, and a number of men from the "Rail Splitters" club carrying "beetle and wedge."

Following these lead groups came large contingents from each town in the county, including "little Wilmurt." Interspersed amongst the throng of people were fifteen brass bands, hundreds of banners and dozens of floats. Among the most popular floats (of which there were six), was the standard scene of thirty-four young maidens representing the thirty-four states of the Union. Fairfield and Frankfort remembered that West Virginia had recently been made a state, and only their floats carried thirty-five girls. Other favorite displays were Litchfield's wooden model of a rail-splitter that moved by clock work, Columbia's wagon presenting a blacksmith, a cooper and other artisans at work underneath a banner intoning "Free Labor," and Fairfield's twelve-foot-high likeness of Abraham Lincoln.

Each township contingent also carried a number of banners. Most of the pennants either displayed a kindly portrait of Lincoln, a derisive caricature of McClellan or an "American Eagle" with the requisite rattlesnake or copperhead in its talons. Some of the banners displayed combinations of all three representations. All of the banners bore mottoes with inscriptions such as: "Grant, Sherman and Sheridan will give terms of Peace"; "We prefer Black Patriots to White Traitors"; and "Peace under the Stars and Stripes, not under the White Flag."

Somehow the parade marshals and the rally's officials, which included three "Presidents" and twenty "Vice Presidents," got the huge crowd in order and the speeches began. Three speaker stands were set up around the fairgrounds and from these, six featured orators spoke. The speechmakers included: Col. James Jaquess, a Methodist clergyman from Illinois who had recently visited Richmond on an unauthorized peace mission; Prof. W.W. Hegeman of Rochester; Judge James Barker of Maine; Lyman Tremaine of Albany; Gen. Benjamin Bruce of Madison; and Col. John Spofford from Brockett's Bridge. Thankfully, the speeches were given concurrently from the three stands, so that the multitude of listeners did not have to remain forever in the rain that fell unabated throughout the day.

Of the success of the day the *Journal* noted:

> "During the day it rained considerably at intervals, yet there was manifested on every hand the greatest enthusiasm. Cheers from one part of the field were answered by those from another and every one's eye and countenance told a story of confident determination to work and win between this and the eight proximo [Election Day.]" [31]

But the Unionist's rally had not proceeded without interference by the Democrats. Anonymous "Copperheads" had circulated a handbill throughout Herkimer County urging people to stay away from the rally and Democratic storekeepers had kept their stores open hoping to draw people from the meeting. On the day of the rally itself, "Copperhead" agitators attempted to disrupt the proceedings. In an article titled, "Meanness Personified," the *Journal* reported:

> "It is a fact, exemplified every day almost, that latter-day Democrats, having abandoned principles, do most delight in insulting and misusing their opponents and demeaning and belittling themselves! Who ever heard of a Democratic political meeting being disturbed by Unionists? Yet, it is very uncommon for the latter to engage a speaker and attend a meeting without being insulted by Democratic rowdies, set on by Democratic leaders. One of the leading features of the Mass Meeting on Saturday was an illustration of this very thing. Before the train left Little Falls, the plan was formed and a number of fellows were deputized to hang around and hurrah for 'Little Mac.' After the speaking began on the Fair Grounds another gang, half drunk and noisy, tried a continuance of the same plan, desisting only when it began to be evident that they might get a little more than they bargained for. But in the evening the scheme culminated. The spirits of rum

and rowdyism had full sweep under the lead of 'Charles Spinner's Band' marching through the streets with Copperhead transparencies, shouting, yelling, screaming, swearing and fighting among themselves—with a pack of drunken Irish women bringing up the rear. After a speech by Samuel Earl Esquire, a speech which we do not care to report in our columns, the mob—Governor Seymour's friends—filed past the Railroad House hurling a stone through its windows and swearing forth the most ridiculous blasphemy we ever heard. To this depth has Democracy fallen." [32]

Prior to 1864, soldiers in the field were not able to vote because state constitutions did not allow absentee balloting. The Lincoln government, believing many pro-Union votes lay with the soldiers, urged the state governments to amend this law. The Peace Democrats, on the other hand, viewed the soldier vote as harmful to their prospects and therefore pressed the states to retain their no absentee ballot laws. In the end the Unionists won out. With the exception of New Jersey, Delaware and Indiana, the Northern states amended their constitutions to permit soldiers in the field to vote. As evidenced by letters to the *Journal* from the men in the war zone, the popular sentiment of the troops was with the Union party. Excerpts from these letters read:

From "Mike" of the 152nd New York:

"A few men here endeavored to resuscitate their old idol when the news of the result of the Chicago Convention was received, but Little Mac won't go down with us. If he had been placed on a soldier's platform or had placed himself there he might receive a fair share of the soldiers' vote, but if Grant himself was a candidate on the platform where McClellan now stands he couldn't carry the popular vote in the army, and he is more of a favorite with the boys than Little Mac would be if he had command of the army for a thousand years. The actions of the Peace-Democratic party have disgusted the soldiers and, thank God, we are enabled this fall to show our disapprobation of their policy in spite of Seymour's veto and Copperhead opposition." [33]

From Salisbury's Moses Bliss of the 44th New York:

"The friends of 'Little Mac' are troubled to harmonize his letters of acceptance, and the Chicago Platform. A political game is too apparent. One cannot serve two masters. Pendleton is a dead weight on McClellan's prospects. Many who wish to vote for him refuse to do so unless he utterly repudiates the Platform, and the nominee for Vice President. On the other side there is no chance to cavil. Lincoln's cause is definitely picked out, and there is no turning. We feel confident of Union successes here in the field, and we look to it that you secure the same at the ballot box." [34]

From Orrin Beach of Little Falls, a member of the 16th New York H.A.:

"I trust that while we poor soldiers are fighting in the field for the restoration of peace, that you at the North will show your ballots on the 8th of November next that you are determined not to submit to any Copperheadisms in the choice of the next President. In my estimation there is but one true way to quell the riotous despotism of the South. That is, total sub-jugation. I, for one, am willing to fight with both my sword and vote for the restoration of peace. I know of many others of the same stamp." [35]

As further confirmation of the soldiers' opinions on the upcoming election, the *Journal* published the results of two "straw votes." From the Officers' Hospital in Annapolis, the 44th New York's Lt. John Hardenburgh of Little Falls reported, "For Lincoln - 237, For McClellan - 32, For Fremont - 1; and from "Mike" of the 152nd New York came, "Lincoln - 13, McClellan - 4, Fremont - 'not there.' " [36]

As October rolled on, the momentum of the Union cause continued to grow. State elections in Vermont, Maine, Pennsylvania, Ohio, and even in Democratic Indiana, saw Union candidates winning by large margins. In Ohio, the Union ticket won by fifty thousand votes; in Indiana, which had disallowed the soldier vote, the Democrats majority in the Legislature was reversed, and in Pennsylvania, of the twenty-four seats open in that state's Congress, nineteen were filled by Union men. As an extra boost to the Unionists' fortunes, news came of Sheridan's victories in the Shenandoah Valley.

Election Day, Tuesday, November 8th, finally arrived and when it was over, the polls showed that Abraham Lincoln had been returned for a second term. Lincoln's plurality of four hundred thousand votes out of the over four million votes cast, translated into fifty-five percent of the popular vote for Lincoln and forty-five per-cent for McClellan. In the all important electoral college vote, Lincoln's victory over McClellan was a more substantial two hundred and twelve to twenty-one. [37]

New York State had gone for Lincoln by a margin of less than ten thousand votes out of the over seven hundred thousand cast. The huge pluralities gained by McClellan in the southeastern part of the state, (New York City, having favored "Little Mac" by almost forty thousand votes) were offset by Lincoln victories in the northern, western, and central counties.

The gubernatorial race in New York mirrored the Lincoln victory. Reuben Fen-ton defeated the incumbent Horatio Seymour (of Utica) by almost the same margin that Lincoln had bested McClellan in the state. The other state positions, Lieutenant Governor, Canal Commissioner and Inspector of Prisons, also went to the Unionist candidates.

Herkimer County had gone for Lincoln by a majority of nearly nine hundred votes from the nine thousand cast. Little Falls, Herkimer, Manheim and Warren had given the nod to McClellan and Seymour, but the rest of the county had been swept by the Unionists. In addition, all of the county positions, from Assemblyman to Coroner, were filled by Union men. In the race for Congress, Herkimer's Addison Laflin easily beat the Democratic candidate, Frederick Hubbard. [38]

A major battle of the war had been won. The people of the North had given Lincoln their mandate, albeit not by an overwhelming margin, to continue the con-flict until the peace was won. In northern Georgia, Sherman, who had been poised near Atlanta awaiting the results of the election, stepped off on his march through the South's underbelly. Along the Petersburg front in Virginia, there was no need to resume the fight, for the struggle had never ceased in that quarter.

CHAPTER XX

"Let us all have a fair start with Father Abraham"

*Fall/Winter 1864 - Hatcher's Run - Petersburg Winter
Prison Camps - Hicksford*

On the eve of the Presidential election, Ulysses S. Grant decided to take another stab at Petersburg's supply lines in the hope that such a stroke would prove fatal to Lee's besieged army. Grant's objective was the South Side Railroad, which entered Petersburg from the west and communicated with the port of Wilmington, North Carolina, and the rail center at Lynchburg, Virginia. With major portions of the Weldon Railroad now in Union hands, the South Side Railroad was Lee's last lifeline to the rest of the South and its loss would probably result in the evacuation of Petersburg and consequently the loss of Richmond, within forty-eight hours. Grant knew that a Union victory of this magnitude would insure Lincoln's re-election and a speedy termination of the war.

The actual battle plan was designed by General Meade, who was chafing under ridicule from the Northern press that he was a "deadweight" in the Union camp. The sector selected by Meade for the attack was an area on the rebel right flank just to the west of a small stream called Hatcher's Run. Meade's scouts described the enemy's defenses in this section, roughly seven miles southwest of Petersburg, as being largely unfinished with only a small garrison. Targeting this supposed soft spot, Meade proposed to attack with three infantry corps—Hancock's 2nd, Warren's 5th and Parke's 9th, and with General Gregg's division of cavalry. The order of attack called for the 9th Corps, already encamped along the west side of Hatcher's Run, to assault the rebel works along the Boydton Plank Road, which came up to Petersburg from the south before turning east to parallel the South Side Railroad. If Parke's men failed to break through to the railroad, they would at least hold the enemy in position while the 2nd Corps, maneuvering further to the southwest, could swing around the rebel flank and strike the track line. The 5th Corps would advance westerly guarding Hancock's right flank and as the situation presented itself would be available to support either of the other two corps. Gregg's cavalry would be used to screen the Federal moves and to protect the 2nd Corps' exposed left flank. In addition to these movements, Butler's Army of the James would feint against the rebel line on Petersburg's northeast perimeter, preventing Lee from sending reinforcements south. Meade set the time of attack for the morning of October 27th.

The 152nd New York, moving with its 2nd Corps, broke camp at Fort Haskell early on the evening of October 26th and started on the march towards Hatcher's Run. During the all night march heavy rains, that would persist through most of the next day, began to fall. Hatcher's Run was reached early the next morning and crossed after the 152nd, with the rest of its brigade, charged across to drive off a small band of rebel pickets. Continuing on, the 2nd Corps struck the Boydton Plank Road at a point five miles south of the South Side Railroad at noon.

The 5th and 9th Corps, having much shorter routes to travel than the 2nd Corps, stepped off at 5 a.m. on that morning of October 27th. The 9th Corps travelled only a short distance before reaching the enemy's works on the Boydton Plank Road and the fight began. The 97th New York with the 5th Corps, marching to the south of the 9th Corps, crossed Hatcher's Run and began what would be a daylong meander through the labyrinth of thickets and swamps in their line of march. As described by Isaac Hall of the 97th New York, this area of the Confederate line was not as "soft" as had been reported. Hall wrote:

> "The movement was intended to be a surprise; but the morning was dark and rainy, which with other impediments . . . so caused delay that the enemy had ample time to avail himself of every advantage. His works at Hatcher's Run were quite formidable, their approaches being guarded by slashings and abatis." [1]

A few miles to the southwest of the 5th Corps, the 152nd New York and its brigade, forming the extreme left of the 2nd Corps' line, crossed the Boydton Plank Road and began to advance through an open field. Confederate artillery quickly opened on the Federal line and sent the men scurrying for cover back across the road. One cannon shot landed amidst the men of the 152nd, instantly killing Charley Watson of Herkimer and wounding Matt House of Mohawk. House was left on the field and later taken prisoner.

Seeking refuge at the rear of a nearby mansion, the men were surprised to learn that they were on the farm of William Burgess, a former resident of West Winfield. As the rebel cannoneers found the range of the 152nd's new position, Burgess and his slaves broke from the mansion and headed for the rear of the Union lines, the slave owner seeking protection and his slaves freedom. The artillery barrage increased in intensity and Capt. Willard Musson, temporarily commanding the 152nd, ordered the men to lie down. For thirty minutes, the shelling continued but miraculously no one was hit.

Ordered to support a battery of Union artillery stationed near a barn on the Burgess farm, the 152nd advanced to a small rise near the guns and once again laid down. Capt. Musson, who had moved off a short distance to gauge the accuracy of the Federal gunners, was struck by a return shot from rebel artillery and instantly killed. During a lull in the firing, Musson's body was dragged from the field and buried.*

A feeble rebel charge was made against the battery that the 152nd was guarding and was easily repelled. The artillery fire quieted on both sides and the men used this time to inspect their surroundings. An unnamed new recruit to the 152nd quickly recognized the home of his grandparents in which he had lived five years previous. Entering the now vacant house, the young soldier gathered up the family bible, photographs and a small powder horn that he had crafted.

With darkness coming on and the level of rebel musketry increasing, the men built a line of low breastworks and huddled behind them for protection. Unbeknownst to the men of the 152nd, their regiment and for that matter much of the 2nd Corps, was nearly surrounded and the fire to their front would soon be matched by fire from their rear. The 5th Corps, which had been directed to link up with the 2nd Corps and thereby guard Hancock's right flank, had lagged far behind and had left a huge gap in the Federal line. The enemy had quickly discovered this opening and exploited it. The 2nd Corp's right wing was overwhelmed and the rebels continued down Hancock's line, attacking from both the front and rear.

The fortifications that the 152nd New York had built were now providing little protection as the Confederate fire was seemingly coming in from all sides. In evidence of this vicious fire, the 152nd's Chauncey Kelsey of Otsego County, was shot in the chest and killed while sitting with his back to the breastworks.

In describing this crossfire, Henry Roback of the 152nd wrote:

> "The front was the rear, and the rear the front. Perforations of the physical system were very apt to take place without consulting us, as to the parts preferred." [2]

Fortunately for the 2nd Corps, nightfall came before the enemy could complete the encirclement and Hancock was able to withdraw his troops back over Hatcher's Run. To the north, the 5th and 9th Corps also disengaged from their battle lines and pulled back. The grand move to capture the South Side Railroad was over.

In the battle known as Hatcher's Run, or the Boydton Plank Road, of the forty-three thousand Federals engaged, almost two thousand men were lost. The Confederates suffered almost thirteen hundred casualties from the estimated twenty thousand men who went into battle. In addition to the Union losses south of Petersburg, the Army of the James lost sixteen hundred men when Butler blundered into a trap. In this action, Lee lost an unbelievably low count of sixty-four men. [3]

Of the Mohawk Valley regiments engaged, the 97th New York came out of the fight unscathed, while the 152nd New York lost three men killed, four wounded and one missing. [4] In addition to the 152nd's battlefield casualties, Herman Delong was taken sick on the return march and fell by the side of the road. Delong, a resident of

---

* One year later Musson's father had the body disinterred and sent back to Gilbertsville, N.Y.

the town of Stark, was found four days later by cavalry scouts and sent to a Washington hospital where he died soon after.

Meade's master plan was a dismal failure. Although the people of the North were told the move was simply a large "reconnaissance in force" and that valuable ground had been gained, the common soldier knew otherwise. As to the cause of the defeat, Isaac Hall of the 97th New York provided his opinion. Hall wrote:

> "The movement to the left developed the inefficiency of raw recruits and substitutes with which the several corps had been supplied to fill the vacancies that occurred during the summer. These high bounty men were of different material from those who volunteered at the beginning of the war. Lured to join the service by the $500 to $1,200 or more bounty paid at that time, many sought an opportunity to desert, and if compelled to remain, they were in many instances, in battle, but a dead weight on the remnant left of the army's former power. In fact many were mere bounty jumpers, mustered under assumed names, some of whom escaped before they could be brought to the front." [5]

The reverse of October 27th so disgusted Gen. Winfield Hancock that he took a leave of absence from the service, never to return to his beloved 2nd Corps. Gen. Andrew Humphreys took over command of the 2nd Corps in November 1864.

After the move against the Confederate right, the action quieted along the Petersburg front except for the occasional artillery duel and the constant deadly hum of the sharpshooter's bullet. With the season of bad weather and muddy roads coming on, both armies began to prepare their winter quarters.

No major military operations occurred along the Petersburg line in November, but the work of war and the killing continued. The 97th New York encamped along the Jerusalem Plank Road and the 152nd New York, at Fort Stedman, spent the month, as did the rest of the army, improving the trench lines and serving time at the forward picket stations.

Life in the trenches was hard to begin with, but the rain, sleet, snow and cold winds that visited Petersburg this November made it doubly miserable for the men. The seemingly constant precipitation turned the trenches into quagmires and at times filled the ditches waist deep in water. In one instance, men from the 152nd New York swam to safety when their picket post was surrounded by a surprise rebel raid.

The cold and damp seemed to permeate everything and the warmth of a fire was precious. Firewood was becoming increasingly scarce and what was still available was difficult to gather. The sound of wood being chopped was sure to bring a deadly volley from the ever vigilant sharpshooters.

When not huddled in their trenches trying to keep warm, the men were often ordered out on work details. The breastworks and abatises were always in need of repair, bombproofs and covered ways continually required reinforcement, and trenches and traverses were constantly being extended as the army slowly wormed its way closer to the rebel lines. In cutting a new trench, some men of the 152nd New York unearthed the body of a Confederate soldier killed in the June battles. A sergeant in the group rifled the corpse's pockets for souvenirs and found three cents which he confiscated as trophies of war. Not surprisingly the new picket station was named "Dead man's post."

The 152nd also were given the task of driving a twenty foot underground shaft between the lines. Fearing retaliation from the enemy for the July blast at the "Crater," this countermine was dug as a "listening post" for any rebel mining activity. Men from the 152nd drew the unenviable duty of standing sentry at the shaft's terminus.

While living and working in the trenches was certainly no joy, serving on picket duty was much worse. Spread out at three hundred foot intervals, most of the picket posts were situated in open fields and provided little or no cover from the elements. Typically ordered out for three or four days, the three privates and the non-commissioned officer detailed to each station survived as best they could. Each man was expected to stand "on post" sixteen hours each day, using the balance of his time to sleep, cook and obtain firewood.

At all times, the lonely pickets had to maintain their vigilance, for one slip-up on their part could mean death from the sharpshooter's bullet. Henry Roback of the 152nd New York described the picket's lot on his regiment's line. Roback wrote:

> "The deadly picket trench and every spot in and around the fort was extremely hazardous, every minute, both day and night. Why so many lives were preserved was indeed one of the mysteries of war. A comrade while pacing his 'beat' on the parapet of the fort, came suddenly to a halt; instantly a bullet descended, burying deep in the hard ground between his feet.
>
> Just back of a portion of the picket trench was a piece of woods. The bullets had completely riddled them. It was a handy place to obtain fuel and many risks were taken, the sharpshooters' bullets keeping time with the blows of the axe.
>
> There was some in the ranks of our friends over the way who were humorously inclined. They would call over, inviting us to hold up our hands and get a six-months furlough. Doubtless there were some who would fire high but as a general practice they shot to kill."[6]

From the 152nd New York, three men were killed in November on picket duty at Fort Stedman. Oscar Avery, George Bush and James Hubbard of Otsego County were slain by sharpshooters.

Artillery duels were quite frequent all along the lines, but as related by Henry Roback, they were little feared and in fact provided the men a source of entertainment. Roback wrote:

> "The artillery duels at night were beautiful to those who viewed them from afar, or saw the pictures in an illustrated paper. The enemy had one battery on our front. We christened it the terror, as it would drop a bomb in the ditch outside the fort. Our position was taken at the parapets, where we would remain watching the bright meteors late in the night. Shells were continually dropping between the fort and the creek in the rear, although it did not in any way deter the men from keeping up a continual travel, for the purpose of obtaining wood, water, and washing clothes."[7]

The only serious casualty in the 152nd New York from the cannon fire was Pat Curtin of Schuyler. Curtin, who had in civilian life been employed by the 152nd's surgeon, Silas Ingham, had a leg mangled by a cannon ball. During an amputation performed by Dr. Ingham himself, Curtin died.

Throughout November, deserters from the rebel army were increasingly coming into the Union lines. On dark, dreary nights, great numbers of ragged, barefoot and emaciated men would brave the fire from their own pickets to "give themselves to the care of Uncle Sam." One individual of note that came into the 152nd's line was deserting, not from the Confederate army, but from the Union side. The wayward soldier, a member of the 184th Pennsylvania, had deserted from his regiment, gotten lost between the lines and stumbled into the camp of the 152nd New York asking to see Gen. Lee. Taken to the Provost Marshal, the misguided man was summarily court-martialed and one month later was executed in the presence of the brigade.

Thanksgiving Day, 1864, brought boxes of turkeys and "extra viands" to the 97th and 152nd in Petersburg and to the 121st New York in the Shenandoah Valley. The eatables were supplied by the Sanitary Commission and from the ladies of Herkimer, Otsego and Oneida counties. Unfortunately, not all of the food sent reached the private soldier. John Ingraham, with the 121st New York, voiced his displeasure at the liberties taken by many officers with the Thanksgiving foodstuffs sent from home. Ingraham wrote:

> "I suppose the people North think the Soldiers at the Front are having a Feast today on what was contributed for them for Thanksgiving. They would not call it a very large feast if they were here to see how the thing was carried on. I know of some Tents in our Regt that had given them one wing of a Turkey and others a neck of a fowl and just so throughout the whole Regt if that is what they call a Feast. I care little for a Feast but we shouldn't complain. The people North are not to blame. All that is sent to the soldiers has to go through too much red tape. All the officers have the handling over of such articles and take such as they want and all they want and the rest if any left go to the soldiers." [8]

Life in the trenches and picket posts of Petersburg was indeed miserable, but in no way could it compare with the suffering evidenced by Union prisoners of war interred in Confederate prison camps.

Grant's push through the Wilderness, Spotsylvania and Cold Harbor and the fights around Petersburg had produced numbers of prisoners from both sides that were unimaginable. With the prisoner exchange system having broken down, the Confederate prisons that had sprung up at Salisbury, North Carolina; Andersonville, Georgia and Florence, South Carolina were quickly overwhelmed by the innumerable Federal captives sent to them. Filled far beyond capacity with little or no sanitation, these camps were no more than open stockades and were perfect arenas for disease, starvation and death. Sadly, much of this depravation was really no one's fault. At this point of the war, the South was barely able to feed, clothe and doctor their own troops, much less care for a vast number of Federal prisoners. Combining all of these elements, it was not surprising that untold thousands of Union boys died in the Confederate prison camps.

In the latter months of 1864 alone, thirty-two men from Herkimer County died in rebel custody. The men were: from Little Falls - George Eaton (121st), William Turner (121st), Henry Alfreds (152nd), Israel Youker (97th), Alonzo Starring (57th) and Thomas Boussha (2nd HA); from Danube - Ben Covel (121st) and Delos Fox (152nd); from Fairfield - Norman Zoller (121st) and William Morey (152nd); from German Flatts - James Chismore (2nd HA), Abram Squires (14th Cav) and Daniel Mott (6th Cav); from Stark - Lorenzo Eldridge (152nd), Solomon Hollenbeck (152nd) and John McNeil (152nd); from Litchfield - Addison Eldred (152nd), Oscar West (97th) and Montraville Platt (152nd); from Newport - Franklin Terry (3rd HA); from Columbia - James Maxfield (152nd) and Joseph Mead (16th Cav); from Schuyler - Charles Brown (152nd); from Frankfort - Harvey Van Alystyne (152nd) and Rudy Devendorf (2nd HA); from Salisbury - James Benjamin (121st) and George Somers (81st); from Herkimer - Melchert Holler (152nd); from Manheim - Adam Grofs (152nd) and August Johnson (97th); and from Warren - William Lewis (2nd HA).

Prominent among these men was the 121st's George Eaton, a frequent correspondent to the *Journal*. Of Eaton's death, J.R. Stebbins wrote in the *Journal*:

> "Our citizens are again called upon to mourn the loss of a noble and brave young man, George Eaton, a member of Co. A, 121st regiment, who died a prisoner in the hands of the rebels, at Florence, Ga. [South Carolina], on the 15th ult. [November 15th], of chronic dysentery. George, although thought to be a boy at the time of his enlistment soon proved himself a man in the virtues and duties of a soldier. The very first day upon which the enlistment books were opened, in this village by Capt. Galpin, and after a hard day's work in the hayfield, he came down and enrolled his name on the 19th of July 1862, then being but seventeen years of age. He was a youth loved by all who knew him for his amiable disposition and quiet manner, and we are assumed by many of his old comrades in the regiment that he made friends wherever he went in the army. He went to battle for the country because he thought it his duty to do it, and his death is but another willful murder to be charged in the long account against cruel, hard-hearted rebels. We shall publish a letter next week giving something of the life and privations of the thousands of prisoners of whom he was one. At the time of his death he was aged 19 years, 5 months and 9 days."[9]

The letter alluded to in the *Journal* article was from Sgt. Joe Hoover of Little Falls, a member of the 121st New York, who had been captured in the Wilderness in May. Hoover's letter, which detailed his experiences as a prisoner and gave the particulars of his escape, was too long for publication so it was paraphrased by Stebbins. The story that appeared in the *Journal* read:

> "He [Hoover] was taken to Orange Court House, thence successively to Gordonsville, Charlottesville, Lynchburg, Danville, Charlotte, Augusta, Macon and finally to Andersonville, Ga. They were here kept in a sort of stockade about four months together with many thousands of other prison-

ers, among whom were L. Hemmingway, C. Young, Geo. Eaton, B. Covel, W.P. Smith* and others whose names he does not mention, of the 121st. While here, their rations were a pound of corn bread and four ounces of bacon per day, and the average number of deaths per day was from forty to sixty. On the 15th of September most of the prisoners were taken to Charleston, Savannah and Florence, S.C. on account of the capture by our forces of Atlanta and the fears of the rebels that Sherman might recapture them. He, with most of the others from the 121st, was among those taken to Florence, and soon after reaching that place on the 20th of September he contrived to get away with a companion named Thomas J. Ryan to the swamps in the rear of the stockade in which they were confined.

From this time until the 24th of October they were constantly on the march, sleeping in the woods during the day and walking as rapidly and as circumspectly as possible during the nights-sustaining themselves upon berries and fruits and with the food kindly furnished them in every instance when they dared go near enough to habitation to ask food of the negroes. Indeed the slaves not only fed them, but in several instances helped them forward materially upon their journey, giving them directions how to avoid rebel pickets and towns and in every possible way lending material assistance. They could always rely upon friends in the negroes. The details of this journey are most interesting and wonderful. They were several times very near capture, and twice came near being drowned in attempting to cross rivers, and were often on the verge of starvation. But they persevered boldly and hopefully all through these thirty three days of weariness and privations and at last reached our lines almost exhausted. They slept in the rain, usually without fires and always upon the alert for rebel soldiers who were frequently all about them. They were chased not only by soldiers, but by men, boys and blood-hounds and no doubt whether a more perilous and successful march through an enemy's country was ever made and we sincerely congratulate Serg. Hoover upon his good fortune. He is now with his regiment at the front."[10]

Sergeant Hoover, in a letter to Joe Heath of the 121st, made mention that two of the regiment's prisoners of war, Milo Tanner of Schuyler and P. Lettus of Otsego County, had been released by the rebels after having disgracefully taken an oath of allegiance to the Southern Confederacy.[11]

At just about the time that Joe Hoover returned to the 121st, the regiment broke camp in the Shenandoah Valley and began the journey back to Petersburg.

The 121st, which had been doing picket and guard duty since the Battle of Cedar Creek, left their camp at Kernstown, Virginia, on December 1st and entrained to Washington. From there, the regiment, numbering one hundred and seventy-five men, travelled by steamer to City Point on the James River, arriving on December 4th. Transported by troop train to Parke's Station on the outskirts of Petersburg, the 121st, under the command of Lt. Col. Olcott, marched to a ready-made camp. The camp, with newly built winter quarters and neatly laid out streets, had just recently

* Young and Hemmingway were from Salisbury, Covel from Danube, Eaton and Smith from Little Falls.

been occupied by the 3rd Division of the 5th Corps. The unfortunate 5th Corps boys, among whom the men of the 97th New York were included, had painstakingly erected their winter homes only to be ordered out on a mission by General Grant.

Grant had been receiving reports from his cavalry patrols that the rebels were building a branch line from the Weldon Railroad, at a point just below Union-held Stoney Creek Station, to the South Side Railroad. Fearing that winter would set in before he could destroy this new Confederate supply line Grant decided to act.

Having lost faith in the 2nd Corps after its failures at Reams Station and Hatchers Run, Grant called on Warren's 5th Corps to perform the job. Warren's orders were to destroy the Weldon Railroad from Stoney Creek Station to Hicksford, a distance of some twenty miles. At the completion of this mission not only would the enemy's new spur line be disrupted, but a total of forty miles of the Weldon's track from Petersburg to Hicksford would be obliterated.

The 97th New York reluctantly moved out of its freshly erected quarters on the morning of December 7th. The line of march that day took them nineteen miles south along the Jerusalem Plank Road, where they turned to the southwest, crossed the Nottoway River and bivouacked for the night at Sussex Court House. Resuming the march the next morning, the 97th advanced to a point on the Weldon Railroad, six miles south of Stoney Creek Station, where they joined the rest of the 5th Corps. Working until 11 o'clock that night, the men lifted sections of track, built fires of the ties and heated the rails before bending them into unusable shapes around convenient trees. All the next day, from sunup until well after dark, the work continued until sixteen miles of the Weldon track was destroyed. On the morning of December 10th, the work stopped just north of Hicksford, when a sizable rebel force drawn down from Petersburg confronted the 5th Corps. General Warren, believing his mission was nearly completed and realizing his rations were running low, turned his troops to withdraw rather than risk an engagement with the enemy.

The 97th New York, with its brigade and a detachment of cavalry, was detailed to guard the rear of the 5th Corps' column. Almost as soon as the Federal line began the march to Petersburg, the Confederate cavalry appeared and began to harass the rear guard. "J.W." of the 97th New York, in a letter to the *Journal*, described the Federals' solution to this problem, writing:

> "It was nearly noon before the corps had passed, and we were on the road. We had marched some four or five miles when this detachment of [Union] cavalry came rushing down upon us in the greatest confusion: we little suspecting anything of the kind endeavored to halt them but soon discovered that the 'Johnnies' were chasing in our much frightened and sadly demoralized cavalry. Our regiment, which was the rear regiment of the brigade, immediately filed to the left, and with a sharp volley of musketry soon stopped their further progress, and set them skedaddling. I could not but admire their bravery as some of them rode up within a few feet of our line.
>
> . . . Their intention was undoubtedly to create a panic and stampede us —but the game would not work with troops of three years service. We resumed the march with these fellows still hanging on our flanks and rear.

After it had become quite dark, and we had arrived to within a short distance of the place of encampment, the General commanding the Division [Crawford] laid a trap for them. He placed the 11th Pennsylvania behind a fence running parallel with the road on the right: the 97th along another fence at right angles with the road on the left. The officer commanding the detachment of our cavalry was to entice them in. In a few moments our boys came rushing in at a full gallop with the 'Johnnies' close upon them, crying 'halt', 'surrender' &c.. The moment they arrived inside the lines, the two regiments opened a cross fire on them: and it was really amusing to see the confusion scattering among them when they discovered their situation. Only their advance guard ventured inside the lines, and of these seven were killed, seven prisoners were captured, four of whom were wounded. Two horses now in possession of persons in this regiment and several others found dead, show that still more were disabled. Several rebel sabres were also captured: the Colonel, Lieut. Colonel and Adjutant, being between the two regiments, narrowly escaped being shot. During the melee, a Johnny rode up to Colonel Wheelock and demanded 'who are you?' Receiving no reply, he raised his sabre to strike him, but before the blow fell a ball pierced his head killing him instantly." [12]

The 5th Corps rear guard was not seriously molested for the remainder of the march back to Petersburg. In the Hicksford raid the 97th New York would suffer no casualties.

The 97th New York reached Petersburg on December 11th and with the rest of the 5th Corps, dejectedly began building new winter quarters within sight of their former camp, now occupied by the 121st New York and the other 6th Corps regiments. The other Mohawk Valley regiment, the 152nd New York, set up their winter camp at Patrick's Station, the terminus of the army's rail line.

Christmas 1864 brought parcels from home to the Herkimer County boys, but as usual many of the packages had been rifled somewhere en route. The Sanitary Commission could be counted on though, making presents of a pair of woolen socks and mittens to each soldier.

As 1864 neared its end and a new year loomed, the men looked optimistically towards the war's end. Everywhere but Petersburg, the Southern Confederacy had been for the most part subdued. Down in the South's underbelly, Sherman had cut a swath through Georgia, had taken Savannah and was preparing to start north to join forces with Grant. In Tennessee, Hood's army, the only other viable rebel force besides Lee's, had been routed by General Thomas at Nashville and for all practical purposes, ceased to exist. But most of all, the men of Grant's army believed the end of Lee's invincible Army of Northern Virginia was near. Even the common soldier, who daily saw the ragged, half-starved deserters from the rebel army come ever increasingly into the Union camps, knew that the Federal noose was being pulled tighter and that the Petersburg garrison was strangling. As 1865 began, all signs pointed to an end to the rebellion before the year was out.

Back in Herkimer County, the first heavy snowstorm of the winter season of

1864 struck on the day before Thanksgiving and brought unseasonably cold temperatures that settled in the Mohawk Valley. Many of the county's homeowners and businessmen were unprepared for this early onset of winter-like weather, and the stocks of firewood in most towns were quickly exhausted. With the snow too deep for the passage of wagon loaded teams but not deep enough for the use of sleighs, the price per cord of wood jumped from $6 to $20. In addition to this increase in price, a set of unscrupulous woodcutters, that the *Journal* labeled as "ravenous land sharks," were passing off loosely piled loads of short length wood to unwary buyers as full cords. In evidence to the value of firewood, the *Journal* informed its readers that subscriptions to the newspaper could now be paid off with wood.

As the snowfall continued, the snow pack built up and became conducive to sleighing. Large supplies of firewood began to come in to the towns and villages, but the price remained inflated. Only after many people turned to coal, at a now comparatively reasonable $13 to $15 per ton, did the price of firewood drop below $10 per cord.

While the greedy woodcutters had really done nothing illegal, *Journal* articles reported on those that truly had transgressed the law. On Main St. in Herkimer, John Cave of that village, was struck senseless by an "unknown ruffian" wielding a club and robbed of $40. The Herkimer Police took three suspects into custody. In Little Falls, Henry Hallings was arrested for manufacturing cigars without an Internal Revenue permit and was released on $110 bail. But the most senseless of the crimes involved three Little Falls youths that vandalized a private home and a Little Falls schoolhouse. Under the title "A Dastardly Outrage," the *Journal* reported on the boys' rampage":

> "During several days of last week, three young lads of this village, whose names we withhold, from respect for their parents, were engaged in 'playing confiscation' as they termed it. They entered the house of Mrs. Geo. W. Davis, who was absent from home for a week or two, and spent the most of two whole days in destroying and mutilating everything within reach. They ripped open and broke in pieces sofas and chairs, broke bureaus and mirrors, went down cellar, taking all its contents in the way of preserves, molasses, vinegar, &c. up into the front parlor and there spreading these out upon the Brussels carpet and mixing them up with flour, meal, feathers (from the beds) and almost every imaginable thing in the house. They took up handfuls of butter and lard and threw them all over the walls and furniture and in fact exhausted all their ingenuity to perfectly destroy everything they could find.
>
> Then they proposed to 'confiscate' the school house on this side of the river, entering it through a window. They took down the large maps, tearing them and throwing them into the furnaces, broke the school-room lamps in pieces, poured pails of water into the melodeons, broke the locks from the doors and did other damage to a large amount. After considerable search, the affair was traced to the three boys who were arrested and they soon confessed the whole thing. The story they told of the crimes they had committed and those they had planned for future perpetration, including the murder of Mr. Champion, the schoolteacher, for which two of them had

provided themselves with pistols, is too awful to be believed of boys, two of whom are not twelve years of age and the other only fifteen. It is difficult to understand by what motives short of pure 'deviltry' they could have been actuated. It is some satisfaction that their parents are not only able but perfectly willing to pay for the damage done and to take such course with their sons as will, we trust, yet redeem them from the evil ways into which they have fallen." [13]

In the autumn of 1864, Herkimer County evidenced its first major bout with the crime of bounty jumping. Bounty jumping, which was more common in larger cities than in rural areas such as Herkimer County, was typically accomplished by a man enlisting, collecting his bounty money and deserting at the first opportunity. Some individuals carried on this practice a number of times and with the bounty money being fairly substantial, could become relatively wealthy. While bounty jumpers often acted alone, on occasion, as was the case in Herkimer County, well organized rings would develop.

In late November, a large number of bounty jumpers were arrested in Buffalo and included among the catch were twenty men from Herkimer County. One of these men, Addison Countryman of Little Falls, implicated two Little Falls bounty brokers, John Kosboth and Albert Fralick Jr., as the heads of the bounty jumping scheme in Herkimer County. In a sworn affidavit, Countryman outlined the ring's methods, which the *Journal* described to its readers:

> "In his affidavit, Countryman swore that he lived at Little Falls, and in Sept. last he, with thirteen others, went to Buffalo to enlist. Himself and two others did enlist with Captain Mackey, in the 7th U.S. Infantry, under assumed names, were mustered and sworn in but not clothed, and received $100 bounty from Fralick.
>
> The brokers told them they had an arrangement with the official: that it was a soft thing. After paying them, the [brokers] told them to take the next train and go home, and look out for themselves, which they did. Kosboth and Fralick said they had it all fixed with the officers to let Countryman and the others off. All the men that went up with Countryman enlisted, but he only saw two of them do so.
>
> About the 15th of September the same parties went up with Albert Fralick and John Kosboth to Buffalo to enlist again. They were again enlisted and mustered and by the same officer. This time, after having enlisted, they were put into a room, from which they escaped. Fralick coming and beckoned them to do so. After dusk they were met by Fralick and Kosboth, paid $100 each and told to shift for themselves.
>
> Then they went home. Countryman enlisted twice, other of his companions from four to seven or eight times each. Seven of these parties at one time jumped off a train and thus deserted." [14]

John Kosboth and Albert Fralick Jr., along with two other Little Falls brokers, James Rowe and Albert's brother Levi, were arrested and brought before Judge Boyce in Utica for examination. Set free on bail, two months later the four men were brought before the U.S. Circuit Court in Albany, where they were convicted of harboring deserters and enticing soldiers to desert.

As 1864 wound down to its last few weeks, most of the Herkimer County schools ended their fall terms and the students were freed for the holidays. At the Little Falls Academy, the three days of examinations and exercises were, as was the norm, open to the public. The students gave declamations in English and German and presented compositions and recitations in French and English. It was announced that starting with the academy's next term, Spanish and Italian would be added to the school's required curriculum.

Year end was also a time for closing accounts. The school libraries of Herkimer County requested that all persons having library books on loan return them immediately. Failure to do so would result in the patron being charged full value for the book. The *Journal's* J.R. Stebbins reminded the newspaper's subscribers that it was time to renew. To those people that had fallen behind on paying their subscriptions, Stebbins declared:

> "The country printer never was compelled to paddle his way against so many adverse currents as at the present time. The prices of white paper, labor, &c. are so ruinously high, that unless the patrons pay promptly, he must soon run ashore. Credit it is 'played out,' though we are sorry to say that the higher prices have risen, the more some of our friends forget to tender us their compliments!
>
> The close of the year is a good time to change this habit, and the sooner the 'change'—and the more of it—the better for us.
>
> There are a large number of names on our list whose owners are indebted to us for two, three or even four and five years. To go on in this way, in these times, is little better than downright swindling. Wipe out the old scores, friends and let us all have a fair start with Father Abraham, on the new Presidential term." [15]

On December 20th, Abraham Lincoln gave the Union war effort a "fair start" for 1865 by issuing a new call for three hundred thousand men. The quota for the 20th Senatorial District was set at sixteen hundred and thirty-five men by Provost Marshal, General Fry, of which the townships of Herkimer County were required to supply four hundred and sixteen men. By the Conscription Act of 1864, fifty days after the President's call, a draft would be held to cover any deficiencies. February 8th, 1865 would be the draft day under this call.

The township quotas in Herkimer County ranged from seventy-eight for Little Falls to two for Wilmurt.[16] Deducted from each township's quota and from the county as a whole were credits for men that had enlisted since the last draft in September.

With the holiday season in full swing, the work of filling the new quotas was put on hold for the moment and the festivities of Christmas and New Years took command.

In brightly lit churches throughout Herkimer County, people gathered on Christmas Eve around Christmas trees adorned with bulbs, garlands and candles to sing carols and enjoy Yuletide refreshments. As a culmination to the evening, the congregation often presented their rector with a monetary gift that served to partially compensate the minister for his services. The parishioners of the Baptist Church in

Frankfort gave their clergyman, Rev. J.C. Ward, a pair of gloves with $101 stuffed inside of them.

Christmas Day was spent exchanging gifts, feasting on turkey or goose and oysters, visiting family and friends and perhaps by attending a performance by one of the troupes passing through Herkimer County. The Peak Family of Swiss Bell Ringers, banjoist Charles Dobson, Father Kemp's Old Folk Singers, and Duprez and Green's Theatrical Troupe, all put in an appearance at Concert or Keller Hall in Little Falls during Christmas week.

As 1864 wound down to its last night, congregations met at their churches for the annual "Watch Meeting." After a sumptuous banquet, the members bade the old year goodbye with song and welcomed in the new year with prayer.

The year past had not been kind to the Herkimer County folk. The county's favored regiments, the 97th, 121st and 152nd New York, had absorbed over eleven hundred casualties (including two hundred and fifty-eight killed) in Grant's campaign to the gates of Petersburg and in the Shenandoah Valley fights. The losses had been taken hard, for even with all the bloodshed, the end of the rebellion had appeared no nearer.

But now, after important Union victories in the west, the war had been distilled down to a single point, Petersburg, and this last rebel citadel was tottering. As 1865 dawned, the disappointments of the past were fading and the prospects for peace were clearly in sight.

Col. George Thompson,
34th & 152nd New York

History of the 34th Regiment

Col. Timothy O'Brien, 152nd New York

Courtesy of the Little Falls Historical Society

Courtesy of the Little Falls Historical Society

Main Street, Little Falls, 1862

*Mrs. Seth Richmond, head of the
Herkimer County Ladies Aid Societies*

Courtesy of the Little Falls Historical Society

CHAPTER XXI

"Along most of the line all is quiet"

Winter 1864/1865 - Winter Quarters - 2nd Hatcher's Run - The Draft

In January of 1865, the Union envelopment around Petersburg stretched fifty miles from northeast of Richmond to Fort Welch on Petersburg's southwest perimeter. In most places the Federal line was so close to the city that the spires of tall churches were clearly visible, and in still times the chimes of Petersburg's town clock could be heard. The opposing trenches along the line were usually no more than a stone's throw apart and at a few positions were separated by the length of a musket.

With the lines in such proximity, to keep the men fresh and vigilant, picket details were changed every twenty-four hours. While on picket duty, not only were the front line soldiers prohibited from sleeping, but the men at the reserve posts were also under orders to stay awake. All intercourse with the enemy was strictly forbidden, but as described by Salisbury's A.N. Jennings, a member of the 121st New York, friendly and not so friendly banter was frequent along the picket line. Jennings wrote:

> "Along most of the line all was quiet, the firing is only kept up nights, through the day the guns being stuck up and the men lounge about at their ease, but as soon as it begins to get dark you may hear them calling to one another—'Hallo Yanks, or Johnnys, look out!' we are going to shoot! lay low! When like the prairie dogs, they take to their holes, and not so much as a nose can be seen above their little breastworks, and only, pop, pop, tells of their whereabouts: but as soon as it gets to be daylight all becomes silent.

There was a detail made from our regiment for picket. They said there was only one shot fired from their part of the line while out, and that by a Reb who fancied his feelings hurt by one of our boys, who, feeling rather musical, commenced singing 'We'll hang Jeff Davis from a sour apple tree.' [The rebel] let his Ebeneezer get the better of him and fired at the offending Yank, but the shot was not returned and all remained quiet the remainder of the time." [1]

The rebel fire that was kept up at night was not so much directed at the Union boys as it was intended to discourage desertions from the Confederates' own ranks. Circulars offering $16 to each rebel that brought his musket into Union lines were passed to enemy pickets and before long the tide of rebel deserters increased dramatically. Each night, singly or in groups numbering as many as forty, Confederate enlisted men and officers braved their own picket fire and made their way to the Union trenches. Increasingly noted among these deserters were graybeards and young boys dragging muskets too heavy for them to carry. While most of the desertions occurred at night, the Union boys also devised ways to aid rebel deserters in broad daylight. John Ingraham described such a scheme developed by the men of the 121st New York Ingraham wrote:

"Our Corps are building a very long Fort, the longest one along the entire line. It is called Fort Fisher. It is customary for the Rebs & also our men to pass through the picket line & pick up wood & we are careful not to get near each other's pickets. Well, as it happened the other day both our men and theirs were out in front and in fact got among each other pretty thickly, and the Johnnys thought it a pretty good opportunity to desert and to shield themselves from being fired upon by their own men when they attempted to gain our lines. They hit upon a plan like this. Our boys took off their overcoats and threw them over their—the Johnnys—shoulders and then they would walk unmolested right into our lines. The Reb pickets would see the blue overcoat of course, and think they were our men and would not fire. Our boys worked in that way and got quite a number in all. This was in the daytime." [2]

To a much lesser extent there were Union soldiers deserting to the Confederate lines. Typically, these were high bounty men who had failed to run off on the trip south and now saw their chance to do so. Deserting into the rebel camps, these men would take the Confederate oath of allegiance with every intention of also escaping from the rebel army. Many times these men would be recaptured by the Federals and would face the penalty of death by hanging. In the 2nd Corps, a large gallows was constructed and each Friday six of these turncoats were hung in the presence of the corps. For those deserters who had turned north, the penalty if caught was a little more lenient—death by the firing squad.

The weather of southern Virginia, in January of 1865, featured rain followed by more rain. Virginia's "sacred soil" quickly turned into a sticky paste and as the ground became thoroughly saturated with water, campgrounds changed from quagmires to small lakes. On many mornings men awoke to find the contents of the huts, pots, pans, canteens and other paraphernalia, floating about their bunks. Railroad beds turned into canals, roads into rivers, and country lanes into streams. Travel outside of the campgrounds was nearly impossible and all active campaigning was out of the question until the rain subsided and the waters drained off.

Stuck in their quarters with nowhere to go and little to do, boredom was the men's chief enemy. The only rays of sunshine in this dreary existence were the infrequent parcels from home that somehow found their way to the camps. Unfortunately, many of the packages were rifled en route and what was not taken was often damaged. But, as evidenced by John Ingraham's letter to his parents, the soldiers didn't expect much and any item from home was a godsend. Ingraham wrote:

> "We'd rec'd the last box you sent us yesterday morning. The eatables turned out much better than we expected they would, being on the route so long. You can think it did not take us but a very few minutes to inspect it. Everything was in good order except the longest roll of sausage. They were furred some but not too hurt. The vinegar leaked off from the pickles & kraut which soaked the . . . cake. There is just twang enough in it to give a fellow an appetite to eat another just like it. The pies were pressed pretty solid together but not so but what we can pry them apart to eat them."[3]

Of another box from home, and of a comrade's pilfered parcel, Ingraham noted:

> "It is gratifying to tell you our box came in very good order. The books were a little furred on the outside but no material damage done in the least. The can pickles were spoiled and the apples are what we call rotten. The butter smells quite rancid but will answer for a soldier. The other fellow rec'd his this morn but it had been opened and his boots and a great many other articles had been taken out so the poor fellow is rather disappointed in his. Any man that will rob a soldier's box sent to him by his friends ought to be shot for there is no manly principle about them."[4]

During the winter months of 1865, significant organizational changes were made in the three Mohawk Valley regiments.

In the 152nd New York, Lt. Col. Timothy O'Brien of Little Falls was unable to continue as commander of the regiment due to frequent flare-ups of wounds he had received in the Wilderness and at Deep Bottom. Mohawk resident, James Curtiss, was brevetted to lieutenant colonel and given command of the 152nd. Not long after assuming command, Curtiss learned that the War Department was considering a breakup of the 152nd. The manpower level of the regiment had fallen below two hundred men and the Union high command proposed a transfer of the 152nd's men to other regiments. In such a move, the 152nd's colors would be lost, its officers would lose their commands and the common soldiers would be deprived of their unit identity. Before any action could be taken, Curtiss filed a request with the adjutant general's office for three hundred new recruits from New York State's quota. The Secretary of the Treasury, Francis Spinner of Mohawk, interceded once more on the behalf of a Herkimer County regiment and addressed a note to the Secretary of War, Edwin Stanton, recommending maintenance of the 152nd. In early March, the adjutant general approved Curtiss's request and before the winter was over, three hundred bounty men were detailed to the 152nd's ranks.[5] The crisis had passed and the

152nd New York was given new life.

Although there was no talk of disbanding the 121st New York, the ranks of this regiment—now numbering less than two hundred and seventy-five muskets—had been so decimated that its effectiveness as a fighting force was questionable. Brevet Col. Egbert Olcott, commanding the 121st ever since Emory Upton's promotion to brigadier general, requested four hundred new recruits for the regiment. The army's high regard for the 121st New York was evident as Olcott's petition quickly passed through channels and was heartily endorsed by Secretary of War Stanton. Unfortunately, no men were immediately available and the 121st did not get its additional manpower consignment until early summer. While waiting for his request to be filled, Olcott, Maj. James Cronkite of Milford and Brevet Lt. Col. John Kidder, of Otsego County, travelled through Herkimer and Otsego counties trying to drum up new enlistees to the 121st. The trio of officers were unsuccessful and returned to Petersburg with only a handful of recruits.

In the 97th New York, the command structure changed dramatically with the death of the regiment's commander, Col. Charles Wheelock. Wheelock, a prominent produce dealer from Boonville, was a great bear of a man—standing over six feet tall and weighing well over two hundred pounds—who was accursed with a weak constitution. On many occasions Wheelock put himself on sick leave, but after a few weeks of rest and recuperation he always dutifully returned to his regiment. Soon after Lt. Col. John Spofford rejoined the 97th in January, Wheelock once more became sick and was transported from Petersburg to a Washington hospital. The men felt no special cause for concern, but on January 21st, Charles Wheelock died at the age of forty-nine of unspecified causes. The news of Wheelock's death shocked the 97th and the rest of the brigade. Upon hearing the news, Isaac Hall of the 97th wrote:

> "The official announcement of his death created a profound sensation of grief among the officers and men of his regiment; no commandant of a regiment was more beloved by his men or possessed more respect among subordinate officers; besides he was well known and much respected throughout the brigade and division." [6]

Soon after Wheelock's death, it was learned by the men that he had been breveted a brigadier general back in August and offered the command of a brigade, but that he had turned down the position to stay with the boys of the 97th. As a return show of affection for their departed leader, the officers and men of the 97th New York resolved that their regimental colors be suitably draped and that the officers would wear a badge of mourning in honor of Wheelock for the remainder of the 97th's service.

Colonel Wheelock's body was transported back to Boonville, where on January 26th his funeral service was conducted. So numerous were the mourners that came to pay homage that an extra train had to be scheduled from Utica to Boonville that day.

With the death of Wheelock, the command of the 97th New York passed to Brockett's Bridge's John Spofford. Spofford was promoted to a full colonel, while Rouse Egelston, also of Brockett's Bridge, and Delos Hall of Salisbury, respectively moved up to lieutenant colonel and major. It was singular that the 97th New York, which bore as its nickname "The Third Oneida," now had three Herkimer County men as its top field officers.

At the end of January, the rains let up and warm sunshine dried the roads and campgrounds around Petersburg. In early February, General Grant received information that a large Confederate wagon train was approaching Petersburg from the southwest laden with supplies for the city's beleaguered defenders. With the intent of destroying this supply train, Grant detailed Gen. David Gregg's cavalry to strike out after the rebel convoy. In support of Gregg's troopers, the 5th Corps was ordered to march along in the trail of the cavalry, while the 2nd Corps was directed to sidle westward along the Petersburg front, screening the 5th Corps' move.

Early on the morning of February 5th, the 97th New York left their winter quarters and marched south along the Weldon Railroad as the tail of the 5th Corps column. After travelling three miles, the line of march left the tracks and veered southwest to Hatcher's Run. The stream was crossed without opposition, for the way had been cleared by cavalry and the vanguard of the 5th Corps column. The march continued on another mile, at which point the men were allowed to break ranks and prepare lunch. Cookfires were quickly lit, but before the bacon began to fry, the sound of cannon fire and the rattle of musketry from the rear brought the order to reform ranks. General Warren soon appeared and the 97th was ordered to about face and lead the 5th Corps back to Hatcher's Run. On reaching the stream, the men of the 97th were ordered to build defensive breastworks facing northeast. The position was held throughout the night as the rest of the 5th Corps tramped by. Just past midnight on the morning of February 6th, the 97th crossed back over Hatcher's Run and fell in line once more as the 5th Corps' tail.

The sounds of guns that had caused the 97th New York to miss lunch and reverse their march had arisen from a clash between elements of the 2nd Corps and a rebel probe sent down from Petersburg. With an enemy force threatening to intersperse itself between the 2nd and 5th Corps, General Meade ordered the 5th Corps to return from beyond Hatcher's Run and link up with the left wing of the 2nd Corps. What had started out as a simple raid on a Confederate wagon train was now threatening to turn into a major engagement as units from both sides were being drawn into the arena.

The 97th New York, with its brigade, made contact with the 2nd Corps line at noon on the 6th. Ordered into battleline, the brigade was directed to attack a thin line of rebel skirmishers near a ruined sawmill at Dabney's Mill. Attacking en masse, the Union boys easily pushed back the meager enemy force and approached what appeared to be a rebel earthen fort adjacent to the sawmill. The command to charge was given, and a race between the regimental color bearers to be the first to reach the rebel works ensued. John Hartman of the Salisbury described the contest, writing:

"The order was given to charge and our boys moved forward in gallant style. The color bearers of the 16th Maine and of the 97th rushed forward, each with the same intent to be the first to plant his colors upon the supposed works: but Corporal Mortimer of the 97th outran the other and was first to plant the stars and stripes upon fort 'sawdust.' " [7]

To the dismay of Cpl. Charles Mortimer of Utica, the prize he had won was not a Confederate fort, but simply an old pile of sawdust left over from the sawmill's workings.

Before the men could catch their breath, the 97th's brigade was counterattacked by a large and very real enemy force. The first assault was repulsed, but the rebels moved artillery into position and attacked once more. Cartridge boxes soon emptied along the Union line and with no ammunition wagons in sight, the 97th, with its brigade, melted back in retreat. Driven back over a mile, the routed 5th Corps men emerged into an open field and were welcomed by a division from the 6th Corps waiting behind newly constructed breastworks. The 6th Corps boys had been providentially ordered down from the Petersburg line by General Meade just that morning in case Warren got in trouble. Numbered among the 6th Corps units was the 121st New York and, fittingly, it was along their section of breastworks that the 97th New York sought refuge. John Ingraham of the 121st wrote of this meeting with a brother Mohawk Valley regiment:

> "The 5th Corps began to fall back before our Div. could form and came through our ranks. There was a perfect stampede for about 1/2 an hour but the men soon rallied and checked the Rebs. You can't imagine what a sight it is when there is a stampede. Our troops fell back a short distance and formed behind some works. I saw the old 97th rallying and went to see if Col Spofford & Capt Eggleston & Judd were all right but they were not with that part of the Regt. I stopped a while with them and soon Col Spofford & Capt Eggleston came up with another squad of the 97th. I shook hands with Col & Capt and was glad they came out all right." [8]

The enemy attacks were stemmed by the show of Federal force behind the breastworks and the Union boys settled down to a miserable night of sleet and rain.

At first light the next morning, February 7th, the 97th New York, with its brigade, was ordered out onto a now ice-slicked field to attack the rebel's picket line. The pickets were easily driven in, but advancing further, the brigade came up against a formidable enemy line of fortifications. The Federals hurriedly built their own works and for the bulk of the day, the two sides exchanged shots. At 1 a.m. the next morning, the 97th's brigade received the order to withdraw. Gregg's horsemen were back from their raid and the 5th Corps' mission was completed.

Materially, General Gregg's foray had been a complete failure. Although the blue cavalry had fanned out through the countryside, no substantial Confederate wagon train was found. Eighteen wagons and fifty prisoners had been captured, but balanced against the over fifteen hundred casualties taken by the Union army, the cost had been enormous. [9] Tactically, some gains had been made. As a result of the maneuver new ground had been gained and the further extension of the Union line had stretched the already thin Confederate defenses a bit more.

The price paid by the Mohawk Valley regiments involved was relatively light.

The 121st New York had four men wounded,[10] and the 152nd New York, which had moved with the 2nd Corps but had not been actively engaged, showed no casualties. The 97th New York, which bore the brunt of the fight, counted eleven men killed and twenty-three wounded.[11] Notable to the Herkimer County folk, among the 97th's casualties were: Colonel Spofford who was struck in the side by a spent ball and suffered broken ribs; William Burberry of Russia who was killed; William McGowan of Russia who died soon after his leg was amputated; and Adj. Willard Judd of Brockett's Bridge who was shot in the knee and died after amputation. Of the death of Judd, the *Journal* noted:

> "In the bloody fight of Hatcher's Run about the 5th of last month he was severely wounded in the leg and was conveyed to City Point when his leg was amputated. While in the hospital he wrote to his friends in this county that he was doing well and expected to be home on Friday of last week. On Friday he did come home-a corpse. It seems that the amputation of his limb was imperfect and by some start or over exertion an artery was burst open, and all efforts to save his life wore vain. He died at City Point, Feb. 20th.
>
> . . . His remains were interred at Brockett's Bridge on Sunday last with a large concourse of his old friends and acquaintances. The discourse was delivered by Rev. Ferguson, formerly Chaplain of the regiment to which he belonged."[12]

After this latest battle of Hatcher's Run, the 121st New York returned to their cozy winter quarters along the Weldon Railroad. The 97th New York and the 152nd New York, on the other hand, remained in the vicinity of the stream and had to construct new quarters.

For the remainder of the month and well into March, the action around Petersburg was quiet. The weather turned warm and mild, the men received many months of back pay, and new regiments and new recruits were arriving from the North. Among the new units arriving at Petersburg was the 186th New York which had been raised in Sackett's Harbor and included a smattering of men from Graysville and Herkimer. Among the 186th's officers were Capt. Judson Legg and Lt. Amos Morse of Graysville.

With the military machines of both sides seemingly having gone into neutral, the daily routine of camp life turned into drudgery. Besides the nightly pyrotechnic displays of the artillery and the one hundred gun salutes that followed the announcements of major Union victories, there was little excitement for men that had been living on the razor's edge since last May. It was therefore not surprising that when the Irish Brigade of the 2nd Corps held their St. Patrick's Day celebration, the men flocked to it. The Irishmen's festivities, which included all sorts of games, horse races and general "merriment," drew not only privates but also many generals. A work detail from the 121st New York was sent out to gather pine poles, got waylaid at the Irish Brigade's camp, and did not arrive home until late in the day. The by now thoroughly drunken men were reprimanded by Major Cronkite and made to carry logs around the camp for the rest of the night.

As the end of March neared, all extra baggage was sent to the rear. The veterans knew this was a sure sign that the final campaign was about to begin, a campaign that the men looked forward to. A.N. Jennings of the 121st, in a letter to the *Journal*, eloquently expressed the men's attitude. Jennings wrote:

> "The health of the regiment is first rate, and the men are feeling quite jolly over the victories of Sherman and the capture of Fort Fisher. . . . Most of them have seen enough of fighting, and are ready for peace on the right ground, but none of that peace that the followers of Geo. B. McClellan, and Seymour proposed, or their constituents; and with such leaders as Grant, Sherman and Sheridan they feel that victory is sure, and that they will yet conquer a peace that will be glorious and honorable, and one that will let them sit down under the folds of the Glorious old flag feeling a still small voice whispering to their hearts as they witness the sport of their bright eyed and golden haired sons and daughters, that for these they have shed their blood and wasted their youth on the gory fields of the south. And tears of pleasure will chase each other down the cheek, all smeared and wrinkled, that theirs has been the honor to give them so rich a boon as a free land and a lasting peace.
>
> The boys are looking anxiously forward for the next seven months to pass [scheduled for muster-out in August, 1865], when they can once more meet old friends and associates and renew old friendships that have so long been severed. Many of them have not been home since they first left old Herkimer Co. and anticipate much of happiness and joy in the glad reunion, and a feeling that they have done their duty as men and soldiers, before whom the mean nasty Copperheads will look small." [13]

The Winter of 1864-1865 was long and harsh in the Mohawk Valley. Throughout most of January and February, Herkimer County was locked in a deep freeze with nighttime temperatures dropping to twenty degrees below zero and the thermometer rarely climbing to double digits during the day. The intense cold was often augmented by chilling winds and blinding snowstorms that frequently brought all forms of travel to a standstill. The snow that had begun back in early November seemingly never let up and by mid-January, over five and one-half feet had fallen. February brought no reprieve as massive storms continued to pound the area. The snow became such a problem in Little Falls that the *Journal* regularly reminded the residents of that village that they were liable by village by-laws to keep their sidewalks shoveled. Little Falls policemen were regularly on the prowl, ready to hand out fines of $2 per day to homeowners or shopkeepers with uncleared walks. Of this winter, the *Journal* noted:

> "This has been an extraordinary winter and one that will be long remembered. From the time of the first real snow storm we have had uninterrupted sleighing, it is only interrupted by drafts and severe blows.
>
> We have not even been favored with the usual January thaws, but on the contrary there have been but few days that snow even melted on our sidewalks under the rays of the sun.

The thermometer has ranged most of the time from the freezing point downward-seldom if ever, for more than an hour or two during mid-day has it been found above that point. During the past two weeks, it has ranged from a few degrees above to eighteen or twenty degrees below zero. The wind has been sharp and cutting, and the country roads have been filled with drifts piled many feet high. The rail roads have found it almost impossible to withstand the effects of such weather, and trains, even now, are not running with much regularity." [14]

Notwithstanding the severe weather, Herkimer County still had its quota of four hundred and sixteen men from Lincoln's December call to fill. In responding to this call, the county townships dropped all pretenses of recruiting locally and wholly sought to buy their "volunteers" in metropolitan areas such as Buffalo and New York City. The ability to raise a quota had by now made the complete transition from relying on the people's patriotic fervor to relying on the depth of their pocketbooks. In Little Falls, the level of bounty money to be offered was put to a straw vote among the village's residents. At a town meeting held at the Nelson House, votes were cast which ranged from a $2,000 bounty for a one-year-man to no bounty at all. The majority opted for a bounty "without specification," the amount to be left to the discretion of the Little Falls recruiting committee, headed by town Supervisor Zenas Priest. In a *Journal* editorial, J.R. Stebbins derided the five people that had campaigned and voted against a town bounty, writing:

"We would not say a word further as to the necessity for immediate action in offering some local inducements to volunteers, were it not that there seems to be an evident purpose on the part of a few men who are not liable to the coming draft, either through physical disability or because the town has furnished substitutes for them, to prevent by fair or foul means, the offering of a town bounty. They are doubtless endeavoring to see the justice of refusing to assist in providing substitutes for those who are now paying heavy taxes in their behalf - for their substitutes. If these men have fully determined to resort to such means as were tried last Saturday to defeat popular expression, it may as well be known to the public. It may be policy to wait, as we have too often done heretofore, till the draft is right upon us, and then pay exorbitant prices for volunteers, after towns about us (as Salisbury and some others have already done) have secured their men at low rates - but we fail to see it in that light. The men must be had either by volunteering or by draft. It is hardly to be supposed that seventy-five or a hundred men, most of whom are already paying large sums to secure the exemption of other men, will deem it quite the fair thing that now the town shall refuse to render them like assistance. In our opinion it will still be found to be necessary to offer further bounties, and the sooner the better." [15]

With bounty money coming principally from tax dollars and township bonding, the taxpayers of Herkimer County were pleasantly surprised to learn that "volunteers" could be bought for less money this call than they could under the previous call. In August of 1864, after the bitter fighting in the Wilderness and at Spotsylvania and Cold Harbor, bounty men commanded $900 to $1300, now with the war apparently winding down, a man could be got for $550 to $775.

Working through agents that enrolled principally Canadians or Britons, most of the Herkimer County towns had either filled their quotas or were very close to doing so as the draft day, February 9th, approached.

A number of the new recruits were being shuttled to the area's newest regiment, the 193rd New York. Organized in Albany, the 193rd was commanded by Fairfield Academy Principal Col. John Van Petten, formerly Chaplain of the 34th New York and most recently a lieutenant colonel in the 160th New York. Other Herkimer County officers in the 193rd were, Lt. James Haile of Little Falls, Lt. Julius Townsend (formerly with the 152nd New York) from Newport and Lt. John Wilson (formerly with the 34th) from Herkimer.

Bounty brokers were still in the area, but theirs was a dying profession—the New York State Senate would, for all practical purposes, outlaw bounty brokering in mid-February. One bounty broker, apparently low on willing customers, attempted to shanghai an unnamed Herkimer farmer and pass him off as a volunteer. The farmer had come into Herkimer to sell some produce and, while hitching up his team, was approached by a stranger who struck up a conversation. Invited to partake of a little refreshment, the farmer entered a local saloon with the stranger and had one—obviously doctored—drink. The next thing the farmer could recollect was waking up in a locked room in Oswego. Fortunately, the "scoundrel" was out negotiating his prisoner's sale and the farmer was able to escape and make his way to the authorities. The unscrupulous broker could not be located by the police and the farmer took the first train home, expressing great concern for his team and the fifty unattended cows on his farm.

The people of Herkimer County paid little attention when the February 9th draft date was changed to March 15th since they believed each town had already met its quota. But to their surprise, word came from the provost marshal in Watertown that his records showed the county still to be deficient by over two hundred men. Herkimer County officials argued to no avail that many of the recruits had enrolled in Albany and their records had not been transferred to Watertown. The provost marshal remained steadfast, discounting the Albany records as false. To this turn of events, J.R. Stebbins wrote in the *Journal*:

> "So far as the towns in this county are concerned, we had supposed the quotas already filled, with one or two exceptions. But the recent developments . . . have led to the retention of the papers by the authorities at Albany and consequently to a failure to receive the proper credits on the books of the Provost Marshal at Watertown. Indeed it is found impossible, so far, to ascertain how many of these papers so retained at Albany, are forged or bogus and how many are genuine. If the government shall insist upon proceeding with a draft in a county which has always furnished its full quotas and more too, under circumstances like these, after the efforts that have been put forth to obtain men, and after the supposition had generally obtained that the quotas were full, it will do an act of injustice for which we believe it is hardly prepared. We trust that we may at least be able to learn, before the day of the draft, how many conscripts will be drawn on the respective towns. Nobody seems to know anything about it now." [16]

The draft drum did turn in Watertown, but not until March 20th. Seventy-two names were drawn from the town of Adams in Jefferson County before the order for the draft was countermanded by telegraph. The draft in Herkimer County's 20th Senatorial District was postponed indefinitely and as military events turned favorable down south it was suspended altogether.

Although recruiting and the draft were in the forefront of the news, the *Journal* also reported on other interesting happenings in Herkimer County.

On the business front, the Salisbury Iron Company was formed with Ilion's Samuel Remington as president and Zenas Priest of Little Falls as vice president. Remington and Priest, along with a number of other investors, had purchased an old iron mine near the John Gifford farm in the northern part of Salisbury. Years before iron ore had been found on the land, but attempts at mining it on a cost efficient basis had proved unsuccessful. But now with the price of iron advanced, the Salisbury iron company's directors believed that a good return could be realized on their money and offered $150,000 in capital stock to the public. Mining operations were planned to commence when the weather broke in the spring.

Also newly formed was the Little Falls Petroleum Company. Headed by Herkimer County men Oliver LaDue, H.M. Burch and Albert Story, the company had purchased one hundred acres of land in Lambton County in the southwestern corner of Ontario. The land contained five active oil wells pumping over two hundred barrels of crude oil a week, machine shops, refineries and a railhead. A geological survey had pronounced the supply of oil from these wells as "inexhaustible" and rated its quality for "illuminating purposes" as far superior to the oil produced by Pennsylvania wells. The Little Falls investment group offered to investors one hundred thousand shares in their new company at the price of $5 per share.

For the real estate entrepreneur, the *Journal* advertised a "Confiscation Sale" to be held in Norfolk, Virginia. Rebel land valued at five million dollars had been seized by the Federal government and was being proffered for sale to loyal citizens. As stated in a *Journal* ad, the property afforded rare opportunities for profitable investment and where similar sales had been made, the introduction of northern citizens had resulted in "a complete change and reorganization of society and the foundation of future prosperity is permanently laid."

In other business news, the *Journal* noted that Lieut. Col. Henry Galpin, recently discharged from the 121st by reason of disability, had reopened his store in the Bucklin Block in Little Falls. Galpin's store, the *Journal* stated, sold the finest in stoves and furnaces and that a "run in trade" was expected from an appreciative public.

J.R. Stebbins also gave a plug to his sister, Irene, who was starting a new oil painting class in Little Falls.

Passing through Herkimer County on the lecture circuit this winter were Thurlow Brown of Wisconsin, also known as the "Cayuga Chief," who was discoursing on temperance. Also in the county was Miss Highgate, a missionary working with freed blacks on Roanoke Island. Miss Highgate's speech at the Methodist-Episcopal Church in Little Falls was so inspiring that the ladies of that village immediately formed a "Freedmen's Committee." The committee, headed by Misses Story, Shaw, and Burch, asked for donations of cast-off clothing, cloth, bed quilts and ticks, dishes, knives and forks, tongs, bellows, candlesticks, dried apples and of course money. All contributions would be forwarded to Miss Highgate's colony on Roanoke Island.

In entertainment news, the *Journal* reported that Battery A of the Little Falls militia were holding their first annual military ball. The members of the battery were to appear in full dress uniform and the public was cordially invited to attend.

At Keller Hall in Little Falls, a troupe of orphans, "Colonel Young's Zouaves," put on a performance of which the *Journal* noted:

> "The entertainments given by Col. Young's Zouaves on Monday and Tuesday evenings were quite well attended and with collections taken must have realized quite a respectable sum, to be applied to the maintenance of the little fellows, sons of deceased soldiers, who have been received in the school founded by him in Niagara. The young lads went through their various military maneuvers so creditably as to draw praise even from many veteran soldiers who were present. During the stay of Col. Young here the ladies of the village assisted in making a large number of garments for the little fellows under his charge, and everyone manifested a hearty sympathy and willingness to assist in the work which he has commenced. We commend him and his young 'Zouaves' to the charitable of all the places he may visit." [17]

One week later, under the title, "An Outrageous Swindle," the *Journal* reported on the true identity of Colonel Young's troupe:

> "There is every reason for believing that Col. W.H. Young and Mrs. Llewellyn Young who exhibited here with their young Zouaves are swindlers. A card is published in many of our exchanges and signed by nine prominent citizens of Niagara Falls which states that these children of the institution which these imposters pretend to have founded, are supported during the absence of their 'father and mother,' as they styled themselves here, at the county poorhouse, and that this Col. Young and his wife Llewellyn, are 'unworthy of the public confidence and support.' Their enterprise as explained by them here, seemed most charitable and deserving support, and we endeavored to do our share towards helping it along. We hope that they may be able to refute the charges made against them, but fear they will hardly attempt to do so. Their neglect to pay a small bill for printing—done at half rates—even after we have reminded them of it by letter, does not greatly increase our confidence in their honesty, and we cannot but feel it our duty to warn the people to look out for and to avoid them." [18]

In articles of general interest, the *Journal* reminded parents to have their young ones inoculated against smallpox, reported on a billiard match in Utica attended by hundreds of Herkimer County people—Gates of Utica bested Steele of Herkimer 1,000 to 950—and noted that the next mintage of national coins would bear the motto "In God We Trust."

In the early part of March, the winter long cold spell abruptly broke and the weather turned unseasonably warm and mild. The great heaps of snow began to melt and heavy rains struck the valley towards the middle of the month. The still frozen ground could not absorb this water and the resulting runoff cascaded down innumerable small creeks and rivulets into a rapidly rising ice covered Mohawk River. On the night of March 16th, the ice broke on the swollen river and a flood of immense volume and power surged through the Mohawk Valley. The "freshet," complemented by "ice logs" and timber, tore down small bridges in Frankfort and Ilion and the large West Canada Creek bridge in Herkimer. A major break in the canal occurred near Mohawk and the Farmer's Club building between Herkimer and Little Falls was swept away. But the flood's devastation was not fully realized until the torrent hit Little Falls.

The flood tide, which at its crest covered the upper span of the stone bridge at the foot of Ann Street, wreaked havoc with the mills at the river's edge in Little Falls. The southwest corner of Ligneon's Paper Mill, just recently purchased by the Mohawk Mill, was entirely torn out and brand new machinery, some of which was still in crates, was washed away. Farnam's axe shop was carried off, as were several tenement houses and offices. One of these buildings floated down the river in perfect condition only to be smashed to kindling against the stone bridge. The stone bridge itself stood fast but acted as a perfect dam for the ice floes and lumber. For a considerable distance behind this dam, the waters rose and inundated buildings well back from the river.

Two miles east of Little Falls, the roaring waters, now laden with all sorts of debris, blasted through the Fink's Basin area. Fink's Bridge, which had been constructed less than a year before at a cost of $9,000, was completely swept off its piers. All of the homes adjacent to the Mohawk near the bridge were flooded to such an extent that the inhabitants could only be saved by boatmen that braved, not only the raging water, but also a blinding snowstorm that had sprung up. One of the rescued Fink's Basin residents was old Mrs. Van Etten, who had been confined to her bed for a number of years by consumption. Mrs. Van Etten, whose condition was such that her physician forbade even mopping floors while she was in a room, was pulled from her floating bed by men in a skiff and carried in a chair to Little Falls.

Miraculously the only loss of life from the flood was a horse owned by Mr. Fink, who judged the waters to be six feet higher than any flood he had seen since 1804. In terms of material damage the water had not been so kind. Besides the damage done to bridges, factories and homes—in Little Falls alone the damages were estimated at $130,000—roads, railroad beds and the canal were in many places washed out.

In a little more than a week, most of the bridges were back in place— temporarily strung up with rope—and one track was open on the railroad. The damage to the canal was more severe and it would be closed until well into June. The cleanup efforts in the valley towns was completed fairly quickly, for much of the flood's debris had been washed downstream. Andrew Van Valkenburg of Fink's Basin would advertise in the *Journal*, that if the logs, lumber, and driftwood deposited on his land by the flood, were not removed by the owners by May 1st, he would take possession of them.

While the attention of the people of Herkimer County was obviously focused on the effects of the flood, events were transpiring down south that would soon make the night of the deluge all but forgotten. On the Petersburg front, the expected spring offensive had begun, but unbelievably the initiative had been taken by Lee and not by Grant.

CHAPTER XXII

"At last the day of Jubilee had arrived"

Spring 1865 - Fort Stedman - Five Forks - The Fall of Petersburg
Lee Surrenders - Victory - Lincoln Assassinated

On March 24th, Ulysses Grant issued orders to his corps commanders to prepare for a move against the Confederate right flank, Lee's sole escape route. Above all else, Grant feared that Lee's army would slip out of Petersburg via the South Side Railroad and unite with Joe Johnston's small army in North Carolina. In accordance with Grant's orders the troops assumed a "light marching" attitude and excess baggage, such as heavy winter coats and personal belongings, were gathered up for transportation to the rear. A few camps were broken up as preliminary troop movements began, but before the bulk of the Union army went into motion, Robert E. Lee beat Grant to the punch and launched an offensive of his own.

Lee, with the uncanny ability to predict his counterpart's moves, saw through Grant's plans and sought to delay any Federal action on his right by sending Gen. John Gordon and twenty thousand troops against the extreme Union right flank.

In the early hours of the morning of March 25th, small bands of rebels under the guise of deserters crossed the two hundred yards of no-man's land between their base at Colquitt's Salient and Union held Fort Stedman, and quickly overwhelmed the front line pickets and the fort's garrison. Rebel reinforcements soon came up and fanned out to the north and south of Fort Stedman capturing three Federal batteries and opening a thousand yard gap in the Union line. Gordon hurried more troops forward and the Confederate thrust started off towards the massive Federal supply depot at City Point.

By now the sun had risen and the startled and confused men of the 9th Corps, who had the responsibility of guarding this section of the line, rallied under the leadership of Gen. John Parke. With further rebel reinforcements delayed by a fortuitous breakdown in a Confederate troop train, Parke was able to arrest the rebel advance and slowly began pushing Gordon's men back to Fort Stedman. The perimeters of the rebel breakthrough were sealed and the Confederate incursion contracted to a pocket in and around Fort Stedman. Union artillery quickly zeroed in on the fort and with a deadly fire blasted the rebel troops from three sides. Unable to withstand this fire, the Confederate offensive soon collapsed and in the retreat back over the open ground to their lines, many men in gray fell to Union muskets and cannon fire. By 8 a.m. Gordon's attack was over and Fort Stedman was back in Federal hands.

The three Herkimer County regiments were not directly involved in the fighting at Fort Stedman. The 97th, the 121st and the 152nd had all been ordered out, but after marching a short distance, the sounds of the struggle to the east ceased and the three regiments were ordered back to their camps. But the 121st and the 152nd had no more than settled into their camps when the order to fall in was once more given.

The Federal high command, assuming that other points on the rebel line may have been thinned by the attack on Fort Stedman, ordered the 2nd and 6th Corps to "feel" the enemy's strength at their fronts. The 121st New York with the 6th Corps, and the 152nd New York with the 2nd Corps, moved out of their camps at around noon and advanced toward the Confederate lines in their sector. Heavy musket fire to the front of both regiments showed the enemy defenses to be as strong as ever. While the 152nd was permitted to withdraw without becoming engaged, the 121st was ordered to continue the advance. After pushing in the rebel picket line, the 121st met a heavier rebel force and engaged in a brief skirmish before falling back.

In the reconnaissance in the aftermath of the battle of Fort Stedman, the 121st New York suffered four casualties including one man, Lt. Horatio Duroe of New Lisbon (Otsego County), killed.[1] Among the severely wounded men were Lt. Langford Burton of Schuyler, and Sgt. William Barnes and Timothy Deasy of Little Falls. Another Herkimer County man, Jerome Sixbey of Salisbury, was killed at Fort Stedman fighting with the 69th New York.

The Confederate offensive against Fort Stedman had not changed Grant's plan of attack nor his timetable for cutting the South Side Railroad. With General Sheridan back from a successful raid in northern Virginia, Grant gave "Little Phil" the responsibility of leading the attack force which would include not only thirteen thousand cavalrymen but the 2nd and 5th Corps as well.

Sheridan, on schedule, began his move on March 29th with the mounted troopers leading the way for the infantry columns. Advancing in a northwesterly direction from near Globe Tavern, the going was slow as heavy rains rendered many of the roads almost impassable. Lead cavalry units reached Dinwiddie Court House, ten miles south of the South Side Railroad, on the afternoon of March 30th and halted.

On the same day the 97th New York, marching with Warren's 5th Corps, arrived at the Holliday House on the south side of a branch of Gravelly Run and encamped. Three miles to the west of the 97th's position was Dinwiddie Court House and Sheridan's cavalry.

The 152nd New York, moving with Humphrey's 2nd Corps, had proceeded on a line of march to the north of and slightly to the rear of the 5th Corps' path. Reaching Hatcher's Run late in the day on the 30th, the 152nd went into bivouack. While on the march, the 152nd had temporarily been checked near Dabney's Mill by an obstacle that the boys of the 97th New York knew quite well. Upon approaching the Mill, the 152nd's brigade was confronted by a Confederate fort bristling with cannon. No enemy soldiers were in sight, but suspecting an ambush, the men were ordered to conceal themselves in a set of nearby woods. While the regimental commanders met to discuss a plan of attack—Lieutenant Colonel Curtiss offered his regiment, the 152nd New York to lead the charge—a private soldier of the 152nd took it upon himself to assault the fort. Henry Roback of the 152nd described the one-man "charge."

> "While the [officers'] conference was continued, Roselle Woodhull [of Otsego Co.], a veteran who had served under Gen. McClellan, proceeded without orders, his gun at right shoulder shift, and walked leisurely toward the fort. He mounted the parapets, and found it deserted. We advanced, and upon examination found a pile of saw dust the color of Virginia soil. Mounted upon wagon wheels was placed burnt logs, which resembled cannon." [2]

The pile of sawdust that had stymied the 2nd Corps men was the same "fort" that had precipitated a race for honor between the color-bearers of the 97th New York and the 16th Maine back in February.

The remainder of the 152nd's march to Hatcher's Run was passed without note save for the sheepish grin on many of the officer's faces.

On the morning of March 31st, with the roads having dried sufficiently, Sheridan's cavalry began an advance towards Five Forks, an important crossroads on White Oak Road two miles south of the South Side Railroad. On reaching a point about three miles below Five Forks, the Union cavalry column was struck on its western flank by rebel cavalry supported by infantry and slowly pushed back. Warren's 5th Corps, to the east of Sheridan's men, was also attacked and after a futile stand by a few regiments, which included the 97th New York, was also driven off.

Anticipating Grant's move against the Confederate right flank, Lee had dispatched nineteen thousand men under Gen. George Pickett to protect the South Side Railroad. Pickett's army had shadowed Sheridan's force for the last few days and now had struck it while it was vulnerably stretched out on the march.

Sheridan's cavalry, which at one point was on the verge of disaster, was saved by reinforcements from Warren who stopped the rebel advance. The 5th Corps itself was stabilized by troops hustled over from the 2nd Corps. Pickett, realizing that his force was now outnumbered and in danger of being outflanked itself, withdrew his men back to Five Forks. Sundown put an end to the fighting and the men of both armies slept on their guns that night.

On the morning of April 1st, Sheridan, now in total command of the 5th and 2nd Corps besides his own cavalry, began to reposition his troops for an assault on Pickett's line. Having detected a three mile wide gap between Pickett's left flank and the main rebel defenses, Sheridan ordered an attack to hit that area late that afternoon. Notwithstanding a delay by some of Warren's men in joining the attack, a delay which would lead Sheridan to relieve Warren of command, the Confederate left flank was quickly crushed and the rest of the rebel line was subsequently rolled up. Elements of the 5th Corps, including the 97th New York, crossed White Oak Road into Pickett's rear and routed a rebel force near Gilliam Field. The remnant's of Pickett's army hightailed it back toward the Petersburg defenses and if it were not for reinforcements sent down to the main line by Lee, Federal forces would have struck the South Side Railroad that evening.

As it was, Sheridan's victory had been complete. At a cost of fewer than two thousand casualties, Sheridan had captured between five and six thousand rebels and had killed or wounded an indeterminate number more.[3] In addition, his force was positioned to pounce on the South Side Railroad. Lee's army had suffered its most grievous defeat of the campaign, and the fall of Petersburg and thence Richmond could be no more than momentarily away.

The losses to the 97th New York in the Five Forks Campaign amounted to four killed, eighteen wounded and seven missing.[4] Among the 97th's casualties Sgt. Ira Avery of Manheim was killed and Lt. Col. Rouse Egelston of Brockett's Bridge was wounded in the right arm.

The 152nd New York had taken no casualties at Five Forks. Detailed to a holding position while the rebel line was flanked, it had only been lightly engaged.

In the fighting around Dinwiddie Court House, Capt. Eli Morse of Little Falls, a member of the 2nd New York Mounted Rifles, was slain.

Ulysses Grant received the news of Sheridan's decisive victory at Five Forks with no outward show of emotion. Retiring to his tent to write orders to his corps commanders, he soon emerged and calmly announced to his staff that he had ordered a general assault all along the Petersburg line. Zero hour was set for the next morning, April 2nd, at 4 a.m.

With but little time to spare, the headquarter staffs of the units designated to lead the assault, the 6th, 9th and 24th Corps, rushed to select a target area and to develop a plan of attack. Working with diligence, attack points were chosen, battle plans were set, and troop movements were begun well before midnight. General Parke positioned his 9th Corps men opposite a ring of rebel batteries surrounding Fort Mahone near Petersburg's southeastern tip. The 24th Corps, under General Gibbon, moved into place fronting Fort Gregg and Fort Whitworth, one mile to the west of the city. General Wright formed his 6th Corps into an attack wedge pointed at a section of the rebel line two miles to the west of the 24th Corps' target. With troop dispositions set, the Union infantrymen lay down for a sleepless night awaiting the cannon barrage that would signal the start of the attack.

The 121st New York received orders at 10 p.m. that night to stand ready for a move. Knapsacks, bed rolls and all other unnecessary equipment were thrown into a pile to be left under camp guard, cartridge boxes were filled with sixty rounds of ammunition, and muskets were double-checked. Shortly thereafter the regiment was ordered to form ranks and was directed to quietly file out of camp. Assigned a position on the right (eastern) wing of the 6th Corps' wedge, the 121st marched to within two hundred yards of the rebel line. At this point the men were ordered to lie down and keep quiet. Union picket fire, intended to muffle the sound of the moving troops, soon brought a deadly return fire on the prone men. Of this trial, Clinton Beckwith of the 121st related:

> " . . . we formed in line of battle in [the] rear of the 2d Connecticut and had scarcely gotten into position when we were ordered to lie down. At the same time the pickets began firing, as we supposed, to cover the noise of our forming, and we were treated to the sensation of lying upon a field for a long time exposed to the fire of the enemy's skirmishers without any shelter. Every once in a while some one would get hit with a ball, and we could hear his cry of anguish as the lead tore through. Finally our men, by stopping their fire and crying, 'April Fool, Johnnies,' restored quiet, and for a long time we lay perfectly quiet, waiting for the time to come when we could move forward. The night was cold and damp and we were chilled and numb." [5]

On what seemed to be an endless night, thousands of silent men in blue lay with their own thoughts, praying that the signal to attack would come and end the tension. Jump-off time, 4 a.m., came and went and the Union cannons remained quiet. The sun finally began to rise at 4:45 a.m. and with it the Federal guns opened up. The "ball had opened" and the order to charge rang out all along the Union line. As narrated by Clinton Beckwith, the 121st New York was soon up and moving:

> "As the first gray dawn began to show, out belched the guns, and we could mark the course of the shells as their fuse left a dim spark passing to the Rebel works. We were up in another moment, in closed ranks, feeling for the man on our right we plunged forward in the darkness. In another instant the Reb skirmishers delivered their fire and their battery in our front opened. Almost its first shot cut Jimmie Hendricks of Company A in two. A little farther on, and the Rebel works were marked by the jets of flame from their rifles as they fired upon us. Another instant and we were up to their abatis, and we got into a tangle looking for a place to get through. Finally some fellow to our left sang out, 'Here's a road,' and a lot of us made for it and followed it on a run to the Rebel works, at that point a fort. Climbing up the sides, it being now light enough to see a few paces ahead, I went in through the embrasure of the guns, one of which had been firing at us. The Johnnies had run back among the huts and were firing back at us. We ran down toward them and they ran back into the field. Quite a number hid in the huts, and our fellows hunted them out. Afterwards a lot of us fellows charged over the field to the road, and fired into the running Rebs, and also into some wagons which were passing. We also twisted off the telegraph wires with our bayonets, continuing our firing at everything in sight." [6]

Having torn a huge hole in the Confederate line, the right flank of the 6th Corps wedge was now ordered to advance easterly behind the enemy's defenses and link up with the 24th Corps. The 121st New York marched two miles with negligible resis-

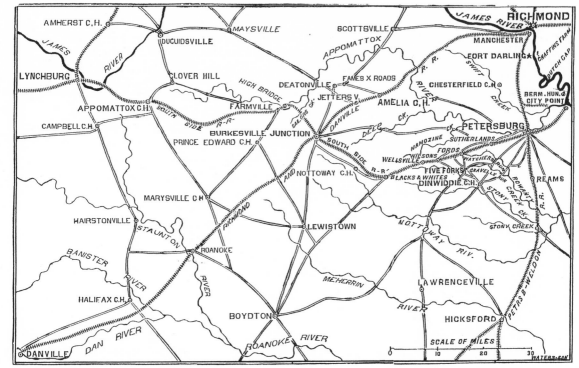

The History of the Civil War, Schmucker

Petersburg to Appomattox

tance before coming under an enfilading fire thrown from Fort Whitworth. A division of the 24th Corps soon arrived on the scene and the 121st, with the rest of its brigade, was ordered back to their starting point of that morning, Fort Fisher.

At Fort Fisher each regiment was given a chance to reassemble, before the brigade was ordered to march east to support the 9th Corps' attack. By the time the 6th Corps boys reached Fort Sedgwick in the 9th Corps' sector, the fighting on that part of the field was over. For the rest of the day and well into the night, the 121st New York drew the grisly duty of standing guard in captured rebel works strewn with dead and dying Confederates.

Nightfall and exhaustion—some of the Union troops would fight for eighteen hours this day—brought an end to the fighting. At all points the Federal troops had been victorious. The rebel line that had held back Grant's men for nearly three hundred days had not been simply pierced, but had been shattered. Furious and tenacious fighting had marked many points on the Petersburg line, but the threadbare and half-starved men of Lee's army had eventually yielded to Yankee pressure at every turn. Under the cover of darkness, Lee evacuated what remained of his army from Petersburg and headed off to the west.

Confederate losses in the April 2nd assault on Petersburg were not known whereas Federal records counted nearly four thousand casualties among Grant's army.[7]

In the Herkimer County regiments only the 121st New York showed losses. The

97th New York and the 152nd New York had participated in a Union drive from the Five Forks area, but had not been actively engaged. In the 121st, one man, the afore-mentioned James Hendrix of Danube, had been killed and twelve men had been wounded.[8] Included among the wounded was Anson Ryder of Litchfield. Of Ryder's wound, Clinton Beckwith wrote:

> "The wounded were carried back to the hospital near the observatory where we found Anse Ryder. Doctor Slocum said it would kill him to am-putate his leg, and that he would die if it was not done, and Anse wanted to die with it on; so the doctor fixed him up* and sent him to the hospital, and he is living to-day with the Rebel bullet and the bone of his leg cemented together like old friends."[9]

Another regiment with a Herkimer County flavor, the 186th New York, saw its first action on April 2nd. The 186th was formed in Sackett's Harbor as a one-year regiment in September, 1864, and drew men principally from Lewis and Jefferson counties. Company G, recruited in Herkimer and Graysville, contained nearly fifty Herkimer County boys. The 186th left New York State on September 28, 1864, and was placed in the 2nd Brigade, 2nd Division, of the 9th Corps. In the April 2nd attack on Petersburg, the green regiment struck the enemy's fortifications with a blind courage and suffered a fearful beating. In this engagement, which would be the 186th's first and last bloodletting, the regiment realized one hundred and eighty ca-sualties, including forty-eight men killed.[10] Among the mortally wounded were Charles Platt of Manheim and forty-eight-year-old John Alexander of Salisbury. Alexander would leave behind a wife and five children.

With Lee's troops gone, the fall of Petersburg and Richmond was a given. Dur-ing the early morning hours of April 3rd, Federal troops began to enter Petersburg and prominent among the first units to set foot in the city was the 121st New York.

At 3 a.m. that morning, the men of the 121st were roused from their sleep among the Confederate dead and ordered to form ranks and fall in line with their brigade. The line of march took them through the Petersburg suburbs, past vacant enemy trenches and camps, and into the heart of the city. On nearing the Court House, a knot of men from the brigade broke ranks and raced into the building. Moments later, the Stars and Stripes were thrust out of a window in the Court House dome and unfurled to the breeze.

The neat brigade column soon disintegrated as curiosity and the hunger for spoils overcame the men. Small groups of roving explorers broke ranks and fanned out through the city in search of "treasures." Clinton Beckwith of the 121st wrote:

> "We secured a lot of Confederate currency and postage stamps, and routed out a lot of stragglers and sneaks, hid about the city. At the Commis-sary we secured some nice hams and some apple jack that was quite smooth, and under its softening influence we forgave a good many of our foes. Some of the women, whose houses we entered, to get the Johnnies the

---

* Dying men would often ask to be put in a proper death pose which was termed "fixed up."

darkies told us were hidden there, gave us a startling exhibition of their ability to blackguard us. About noon we were in line again and on our way to our old camp. Passing along through the city we saw President Lincoln and General Grant, and gave them a marching salute. Soon reaching camp, we slung our traps, and the same night reached our division fagged out, but ready to push on after Lee's broken columns." [11]

Ulysses Grant was not about to linger in Petersburg. Although Federal troops would march north and take Richmond, Grant's prize was off to the west. Sheridan had taken possession of the South Side Railroad and Lee's battered army had taken off on foot in its attempt to link up with Johnston's army. Grant had not fought all of these months simply to gain Richmond, but to capture the Army of Northern Virginia, and now with his quarry in reach, he was not about to let it get away. Giving his men little time to catch their breath and no chance to revel in their victory, Grant had his legions marching after Lee. However, Grant was not content with simply following Lee, his intention was to get ahead of and cut off the gray column.

Robert E. Lee's ultimate destination was Danville, Virginia, situated on the North Carolina border, one hundred miles southwest of Petersburg. The Confederate government had fled from Richmond to Danville and the city was in easy reach of Joe Johnston's army.

On leaving Petersburg on the night of April 2nd, Lee headed his thirty thousand men towards Amelia Court House some thirty-five miles to the west. At Amelia Court House, Lee expected to find a stockpile of rations—many of his men hadn't eaten in two days—and trains waiting to take him south to Danville along the Richmond & Danville Railroad. Leaving a trail of abandoned wagons and artillery, pots, pans, piles of tobacco—which the Union boys quickly scooped up—broken down horses, and broken down men, the rebel army reached Amelia Court House on April 4th and found neither provisions nor locomotives awaiting them. Faced with starvation, Lee reluctantly halted his army and sent foraging parties into the countryside, hoping that in the meantime a supply train would come up from Danville.

Lee's head start out of Petersburg had been lost by his stop at Amelia Court House. Phil Sheridan's cavalry with the 2nd, 5th and 6th Corps in tow were rapidly marching on a parallel course to the south of Lee. While Lee searched for food to the north, Sheridan's force struck the Richmond and Danville Railroad at Jetersville, six miles below Amelia Court House. At the same time, the 9th Corps was on the rail line at Burkesville, six miles further to the south. All told, Grant now had eighty thousand men in pursuit of Lee and the majority of them were positioned between Lee and Danville.

The 152nd New York, with the 2nd Corps, left Petersburg on the morning of April 3rd, marching in the immediate rear of Sheridan's cavalry. Advancing westerly ten miles through dense swamps and forests, they passed by the mansion of former Winfield native William Burgess, which had been reduced to ashes the previous night. That night was spent bivouacked near the 5th Corps. The next morning, the march was resumed and Jetersville was reached at about 5 p.m. Breastworks were hurriedly thrown up across the Danville rail line and the men bedded down for the night. At daybreak on April 5th, the line of march started northward as the 2nd Corps sought to make contact with Lee's rear guard. During this march, the men of the 152nd took notice of a number of bee hives while they were passing a large mansion. The column halted, arms were stacked and the hives were charged. A goodly amount of honey was retrieved and the bees were left in "an utterly demoralized condition." The march continued on until 10:00 p.m. before a halt was called to permit the men a few hours rest.

Lead units of the 2nd Corps did have a brush with the tail of Lee's main column. Rebel forage parties had come up empty at Amelia Court House so Lee started his columns off down the Dansville Railroad towards Jetersville. Finding his path blocked by the 2nd, 5th and 6th Corps, he reversed direction and put his men on the road for Farmville. At Farmville, twenty miles further to the west, Lee hoped to reach the South Side Railroad and much needed supplies. Marching in a cold rain, the rebel column got within six miles of Farmville before its rear guard was attacked on April 6th by the 6th Corps at a place called Sayler's Creek.

The 121st New York, moving with the 6th Corps, broke camp at Jetersville on the morning of April 6th and headed toward Deatonville. Couriers soon appeared and the officers began galloping up and down the line urging the already footsore men to quicken their pace. Unbeknownst to the common soldiers, the rear third of Lee's army had become separated from the main body and was in a position to be surrounded and destroyed. Of the race to Sayler's Creek, Clinton Beckwith of the 121st wrote:

> "Everything and everybody now seemed to be in a hurry. Everything on wheels was halted in the open places except the artillery and ambulances, which were making desperate efforts to keep up with the infantry, and it became evident to us that at the rate we are going we should soon catch up with the enemy." [12]

The 121st crossed Flat Creek, and with the sound of musketry and artillery rising to their front, increased their step. Reports came on back down the line that Sheridan's cavalry had captured a portion of the enemy's wagon train and that rebel infantry were nearby. Emerging into an open field that looked down into the valley of Sayler's Creek, the 121st rushed to join its division's battleline. Across the way the men could see the enemy ready and waiting for the 6th Corps' charge. As soon as the 121st fell into line the order to go forward was given and the blue wave moved down into the valley. Of the 121st's part in the action, Beckwith related:

> "The troops on our left had deployed first and we had to run to get into line with them, but we were on good ground and got along all right until we came into the vicinity of the creek and into the range of the enemy's fire, which now was rapid and heavy, but on account of the conformity of the ground not very destructive. Here after halting for a short time to reform we were ordered to charge, and drive the enemy from their works. Forward on a run we went as rapidly as the steep hill would permit, and in a moment we were up to, and over their slight earthworks, the occupants offering no further resistance, after emptying their guns in our faces. On our right the 37th Massachusetts did not get on as well. They were more exposed, had a farther distance to go and suffered very heavily. Colonel Olcott, finding

the ground in front of him clear and the enemy holding on to the works on the right, half wheeled the 121st to the right and moved lengthwise and partly in the rear of the enemy's line and they immediately abandoned their works and surrendered. These last troops we encountered were Marines, or land sailors, and had never before been in battle. They were mostly boys and were commanded by G.W. Custis Lee who fell into our hands with a large number of prisoners and several stands of colors." [13]

The Battle of Sayler's Creek, which became known as "Black Thursday" in the Confederate army, had been a one-sided Union victory. At a cost of twelve hundred casualties to the 6th Corps, Lee had lost one third of his army, nearly eight thousand men.[14] Among the five thousand rebels captured were six Confederate generals, including Ewell, Kershaw and Lee's eldest son, Custis. Custis Lee was taken prisoner by Sgt. Hawthorne Harris of the 121st New York. Harris, from Otsego County, was awarded the Medal of Honor for this act. Two other members of "Upton's Regulars," Benjamin Gifford of Salisbury and Warren Dockum from Otsego County, would also win the Medal of Honor at Sayler's Creek for the capture of Confederate battle flags.[15]

Losses in the 121st New York numbered eight killed and thirteen wounded.[16] Included among those killed were Isaac Basset of Russia and Nathaniel Lamphere of Fairfield. Two Otsego County officers, Capt. Ten Eyck Howland from Westford and Lt. Tracy Morton of Edmeston were also slain. Maj. James Cronkite of Milford was accidentally wounded after the battle when a stacked musket fell to the ground and discharged. The ball tore into Cronkite's leg injuring it so severely that amputation was necessary.

Union cavalry and elements of the 2nd Corps beat Lee to Farmville and once more blocked his access to a rail line. In a clash at Farmville between a division of the 2nd Corps and Lee's rear guard, two Herkimer County members of the 2nd New York Heavy Artillery were slain. Killed were Julius Clapsaddle of German Flatts and forty-three-year-old John Davis of Litchfield. Davis left a wife and seven children.

Turning to the northwest, Lee crossed the Appomattox River and ordered the bridges behind him to be fired. As a last ditch effort, Lee hoped to buy some time for his troops to regroup by forcing the pursuing Federals to take a round-about route in crossing the Appomattox. Lee's engineers were able to set the one-half mile long, sixty-foot-high, railroad trestle at High Bridge ablaze, but thanks to units of the 2nd Corps, was not able to destroy the wagon bridge below it.

The 152nd New York was among the 2nd Corps regiments that was instrumental in saving the wagon span at High Bridge. On the morning of April 7th, the 152nd, encamped only ten minutes from High Bridge, was ordered to double-time to the bridge crossing. Upon arrival, the railroad trestle was already wrapped in flames but the fire on the wagon bridge was still just smouldering. Along with other regiments from the brigade, the 152nd New York charged through the water below the bridges and drove the enemy up the heights on the other side. The fire on the wagon bridge was doused and the Federal path to Lee remained unbarred.

With no further obstacles in its way, Grant's army raced ahead of Lee and blocked his last lane of escape. With overwhelming numbers of Federal troops on his flanks and now at his front, Lee sent up the white flag and asked Grant for terms of surrender. At a private home in Appomattox Court House on Palm Sunday, April 9th, Lee officially surrendered his Army of Northern Virginia to Grant.

News of the surrender soon reached the Federal camps, setting off wild celebrations. Henry Roback of the 152nd New York and Isaac Best of the 121st New York, described the scenes at their camps. Best wrote:

> "Late in the afternoon General Hamblin was seen coming towards the camp, his splendid black horse on the dead run, his hat in his hands, his cheek bloody where he had failed to escape the limb of a tree, and as soon as his voice could be heard he shouted, 'Lee has surrendered.' And then what a tumult broke out among the troops. Cheers, shout, laughter, hats and countless other things flung into the air. Some were too affected to cheer and stood with tears running down their faces. The excitement communicated itself to the animals. The mules brayed, the horses neighed and the author's dog leaped up and with his fore paws on his breast barked joyously. It seemed as though all nature was glad. It meant to us all, no more fighting, no more long, weary marches, home, friends, peace, a saved country, a triumphant flag." [17]

While Roback related:

> "All eyes were strained when we heard the clattering of hoofs. Gen. Meade, accompanied by officers in blue and grey, rode by bowing and smiling and waving a token of peace. At last the day of jubilee had arrived. No pen can describe the joy and feeling of the forty thousand men assembled. The air resounded with cheers and shouts. Caps were thrown in the air, blank cartridges were fired by the artillery and all was rejoicing." [18]

So the army of Northern Virginia was no more and for all practical purposes the war was over. The end had come, not in a cataclysmic battle to end all battles, or, as some predicted, after years of guerrilla warfare, but it had come when the men in gray simply laid down their guns and went home.

The news of the fall of Richmond started the people of Herkimer County on an emotional roller coaster ride. Within hours of the taking of the rebel capital, telegraphs all across the North clicked off the news igniting festivities in every village and town. As to the reception of the news in Little Falls, the *Journal* noted:

> "Our village was never more alive with wild enthusiasm than on the announcement of the capture of Richmond on Monday. Throngs of people gathered upon the streets, the Band, at the head of a large procession, paraded with flags and cheers, and the Little Falls Battery [N.Y. State militia] fired a hundred guns in honor of the event. As this was the occasion of their first appearance it is due to them to say that the manner and rapidity of the firing elicited general commendation.
> In the evening a large bonfire was lighted, fireworks were let off and general jubilation prevailed.

The sorrrow-stricken visages of two or three secesh-sympathizers, who hung around disconsolately on Monday, were pitiable to behold. Not a ray of comfort could they extract from the glorious dispatches of victory, Democrats and Republicans rejoiced together, but over this select circle hung a terrible cloud of grim despair." [19]

One week later, the *Journal* headlines and subtitles blared the news of Lee's surrender:

"Glorious News - 'Peace and Joy to All' - Gen. Lee's Surrenders - His Army Prisoners - The Prisoners Paroled - The Last Ditch Found - The Result of 'Pressing' - The Confederacy Snuffed Out - The Biggest Accident of the War" [20]

The same edition of the *Journal* under the title "The Day of Jubilee," detailed the raucous celebration in Little Falls, reporting:

"The reception of the glorious news of Monday morning threw our village into a perfect fervor of excitement. Everybody shook hands, smiled, laughed, hurrahed and was happy. A 'Band of Freemen' from Mill St. with sticks and wooden guns, gave swift chase after every citizen as he appeared from his house, and amid the shouts and laughter of a great crowd, conducted him with mock ceremony, to an improvised Provost Marshals' office where he was expected to 'take the oath of allegiance'—a glass of ale, a cigar, a shake of hands all around as he might prefer. For two hours or more this fun went on, each new-comer swelling the crowd and laughing heartily at the sight of his successors under similar chase, arrest and pilotage to the grand rendezvous.

About ten o'clock the band appeared and a laughing procession formed and paraded till noon the principal streets, with cheers and uninterrupted hilarity.

Many of our citizens were brought forward and made brief remarks to the crowd.

After noon a large procession of cart teams with vehicles filled with men and boys had a similar parade. The places of business were closed and everybody was out upon the streets each congratulating his neighbor and all 'Merry as a marriage bell.'

Preparations were immediately made for a grand celebration to come off in the evening. The old 'Little Giant' and 'Wide Awake' torches were collected without reference to their former party uses, and citizens were actively engaged in the work of preparing illuminations for their residences.

About half past seven o'clock the torch-light procession formed on Main St. and thence marched through nearly every principal street of the village. Along the entire distance Roman candles were fired from the procession and from many of the houses: reports of cannon were echoed from hill to hill and small arms and fire-crackers resounded from knots of boys at every corner. The Stars and Stripes were everywhere spread to the breeze, were unfurled from windows by ladies' hands, were waved by boys and girls along the streets and were carried on tops of umbrellas. No. 2 Fire

Company appeared on horse-back, the others on foot in the procession.

The houses of nearly all our citizens were very brilliantly illuminated with Chinese lanterns, transparencies, &c. and the effect of the entire celebration was most pleasing and satisfactory. The march was conducted in much better order than could have been anticipated. It was under the direction of Col. Galpin, as Marshal and the ranks were kept full for more than two hours and until the procession halted when cheer after cheers were again given and the crowd began to disperse.

As soon as the exercises were concluded, the Band appeared upon the roof of the Journal & Courier office [on Main St.] whence were let off a large number of rockets, wheels and other fireworks.

There was less than the usual rowdyism incident to the close of such celebrations most citizens retiring quietly to their homes. Indeed four years of trial such as no nation has lived through, four years of unequalled financial pressure, of armies till now unknown in history for numbers, for courage, for endurance, for achievement; four years of wrestling with a foe of our own blood and birth; four years in which no sun has set that did not pale its fire over newly bereaved hearthstones, and rekindle its morning rays amid the tears of widows and orphans—four such years should (and they have) chasten and sober our hearts more in accordance with our sufferings and hopes than can be expressed in any wild drunken revelry."[21]

Five days after the celebration in Little Falls, the roller coaster ride took the townsfolk of Herkimer County hurtling into despair with the news of the assassination of Abraham Lincoln. For a week the stunned citizens of the county awoke each morning hoping that the news had been just a bad dream, but on the night of April 26th, Lincoln's funeral train pulled into Little Falls, and the nightmare became a reality.

Long before the arrival of the train, an immense crowd had gathered at the Little Falls Depot. The depot itself and other trackside buildings were decorated in black and white crepe and trimmed with emblems of mourning. Of the mood of the throng, J.R. Stebbins of the *Journal* related:

"On the 18th day of February, 1861 at 12 1/4 o'clock, Abraham Lincoln President elect, stepped from the platform of the car in which he was traveling to Washington, and made a short humorous address to the immense crowd who had gathered at the depot to see and welcome him. On the 26th day of April, 1865, at 7 1/2 o'clock p.m. his remains with the funeral cortege, passed the same depot, on their way to their last resting place in Springfield, greeted with tears and the sorrow of nearly the same people. In 1861 the bells were rung right joyously, cannon pealed forth their welcoming echoes, 'Hail Columbia' burst from the Band, and glad shouts and hurrahs of the multitude made the old valley of the Mohawk ring as with festive joy. Last evening, how different! The bells tolled with solemn cadence: minute guns of distress broke upon the ear from the surrounding bluffs: a mournful dirge and muffled drum-beat were the only music: and sad, deep silence and uplifted hats of the immense assemblage bespoke how sincere, how heartfelt and how universal was the peoples' sorrow, as they beheld the slowly moving train pass onward with all that is left upon earth of him they had learned to love so well."[22]

The funeral train consisted of the engine with brightly lit headlamps, a baggage car, and eight coaches draped in mourning. On the sides of the seventh coach, which carried the President's remains, were a large eagle and the words 'United States.'

As the funeral train came to a halt in front of the depot, eight ladies dressed in black presented to Col. James Bowen—a former resident of Little Falls who was in charge of the President's remains—a woven wreath of wildflowers designed in the shape of a shield and a cross.

The committee of women, along with four men—of whom J.R. Stebbins was one —were invited to enter the funeral car. In describing the contents of the car, Stebbins reported:

> "The flowers were deposited upon the coffin, around which the few present stood with tears and sobs for a moment, and then passed out at the other end of the car. The interior of the car had been finished in the highest style of art, and at every hand were wreaths and bouquets of flowers. We saw no prettier or more appropriate collections than the offering of wild flowers presented here. The splendor and magnificence of the coffin could not well be surpassed. Its entire cost was about $2000, and it is probably the most perfect and finished of the kind ever manufactured in this country. The timber used in the construction is mahogany, which is lined in lead. The inside of the coffin is lined with plaited satin, the pillow and lower surface are of the finest description of white silk, and the whole is surrounded with chennile as in fringe. In front of the car were the remains of 'Little Willie,' the President's son."[23]

After a stop of about five minutes, the train pulled slowly away and the large crowd dispersed.

Through all of this sorrow and despair, there shone one consoling factor—the terrible war was over and the hometown boys would soon be coming home. The rebellion would not officially end until April 26th, when General Johnston surrendered to General Sherman, but by that time the Herkimer County regiments had already shifted into a peacetime posture.

CHAPTER XXIII

"Faithfully they have fulfilled their mission"

Spring/Summer 1865 - The Grand Review - The 121st in Little Falls
The 97th and the 152nd Come Home - Muster-out

Within two days after Lee's surrender on April 9th, the 97th, 121st and 152nd New York regiments had left the vicinity of Appomattox Court House and were on the road east to Burksville. With no one left to fight, the Army of the Potomac was being withdrawn from the field and consolidated around rail centers to ease communication and supply problems. Along the route the Union boys often met and conversed with the inhabitants of this section of war-ravaged Virginia. To their chagrin, the men learned that although they had subdued the rebellion materially, the spirit of the Southern people remained as defiant as ever. Clinton Beckwith of the 121st wrote:

> "We met a great many more of the citizens of the country than we had in the pursuit of Lee, and had opportunity to talk with them. They claimed that they had been impoverished, had no negroes, no stock and no seed to put in a crop, and saw nothing before them but starvation. Many of them availed themselves of the generosity of the government to draw supplies from our commissaries. Most of them had been at one time or another in the Confederate army, and some had been disabled by wounds or broken down by disease contracted in camp. These men were the most steadfast in their allegiance to the Rebel cause. Some went so far as to predict a renewal of the war, saying that the South was not conquered, but worn out." [1]

At Burksville the 121st and 152nd halted and went into bivouack while the 97th continued its eastward march towards Richmond.

Shortly after reaching Burksville, the 121st New York received the allotment of recruits that it had requested back in early March. Four hundred and thirteen draftees and substitutes from throughout New York State were added to the 121st's roster, swelling the ranks of the regiment to over one thousand men. To the veterans of the regiment it seemed nonsensical to finally bring the 121st to fighting strength with the fighting now over.

While at Burksville, military order and discipline were maintained, "to retain the high moral standard of the men." Much of each day was spent on the drill field, on guard duty, or in camp maintenance. It was at Burksville that the men received word of President Lincoln's assassination. Clinton Beckwith remarked:

> "A thrill of horror and rage ran through the ranks and it would have
> fared badly for any armed Rebels who fell into our hands at that time." [2]

Notwithstanding Lee's capitulation to Grant, the war was technically not over and there were still armed rebels about. Down near Hillsboro, North Carolina, Joseph Johnston's army was still a viable force. Although formal peace negotiations between Johnston and Sherman were underway, until the surrender was ratified, Johnston's rebels would have to be treated as potentially dangerous. Fearing that Johnston might reconsider and escape with his army into the hills of Virginia, the Federal high command ordered the 6th Corps from Burksville to Danville, Virginia to block any move that the rebels might make in that direction.

The 121st New York broke camp at Burksville on April 23rd, and with the rest of the 6th Corps, began the one hundred-mile trek to Danville along the bed of the Danville & Richmond Railroad. The track had recently been used by Confederate supply trains chugging to Lee's garrison at Petersburg, but due to the poor condition of the rails, it was judged to be unsuitable for troop transport. In a hard driving march the 6th Corps covered the distance in four days, arriving in Danville on April 27th.

Danville had been an important supply center for the Confederate army defending Richmond and Petersburg and also boasted a large prison camp and a hospital. Consequently, when the 6th Corps entered the city, considerable stocks of military and hospital supplies fell into Union hands. Unfortunately for the Federal boys, Danville's most important citizen of late, Jefferson Davis, had left the city weeks earlier and was not among the 6th Corps' haul. (Davis would be captured on May 10th in Irwinsville, Georgia.)

While in Danville, the Union troops toured the city and appropriated former Confederate property for their own use. John Ingraham of the 121st in a letter to his parents wrote:

> "As soon as our advance arrived here they took possession of the Print-
> ing Office and all public buildings. Our boys printed a paper called the 6th
> Corps Sheet, a big thing for soldiers. We passed through a street just to the
> left of where the prisons were, where they held our men as prisoners of war.
> We little thought the other day when we were talking with Frank Faville
> about his prison life* that we would soon see his paradise. I can say

* Frank Faville of Brockett's Bridge, a member of the 97th, was captured at Gettysburg and later paroled.

Danville is a pretty nice little town situated along the River Dan. We captured quite a large amount of rolling stock, cars &c. We happened to halt for a short rest at the Depot just before we crossed the river, and such a ringing of bells you can hardly imagine. The boys mounted upon the engines went to ringing the car bells and hollering all aboard for Herkimer and Mohawk. . . . A great number of the inhabitants were greatly disappointed when they saw us. They thought the Yankees had cloven feet & horns. They concluded they are all a very good looking set of men."[3]

Johnston's surrender to Sherman, on April 27th, released the 6th Corps from their duty at Danville. On May 1st, the 121st New York boarded cars at the Danville Depot—the Danville & Richmond Railroad had been repaired in the interim—and travelled back to Burksville, where they set up a temporary camp. While at Burksville, John Ingraham had the opportunity to witness the repatriation of the Southern citizens of that town. In a letter home, Ingraham wrote:

"I am stopping in a large Hotel with a couple of our Boys that are sick. Just below my room is the Provost Marshal's office. You can hardly imagine how the citizens are packing in to take the Oath of Allegiance and are getting orders to get Commissary stores &c., and there are any amount of Ladies and Rebel soldiers applying for aid and passes, some going North. There seems to be a great rejoicing among the whole of them. They are glad the war is at an end. There is a perfect cloud of Contrabands here, all the while trying to go North. A great many want to go to Richmond & Petersburg. They carry their Bed and Board with them, always on their heads. They generally have a pickininny, as they call them, under each arm (little wooly heads) and a bundle as large as a well stuffed straw tick on their heads. It is fun to hear them talk on. Lord bless your soul I knew the Yankees would come. I told em so. I has been praying for you all de while &c.. They have all got a great long lingo to tell you."[4]

On May 5th, the 121st New York left Burksville and began the seventy-two mile march to Richmond. On that same day the 152nd New York moved into camp in Manchester, a suburb of Richmond, having just completed the trip now being taken up by the 121st.

The 152nd, after spending the last two weeks in April on guard duty in Burksville, began their march to Richmond on the afternoon of May 2nd. The first day's march of nine miles brought them to Jetersville where they encamped for the night. On May 3rd and 4th the intervening sixty odd miles to Richmond were covered with the weary soldiers pulling into Manchester on the morning of May 5th. All along the route from Burksville to Richmond the boys in blue received "encouragement" from Southern spectators. Henry Roback of the 152nd noted:

"The planters viewed the procession from the roadside and answered numberless questions, and laughed at the boys who traded their regulation caps with the scare crows in the corn field for the broad-brimmed sombrero. One farmer, to expedite the answer to so many questions, kindly chalked upon a board, 12 miles to Richmond. Ten miles farther on the road the guide board gave the correct distance, which was 16 miles. The average

Virginian measured distances according to their ability to perform the journey, either on foot or horseback, each individual having a different scale."[5]

Each of the Mohawk Valley regiments remained for a week or two at Richmond before proceeding on to Washington. The 97th New York had left Manchester at the end of April and marched to Washington, encamping at Ball's Cross Roads; the 152nd New York departed on May 7th and set up camp on Munson's Hill, and the 121st New York moved out on May 23rd and marched to Hall's Hill. Of the 121st's journey from Richmond to Washington, Clinton Beckwith reported:

"Reveille sounded every morning at 3:30 a.m. and sometimes the march was prolonged till after dark. It rained frequently and the most of the streams had to be forded. The march was through the section over which the corps had fought during the entire war, past the battle fields of Cold Harbor, Chancellorsville, Spotsylvania, The Wilderness, Fredericksburg, Bull Run—names that recall terrible experiences and bloody scenes."[6]

The urgency in the 6th Corps' forced march was due in part to the desire of the corps' generals to participate in the Grand Review of troops scheduled in Washington. Unfortunately for the 6th Corps boys, the parade stepped off at about the time that their column was leaving Richmond. Held on May 23rd and 24th, the Grand Review showcased the Army of the Potomac and Sherman's Army of the Tennessee (the 97th New York and the 152nd New York marched on the first day). Over one hundred and fifty thousand men in blue paraded past throngs of grateful onlookers lining the streets, and strutted in front of a reviewing stand occupied by President Johnson, Generals Grant and Sherman, cabinet members and other dignitaries.

The 6th Corps belatedly reached Washington at the end of May. Having been deprived of their chance to march in the Grand Review, the 6th Corps boys were given their own parade on June 8th. While the display was enjoyed by the spectators, the marching men of the 6th Corps viewed the day with displeasure. Clinton Beckwith of the 121st related:

"Leaving camp at 4 o'clock in the morning, marching the five miles to Washington over Long Bridge, up Maryland Avenue to mass at the foot of the Capital grounds, was the first portion of the long and tedious process of review.

Then at 9 o'clock passing down Pennsylvania Avenue at wheeling distance, past the reviewing stand before President Johnson, General Grant and other dignitaries, and crossing Acquaduct Bridge march back again to camp, was the second part of the proceeding. All this on a hot day in June made this review an experience more pleasant to look back upon than to participate in. I have never heard an enlisted man enthuse over the memory of that review."[7]

One of the admirers of the 121st New York that day was General Meade, who, according to the *Journal*, remarked that if he could retain one regiment from New York, he would prefer the 121st above all others.

To men accustomed to living at the razor's edge, life in the camps around Washington was sheer tedium. With the war over, there was very little for them to do and each day was as boring and wearisome as the next. Camp duties and drills were performed half-heartedly and discipline was lax. The expectation of going home stretched the time out even further, and the interminable mustering-out process protracted the wait.

The order of mustering-out began with the one year's men (the War Department in its wisdom realized that the timely release of these men would free the government from paying such men their full bounty). Next in order came the veterans that had re-enlisted, followed by the regiments that had been mustered in prior to October 15, 1862. At the end of the muster-out chain were the regiments that had entered Federal service after the October 1862 date.

Prior to being mustered out, the War Department offered to let the men buy their arms. Muskets were available for $6, Spencer carbines for $10, revolvers could be purchased for $8, and sabers and swords were priced at $3. Of the worth of the muskets, Henry Roback of the 152nd remarked:

> "Our regiment had preserved and used them and helped to settle the great difficulty from the Wilderness to the Appomattox, a period of 340 days. We had encountered the missiles of death hurled at us from the enemy, more than 200 days, and marched many weary miles and performed a large amount of hard labor. One thousand days we had the old army musket by our side. Now it was ours. To the veteran volunteer the value will be greater than the highest work of art America ever produced." [8]

The unfortunate inmates of the Confederate prisoner of war camps were sent north well in advance of any other troops. After the Confederacy's surrender, one of the first priorities of the Federal government was to get these men, most of whom were now little more than physical wrecks, transferred to northern hospitals. From DeCamp Hospital on David's Island in New York Harbor, a correspondent to the *Journal*, who wrote under the pseudonym "Tyro," provided a graphic and grisly description of the physical condition of these former prisoners. "Tyro" also voiced his indignation against the Confederate leaders that permitted such atrocities, writing:

> "I wish the persons who are ready to offer Gen. Lee a dinner, or who are holding friendly communication with Campbell—lately Davis's Asst. Sec. of War—Hunter and other rebel leaders could see these poor fellows who were, when they fell into the hands of Davis, and his confederates, stout, hearty men, but who returned to us by Davis were wrecks and skeletons, maimed and crippled for life even if they ever arise from the beds in the Hospital.
>
> I have seen these men, one of them of stout frame but gaunt and thin, with a foot sticking out from the bed-clothes—or rather the remains of a foot—a greater part which had rotted away in the rebel prison at Salisbury.
>
> Beyond the bandage, which covers the wasted heel and instep, protrude the dry, bare bones of the toes—the skeleton of this part of his foot—a ghastly sight—which ought to form the centre-piece of the table at the dinner to which Gen. Lee is to be invited in New York.
>
> As you walk through the ward in which the Union soldier and his comrades lay, upon either side are half a dozen other equally ghastly evidences

of this devilish cruelty of Davis and his companions. These poor fellows have lost one and some both feet entirely: the whole foot had rotted off, and out of the bandages which covered the ends of the shrunken and withered limbs, protruded the dry, bare bones of the leg.

These men say their limbs were frost-bitten, and then as they received no care, and suffered and suffered continually from lack of food and exposure—having even in the prison hospitals only a little straw upon the damp ground for a bed, of course the flesh began to drop off.

. . . What the country demands and expects, is that such men as Campbell, RMT Hunter once Davis's Secretary of State, and others now in Richmond be seized and brought to trial for their crimes. But some protest against degrading a great conflict of ideas and principles into a paltry matter of detected felony and legal retribution, we should like to have them make a visit to David's Island, and look at the victims of the conflict. Not 'ideas and principles' but the demoniac malice, the principle of hellish torture could subject those poor fellows to such suffering as they have endured.

. . . That the rebellion grew out of a conflict of principles no one will deny, that it involved such a conflict is equally clear,—but the men who instigated the appeal to arms, who have conducted the war in a spirit of dishonorable rancor and revenge, who have inflicted remediless evils upon the nation, and tortures that would disgrace wild Indians upon our soldiers must be held to a proper legal retribution."[9]

During their terms of service, three hundred and ninety-four men from the 97th, 121st and 152nd New York regiments were taken prisoner. Of this total, one hundred and two men died in rebel custody.[10] Making this figure even more horrific was the fact that of the one hundred and twenty-seven men from the 121st and 152nd captured after the prisoner exchange program had broken down, nearly forty percent (forty-eight) perished in Confederate prison pens. Among the Herkimer County boys who died in rebel prisons during the early months of 1865 were: Levi Hemingway (121st) of Salisbury; Vernon Harvey (2nd HA) from Schuyler; Sgt. William Fralick (97th) of Little Falls; Henry Cooley (97th) from Newport; Ceylon Walby (76th) of Herkimer, and Hiram Potter (97th) from the town of Ohio.

The 121st New York was the first of the Mohawk Valley regiments to be mustered out, receiving their discharge from Federal service on June 25th. Of the three hundred and twenty men mustered out of the 121st on that day, two hundred and seventy-five were original members of the regiment. The balance of those discharged—forty-five men—were transfers and recruits. The four hundred and thirteen recruits added to the 121st at Burksville were transferred to the 65th New York.

On June 27th, the 121st left their camp at Hall's Hill, Virginia, and travelled by rail to New York City, arriving on June 30th. The next morning the regiment marched down Broadway proudly displaying the seven stands of Confederate regimental colors captured at Rappahannock Station and Sayler's Creek. All along the way people lining the street gave the men of "Upton's Regulars" a tremendous ovation. The march terminated at the train station, where the regiment loaded on cars for Albany. Lying ahead of the 121st was an invitation to a homecoming celebration in

Little Falls, a visit from the paymaster, and dissolution of the regiment.

The end of the war had an immediate and definite effect on the economy of Herkimer County.

On the downside, the value of two Herkimer County commodities, hay and cheese, dropped sharply. As thousands of horses were removed from government service and returned to private interests, the subsequent loss of Federal fodder expenditures tumbled the price of hay from $35 per ton down to $12 per ton in a matter of weeks. The loss in revenue caused by the devaluation of hay—which the *Journal* labeled as "legal tender in this vicinity"—had a decidedly adverse effect on the pocketbooks of many Herkimer County farmers. To make matters worse, the price of cheese also fell, although not as dramatically as that of hay. From a late spring high of twenty cents per pound, the price fell to less than fifteen cents per pound by early summer. The demand for cheese was still there—as was evidenced by a record one half million pounds shipped in one week in early July from the Little Falls Depot —but enigmatically the value of it had fallen.

On the economic upside, with trade opening up with the South, prospects for increased business in the manufacturing industry looked favorable. The Garner & Co. Cotton Factory in Little Falls believed so strongly in the return of prosperity that it began erecting a major addition to its mill.

Among the other items reported on by the *Journal* in the late spring and early summer of 1865 were:

. . . The Rockton "nine" challenged all comers to a match game of Base Ball. The game was to be played according to the rules of the New York Base Ball Congress of 1863.

. . . *Journal* editor J.R. Stebbins had returned from Piseco Lake with a prize three and one-half pound brook trout caught with a "fly-hook."

. . . The people of Booth in the town of Russia had changed the name of their community to Grant in honor of the Union Army's commander.

. . . A pack of wolves were terrorizing the people of Graysville. In a three week period, sixty sheep and lambs had been killed. Although a large sum had been offered for their skins, none of the "ravenous beasts" had been shot yet.

. . . Mr. John Rathbun and his wife were struck by lightning while sitting on their porch in Norway. Mr. Rathbun was severely injured but his wife escaped harm "doubtless in measure due to her steel spring dress hoops."

. . . A reminder that June 1st had been designated as a national day of "Humiliation and Prayer" in memory of Abraham Lincoln.

The *Journal* also carried a tongue-in-cheek story under the title "Big Fishing" which stated:

> "Dr. Rose of [West Winfield], caught three Eells on Saturday last which weighed 14 pounds. Two are females and one male. The father of this little group is Mr. C.B. Eells. The mother and children are doing well." [11]

Overshadowing all other events in Herkimer County this summer was the reception given to the men of the 121st New York on July 4th.

Back in late May, planning for the event, which initially was to include the 152nd New York, had begun with the formation of a Reception Committee made up of both Herkimer and Otsego County men. Little Falls was selected as the site—in part for the fine job it had done in hosting the 34th's reception—but the date of the event was still up in the air. Correspondence passed back and forth between the committee and the 121st's Colonel Olcott in an attempt to learn the regiment's muster-out date—reports ranged from the second week in June to the end of August. Olcott finally wrote on June 19th that the 121st would be available for an Independence Day celebration. Working under the supervision of the Reception Committee, separate township groups enlisted their citizens to donate food, build picnic tables, make decorations and most importantly donate money to the reception fund. A total of $731.16 was collected by "subscription" of which $631.76 was spent. The balance of the money was "appropriated" by the Reception Committee.

July 4th, 1865, the country's eighty-ninth birthday, finally arrived and was announced in Little Falls by the firing of a signal cannon at daybreak and a "national salute" at sunrise. The morning broke cool, dry and comfortable, and by 9 a.m. hundreds of wagons and carriages were pouring into the village from all directions. Throughout the forenoon, trains arrived at Little Falls bringing still more people and swelling the already massive crowd. Amidst the hustle and bustle, the citizens of Little Falls were putting the finishing touches to decorations, setting up picnic tables, polishing fire engines, tuning up band instruments and doing the myriad of other things that needed to be done to make the day perfect. But at this point in the day, Western Square was the center of activity. The *Journal* described the action:

> "The great, astonishing scene of the morning was at the Park towards which from 8 o'clock to 10 poured a continuous crowd of men, women and children on foot and in vehicles, bearing pails, baskets and arms full of provisions. The arrangements for the reception of these were perfect and it soon became evident that there would be provided several times as many eatables as would be wanted. There were sent in at least two large washtubs full of pickles, more than two bushels of cold boiled eggs, quarters of mutton, boiled hams, dried beef, fifty cold chickens, cold tongue, fifty lbs of sugar, one-hundred and fifty loaves of cake, a cart load of cookies, more than two hundred pies, many pounds of butter, sixty gallons of fresh milk, more than two hogsheads full of biscuits and bread, and large quantities of a score of other articles of which we had no time to take particular notice. But we do honestly believe that there was provender enough provided to feed five times the number in the 121st regiment: and it all looked as though each lady had taken special pains to send to the brave boys the very best her house could afford." [12]

The train bearing the 121st pulled into the Little Falls Depot shortly before eleven o'clock. The surging and pushing of the huge crowd in trying to get a better look at their heroes forced a number of people onto the track in front of the still moving train, but miraculously no one was run over. To the roar of the crowd, the men of the 121st New York stepped from the cars and were joined by over one hundred of their comrades who had been furloughed the previous day and had spent the night in their Herkimer County homes. All told, three hundred and thirty-eight members of the 121st were in Little Falls to enjoy the festivities.

While the regiment was falling into line, H.L. Greene of Herkimer welcomed the men on behalf of the people of Herkimer and Otsego counties. Colonel Olcott's reply of gratitude brought on loud cheers, and with that the procession stepped off.

Leading the parade was the Little Falls Citizen's Brass Band, followed by the Reception Committee. The 121st was next in line with its line officers to the front and then came the Little Falls National Guard Battery with their six horse drawn cannons and caissons. The Brockett's Bridge Drum Corps preceded the Little Falls Academy Cadets who were followed by fifteen veterans of the War of 1812. The day's orators, the Officers of the Day, and other prominent Herkimer and Otsego County citizens, completed the parade's first division. The Newville Band led the second division which was composed of the Little Falls fire companies, Cascade Hose Co. No. 1, Protection Hose Co. No. 2, and Gen. Herkimer Hose Co. No. 3.

The line of march from the depot wended its way through the principal streets of the village's north side, Eastern Avenue, Main Street and Canal Street, before crossing to the south side on Bridge Street. The parade tramped along German and Jefferson Streets, recrossed the river and the canal and made its way up Ann Street to Monroe Street. At this point, the column turned east and circled Western Square via Monroe, William and Gansevoort Streets before halting at the park. All along the route all eyes were on the soldiers in blue. Of the spectacle the *Journal* related:

> "The streets and house-tops along the entire march were literally thronged with people and upon every side were the waving of handkerchiefs and hearty cheers for the war-torn veterans. The regiment . . . marched with that long step which has won for them Gen. Sheridan's highest praise. Sun-browned and war-beaten though they were, they looked every inch of them, the valiant men they had proved themselves to be. With them they bore their battle-flags, torn and cut with a thousand bullets —proud monuments of their heroism and bravery. They also had with them three rebel flags, captured from the 'Louisiana Tigers' at Rappahannock Station. But the most interesting of these mementoes was a rebel silk flag inscribed on one side 'Savannah Volunteer Guards, 1802' and on the other 'Our altars and our hearths' in letters of silver. It was lined with silk and dotted with stars and emblems. It was captured by Warren Dockum, Co. H, in the engagement at Sailor's Creek, April 6th, 1865, and was, we believe, borne by him in the procession." [13]

Soon after reaching Western Square, the men of the 121st were escorted to their tables. However, as related by the *Journal*, the habits gained during army life were hard to break:

> "They had but just stacked arms when one of them espied the little stream which runs through the Park, between high stone walls. Without a word of ceremony over the wall went the soldier, and after him amid the laughter and rich enjoyment of the people, followed almost the entire regi-

ment: and then commenced a scene which gave those who have not witnessed the details of camp life, some idea of a soldier's manner of living. Hands and faces were washed in the running stream with a gusto, and wiped upon handkerchiefs, and soon the boys were over the wall again and ready for their dinner. We imagined a shades' difference, however, between the faces of those who washed above and those who stood below the stream." [14]

Now cleaned up a bit, the men of the 121st sat down to eat, and as reported by the *Journal*, "did themselves proud":

"Indeed, we judged from the remarks of several who had been away from home society nearly three years, that the sight of nearly a hundred beautiful young ladies, dressed in white, with blue scarfs and red bows upon the shoulders, and beaming with glad welcoming smiles, was not the least pleasing feature of the repast. The boys eat nearly as well as they fight, and provisions disappeared from the table at a double-quick. But the ladies brought forward fresh supplies and plied the veterans with charges of biscuits, cold meat and pickles, with cakes, pies and coffee, till the lads were at last compelled to surrender at discretion. They stood up to the hand-to-mouth contest bravely, and long hung the issue doubtful: but the odds against them were too great, and we may now privately tell them that the ladies had provisions enough to have continued the fight to this time, had the boys' appetites not 'gone back on them.' " [15]

After the meal the men of the 121st mingled with the crowd and many "hands were clasped and lips pressed." Special policemen and the village firemen guarded the eating area so that no riotous scene, as was evidenced when the crowd rushed the tables in 1863 after the 34th New York's homecoming dinner, would occur. The leftover food, which filled twelve two-bushel baskets, was later distributed to the families of soldiers.

Following a medley of tunes played by the Citizen's Brass Band that were suitable to the occasion, the Independence Day program began. The Invocation was delivered by Rev. M.L.P. Hill of the Presbyterian Church in Little Falls, Henry Petrie read the Declaration of Independence, and after more music, the Reception Committee President, Judge George Hardin, introduced the principal orator of the day, Rev. B.I. Ives of Auburn. After Reverend Ives' speech, which consumed over an hour (and for which the Reverend was paid $40), the Benediction, which concluded the program, was performed by Rev. J.L. Humphrey of the Little Falls Methodist-Episcopal Church.

The huge crowd—some estimates put its number at fifteen thousand—now poured down Ann Street and gathered as best they could at its intersection with Main Street. The featured entertainment, a rope walking exhibition by Mr. Dernier, was about to begin and no one wanted to miss it. High above the crowd's head a rope stretched from the Benton House to the Alexander Block. The high wire artist soon appeared and the crowd quieted. Of the acrobat's daring feat, the *Journal* related:

"Mr. Dernier is not the man to keep people waiting, and attired in the close fitting costume of his profession, holding a balancing pole in his hands, he soon made his appearance amid the profoundest stillness and anxiety for his safety. But by the time he was at the center of the rope, fear for him was lost in the admiration of the people at his cool self-possessed and evident familiarity with what he was about. His various feats with the wheelbarrow and upon the flying bar were most wonderful and gave the most complete satisfaction to those who take pleasure in such daring exhibitions. He did what he advertised to do, and did it in a manner to convince the most skeptical of his ability to perform anything that any man would dare attempt." [16]

For his performance, Mr. Dernier was paid $100 by the Reception Committee.

As darkness began to fall, goodbyes were said to the men of the 121st as they boarded the train back to Albany and the crowd started off for Eastern Square and the fireworks display. The pyrotechnic exhibit, which cost the committee an unheard of sum of $150, was judged to be the most spectacular ever seen in the area.

With the day come to an end, thousands of sleepy folk climbed aboard their wagons and carriages or mounted rail cars for the ride home. The Reception Committee had done their job well, the 121st had been properly welcomed home and the Independence Day pageant would be long remembered.

The return to Albany and the settling of all pay due to the men marked the dissolution of the 121st Regiment of New York State Volunteers. As soon as the men were paid off, they said their goodbyes and slipped away singly or in small groups for their journey home. The official muster-out date of the 121st New York was given as June 25, 1865, but the regiment did not formally disband until July 17th.

For the record, 1,815 men served in the 121st New York. Of this total:

> 976 men left Camp Schuyler in August of 1862
> 426 men transferred to the 121st New York (primarily from the 16th, 18th, 27th, 31st and 32nd New York Regiments)
> 413 men joined the 121st after Appomattox.

Losses in the 121st New York were:

> Killed in action or mortally wounded....226
> Died in Confedrate prisons.....................20
> Wounded but recovered.........................454
> Died of disease or other causes..............100
> Total casualties of war..........................800

Discounting the four hundred and thirteen men that joined the 121st after Lee's surrender, nearly three out of every five men in the regiment reached the casualty roll and about one of every four men died. Counting battlefield deaths alone, over sixteen percent of the regiment fell to Confederate guns. This percentage of fatalities to men served certainly ranked the 121st New York among the most bloodied regiments in the Union Army.

At muster-out the staff officers of the 121st New York (all Otsego County men) were:

Colonel - Egbert Olcott
Lieut. Colonel - John Kidder
Major - James Cronkite
Adjutant - Francis Lowe
Quartermaster - Theodore Sternberg
Chief Surgeon - John Slocum

While the 121st was being feted in Little Falls, the 152nd New York was holding a July 4th celebration of their own at their camp on Munson's Hill outside of Washington. As was the tradition on this day, the private soldiers and the officers exchanged positions. From within their own ranks, the enlisted men elected new officers and affixed shoulder straps made of pasteboard and tinsel to the uniforms of the "one-day wonders." Assuming a farcical display of pomp and ceremony, the mock-officers mounted mules and went out to take command of the regiment.

The first order of business was the assignment of camp duties, and to this task the new "officers" enthusiastically applied themselves. Moving from tent to tent, the erstwhile privates rousted the old officers, from Colonel Curtiss on down to the most junior 2nd lieutenant, and put them to work as guards, orderlies, or assigned them to "police" the campgrounds. After getting their former officers properly detailed, the new headquarters staff of the 152nd, astride their mules, visited the other area regiments that had undergone the same transformation. At each camp that they visited, the erzatz officers stopped for refreshments. Henry Roback of the 152nd related:

> ". . . both the mules and the officers were received with all due hospitality, the mules partaking of a mess of corn, the men a potion of corn extract, surnamed Kentucky bourbon." [17]

Thus fortified, the "officers" of the 152nd returned to their camp and in the spirit of fun began to mete out punishment to the old officers who had failed to satisfactorily perform the duties assigned them. Captain Beebe was made to carry on his back a large placard that had written on it, "$1,000 B" (bounty), Lieutenant Lee was confined to quarters, and Lieutenant Colonel Gilbert and Adjutant Gallaher were made to stand on barrel heads. The term of the punishment was relatively short, for the "July 4th officers" knew that on July 5th they would go back to being privates.

Towards mid-afternoon, a grand dinner was served up to which the old officers were invited. With the day being quite warm, the effects of the large meal and the "corn extract" were enhanced and the remainder of the afternoon was given to a siesta.

As the sun dropped lower in the sky and the day cooled off, the men of the 152nd roused for some Independence Day games. The day's contests included the ever popular sack race, a boxing match with soft gloves, a three-heat one-third-mile foot race and, of course, a greased pole. Aptly named Peter Tallman of Schuyler was the first man to scale the slick twenty-five-foot pole and snatch the ten dollar greenback atop it. The greased pig chase had to be cancelled because the pig was "absent without leave." For the black children that were watching the soldiers' revelry, the men of the 152nd buried a silver dollar in a tub of flour and challenged the children to extract it with only their teeth. The first boy to try recovered the prize and walked away leaving the rest "to chew snuff and hunt in vain."

The day ended with a torchlight dress parade and a fireworks display.

On the next day, July 5th, the filling out of the 152nd's muster rolls began. The mass of paperwork took over one week to finish and upon its completion on July 13th, the 152nd Regiment of New York State Volunteers, numbering all of two hundred and thirty-three men, was mustered-out of Federal service.

Boarding trains in Washington on July 14th, the 152nd rode to Philadelphia where they were treated to a meal at the Cooper's Shop, a favorite hospitality station for travelling soldiers. From Philadelphia, cars were taken to Perth Amboy, New Jersey, at which point the men boarded a river steamer to take them past New York City and up the Hudson to Albany. Albany was reached on the morning of July 16th, whereupon the men were paraded to the Executive Mansion to partake of a meal of "lamb and green peas" with Governor Fenton. From there the 152nd marched out three miles on the Troy Road and encamped. On July 20th, after receiving their final pay and their discharge papers, the men started for home; the 152nd New York quietly dissolved.

No grand celebration like those that were given the 34th New York and 121st New York greeted the return of the 152nd, but as J.R. Stebbins explained in the *Journal*, circumstances beyond control prevented it. Stebbins wrote:

> "We had hoped for and attempted preparations for a suitable reception of the Regiment. Meetings of citizens have been held at Herkimer and Mohawk to prepare for their coming and for proper public honors to be given them. But on Tuesday [July 18th] a dispatch was received from some of the officers of the regiment, stating that as the men were to be paid off and mustered out immediately, it would be impossible to keep them together for a reception. The attempt has, therefore, been for the present abandoned: but we shall hope to see it renewed, at least so far as to include the members from this county, at no distant day. But whether this can be done or not, the brave boys may rest assured that they have won warm places in the hearts of every patriot of this county." [18]

So without fanfare, the men of the 152nd simply melted back into civilian life. For the record, 1,457 men served in the 152nd New York, of which:

857 men left Camp Schuyler in October of 1862
600 men transferred to the 152nd New York or were later recruited

Losses in the 152nd New York during their term of service were:

Killed in action or mortally wounded...................73
Died in Confederate Prisons...............................28
Wounded but recovered.....................................159
Died of disease or other causes...........................65
Total Casualties of War......................................325

The casualty rate in the 152nd New York was roughly one in four men while the mortality rate was about one in nine men. Combat wounds claimed the lives of approximately five percent of the 152nd's men.

At muster-out the staff officers of the 152nd New York were:

Colonel - James Curtiss of Mohawk

Lieut. Colonel - Edmund Gilbert of Mohawk

Major - Charles Dygert of Herkimer

Adjutant - Benjamin Gallaher of Little Falls

Quartermaster - George Ernst of Otsego County

Chief Surgeon - James Hughes of Russia

With the 121st and 152nd having mustered-out, the 97th New York became the last Mohawk Valley regiment still in Federal service.

Regiment after regiment—including all of the other units in the 97th's Brigade — had broken camp and headed home, yet the old "Third Oneida" remained at Ball's Cross Roads. Watching the other troops leave made the 97th's wait seem interminable and, as the surrounding campsites emptied, a feeling of loneliness and isolation crept over the men.

Making good use of this time, Col. John Spofford led a group of the 97th's officers to the old Bull Run Battlefield to search for the remains of their comrade Lt. Dwight Faville, who had been slain on August 30th, 1862, at Second Manassas. Spofford was able to recover the bones of his friend Faville and have them sent to Brockett's Bridge for burial. The reason for Spofford's special mission to retrieve Faville's remains were explained in a *Journal* article which read:

> "The funeral services of Lieut. Dwight Faville, of the 97th regiment,
> were held at Brockett's Bridge last Sabbath. Lieut. Faville was killed in the
> second Bull Run fight, and his remains have lain, until a week or two since,
> upon the spot where he fell. Before going into battle he earnestly requested
> of several friends that, if he fell, they would see that his remains be brought
> to rest 'in the old burying-ground at Brockett's Bridge.' For many months
> after the battle, the ground where he lay was held by the rebel forces, and
> it was found impossible to remove the remains, until a few days ago several
> of the officers of the regiment succeeded in doing so. The body had not
> been buried and the bones of the fallen hero were literally whitened by
> exposure." [19]

The 97th New York finally received its muster-out orders on July 18th. It was noted with indignation by the men that the orders had been signed on July 7th, but because of some foul-up at headquarters, the 97th's stay at Ball's Cross Roads had been needlessly extended. Since the regiment's muster rolls had been prepared for some time, the 97th was able to leave for home that day. Boarding a train in Washington, the 97th travelled through Philadelphia and Binghamton and arrived in Syracuse in the last week of July. While waiting for their final installments of army pay and their discharge papers, the men of the 97th were invited to Utica for a reception in their honor.

The 97th New York, numbering two hundred and seventy men, travelled by rail to Utica on the morning of August 1st. Met at the rail station by a large crowd, which included many people from Boonville, Salisbury and Brockett's Bridge, the 97th was officially welcomed by Bvt. Brig. Gen. Rufus Daggett of the 117th New York. A procession formed and the 97th New York, preceded by a drum corps and escorted by the 45th New York and Utica fire companies, paraded through the city's principal streets to the banquet tables set up in Chancellor Square. After the playing of "Home Sweet Home" by the "old band" and a few well chosen words from Reception Chairman Hubbell, the main address, extolling the reputation of the gallant 97th, was delivered by Rev. S. Hanson Coxe.

After Reverend Coxe's speech, Colonel Spofford rose to the roar of the crowd and responded on the behalf of the men of the 97th. The *Utica Herald's* description of Spofford's reply, which was reprinted by the *Journal*, reported:

> "Col. Spofford replied briefly but appropriately. He regretted that the force of circumstances compelled his men to appear without arms and equipments. His soldiers, he said if not handsome were much better than they appeared to be. Hard fought battles, also had worn through their clothing. He closed by saying that 'our late Colonel Brevet Brig. Gen. Wheelock, when he raised his regiment did not fill it with holiday, Fourth of July soldiers but with men who were expected to receive hard knocks, and the tattered remains of 2,200 men which you see before you show how faithfully they have fulfilled their mission. Their hearts are right. We believe you sympathize with us, and are satisfied with our conduct on the bloody field. Permit me, in behalf of my officers and men to return to you our sincere thanks.' "[20]

Mr. Hubbell led the crowd in three cheers for the 97th and the men were escorted "to well laden tables." Shortly after three o'clock, the regiment mounted rail cars and travelled back to Syracuse.

The last days of the 97th were marked by one more battle, of which the *Journal* reported:

> "The Syracuse Courier says that some members of the 97th, and of the 1st New York Provisional Cavalry, had a bloody fight in that city Saturday. The Prov's, were a quarrelsome set, and the Syracusans congratulate themselves that most of them have left that city."[21]

On August 5th, the men were paid and handed their discharge papers and the 97th Regiment of New York State Volunteers was officially dissolved.

During the 97th New York's nearly three and one half years in Federal service, 2,105 men appeared on the regiment's rolls. On mustering-in, in February of 1862, the 97th numbered 918 men. Additions to the 97th came primarily from transfers from the 26th, 83rd and 94th New York regiments.

Losses in the 97th New York were:

Killed in action or mortally wounded....180
Died in Confederate Prisons...................54
Died of disease or other causes.............105

Wounded but recovered.........................444
Total casualties of War.........................783

The casualty rate in the 97th New York was better than one in three men and the mortality rate was approximately one in six men. Death in battle came to about nine percent of the 97th's men.

At muster-out the staff officers of the 97th New York were:

Colonel - John Spofford of Brockett's Bridge
Lieutenant Colonel - Rouse Egelston of Brockett's Bridge
Major - Delos Hall of Salisbury
Adjutant - Charles Caron of Rochester
Quartermaster - Thomas Sayers of Cold Brook
Chief Surgeon - George Little of Oneida County

Also returning to the Mohawk Valley were Herkimer County men from other mustered-out Federal units, most notably the 186th New York Infantry, the 16th New York Heavy Artillery and the 2nd New York Mounted Rifles. These regiments did not have as high a concentration of Herkimer County men as did the 97th New York, 121st New York and 152nd New York—approximately two hundred county men served in these units—so their return was marked by little public acknowledgement. It was notable that the last Herkimer County man to die by gunshot wound should come from one of these regiments. In late May, Joseph Perry of Little Falls, a member of the 16th New York Heavy Artillery, was accidentally shot and killed at his camp in Keysville, Virginia. Lt. E.T. Curtis' letter of condolence to Joseph Perry's father, Henry, was published in the *Journal* and read in part:

"It is my painful duty to inform you of the death of your son Joseph. He was shot about six and a half this a.m. by the accidental discharge of a revolver in the hands of one of the men in the regiment and expired at twenty-six minutes of eleven. The ball entered his brain just above the forehead.

It is indeed a sad task for me thus to inform you of the sudden departure from this world of one whom I doubt not, both you and your family have followed with anxious hearts through the past year of bloodshed and danger. And now, when the terrible strife is well nigh ended, and the load of anxiety lifted from the hearts of thousands of friends at the North, the intelligence of the unexpected death of so promising a young man as your son must necessarily fall upon yourself and family with ten fold severity, even in the most consoling manner my pen can present it."[22]

Joseph Perry had been well thought of in his regiment and in consequence his comrades collected $115 to have his body embalmed and shipped to Little Falls for burial.

In the War of the Rebellion three hundred and sixty thousand Union boys lost their lives (Confederate deaths were estimated at less than half this number), and of this total the State of New York contributed fifty-three thousand men.[23] From

Herkimer County four hundred and forty-four men perished in the war. An analysis of these mortalities reveals:

Killed in action or mortally wounded....234
Died of sickness or disease....................148
Died in Confederate custody....................43
Other or Unknown causes........................19

History of the 34th Regiment

Dedication of the 34th's Monument at Antietam, 1902

History of the 97th Regiment

Dedication of the 97th's Monument at Gettysburg, 1889

Report of the 121st New York's Monument Committee

Dedication of the 121st's Monument at Gettysburg, 1889

Courtesy of the Little Falls Historical Society

Veterans on Parade, Little Falls

CHAPTER XXIV

"Never shall their memory be forgotten"

Afterwards - Regimental Histories - Memorials - The GAR

In the war's early years men from all walks of life and from every corner of Herkimer County were drawn together by the call to arms. In the oneness of their regiments these men surrendered their individuality and took up the mantle of a common soldier. Now after four long years of war, the regiments dissolved and the men returned home to once more regain their identities.

The returning soldiers spread to the north woods or to the valleys of the Mohawk River and the Canada Creeks. They went to homes in crossroad hamlets, or the larger canal towns, to lumber camps and most often to small farms. After attending to family matters and renewing old acquaintances, the ex-soldiers once again took up the pen or the plowshare and went back to earning a living. Numbered among the occupations of the returning men were the makers of shoes, wagons, harnesses, and axes. Other men made a living as sawyers, lawyers, coopers, barbers, potters, boatmen, grocers, masons, stonecutters, and blacksmiths. Also back to work were druggists, carpenters, teamsters, tinsmiths, grocers, innkeepers, printers, accountants, railmen, tanners, tailors, musicians, a liquor dealer, a copper plate painter and even a hunter. Included in the callings were the requisite butchers, bakers, and a soap and candlestick maker. But the majority of the men regained their former mundane positions as mechanics, day laborers and most especially, farmers.

The returning men had little problem finding work, for the war had put a severe drain on the manpower of Herkimer County and the job market was wide open. Whereas the census of 1860 showed 40,561 people to be residing in Herkimer

County, a head count taken in 1865 only realized 39,154 souls.[1] Not until 1875 would the population of the county exceed the pre-war figures. In addition to this loss in the work force—the majority of which could be attributed to war casualties— a significant number of the homecoming soldiers were disabled by wounds or disease and were unfit for most work. The old men, women and children that had run the farms, operated the factories, and maintained the businesses of Herkimer County while the men were off to war, for the most part, happily gave up their jobs.

So the boys were home again and were back to their serious life's work of raising families, or in the case of the bachelors, starting new ones. For these men there would be no more marching from dawn to dusk, no more subsisting on hard tack and salt pork, no more sleeping on the wet earth shivering in a thoroughly soaked blanket, and certainly no more of the shock, terror and carnage of battle. But there was one aspect of army life that the men would miss, for with the return to civilian life, gone was the camaraderie that only a soldier could know and understand.

A strong fraternal bond was born at the formation of the regiment and was nurtured around countless campfires, during many a long march, by the teamwork of the drill field, and from the shared horror of the battlefield. From a need to remain in contact with their comrades and as a means of keeping the memories of their regiments alive, each of the Mohawk Valley regiments formed regimental associations. The formation of the "Social Union of the 97th Regiment, New York Volunteers" provides an example of the pattern that was also followed by men of the 34th, 121st and 152nd New York's in the creation of their own associations.

The birth of the 97th's "Social Union" resulted from a meeting of twenty-four of the regiment's officers in Boonville in 1867. Col. John Spofford—now brevetted to brigadier general—was chosen as temporary chairman and a committee was appointed to draft rules for a permanent organization. Among the articles approved were a requirement that further members could only be elected by a four-fifths vote, and that an annual reunion would be held on or around the 12th of March. (On March 12, 1862 the 97th had left Boonville for the seat of war).

At the second meeting of the 97th's Social Union, held in Brockett's Bridge in 1868, the officers eliminated their exclusive membership rule—by a single vote— and made membership in the association open to all honorably discharged members of the 97th New York (the following year the sons of the 97th men would also be made eligible).

From that year on the annual reunions of the 97th became grander and grander affairs. As the dinner meetings rotated among villages in Oneida and Herkimer Counties, each host-town tried to outdo its predecessor. The simple meetings evolved into all day affairs complete with brass bands, parades and well-staged campfires. Besides the old standbys, Boonville and Brockett's Bridge, the events were hosted by GAR posts in Utica, Little Falls, Rome, and Ilion.

The actual reunion portion of the ceremonies typically began with a lavish banquet, which was followed by the meeting portion of the agenda, and closed with an appropriate oration—General Spofford being the favored speaker. Afterwards there was music and dancing which usually went on into the small hours of the morning. With a gift of foresight, the original officers of the 97th's Social Union passed a rule

358 / DISTANT DRUMS

prohibiting "spirituous beverages" from the meetings and the reunions therefore did not degenerate into drunken affairs.

The reunions of the 97th continued on through the 1870's and 1880's but at each meeting fewer and fewer members attended as the list of departed comrades lengthened. The last "separate" reunion of the 97th was held in the early 1890's and from that point on reunions were held in conjunction with those of other area regiments.

Initially the regimental associations' primary function was to promote fellowship, (and to plan next year's reunion), but as the years went by and the men recognized their mortality, ways of preserving the regiment's history were sought. A major endeavor of these organizations now turned to the writing of regimental histories and to the erection of battlefield monuments in the hopes that future generations would remember the regiments and their accomplishments.

In regard to regimental histories, each of the four Mohawk Valley regiments appointed a member of the regiment to write a chronicle of the regiment's life. To this end there were written: *The History of the 152nd New York Volunteers*, by Henry Roback, published in 1888; *The History of the Ninety-Seventh Regiment New York Volunteers*, by Isaac Hall, published in 1890; *A Brief History of the Thirty-Fourth Regiment New York S.V.*, by L.N. Chapin, published in 1903; and *The History of the 121st New York State Infantry*, by Isaac Best, published in 1921. While numberless volumes had been written that told the story of the War of the Rebellion, only in these regimental texts could the personal tale of each regiment's history be related.

The placing of battlefield monuments provided a much more visible and enduring means of recognizing a regiment than could the regimental history books. Three of the Mohawk Valley regiments, the 34th, 97th and 121st New York, were able to acquire the funds necessary to erect battlefield memorials to their fallen comrades.

In 1887 an act was passed by the New York State Legislature that directed the state to erect monuments on the Gettysburg battlefield to each New York regiment or battery that had been engaged in that battle. Among the eighty-two units that were authorized to draw up to $1,500 in state funds for this purpose were the 97th New York and the 121st New York. While the paths taken by these two regiments in procuring their monuments were similar, the course followed by the 121st provides the better example, for it was more thoroughly documented.

The initial steps taken by the 121st's monument committee (consisting of John Kidder, J.W. Cronkite, Frank Lowe and Clinton Beckwith) towards erecting a Gettysburg monument began in 1886. That year a State Monument Commission was given the task of placing markers at the positions taken by New York State units in the Gettysburg fight. To aid in this endeavor, the commission asked that representatives from each unit engaged in the battle meet with them in Gettysburg to verify their position on the battlefield. While in attendance at one of these meetings, the committeemen of the 121st were able to gain valuable information on the best methods of monument construction, possible designs, and the comparative durability of various building materials. Armed with this knowledge, the 121st was well prepared the following year when the state offered subsidies for the Gettysburg regimental monuments.

Working under the guidelines of the Monument Commission, which covered everything from monument design and materials, to the style of lettering, the 121st's committee developed a set of specifications for their memorial stone. After attaching a $2,500 maximum cost stipulation to the specifications, the committee began seeking bids. Over the course of the next year numerous proposals were submitted to the committee and rejected before the design and the $2,900 price tag of Frederick & Field Co. of Quincy, Massachusetts was accepted. During this interval, the 121st was able to raise nearly $4,500 through a fund drive that was added to the state's $1,500 grant. The design selected by the 121st, which was submitted to the New York State Monument Commission for final approval, consisted of a ten-foot-high granite base topped by a seven-foot bronze figure of a soldier at "place rest." Bronze plaques giving a brief sketch of the 121st's history were on two sides of the base, a bronze likeness of Emory Upton was on a third, and the fourth facing bore an etched inscription marking the site as the 121st's position during the Gettysburg battle.

The monument was constructed in Quincy, transported to Gettysburg, and assembled on the northwestern slope of Little Round Top near the end of August 1889. The plot of land on which the monument was set and upkeep on the memorial was at that point ceded to the Gettysburg Battlefield Memorial Association.

On October 10, 1889, the 121st New York's Gettysburg monument was dedicated in the presence of over fifty members of the regiment, along with numerous friends, relatives, and distinguished guests. After the Rev. J.R. Dunkerley of Gettysburg gave the invocation, Mrs. Maria Upton Hanford, the sister of Emory Upton,* pulled the drawstring and unveiled the stone. Judge A.M. Mills of Little Falls delivered the main address, which was followed by Professor J.H.J. Watkins of Frankfort reading a poem of his own composition. Monument chairman J.W. Cronkite then read letters of commendation from Generals Wright and Slocum, after which the assemblage joined in the singing of "America." Rev. Dunkerley's benediction closed the ceremonies. Afterwards the veterans posed for pictures and toured parts of the battlefield by wagon.

The dedication of the 97th New York's monument on Seminary Ridge took place on July 2, 1889, forty-six years and one day after the regiment's bloody fight at Gettysburg. The 97th's ceremony was similar to that of the 121st. The 97th's Chaplain, J.V. Ferguson, gave the invocation, a poem was recited by Capt. John Norcross, Judge C.D. Prescott of Rome provided the oration and Chaplain Ferguson spoke the Benediction. The ceremony closed with the placing of a wreath on the monument by Mrs. Seymour Scott of Oneonta. About thirty members of the 97th were in attendance.

The tale of the 34th New York's battlefield monument was quite different from that of the 97th New York and the 121st New York. The 34th, having mustered-out prior to Gettysburg, had not taken part in the battle and therefore was not eligible for funding under the Monument Act of 1887. Nevertheless, the members of the 34th's regimental association resolved to have a monument of their own and in 1895 began to seek funding. With a design for a monument chosen and with an expense of

* Upton, suffering from an incurable disease, committed suicide in 1881.

$5,000 projected, the 34th's monument committee approached the Supervisors of Herkimer County for money, but were turned down. The next step was to request funds from New York State. Sen. James D. Feeter of Little Falls, an honorary member of the 34th's association, introduced a bill in the New York State Senate requesting that $5,000 be given by the state towards the 34th's monument. Feeter's bill was cut in half by the State Finance Committee before it was voted on and approved by the State Legislature. The Herkimer County Supervisors, presumably embarrassed by their stinginess, promptly allocated $500 to the 34th's monument fund. Private donations trickled in over the next several years and by the turn of the century, the required money was in hand.

The site selected for the 34th's monument was on the Antietam battlefield alongside the Dunker Church where the regiment had done its heaviest fighting. Since this plot of ground was on private property, the necessary real estate, a sixty foot by sixty foot parcel owned by Sharpsburg farmer, George Poffenberger, had to be purchased for the outrageous price of $160.

The monument itself was built and erected for a cost of nearly $2,500. Constructed of Quincy granite by Maslen Company of Hartford, Connecticut, the multi-tiered stone stood twenty feet high and was faced with four bronze plaques. Two of the plaques gave a brief history of the 34th, a third listed the regiment's officers at the time of the Antietam battle, and the fourth plaque gave an account of the 34th's role in the fight.

The dedication of the 34th's monument took place on September 17, 1902, forty years to the day after the battle outside of Sharpsburg. The thirty aged veterans of the 34th that had come for the ceremony were transported to the monument site by wagon. Approaching the old killing ground, where so many of their comrades had fallen, many of the men were overcome with emotion. Louis Chapin related:

> "Arriving at the same little old Dunkard Church which did not seem to have changed much in all the long interval, the veterans looked around them on scenes vastly different from those with which they had once been familiar. Then all this vast tract was covered with dead men and dead horses, and all the dreadful detritus of a great battle; while the air was rank with villainous odors. Now there were 'orchard lawns, and bowery hollows, crowned with summer sea.' The faces of many of the comrades were bathed in tears, as it all came back." [2]

The dedication program began with a welcome by the 34th's monument committee chairman, Nathan Easterbrook, after which James A. Suiter Jr., the son of the 34th's commander Col. James Suiter, unveiled the monument. Colonel Suiter, who was 86 years old at the time, was too infirm to make the trip to Sharpsburg. Judge John Henderson of Herkimer delivered the main address and was followed to the dais by Mrs. Donald McLean, the Regent of the New York City Chapter of the DAR. Former officers of the 34th, Wells Sponable, Irving Clark and Henry Sanford delivered short speeches and a letter from Colonel Suiter was read. Chairman Easterbrook formally transferred the monument and site to the American people and Gen. E.A. Carman accepted the gift on behalf of the government. Afterwards the veterans posed for pictures with their families and friends before touring the battlefield.

To help fill the void between the annual regimental reunions many of the Herkimer County veterans joined local GAR posts.

The GAR, or Grand Army of the Republic, was formed in 1866 as a fraternal organization for Union veterans and was dedicated to the principles of "fraternity, charity and loyalty." Reaching a peak membership of over four hundred thousand in 1890, the GAR would have a tremendous influence on the writing of legislation that affected the Union veterans. Although the GAR portrayed itself as apolitical, during its glory days it helped sway many Presidential elections. The GAR would survive for ninety years, until the death of its last member, 109-year-old Albert Woolson, in 1956.

Eight GAR posts were formed in Herkimer County: Chismore Post #110 in Ilion in 1869, Galpin Post #19 in Little Falls in 1873, Wendell Post #40 in Van Hornesville, Aaron Helmer Post #404 in Herkimer in 1883, Burrell Post #503 in Salisbury in 1884, Mann Post # 604 in Frankfort in 1886, S.G. Button Post #364 in West Winfield in 1891, and Spofford Post #664 in Dolgeville in 1892. With the exception of the Spofford and Galpin Posts, the Herkimer County GAR posts were named in honor of local boys that lost their lives in the war.

The Herkimer County GAR posts held monthly or semi-monthly meetings in rooms set aside for them at locations such as the Royal Arcanum in Dolgeville, Grange Halls in Herkimer and Salisbury, Odd Fellows Hall in Ilion, the Knights of Pythias Hall in Frankfort and Wilcox Hall in West Winfield. The Galpin Post in Little Falls rented rooms formerly occupied by the Hunter's Club in the Wheeler block at the northeast corner of Main and Ann Streets. Later the Galpin Post would take up temporary quarters in the Baptist Church on Mary Street, before moving to a three room suite on the third floor of the then brand new Little Falls City Hall on July 4th, 1918. Upon receiving the keys to the GAR rooms from Mayor Zoller, Galpin Post Commander Martin Burney remarked:

> "If the time ever comes, we are willing to do anything as an organiza-
> tion to help out our beloved and picturesque city. I think, Mr. Mayor, that
> you have built wiser than you knew. Before long we will all have passed
> away, but there will be a new generation of veterans who have served their
> country well, and they will use these rooms. They might be too small at the
> start but I hope the things that we assemble here will remain for them."[3]

The GAR functioned primarily as a social club for Union veterans, but as time passed and the membership became more and more involved in civic-minded projects, the GAR evolved into a true service organization. Working in conjunction with two auxiliary organizations, the Women's Relief Corps and the Sons of Union Veterans, the GAR helped fund relief for indigent veterans and their families, hosted regimental reunions, and encouraged and contributed to the raising of soldiers' monuments in their communities. But it was on Memorial Day that the GAR was most evident. Prior to the holiday, the members of the GAR posts, accompanied by the ladies of the Relief Corps, would visit the local cemeteries. The women would decorate the veterans' graves with fresh floral bouquets while the men would plant flags at the tombs or erect one of the GAR's distinctive star-shaped markers near the stone of a newly fallen comrade. On Memorial Day itself, the veterans would don their GAR uniforms and march proudly in their villages' parade. Afterwards the GAR men might host a banquet in their club rooms or else attend a special Memorial Day church service.

As time wore on the roll of veterans in the GAR posts began to shrink. The Galpin Post in Little Falls presented a prime example. At its peak in 1893 the Galpin Post boasted a membership of one hundred and nineteen veterans, fifteen years later, in 1908, the club's roster was almost halved to sixty-five men, in 1918 there were only seventeen members, and in 1929 six men answered the roll call. In December of 1942, Charles Jennett of Ilion passed away, leaving Martin Burney of Little Falls as the last Civil War veteran in Herkimer County. Soon after Jennett's death, *The Little Falls Evening Times*, in recognition of the passing of the old guard, noted:

"Many men now living remember the GAR in the days when it was a flourishing organization. These veterans were the ideals of the boys who grew up in the latter part of the last century. Their idea of a soldier was a grand army man with his blue uniform and his gilt buttons and his black campaign hat with the insignia of the order on the front of the hat. Many have seen them march and noted the erect bearing and the quick steps as they followed the drum corps to the tune of 'Marching Thro Georgia.' And even as time began to take its toll there was something in the uniform and the drums which served to straighten the shoulders and quicken the step even if afterwards there was a let-down which aging limbs could not hide. We owe a great deal to the GAR for its preservation of the martial spirit. Political campaigns were conducted along military lines, with thousands of caped and torched 'wide-awakes' marching in line, by company and regiment. Most, if not all, of this military training was done by men of the GAR. It was not until the turn of the century that this picturesque form of political endeavor was abandoned.

But Memorial day was the great day for the GAR. Here it came into its very own for it was conceived by the army, and its tenets preserved by the army. Here they come marching down the street in solemn parade, dress uniform, eyes fixed on the flag which they truly saved. Tramp, tramp, tramp, the boys marched—for the Civil War was fought on foot. And over the familiar street they tread. Here in Little Falls the line of march was over historic ground. Men of the Revolution had marched here, before them, to erect a country. The men of the Civil War marched to preserve it.

Great changes have come since those days. They marched down an unpaved street, past mostly wooden buildings. The people were dressed differently, but the street, after all is the same and the people are the same. We are again fighting for the same great principles, because, after all, democracy has to be fought for every so often. And as we march, whether it be Spanish war, World war or global war, let us pause long enough to pay tribute to the men of '61-'65, and the things they fought for and to congratulate Commander Burney and his phantom company for what they did, and to assure them they did not march, they did not make their sacrifices in vain. And it is now our turn to see to it that never shall their memory be forgotten, and that their duties are now our duties. May we give as good account as they did - these men of '61-'65."[4]

Martin Burney died on January 18, 1943, at the age of ninety-five at his son's home in Richmond, Virginia. The old soldier's body was transported to Little Falls for the funeral and was briefly interred in the Fairview Cemetery's mausoleum before it was sent on to the Burney family's burial plot in Gouverneur.

With the death of Martin Burney—a member of the 26th New York Cavalry—Herkimer County lost its last living link with the men who had fought in the War of the Rebellion. Granite monuments would remain to honor these men and the printed word would tell of their deeds, but with the flesh and blood men gone the memory of the men themselves would fade. Future generations would live their lives, fight their wars and add their own pages to the history of Herkimer County, but the boys in blue, through their struggle to keep the United States truly whole, had written the most significant chapter of all.

APPENDIX A

34th NEW YORK

| Place/Date | Killed | Wounded | | Missing | Aggregate |
		Died	Recovered		
Seneca Mills, Md 9/1/61		1			1
Seneca Mills, Md 9/16/61	1				1
Dranesville, Md 9/17/61	1				1
Tyler House, Va 5/24/62		1			1
Fair Oaks, Va 5/31 - 6/1/62	23	6	65	3	97
White House, Va 6/16/62	1				1
Seven Days Battle, Va 6/25 - 7/2/62	4	3	20	35	62
Sharpsburg, Md 9/17/62	33	13	98	10	154
Fredericksburg, Va 12/11 - 12/15/62	3	4	8	18	33
Fredericksburg, Va 5/3/ - 5/4/63			2	1	3
Total	66	28	193	67	354

97th NEW YORK

| Place/Date | Killed | Wounded | | Missing | Aggregate |
		Died	Recovered		
Cedar Mt., Va 8/9/62			1		1
Manassas, Va 8/16 - 9/2/62	10	6	36	59	111
South Mt., Md 9/14/62	2		3		5
Sharpsburg, Md 9/17/62	24	15	59	9	107
Fredericksburg, Va 12/11 - 12/15/62	4	4	30	4	42
Gettysburg, Pa 7/1 - 7/3/63	14	4	32	76	126
Bristoe Sta., Va 10/14/63			1		1
Mine Run, Va 11/26 - 12/2/63				4	4
Wilderness, Va 5/5 - 5/7/64	19	9	62	9	99

97th NEW YORK (continued)

Place/Date	Killed	Wounded		Missing	Aggregate
		Died	Recovered		
Spotsylvania, Va 5/8 - 5/21/64	6	9	58	2	75
North Anna, Va 5/22 - 5/26/64	1		6		7
Cold Harbor, Va 6/1 - 6/12/64	4	2	14	1	21
White Oak, Va 6/13/64	1				1
Before Petersburg, Va 6/16/64 - 6/19/64	3	13	47		63
Assault Petersburg, Va 6/16 - 6/19/64	3	7	42	2	54
Weldon Road, Va 8/18 - 8/19/64	6	1	12	92	111
Hatcher's Run, Va 2/5 - 2/7/65	5	6	23		34
Appomattox Campaign 3/28 - 4/9/65	2	2	18	7	29
Total	104	78	444	265	891

121st NEW YORK

Place/Date	Killed	Wounded		Missing	Aggregate
		Died	Recovered		
Fredericksburg, Va 12/11 - 12/15/62	4		12		16
Salem Church, Va 5/3 - 5/4/63	80	16	157	23	276
Gettysburg, Pa 7/2 - 7/3/63			2		2
Rappahannock Sta., Va 11/7/63	4	3	18		25
Wilderness, Va 5/5/ - 5/7/64	15	6	31	21	73
Spotsylvania, Va 5/8 - 5/21/64	49	14	92		155
Cold Harbor, Va 5/31 - 6/12/64	1		6		7
Before Petersburg, Va 6/17/64 - 4/2/65			18	1	19
Assault Petersburg, Va 6/17 - 6/23/64	1		8		9
Washington, D.C. 7/12 - 7/13/64	3	2	19	2	26
Charleston, W Va 8/21 - 8/22/64	2		5		7
Opequon Creek, Va 9/13/64			2		2

121st NEW YORK (continued)

Place/Date	Killed	Wounded		Missing	Aggregate
		Died	Recovered		
Opequon Creek, Va 9/19/64	2		13		15
Fisher's Hill, Va 9/22/64			5		5
Cedar Creek, Va 10/19/64	10	5	37	5	57
Newtown, Va 11/12/64			1		1
Hatcher's Run, Va 2/5 - 2/7/65		1	3		4
Petersburg, Va 3/25/65	1		3		4
Appomattox Campaign 3/28 - 4/9/65	9		25		34
Total	181	47	457	52	737

152nd NEW YORK

Place/Date	Killed	Wounded		Missing	Aggregate
		Died	Recovered		
Mine Run, Va 11/26 - 12/2/63			2		2
Wilderness, Va 5/5 - 5/7/64	13	4	32	2	51
Spotsylvania, Va 5/8 - 5/21/64	16	7	45	2	70
North Anna, Va 5/22 - 5/31/64	2	1	13		16
Cold Harbor, Va 6/1 - 6/12/64	8	3	20	1	32
Before Petersburg, Va 6/15/64 - 4/2/65	3	3	19	14	39
Assault Petersburg, Va 6/15 - 6/23/64	2	1	7	30	40
Strawberry Plains, Va 8/14 - 8/18/64	1	2	8	16	27
Ream's Sta., Va 8/25/64	4	1	9	6	20
Boydton Plank Rd., Va 10/27 - 10/18/64	3		4	1	8
Total	52	22	159	72	305

Source: *New York in the War of the Rebellion*, Pfisterer, p. 2126 (34th), pp. 3111, 3112 (97th), p. 3424 (121st), pp. 3767, 3768 (152nd).

APPENDIX B

	34th NY	97th NY	*P	121st NY	*P	152nd NY	*P
Killed in Action							
Officers	1	7		10		4	
Enlisted	65	97		171		48	
Mortally Wounded							
Officers	2	5		5			
Enlisted	26	71	2	40	2	21	1
Died of Disease							
Officers	1	1		4		1	
Enlisted	58	97	46	92	16	57	23
Accidentally Killed							
Officers							
Enlisted	2	3	1			1	
Drowned							
Officers							
Enlisted				1		1	
Killed after Capture							
Officers							
Enlisted		1					
Died of Sunstroke							
Officers							
Enlisted						1	
Died of Other Causes							
Officers							
Enlisted		3		1			
Died of Unknown Causes							
Officers							
Enlisted	7	3	2	2	2	4	4
Deaths of Non-POWs							
Officers	4	13		19		5	
Enlisted	158	272		307		133	
Deaths of POWs							
Officers							
Enlisted			54		20		28
Aggregate	162	339		346		166	
Wounded, Recovered							
Officers	9	26		19		7	
Enlisted	184	418		435		152	
Captured, Returned							
Officers	2	12		4		5	
Enlisted	65	201		30		40	
Aggregate Loss	422	996		834		370	
Number in Regiment	1110	1950		1380		930	

Source: Pfisterer, pp. 297, 299, 300, 301

* Prisoners

APPENDIX C

HERKIMER COUNTY CIVIL WAR MORTALITIES (444)

Columbia (13)

Ackler, Meather	34th NY Killed in Action. Date and place unknown.
Crewell, John	34th NY Died of sickness, 8/22/62, in Philadelphia.
Crouch, David	34th NY Killed in Action, 9/17/62, at Antietam.
Curley, Patrick	125th NY Died of sickness, 5/29/64, in prison at Andersonville, Ga.
Fasket, Orlando	34th NY Killed in Action, 12/13/62, at Fredericksburg.
Fox, Robert	121st NY Killed in Action, 5/3/63, at Salem Church, Va.
Gaye, Elias	121st NY Died of sickness. Date and place unknown.
Huntly, Lester	152nd NY Killed in Action, 8/25/64, at Ream's Station, Va.
Maxfield, James	152nd NY Died of sickness in prison at Andersonville, Ga. Date unknown.
Mead, Joseph	16th NY Cav. Died of sickness, 10/1/64, in prison at Columbia, NC.
Pierce, Wash.	2nd NY HA Died of sickness, 2/7/63, in Washington.
Wheeler, Peter	2nd NY HA Died of sickness, 7/28/65, in Washington.
Young, Floyd	44th NY Died of wounds, 6/5/62, at Hanover Court House, Va.

Danube (14)

Baum, Lester	121st NY Killed in Action, 5/6/64, at the battle of the Wilderness.
Brin, Nicholas	152nd NY Killed in Action. Date and place unknown.
Covell, Ben	121st NY Died of sickness in prison at Florence, SC. Date unknown.
Eckler, Norman	152nd NY Killed in Action, 5/6/64, at the battle of the Wilderness.
Fox, Delos	152nd NY Died of sickness, 10/19/64, in prison at Andersonville, Ga.
Fox, Thomas	152nd NY Died of sickness, 10/30/63, in Washington.
Hale, William	152nd NY Killed in Action, 5/10/64, at Spotsylvania, Va.
Hendrix, James	121st NY Killed in Action, 4/2/65, at Petersburg, Va.
Hewitson, Geo.	121st NY Died of wounds, 5/64, at Salem Church, Va.
Hewitson, Robt.	121st NY Died of sickness at White Oak, Va. Date unknown.
Lanz, Andrew	152nd NY Killed in Action, 5/6/64, at the batttle of the Wilderness.
Lightheart, Jas.	57th NY Died of sickness at Falmouth, Va. Date unknown.
O'Brien, Nich.	152nd NY Killed in Action, 6/3/64, at Cold Harbor, Va.
Rourke, Walter	97th NY Killed in Action, 8/31/62, at Manassas, Va. (2nd Bull Run)

Fairfield (17)

Cameron, Angus	121st NY Died of sickness, 11/10/62, at Bakersville, Md.
Evans, Thomas	152nd NY Killed in Action, 6/3/64, at Cold Harbor, Va.
Ford, Fred.	121st NY Killed in Action, 5/3/63, at Salem Church, Va.
Ford, J. Edwin	121st NY Died of wounds, 10/8/64, at Winchester, Va.
Gardener, Jas.	115th NY Died of wounds, 3/18/64, at Hilton Head, SC.
Hackman, Jacob	Unit unknown Date, place and cause of death unknown.
Harris, Edwin	34th NY Died of sickness, 8/10/62, at Harrison's Landing, Va.
Helmer, Aaron	34th NY Killed in Action, 9/17/62, at Antietam.
Lamberson, Wilbur	121st NY Died of sickness, 10/28/62, at Bakersville, Md.
Lamphere, Nathan	121st NY Killed in Action, 4/6/65, at Sailor's Creek, Va.
Morey, William	152nd NY Died of sickness in prison at Andersonville, Ga.. Date unknown.
Rees, Harlem	152nd NY Died of sickness, 9/27/64, at David's Island, NY.
Rice, Adam C.	121st NY Died of sickness, 9/19/63, in Washington.
Rockwood, James	34th NY Died of sickness, 5/25/62, at Fortress Monroe, Va.

Smith, Seymour	152nd NY Accidentally killed, 10/28/62, at Havre De Grace, Md.
Williams, Chas.	121st NY Killed in Action, 5/3/63, at Salem Church, Va.
Zoller, Norman	121st NY Died of sickness, 10/18/64, in prison at Andersonville, Ga.

Frankfort (33)

Alexander, Reub.	2nd NY HA Died of wounds, 9/8/64. Place unknown.
Archer, James	2nd NY HA Died of sickness, 7/3/64, in Washington.
Austin, Steven	121st NY Died of sickness, 9/2/63, in Washington.
Brown, Burton	2nd NY HA Died of sickness, 12/65. Place unknown.
Brown, Darin	121st NY Killed in Action, 5/10/64, at Spotsylvania, Va.
Church, Foster	57th NY Died of wounds, 7/64, at Petersburg, Va.
Churches, Oliver	2nd NY HA Died of sickness, 6/26/64, at City Point, Va.
Davis, David	2nd NY HA Died of accidental wounds, 12/18/64, at Newark, NJ.
Devendorf, Rudy	2nd NY HA Died of sickness, 8/6/64, in prison at Andersonville, Ga.
Edicks, Samuel	Reg. Army Died of sickness, 12/18/64, at Frankfort, NY.
Eitelby, John	152nd NY Killed in Action, 5/13/64, at Spotsylvania, Va.
Farrington, John	2nd NY HA Killed in Action, 6/64, at Cold Harbor, Va.
Fish, John	121st NY Killed in Action, 5/12/64, at Spotsylvania, Va.
Gafney, Timothy	26th NY Accidentally killed, 1/7/62, at Fort Lyon, Va.
Gebney, James	2nd NY HA Died 7/16/64. Place and cause unknown.
Green, Gilbert	2nd NY HA Died of sickness, 10/4/62, at Washington.
Green, H. J.	44th NY Date, place and cause unknown.
Hartley, John	121st NY Date, place and cause unknown.
Hyer, John	152nd NY Died of wounds, 5/10/64, at Spotsylvania, Va.
Inman, Asa	152nd NY Died of wounds, 6/64, place unknown.
James, William	2nd NY HA Died of sickness, 8/64, at David's Island, NY.
Johnston, Robert	121st NY Died of wounds, 11/17/63, in Washington.
Kuck, George	2nd NY HA Died of wounds in Washington. Date unknown (1862).
Loftis, James	2nd NY HA Died of sickness, 7/29/64, in Washington.
Miller, Aaron	121st NY Missing in Action, 6/64, at Cold Harbor, Va.
Newsham, George	2nd NY HA Died of sickness 9/16/64. Place unknown.
Rodgers, Rosell	2nd NY HA Died of wounds, 9/64. Place unknown.
Rowland, John	121st NY Killed in Action, 10/18/64, at Cedar Creek, Va.
Van Alystyne, H.	152nd NY Died of sickness, 9/14/64, in prison at Richmond, Va.
Vanort, Daniel	2nd NY HA Died of sickness, 2/10/65, at City Point, Va.
Watson, William	121st NY Killed in Action, 11/7/63, at Rappahannock Station, Va.
Woodbridge, Hen.	15th NY Cav. Accidentally killed, 2/20/65, at Winchester, Va.
Zoller, Jonas	2nd NY HA Died of wounds, 2/16/65, in Washington.

German Flatts (29)

Bourshay, Thos.	Unit unknown. Died of sickness. Date and place unknown.
Carpenter, Cyrus	121st NY Died of sickness, 11/22/62, at Hagerstown, Md.
Cassens, Nich.	152nd NY Killed in Action, 5/6/64, at the battle of the Wilderness.
Chismore, James	2nd NY HA Died of sickness, 11/1/64, in prison at Florence, SC.
Clapsaddle, P.J.	2nd NY HA Killed in Action, 4/7/65, at Farmsville, Va.
Cookley, Jer.	2nd NY HA Died of sickness, 1/10/65, at Point Lookout, Md.
Cristman, Jacob	121st NY Killed in Action, 5/3/63, at Salem Church, Va.
Crittenden, Hen.	121st NY Killed in Action, 5/3/63, at Salem Church, Va.
Davis, George	2nd NY HA Died of wounds, 9/29/64, in Washington.
Dennison, Corn.	152nd NY Died of sickness (diphtheria), in Philadelphia. Date unknown.
Doxtater, Levi	121st NY Killed in Action, 12/13/62, at Fredericksburg, Va.
Douw, John	121st NY Died of wounds, 11/11/64, at Cedar Creek, Va.
Farrell, Jer.	USS Vanderbilt Died of sickness, 4/5/65, at German Flatts, NY.
Frazier, James	81st NY Died of wounds, 6/62, Chapin Farm, Va.

Gardner, Amos — 152nd NY Died of sickness at Fortress Monroe, Va. Date unknown.
Goodrich, Silas — 121st NY Killed in Action, 5/3/63, at Salem Church, Va.
Harter, Mill. — 121st NY Killed in Action, 5/3/63, at Salem Church, Va.
Howell, Henry — 44th NY Killed by lightning, 6/2/62, at Gaines's Mills, Va.
Judge, Daniel — 121st NY Killed in Action, 5/10/64, at Spotsylvania, Va.
Judge, James — 121st NY Killed in Action, 5/10/64, at Spotsylvania, Va.
Kirck, Robert — 34th NY Killed in Action, 5/31/62, at Fair Oaks, Va.
Kirk, Daniel — 50th NY Died of wounds, 9/18/64, at Petersburg, Va.
Mott, Daniel — 6th NY Cav. Died of sickness, 11/21/64, in prison at Salisbury, NC.
Murdent, John — 9th Minn. Died of wounds, 4/3/65. Place unknown.
Norris, Enoch — 34th NY Killed in Action, 5/31/62, at Fair Oaks, Va.
Squires, Abram — 14th NY Cav. Died of sickness, 11/21/64, in prison at Salisbury, NC.
Steele, William — 2nd NY HA Died of wounds, 11/8/64, at City Point, Va.
Swart, Dominick — 2nd NY HA Died of wounds, 11/20/64, in Washington.
West, Benton — 121st NY Killed in Action, 5/3/63, at Salem Church, Va.

Herkimer (24)

Addy, Charles — 97th NY Died of sickness (Typhoid), 7/15/62, at Warrenton, Va.
Beardsley, John — 34th NY Killed in Action, 9/17/62, at Antietam.
Brown, Charles — 34th NY Died of wounds, 6/3/62, at Malvern Hill, Va.
Crawford, Geo. — 152nd NY Died of sickness, 1/20/64, at Brandy Station, Va.
Dixon, John — 34th NY Killed in Action, 9/17/62, at Antietam.
Harter, John — 152nd NY Killed in Action, 8/14/64, at Petersburg, Va.
Holler, Melchert — 152nd NY Died of sickness, 8/20/64, in prison at Andersonville, Ga.
Kast, Daniel — 16th NY HA Killed in Action, 8/64, at Petersburg, Va.
Little, Frank — 44th NY Died of sickness, 1/15/62, at Hall's Hill, Va.
Martin, Henry — 34th NY Missing in Action, 7/1/62, at Nelson's Farm, Va.
Mosher, Richard — 34th NY Killed in Action, 6/16/62, at White Oak, Va.
Myers, John — 34th NY Died of wounds, 6/28/62, at Portsmouth, Va.
Richardson, S. — 14th NY Died of sickness, 7/24/62, in prison at Richmond, Va.
Rubbins, William — 34th NY Killed in Action, 9/17/62, at Antietam.
Schossler, Jos. — 14th NY HA Died of wounds, 8/26/64, at Petersburg, Va. (Weldon R.R.)
Schwiniger, Con. — 97th NY Died of sickness, 12/10/63, in prison. Place unknown.
Shoemaker, Jos. — Unit unknown Died of sickness in prison at Andersonville, Ga. Date unknown
Stevens, Frank — Unit unknown Killed in Action, 12/13/62, at Fredericksburg, Va.
Swart, John — 152nd NY Died of sickness. Date and place unknown.
Syllbach, Wm. — 152nd NY Killed in Action, 7/27/64, at Petersburg, Va. (Deep Bottom).
Walby, Ceylon — 76th NY Died of sickness in rebel prison. Date and place unknown.
Watson, Charles — 152nd NY Killed in Action, 10/27/64, at Petersburg, Va. (Hatcher's Run).
Wilcott, Wilford — 34th NY Died of sickness, 8/31/62, at Fortress Monroe, Va.
Vedder, Nicholas — 152nd NY Died of sickness. Date and place unknown.

Litchfield (16)

Bennett, Charles — 121st NY Died of sickness, 5/2/63, in Washington.
Burry, John — 121st NY Died of sickness (Typhoid), 12/13/62, at Hagerstown, Md.
Carran, Francis — 121st NY Died of wounds, 6/5/63, in Washington.
Champney, Wilber — 121st NY Killed in Action, 8/21/64, at Charlestown, Va.
Davis, John — 2nd NY HA Killed in Action, 4/7/65, place unknown.
Eldred, Addison — 152nd NY Died of sickness in rebel prison. Date and place unknown.
Evans, William — 152nd NY Died of sickness, 11/2/63, at Alexandria, Va.
Hulser, Wash. — 152nd NY Killed in Action, 5/5/64, at the battle of the Wilderness.
Matthews, Rich. — 121st NY Killed in Action, 5/3/63, at Salem Church, Va.
Mead, Garland — 34th NY Killed in Action, 9/17/62, at Antietam.
Mead, George — 18th NY Cav. Died of sickness, 12/31/64, New Orleans, La.

Millan, Aaron	152nd NY Died of wounds, 5/64, in Washington.
Murphy, John	121st NY Died of sickness, 10/14/62, at Bakersville, Md.
Platt, Mont.	152nd NY Died of sickness in rebel prison. Date and place unknown.
Robinson, John	117th NY Died of sickness, 11/62, at Jersey City, NJ.
West, Oscar	152nd NY Died of sickness in rebel prison. Date and place unknown.

Little Falls (70)

Alfreds, Henry	152nd NY Died of sickness, 10/20/64, in prison at Andersonville, Ga.
Allen, Henry	Signal Corps Died of sickness, 9/28/64, at Newbern, NC.
Armstrong, Wm.	4th NY HA Died of sickness, 1/65, in Little Falls, NY.
Arnold, Thomas	121st NY Died of wounds, 5/63, at Salem Church, Va.
Ashley, Hilo	2nd NY Cav. Died of sickness in Baton Rogue, La. Date unknown.
Babcock, Wash.	121st NY Killed in Action, 5/4/63, at Salem Church, Va.
Ballard, Stephen	34th NY Killed in Action, 5/31/62, at Fair Oaks, Va.
Boussha, Thomas	2nd NY HA Died of sickness, 8/64, in prison at Richmond, Va.
Brazamber, Henry	110th NY Died of sickness, 10/14/64, in Oswego Co., NY.
Brazamber, John	121st NY Killed in Action, 5/3/63, at Salem Church, Va.
Cary, William	121st NY Killed in Action, 10/18/64, at Cedar Creek, Va.
Carr, James	34th NY Died of sickness, 11/12/62, at Harper's Ferry, Va.
Casler, Joseph	121st NY Died of sickness at Hagerstown, Md. Date unknown.
Casler, Orlando	121st NY Killed in Action, 5/3/63, at Salem Church, Va.
Clark, Roswell	97th NY Died of wounds, 9/19/62, at Antietam.
Cleaveland, P.	97th NY Died of wounds, 10/23/64. Place unknown.
Colony, Charles	34th NY Died of sickness, 8/27/62, at Philadelphia.
Cool, Stephen	34th NY Killed in Action, 9/17/62, at Antietam.
Cornell, William	152nd NY Missing in Action, 6/22/64, at Petersburg, Va. (Weldon R.R.).
Cross, Frank	125th NY Died of wounds, 7/2/63, at Gettysburg.
Davis, Daniel	"Griffin's Battery" Died of wounds, 7/7/63, at Annapolis, Md.
Davis, George	121st NY Died of sickness, 10/20/62, at Hagerstown, Md.
Delong, Guy	44th NY Died of wounds, 7/6/62, at Malvern Hill, Va.
Donovan, Timothy	152nd NY Died of sickness, 3/63, White Oak Church, Va.
Eaton, George	121st NY Died of sickness, 10/6/64, in prison at Florence, SC.
Ellis, Thomas	152nd NY Died of sickness. Date and place unknown.
Fagan, Michael	121st NY Killed in Action, 5/3/63, at Salem Church, Va.
Flynn, George	2nd Mounted Rifles Died of sickness, 10/19/64, at Little Falls, NY.
Fralick, William	97th NY Died of sickness (starvation), 2/17/65, in prison at Salisbury, NC.
Gray, William	97th NY Killed in Action, 9/17/62, at Antietam.
Harrington, U.H.	121st NY Killed in Action, 5/3/63, at Salem Church, Va.
Haskins, Homer	8th Ill. Cav. Died of sickness, 5/7/62, in New York City.
Hills, John	121st NY Died of sickness, 1/63, at White Oak Church, Va.
Horrocks, Wm.	2nd US Cav. Died of sickness, 4/21/63, in Washington.
Horton, Daniel	97th NY Killed in Action, 9/17/62, at Antietam.
Kelley, Guy	18th NY Cav. Died of sickness, 3/7/65, at Little Falls, NY.
Kenna, William	2nd NY HA Killed in Action, 5/31/64. Place unknown.
Kennedy, Matthew	34th NY Died of wounds, 6/16/62, at Philadelphia.
Krow, Jeroine	2nd NY HA Died of sickness, 3/9/63, at Little Falls, NY.
Ladew, Warren	34th NY Killed in Action, 9/17/62, at Antietam.
Loomis, John	34th NY Killed in Action, 5/31/62, at Fair Oaks, Va.
Maguire, John	121st NY Killed in Action, 5/3/63, at Salem Church, Va.
Marks, Ebenezer	5th Mich. Cav. Killed in Action, 5/63, at Fredericksburg, Va.
Middlebrooks, A.	34th NY Killed in Action, 5/31/62, at Fair Oaks, Va.
Monk, James	152nd NY Killed in Action, 5/10/64, at Spotsylvania, Va.
Montana, George	Unit unknown Died of sickness, 5/62. Place unknown.
Morse, Eli	2nd Mounted Rifles Died of wounds, 4/65, Dinwiddie Court House, Va.

Nash, Daniel   34th NY Died of sickness, 8/14/62, at Little Falls, NY.
Perry, Joseph   16th NY HA Accidentally killed (gunshot) 5/2/65, at Keysville, Va.
Quigley, Patrick   16th NY HA Died of sickness, 1/65. Place unknown.
Reed, Charles   "Bates Battery" Died of wounds, 5/31/63, at Fortress Monroe, Va.
Reinke, John   152nd NY Died of sickness. Date and place unknown.
Rider, Charles   34th NY Died of sickness, 7/62, at Fredericksburg, Va.
Rooney, Lawrence   34th NY Murdered, 10/15/61, Seneca Mills, Md.
Sherry, Levi   121st NY Killed in Action, 5/12/64, at Spotsylvania, Va.
Shiltwatter, H.   43rd NY Died of wounds at Annapolis, Md. Date unknown.
Smith, William   Unit, date, place and manner unknown.
Staring, Alonzo   57th NY Died of sickness, 7/64, in prison at Andersonville, Ga.
Starring, Fred.   121st NY Killed in Action, 5/3/63, at Salem Church, Va.
Stauring, Amenzo   121st NY Died of wounds, 10/11/64, in Washington.
Tubbs, Samuel   2nd NY HA Killed in Action, 5/19/64, at Spotsylvania, Va.
Turner, William   121st NY Died of sickness, 10/29/64, in prison at Florence, SC.
Vanderwacker, L.   34th NY Died of sickness, 9/11/62, at Philadelphia.
Vosburg, Daniel   152nd NY Died of sickness, 9/64, at Little Falls, NY.
Walby, Ralph   34th NY Killed in Action, 9/17/62, at Antietam.
Watches, Edward   12th NY Died of sickness, 5/19/62, in Washington.
Watches, William   3rd NY Killed in Action, 7/21/61, at Manassas, Va. (1st Bull Run).
Waterhouse, Geo.   34th NY Accidentally killed (gunshot), 7/20/61, in Washington.
Wraught, Homer   34th NY Died of sickness, 8/1/61, in Washington.
Youker, Israel   97th NY Died of sickness, 11/64, in prison at Andersonville, Ga.

Manheim (27)

Avery, Ira   97th NY Killed in Action, 4/1/65, at Petersburg, Va. (Five Forks).
Avery, Warren   97th NY Died of sickness, 9/18/62, at Alexandria, Va.
Brown, James   121st NY Died of wounds, 5/11/64, at Spotsylvania, Va.
Comins, Alex.   34th NY Died of wounds, 12/62, at Fredericksburg, Va.
Dingler, Fred.   121st NY Killed in Action, 5/12/64, at Spotsylvania, Va.
Faville, Dwight   97th NY Killed in Action, 8/30/62, at Manassas, Va. (2nd Bull Run).
Faville, Nathan   121st NY Died of sickness, 12/14/64, at Little Falls, NY.
Fox, Germaine   97th NY Killed in Action, 5/64, at the battle of the Wilderness.
Grofs, H. Adam   152nd NY Died of sickness, 10/21/64, in prison at Andersonville, Ga.
Haur, Monroe   97th NY Died of wounds, 8/62, at Manassas, Va.
Johnson, August   97th NY Died of sickness in prison at Salisbury, NC. Date unknown.
Judd, Willard   97th NY Killed in Action, 2/7/65, at Petersburg, Va. (Hatcher's Run).
Keller, George   97th NY Died of sickness, 7/15/63, at Alexandria, Va.
Keller, Henry   44th NY Died of sickness, 12/23/62, at Hall's Hill, Va.
Lamb, Clinton   34th NY Died of wounds, 5/31/62, at Fair Oaks, Va.
Lewis, William   34th NY Killed in Action, 9/17/62, at Antietam.
McCammon, Elias   152nd NY Killed in Action, 8/64, at Petersburg, Va. (Weldon R.R.).
McClone, Thomas   152nd NY Killed in Action, 5/64, at the battle of the Wilderness.
Mower, James   97th NY Died of wounds, 8/30/62, in Washington.
Moyer, Adam   34th NY Died of wounds, 12/13/62, at Fredericksburg, Va.
Platt, Charles   186th NY Died of wounds, 4/24/65, at Alexandria, Va.
Platt, Delos   121st NY Killed in Action, 11/7/63, at Rappahannock Station, Va.
Rutt, Charles   16th NY HA Died of sickness (Typhoid), 7/7/64, at Point Lookout, Md.
Snell, Edgar   121st NY Died of wounds (Spotsylvania), 1865, at Albany, NY.
Staring, Laverne   2nd NY HA Killed in Action, 5/19/64, at Spotsylvania, Va.
Van Wie, Edw.   Unit unknown Died of sickness, 4/7/64. Place unknown.
Von Garner, Alb.   97th NY Died of wounds, 6/19/64, at Petersburg, Va.

Newport (18)

Cooley, Henry	97th NY Died of sickness, 3/65, in prison at Richmond, Va.
Dailey, Peter	Berdan's Sharpshooters Died of sickness, 2/19/63, at Falmouth, Va.
Feiner, John	116th NY Died of sickness, 1/7/64, in Louisiana.
Finnegan, Pat.	97th NY Killed in Action, 9/17/62, at Antietam.
Hampton, John	14th NY Died of sickness, 8/62, at Harrison's Landing, Va.
Harris, William	1st US Sharpshooters Died of sickness, 8/10/63, at Alexandria, Va.
Herenden, James	10th NY HA Died of sickness, 12/16/64, at Germantown, Pa.
Jedets, John	152nd NY Killed in Action, 5/6/64, at the battle of the Wilderness.
Kelly, Almon	1st US Sharpshooters Died of sickness, 5/20/63, at Falmouth, Va.
Newburn, Joseph	Berdan's Sharpshooters Died of sickness, 1863, at Annapolis, Md.
Norton, Hurlbut	152nd NY Killed in Action, 5/12/64, at Spotsylvania, Va.
Rice, J.	Unit unknown Died of sickness in a rebel prison. Date and place unknown.
Robinson, Anson	97th NY Killed in Action, 12/13/62, at Fredericksburg, Va.
Terry, Franklin	3rd NY HA Died of sickness, 10/18/64, in prison at Newbern, NC.
Torrey, Edward	97th NY Killed in Action, 9/17/62, at Antietam.
Walker, Arnold	97th NY Died of sickness, 8/63, place unknown.
Whiting, Edmund	52nd NY Died of sickness, 6/24/62, at Middleville, NY.
Whitman, William	97th NY Died of wounds, 8/24/64, at Petersburg, Va.

Norway (15)

Austin, Charles	1st US Sharpshooters Died of sickness, 9/2/62, at York, Pa.
Bailey, John	97th NY Killed in Action, 6/18/64, at Petersburg, Va.
Bullock, Chaun.	34th NY Died of sickness, 6/28/62, at Harrison's Landing, Va.
Corp, William	34th NY Died of sickness, 11/11/62, in Philadelphia.
Delevan, Cassius	121st NY Died of sickness, 1/25/63, at Aquia Creek, Va.
Dixon, William	1st US Sharpshooters Died of sickness, 1/63, in Washington.
Hardenburg, Jas.	16th NY HA Died of sickness. Date and place unknown.
McIntosh, James	97th NY Died of wounds, 9/11/62, at Manassas, Va.
Reynolds, John	1st US Sharpshooters Died of sickness, 6/19/63, at Alexandria, Va.
Salisbury, Wm.	34th NY Killed in Action, 9/17/62, at Antietam.
Smith, Allen	81st NY Killed in Action, 6/2/64, at Cold Harbor, Va.
Smith, Elisha	152nd NY Killed in Action, 6/10/64, at Cold Harbor, Va.
Snyder, William	97th NY Died of wounds, 10/7/62, at Antietam.
Tompkins, Daniel	81st NY Died of sickness, 5/25/62, in Washington.
Wilcox, David	152nd NY Died of sickness, 10/29/64, at Annapolis, Md.

Russia (47)

Ashley, Jacob	34th NY Killed in Action, 9/17/62, at Antietam.
Backus, Isaac	121st NY Killed in Action, 5/3/63, at Salem Church, Va.
Barkley, John	121st NY Killed in Action, 5/64, at the battle of the Wilderness.
Bassett, Isaac	121st NY Killed in Action, 4/5/65, at Sailor's Creek, Va.
Bennett, Francis	152nd NY Died of sickness. Date and place unknown.
Bennett, Jason	34th NY Died of sickness, 12/18/61, in Washington.
Burberry, Wm.	97th NY Killed in Action, 2/5/65, at Petersburg, Va. (Hatcher's Run).
Burlingame, B.	121st NY Accidentally killed, 5/25/63, at White Oak Church, Va.
Christman, Benj.	152nd NY Died of sickness. Date and place unknown.
Collins, George	121st NY Missing in Action, 6/10/64, at Spotsylvania, Va.
Downer, Joseph	2nd NY HA Killed in Action, 6/64, at Cold Harbor, Va.
Fralick, Harris.	1st US Sharpshooters Died of sickness, 2/8/65. Place unknown.
Furguson, Julius	117th NY Killed in Action, 7/3/63, at Gettysburg.
Gaefentz, Frank	Unit unknown Died of sickness, 1865. Place unknown.
Griffith, Henry	57th NY Died of sickness, 7/14/62, in Russia, NY.

Griffith, John   81st NY Died of sickness, 5/7/62. Place unknown.
Grinell, George   97th NY Died of wounds, 10/3/62, in Washington.
Halladay, Roland   1st NY HA Died of sickness, 2/6/65, at Alexandria, Va.
Johnson, Edward   121st NY Killed in Action, 5/10/64, at Spotsylvania, Va.
Jones, Edgar   121st NY Died of wounds, 9/26/64, at Winchester, Va.
Jones, Julius   121st NY Killed in Action, 9/19/64, at Winchester, Va.
Lee, Henry   14th NY Died of sickness at Fairfax, Va. Date unknown.
McIntosh, Doug   152nd NY Missing in Action. Date and place unknown.
McNeal, Sidney   1st US Sharpshooters Died of sickness, 12/19/64, at Alexandria, Va.
Maxfield, David   97th NY Died of wounds, 10/27/62, at Frederick, Md.
McGowan, William   97th NY Died of wounds, 3/28/65, at Point Lookout, Md.
Newman, Morris   1st US Sharpshooters Died of sickness, 12/24/62, at Falmouth, Va.
Onderkirk, Jos.   152nd NY Killed in Action, 5/12/64, at Spotsylvania, Va.
Petrie, Hayden   34th NY Killed in Action, 5/31/62, at Fair Oaks, Va.
Potter, Hiram   97th NY Died of sickness, 1/18/65, in prison at Salisbury, NC.
Prindle, Eben   121st NY Died of sickness, 10/23/62, at Bakersville, Md.
Pullman, Ephraim   97th NY Killed in Action, 9/17/62, at Antietam.
Quackenbush, A.   152nd NY Died of wounds, 5/31/64. Place unknown.
Rich, Henry   81st NY Died of wounds, 6/20/64, in Washington.
Ricker, David   97th NY Died of sickness, 2/2/62, at Boonville, NY.
Rust, Abel   2nd NY HA Killed In Action, 6/17/64, at Petersburg, Va.
Simonds, Patrick   97th NY Died of sickness, 11/26/62, at Brook Station, Va.
Smart, William   81st NY Killed in Action, 6/3/64, at Cold Harbor, Va.
Smith, Franklin   121st NY Died of wounds, 7/14/63. Place unknown.
Stancliff, Geo.   26th NY Accidentally killed, 12/14/63, at Fredericksburg, Va.
Stone, George   117th NY Killed in Action, 9/29/64, at Petersburg, Va. (Weldon R.R.).
Theabold, David   97th NY Died of wounds, 6/23/64, at City Point, Va.
Thrasher, Wm.   34th NY Killed in Action, 5/31/62, at Fair Oaks, Va.
Wandour, Benj.   97th NY Killed in Action, 9/17/62, at Antietam.
Westcott, George   121st NY Killed in Action, 5/3/63, at Salem Church, Va.
Wheeler, Edward   97th NY Killed in Action, 8/30/62, at Manassas, Va. (2nd Bull Run).
Wheeler, James   121st NY Accidentally killed, 12/18/62, at Bellplain Landing, Va.

Salisbury (57)

Alexander, John   186th NY Killed in Action, 4/2/65, at Petersburg, Va.
Allen, Walter   "Oneida Cavalry" Died of sickness, 5/62. Place unknown.
Avery, Ashten   "Oneida Cavalry" Died of sickness, 7/8/62, Harrison's Landing, Va.
Bangs, George   34th NY Died of sickness, 11/5/62, at Harper's Ferry, Va.
Benedict, Allan   97th NY Died of sickness, 8/4/62, at Salisbury, NY.
Benjamin, James   121st NY Died of sickness, 12/12/64, in prison at Salisbury, NC.
Bloodough, James   16th NY HA Died of sickness, 8/12/64, at Fortress Monroe, Va.
Burrell, John.   121st NY Died of wounds, 10/31/64, at Winchester, Va.
Burton, Nicholas   97th NY Died of wounds, 11/4/62, in Washington.
Casler, Alphonzo   121st NY Killed in Action, 5/3/63, at Salem Church, Va.
Darling, Francis   97th NY Killed in Action, 7/1/63, at Gettysburg.
Darling, Oliver   34th NY Killed in Action, 9/16/61, at Edward's Ferry, Va.
Dresher, William   97th NY Killed in Action, 5/6/64, at the battle of the Wilderness.
Dye, David   34th NY Died of sickness, 7/21/62, at Fortress Monroe, Va.
Fitzpatrick, H.   97th NY Killed in Action, 8/19/64, at Petersburg, Va. (Weldon R.R.).
Fuller, Albert   97th NY Died of sickness, 4/3/62, in Washington.
Fynn, Michael   121st NY Died of sickness, 11/15/62, in Philadelphia.
Gransbury, O.C.   121st NY Killed in Action, 5/3/63, at Salem Church, Va.
Haar, James   97th NY Died of wounds, 9/5/62, at Manassas. Va.
Hemmingway, Levi   121st NY Died of sickness in rebel prison. Date and place unknown.

Huntley, Abner	121st NY Killed in Action, 5/3/63, at Salem Church, Va.
Kibbe, Eugene	34th NY Missing in Action, 7/2/62, at Savage Station, Va.
Lamphere, Wm.	34th NY Died of sickness, 5/6/62, at Shipping Point, Va.
McConnell, Pat	97th NY Killed in Action, 9/17/62, at Antietam.
McCuen, Dennis	97th NY Died of wounds, 9/62, in New York City.
McLaughlin, R.	34th NY Killed in Action, 5/31/62, at Fair Oaks, Va.
Miner, George	16th NY HA Died of sickness, 7/12/65, at Smithville, NC.
Montancy, Well.	16th NY HA Died of sickness, 1864, in New York City.
Munson, Fred.	97th NY Killed in Action, 7/1/63, at Gettysburg.
Nichols, David	97th NY Died of sickness, 7/21/62, at Boonville, NY.
Nichols, John	34th NY Killed in Action, 6/31/62, at Nelson's Farm, Va.
Peck, William	34th NY Died of wounds, 6/5/62, at Fair Oaks, Va.
Perkins, Jenks	121st NY Died of sickness, 5/29/63, in Washington.
Porter, Henry	34th NY Died of sickness, 10/30/62, at Salisbury, NY.
Reynolds, Wm.	121st NY Killed in Action, 10/19/64, at Cedar Creek, Va.
Richardson, P.	16th NY HA Died of sickness, 2/65, at Wilmington, NC.
Roback, Swift	152nd NY Killed in Action, 5/7/64, at the battle of the Wilderness.
Sashagra, Edw.	34th NY Died of sickness at Potomac Creek, Va. Date unknown.
Satterlee, Geo.	34th NY Died of sickness, 1/14/62, in Washington.
Sixbey, Jerome	69th NY Killed in Action, 3/29/65, at Petersburg, Va. (Fort Stedman).
Sixbey, John	34th NY Killed in Action, 7/1/62, at Nelson's Farm, Va.
Sixbey, Nicholas	34th NY Killed in Action, 5/31/62, at Fair Oaks, Va.
Smith, Andrew	34th NY Killed in Action, 12/13/62, at Fredericksburg, Va.
Smith, Henry	"Oneida Cavalry" Died of sickness, 11/61, in Washington.
Somers, George	81st NY Died of sickness, 10/64, in prison at Richmond, Va.
Spencer, Warren	121st NY Killed in Action, 5/3/63, at Salem Church, Va.
Stiles, James	97th NY Killed in Action, 7/1/63, at Gettysburg.
Stoddard, Elz.	44th NY Killed in Action, 5/27/62, at Hanover Court House, Va.
Terry, Albert	34th NY Died of wounds, 6/1/62, at Fair Oaks, Va.
Terry, Victor	34th NY Died of wounds, 6/1/62, at Fair Oaks, Va.
Van Hagen, J.	34th NY Killed in Action, 5/31/62, at Fair Oaks, Va.
Wells, Francis	16th NY HA Died of sickness, 5/65, in New York City.
Whitford, Cloth.	97th NY Killed in Action, 5/12/64, at Spotsylvania, Va.
Wiley, Francis	"Oneida Cavalry" Died of sickness, 5/26/62, at Shipping Point, Va.
Williams, John	34th NY Killed in Action, 5/31/62, at Fair Oaks, Va.
Young, James	121st NY Date, place and cause of death unknown.
Young, John	97th NY Killed in Action, 12/13/62, at Fredericksburg, Va.

Schuyler (16)

Baldwin, Lewis	44th NY Died of sickness, 5/27/62, in New York City.
Brown, Charles	152nd NY Died of sickness in a rebel prison. Date and place unknown.
Burdict, Ben.	97th NY Killed in Action, 5/10/64, at Spotsylvania, Va.
Clemons, Boselle	24th NY Cav. Killed in Action, 5/6/64, at the battle of the Wilderness.
Curtin, Patrick	152nd NY Killed in Action, 11/64, at Petersburg, Va.
Evans, Phillip	2nd NY HA Killed in Action, 5/19/64, at Spotsylvania, Va.
Frank, Almond	Unit unknown (Artillery) Died of wounds, 7/8/64, at Alexandria, Va.
Friz, James	152nd NY Killed in Action, 5/6/64, in the battle of the Wilderness.
Graham, Malcolm	121st NY Killed in Action, 5/10/64, at Spotsylvania, Va.
Harvey, Vernon	2nd NY HA Died of sickness, 4/2/65, at Annapolis, Md.
Olds, Orson	121st NY Died of sickness, 10/11/62, at Frederick, Md.
Parkhurst, Geo.	121st NY Killed in Action, 5/10/64, at Spotsylvania, Va.
Parkhurst, Lyman	34th NY Accidentally killed, 5/30/62, at Gaines's Mills, Va.
Souder, Charles	152nd NY Died of sickness, 9/63, in New York City.
Souder, Levi	121st NY Died of sickness, 1/2/63. Place unknown.
Stack, Frank	152nd NY Killed in Action, 5/12/64, at Spotsylvania, Va.

Stark (19)

Ackerman, Clint	97th NY Killed in Action, 9/17/62, at Antietam.
Borst, William	152nd NY Died of wounds, 6/4/64, at Alexandria, Va.
Bronner, Felix	152nd NY Killed in Action, 5/12/64, at Spotsylvania, Va.
Bronner, Horatio	152nd NY Missing in Action, 5/64, at the battle of the Wilderness.
Delong, Herman	152nd NY Died of sickness, 10/10/64, at Petersburg, Va.
Eldridge, L.	152nd NY Died of sickness, 8/14/64, in a rebel prison. Place unknown.
Firl, Albert	2nd NY HA Died of wounds, 5/19/64, at Spotsylvania, Va.
Guywits, Byron	18th NY Died of sickness. Date and Place unknown.
Guywits, Isaac	18th NY Died of sickness, 2/11/65, at Starkville, NY.
Hecks, R.	24th NY HA Died of sickness, 8/14/64, at New Orleans, La.
Holenbeck, Sol.	152nd NY Died of sickness, 8/14/64, in a rebel prison. Place unknown.
Jewell, Hamilton	152nd NY Died of sickness, 4/1/63. Place unknown.
Jones, Clemon	57th NY Died of sickness, 12/62. Place unknown.
McNeil, John	152nd NY Died of sickness in a rebel prison. Date and place unknown.
Shaul, Alfred	152nd NY Killed in Action, 5/12/64, at Spotsylvania, Va.
Shaul, Orlando	76th NY Died of sickness, 5/1/64, at Stark, NY.
Shaul, Paul	Unit unknown Died of sickness, 9/5/62. Place unknown.
Shaw, John	16th NY HA Died of wounds. Date and place unknown.
Wormett, Josia	121st NY Died of wounds, 5/20/64. Place unknown.

Warren (7)

Conklin, John	152nd NY Killed in Action, 5/6/64, in the battle of the Wilderness.
Eastwood, Wm.	121st NY Killed in Action, 11/7/63, at Rappahannock Station, Va.
Houghtaling, J.	Unit unknown Died of sickness, 7/1/64, at City Point, Va.
Lewis, William	2nd NY HA Died of sickness (Starvation), 12/64, in prison at Salisbury, NC.
Peak, Dewitt	2nd NY HA Died of sickness (Starvation), 12/17/63, in prison at Richmond, Va.
Sternberg, A.	Navy Died of sickness, 10/8/64, at Pensacola, Fla.
Wheeler, George	152nd NY Died of sickness, 1864. Place unknown.

Wilmurt (9)

Clough, Francis	152nd NY Died of wounds, 5/29/64, in Washington.
Hathaway, Daniel	81st NY Killed in Action, 9/29/64, at Petersburg, Va.
Paul, John	152nd NY Died of wounds, 7/1/64, in Washington.
Pruyn, James	81st NY Killed in Action, 6/3/64, at Cold Harbor, Va.
Service, Squire	16th NY HA Died of sickness, 7/20/64. Place unknown.
Stevens, George	152nd NY Died of sickness (Typhoid), 7/15/63, in Washington.
Wheeler, Jerome	97th NY Died of wounds, 6/63. Place unknown.
Wheeler, William	16th NY HA Died of sickness, 12/64. Place unknown.
Williamson, R.	81st NY Died of sickness (Typhoid), 7/11/62, in Baltimore.

Winfield (13)

Button, Samuel	121st NY Killed in Action, 5/10/64, at Spotsylvania, Va.
Davis, Ashabel	121st NY Killed in Action, 12/13/62, at Fredericksburg, Va.
Hentz, John	152nd NY Died of sickness, 1864. Place unknown.
Jones, John	121st NY Died of sickness, 6/13/63, at Alexandria, Va.
Jones, Levi	121st NY Died of sickness, 8/13/63, at New Baltimore, Va.
Porter, William	152nd NY Died of sickness, 7/63. Place unknown.
Rounds, Joseph	121st NY Killed in Action, 12/14/64, at Petersburg, Va.
Sessions, Henry	152nd NY Died of sickness, 6/65, in Washington.
Spicer, Oscar	121st NY Killed in Action, 12/13/62, at Fredericksburg, Va.
Thomas, Benjamin	44th NY Died of wounds, 7/2/63, at Gettysburg.

Wendell, Nelson   121st NY Killed in Action, 5/3/63, at Salem Church, Va.
Wing, Fayeth   121st NY Died of wounds, 6/20/64, in Washington.
Wright, Alonzo   152nd NY Died of sickness, 2/21/63, in Washington.

Note: The information contained in this appendix was drawn from Town Clerk's records, the 1865 Herkimer County census report, and regimental and county histories. In many instances this data was found to be incomplete, illegible or conflicting. Although an honest effort was made to compile a complete and accurate listing, the author believes that errors and omissions may exist.

NOTES

Foreword

1   Hardin, George A., *History of Herkimer County, New York*, (Syracuse: D. Mason, 1893), pp 111, 112

2   Fisher, Richard Swainson, *Statistical Gazetteer of the United States of America*, (New York: Colton, 1856), p 287

Prologue

1   *Herkimer County Journal*, (Little Falls, N.Y.), October 11, 1860

2   *Utica Herald*, (Utica, N.Y.), October 12, 1860

3   Ibid.

4   *HCJ*, October 25, 1860

5   Ibid.

6   *HCJ*, November 8, 1860

7   *HCJ*, February 21, 1861

8   Ibid.

I. "We are in fighting condition"

1   *HCJ*, January 17, 1861

2   *HCJ*, April 18, 1861

3   *HCJ*, April 25, 1861

4   Ibid.

5   *HCJ*, May 9, 1861

6   Chapin, Lieut. L.N., *A Brief History of the Thirty-Fourth Regiment N.Y.S.V.*, (Privately Printed: 1903), p 12

7   *HCJ*, May 2, 1861

8   *HCJ*, May 9, 1861

9   *HCJ*, May 23, 1861

10 *HCJ*, May 30, 1861

11 Ibid.

12 *History of the Thirty-Fourth N.Y.S.V.*, p 18

13 *HCJ*, July 11, 1861

14 *HCJ*, July 18, 1861 .

15 *HCJ*, August 1, 1861

16 *HCJ*, August 8, 1861

17 *HCJ*, September 12, 1861

18 *HCJ*, August 22, 1861

19 *HCJ*, September 19, 1861

20 *HCJ*, October 17, 1861

21 *HCJ*, October 24, 1861

II. "The enemy and victory before us"

1   *HCJ*, October 31, 1861

2   White, Col. E.V., *History of the Battle of Ball's Bluff*, (Leesburg, Va.: The "Washingtonian" Print)

3   *History of the Thirty-Fourth N.Y.S.V.*, p 25

4   Greeley, Horace, *The American Conflict*, Vol. I (Hartford: O.D. Case, 1864), p 624

5   *HCJ*, November 7, 1861

6   Hall, Isaac, *History of the Ninety-Seventh Regiment New York Volunteers*, (Utica, N.Y.: L.C. Childs & Sons, 1890), p 21

7   *HCJ*, December 19, 1861

8   *HCJ*, January 16, 1862
9   *HCJ*, February 27, 1862
10 *HCJ*, December 26, 1861
11 *HCJ*, January 16, 1862
12 *HCJ*, November 14, 1861
13 *HCJ*, February 27, 1862
14 *HCJ*, February 13, 1862
15 *HCJ*, January 30, 1862
16 *HCJ*, December 26, 1861
17 *HCJ*, March 6, 1862
18 *HCJ*, March 19, 1862
19 *HCJ*, April 10, 1862
20 *HCJ*, April 17, 1862
21 Ibid.
22 Ibid.
23 Ibid.
24 *HCJ*, May 1, 1862
25 *HCJ*, May 15, 1862
26 Ibid.
27 *HCJ*, May 22, 1862
28 *History of the Thirty-Fourth N.Y.S.V.*, p 38
29 *HCJ*, June 19, 1862
30 *HCJ*, March 13, 1862

III. "Our boys behaved like veterans"

1   *HCJ*, June 19, 1862
2   Ibid.
3   Boatner, Mark III, *The Civil War Dictionary*, (New York: Vintage Books, 1988), p 273
4   Phisterer, Frederick, *New York in the War of the Rebellion, 1861 - 1865*, (Albany: 1912), p 2126
5   *History of the Thirty-Fourth N.Y.S.V.*, p 43
6   *HCJ*, June 19, 1862
7   *HCJ*, June 12, 1862
8   Ibid.
9   *History of the Thirty-Fourth N.Y.S.V.*, pp 173 - 175
10 *HCJ*, June 19, 1862
11 Ibid.
12 *HCJ*, June 12, 1862
13 *HCJ*, June 19, 1862
14 Ibid.
15 *HCJ*, June 26, 1862
16 *HCJ*, July 17, 1862
17 *HCJ*, July i0, 1862
18 *History of the Thirty-Fourth N.Y.S.V.*, p 52
19 *HCJ*, July 17, 1862
20 *HCJ*, July 10, 1862
21 Ibid.
22 *History of the Thirty-Fourth N.Y.S.V.*, pp 52, 53
23 *HCJ*, September 11, 1862
24 *HCJ*, July 31, 1862
25 Ibid.
26 Ibid.

IV. "The balls flew like hailstones." Autumn 1862

1   *HCJ*, August 14, 1862

2   *HCJ*, August 28, 1862
3   *HCJ*, August 14, 1862
4   Ibid.
5   *HCJ*, July 17, 1862
6   *HCJ*, July 24, 1862
7   *History of the Ninety-Seventh Regiment*, p 46
8   Ibid., p 50
9   Ibid., p 53
10   Ibid., p 61
11   Ibid., pp 63, 64
12   Ibid., p 62
13   Ibid., pp 74, 75
14   *Civil War Dictionary*, p 105
15   *New York in the War of the Rebellion*, p 3111
16   *HCJ*, September 11, 1862
17   *HCJ*, September 18, 1862
18   *History of the Ninety-Seventh Regiment*, p 46

V. "The fury of a hurricane storm"

1   *History of the Thirty-Fourth N.Y.S.V.*, p 56
2   Ibid., p 58
3   *HCJ*, September 4, 1862
4   *HCJ*, October 9, 1862
5   *HCJ,* September 18, 1862
6   *History of the Ninety-Seventh*, pp 82, 83
7   Ibid., p 87
8   *New York in the War of the Rebellion*, p 3111
9   *HCJ*, October 16, 1862
10   Best, Isaac O., *History of the 121st New York State Infantry*, (Chicago: Lieut. Jas. H. Smith, 1921)
     p 21
11   *History of the Ninety-Seventh*, pp 91 - 93
12   *HCJ*, October 2, 1862
13   Sears, Stephen. *Landscape Turned Red*, (New Haven: Ticknor & Fields, 1983) p 225
14   *HCJ*, October 2, 1862
15   *HCJ*, October 9, 1862
16   *Civil War Dictionary*, p 21
17   *New York in the War of the Rebellion*, p 3111
18   Ibid., p 2126
19   *HCJ*, October 9, 1862
20   *History of the Ninety-Seventh*, pp 92, 93
21   *HCJ*, October 2, 1862
22   *History of the Ninety-Seventh*, p 92
23   *History of the Thirty-Fourth N.Y.S.V.*, p 69
24   *History of the 121st New York*, pp 23 - 25
25   *HCJ*, October 16, 1862
26   *HCJ*, October 2, 1862

VI. "It was naught but murder"

1   *HCJ*, August 28, 1862
2   Roback, Henry. *History of the 152nd New York Volunteers*, (Little Falls, N.Y.: Henry Roback,
     1888) p 15
3   Ibid., p 17
4   *HCJ*, October 16, 1862
5   *HCJ*, October 23, 1862

6   *HCJ*, October 16, 1862
7   *HCJ*, October 23, 1862
8   Ibid.
9   *HCJ*, November 6, 1862
10 Ibid.
11 *HCJ*, November 20, 1862
12 *HCJ*, November 27, 1862
13 *HCJ*, November 20, 1862
14 *HCJ*, November 6, 1862
15 *HCJ*, November 13, 1862
16 *HCJ*, November 27, 1862
17 Ibid.
18 *History of the Thirty-Fourth N.Y.S.V.*, p 75
19 *HCJ*, December 11,1862
20 Ibid.
21 *HCJ*, December 25, 1862
22 Ibid.
23 *HCJ*, January 1, 1863
24 *New York in the War of the Rebellion*, p 3112
25 *HCJ*, December 25, 1862
26 Ibid.
27 Ibid.
28 *New York in the War of the Rebellion*, p 2126
29 *History of the 121st New York*, pp 45 - 48
30 *New York in the War of the Rebellion*, p 3424
31 *Civil War Dictionary*, p 313
32 *HCJ*, November 27, 1862
33 *HCJ*, December 25, 1862
34 *HCJ*, January 1, 1863
35 *HCJ*, February 5, 1863

VII. "Uncle Abraham looked very much worn out"

1   *HCJ*, December 25, 1862
2   *History of the Thirty-Fourth N.Y.S.V.*, p 85
3   *History of the Ninety-Seventh*, p 116
4   *HCJ*, February 5, 1863
5   *HCJ*, March 26, 1863
6   *HCJ*, April 23, 1863
7   *HCJ*, March 5, 1863
8   *HCJ*, February 19, 1863
9   *HCJ*, February 5, 1863
10 *HCJ*, February 19, 1863
11 *HCJ*, March 19, 1863
12 Ibid.
13 Ibid.
14 *HCJ*, November 27, 1862
15 *HCJ*, December 11, 1862
16 *HCJ*, February 26, 1863
17 *HCJ*, December 4, 1862
18 *HCJ*, December 25, 1862
19 *HCJ*, January 1, 1863
20 *HCJ*, March 19, 1863
21 Ibid.
22 HCJ, March 5, 1863

23 *History of the Thirty-Fourth N.Y.S.V.*, p 88
24 *HCJ*, April 16, 1863
25 *HCJ*, March 19, 1863
26 *History of the 152nd New York*, p 25
27 Ibid.
28 Ibid., p 21
29 *HCJ*, April 2, 1863
30 *HCJ*, March 5, 1863
31 *HCJ*, April 9, 1863

VIII. "It was a bloody and sorrowful baptism"

1 *HCJ*, January 22, 1863
2 *HCJ*, April 16, 1863
3 *History of the 152nd New York*, p 26
4 *HCJ*, May 7, 1863
5 *HCJ*, May 14, 1863
6 Ibid.
7 *History of the Thirty-Fourth N.Y.S.V.*, p 90
8 *History of the Ninety-Seventh Regiment*, pp 123, 124
9 Ibid., p 124
10 *History of the Thirty-Fourth N.Y.S.V.*, p 91
11 Ibid., p 92
12 Ibid.
13 *HCJ*, May 21, 1863
14 *HCJ*, May 14, 1863
15 *History of the 121st New York*, pp 68 - 70
16 *HCJ*, May 14, 1863
17 *History of the 121st New York*, p 81
18 Rice, C.E., *The Letters and Writings of the Late Lieut. Adam Clarke Rice*, (Little Falls, N.Y.: *Journal & Courier*, 1864), pp 67, 68
19 Ibid., p 68
20 Ibid., p 69
21 *History of the Ninety-Seventh Regiment*, p 127
22 *Civil War Dictionary*, p 140
23 *New York in the War of the Rebellion*, p 2126
24 Ibid., p 3112
25 Ibid., p 3424
26 *HCJ*, May 21, 1863

IX. "Brave Defenders, Home Again!"

1 *HCJ*, May 21, 1863
2 *HCJ*, June 4, 1863
3 Ibid.
4 Ibid.
5 Ibid.
6 *Adam Clarke Rice*, p 79
7 *History of the 152nd New York*, p 31
8 *HCJ*, May 28, 1863
9 *HCJ*, June 4, 1863
10 Ibid.
11 *HCJ*, July 2, 1863
12 *HCJ*, June 4, 1863
13 *History of the Thirty-Fourth N.Y.S.V.*, p 95
14 *HCJ*, June 18, 1863

15 Ibid.
16 Ibid.
17 Ibid.
18 Ibid.
19 Ibid.
20 Ibid.
21 Ibid.
22 Ibid.
23 *New York in the War of the Rebellion*, p 2126

X. "What a glorious day for us was the 3rd of July"

 1 *HCJ*, July 2, 1863
 2 Ibid.
 3 *HCJ*, July 23, 1863
 4 Ibid.
 5 *History of the Ninety-Seventh Regiment*, p 129
 6 Ibid., pp 130, 131
 7 *Adam Clarke Rice*, p 87
 8 *History of the Ninety-Seventh Regiment*, p 133
 9 Ibid., p 137
10 Ibid., p 156
11 Ibid., p 142
12 *HCJ*, July 23, 1863
13 *New York in the War of the Rebellion*, p 3112
14 *HCJ*, July 16, 1863
15 *HCJ*, July 23, 1863
16 *HCJ*, July 16, 1863
17 *HCJ*, July 23, 1863
18 *History of the Ninety-Seventh Regiment*, pp 145, 146
19 *HCJ*, July 16, 1863
20 *HCJ*, July 9, 1863
21 Ibid.
22 Ibid.
23 *HCJ*, July 16, 1863
24 Ingraham, Edward. *John James Ingraham's Civil War Letters 1862 - 1865*, (Frankfort, N.Y.: Phoenix Printing, 1986), 7/17/63
25 Thomas, Howard. *Boys in Blue from the Adirondack Foothills*, (Prospect, N.Y.: Prospect Books, 1960) pp 171, 172

XI. "We live on the fat of the land now"

 1 *HCJ*, August 27, 1863
 2 *HCJ*, July 16, 1863
 3 *HCJ*, May 28, 1863
 4 *HCJ*, August 13, 1863
 5 *HCJ*, November 12, 1863
 6 *HCJ*, July 23, 1863
 7 *HCJ*, August 6, 1863
 8 *HCJ*, July 23, 1863
 9 Ibid.
10 *HCJ*, August 20, 1863
11 *History of the 152nd New York*, pp 47, 48
12 *HCJ*, September 10, 1863
13 *John Ingraham's Civil War Letters*, 7/11/63
14 *HCJ*, August 13, 1863

15   *HCJ*, September 17, 1863
16   *HCJ*, September 3, 1863
17   *Adam Clarke Rice*, p 108
18   *HCJ*, August 6, 1863
19   Ibid.
20   *John Ingraham's Civil War Letters*, 8/15/63

XII.   "Some of you may fall, but you'll all go to heaven"

 1   *HCJ*, August 27, 1863
 2   Ibid.
 3   Ibid.
 4   *HCJ*, July 16, 1863
 5   *HCJ*, July 9, 1863
 6   *HCJ*, September 3, 1863
 7   *New York in the War of the Rebellion*, p 66
 8   *HCJ*, October 1, 1863
 9   *John Ingraham's Civil War Letters*, 10/9/63
10   *History of the Ninety-Seventh Regiment*, p 343
11   *History of the 152nd New York*, p 50
12   Ibid., pp 50, 54
13   *John Ingraham's Civil War Letters*, 10/27/63
14   *History of the 152nd New York*, p 56
15   Ibid., p 53
16   Ibid., pp 100, 101
17   *HCJ*, November 19, 1863
18   Ibid.
19   Ibid.
20   *New York in the War of the Rebellion*, p 3424
21   *HCJ*, November 12, 1863

XIII.   "We waited in suspense to start for the next world"

 1   *HCJ*, September 17, 1863
 2   *HCJ*, September 24, 1863
 3   *HCJ*, August 27, 1863
 4   *HCJ*, December 10, 1863
 5   Ibid.
 6   *History of the 121st New York*, pp 109, 110
 7   *History of the 152nd New York*, p 58
 8   *History of the Ninety-Seventh Regiment*, p 169
 9   *History of the 152nd New York*, p 59
10   *New York in the War of the Rebellion*, p 3767
11   Ibid., p 3112
12   Ibid., p 3424
13   *HCJ*, December 24, 1863
14   HCJ, December 17, 1863
15 · Ibid.

XIV.   "I have staked my all in favor of Union and Freedom"
 1   *History of the 121st New York*, p 112
 2   *Herkimer County Journal & Courier*, March 3, 1864
 3   *HCJ*, December 31, 1863
 4   *HCJC*, January 14, 1864
 5   Ibid.
 6   *HCJC*, March 10, 1864

7   *HCJC*, February 18, 1864
8   *John Ingraham's Civil War Letters*, 1/1/64
9   *HCJC*, April 14, 1864
10 *HCJ*, December 31, 1863
11 Ibid.
12 *HCJC*, February 18, 1864
13 *HCJC*, February 11, 1864
14 Ibid.
15 *HCJC*, February 18, 1864
16 *HCJ*, December 3, 1863
17 *HCJC*, March 17, 1864
18 *HCJC*, March 10, 1864
19 *HCJC*, March 17, 1864
20 *HCJC*, April 28, 1864
21 *HCJ*, December 17, 1863

XV. "With a cheer and a yell like fiends incarnate we rush forward"

1   *HCJC*, June 2, 1864
2   *History of the 152nd New York*, p 67
3   Ibid., pp 67, 68
4   *HCJC*, June 2, 1864
5   *HCJC*, June 16, 1864
6   *HCJC*, June 2, 1864
7   *History of the 152nd New York*, p 68
8   Ibid., p 69
9   *HCJC*, June 2, 1864
10 *History of the Ninety-Seventh Regiment*, pp 179, 180
11 *History of the 121st New York*, pp 121 - 123
12 *HCJC*, June 23, 1864
13 *HCJC*, June 2, 1864
14 *Civil War Dictionary*, p 925
15 *New York in the War of the Rebellion*, p 3112
16 Ibid., p 3424
17 Ibid., p 3767
18 *History of the Ninety-Seventh Regiment*, p 182
19 *HCJC*, June 2, 1864
20 *History of the Ninety-Seventh Regiment*, pp 183, 184
21 *History of the 121st New York*, pp 129 - 132
22 *New York in the War of the Rebellion*, p 3424
23 *HCJC*, June 2, 1864
24 *History of the 152nd New York*, pp 77, 78
25 *HCJC*, June 2, 1864
26 *History of the 152nd New York*, pp 80, 81
27 *New York in the War of the Rebellion*, p 3112
28 Ibid., p 3424
29 Ibid., p 3767
30 *HCJC*, May 19, 1864
31 *Civil War Dictionary*, p 788
32 *History of the 152nd New York*, p 83
33 *New York in the War of the Rebellion*, p 1236

XVI. "Many believed their hour was nigh"

1   *HCJC*, May 26, 1864
2   *History of the Ninety-Seventh Regiment*, p 109

3   *HCJC*, June 16, 1864
4   *History of the 152nd New York*, p 91
5   *Civil War Dictionary*, p 163
6   *History of the 152nd New York*, p 92
7   *New York in the War of the Rebellion*, p 3767
8   *History of the 152nd New York*, p 94
9   *HCJC*, June 23, 1864
10 *History of the 152nd New York*, p 96
11 *John Ingraham's Civil War Letters*, 6/21/64
12 *History of the 152nd New York*, p 100
13 Ibid., pp 100, 101
14 *History of the Ninety-Seventh Regiment*, p 200
15 *Civil War Dictionary*, p 646
16 *New York in the War of the Rebellion*, p 3112
17 Ibid., p 3767
18 Ibid., p 3424
19 *History of the 152nd New York*, pp 101 - 103

XVII. "The leaden hail showering over and around us"

1   *HCJC*, June 16, 1864
2   *HCJC*, June 23, 1864
3   *HCJC*, July 7, 1864
4   Ibid.
5   Ibid.
6   Ibid.
7   *HCJC*, August 8, 1864
8   *HCJC*, July 7, 1864
9   *History of the 152nd New York*, pp 103, 104
10 *New York in the War of the Rebellion*, p 3767
11 *History of the 152nd New York*, p 105
12 *Civil War Dictionary*, p 900
13 *New York in the War of the Rebellion*, p 3424
14 *John Ingraham's Civil War Letters*, 6/21/64
15 Ibid., 7/6/64
16 *History of the 121st New York*, p 171
17 *New York in the War of the Rebellion*, p 3424
18 *HCJC*, July 14, 1864

XVIII. "They arose like demons from the bowels of the earth"

1   *History of the 152nd New York*, pp 110, 111
2   *History of the Ninety-Seventh Regiment*, pp 211, 212
3   *Boys in Blue*, pp 214, 215
4   *New York in the War of the Rebellion*, p 1477
5   *HCJC*, July 14, 1864
6   *HCJC*, August 25, 1864
7   *History of the 152nd New York*, p 114
8   Ibid., p 115
9   *New York in the War of the Rebellion*, p 3767
10 *History of the Ninety-Seventh Regiment*, pp 219, 220
11 Ibid., p 226
12 Ibid.
13 *Civil War Dictionary*, p 346
14 *New York in the War of the Rebellion*, p 3112
15 *History of the 152nd New York*, p 118

16   Ibid., pp 119, 120
17   *Civil War Dictionary*, p 683
18   *New York in the War of the Rebellion*, p 3767
19   *History of the 152nd New York*, pp 120, 121

XIX. "It is a big victory although we suffered severely"

1 *HCJC*, August 18, 1864
  2   *HCJC*, August 25, 1864
  3   *HCJC*, September 29, 1864
  4   *New York in the War of the Rebellion*, p 2290
  5   *HCJC*, August 25, 1864
  6   Ibid.
  7   *HCJC*, September 8, 1864
  8   *HCJC*, September 15, 1864
  9   *John Ingraham's Civil War Letters*, 8/1/64
10   Ibid., 8/26/64
11   *History of the 121st New York*, p 179
12   Ibid., p 181
13   *Civil War Dictionary*, p 940
14   *New York in the War of the Rebellion*, p 3424
15   *HCJC*, October 27, 1864
16   *Civil War Dictionary*, p 281
17   *New York in the War of the Rebellion*, p 3424
18   *John Ingraham's Civil War Letters*, 10/12/64
19   Ibid., 10/23/64
20   Ibid.
21   Ibid.
22   *Civil War Dictionary*, p 134
23   *New York in the War of the Rebellion*, p 3424
24   *HCJC*, October 27, 1864
25   National Archives, Washington, D.C.: Records of Joseph H. Heath, Box 42465, Certificate #434689, Bundle #1
26   *HCJC*, September 8, 1864
27   Ibid.
28   Ibid.
29   *HCJC*, September 29, 1864
30   *HCJC*, October 6, 1864
31   *HCJC*, October 20, 1864
32   Ibid.
33   *HCJC*, September 22, 1864
34   *HCJC*, October 6, 1864
35   *HCJC*, October 27, 1864
36   *HCJC*, September 8, 1864
37   *HCJC*, November 14, 1864
38   Ibid.

XX. "Let us all have a fair start with Father Abraham"

  1   *History of the Ninety-Seventh Regiment*, pp 231, 232
  2   *History of the 152nd New York*, p 130
  3   *Civil War Dictionary*, p 385
  4   *New York in the War of the Rebellion*, p 3767
  5   *History of the Ninety-Seventh Regiment*, p 232
  6   *History of the 152nd New York*, pp 132, 133
  7   Ibid., pp 131, 132

8   *John Ingraham's Civil War Letters*, 11/24/64
9   HCJC, December 15, 1864
10 *HCJC*, December 22, 1864
11 Ibid.
12 *HCJC*, December 29, 1864
13 *HCJC*, November 24, 1864
14 *HCJC*, December 22, 1864
15 *HCJC*, December 29, 1864
16 *HCJC*, February 2, 1865

XXI. "Along most of the line all is quiet"

1   *HCJC*, February 2, 1865
2   *John Ingraham's Civil War Letters*, 2/23/65
3   Ibid., 2/27/65
4   Ibid., 3/17/65
5   *History of the 152nd New York*, pp 142, 143
6   *History of the Ninety-Seventh Regiment*, p 237
7   *HCJC*, February 2, 1865
8   *John Ingraham's Civil War Letters*, 2/10/65
9   *Civil War Dictionary*, p 217
10 *New York in the War of the Rebellion*, p 3424
11 Ibid., p 3112
12 *HCJC*, March 2, 1865
13 *HCJC*, February 2, 1865
14 *HCJC*, February 14, 1865
15 *HCJC*, December 29, 1864
16 *HCJC*, March 3, 1865
17 *HCJC*, April 27, 1865
18 *HCJC*, May 4, 1865

XXII. "At last the day of Jubilee arrived"

1   *New York in the War of the Rebellion*, p 3424
2   *History of the 152nd New York*, p 147
3   *Civil War Dictionary*, p 284
4   *New York in the War of the Rebellion*, p 3112
5   *History of the 121st New York*, pp 209, 210
6   Ibid., pp 210, 211
7   *Civil War Dictionary*, p 647
8   *New York in the War of the Rebellion*, p 3424
9   *History of the 121st New York*, pp 211, 212
10 *New York in the War of the Rebellion*, p 4067
11 *History of the 121st New York*, pp 212, 213
12 Ibid., p 214
13 Ibid., pp 215, 216
14 *Civil War Dictionary*, p 724
15 *New York in the War of the Rebellion*, pp 438, 439
16 Ibid., p 3424
17 *History of the 121st New York*, p 220
18 *History of the 152nd New York*, p 153
19 *HCJC*, April 6, 1865
20 *HCJC*, April 13, 1865
21 Ibid.
22 *HCJC*, April 27, 1865
23 Ibid.

XXIII. "Faithfully they have fulfilled their mission"

1 *History of the 121st New York*, p 221
2 Ibid., p 222
3 *John Ingraham's Civil War Letters*, 4/28/65
4 Ibid., 5/15/65
5 *History of the 152nd New York*, p 156
6 *History of the 121st New York*, p 223
7 Ibid., pp 224, 225
8 *History of the 152nd New York*, p 162
9 *HCJC*, May 4, 1865
10 *New York in the War of the Rebellion*, pp 299, 300, 301
11 *HCJC*, July 13, 1865
12 *HCJC*, July 6, 1865
13 Ibid.
14 Ibid.
15 Ibid.
16 Ibid.
17 *History of the 152nd New York*, p 164
18 *HCJC*, July 20, 1865
19 *HCJC*, July 13, 1865
20 *HCJC*, August 3, 1865
21 *HCJC*, August 10, 1865
22 *HCJC*, June 1, 1865
23 *Civil War Dictionary*, p 602

XIV. "Never shall their memory fade"

1 Hardin, *History of Herkimer County*, p 111
2 *History of the Thirty-Fourth N.Y.S.V.*, p 158
3 *The Evening Times*. Little Falls, N.Y.: Files with the Little Falls Public Library, July 15, 1918
4 Ibid., January 1, 1943

SOURCES

Ambrose, Stephen E. *Upton and the Army*. Baton Rouge: Louisiana State University Press, 1964

Beers, F.W. *History of Herkimer County, N.Y.*. New York: Beers & Co., 1879

Best, Isaac O. *History of the 121st New York State Infantry*. Chicago: Lieut. Jas. H. Smith, 1921

Beyer, W.F. *Deeds of Valor*. Stamford, Conn.: Longmeadow Press, 1903

Boatner, Mark M. III. *The Civil War Dictionary*. New York: Vintage Books, 1988

Cable, G.W. *Famous Adventures and Prison Escapes of the Civil War*. Unknown

Chapin, Lieut. L.N. *A Brief History of the 34th Regiment N.Y.S.V.*. Privately Printed: 1903

Cronkite, Lt. Col. J.W. *Report of the Gettysburg Monument Committee of the 121st New York Volunteers*. Cooperstown, N.Y.: *The Otsego Republican*

Fisher, Richard Swainson. *Statistical Gazetteer of the United States of America*. New York: Colton, 1858

Foote, Shelby. *The Civil War*. New York: Vintage Books, 1986

Greeley, Horace. *The American Conflict*. Vol. I. Hartford, Conn.: O.D. Case, 1864

Hall, Isaac. *History of the Ninety-Seventh Regiment, New York Volunteers*. Utica: L.C. Childs & Sons, 1890

Happel, Ralph. *Salem Church Embattled*. National Parks Service: 1980

Hardin, George A. *History of Herkimer County, New York*. Syracuse: D. Mason, 1893

Headley, J.T. *The Great Rebellion: A History of the Civil War in the United States*. Hartford: American Publishing, 1866

Ingraham, Edward. *John James Ingraham's Civil War Letters 1862 - 1865*. Frankfort, N.Y.: Phoenix Printing, 1986

Moe, Richard. *The Last Full Measure*. New York: Holt, 1993

Nichols, B. *Atlas of Herkimer County*. New York: Stranahan & Nichols, 1868

O'Donnell, Thomas C. *Tip of the Hill*. Boonville, N.Y.: Black River Books, 1953

Phisterer, Frederick. *New York in the War of the Rebellion, 1861 - 1865*. Albany: 1912

Rice, C.E. *The Letters and Writings of the Late Lieut. Adam Clarke Rice*. Little Falls, N.Y.: *Journal & Courier*, 1864

Roback, Henry. *History of the 152nd New York Volunteers*. Little Falls, N.Y.: Henry Roback, 1888

Sandburg, Carl. *Abraham Lincoln, The Prairie and the War Years*. New York: Harcourt, Brace & World, 1954

Schmucker, Samuel M. *The History of the Civil War in the United States*. Philadelphia: Jones Bros., 1865

Sears, Stephen. *Landscape Turned Red*. New Haven: Ticknor & Fields, 1983

Thomas, Howard. *Boys in Blue from the Adirondack Foothills*. Prospect, N.Y.: Prospect Books, 1960

Trudeau, Noah Andre. *Bloody Roads South*. Boston: Little, Brown & Co., 1989

Trudeau, Noah Andre. *The Last Citadel*. Baton Rouge: Louisiana State University Press, 1991

Walker, Francis. *Second Army Corps*. New York: Scribner, 1887

White, Col. E.V. *History of the Battle of Ball's Bluff.* Leesburg, Va.: The "Washingtonian" Print

Wiley, Bell Irvin. *The Life of Billy Yank.* Baton Rouge: Louisiana State University Press, 1978

Herkimer County Journal. Little Falls, N.Y., Files with the Little Falls Public Library

1865 Herkimer County Census. Herkimer, N.Y., Files with the Herkimer County Clerk

Herkimer County Township Clerks' Registers. Albany, N.Y.. Files in the New York State Archives

Proceedings of the Forty-Second Encampment Department of New York, G.A.R.. Albany: J.B. Lyon Co., 1908

The Evening Times. Little Falls, N.Y., Files with the Little Falls Public Library

INDEX

Larabee, Capt. Lucius, 39
Lee, Lt. Adrian, 348
Legg, Capt. Judson, 315
Leland, William, 247
Leslie, Capt. J.P., 14, 16, 18, 172
Lettus, P., 300
Lewis, D.H., 235
Lewis, Henry, 103
Lewis, William, 68
Lewis, William J., 299
Little, Dr. George, 352
Lloyd, Reese, 140
Loomis, John, 34
Lowe, Adj. Francis, 161, 171, 233, 348, 358

MacElroy, William, 216
Maguire, John, 103
Maguire, Thomas, 103
Manchester, Capt. J.R., 140
Marden, Jack, 176
Martin, Henry, 37
Mason, Fred, 201, 202
Mather, Capt. Andrew, 118
Matteson, H.R., 213
Matthews, Richard, 120
Maxfield, David, 68
Maxfield, James, 299
McCammon, Elias, 268
McClone, Thomas, 228
McConnell, Patrick, 68
McCuen, Dennis, 56
McGowan, William, 315
McIntosh, James, 56
McLaughlin, John, 11
McLaughlin, Robert, 11, 34
McLean, William, 19, 37, 41, 67, 69, 88
McNeil, John, 299
Mead, Garland, 68
Mead, Joseph, 299
Middlebrook, QM Allan, 34, 35
Millan, Aaron, 229
Miller, Aaron, 236
Monk, James, 229
Moon, Capt. Clinton, 49, 50
Morey, William, 299
Morse, Lt. Amos, 315
Morse, Capt. Eli, 156, 326
Morse, Adj. Francis, 96, 120, 222
Morse, George, 18, 26, 38
Mortimer, Charles, 314
Morton, James, 261, 264
Morton, Lt. Tracy, 332
Mott, Daniel, 299
Moyer, Adam, 88
Munson, Frederick, 142, 143

Murphy, Lt. Frank, 142, 146, 147
Musson, Capt. Willard, 295
Myers, John, 34

Nau, J.J., 235
Nichols, John, 37
Michols, (43rd Mass), 182
Norcross, Capt. John, 359
Norris, Enoch, 34
Northrup, Maj. Charles, 16, 65
Northrup, Capt. Emerson, 37, 40, 93
Norton, Hurlbut, 224, 228
Norton, Lt. John, 146

O'Brien, Nicholas, 234, 236
O'Brien, Col. Timothy, 74, 75, 156, 248, 267, 311
Olcott, Col. Egbert, 50, 95, 216, 226, 270, 284, 300, 312, 331, 344, 345, 348
Onderkirk, Josephus, 229
Oswald, Capt. William, 5, 6, 28

Parkhurst, George, 228
Parsons, Capt. William, 87
Peck, William, 34
Perry, Joseph, 352
Petrie, Chauncey, 146
Petrie, Hayden, 34
Phelps, George, 122
Platt, Charles, 329
Platt, Delos, 178
Platt, Montraville, 299
Potter, Hiram, 342
Prame, Jacob, 78
Proctor, Arthur, 116
Pruyn, James, 236
Pullman, Ephraim, 68

Quaiffe, Capt. Alfred, 135, 228, 268

Ramsey, Capt. John, 49, 50
Redway, Capt. Sheldon, 72, 226
Reynolds, John, 216
Reynolds, William, 284
Rice, Lt. Adam C., 118, 119, 124, 138, 162, 171
Rich, Capt. Davis, 6, 28
Rich, Henry, 239
Rider, Charles, 40
Riley, Capt. Charles, 6
Roback, Henry, 75, 76, 102, 108, 125, 158, 172, 175, 185, 186, 212, 214, 224, 225, 226, 234, 235, 236, 238, 240, 248, 257, 261, 267, 268, 295, 297, 325, 333, 339, 341, 348, 358
Roback, Swift, 229